♻ NatWest
PLAYFAIR
CRICKET ANNUAL

All statist~~~~~*ted*

PLAYFAIR CRICKET COMPETITION 1998

CRICKET QUIZ

£1500 TO BE WON

**PLUS NATWEST FINAL TICKETS AND HOSPITALITY
PLUS 25 CONSOLATION PRIZES**

First Prize   £500 + overnight accommodation (B and B) at the Regents Park Hilton Hotel (opposite Lord's) on 4 and 5 September + TWO tickets to the 1998 NatWest Trophy Final + NatWest hospitality

Second Prize £400 + TWO tickets to the 1998 NatWest Trophy Final

Third Prize   £300 + TWO tickets to the 1998 NatWest Trophy Final

Fourth Prize £200

Fifth Prize   £100

Consolation prizes

Senders of the next 25 correct entries will each receive a copy of

FRASER'S TOUR DIARIES

by Angus Fraser, published by Headline at £16.99

Closing date for entries
12.00 noon on 21 July 1998

Winning entries will be drawn by the Man of the Match Adjudicator
at one of the NatWest semi-finals on 11/12 August.

PLAYFAIR CRICKET COMPETITION 1998
CRICKET QUIZ
ENTRY FORM

Please PRINT your answers in the spaces provided and answer every question.

The answers to all ten questions can be found within this Annual

1 Who is the longest-serving umpire on the 1998 First-Class List? ....

2 Which counties have not won the County Championship since it was officially constituted in 1890? ....

3 Who had the highest batting average in Britannic Assurance Championship matches in 1997? ....

4 Which county plays some of its home matches at Brockhampton? ....

5 Who, in 1997, returned a record bowling analysis for his county in first-class matches? ....

6 Which Danish cricketer made his county debut in 1997? ....

7 Who took most wickets in Britannic Assurance Championship matches in 1997? ....

8 Who was the last batsman to score a triple century in English first-class cricket? ....

9 Which county recorded its highest total in 1997? ....

10 Who, at the start of the 1998 season, were the longest-serving county captains? ....

Your name and address:

....

....

....

Your daytime telephone number: ....

Post to: PLAYFAIR CRICKET COMPETITION, Brand Communication, Level 12, Drapers Gardens, 12 Throgmorton Avenue, LONDON EC2N 2DL.

Entries must be received before noon on 21 July 1998. All-correct entries will go into the prize-winning draw on 11/12 August and an announcement detailing all prize-winners will appear in the October edition of *The Cricketer* magazine. A list of winners is available on request by writing to Mrs B.J.Quinn at the above address and enclosing a stamped addressed envelope.

Rules: All entries must be on this official form. Proof of posting is not proof of entry. The decision of the editor regarding the answers to this quiz shall be final and binding; no correspondence may be entered into.

1997 PLAYFAIR CRICKET COMPETITION
CRICKET QUIZ ANSWERS

1 After whom is this Annual named?	SIR NIGEL PLAYFAIR
2 Who is the only English batsman to score 2000 Test match runs in Australia?	J.B./Sir Jack HOBBS
3 In which city could you watch international cricket at the R. Premadasa Stadium?	COLOMBO
4 Who has been elevated to the first-class list of umpires this season?	J.F. (John) STEELE
5 Which currently registered county cricketer was born in Yokohama?	G.J. (Gregor) KENNIS
6 Who was the last bowler to take a hat-trick in an Ashes Test match?	S.K. (Shane) WARNE
7 Which country is sending an 'A' touring team to England this season?	PAKISTAN
8 Who is alone in scoring a century and taking four wickets with successive balls in a first-class match?	K.D. (Kevan) JAMES
9 Which bowler returned an analysis of six for 18 in a Lord's final?	G. (Glen) CHAPPLE
10 Who, in 1973, became the first holders of the Lord's Taverners' Trophy?	HAMPSHIRE

There were a record **1954** sets of correct answers from a record total of **2273** entries. The winners were drawn by Rachael Heyhoe Flint MBE at the 1997 semi-final between Warwickshire and Sussex at Edgbaston.

First Prize:	£500 + two nights' accommodation + two tickets to include hospitality at the 1997 NatWest Trophy Final	K. NEWBERY (Stratford)
Second Prize:	£400 + two tickets to the 1997 NatWest Trophy Final	A.G. DODGSON (Sheffield)
Third Prize:	£300 + two tickets to the 1997 NatWest Trophy Final	T. BURFORD (Great Yarmouth)
Fourth Prize:	£200	D. SCOTT (Dover)
Fifth Prize:	£100	G. DUNCAN (Stafford)

25 Runners-up: each winning a signed copy of *A LOT OF HARD YAKKA* by Simon Hughes, published by Headline at £16.99.

B.S.Barnard	(Brockbeare, Devon)	C.Hood	(Blenheim, New Zealand)
J.M.Brown	(Hinckley)	T.Hopkins	(Long Harborough)
S.Essam	(Ilford)	M.W.Kennedy	(Chesham)
J.Fisher	(Newcastle upon Tyne)	T.Lakey	(Blockley, Glos)
J.R.Franks	(Manchester)	G.McArdle	(Bracknell)
J.T.Golby	(Churchdown, Glos)	C.S.Mitchell	(Stockport)
S.Goodwin	(Stoke on Trent)	C.F.Oliver	(Canterbury)
K.Graham	(Stoke on Trent)	A.Riddle	(London)
C.N.Hamblet	(Stoke on Trent)	I.Ross	(Newcastle upon Tyne)
R.T.Harper	(St Austell)	M.Sharp	(Sheffield)
D.Harwood	(Winchester)	D.Woodford	(Llanyrafon, Wales)
R.Hill	(Golders Green)	D.P.Woods	(Romford)
R.J.Holdsworth	(Northampton)		

SPONSOR'S MESSAGE FROM

♻ NatWest

In 1998 NatWest celebrate the eighteenth year of sponsorship of the NatWest Trophy competition. Since we began our sponsorship in 1981, NatWest has shown an ever-increasing commitment to the domestic game. Next year, our commitment to cricket will reach a much wider audience, with NatWest an Official Partner of the 1999 Cricket World Cup. In 1999 we will also see a new-look NatWest Trophy competition – it will become cricket's equivalent to the FA Cup; 60 teams will compete for the coveted NatWest Trophy.

The NatWest Development of Excellence has continued to blossom since the beginning of our sponsorship in 1996. On 1 February, the NatWest England Under-19 team became the Under-19 Cricket World Cup champions with a wonderful seven-wicket victory over New Zealand in Johannesburg. Congratulations and very well done to the squad and the management of the team. With their excellent achievements, the NatWest England Under-19 team have shown there is a very bright future for English cricket.

Our support for the game remains strong, both on and off the field, with our sponsorship of the *NatWest Playfair Cricket Annual* and the NatWest Media Centre at Lord's. The construction of the Centre is well underway and NatWest, in partnership with the MCC, look forward to helping the world's media broadcast World Cup coverage all over the globe.

The year 1998 is one of anticipation – the final season of the traditional-look NatWest Trophy, the summer arrival of the South African and Sri Lankan teams, plus the excitement of the build-up to the World Cup in 1999. Let us hope it will be a year of celebration for the senior national team as they try to emulate the success of the Under-19s. Perhaps we can even hope that the Millennium edition of the Playfair Annual will be hailing England as the new champions of the world.

Martin Gray
Chief Executive, NatWest UK

FOREWORD

by Bob Woolmer

Before I start writing on a variety of topics relating to this great game, I must say that I am deeply privileged to be asked to make a contribution to the Annual. That feeling was increased when Bill Frindall told me that the last person to write a foreword was C.B.Fry, from whom I have gained a lot of my coaching techniques and ideas. Furthermore, if one reads his work, *C.B.Fry on Batting*, one will also see how far ahead of his time he was.

As a coach and certainly as a player, the search for the Holy Grail of batting is never ending. The cricketer that came the closest to the cup was, of course, Sir Donald Bradman. I was particularly struck by his recent answer to the question 'why his average was so much greater than the next great Australian batsman, Allan Border?' He replied, 'I really can't answer the question; I do not know why Border got himself out so much!'

I will never be able to see him live and to judge the standards of today with then. Nor do I particularly want to. I hold very little truck with players of yesteryear denigrating the players of today. My own experiences tell me that current players work every bit as hard as in my era and the majority far harder. What people who criticise the players of today fail to remember is the vast differences in the game.

Uncovered wickets and limited-overs matches are the two areas of the game that have created the most change. Having sampled both eras, and as I travel with the South African cricket team around the world, playing in so many different competitions, I am only too aware of the differences and the problems that today's cricketers encounter. Travelling by plane is different to journeying by train. Yet stories from the past of touring sides getting off the train and playing the same day are more horrendous even than today's hurly-burly of one-day cricket 'play plane and play'. The effect of jet-lag is debilitating.

Traditionalists forget that there is no doubt the pace of the game has changed. I remember diving to stop a ball at mid-off in 1969 and soiling my trousers! Two things happened which would cause astonishment today and possibly ridicule. I was told to go off and change my trousers so that I looked smart and secondly my captain came up to me and said. 'Well done but you have a long season in front of you – you must learn to pace yourself!' Imagine a coach going up to a player before a Test match and saying 'pace yourself guys we've got eleven Test matches in six months!' This, in fact, was South Africa's itinerary between October and March during the 1997-98 season, not to mention limited-overs internationals. No wonder the questions arise: Do the players play too much cricket? Is there the danger of overkill? Will the public support so many games? Can the players maintain their level of performance? South Africa and England will play a five-Test series this summer following hectic schedules. I wonder how many players will fall by the wayside due to injury brought on by fatigue?

As an ex-Kent and England player, and then coach of both Kent and Warwickshire, I am always interested to follow the game in England. I have obviously been intrigued and sometimes baffled by the attempted changes to the county system. However, the dilemma that English cricket now faces is how can their national team compete unless the county system is altered to provide better training for the Test match arena. Australia is of course the major factor in the perception that England is slipping behind. Nobody wants to lose to the Aussies, but is this dilemma exclusive to England? The simple answer is no!

Not so long ago, English cricket changed from a three-day to four-day format – this was to be the saviour of the game. Previously, limited-overs cricket brought big money to keep the counties afloat and was the saviour for the game. Why then did English cricket fall behind its competitors despite this? Why did England stop beating the Australians? I believe it is because Australians for years have produced exciting batsmen brought up on excellent batting-friendly wickets. This meant that their bowlers had to learn the value of line and length. Furthermore, they are not all professionals; they have jobs to go to and cricket is a passion for them.

While the England team and its coaching staff are making strides and have, in my opinion, improved a lot in the last two years, I might humbly suggest that English cricketers, by being so-called professional (paid to play), must regain their passion for the game. Too many players look at cricket as a means to making ends meet! The attitude that 'If I can get through to a benefit I can have a nest-egg for the future' is the only major difference between English cricket and its competitors. Of course cricketers should earn good money, and they can only display their talents for a limited period so they should be set up for the future. The benefit system means there are too many cricketers in England who are not prepared to eradicate faults, to strengthen their weaknesses, to have pride in their county and their country. Instead, there are plenty of cricketers who want a rise at the end of the season after they have averaged 30-something with the bat or taken 30 wickets. The focus is not aimed at improving, it is aimed at being 'all right jack' and ensuring that they get a sponsored car.

The problem is much more with the management of the game. They should realise that any sport is an insecure career, yet the players need to feel secure to perform at their best. Which is why I am in favour of any system that reduces stress on a player. The best way to do this, I believe, would be for players to have alternative employment, with a guaranteed job at the end of their cricketing career. Many firms sponsor counties, but this would be a better way of supporting them. It would also mean that cricketers could play with greater freedom, and concentrate on the good of the team, rather than their own narrow interests. It would also help to avoid the jam of players at the end of their careers hanging on for a testimonial, so allowing younger cricketers to come through.

If this plan was set up, the system of county cricket would be good enough because the players' motivation would be higher and standards would rise all round.

I wonder if English cricket would be suffering the same microscopic examination if they had a similar attitude to the Australians. The Australians are proud to play for their country, are provincially parochial, and practise and play with passion, admittedly backed up by terrific facilities and the security of a job. At least one limited-overs competition needs to be trimmed from the English calendar to create more room for skill improvement. Again, it is these areas where the Australians are more advanced: the use of state-of-the-art computerised, video editing systems and 'stats' analysis programmes gives them a crucial edge.

The idea of a two-division County Championship has been much discussed as a solution to England's problems at international level. While not entirely against the idea, I doubt such a system will work because it will lead to a transfer system where the rich will become richer and the poor poorer. This might lead to some counties going under, which would be a pity as potential breeding grounds for Test players would be lost. No wonder some counties are against it.

Internationally too, the ICC will have to address various matters, especially standards of umpiring. While understanding that all umpires have a difficult job, more so now that they are constantly under the scrutiny of the TV cameras, it must be said that there is need for improvement in standards. Players' and (dare I say it?) coaches' careers are on the line day after day. The public, the media and sponsors all want to be associated with a winning team, which creates much more pressure than ever before.

Cricket is without doubt the only game that really mirrors life. In modern society people expect to be treated better than in the past; I often have a quiet chuckle when I think of how I was spoken to by my first cricket coaches and how I was scolded and punished when things went wrong. If that happened now, the coach would be sacked by player pressure. Now there are team-building seminars to get the best out of each player and thus the team. It is all a far cry from 1968 when six Kent second XI players turned up to a game in an Austin A40 Somerset costing £50, with all their kit paid for out of their own pockets!

Yes, the game has changed in all areas. It is still the wonderful game that we all love to watch, but we would do well to heed the words of Lord Harris, especially in these times of constant pressure: 'Foster it, my brothers, so that it may attract all who can find the time to play . . .'

Bob Woolmer
February 1998

(Bob Woolmer, South Africa's coach, played for Kent between 1968 and 1984, and won 19 caps for England, scoring three hundreds against Australia.)

EDITORIAL PREFACE

Mention of C.B.Fry's foreword to the inaugural edition of *Playfair* in 1948 provoked the idea of re-establishing this feature. With his unique background combining a distinguished playing career for Kent and England with a current high-profile role as coach to South Africa's national team, Bob Woolmer was easily my first choice of victim. Assisted by the modern miracles of fax and e-mail, his contribution sped from Melbourne to Wiltshire. His comments on the English professional system are especially pertinent; significantly he does not seize on the much-bandied concept of a two-division County Championship as the instant panacea for all the ills of our professional game.

One of the main disappointments of the ECB's Blueprint *Raising the Standard* was its failure to tackle the feudal county benefit system. Replace that with a finely tuned pension fund, perhaps based on that which Essex employ to reward players who fail to qualify for a full benefit and which is the subject of their fund-raising this season, and you will remove a backlog of dead wood that is cluttering up the county registers. There has to be a severe culling to streamline county staffs to a hardcore of ambitious, enthusiastic, mentally tough, talented cricketers. Rather than offload half the counties, one could do much to eliminate the current mediocrity of playing standards by reducing the full-time workforce from 25 to a maximum of 17, that elite being contracted by their counties, possibly supported individually by various sponsors, for the entire year, as Lancashire are now doing.

The most ridiculous feature of the Blueprint is the plan to reward the top echelon of this season's Britannic Assurance Championship table with the excruciating prospect of competing in a nebulous limited-overs tournament. When a great many of our current players' technical shortcomings have been attributed to over-exposure with the instant format, this proposal defies all logic. Better by far to introduce a regional competition organised on Duleep Trophy lines which would pit the best county players against each other in a four-day or even five-day format. This could replace the suggested extra one-day bash and such useless phantom Test trials as England A v The Rest.

England's investment in the 'A' team concept, now emulated by all the Test-playing boards, is paying rich dividends. The success at first-class level of the recent expedition to Sri Lanka and Kenya appears to have sped the development of Ben Hollioake, Ashley Giles and Darren Maddy into top-class players who will soon be gracing major arenas. Unless the county system is dramatically revamped, it will be from 'A' and Under-19 appearances that our Test cricketers are fine-tuned.

The Blueprint's proposal to reduce the domestic limited-overs competitions from three to two is brave and highly commendable. Fortunately the oldest of all the one-day competitions will survive. Introduced in 1963, the Knock-Out Competition (as it had to be called!) with its 60-over format does not impose such pressures as the more bucolic 50-over pattern that has become standard at international level because of the reduced playing hours possible in some countries. It is a doubly fortunate survival as its current sponsors, NatWest, remain the well-established benefactors of this Annual. We are again indebted to Barbara Quinn and her colleagues for administering our competition. Despite my attempts last year to set more challenging questions, the record number of entries was extended from 1382 to 2273, with 1954 (86%) sets of correct answers. The answers to this year's quiz can again be found within the following pages – but extended research of the sections relating to county captains, County Championship performances and umpires' seniority will be necessary! May we wish 'Dickie' Bird an enjoyable final season on the first-class list.

Last season's Championship provided rich entertainment and most worthy winners in Glamorgan. Their talented captain, Matthew Maynard, inspired self-belief throughout his team and, with the supreme advantage of a consistent pair of opening batsmen

8

and a well-balanced attack, they were able to overcome the loss of almost 2,000 overs to rain and win their first title for 28 years. It is a sign of the pressures on modern captains that, after just two seasons at the helm, Maynard is one of the most senior. None was appointed prior to 1995 and no fewer than six (one third) will start their tenures this summer. One of those is Brian Charles Lara, whose previous efforts for Warwickshire produced three trophies and an abundance of runs and records. His tactics in the current Test series against England reveal a mind that ranges from the inventive to the bizarre and Warwickshire supporters should prepare themselves for an intriguing season.

On the international front, we offer the warmest welcome to the South Africans for their first full tour since 1960. 'Hansie' Cronje will lead a team which is expected to include such exciting new players as Paul Adams and Makhaya Ntini. Neither would have been eligible for selection had they been around in 1960. The Protea's captain adorns the spine and back cover of this edition. The dubious honour of being portrayed on the front has been bestowed upon Nasser Hussain. Promoters of the *Playfair* hex will seize upon his lack of runs in the Caribbean. Hopefully he will swiftly regain his form and destroy this silly myth. Sri Lanka, who visit for a one-off Test and a triangular limited-overs series in August, will be relieved to find that none of their players appears on our cover.

The proliferation of international tours continues despite a conference of Test captains agreeing guidelines for a maximum quota of Tests and limited-overs internationals per country each year. The ICC is very conscious of this problem and is working with the national boards to bring it under control. Apart from inflicting stress injuries on players, the faster bowlers in particular, it has demanded more space for Test match scores and series averages in this annual. That pressure, allied to the fact that the structure of the university first-class programme is likely to change shortly, has led to my reducing the space devoted to Oxbridge cricket from six pages to a basic register of players. Full details of the seven blues who played first-class county cricket last season appear within their county registers.

Thank you to all those who sent kind messages concerning *Playfair's* 50th birthday. I am delighted to record that Peter West, our founding editor, now in his 78th year, is in fine fettle and survived my recent appearance as guest speaker during an evening hosted by the Cheltenham Cricket Society, of whom he is the energetic president.

This publication relies heavily on support from many sources, particularly from the county clubs' administrators, scorers and statisticians who supply data and circulate my 'Newcomers' Forms' for the County Registers; from Kate Hanson (née Jenkins) and Alan Fordham (née Northamptonshire opening batsman!) at the ECB; from Clive Hitchcock at the ICC; from David Armstrong, ever-enthusiastic controller-general of the Minor Counties; and from numerous overseas correspondents who check Test match and other first-class scores.

Philip Bailey has once more provided the first-class career records and researched the birth registrations of new players. There does not seem much point in publishing any data unless every effort is made to ensure its accuracy; whether or not a player is trying to conceal an unwanted given name or his true date of birth is totally irrelevant.

My wife, Debbie, has returned to teaching, possibly to escape the chore of proof-checking but happily has found time to maintain players' limited-overs county records, compile scorecards and ward off our infant daughter's attacks on my PC.

But, above all, thanks are again due to our publishers, Headline, and in particular to Ian Marshall for his expertise and calm control of the entire operation, and to Chris Leggett and his typesetting team at Letterpart for much technical wizardry.

Bill Frindall
Urchfont
13 March 1998

ENGLAND v SOUTH AFRICA

1888-89 to 1995-96

Season	England	*Captains* South Africa	T	E	SA	D
1888-89	C.A.Smith[1]	O.R.Dunell[2]	2	2	–	–
1891-92	W.W.Read	W.H.Milton	1	1	–	–
1895-96	Lord Hawke[3]	E.A.Halliwell[4]	3	3	–	–
1898-99	Lord Hawke	M.Bisset	2	2	–	–
1905-06	P.F.Warner	P.W.Sherwell	5	1	4	–
1907	R.E.Foster	P.W.Sherwell	3	1	–	2
1909-10	H.D.G.Leveson-Gower[5]	S.J.Snooke	5	2	3	–
1912	C.B.Fry	F.Mitchell[6]	3	3	–	–
1913-14	J.W.H.T.Douglas	H.W.Taylor	5	4	–	1
1922-23	F.T.Mann	H.W.Taylor	5	2	1	2
1924	A.E.R.Gilligan[7]	H.W.Taylor	5	3	–	2
1927-28	R.T.Stanyforth[8]	H.G.Deane	5	2	2	1
1929	J.C.White[9]	H.G.Deane	5	2	–	3
1930-31	A.P.F.Chapman	H.G.Deane[10]	5	–	1	4
1935	R.E.S.Wyatt	H.F.Wade	5	–	1	4
1938-39	W.R.Hammond	A.Melville	5	1	–	4
1947	N.W.D.Yardley	A.Melville	5	3	–	2
1948-49	F.G.Mann	A.D.Nourse	5	2	–	3
1951	F.R.Brown	A.D.Nourse	5	3	1	1
1955	P.B.H.May	J.E.Cheetham[11]	5	3	2	–
1956-57	P.B.H.May	C.B.van Ryneveld[12]	5	2	2	1
1960	M.C.Cowdrey	D.J.McGlew	5	3	–	2
1964-65	M.J.K.Smith	T.L.Goddard	5	1	–	4
1965	M.J.K.Smith	P.L.van der Merwe	3	–	1	2
1994	M.A.Atherton	K.C.Wessels	3	1	1	1
1995-96	M.A.Atherton	W.J.Cronje	5	–	1	4

	T	E	SA	D
Lord's	11	6	2	3
Leeds	9	5	1	3
The Oval	11	4	–	7
Birmingham	3	2	–	1
Manchester	7	3	1	3
Nottingham	6	2	2	2
In England	47	22	6	19
Port Elizabeth	7	4	1	2
Cape Town	16	9	3	4
Johannesburg	24	7	8	9
Durban	15	5	2	8
Pretoria	1	–	–	1
In South Africa	63	25	14	24
Totals	110	47	20	43

The following deputised for the official touring captain or were appointed for only a minor portion of a home series:

[1]M.P.Bowden (2nd). [2]W.H.Milton (2nd). [3]Sir T.C.O'Brien (1st). [4]A.R.Richards (3rd). [5]F.L.Fane (4th, 5th). [6]L.J.Tancred (2nd, 3rd). [7]J.W.H.T.Douglas (4th). [8]G.T.S.Stevens (5th). [9]A.W.Carr (4th, 5th). [10]E.P.Nupen (1st), H.B.Cameron (4th, 5th). [11]D.J.McGlew (3rd, 4th). [12]D.J.McGlew (2nd).

SERIES RECORDS – ENGLAND v SOUTH AFRICA

HIGHEST INNINGS TOTALS

England	in England	554-8d	Lord's	1947
	in South Africa	654-5	Durban	1938-39
South Africa	in England	538	Leeds	1951
	in South Africa	530	Durban	1938-39

LOWEST INNINGS TOTALS

England	in England	76	Leeds	1907
	in South Africa	92	Cape Town	1898-99
South Africa	in England	30	Birmingham	1924
	in South Africa	30	Port Elizabeth	1895-96

HIGHEST MATCH AGGREGATE 1981 for 35 wickets   Durban   1938-39
LOWEST MATCH AGGREGATE 378 for 30 wickets   The Oval   1912

HIGHEST INDIVIDUAL INNINGS

England	in England	211	J.B.Hobbs	Lord's	1924
	in South Africa	243	E.Paynter	Durban	1938-39
South Africa	in England	236	E.A.B.Rowan	Leeds	1951
	in South Africa	176	H.W.Taylor	Johannesburg	1922-23

HIGHEST AGGREGATE OF RUNS IN A SERIES

England	in England	753 (av 94.12)	D.C.S.Compton	1947
	in South Africa	653 (av 81.62)	E.Paynter	1938-39
South Africa	in England	621 (av 69.00)	A.D.Nourse	1947
	in South Africa	582 (av 64.66)	H.W.Taylor	1922-23

RECORD WICKET PARTNERSHIPS – ENGLAND

1st	359	L.Hutton (158), C.Washbrook (195)	Johannesburg	1948-49
2nd	280	P.A.Gibb (120), W.J.Edrich (219)	Durban	1938-39
3rd	370	W.J.Edrich (189), D.C.S.Compton (208)	Lord's	1947
4th	197	W.R.Hammond (181), L.E.G.Ames (115)	Cape Town	1938-39
5th	237	D.C.S.Compton (163), N.W.D.Yardley (99)	Nottingham	1947
6th	206*	K.F.Barrington (148*), J.M.Parks (108*)	Durban	1964-65
7th	115	J.W.H.T.Douglas (119), M.C.Bird (61)	Durban	1913-14
8th	154	C.W.Wright (71), H.R.Bromley-Davenport (84)	Johannesburg	1895-96
9th	71	H.Wood (134*), J.T.Hearne (40)	Cape Town	1891-92
10th	92	C.A.G.Russell (111), A.E.R.Gilligan (39*)	Durban	1922-23

RECORD WICKET PARTNERSHIPS – SOUTH AFRICA

1st	260	B.Mitchell (123), I.J.Siedle (141)	Cape Town	1930-31
2nd	198	E.A.B.Rowan (236), C.B.van Ryneveld (83)	Leeds	1951
3rd	319	A.Melville (189), A.D.Nourse (149)	Nottingham	1947
4th	214	H.W.Taylor (121), H.G.Deane (93)	The Oval	1929
5th	157	A.J.Pithey (95), J.H.B.Waite (64)	Johannesburg	1964-65
6th	171	J.H.B.Waite (113), P.L.Winslow (108)	Manchester	1955
7th	123	H.G.Deane (73), E.P.Nupen (69)	Durban	1927-28
8th	109*	B.Mitchell (189*), L.Tuckett (40*)	The Oval	1947
9th	137	E.L.Dalton (117), A.B.C.Langton (73*)	The Oval	1935
10th	103	H.G.Owen-Smith (129), A.J.Bell (26*)	Leeds	1929

BEST INNINGS BOWLING ANALYSIS

England	in England	9- 57	D.E.Malcolm	The Oval	1994
	in South Africa	9- 28	G.A.Lohmann	Johannesburg	1895-96
South Africa	in England	7- 65	S.J.Pegler	Lord's	1912
	in South Africa	9-113	H.J.Tayfield	Johannesburg	1956-57

BEST MATCH BOWLING ANALYSIS

England	in England	15- 99	C.Blythe	Leeds	1907
	in South Africa	17-159	S.F.Barnes	Johannesburg	1913-14
South Africa	in England	10- 87	P.M.Pollock	Nottingham	1965
	in South Africa	13-192	H.J.Tayfield	Johannesburg	1956-57

HIGHEST AGGREGATE OF WICKETS IN A SERIES

England	in England	34 (av 8.29)	S.F.Barnes	1912
	in South Africa	49 (av 10.93)	S.F.Barnes	1913-14
South Africa	in England	26 (av 21.84)	H.J.Tayfield	1955
		26 (av 22.57)	N.A.T.Adcock	1960
	in South Africa	37 (av 17.18)	H.J.Tayfield	1956-57

1998 TOURING TEAMS

Neither the South African nor the Sri Lankan touring teams had been selected at the time of going to press in mid-March. The following players either represented those countries in international cricket during the 1997-98 season or have enjoyed success on recent 'A' or U19 tours:

SOUTH AFRICA

Full Names	Birthdate	Birthplace	Team	Type	F-C Debut
ACKERMAN, Hylton Deon	14. 2.73	Cape Town	W Province	RHB/RM	1993-94
ADAMS, Paul Regan	20. 1.77	Cape Town	W Province	RHB/SLC	1995-96
BACHER, Adam Marc	29.10.73	Johannesburg	Transvaal	RHB	1993-94
BOUCHER, Mark Verdon	3.12.76	East London	Border	RHB/WK	1995-96
CRONJE, Wessel Johannes ('Hansie')	25. 9.69	Bloemfontein	Free State	RHB/RM	1987-88
CULLINAN, Daryll John	4. 3.67	Kimberley	Transvaal	RHB/OB	1983-84
DONALD, Allan Anthony	20.10.66	Bloemfontein	Free State	RHB/RF	1985-86
GIBBS, Herschelle Herman	23. 2.74	Cape Town	W Province	RHB/RFM/LB	1990-91
HAYWARD, Mornantau ('Nantie')	6. 3.77	Uitenhage	E Province	RHB/RF	1995-96
HUDSON, Andrew Charles	17. 3.65	Eshowe	Natal	RHB/RM	1984-85
KALLIS, Jacques Henry	16.10.75	Cape Town	W Province	RHB/RM	1993-94
KIRSTEN, Gary	23.11.67	Cape Town	W Province	LHB/OB	1987-88
KLUSENER, Lance	4. 9.71	Durban	Natal	LHB/RFM	1993-94
LIEBENBERG, Gerhardus Frederick Johannes	7. 4.72	Upington	Free State	RHB/RFM/WK	1989-90
McMILLAN, Brian Mervin	22.12.63	Welkom	W Province	RHB/RFM	1984-85
NTINI, Makhaya	6. 7.77	Zwelitsha	Border	RHB/RF	1995-96
POLLOCK, Shaun Maclean	16. 7.73	Port Elizabeth	Natal	RHB/RF	1991-92
POTHAS, Nic	18.11.73	Johannesburg	Transvaal	RHB/WK	1993-94
RHODES, Jonathan Neil ('Jonty')	27. 7.69	Pietermaritzburg	Natal	RHB/RM	1988-89
SYMCOX, Patrick Leonard	14. 4.60	Kimberley	Natal	RHB/OB	1977-78

SRI LANKA

Full Names	Birthdate	Birthplace	Team	Type	F-C Debut
ANURASIRI, Sangarange Don	25. 2.66	Panadura	Panadura	RHB/SLA	1984-85
ARNOLD, Russel Premakumaran	25.10.73	Colombo	Nondescripts	LHB/OB	1993-94
ATAPATTU, Marvan Samson	22.11.72	Kalutara	Sinhalese	RHB/OB	1988-89
CHANDANA, Umagilya Durage Upul	7. 5.72	Galle	Tamil Union	RHB/LB	1991-92

DE SILVA, Karunakalage Sajeewa Chanaka 11. 1.71 Kalutara Sebastianites LHB/LFM 1990-91
DE SILVA, Pinnaduwage Aravinda 17.10.65 Colombo Nondescripts RHB/OB 1983-84
DE SILVA, Sanjeewa Kumara Lanka 29. 7.75 Kurunegala Kurunegala RHB/WK/OB 1991-92
DHARMASENA, Handunettige 24. 4.71 Colombo Bloomfield RHB/RM/OB 1988-89
  Deepthi Priyantha Kumara
JAYASURIYA, Sanath Teran 30. 6.69 Matara Bloomfield LHB/SLA 1988-89
KALPAGE, Ruwan Senani 19. 2.70 Kandy Bloomfield LHB/OB 1988-89
KALUWITHARANA, Romesh Shantha 24.11.69 Colombo Galle RHB/WK 1988-89
MAHANAMA, Roshan Siriwardene 31. 5.66 Colombo Bloomfield RHB 1984-85
MURALITHARAN, Muttiah 17. 4.72 Kandy Tamil Union RHB/OB 1989-90
PUSHPAKUMARA, Karuppiahyage 21. 7.75 Panadura Nondescripts RHB/RFM 1992-93
  Ravindra
RANATUNGA, Arjuna 1.12.63 Colombo Sinhalese LHB/RM 1981-82
SILVA, Kelaniyage Jayantha 2. 6.73 Kalutara Sinhalese RHB/SLA 1991-92
TILLEKERATNE, Hashan Prasantha 14. 7.67 Colombo Nondescripts LHB/RM/WK 1984-85
VAAS, Warnakulasooriya Patabendige 27. 1.74 Colts LHB/LFM 1990-91
  Ushantha Chaminda Joseph Mattumagala
WICKREMASINGHE, Gallage Pramodya 14. 8.71 Matara Sinhalese RHB/RFM 1988-89
ZOYSA, Demuni Nuwan Tharanga 13. 5.78 Colombo Sinhalese LHB/LFM 1996-97

ENGLAND v SRI LANKA
1881-82 to 1992-93

Captains

Season	England	Sri Lanka	T	E	SL	D
1981-82	K.W.R.Fletcher	B.Warnapura	1	1	–	–
1984	D.I.Gower	L.R.D.Mendis	1	–	–	1
1988	G.A.Gooch	R.S.Madugalle	1	1	–	–
1991	G.A.Gooch	P.A.de Silva	1	1	–	–
1992-93	A.J.Stewart	A.Ranatunga	1	–	1	–
		Lord's	3	2	–	1
		In England	3	2	–	1
		Colombo (PSS)	1	1	–	–
		Colombo (SSC)	1	–	1	–
		In Sri Lanka	2	1	1	–
		Totals	5	3	1	1

SERIES RECORDS – ENGLAND v SRI LANKA
HIGHEST INNINGS TOTALS

England	in England	429	Lord's	1988
	in Sri Lanka	380	Colombo (SSC)	1992-93
Sri Lanka	in England	491-7d	Lord's	1984
	in Sri Lanka	469	Colombo (SSC)	1992-93

LOWEST INNINGS TOTALS

England	in England	282	Lord's	1991
	in Sri Lanka	223	Colombo (PSS)	1981-82
Sri Lanka	in England	194	Lord's	1988
	in Sri Lanka	175	Colombo (PSS)	1981-82

HIGHEST MATCH AGGREGATE 1219 for 35 wickets Colombo (SSC) 1992-93
LOWEST MATCH AGGREGATE 787 for 33 wickets Colombo (PSS) 1981-82

HIGHEST INDIVIDUAL INNINGS

England	in England	174	G.A.Gooch	Lord's	1991
	in Sri Lanka	128	R.A.Smith	Colombo (SSC)	1992-93
Sri Lanka	in England	190	S.Wettimuny	Lord's	1984
	in Sri Lanka	93*	H.P.Tillekeratne	Colombo (SSC)	1992-93

HIGHEST AGGREGATE OF RUNS IN A SERIES

England	in England	212 (av 106.00)	G.A.Gooch	1991
	in Sri Lanka	163 (av 81.50)	R.A.Smith	1992-93
Sri Lanka	in England	205 (av 102.50)	L.R.D.Mendis	1984
	in Sri Lanka	129 (av ∞)	H.P.Tillekeratne	1992-93

RECORD WICKET PARTNERSHIPS – ENGLAND

1st	78	G.A.Gooch (174), H.Morris (23)	Lord's	1991
2nd	139	G.A.Gooch (174), A.J.Stewart (43)	Lord's	1991
3rd	112	R.A.Smith (128), G.A.Hick (68)	Colombo (SSC)	1992-93
4th	122	R.A.Smith (128), A.J.Stewart (63)	Colombo (SSC)	1992-93
5th	40	A.J.Stewart (113*), I.T.Botham (22)	Lord's	1991
6th	87	A.J.Lamb (107), R.M.Ellison (41)	Lord's	1984
7th	63	A.J.Stewart (113*), R.C.Russell (17)	Lord's	1991
8th	20	J.E.Emburey (59), P.W.Jarvis (3)	Colombo (SSC)	1992-93
9th	37	P.J.Newport (26), N.A.Foster (14*)	Lord's	1988
10th	40	J.E.Emburey (59), D.E.Malcolm (8*)	Colombo (SSC)	1992-93

RECORD WICKET PARTNERSHIPS – SRI LANKA

1st	99	R.S.Mahanama (64), U.C.Hathurusinghe (59)	Colombo (SSC)	1992-93
2nd	83	B.Warnapura (38), R.L.Dias (77)	Colombo (PSS)	1981-82
3rd	101	S.Wettimuny (190), R.L.Dias (32)	Lord's	1984
4th	148	S.Wettimuny (190), A.Ranatunga (84)	Lord's	1984
5th	150	S.Wettimuny (190), L.R.D.Mendis (111)	Lord's	1984
6th	138	S.A.R.Silva (102*), L.R.D.Mendis (94)	Lord's	1984
7th	74	U.C.Hathurusinghe (66), R.J.Ratnayake (52)	Lord's	1991
8th	29	R.J.Ratnayake (17), C.P.H.Ramanayake (34*)	Lord's	1991
9th	83	H.P.Tillekeratne (93*), M.Muralitharan (19)	Colombo (SSC)	1992-93
10th	64	J.R.Ratnayeke (59*), G.F.Labrooy (42)	Lord's	1988

BEST INNINGS BOWLING ANALYSIS

England	in England	7-70	P.A.J.DeFreitas	Lord's	1991
	in Sri Lanka	6-33	J.E.Emburey	Colombo (PSS)	1981-82
Sri Lanka	in England	5-69	R.J.Ratnayake	Lord's	1991
	in Sri Lanka	4-70	A.L.F.de Mel	Colombo (PSS)	1981-82

BEST MATCH BOWLING ANALYSIS

England	in England	8-115	P.A.J.DeFreitas	Lord's	1991
	in Sri Lanka	8- 95	D.L.Underwood	Colombo (PSS)	1981-82
Sri Lanka	in England	5-160	R.J.Ratnayake	Lord's	1991
	in Sri Lanka	8-188	K.P.J.Warnaweera	Colombo (SSC)	1992-93

HIGHEST WICKET AGGREGATE IN A SERIES

England	in England	8 (av 14.37)	P.A.J.DeFreitas	1991
	in Sri Lanka	8 (av 11.87)	D.L.Underwood	1981-82
Sri Lanka	in England	5 (av 32.00)	R.J.Ratnayake	1991
		5 (av 36.00)	S.D.Anurasiri	1991
	in Sri Lanka	8 (av 23.50)	K.P.J.Warnaweera	1992-93

THE FIRST-CLASS COUNTIES
REGISTER, RECORDS AND 1997 AVERAGES

Career statistics: Test and L-O Internationals to end of 1997 season but including the 1997-98 Asia Cup (July), Sri Lanka v India series (August) and the 1997 Sahara series involving India and Pakistan in Toronto (September).

ABBREVIATIONS
General

*	not out/unbroken partnership	f-c	first-class
b	born	HS	Highest Score
BB	Best innings bowling analysis	LOI	Limited-Overs Internationals
Cap	Awarded 1st XI County Cap	Tests	Official Test Matches
Tours	Overseas tours involving first-class appearances		

Awards

BHC	Benson and Hedges Cup 'Gold' Award
NWT	NatWest Trophy/Gillette Cup 'Man of the Match' Award
Wisden 1997	One of *Wisden Cricketers' Almanack*'s Five Cricketers of 1997
YC 1997	Cricket Writers' Club Young Cricketer of 1997

Competitions

BHC	Benson and Hedges Cup
GC	Gillette Cup
NWT	NatWest Trophy
SL	Sunday League

Education

BHS	Boys' High School
BS	Boys' School
C	College
CE	College of Education
CFE	College of Further Education
CHE	College of Higher Education
CS	Comprehensive School
GS	Grammar School
HS	High School
IHE	Institute of Higher Education
LSE	London School of Economics
RGS	Royal Grammar School
S	School
SFC	Sixth Form College
SM	Secondary Modern School
SS	Secondary School
TC	Technical College
T(H)S	Technical (High) School
U	University
UMIST	University of Manchester Institute of Science and Technology

Playing Categories

LBG	Bowls right-arm leg-breaks and googlies
LF	Bowls left-arm fast
LFM	Bowls left-arm fast-medium
LHB	Bats left-handed
LM	Bowls left-arm medium pace
LMF	Bowls left-arm medium fast
OB	Bowls right-arm off-breaks
RF	Bowls right-arm fast
RFM	Bowls right-arm fast-medium
RHB	Bats right-handed
RM	Bowls right-arm medium pace
RMF	Bowls right-arm medium-fast
RSM	Bowls right-arm slow-medium
SLA	Bowls left-arm leg-breaks
SLC	Bowls left-arm 'Chinamen'
WK	Wicket-keeper

Teams (see also p 118)

Cav	Cavaliers	NT	Northern Transvaal
CD	Central Districts	OFS	(Orange) Free State
DHR	D.H.Robins' XI	PIA	Pakistan International Airlines
Eng Co	English Counties XI	Q	Queensland
EP	Eastern Province	RW	Rest of the World XI
GW	Griqualand West	SAB	South African Breweries XI
Int XI	International XI	SAU	South African Universities
IW	International Wanderers	WA	Western Australia
ND	Northern Districts	WP	Western Province
NSW	New South Wales	Z	Zimbabwe (Rhodesia)

DERBYSHIRE

Formation of Present Club: 4 November 1870
Colours: Chocolate, Amber and Pale Blue
Badge: Rose and Crown
Championships: (1) 1936
NatWest Trophy/Gillette Cup Winners: (1) 1981
Benson and Hedges Cup Winners: (1) 1993
Sunday League Champions: (1) 1990
Match Awards: NWT 39; BHC 66

Secretary/General Manager: J.Smedley.
County Cricket Ground, Nottingham Road, Derby DE2 6DA (Tel 01332 383211)
Captain: D.G.Cork. **Vice-Captain:** K.M.Krikken. **Overseas Player:** M.J.Slater.
1998 Beneficiary: None. **Scorer:** S.W.Tacey

ALDRED, Paul (Lady Manner's S, Bakewell), b Chellaston 4 Feb 1969. 5'10". RHB,
RM. Debut 1995. Cheshire 1994. HS 83 v Hants (Chesterfield) 1997. BB 3-28 v Notts
(Nottingham) 1997. **NWT:** HS 4. BB 4-30 v Lincs (Lincoln) 1997. **BHC:** HS 7 and BB
2-35 v Warwks (Birmingham) 1996. **SL:** HS 17 v Warwks (Birmingham) 1997. BB 4-41
v Leics (Derby) 1996. Hockey for Derbyshire.

BARNETT, Kim John (Leek HS), b Stoke-on-Trent, Staffs 17 Jul 1960. 6'1". RHB, LB.
Debut 1979; cap 1982; captain 1983-95; benefit 1992. Boland 1982-83 to 1987-88.
Staffordshire 1976. *Wisden* 1988. **Tests:** 4 (1988 to 1989); HS 80 v A (Leeds) 1989. **LOI:**
1 (1988; HS 84). Tours: SL 1989-90 (Eng XI); NZ 1979-80 (DHR); SL 1985-86 (Eng B).
1000 runs (14); most – 1734 (1984). HS 239* v Leics (Leicester) 1988. BB 6-28 v Glam
(Chesterfield) 1991. Awards: NWT 3; BHC 11. **NWT:** HS 113* v Glos (Bristol) 1994. BB
6-24 v Cumberland (Kendal) 1984. **BHC:** HS 115 v Glos (Derby) 1987. BB 3-52 v Notts
(Derby) 1996. **SL:** HS 131* v Essex (Derby) 1984. BB 3-26 v Worcs (Chesterfield) 1996.

BLACKWELL, Ian David (Brookfield Community S), b Chesterfield 10 Jun 1978. 6'1".
LHB, SLA. Debut 1997. HS 42 and BB 1-27 v Lancs (Derby) 1997. **BHC:** HS –. **SL:** HS
29 v Hants (Chesterfield) 1997.

CASSAR, Matthew Edward (Sir Joseph Banks HS, Sydney), b Sydney, Australia 16 Oct
1972. Husband of Jane Cassar (England). 6'0". RHB, RFM. Debut 1994. Qualified for
England/BAC debut 1997. HS 78 v Somerset (Derby) 1997. BB 4-54 v OU (Oxford) 1995.
BAC BB 3-31 v Northants (Derby) 1997. **SL:** HS 33 and BB 1-15 v Middx (Lord's) 1997.

CLARKE, Vincent Paul (Sacred Heart C, Perth, Australia; Perth C), b Liverpool, Lancs
11 Nov 1971. 6'3". RHB, RM/LB. Somerset 1994. Leicestershire 1995-96. Derbyshire
debut 1997. HS 99 v Warwks (Birmingham) 1997. BB 3-47 v CU (Cambridge) 1997.
BAC BB 3-72 Le v Worcs (Worcester) 1995. Award: BHC 1. **NWT:** HS 24* and BB 1-38
v Northants (Derby) 1997. **BHC:** HS 52 v Worcs (Worcester) 1997. BB 4-49 v Warwks
(Derby) 1997. **SL:** HS 77* and BB 2-28 v Yorks (Derby) 1997.

CORK, Dominic Gerald (St Joseph's C, Stoke-on-Trent), b Newcastle-under-Lyme,
Staffs 7 Aug 1971. 6'2". RHB, RFM. Debut 1990; cap 1993; captain 1998. *Wisden* 1995.
Staffordshire 1989-90. **Tests:** 19 (1995 to 1996-97); HS 59 v NZ (Auckland) 1996-97; BB
7-43 v WI (Lord's) 1995 – on debut (record England analysis by Test match debutant);
hat-trick v WI (Manchester) 1995 – the first in Test history to occur in the opening over of
a day's play. **LOI:** 25 (1992 to 1996-97; HS 31*; BB 5-27). Tours: A 1992-93 (Eng A);
SA 1993-94 (Eng A), 1995-96; WI 1991-92 (Eng A); NZ 1996-97; I 1994-95 (Eng A). HS
104 v Glos (Cheltenham) 1993. 50 wkts (3); most – 90 (1995). BB 9-43 (13-93 match) v
Northants (Derby) 1995. Took 8-53 before lunch on his 20th birthday v Essex (Derby)
1991. 2 hat-tricks: 1994 and 1995 (*see Tests*). Awards: NWT 2; BHC 3. **NWT:** HS 62 v
Kent (Derby) 1994. BB 5-18 v Berks (Derby) 1992. **BHC:** HS 92* v Lancs (Lord's)
1993. BB 5-49 v Lancs (Chesterfield) 1996. **SL:** HS 66 v Sussex (Eastbourne) 1994. BB
6-21 v Glam (Chesterfield) 1997.

DEAN, Kevin James (Leek HS; Leek C), b Derby 16 Oct 1975. 6'5". LHB, LMF. Debut 1996. HS 21* v A (Derby) 1997. BAC HS 16 v Glos (Cheltenham) 1997. BB 4-39 v CU (Cambridge) 1997. BAC BB 3-21 v Surrey (Derby) 1997. **NWT:** HS 0*. BB 3-52 v Staffs (Stone) 1996. **BHC:** HS 6. BB 1-16. **SL:** HS 8*. BB 5-32 v Glos (Derby) 1996.

DeFREITAS, Phillip Anthony Jason (Willesden HS, London), b Scotts Head, Dominica 18 Feb 1966. 6'0". RHB, RFM. UK resident since 1976. Leicestershire 1985-88; cap 1986. Lancashire 1989-93; cap 1989. Boland 1993-94 and 1995-96. Derbyshire debut/cap 1994; captain 1997 (part). *Wisden* 1991. MCC YC. **Tests:** 44 (1986-87 to 1995-96); HS 88 v A (Adelaide) 1994-95; BB 7-70 v SL (Lord's) 1991. **LOI:** 103 (1986-87 to 1997; HS 67; BB 4-35). Tours: A 1986-87, 1990-91, 1994-95; WI 1989-90; NZ 1987-88, 1991-92; P 1987-88; I 1992-93; Z 1988-89 (La). HS 113 Le v Notts (Worksop) 1988. De HS 108 v Leics (Derby) 1994. 50 wkts (10); most – 94 (1986). BB 7-21 La v Middx (Lord's) 1989. De BB 7-64 v Kent (Canterbury) 1997. Hat-trick 1994. Awards: NWT 5; BHC 4. **NWT:** HS 69 Le v Lancs (Leicester) 1986. BB 5-13 La v Cumberland (Kendal) 1989. **BHC:** HS 75* La v Hants (Manchester) 1990. BB 5-16 La v Essex (Chelmsford) 1992. **SL:** HS 72* v Kent (Derby) 1996. BB 5-26 La v Hants (Southampton) 1993.

GRIFFITHS, Steven Paul (Beechen Cliff S, Bath; Brunel C of Art & Technology, Bristol), b Hereford 31 May 1973. RHB, WK. 5'11". Debut 1995. HS 20 v Surrey (Derby) 1995. **SL:** HS –.

HARRIS, Andrew James (Hadfield CS; Glossopdale Community C), b Ashton-under-Lyne, Lancs 26 Jun 1973. 6'1". RHB, RM. Debut 1994; cap 1996. Tour: A 1996-97 (Eng A). HS 36 v Worcs (Worcester) 1997. BB 6-40 (12-83 match) v Middx (Derby) 1996. 50 wkts (1): 72 (1996). **NWT:** HS 11* and BB 3-58 v Kent (Derby) 1996. **BHC:** HS 5. BB 3-41 v Warwks (Derby) 1997. **SL:** HS 10* v Lancs (Derby) 1997. BB 4-22 v Yorks (Derby) 1997.

KRIKKEN, Karl Matthew (Rivington & Blackrod HS & SFC), b Bolton, Lancs 9 Apr 1969. Son of B.E. (Lancs and Worcs 1966-69). 5'9". RHB, WK. GW 1988-89. Derbyshire debut 1989; cap 1992. HS 104 v Lancs (Manchester) 1996. **NWT:** HS 55 v Kent (Derby) 1996. **BHC:** HS 42* v Lancs (Manchester) 1997. **SL:** HS 44* v Essex (Chelmsford) 1991.

LACEY, Simon James (Aldercar CS; Ripley Mill Hill SFC), b Nottingham 9 Mar 1975. 5'11". RHB, OB. Debut 1997. HS 50 v Somerset (Derby) 1997. BB 3-97 v Essex (Southend) 1997. **SL:** HS 9. BB 1-38.

MAY, Michael Robert (The Bolsover S; NE Derbyshire CFE), b Chesterfield 22 Jul 1971. 5'9". RHB, OB. Debut 1996. HS 116 v Glam (Chesterfield) 1997. **NWT:** HS 5.

ROBERTS, Glenn Martin (King James's HS and Greenhead C, Huddersfield; Leeds Met U), b Huddersfield, Yorks 4 Nov 1973. 5'11". LHB, SLA. Debut 1996. HS 52 and BB 1-55 v Somerset (Taunton) 1996 – on debut. **BHC:** HS 12 v Warwks (Derby) 1997. BB 3-45 v Lancs (Manchester) 1997. **SL:** HS 9. BB 2-28 v Worcs (Chesterfield) 1996.

ROLLINS, Adrian Stewart (Little Ilford CS), b Barking, Essex 8 Feb 1972. Brother of R.J. (*see* **ESSEX**). 6'5". RHB, WK, occ RM. Debut 1993; cap 1995. 1000 runs (3); most – 1142 (1997). HS 200* v Glos (Bristol) 1995. BB 1-19. **NWT:** HS 56 v Sussex (Hove) 1995. **BHC:** HS 70 v Lancs (Derby) 1994. **SL:** HS 126* v Surrey (Derby) 1995.

SMITH, Trevor Mark (Friesland S, Sandiacre; Broxtowe C, Chilwell), b Derby 18 Jan 1977. 6'3". LHB, RFM. Debut 1997. HS – and BB 1-27 v Yorks (Derby) 1997.

SPENDLOVE, Benjamin Lee (Trent C), b Belper 4 Nov 1978. 6'1". RHB, OB. Debut 1997. HS 15* v Yorks (Derby) 1997. **SL:** HS 4.

STUBBINGS, Stephen David (Frankston HS; Swinburne U), b Huddersfield, Yorks 31 Mar 1978. 6'3". LHB, OB. Debut 1997. HS 22 v Worcs (Worcester) 1997.

TWEATS, Timothy Andrew (Endon HS; Stoke-on-Trent SFC), b Stoke-on-Trent, Staffs 18 Apr 1974. 6'3". RHB, RM. Debut 1992. HS 189 v Yorks (Derby) 1997. BB 1-23. **NWT:** HS 16 v Warwks (Derby) 1995. **BHC:** HS 10 v Lancs (Chesterfield) 1996. **SL:** HS 19 v Glam (Derby) 1995 and v Worcs (Worcester) 1997.

NEWCOMER

SLATER, Michael Jonathon (Wagga Wagga HS), b Wagga Wagga, NSW, Australia 21 Feb 1970. 5'9". RHB, RM. NSW 1991-92 to date. **Tests** (A): 34 (1993 to 1996-97); HS 219 v SL (Perth) 1995-96; BB 1-4. **LOI** (A): 42 (1993-94 to 1997; HS 73). Tours (A): E 1993, 1995 (NSW), 1997; SA 1993-94; WI 1994-95; I 1996-97; P 1994-95. 1000 runs (1+3); most – 1472 (1994-95). HS 219 (see Tests). UK HS 152 A v E (Lord's) 1993. BB 1-4 (see Tests).

DEPARTURES (who made first-class appearances in 1997)

ADAMS, C.J. – see SUSSEX.

HAYHURST, Andrew Neil (Worsley Wardley HS; Eccles SFC; Leeds Poly), b Davy-hulme, Manchester 23 Nov 1962. 5'11". RHB, RM. Lancashire 1985-89. Somerset 1990-96; cap 1990; captain 1994-96. Derbyshire 1997. Tours: WI 1986-87 (La); Z 1988-89 (La). 1000 runs (3); most – 1559 (1990). HS 172* Sm v Glos (Bath) 1991. De HS 6. BB 4-27 La v Middx (Manchester) 1987. De BB 1-12. Awards: NWT 2; BHC 2. **NWT:** HS 91* and BB 5-60 v Warwks (Birmingham) 1991. **BHC:** HS 95 v Notts (Nottingham) 1992. **SL:** HS 84 La v Leics (Manchester) 1988. BB 4-37 La v Glam (Pontypridd) 1988 and Sm v Sussex (Hove) 1990. Appointed Derbyshire's Director of Cricket.

JONES, Dean Mervyn (Mount Waverley HS), b Coburg, Victoria, Australia 24 Mar 1961. 6'1". RHB, OB. Victoria 1981-82 to date; captain 1993-94 to 1995-96. Durham 1992; cap 1992. Derbyshire 1996-97; cap 1996; captain 1996-97. *Wisden* 1989. **Tests** (A): 52 (1983-84 to 1992-93); HS 216 v WI (Adelaide) 1988-89; BB 1-5. **LOI** (A): 164 (1983-84 to 1993-94); HS 145; BB 2-34). Tours (A): E 1987 (RW), 1989, 1991 (Vic); WI 1983-84, 1990-91; NZ 1989-90; I 1986-87; P 1988-89; SL 1992-93; Z 1985-86 (Young A). 1000 runs (3+5); most – 1510 (1989). HS 324* Victoria v S Australia (Melbourne) 1994-95. De/BAC HS 214* v Yorks (Sheffield) 1996. BB 5-112 v Hants (Southampton) 1996. Award: BHC 1. **NWT:** HS 100* v Lancs (Manchester) 1996. BB 2-0 v Staffs (Stone) 1996. **BHC:** HS 142 v Minor C (Derby) 1996. BB 2-34 Du v Comb Us (Cambridge) 1992. **SL:** HS 118 v Middx (Derby) 1996. BB 2-15 v Northants (Northampton) 1996.

KHAN, Gul Abbass (Valentine S, Ilford; Ipswich S; Swansea U; Keble C, Oxford), b Gujrat, Pakistan 31 Dec 1973. 5'8". RHB, LBG. Essex staff 1993-95. Debut (Oxford U) 1996, scoring 94 v Leics (Oxford); blue 1996. Derbyshire 1996-97. HS 101* OU v Kent (Canterbury) 1996. De HS 62* v Surrey (Derby) 1997. BB 2-48 OU v Hants (Oxford) 1996. **NWT:** HS 19 v Northants (Derby) 1997. **BHC** (Brit Us): HS 147 v Glam (Cambridge) 1996. **SL:** HS 71* v Kent (Canterbury) 1997.

MALCOLM, D.E. – see NORTHAMPTONSHIRE.

OWEN, John Edward Houghton (Spondon S, Derby), b Derby 7 Aug 1971. 5'10". RHB, occ OB. Derbyshire 1995-97. HS 105 v Glam (Cardiff) 1996. **NWT:** HS 7. **BHC:** HS 49 v Warwks (Birmingham) 1996. **SL:** HS 45 v Surrey (Derby) 1995.

VANDRAU, Matthew James (St Stithian's C, Johannesburg; St John's C, Jo'burg; Witwatersrand U), b Epsom, Surrey 22 Jul 1969. Son of B.M. (Transvaal B 1963). 6'3½". RHB, OB. Transvaal/Transvaal B 1990-91 to date. Derbyshire 1993-97. HS 66 v Kent (Derby) 1994. BB 6-34 v Hants (Southampton) 1996. **NWT:** HS 27 v Kent (Derby) 1994. BB 2-36 v Durham (Darlington) 1994. **BHC:** HS 12* v Lancs (Chesterfield) 1996. BB 1-46. **SL:** HS 32* v Kent (Canterbury) 1993. BB 3-25 v Leics (Derby) 1994.

DERBYSHIRE 1997

RESULTS SUMMARY

	Place	Won	Lost	Tied	Drew	No Result
Britannic Assurance Championship	16th	2	9	–	6	–
All First-Class Matches		5	9	–	6	–
NatWest Trophy	Quarter-Finalist					
Benson and Hedges Cup	3rd in Group A					
Sunday League	14th	4	9	–	–	4

BRITANNIC ASSURANCE CHAMPIONSHIP AVERAGES

BATTING AND FIELDING

Cap		M	I	NO	HS	Runs	Avge	100	50	Ct/St
–	T.A.Tweats	7	13	2	189	590	53.63	1	1	7
1982	K.J.Barnett	15	24	3	210*	1055	50.23	3	5	3
1995	A.S.Rollins	14	24	3	210	854	40.66	3	2	10
1996	D.M.Jones	5	9	1	99*	312	39.00	–	3	6
–	V.P.Clarke	16	25	5	99	728	36.40	–	4	8
–	M.E.Cassar	7	8	1	78	227	32.42	–	2	2
–	M.R.May	7	13	1	116	383	31.91	1	2	2
–	S.J.Lacey	5	7	3	50	126	31.50	–	1	1
1992	C.J.Adams	12	21	1	108	611	30.55	2	2	14
–	M.J.Vandrau	4	7	1	54	168	28.00	–	1	4
–	P.Aldred	6	5	1	83	111	27.75	–	1	4
1993	D.G.Cork	6	9	1	55*	192	24.00	–	2	4
1992	K.M.Krikken	17	24	3	72	492	23.42	–	3	51/2
1994	P.A.J.DeFreitas	16	20	1	96	417	21.94	–	2	4
–	J.E.H.Owen	4	6	–	22	83	13.83	–	–	3
1996	A.J.Harris	16	22	3	36	140	7.36	–	–	9
–	K.J.Dean	7	9	3	16	41	6.83	–	–	1
1989	D.E.Malcolm	13	18	8	21*	61	6.10	–	–	–

Also played: I.D.Blackwell (3 matches) 2, 42, 2; A.N.Hayhurst (1) 6 (1 ct); G.A.Khan (2) 62*, 4, 11; G.M.Roberts (1) 2, 13; T.M.Smith (1) did not bat (1 ct); B.L.Spendlove (1) 15* (1 ct); S.D.Stubbings (1) 5, 22.

BOWLING

	O	M	R	W	Avge	Best	5wI	10wM
D.E.Malcolm	373.3	52	1262	60	21.03	6-23	5	2
P.Aldred	123	38	291	10	29.10	3-28	–	–
P.A.J.DeFreitas	486.1	104	1574	54	29.14	7-64	5	2
K.J.Dean	158.4	32	541	14	38.64	3-21	–	–
D.G.Cork	132	28	457	11	41.54	4-48	–	–
A.J.Harris	434.3	89	1531	33	46.39	3-66	–	–

Also bowled: C.J.Adams 2.5-0-16-0; I.D.Blackwell 28-8-121-1; M.E.Cassar 52.1-6-224-8; V.P.Clarke 171.4-35-668-7; D.M.Jones 2-2-0-0; S.J.Lacey 94-19-291-7; M.R.May 4.1-0-50-0; G.M.Roberts 6-1-8-0; A.S.Rollins 1-0-9-0; T.M.Smith 18-6-51-1; M.J.Vandrau 44-6-182-4.

The First-Class Averages (pp 118-133) give the records of Derbyshire players in all first-class county matches (their other opponents being the Australians, Pakistan A and Cambridge University), with the exception of:

C.J.Adams 14-24-1-108-732-31.82-2-3-17ct. 2.5-0-16-0.
A.J.Harris 17-24-4-36-171-8.55-0-0-9ct. 468.3-94-1650-35-47.14-3/66.
D.E.Malcolm 15-19-8-21*-80-7.27-0-0-0ct. 433.1-62-1454-69-21.07-6/23-5-2.

DERBYSHIRE RECORDS

FIRST-CLASS CRICKET

Highest Total	For 645		v	Hampshire	Derby	1898
	V 662		by	Yorkshire	Chesterfield	1898
Lowest Total	For 16		v	Notts	Nottingham	1879
	V 23		by	Hampshire	Burton upon T	1958
Highest Innings	For 274	G.A.Davidson	v	Lancashire	Manchester	1896
	V 343*	P.A.Perrin	for	Essex	Chesterfield	1904

Highest Partnership for each Wicket

1st	322	H.Storer/J.Bowden	v	Essex	Derby	1929
2nd	417	K.J.Barnett/T.A.Tweats	v	Yorkshire	Derby	1997
3rd	316*	A.S.Rollins/K.J.Barnett	v	Leics	Leicester	1997
4th	328	P.Vaulkhard/D.Smith	v	Notts	Nottingham	1946
5th	302*†	J.E.Morris/D.G.Cork	v	Glos	Cheltenham	1993
6th	212	G.M.Lee/T.S.Worthington	v	Essex	Chesterfield	1932
7th	241*	G.H.Pope/A.E.G.Rhodes	v	Hampshire	Portsmouth	1948
8th	198	K.M.Krikken/D.G.Cork	v	Lancashire	Manchester	1996
9th	283	A.Warren/J.Chapman	v	Warwicks	Blackwell	1910
10th	132	A.Hill/M.Jean-Jacques	v	Yorkshire	Sheffield	1986

† 346 runs were added for this wicket in two separate partnerships

Best Bowling	For 10- 40	W.Bestwick	v	Glamorgan	Cardiff	1921
(Innings)	V 10- 45	R.L.Johnson	for	Middlesex	Derby	1994
Best Bowling	For 17-103	W.Mycroft	v	Hampshire	Southampton	1876
(Match)	V 16-101	G.Giffen	for	Australians	Derby	1886

Most Runs – Season	2165	D.B.Carr	(av 48.11)	1959
Most Runs – Career	22625	K.J.Barnett	(av 40.83)	1979-97
Most 100s – Season	8	P.N.Kirsten		1982
Most 100s – Career	52	K.J.Barnett		1979-97
Most Wkts – Season	168	T.B.Mitchell	(av 19.55)	1935
Most Wkts – Career	1670	H.L.Jackson	(av 17.11)	1947-63

LIMITED-OVERS CRICKET

Highest Total	NWT	365-3	v	Cornwall	Derby	1986
	BHC	366-4	v	Comb Us	Oxford	1991
	SL	292-9	v	Worcs	Knypersley	1985
Lowest Total	NWT	79	v	Surrey	The Oval	1967
	BHC	80	v	Worcs	Derby	1994
	SL	61	v	Hampshire	Portsmouth	1990
Highest Innings	NWT 153	A.Hill	v	Cornwall	Derby	1986
	BHC 142	D.M.Jones	v	Minor C	Derby	1996
	SL 141*	C.J.Adams	v	Kent	Chesterfield	1992
Best Bowling	NWT 8-21	M.A.Holding	v	Sussex	Hove	1988
	BHC 6-33	E.J.Barlow	v	Glos	Bristol	1978
	SL 6- 7	M.Hendrick	v	Notts	Nottingham	1972

DURHAM

Formation of Present Club: 10 May 1882
Colours: Navy blue, yellow and maroon
Badge: Coat of Arms of the County of Durham
Championships: (0) 16th 1994
NatWest Trophy/Gillette Cup Winners: (0) Quarter-Finalist 1992
Benson and Hedges Cup Winners: (0) Second Round 1994
Sunday League Champions: (0) Seventh 1993
Match Awards: NWT 19; BHC 9.

Chief Executive: M.Candlish
County Ground, Riverside, Chester-le-Street, Co Durham DH3 3QR
(Tel 0191 387 1717)
Captain/Overseas Player: D.C.Boon. **Vice-Captain:** J.E.Morris.
1998 Beneficiary (testimonial): T.Flintoft (head groundsman). **Scorer:** B.Hunt

BETTS, Melvyn Morris (Fyndoune CS, Sacriston), b Sacriston 26 Mar 1975. 5'10". RHB, RMF. Debut 1993; cap 1994. HS 57* v Sussex (Hove) 1996. BB 9-64 (Durham record; 13-143 match) v Northants (Northampton) 1997. **NWT:** HS 11 v Essex (Chelmsford) 1996. BB 3-33 v Scot (Chester-le-St) 1996. **BHC:** HS 5*. BB 2-36 v Minor C (Chester-le-St) 1996. **SL:** HS 21 v Hants (Chester-le-St) 1997. BB 3-22 v Derbys (Chester-le-St) 1997.

BOILING, James (Rutlish S, Merton; Durham U), b New Delhi, India 8 Apr 1968. 6'4". RHB, OB. Surrey 1988-94. Durham debut/cap 1995. Tour: A 1992-93 (Eng A). HS 69 v WI (Chester-le-St) 1995. BAC HS 62 v Derbys (Chester-le-St) 1997. BB 6-84 (10-203 match) Sy v Glos (Bristol) 1992. Du BB 5-73 v Notts (Chester-le-St) 1995. Award: BHC 1. **NWT:** HS 46* v Essex (Chelmsford) 1996. BB 4-22 v Herefords (Chester-le-St) 1995. **BHC:** HS 15 v Derbys (Chesterfield) 1996. BB 3-9 Comb Us v Surrey (Cambridge) 1989. **SL:** HS 27 v Warwks (Birmingham) 1996. BB 5-24 Sy v Hants (Basingstoke) 1992.

BOON, David Clarence (Launceston GS), b Launceston, Australia 29 Dec 1960. 5'7½". RHB, OB. Tasmania 1978-79 to date; captain 1992-93 to date. Durham debut/cap 1997; captain 1997 to date. MBE. **Tests** (A): 107, inc 60 in succession (1984-85 to 1995-96); HS 200 v NZ (Perth) 1989-90. **LOI** (A): 181 (1983-84 to 1994-95; HS 122). Tours: E 1985, 1989, 1993; SA 1993-94; WI 1990-91, 1994-95; NZ 1985-86, 1989-90, 1992-93; I 1986-87; P 1988-89, 1994-95; SL 1992-93; Z 1995-96 (Tas – captain). 1000 runs (3+7); most – 1437 (1993). HS 227 Tasmania v Victoria (Melbourne) 1983-84. Du HS 117 v Northants (Northampton) 1997. BB 2-18 v Kent (Darlington) 1997. **NWT:** HS 57 v Surrey (Oval) 1997. **BHC:** HS 103 v Northants (Chester-le-St) 1997. **SL:** HS 76 v Sussex (Chester-le-St) 1997.

BROWN, Simon John Emmerson (Boldon CS), b Cleadon 29 Jun 1969. 6'3". RHB, LFM. Northamptonshire 1987-90. Durham debut/cap 1992; captain 1996 (part). **Tests:** 1 (1996); HS 10* and BB 1-60 v P (Lord's) 1996. HS 69 v Leics (Durham) 1994. 50 wkts (5); most – 79 (1996). BB 7-70 v A (Durham) 1993. BAC BB 7-105 v Kent (Canterbury) 1992. Awards: NWT 1; BHC 1. **NWT:** HS 7*. BB 5-22 v Cheshire (Bowdon) 1994. **BHC:** HS 12 v Warwks (Birmingham) 1995. BB 6-30 v Northants (Chester-le-St) 1997. **SL:** HS 18 v Derbys (Derby) 1996. BB 4-20 v Yorks (Leeds) 1995.

CAMPBELL, Colin Lockey (Blaydon CS & SFC), b Newcastle-upon-Tyne, Northumb 11 Aug 1977. 6'6". RHB, RFM. Debut/cap 1996. HS 7. BB 1-29. **SL:** HS 0. BB 2-45 v Glos (Chester-le-St) 1996.

COLLINGWOOD, Paul David (Blackfyne CS; Derwentside C), b Shotley Bridge 26 May 1976. 5'11". RHB, RMF. Debut 1996 v Northants (Chester-le-St) taking wicket of D.J.Capel with his first ball before scoring 91 and 16. Cap 1996. HS 107 v OU (Oxford) 1997. BAC HS 91 v Northants (Chester-le-St) 1996 (on debut). BB 3-46 v Lancs (Manchester) 1997. **NWT:** HS 28 v Essex (Chelmsford) 1996. **BHC:** HS 49 v Notts (Nottingham) 1997. BB 3-38 v Minor C (Chester-le-St) 1996. **SL:** HS 61* v Kent (Maidstone) 1996. BB 1-2.

COX, David Mathew (Greenford HS), b Southall, Middx 2 Mar 1972. 5'10". LHB, SLA. Staff/cap 1993; debut 1994. Hertfordshire 1992. MCC YC. HS 95* v Somerset (Weston-s-M) 1996. BB 5-97 (10-236 match) v Warwks (Birmingham) 1995. **SL:** HS 7. BB 2-34 v Essex (Hartlepool) 1996.

DALEY, James Arthur (Hetton CS), b Sunderland 24 Sep 1973. 5'10". RHB, RM. Debut/cap 1992. MCC YC. HS 159* v Hants (Portsmouth) 1994. **BHC:** HS 33 v Lancs (Manchester) 1996. **SL:** HS 98* v Kent (Canterbury) 1994.

FOSTER, Michael James (New C, Pontefract), b Leeds, Yorks 17 Sep 1972. 6'1". RHB, RFM. Yorkshire 1993-94. Northamptonshire staff 1995. Durham debut/cap 1996. HS 129 v Glam (Cardiff) 1997. BB 4-21 v Middx (Lord's) 1996. **NWT:** HS 56* and BB 2-37 v Surrey (Oval) 1997. **BHC:** HS 73* v Scot (Forfar) 1997. BB 2-52 v Derbys (Chesterfield) 1996. **SL:** HS 118 Y v Leics (Leicester) 1993. BB 3-52 v Glos (Cheltenham) 1997.

HARMISON, Stephen James (Ashington HS), b Ashington, Northumb 23 Oct 1978. 6'3". RHB, RFM. Debut 1996; uncapped (not on staff). Northumberland 1996. HS 6.

HUTTON, Stewart (De Brus S, Skelton; Cleveland TC), b Stockton-on-Tees 30 Nov 1969. 6'0". LHB, RSM. Debut 1992. HS 172* v OU (Oxford) 1996. BAC HS 101 v Northants (Hartlepool) 1994. Award: NWT 1. **NWT:** HS 125 v Herefords (Chester-le-St) 1995. **BHC:** HS 36 v Derbys (Chesterfield) 1996. **SL:** HS 81 v Leics (Chester-le-St) 1996.

KILLEEN, Neil (Greencroft CS; Derwentside C; Teesside U), b Shotley Bridge 17 Oct 1975. 6'2". RHB, RFM. Debut/cap 1995. HS 48 v Somerset (Chester-le-St) 1995. BB 5-118 v Sussex (Hartlepool) 1995. **NWT:** HS –. BB 1-46. **BHC:** HS 8 and BB 2-43 Comb Us v Hants (Oxford) 1995. **SL:** HS 32 v Middx (Lord's) 1996. BB 5-26 v Northants (Hartlepool) 1995.

LEWIS, Jonathan James Benjamin (King Edward VI S, Chelmsford; Roehampton IHE), b Isleworth, Middx 21 May 1970. 5'9½". RHB, RSM. Essex 1990-96; cap 1994; scored 116* on debut v Surrey (Oval). Durham debut/cap 1997. 1000 runs (1): 1252 (1997). HS 210* v OU (Oxford) 1997 – on Du debut. BAC HS 160* v Derbys (Chester-le-St) 1997. **NWT:** HS 24* Ex v Sussex (Hove) 1994. **BHC:** HS 47 v Northants (Chester-le-St) 1997. **SL:** HS 102 v Glos (Cheltenham) 1997.

LUGSDEN, Steven (St Edmund Campion S, Low Fell), b Gateshead 10 Jul 1976. 6'2". RHB, RFM. Debut 1993 aged 17yr 27d (youngest Durham f-c player); cap 1994. HS 9. BB 3-45 v Lancs (Chester-le-St) 1996. **SL:** HS –. BB 1-55.

MORRIS, John Edward (Shavington CS; Dane Bank CFE), b Crewe, Cheshire 1 Apr 1964. 5'10". RHB, RM. Derbyshire 1982-93; cap 1986. GW 1988-89 and 1993-94. Durham debut/cap 1994. **Tests:** 3 (1990); HS 32 v I (Oval) 1990. **LOI:** 8 (1990-91; HS 63*). Tour: A 1990-91. 1000 runs (11); most – 1739 (1986). HS 229 De v Glos (Cheltenham) 1993. Du HS 204 v Warwks (Birmingham) 1994. BB 1-6. Du BB 1-37. Awards: NWT 2; BHC 2. **NWT:** HS 109 v Scot (Chester-le-St) 1996. **BHC:** HS 145 v Leics (Leicester) 1996. **SL:** HS 134 De v Somerset (Taunton) 1990.

PRATT, Andrew (Willington Parkside CS; Durham New C), b Helmington Row, Crook 4 Mar 1975. 6'0". LHB, WK. Debut 1997; cap 1996. MCC YC. HS –.

ROSEBERRY, Michael Anthony (Durham S), b Sunderland 28 Nov 1966. Elder brother of A. (Leics and Glam 1992-94). 6'1". RHB, RM. Middlesex 1986-94; cap 1990. Durham debut/cap 1995; captain 1995-96. Tour: A 1992-93 (Eng A). 1000 runs (4) inc 2000 (1): 2044 (1992). HS 185 M v Leics (Lord's) 1993. Du HS 145* v OU (Oxford) 1996. BB 1-1. Awards: NWT 1; BHC 1. **NWT:** HS 121 v Herefords (Chester-le-St) 1995. BB 1-22. **BHC:** HS 84 M v Minor C (Lord's) 1992. **SL:** HS 119* M v Surrey (Oval) 1994.

SAGGERS, Martin John (Springwood HS; King's Lynn; Huddersfield U), b King's Lynn, Norfolk 23 May 1972. 6'2". RHB, RMF. Debut/cap 1996. Norfolk 1995-96. HS 18 v Somerset (Weston-s-M) 1996. BB 6-65 v Glam (Chester-le-St) 1996. Award: BHC 1. **BHC:** (Minor C) HS 34* v Leics (Jesmond) 1996. BB 2-49 v Durham (Chester-le-St) 1996. **SL:** HS 13 v Warwks (Birmingham) 1996. BB 4-35 v Essex (Chelmsford) 1997.

SEARLE, Jason Paul (John Bentley S, Calne; Swindon C), b Bath, Somerset 16 May 1976. 5'9". RHB, OB. Staff/cap 1993; debut 1994. HS 5*. BB 2-126 v Surrey (Oval) 1995. **BHC:** HS –. **SL:** HS –.

SPEAK, Nicholas Jason (Parrs Wood HS, Manchester), b Manchester 21 Nov 1966. 6'0". RHB, RM/OB. Lancashire 1986-87 to 1996; cap 1992. Durham debut/cap 1997. Tours (La): WI 1986-87, 1995-96. 1000 runs (3); most – 1892 (1992). HS 232 La v Leics (Leicester) 1992. Du HS 124* v CU (Cambridge) 1997. BB 1-0. Award: BHC 1. **NWT:** HS 83 La v Oxon (Aston Rowant) 1996. **BHC:** HS 82 La v Hants (Manchester) 1992. **SL:** HS 102* La v Yorks (Leeds) 1992.

SPEIGHT, Martin Peter (Hurstpierpoint C; Durham U), b Walsall, Staffs 24 Oct 1967. 5'9". RHB, WK. Sussex 1986-96; cap 1991. Wellington 1989-90 to 1992-93. Durham debut/cap 1997. 1000 runs (3); most – 1375 (1990). HS 184 Sx v Notts (Eastbourne) 1993. Du HS 73* v Kent (Darlington) 1997. BB 1-2. Awards: BHC 2. **NWT:** HS 50 Sx v Warwks (Lord's) 1993. **BHC:** HS 83 Comb Us v Glos (Bristol) 1988. **SL:** HS 126 Sx v Somerset (Taunton) 1993.

SYMINGTON, Marc Joseph (St Michaels, Billingham; Stockton SFC), b Newcastle upon Tyne, Northumb 10 Jan 1980. 5'8". RHB, RM. Durham Academy (uncapped). Awaiting f-c debut. **SL:** HS 7. BB 1-51.

WALKER, Alan (Shelley HS), b Emley, Yorks 7 Jul 1962. 5'11". LHB, RFM. Northamptonshire 1983-93; cap 1987. Durham debut/cap 1994. Tour: SA 1991-92 (Nh). HS 41* Nh v Warwks (Birmingham) 1987. Du HS 29 v WI (Chester-le-St) 1995. 50 wkts (1): 54 (1988). BB 8-118 (14-177 match) v Essex (Chelmsford) 1995. Award: NWT 1. **NWT:** HS 13 v Derbys (Darlington) 1994. BB 4-7 Nh v Ire (Northampton) 1987. **BHC:** HS 15* Nh v Notts (Nottingham) 1987. BB 4-42 v Minor C (Jesmond) 1995. **SL:** HS 30 Nh v Durham (Northampton) 1993. BB 4-18 v Kent (Darlington) 1997.

WOOD, John (Crofton HS; Wakefield District C; Leeds Poly), b Crofton, Yorks 22 Jul 1970. 6'3". RHB, RFM. GW in Nissan Shield 1990-91. Debut/cap 1992. HS 63* v Notts (Chester-le-St) 1993. BB 6-110 v Essex (Stockton) 1994. **NWT:** HS 1. BB 2-22 v Ireland (Dublin) 1992. **BHC:** HS 27 v Leics (Stockton) 1995. BB 3-50 v Warwicks (Birmingham) 1995. **SL:** HS 28 v Worcs (Worcester) 1994. BB 4-17 v Kent (Darlington) 1997.

NEWCOMERS

GOUGH, Michael Andrew (English Martyrs CS, Hartlepool), b Hartlepool 18 Dec 1979. Son of M.P. (Durham 1974-77). RHB, OB.

GRAHAM, John Alexander (Seaton Burn HS), b Newcastle upon Tyne, Northumb 4 Mar 1978. RHB, RM.

DEPARTURE (who made first-class appearances in 1997)

WESTON, Robin Michael Swann (Durham S; Loughborough U), b Durham 7 Jun 1975. Brother of W.P.C. (*see WORCESTERSHIRE*). 5'10". RHB, LB. Durham 1995-97; cap 1994. Minor C debut 1991 when aged 15yr 355d (Durham record). HS 36 v Middx (Chester-le-St) 1997. BB 1-41. **SL:** HS 13 v Warwks (Birmingham) 1996 and v Glos (Cheltenham) 1997.

DURHAM 1997

RESULTS SUMMARY

	Place	Won	Lost	Tied	Drew	No Result
Britannic Assurance Championship	17th	2	8	–	6	1
All First-Class Matches		3	8	–	7	1
NatWest Trophy	1st Round					
Benson and Hedges Cup	3rd in Group B					
Sunday League	17th	3	13	–	–	1

BRITANNIC ASSURANCE CHAMPIONSHIP AVERAGES

BATTING AND FIELDING

Cap		M	I	NO	HS	Runs	Avge	100	50	Ct/St
1997	J.J.B.Lewis	16	29	3	160*	1034	39.76	2	5	10
1997	D.C.Boon	16	28	2	117	981	37.73	2	7	18
1994	J.E.Morris	16	28	1	149	972	36.00	2	4	6
1996	M.J.Foster	14	24	–	129	575	23.95	1	3	2
1997	M.P.Speight	16	27	2	73*	543	21.72	–	3	50
1992	S.Hutton	7	13	1	95	258	21.50	–	1	1
1992	J.Wood	5	8	4	21*	72	18.00	–	–	4
1994	R.M.S.Weston	5	8	–	36	137	17.12	–	–	5
1996	P.D.Collingwood	6	10	–	62	169	16.90	–	1	7
1997	N.J.Speak	10	18	1	93	274	16.11	–	1	6
1995	J.Boiling	15	26	4	62	334	15.18	–	1	13
1995	M.A.Roseberry	3	6	–	45	69	11.50	–	–	3
1994	M.M.Betts	11	18	–	35	201	11.16	–	–	1
1994	A.Walker	12	20	8	16	92	7.66	–	–	–
1996	M.J.Saggers	2	4	2	10*	14	7.00	–	–	2
1992	S.J.E.Brown	15	24	5	30	121	6.36	–	–	2

Also played: C.L.Campbell (cap 1996)(1 match) did not bat; D.M.Cox (cap 1993)(2)
24, 0, 22 (1 ct); J.A.Daley (cap 1992)(1) 7, 39 (1 ct); N.Killeen (cap 1995)(2) 9*, 15, 0*
(1 ct); S.Lugsden (cap 1994)(1) 4, 0*.
Note: Durham award caps on signature of contract and not on merit

BOWLING

	O	M	R	W	Avge	Best	5wI	10wM
M.M.Betts	276.3	63	939	43	21.83	9-64	2	1
S.J.E.Brown	513.4	103	1667	57	29.24	5-58	4	1
A.Walker	341.1	87	1063	33	32.21	7-56	2	–
M.J.Foster	275.4	55	1027	30	34.23	4-58	–	–
J.Wood	102	13	476	11	43.27	4-73	–	–
J.Boiling	280.5	76	849	17	49.94	3-72	–	–

Also bowled: D.C.Boon 12.2-3-39-2; C.L.Campbell 12-0-92-1; P.D.Collingwood
42-4-177-5; D.M.Cox 44.3-8-132-4; N.Killeen 44-9-139-6; S.Lugsden 16.5-2-88-1;
J.E.Morris 1-0-1-0; M.J.Saggers 58-13-160-7; R.M.S.Weston 1-0-5-0.

The First-Class Averages (pp 118-133) give the records of Durham players in all
first-class county matches (their other opponents being Cambridge University and Oxford
University), with the exception of:
S.J.E.Brown 16-24-5-30-121-6.36-0-0-2ct. 550.4-117-1735-63-27.53-5/58-4-1.
J.J.B.Lewis 17-30-4-210*-1244-47.84-3-5-10ct. Did not bowl.

DURHAM RECORDS

FIRST-CLASS CRICKET

Highest Total	For	625-6d	v	Derbyshire	Chesterfield	1994
	V	810-4d	by	Warwicks	Birmingham	1994
Lowest Total	For	67	v	Middlesex	Lord's	1996
	V	73	by	Oxford U	Oxford	1994
Highest Innings	For	210* J.J.B.Lewis	v	Oxford U	Oxford	1997
	V	501* B.C.Lara	for	Warwicks	Birmingham	1994

Highest Partnership for each Wicket

1st	334*	S.Hutton/M.A.Roseberry	v	Oxford U	Oxford	1996
2nd	206	W.Larkins/D.M.Jones	v	Glamorgan	Cardiff	1992
3rd	205	G.Fowler/S.Hutton	v	Yorkshire	Leeds	1993
4th	204	J.J.B.Lewis/J.Boiling	v	Derbyshire	Chester-le-St[2]	1997
5th	185	P.W.G.Parker/J.A.Daley	v	Warwicks	Darlington	1993
6th	152	I.T.Botham/A.C.Cummins	v	Worcs	Stockton	1993
7th	106	I.Smith/D.A.Graveney	v	Somerset	Taunton	1992
8th	134	A.C.Cummins/D.A.Graveney	v	Warwicks	Birmingham	1994
9th	127	D.G.C.Ligertwood/S.J.E.Brown	v	Surrey	Stockton	1996
10th	103	M.M.Betts/D.M.Cox	v	Sussex	Hove	1996

Best Bowling	For	9- 64	M.M.Betts	v	Northants	Northampton	1997
(Innings)	V	8- 22	D.Follett	for	Middlesex	Lord's	1996
Best Bowling	For	14-177	A.Walker	v	Essex	Chelmsford	1995
(Match)	V	12- 68	J.N.B.Bovill	for	Hampshire	Stockton	1995

Most Runs – Season	1536	W.Larkins	(av 37.46)	1992
Most Runs – Career	4278†	W.Larkins	(av 37.52)	1992-95
Most 100s – Season	4	D.M.Jones		1992
	4	W.Larkins		1992
	4	J.E.Morris		1994
Most 100s – Career	10†	W.Larkins		1992-95
Most Wkts – Season	77	S.J.E.Brown	(av 25.87)	1996
Most Wkts – Career	376	S.J.E.Brown	(av 30.73)	1992-97

† J.E.Morris (1994-97) has scored 4111 runs with 9 hundreds

LIMITED-OVERS CRICKET

Highest Total	NWT	326-4		v	Herefords	Chester-le-St[2]	1995
	BHC	287-5		v	Leics	Leicester	1996
	SL	281-2		v	Derbyshire	Durham	1993
Lowest Total	NWT	82		v	Worcs	Chester-le-St[1]	1968
	BHC	162		v	Derbyshire	Chesterfield	1996
	SL	99		v	Warwicks	Birmingham	1996
Highest Innings	NWT	125	S.Hutton	v	Herefords	Chester-le-St[2]	1995
	BHC	145	J.E.Morris	v	Leics	Leicester	1996
	SL	131*	W.Larkins	v	Hampshire	Portsmouth	1994
Best Bowling	NWT	7-32	S.P.Davis	v	Lancashire	Chester-le-St[1]	1983
	BHC	6-30	S.J.E.Brown	v	Northants	Chester-le-St[2]	1997
	SL	5-26	N.Killeen	v	Northants	Northampton	1995

[1] Chester-le-Street CC (Ropery Lane)   [2] Riverside Ground

ESSEX

Formation of Present Club: 14 January 1876
Colours: Blue, Gold and Red
Badge: Three Seaxes above Scroll bearing 'Essex'
Championships: (6) 1979, 1983, 1984, 1986, 1991, 1992
NatWest Trophy/Gillette Cup Winners: (2) 1985, 1997
Benson and Hedges Cup Winners: (1) 1979
Sunday League Champions: (3) 1981, 1984, 1985
Match Awards: NWT 46; BHC 79

Secretary/General Manager: P.J.Edwards
   County Ground, New Writtle Street, Chelmsford CM2 0PG (Tel 01245 252420)
Captain: P.J.Prichard. **Vice-Captain:** N.Hussain. **Overseas Player:** S.G.Law.
1998 Beneficiary: Essex CCC Benefit Association Fund. **Scorer:** C.F.Driver

COUSINS, Darren Mark (Netherhall CS; Impington Village C), b Cambridge 24 Sep 1971. 6'2". RHB, RMF. Debut 1993. Cambridgeshire 1990. HS 18* v Durham (Chelmsford) 1995. BB 6-35 v CU (Cambridge) 1994. BAC BB 3-73 v Leics (Chelmsford) 1995. **NWT:** HS 1*. BB 1-33. **BHC:** HS 12* v Glam (Chelmsford) 1995. BB 1-33. **SL:** HS 6. BB 3-18 v Warwks (Birmingham) 1994.

COWAN, Ashley Preston (Framlingham C), b Hitchin, Herts 7 May 1975. 6'4". RHB, RFM. Debut 1995; cap 1997. Cambridgeshire 1993. HS 77 v Middx (Chelmsford) 1997. 50 wkts (1): 52 (1997). BB 5-45 v Sussex (Hove) 1997. Hat-trick 1996. **NWT:** HS 17 v Notts (Nottingham) 1997. BB 3-29 v Warwks (Lord's) 1997. **BHC:** HS 8. BB 2-35 v Middx (Lord's) 1997. **SL:** HS 22* v Warwks (Birmingham) 1996. BB 4-31 v Middx (Chelmsford) 1997.

FLANAGAN, Ian Nicholas (Colne Community S), b Colchester 5 Jun 1980. 6'0". LHB, OB. Debut 1997. HS 40 v Lancs (Manchester) 1997.

GRAYSON, Adrian Paul (Bedale CS), b Ripon, Yorks 31 Mar 1971. 6'1". RHB, SLA. Yorkshire 1990-95. Essex debut/cap 1996. Tour: SA 1991-92 (Y). 1000 runs (2); most – 1046 (1994). HS 140 v Middx (Lord's) 1996. BB 4-53 v Northants (Northampton) 1997. **NWT:** HS 82* v Worcs (Chelmsford) 1997. BB 3-24 v Lancs (Lord's) 1996. **BHC:** HS 49* v Surrey (Chelmsford) 1997. BB 3-30 v Kent (Chelmsford) 1996. **SL:** HS 69* v Northants (Northampton) 1997. BB 4-25 Y v Glam (Cardiff) 1994.

GROVE, Jamie Oliver (Bury St Edmunds County Upper S), b Bury St Edmunds, Suffolk 3 Jul 1979. 6'1". RHB, RFM. Staff 1996 – awaiting f-c debut.

HIBBERT, Andrew James Edward (St Edward's CS and SFC, Romford), b Harold Wood 17 Dec 1974. 5'11½". RHB, RM. Debut 1995. Awaiting BAC debut. HS 85 v CU (Cambridge) 1996. **SL:** HS 25 v Glos (Colchester) 1996.

HODGSON, Timothy Philip (Wellington C; Durham U), b Guildford, Surrey 27 Mar 1975. Brother of J.S. (Cambridge U 1994); great-nephew of N.A.Knox (Surrey and England 1904-10). 5'10". LHB, RM. Debut 1997. HS 44 v Notts (Worksop) 1997. **NWT:** HS 2. **BHC:** (Brit Us) HS 113 v Hants (Oxford) 1997. **SL:** HS 21 v Glos (Colchester) 1996.

HUSSAIN, Nasser (Forest S, Snaresbrook; Durham U), b Madras, India 28 Mar 1968. Son of J. (Madras 1966-67); brother of M. (Worcs 1987). 5'11". RHB, LB. Debut 1987; cap 1989. YC 1989. **Tests:** 23 (1989-90 to 1997); HS 207 v A (Birmingham) 1997. **LOI:** 12 (1989-90 to 1996-97, 1 as captain; HS 49*). Tours: WI 1989-90, 1991-92 (Eng A), 1993-94; NZ 1996-97; P 1990-91 (Eng A), 1995-96 (Eng A – captain); SL 1990-91 (Eng A); Z 1996-97. 1000 runs (5); most – 1854 (1995). HS 207 (*see Tests*). Ex HS 197 v Surrey (Oval) 1990. BB 1-38. Awards: NWT 3; BHC 2. **NWT:** HS 108 v Cumberland (Chelmsford) 1992. **BHC:** HS 118 Comb Us v Somerset (Taunton) 1989. **SL:** HS 83 v Kent (Canterbury) 1995.

HYAM, Barry James (Havering SFC), b Romford 9 Sep 1975. RHB, WK. Debut 1993. MCC YC. HS 49 v P (Chelmsford) 1996. BAC HS 26 v Glam (Cardiff) 1997. **SL:** HS 3.

ILOTT, Mark Christopher (Francis Combe S, Garston), b Watford, Herts 27 Aug 1970. 6'0½". LHB, LFM. Debut 1988; cap 1993. Hertfordshire 1987-88 (at 16, the youngest to represent that county). **Tests:** 5 (1993 to 1995-96); HS 15 v A (Oval) 1993; 3-48 v SA (Durban) 1995-96. Tours: A 1992-93 (Eng A); SA 1993-94 (Eng A), 1995-96; I 1994-95 (Eng A – part); SL 1990-91 (Eng A). HS 60 Eng A v Warwks (Birmingham) 1995. Ex HS 58 v Worcs (Worcester) 1996. 50 wkts (5); most – 78 (1995). BB 9-19 (14-105 match; inc hat-trick – all lbw) v Northants (Luton) 1995. Hat-trick 1995. Awards: BHC 2. **NWT:** HS 54* v Cheshire (Chester) 1995. BB 2-23 v Cumberland (Chelmsford) 1992. **BHC:** HS 21 v Glam (Chelmsford) 1995. BB 5-21 v Scot (Forfar) 1993. **SL:** HS 56* v Sussex (Hove) 1995. BB 4-15 v Derbys (Derby) 1992.

IRANI, Ronald Charles (Smithills CS, Bolton), b Leigh, Lancs 26 Oct 1971. 6'3". RHB, RMF. Lancashire 1990-93. Essex debut/cap 1994. **Tests:** 2 (1996); HS 41 v I (Lord's) 1996; BB 1-22. **LOI:** 10 (1996 to 1996-97; HS 45*; BB 1-23). Tours: NZ 1996-97; P 1995-96 (Eng A); Z 1996-97. 1000 runs (2); most – 1165 (1995). HS 123* Hants (Chelmsford) 1997. BB 5-19 Eng A v Comb XI (Karachi) 1995-96. Ex BB 5-27 v Notts (Chelmsford) 1996. Awards: NWT 2; BHC 2. **NWT:** HS 124 v Durham (Chelmsford) 1996. BB 4-49 v Sussex (Hove) 1994. **BHC:** HS 82* v Glam (Chelmsford) 1997. BB 4-30 v Brit Us (Chelmsford) 1996. **SL:** HS 101* v Glos (Cheltenham) 1995. BB 3-22 v Worcs (Worcester) 1994.

LAW, Danny Richard (Steyning GS), b Lambeth, London 15 Jul 1975. 6'5". RHB, RFM. Sussex 1993-96; cap 1996. Essex debut 1997. HS 115 Sx v Young A (Hove) 1995. BAC HS 97 Sx v Glos (Bristol) 1996. Ex HS 81 and BB 5-93 v CU (Cambridge) 1997. BB 5-33 Sx v Durham (Hove) 1996. **NWT:** HS 18 and BB 1-2 Sx v Ire (Belfast) 1996. **BHC:** HS 28 v Glam (Chelmsford) 1997. BB 1-44 (Sx). **SL:** HS 82 v Durham (Chelmsford) 1997. BB 3-34 Sx v Worcs (Worcester) 1996.

LAW, Stuart Grant (Craigslea State HS), b Herston, Brisbane, Australia 18 Oct 1968. 6'2". RHB, RM/LB. Queensland 1988-89 to date; captain 1994-95 to date. Essex debut/cap 1996. **Tests** (A): 1 (1995-96); HS 54* v SL (Perth) 1995-96. **LOI** (A): 44 (1994-95 to 1996-97; HS 110; BB 2-22). Tours: E 1995 (Young A); Z 1991-92 (Aus B). 1000 runs (2+1); most – 1545 (1996). HS 179 Q v Tasmania (Brisbane) 1988-89. Ex HS 175 v Leics (Colchester) 1997. BB 5-39 Q v Tasmania (Brisbane) 1995-96. Ex BB 3-27 v Worcs (Chelmsford) 1997. Awards: NWT 4; BHC 1. **NWT:** HS 107 v Hants (Southampton) 1996. BB 2-36 v Devon (Chelmsford) 1996. **BHC:** HS 116 v Somerset (Taunton) 1996. BB 2-57 v Somerset (Taunton) 1996. **SL:** HS 123 v Sussex (Hove) 1997. BB 4-37 v Worcs (Chelmsford) 1997.

NAPIER, Graham Richard (The Gilberd S, Colchester), b Colchester 6 Jan 1980. 5'9½". RHB, RM. Debut 1997. HS 35* v Notts (Worksop) 1997. BB 2-25 v CU (Cambridge) 1997. BAC BB 1-40. **SL:** HS 12 v Kent Canterbury) 1997.

PETERS, Stephen David (Coopers Coborn & Co S), b Harold Wood 10 Dec 1978. 5'9". RHB. Debut 1996 scoring 110 and 12* v CU (Cambridge). HS 110 (*see above*). BAC HS 33 v Surrey (Oval) 1997. **SL:** HS 15 v Yorks (Ilford) 1997.

POWELL, Jonathan Christopher (Chelmsford C), b Harold Wood 13 Jun 1979. 5'10". RHB, OB. Debut 1997. HS 4* and BB 1-109 v Leics (Colchester) 1997. **SL:** HS 2. BB 2-10 v Northants (Northampton) 1997.

PRICHARD, Paul John (Brentwood HS), b Billericay 7 Jan 1965. 5'10". RHB, RSM. Debut 1984; cap 1986; captain 1995 to date; benefit 1996. Tour: A 1992-93 (Eng A). 1000 runs (8); most – 1485 (1992). HS 245 v Leics (Chelmsford) 1990. BB 1-28. Awards: NWT 1; BHC 3. **NWT:** HS 94 v Oxon (Chelmsford) 1985. **BHC:** HS 114 v Somerset (Chelmsford) 1997. **SL:** HS 107 v Notts (Nottingham) 1993.

ROBINSON, Darren David John (Tabor HS, Braintree; Chelmsford CFE), b Braintree 2 Mar 1973. 5'10½". RHB, RMF. Debut 1993; cap 1997. HS 148 v Worcs (Chelmsford) 1997. **NWT:** HS 62 v Glam (Chelmsford) 1997. **BHC:** HS 36 v Glam (Cardiff) 1996. **SL:** HS 80 v Surrey (Southend) 1996. BB 1-7.

ROLLINS, Robert John (Little Ilford CS), b Plaistow 30 Jan 1974. 5'9". RHB, RM, WK. Brother of A.S. (*see* DERBYSHIRE). Debut 1992; cap 1995. HS 133* v Glam (Swansea) 1995. Award: NWT 1. **NWT:** HS 67* v Bucks (Beaconsfield) 1997. **BHC:** HS 18* v Glam (Chelmsford) 1997. **SL:** HS 38 v Somerset (Chelmsford) 1997.

SUCH, Peter Mark (Harry Carlton CS, Ex Leake, Notts), b Helensburgh, Dunbartonshire 12 Jun 1964. 5'11". RHB, OB. Nottinghamshire 1982-86. Leicestershire 1987-89. Essex debut 1990; cap 1991. **Tests:** 8 (1993 to 1994); HS 14* and BB 6-67 v A (Manchester) 1993 – on debut. Tours (Eng A): A 1992-93; SA 1993-94. HS 54 v Worcs (Chelmsford) 1993. 50 wkts (5); most – 82 (1996). BB 8-93 (11-160 match) v Hants (Colchester) 1995. **NWT:** HS 8*. BB 3-56 v Durham (Chelmsford) 1996. **BHC:** HS 10* v Glam (Cardiff) 1996. BB 4-43 v Northants (Northampton) 1992. **SL:** HS 19* v Notts (Ilford) 1994. BB 5-29 v Glam (Cardiff) 1997.

WILLIAMS, Neil FitzGerald (Acland Burghley CS), b Hope Well, St Vincent 2 Jul 1962. 5'11". RHB, RFM. Middlesex 1982-94; cap 1984; benefit 1994. Essex debut 1995; cap 1996. Windward Is 1982-83 and 1989-90 to 1991-92. Tasmania 1983-84. MCC YC. **Tests:** 1 (1990); HS 38 and BB 2-148 v I (Oval) 1990. Tour: Z 1984-85 (EC). HS 77 M v Warwks (Birmingham) 1991. Ex HS 39 v Worcs (Worcester) 1996. 50 wkts (3); most – 63 (1983). BB 8-75 (12-139 match) M v Glos (Lord's) 1992. Ex BB 5-43 v Glos (Colchester) 1996. Award: BHC 1. **NWT:** HS 11* v Lancs (Lord's)`1996. BB 4-36 M v Derbys (Derby) 1983. **BHC:** HS 29* M v Surrey (Lord's) 1985. BB 3-16 M v Comb Us (Cambridge) 1982. **SL:** HS 43 M v Somerset (Lord's) 1988. BB 4-39 M v Surrey (Oval) 1988.

WILSON, Daniel Graeme (St Mary's S, Bishop's Stortford; Cheltenham & Gloucester U), b Paddington, London 18 Feb 1977. 6'2". RHB, RM. Debut 1997 – awaiting BAC debut. Scored 52* and took 2-40 v SA A (limited-overs match) 1996. HS –. BB 1-31. **SL:** HS 7. BB 3-40 v Sussex (Chelmsford) 1996.

NEWCOMER

PHILLIPS, James **Timothy** (Felsted S), b Cambridge 13 Mar 1981. LHB, SLA.

DEPARTURES (who made first-class appearances in 1997)

ANDREW, Stephen Jon Walter (Milton Abbey S; Portchester SS), b London 27 Jan 1966. 6'3". RHB, RMF. Hampshire 1984-89. Essex 1990-97. HS 35 Ex v Northants (Chelmsford) 1990. BB 7-47 Ex v Lancs (Manchester) 1993. Awards: BHC 2. **NWT:** HS 1*. BB 2-34 Ex v Scot (Chelmsford) 1990. **BHC:** HS 4*. BB 5-24 H v Essex (Chelmsford) 1987. **SL:** HS 32 Ex v Yorks (Leeds) 1996. BB 4-50 H v Middx (Southampton) 1988.

GOOCH, Graham Alan (Norlington Jr HS), b Leytonstone 23 Jul 1953. 6'0". RHB, RM. Essex 1973-97; cap 1975; captain 1986-87 and 1989-94; benefit 1985; testimonial 1995. W Province 1982-83 to 1983-84. *Wisden* 1979. OBE 1991. **Tests:** 118 (1975 to 1994-95, 34 as captain); HS 333 and record match aggregate of 456 v I (Lord's) 1990; BB 3-39 v P (Manchester) 1992. **LOI:** 125 (1976 to 1994-95, 50 as captain; HS 142; BB 3-19). Tours (C=captain): A 1978-79, 1979-80, 1990-91C, 1994-95; SA 1981-82 (SAB); WI 1980-81, 1985-86, 1989-90C; NZ 1991-92C; I 1979-80, 1981-82, 1992-93C; P 1987-88; SL 1981-82. 1000 runs (20+1) inc 2000 (5); most – 2746 (1990). HS 333 (*see Tests*). Ex HS 275 v Kent (Chelmsford) 1988. BB 7-14 v Worcs (Ilford) 1982. Awards: NWT 9 (record); BHC 22 (record). **NWT:** HS 144 v Hants (Chelmsford) 1990. BB 5-8 v Cheshire (Chester) 1995. **BHC:** HS 198* v Sussex (Hove) 1982. BB 3-24 v Sussex (Hove) 1982. **SL:** HS 176 v Glam (Southend) 1983. BB 4-33 v Worcs (Chelmsford) 1984.

ESSEX 1997

RESULTS SUMMARY

	Place	Won	Lost	Tied	Drew	No Result
Britannic Assurance Championship	8th	5	6	–	6	–
All First-Class Matches		5	6	–	8	–
NatWest Trophy	Winners					
Benson and Hedges Cup	Quarter-Finalist					
Sunday League	7th	9	6	1	–	1

BRITANNIC ASSURANCE CHAMPIONSHIP AVERAGES

BATTING AND FIELDING

Cap		M	I	NO	HS	Runs	Avge	100	50	Ct/St
1996	S.G.Law	17	28	2	175	1482	57.00	5	8	19
1986	P.J.Prichard	15	25	1	224	1098	45.75	3	8	9
1996	A.P.Grayson	16	25	3	105	876	39.81	1	5	16
1989	N.Hussain	10	17	–	128	650	38.23	2	3	9
1994	R.C.Irani	15	24	1	123*	793	34.47	3	3	4
1997	D.D.J.Robinson	12	20	–	148	664	33.20	2	2	12
1995	R.J.Rollins	12	19	1	82	452	25.11	–	4	24/2
1975	G.A.Gooch	10	17	1	56	369	23.06	–	2	12
1997	A.P.Cowan	16	26	6	77	447	22.35	–	1	7
1993	M.C.Ilott	12	20	5	47	290	19.33	–	–	1
–	T.P.Hodgson	3	6	–	44	101	16.83	–	–	–
1996	N.F.Williams	3	5	1	23	66	16.50	–	–	3
–	D.R.Law	17	28	–	59	411	14.67	–	1	10
–	B.J.Hyam	5	9	1	26	60	7.50	–	–	8
1991	P.M.Such	17	21	10	14	58	5.27	–	–	5

Also batted: S.J.W.Andrew (2 matches) 24, 0, 3; I.N.Flanagan (2) 16*, 16, 40; G.R.Napier (1) 35*, 4*; S.D.Peters (1) 33, 0 (1 ct); J.C.Powell (1) 4*.

BOWLING

	O	M	R	W	Avge	Best	5wI	10wM
M.C.Ilott	317	85	924	40	23.10	7-59	1	–
A.P.Cowan	420	106	1334	52	25.65	5-45	3	–
P.M.Such	627.1	186	1492	56	26.64	6-55	5	1
D.R.Law	239.4	47	854	24	35.58	4-69	–	–
A.P.Grayson	371.5	102	972	27	36.00	4-53	–	–
R.C.Irani	256.5	71	682	18	37.88	3-51	–	–

Also bowled: S.J.W.Andrew 46-14-131-3; G.A.Gooch 2-1-3-0; S.G.Law 116-30-356-5; G.R.Napier 8-3-40-1; J.C.Powell 39.5-5-109-1; N.F.Williams 83-11-281-8.

The First-Class Averages (pp 118-133) give the records of Essex players in all first-class county matches (their other opponents being Cambridge University and Oxford University), with the exception of N.Hussain whose full county figures are as above, and:
A.P.Grayson 18-26-3-105-914-39.73-1-5-17ct. 394.5-112-1009-28-36.03-4/53.
P.M.Such 19-21-10-14-58-5.27-0-0-5ct. 671.1-208-1548-60-25.80-6/55-5-1.

ESSEX RECORDS

FIRST-CLASS CRICKET

Highest Total	For	761-6d		v	Leics	Chelmsford	1990
	V	803-4d		by	Kent	Brentwood	1934
Lowest Total	For	30		v	Yorkshire	Leyton	1901
	V	14		by	Surrey	Chelmsford	1983
Highest Innings	For	343*	P.A.Perrin	v	Derbyshire	Chesterfield	1904
	V	332	W.H.Ashdown	for	Kent	Brentwood	1934

Highest Partnership for each Wicket

1st	316	G.A.Gooch/P.J.Prichard	v	Kent	Chelmsford	1994
2nd	403	G.A.Gooch/P.J.Prichard	v	Leics	Chelmsford	1990
3rd	347*	M.E.Waugh/N.Hussain	v	Lancashire	Ilford	1992
4th	314	Salim Malik/N.Hussain	v	Surrey	The Oval	1991
5th	316	N.Hussain/M.A.Garnham	v	Leics	Leicester	1991
6th	206	J.W.H.T.Douglas/J.O'Connor	v	Glos	Cheltenham	1923
	206	B.R.Knight/R.A.G.Luckin	v	Middlesex	Brentwood	1962
7th	261	J.W.H.T.Douglas/J.Freeman	v	Lancashire	Leyton	1914
8th	263	D.R.Wilcox/R.M.Taylor	v	Warwicks	Southend	1946
9th	251	J.W.H.T.Douglas/S.N.Hare	v	Derbyshire	Leyton	1921
10th	218	F.H.Vigar/T.P.B.Smith	v	Derbyshire	Chesterfield	1947

Best Bowling	For	10- 32	H.Pickett	v	Leics	Leyton	1895
(Innings)	V	10- 40	E.G.Dennett	for	Glos	Bristol	1906
Best Bowling	For	17-119	W.Mead	v	Hampshire	Southampton	1895
(Match)	V	17- 56	C.W.L.Parker	for	Glos	Gloucester	1925

Most Runs – Season	2559	G.A.Gooch	(av 67.34)		1984
Most Runs – Career	30701	G.A.Gooch	(av 51.77)		1973-97
Most 100s – Season	9	J.O'Connor			1934
	9	D.J.Insole			1955
Most 100s – Career	94	G.A.Gooch			1973-97
Most Wkts – Season	172	T.P.B.Smith	(av 27.13)		1947
Most Wkts – Career	1610	T.P.B.Smith	(av 26.68)		1929-51

LIMITED-OVERS CRICKET

Highest Total	NWT	386-5		v	Wiltshire	Chelmsford	1988
	BHC	388-7		v	Scotland	Chelmsford	1992
	SL	310-5		v	Glamorgan	Southend	1983
Lowest Total	NWT	57		v	Lancashire	Lord's	1996
	BHC	61		v	Lancashire	Chelmsford	1992
	SL	69		v	Derbyshire	Chesterfield	1974
Highest Innings	NWT	144	G.A.Gooch	v	Hampshire	Chelmsford	1990
	BHC	198*	G.A.Gooch	v	Sussex	Hove	1982
	SL	176	G.A.Gooch	v	Glamorgan	Southend	1983
Best Bowling	NWT	5- 8	J.K.Lever	v	Middlesex	Westcliff	1972
		5- 8	G.A.Gooch	v	Cheshire	Chester	1995
	BHC	5-13	J.K.Lever	v	Middlesex	Lord's	1985
	SL	8-26	K.D.Boyce	v	Lancashire	Manchester	1971

GLAMORGAN

Formation of Present Club: 6 July 1888
Colours: Blue and Gold
Badge: Gold Daffodil
Championships: (3) 1948, 1969, 1997
NatWest Trophy/Gillette Cup Winners: (0) Finalists 1977
Benson and Hedges Cup Winners: (0) Semi-Finalists 1988
Sunday League Champions: (1) 1993
Match Awards: NWT 39; BHC 50

Secretary: G.R.Stone. **Cricket Secretary:** M.J.Fatkin
Sophia Gardens, Cardiff, CF1 9XR (Tel 01222 343478)
Captain: M.P.Maynard. **Vice-Captain:** P.A.Cottey. **Overseas Player:** Waqar Younis.
1998 Beneficiary: S.L.Watkin. **Scorer:** B.T.Denning.

BUTCHER, Gary Paul (Trinity S; Riddlesdown S; Heath Clark C), b Clapham, London 11 Mar 1975. Son of A.R. (Surrey, Glam and England 1972-92); brother of M.A. (*see SURREY*). 5'9". RHB, RM. Debut 1994. Tours (Gm): SA 1995-96; Z 1994-95. HS 101* v OU (Oxford) 1997. BAC HS 89 v Northants (Northampton) 1996. BB 7-77 v Glos (Bristol) 1996. **NWT:** HS 48 and BB 2-33 v Beds (Cardiff) 1997. **BHC:** HS 17 v Somerset (Taunton) 1997. BB 2-21 v Warwks (Cardiff) 1996. **SL:** HS 47 v Worcs (Worcester) 1997. BB 4-32 v Glos (Bristol) 1996.

COSKER, Dean Andrew (Millfield S), b Weymouth, Dorset 7 Jan 1978. 5'11". RHB, SLA. Debut 1996. HS 24 and BB 4-60 v Lancs (Cardiff) 1996 (on debut). **NWT:** HS 3* and BB 3-26 v Yorks (Cardiff) 1997. **BHC:** HS 0. BB 1-38. **SL:** HS 5. BB 2-38 v Leics (Swansea) 1996.

COTTEY, Phillip Anthony (Bishopston CS, Swansea), b Swansea 2 Jun 1966. 5'4". RHB, OB. Debut 1986; cap 1992. E Transvaal 1991-92. Tours (Gm): SA 1995-96; Z 1990-91, 1994-95. 1000 runs (6); most – 1543 (1996). HS 203 and BB 4-49 v Leics (Swansea) 1996. **NWT:** HS 61* v Leics (Leicester) 1995. BB 1-9. **BHC:** HS 68 v Hants (Southampton) 1989. BB 1-49. **SL:** HS 92* v Hants (Ebbw Vale) 1991. BB 4-56 v Essex (Chelmsford) 1996.

CROFT, Robert Damien Bale (St John Lloyd Catholic CS; W Glam IHE), b Morriston 25 May 1970. 5'10½". RHB, OB. Debut 1989; cap 1992. **Tests:** 10 (1996 to 1997); HS 31 and BB 5-95 v NZ (Christchurch) 1996-97. **LOI:** 14 (1996 to 1997; HS 30*; BB 2-26). Tours: SA 1993-94 (Eng A), 1995-96 (Gm); WI 1991-92 (Eng A); NZ 1996-97; Z 1990-91 (Gm), 1994-95 (Gm), 1996-97. HS 143 v Somerset (Taunton) 1995. 50 wkts (5); most – 76 (1996). BB 8-66 (14-169 match) v Warwks (Swansea) 1992. Award: NWT 1. **NWT:** HS 64 v Beds (Cardiff) 1997. BB 3-30 v Lincs (Swansea) 1994. **BHC:** HS 50 v Middx (Lord's) 1995. BB 4-30 v Essex (Cardiff) 1996. **SL:** HS 68 v Northants (Northampton) 1996. BB 6-20 v Worcs (Cardiff) 1994.

DALE, Adrian (Chepstow CS; Swansea U), b Germiston, SA 24 Oct 1968 (to UK at 6 mths). 5'11½". RHB, RM. Debut 1989; cap 1992. Tours (Gm): SA 1993-94 (Eng A), 1995-96; Z 1990-91, 1994-95. 1000 runs (2); most – 1472 (1993). HS 214* v Middx (Cardiff) 1993. BB 6-18 v Warwks (Cardiff) 1993. Awards: NWT 1; BHC 2. **NWT:** HS 110 v Lincs (Swansea) 1994. BB 3-54 v Worcs (Swansea) 1993. **BHC:** HS 100 v Middx (Cardiff) 1997. BB 5-41 v Middx (Lord's) 1996. **SL:** HS 67* v Derbys (Heanor) 1989. BB 6-22 v Durham (Colwyn Bay) 1993.

DAVIES, Andrew Philip (Dwr-y-Felin CS; Christ C, Brecon), b Neath 7 Nov 1976. 5'11". LHB, RMF. Debut 1995. Wales (MC). HS 11* v P (Pontypridd) 1996. BAC HS –. BB 1-25. **SL:** HS 3 and BB 2-25 v Essex (Cardiff) 1997.

EVANS, Alun Wyn (Fishguard SS; Neath Tertiary C), b Glanamman, Dyfed 20 Aug 1975. 5'8". RHB, RM. Debut 1996 v OU (Oxford), scoring 66* and 71*. MCC YC. HS 71* (*see above*). BAC HS 48* v Notts (Worksop) 1996. **SL:** HS 50* v Glos (Bristol) 1996.

JAMES, Stephen Peter (Monmouth S; Swansea U; Hughes Hall, Cambridge); b Lydney, Glos 7 Sep 1967. 6'0". RHB. Debut 1985; cap 1992. Cambridge U 1989-90; blue 1989-90. Mashonaland 1993-94 to date. Tours (Gm): SA 1995-96; Z 1990-91. 1000 runs (5); most – 1775 (1997). HS 235 v Notts (Worksop) 1996. Awards: NWT 2; BHC 2. **NWT:** HS 123 v Lincs (Swansea) 1994. **BHC:** HS 135 v Comb Us (Cardiff) 1992. **SL:** HS 107 v Sussex (Llanelli) 1993.

JONES, Simon Philip, b Swansea 25 Dec 1978. Son of I.J. (Glamorgan and England 1960-68). RHB, RF. Staff 1997 – awaiting f-c debut.

LAW, Wayne Lincoln (Graig CS; Graig SFC, Llanelli), b Swansea 4 Sep 1978. 5'11". RHB, OB. Debut 1997 – awaiting BAC debut. MCC YC. HS 38* v OU (Oxford) 1997 – on debut. **SL:** HS 15 v Surrey (Oval) 1997.

MAYNARD, Matthew Peter (David Hughes S, Anglesey), b Oldham, Lancs 21 Mar 1966. 5'10½". RHB, RM. Debut 1985 v Yorks (Swansea), scoring 102 out of 117 in 87 min, reaching 100 with 3 sixes off successive balls; cap 1987; captain 1996 to date; benefit 1996. N Districts 1990-91/1991-92. Otago 1996-97. YC 1988. **Tests:** 4 (1988 to 1993-94); HS 35 v WI (Kingston) 1993-94. **LOI:** 10 (1993-94 to 1996); HS 41. Tours: SA 1989-90 (Eng XI), 1995-96 (Gm – captain); WI 1993-94; Z 1994-95 (Gm). 1000 runs (11); most – 1803 (1991). HS 243 v Hants (Southampton) 1991. BB 3-21 v OU (Oxford) 1987. BAC BB 1-3. Awards: NWT 4; BHC 7. **NWT:** HS 151* v Durham (Darlington) 1991. **BHC:** HS 151* v Middx (Lord's) 1996. **SL:** HS 132 v Surrey (Oval) 1997.

PARKIN, Owen Thomas (Bournemouth GS, Bath U), b Coventry, Warwks 24 Sep 1972. 6'2". RHB, RFM. Dorset 1992. Debut 1994. HS 14 v Warwks (Birmingham) 1996. BB 3-22 v Durham (Chester-le-St) 1996. **NWT:** HS 1* and BB 3-23 v Worcs (Cardiff) 1996. **BHC:** HS 8 and BB 3-42 v Somerset (Taunton) 1997. **SL:** HS 1*. BB 5-28 v Sussex (Hove) 1996.

POWELL, Michael John (Crickhowell HS; Pontypool CFE), b Abergavenny 3 Feb 1977. 6'1". RHB. Debut 1997 scoring 200* v OU (Oxford). HS 200 (*see above*). BAC HS 41* v Northants (Abergavenny) 1997. **SL:** HS 42 v Notts (Colwyn Bay) 1997.

SHAW, Adrian David (Neath Tertiary C), b Neath 17 Feb 1972. 5'11". RHB, WK. Wales (MC) 1990-92. Debut 1994. HS 74 v Surrey (Cardiff) 1996. **NWT:** HS 34* v Hants (Southampton) 1997. **BHC:** HS 15 v Essex (Chelmsford) 1997. **SL:** HS 48 v Glos (Swansea) 1997.

THOMAS, Stuart Darren (Graig CS, Llanelli; Neath Tertiary C), b Morriston 25 Jan 1975. 6'0". LHB, RFM. Debut v Derbys (Chesterfield) 1992, taking 5-80 when aged 17yr 217d; cap 1997. Tours (Gm): SA 1995-96; Z 1994-95. HS 78* v Glos (Abergavenny) 1995. 50 wkts (1): 53 (1997). BB 5-24 v Sussex (Swansea) 1997. Award: BHC 1. **NWT:** HS 13 v Yorks (Cardiff) 1997. BB 5-74 v Essex (Chelmsford) 1997. **BHC:** HS 27* v Essex (Cardiff) 1996. BB 6-20 v Comb Us (Cardiff) 1995. **SL:** HS 20* v Northants (Northampton) 1996. BB 3-30 v Notts (Colwyn Bay) 1997.

WAQAR YOUNIS (Government C, Vehari), b Vehari, Pakistan 16 Nov 1969. 6'0". RHB, RF. Multan 1987-88 to 1990-91. United Bank 1988-89 to date. Surrey 1990-91 and 1993; cap 1990. Glamorgan debut/cap 1997. *Wisden* 1991. **Tests** (P): 44 (1989-90 to 1996-97, 1 as captain); HS 34 v NZ (Christchurch) 1995-96; BB 7-76 v NZ (Faisalabad) 1990-91.

WAQAR YOUNIS continued:
LOI (P): 156 (1989-90 to 1996-97, 1 as captain; HS 37; BB 6-26). Tours (P): E 1992, 1996; A 1989-90, 1995-96; WI 1992-93; NZ 1992-93, 1993-94, 1995-96; SL 1994-95. HS 55 P v Natal (Durban) 1994-95. BAC HS 47 v Kent (Canterbury) 1997. 50 wkts (4+3) inc 100 (1): 113 (1991). BB 8-17 v Sussex (Swansea) 1997. Hat-trick 1997. Awards: NWT 3. **NWT:** HS 34* v Yorks (Cardiff) 1997. BB 5-40 Sy v Northants (Oval) 1991. **BHC:** HS 5*. BB 3-29 Sy v Somerset (Taunton) 1991. **SL:** HS 39 Sy v Hants (Oval) 1993. BB 5-26 Sy v Kent (Oval) 1990.

WATKIN, Steven Llewellyn (Cymer Afan CS; S Glamorgan CHE), b Maesteg 15 Sep 1964. 6'3". RHB, RMF. Debut 1986; cap 1989; benefit 1998. *Wisden* 1993. **Tests:** 3 (1991 to 1993); HS 13 and BB 4-65 v A (Oval) 1993. **LOI:** 4 (1993-94; HS 4; BB 4-49). Tours: SA 1995-96 (Gm); WI 1991-92 (Eng A), 1993-94; P 1990-91 (Eng A); Z 1989-90 (Eng A), 1990-91 (Gm), 1994-95 (Gm). HS 41 v Worcs (Worcester) 1992. 50 wkts (9); most – 94 (1989). BB 8-59 v Warwks (Birmingham) 1988. Awards: NWT 1; BHC 1. **NWT:** HS 13 v Worcs (Cardiff) 1996. BB 4-26 v Middx (Cardiff) 1995. **BHC:** HS 15 v Hants (Southampton) 1991. BB 4-31 v Kent (Canterbury) 1996. **SL:** HS 31* v Derbys (Checkley) 1991. BB 5-23 v Warwks (Birmingham) 1990.

NEWCOMER

DAWOOD, Ismail (Batley GS), b Dewsbury, Yorks 23 Jul 1976. 5'8". RHB, WK. Northamptonshire 1994. Worcestershire 1996-97. HS 10* Wo v Pak A (Worcester) 1997. BAC HS 2* (Nh). **SL:** HS 2 (Wo).

DEPARTURES (who made first-class appearances in 1997)

EDWARDS, Gareth John Maldwyn (Brynhyfryd S, Ruthin; University C, London), b St Asaph 13 Nov 1976. 6'2". RHB, OB. Glamorgan 1997 (no BAC appearances). HS –.

METSON, Colin Peter (Enfield GS; Stanborough S, Welwyn Garden City; Durham U), b Goffs Oak, Herts 2 Jul 1963. 5'5½". RHB, WK. Middlesex 1981-86. Glamorgan 1987-97; cap 1987; benefit 1997. Tour: SA 1995-96 (Gm). HS 96 M v Glos (Uxbridge) 1984. Gm HS 84 v Kent (Maidstone) 1991. Award: NWT 1. **NWT:** HS 21 v Notts (Nottingham) 1992. **BHC:** HS 23 v Kent (Swansea) 1990. **SL:** HS 30* v Hants (Bournemouth) 1990.

MORRIS, Hugh (Blundell's S), b Cardiff 5 Oct 1963. 5'8". LHB, RM. Glamorgan 1981-97; cap 1986; captain 1986-89 and 1993-95; benefit 1994. **Tests:** 3 (1991); HS 44 v WI (Oval) 1991. Tours (Eng A)(C=captain): SA 1993-94C, 1995-96 (Gm); WI 1991-92C; SL 1990-91C; Z 1994-95C (Gm). 1000 runs (10) inc 2000 (1): 2276 – inc 10 hundreds – both Gm records (1990). HS 233* v Warwks (Cardiff) 1997. BB 1-6. BAC BB 1-45. Awards: NWT 2; BHC 3. **NWT:** HS 154* v Staffs (Cardiff) 1989. **BHC:** HS 143* v Hants (Southampton) 1989. BB 1-14. **SL:** HS 127* v Surrey (Swansea) 1994. Appointed ECB Technical Director 1997.

WARREN, Paul Michael (Blundell's S; Glamorgan U), b Plymouth, Devon 18 Jan 1978. 6'3". RHB, RM. Glamorgan 1997 (no BAC appearances). Devon 1996 to date. HS –.

BILL FRINDALL'S SCORING SHEETS AND BINDERS

For illustrated instructions and price list send a large S.A.E. to

THE BEECHES, URCHFONT, DEVIZES, WILTSHIRE SN10 4RD

GLAMORGAN 1997

RESULTS SUMMARY

	Place	Won	Lost	Tied	Drew	No Result
Britannic Assurance Championship	1st	8	2	–	7	–
All First-Class Matches		8	3	–	8	–
NatWest Trophy	Semi-Finalist					
Benson and Hedges Cup	3rd in Group D					
Sunday League	13th	5	9	–	–	3

BRITANNIC ASSURANCE CHAMPIONSHIP AVERAGES

BATTING AND FIELDING

Cap		M	I	NO	HS	Runs	Avge	100	50	Ct/St
1992	S.P.James	17	28	4	162	1605	66.87	7	6	14
1987	M.P.Maynard	17	23	6	161*	1106	65.05	3	7	20
1986	H.Morris	16	26	4	233*	1207	54.86	4	3	13
1992	A.Dale	17	25	3	142*	840	38.18	2	5	5
1992	R.D.B.Croft	13	18	1	86	577	33.94	–	4	13
1992	P.A.Cottey	15	19	4	76*	370	24.66	–	1	15
–	A.D.Shaw	17	20	5	53*	352	23.46	–	1	49/2
1997	S.D.Thomas	16	16	4	75*	259	21.58	–	1	7
–	G.P.Butcher	9	9	1	58	172	21.50	–	1	1
1997	Waqar Younis	16	17	1	47	289	18.06	–	–	3
–	M.J.Powell	3	6	2	41*	62	15.50	–	–	1
1989	S.L.Watkin	17	16	3	39	138	10.61	–	–	3
–	D.A.Cosker	13	8	5	7	14	4.66	–	–	4

Also batted: A.W.Evans (1 match) 31 (1 ct).

BOWLING

	O	M	R	W	Avge	Best	5wI	10wM
Waqar Younis	441.4	83	1551	68	22.80	8-17	3	1
S.L.Watkin	508.2	143	1393	61	22.83	7-41	2	–
R.D.B.Croft	504.2	118	1259	54	23.31	5-33	1	–
S.D.Thomas	330.3	49	1160	44	26.36	5-24	2	–
D.A.Cosker	255.3	62	736	20	36.80	4-64	–	–

Also bowled: G.P.Butcher 65.4-14-270-8; P.A.Cottey 3.3-1-19-0; A.Dale 49.1-11-169-0; M.P.Maynard 6.5-0-39-0; M.J.Powell 1-0-3-0.

The First-Class Averages (pp 118-133) give the records of Glamorgan players in all first-class county matches (their other opponents being the Australians and Oxford University), with the exception of R.D.B.Croft whose full county figures are as above, and:

D.A.Cosker 15-9-5-7-16-4.00-0-0-4ct. 343.2-84-1024-28-36.57-4/64.

GLAMORGAN RECORDS

FIRST-CLASS CRICKET

Highest Total	For	597-8d	v	Durham	Cardiff	1997
	V	657-7d	by	Warwicks	Birmingham	1994
Lowest Total	For	22	v	Lancashire	Liverpool	1924
	V	33	by	Leics	Ebbw Vale	1965
Highest Innings	For	287* D.E.Davies	v	Glos	Newport	1939
	V	313* S.J.Cook	for	Somerset	Cardiff	1990

Highest Partnership for each Wicket

1st	330	A.Jones/R.C.Fredericks	v	Northants	Swansea	1972
2nd	249	S.P.James/H.Morris	v	Oxford U	Oxford	1987
3rd	313	D.E.Davies/W.E.Jones	v	Essex	Brentwood	1948
4th	425*	A.Dale/I.V.A.Richards	v	Middlesex	Cardiff	1993
5th	264	M.Robinson/S.W.Montgomery	v	Hampshire	Bournemouth	1949
6th	230	W.E.Jones/B.L.Muncer	v	Worcs	Worcester	1953
7th	211	P.A.Cottey/O.D.Gibson	v	Leics	Swansea	1996
8th	202	D.Davies/J.J.Hills	v	Sussex	Eastbourne	1928
9th	203*	J.J.Hills/J.C.Clay	v	Worcs	Swansea	1929
10th	143	T.Davies/S.A.B.Daniels	v	Glos	Swansea	1982

Best Bowling	For	10- 51	J.Mercer	v	Worcs	Worcester	1936
(Innings)	V	10- 18	G.Geary	for	Leics	Pontypridd	1929
Best Bowling	For	17-212	J.C.Clay	v	Worcs	Swansea	1937
(Match)	V	16- 96	G.Geary	for	Leics	Pontypridd	1929

Most Runs – Season	2276	H.Morris	(av 55.51)		1990
Most Runs – Career	34056	A.Jones	(av 33.03)		1957-83
Most 100s – Season	10	H.Morris			1990
Most 100s – Career	52	A.Jones			1957-83
	52	H.Morris			1981-97
Most Wkts – Season	176	J.C.Clay	(av 17.34)		1937
Most Wkts – Career	2174	D.J.Shepherd	(av 20.95)		1950-72

LIMITED-OVERS CRICKET

Highest Total	NWT	345-2		v	Durham	Darlington	1991
	BHC	318-3		v	Comb Us	Cardiff	1995
	SL	287-8		v	Middlesex	Cardiff	1993
Lowest Total	NWT	76		v	Northants	Northampton	1968
	BHC	68		v	Lancashire	Manchester	1973
	SL	42		v	Derbyshire	Swansea	1979
Highest Innings	NWT	162*	I.V.A.Richards	v	Oxfordshire	Swansea	1993
	BHC	151*	M.P.Maynard	v	Middlesex	Lord's	1996
	SL	132	M.P.Maynard	v	Surrey	The Oval	1997
Best Bowling	NWT	5-13	R.J.Shastri	v	Scotland	Edinburgh	1988
	BHC	6-20	S.D.Thomas	v	Comb Us	Cardiff	1995
	SL	6-20	R.D.B.Croft	v	Worcs	Cardiff	1994

GLOUCESTERSHIRE

Formation of Present Club: 1871
Colours: Blue, Gold, Brown, Silver, Green and Red
Badge: Coat of Arms of the City and County of Bristol
Championships (since 1890): (0) Second 1930, 1931, 1947, 1959, 1969, 1986
NatWest Trophy/Gillette Cup Winners: (1) 1973
Benson and Hedges Cup Winners: (1) 1977
Sunday League Champions: (0) Second 1988
Match Awards: NWT 42; BHC 54

Chief Executive: C.Sextone. **Cricket Secretary:** P.G.M.August County Ground, Nevil Road, Bristol BS7 9EJ (Tel 0117 924 5216)
Captain: M.W.Alleyne. **Vice-Captain:** no appointment. **Overseas Player:** C.A.Walsh.
1998 Beneficiary (testimonial): C.A.Walsh. **Scorer:** H.T.Gerrish

ALLEYNE, Mark Wayne (Harrison C, Barbados; Cardinal Pole S, London E9; Haringey Cricket C), b Tottenham, London 23 May 1968. 5'10". RHB, RM. Debut 1986; cap 1990; captain 1997 to date. Tours (Gs): SL 1986-87, 1992-93. 1000 runs (5); most – 1121 (1991). HS 256 v Northants (Northampton) 1990. 50 wkts (1): 54 (1996). BB 6-64 v Surrey (Oval) 1997. Awards: NWT 1; BHC 1. **NWT:** HS 73 v Herts (Bristol) 1993. BB 5-30 v Lincs (Gloucester) 1990. **BHC:** HS 75 v Hants (Bristol) 1996. BB 5-27 v Comb Us (Bristol) 1988. **SL:** HS 134* v Leics (Bristol) 1992. BB 5-28 v Glam (Ebbw Vale) 1995.

AVERIS, James Maxwell Michael (Bristol Cathedral S; Portsmouth U; St Cross C, Oxford), b Bristol 28 May 1974. 5'11". RHB, RFM. Debut (Oxford U) 1997; blue 1997. Gloucestershire debut 1997. HS 42 OU v Durham (Oxford) 1997 – on debut. Gs HS –. BB 5-98 OU v Hants (Oxford) 1997. Gs BB –. **SL:** HS 2*. BB 2-35 v Essex (Colchester) 1996.

BALL, Martyn Charles John (King Edmund SS; Bath CFE), b Bristol 26 Apr 1970. 5'8". RHB, OB. Debut 1988; cap 1996. Tour (Gs): SL 1992-93. HS 71 v Notts (Bristol) 1993. BB 8-46 (14-169 match) v Somerset (Taunton) 1993. **NWT:** HS 31 v Lincs (Sleaford) 1996. BB 3-42 v Lancs (Gloucester) 1989. **BHC:** HS 28 v Hants (Southampton) 1997. BB 4-23 v Brit Us (Bristol) 1997. **SL:** HS 28* v Worcs (Worcester) 1994. BB 4-26 v Glam (Swansea) 1997.

CAWDRON, Michael John (Cheltenham C), b Luton, Beds 7 Oct 1974. 6'2". LHB, RM. Staff 1994 – awaiting f-c debut. **BHC:** HS – and BB 2-48 v Surrey (Oval) 1996. **SL:** HS 50 v Essex (Cheltenham) 1995. BB 1-23.

CHURCH, Matthew John (St George's C, Weybridge), b Guildford, Surrey 26 Jul 1972. 6'2". RHB, RM. Worcestershire 1994-96. Gloucestershire debut 1997. MCC YC. HS 152 and BB 4-50 Wo v OU (Oxford) 1996. Gs HS 53 v Pak A (Bristol) 1997. BAC HS 38 Wo v Yorks (Worcester) 1994. BAC BB 2-27 Wo v Yorks (Worcester) 1996. **NWT:** HS 35 Wo v Hants (Worcester) 1996. **BHC:** HS –. **SL:** HS 25 v Warwks (Birmingham) 1997.

CUNLIFFE, Robert John (Banbury S; Banbury TC), b Oxford 8 Nov 1973. 5'10". RHB, RM. Debut 1994. Oxfordshire 1991-94. HS 190* v OU (Bristol) 1995. BAC HS 92* v Lancs (Cheltenham) 1995. Awards: BHC 2. **NWT:** HS 40 v Durham (Chester-le-St) 1995. **BHC:** HS 137* v Surrey (Oval) 1997. **SL:** HS 56 v Yorks (Leeds) 1997.

DAWSON, Robert Ian (Millfield S; Newcastle Poly), b Exmouth, Devon 29 Mar 1970. 5'11". RHB, RM. Debut 1992. Devon 1988-91. 1000 runs (1): 1112 (1994). HS 127* v CU (Bristol) 1994. BAC HS 101 v Worcs (Gloucester) 1994. BB 2-38 v Derbys (Chesterfield) 1994. **NWT:** HS 60 v Devon (Bristol) 1994. BB 1-37. **BHC:** HS 38 v Middx (Bristol) and v Somerset (Bristol) 1995. **SL:** HS 85 v Worcs (Worcester) 1996.

HANCOCK, Timothy Harold Coulter (St Edward's S, Oxford; Henley C), b Reading, Berks 20 Apr 1972. 5'10". RHB, RM. Debut 1991. Oxfordshire 1990. Tour: SL 1992-93 (Gs). HS 123 v Essex (Chelmsford) 1994. BB 3-10 v Glam (Abergavenny) 1993. **NWT:** HS 45 v Herts (Bristol) 1993. BB 6-58 v Scot (Bristol) 1997. **BHC:** HS 71* v Sussex (Bristol) 1996. BB 3-13 v Hants (Bristol) 1996. **SL:** HS 57 v Glam (Swansea) 1997. BB 2-6 v Notts (Nottingham) 1996.

HEWSON, Dominic Robert (Cheltenham C), b Cheltenham 3 Oct 1974. 5'8". RHB, occ RM. Debut 1996. HS 87 v Hants (Southampton) 1996 (on BAC debut). **SL:** HS 3.

LAWRENCE, David Valentine **('Syd')** (Linden S), b Gloucester 28 Jan 1964. 6'2". RHB, RF. Gloucestershire 1981-91, 1997; cap 1985; benefit 1993. Missed five seasons (fractured kneecap). YC 1985. **Tests:** 5 (1988 to 1991-92); HS 34 v WI (Nottingham) 1991; BB 5-106 v WI (Oval) 1991. **LOI:** 1 (1991; HS – ; BB 4-67). Tours: NZ 1991-92; SL 1985-86 (Eng B), 1986-87 (Gs). HS 66 v Glam (Abergavenny) 1991. 50 wkts (5); most – 85 (1985). BB 7-47 v Surrey (Cheltenham) 1988. Hat-trick 1990. Awards: NWT 2; BHC 2. **NWT:** HS 5*. BB 5-17 v Norfolk (Bristol) 1991. **BHC:** HS 23 and BB 6-20 v Comb Us (Bristol) 1991. **SL:** HS 38* v Yorks (Scarborough) 1991. BB 5-18 v Somerset (Bristol) 1990.

LEWIS, Jonathan (Churchfields S, Swindon; Swindon C), b Aylesbury, Bucks 26 Aug 1975. 6'2". RHB, RMF. Debut 1995. Wiltshire 1993. Northamptonshire staff 1994. HS 30 v Worcs (Bristol) 1997. 50 wkts (1): 54 (1997). BB 6-50 v Middx (Bristol) 1997. **NWT:** HS 6*. BB 3-27 v Somerset (Taunton) 1996. **BHC:** HS – v Ireland (Dublin) 1996. **SL:** HS 9*. BB 3-27 v Warwks (Birmingham) 1995.

RUSSELL, Robert Charles **('Jack')** (Archway CS), b Stroud 15 Aug 1963. 5'8½". LHB, WK, occ OB. Debut 1981 – youngest Glos wicket-keeper (17yr 307d), setting record for most match dismissals on f-c debut – 8 v SL (Bristol); cap 1985; benefit 1994; captain 1995. *Wisden* 1989. MBE 1996. **Tests:** 49 (1988 to 1996); HS 128* v A (Manchester) 1989; 11 ct v SA (Jo'burg) 1995-96 (Test record); 27 dis 1995-96 series v SA (Eng record). **LOI:** 38 (1987-88 to 1996-97; HS 50). Tours: A 1990-91, 1992-93 (Eng A); SA 1995-96; WI 1989-90, 1993-94; NZ 1991-92, 1996-97; P 1987-88; SL 1986-87 (Gs). 1000 runs (1): 1049 (1997). HS 129* Eng XI v Boland (Paarl) 1995-96. Gs HS 124 v Notts (Nottingham) 1996. BB 1-4. Awards: BHC 2. **NWT:** HS 59* v Suffolk (Bristol) 1995. **BHC:** HS 51 v Worcs (Worcester) 1991. **SL:** HS 108 v Worcs (Hereford) 1986.

SHEERAZ, Kamran Pasha (Licensed Victuallers' S, Ascot; E Berkshire C, Langley), b Wellington, Shropshire 28 Dec 1973. 6'0". RHB, RMF. Debut 1994. Bedfordshire 1992. HS 12* v Glam (Swansea) 1997. BB 6-67 v WI (Bristol) 1995. BAC BB 3-89 v Derbys (Bristol) 1995. **SL:** HS 14* v Surrey (Oval) 1995. BB 2-20 v Middx (Bristol) 1995.

SMITH, Andrew **Michael** (Queen Elizabeth GS, Wakefield; Exeter U), b Dewsbury, Yorks 1 Oct 1967. 5'9". RHB, LMF. Debut 1991; cap 1995. **Tests:** 1 (1997); HS 4*; BB –. Tour: P 1995-96 (Eng A – *part*). HS 55* v Notts (Nottingham) 1996. 50 wkts (3); most – 83 (1997). BB 8-73 (10-118 match) v Middx (Lord's) 1996. Award: BHC 1. **NWT:** HS 13 v Somerset (Taunton) 1996. BB 3-21 v Lincs (Sleaford) 1996. **BHC:** HS 15* Comb Us v Surrey (Oxford) 1990. BB 6-39 v Hants (Southampton) 1995. **SL:** HS 26* v Kent (Moreton-in-M) 1996. BB 4-38 v Leics (Bristol) 1992.

TRAINOR, Nicholas James (St Edmund Campion S, Low Fell), b Gateshead, Co Durham 29 Jun 1975. 6'1". RHB, OB. Debut 1996. Northumberland 1995. HS 121 v A (Bristol) 1997. BAC HS 67 v Surrey (Gloucester) 1996 – on debut. **NWT:** HS 143 and BB 2-25 v Scot (Bristol) 1997. **BHC:** HS 62 v Brit Us (Bristol) 1997. **SL:** HS 22 v Leics (Leicester) 1997.

WALSH, Courtney Andrew (Excelsior HS), b Kingston, Jamaica 30 Oct 1962. 6'5½". RHB, RF. Jamaica 1981-82 to date (captain 1990-91 to date). Gloucestershire 1984-96; cap 1985; captain 1993-94 and 1996; benefit 1992; testimonial 1998. *Wisden* 1986. **Tests** (WI): 93 (1984-85 to 1996-97, 19 as captain); HS 30* v A (Melbourne) 1988-89; BB 7-37 (13-55 match) v NZ (Wellington) 1994-95. **LOI** (WI): 176 (1984-85 to 1996-97, 36 as captain; HS 30; BB 5-1). Tours (WI)(C=captain): E 1984, 1988, 1991, 1995; A 1984-85, 1986-87, 1988-89, 1992-93, 1995-96, 1996-97C; NZ 1986-87, 1994-95C; I 1987-88, 1994-95C; P 1986-87, 1990-91; SL 1993-94; Z 1983-84 (Young WI). HS 66 v Kent (Cheltenham) 1994. 50 wkts (9+3) inc 100 (1): 118 (1986). BB 9-72 v Somerset (Bristol) 1986. Hat-trick 1988-89 (WI). Awards: NWT 2. **NWT**: HS 37 v Herts (Bristol) 1993. BB 6-21 v Kent (Bristol) 1990 and v Cheshire (Bristol) 1992. **BHC**: HS 28 v Comb Us (Bristol) 1989. BB 2-19 v Scot 1985. **SL**: HS 38 v Derbys (Derby) 1996. BB 4-19 v Kent (Cheltenham) 1987.

WILLIAMS, Richard Charles James (**'Reggie'**) (Millfield S), b Southmead, Bristol 8 Aug 1969. 5'8". LHB, WK. Debut 1990; cap 1996. Tour: SL 1992-93 (Gs). HS 90 v OU (Bristol) 1995. **BAC** HS 55* v Derbys (Gloucester) 1991. **SL**: HS 19 v Essex (Cheltenham) 1995.

WINDOWS, Matthew Guy Newman (Clifton C; Durham U), b Bristol 5 Apr 1973. Son of A.R. (Glos and CU 1960-68). 5'7". RHB, RSM. Debut 1992. Combined Us 1995. HS 184 v Warwks (Cheltenham) 1996. BB 1-6 (Comb Us). **NWT**: HS 33 v Devon (Bristol) 1994. **BHC**: HS 16* Comb Us v Lancs (Oxford) 1994. **SL**: HS 72 v Somerset (Bristol) 1994.

WRIGHT, Anthony John (Alleyn's GS) b Stevenage, Herts 27 Jun 1962. 6'0". RHB, RM. Gloucestershire debut 1982; cap 1987; captain 1990-93; benefit 1996. Tours (Gs): SL 1986-87, 1992-93 (captain). 1000 runs (6); most – 1596 (1991). HS 193 v Notts (Bristol) 1995. BB 1-16. Awards: NWT 4; BHC 2. **NWT**: HS 177 v Scot (Bristol) 1997. **BHC**: HS 123 v Ireland (Dublin) 1996. **SL**: HS 96 v Sussex (Bristol) 1996.

NEWCOMER

GANNON, Benjamin Ward, b Oxford 5 Sep 1975. RHB, RFM.

DEPARTURES (who made first-class appearances in 1997)

DAVIS, R.P. – *see SUSSEX*.

LYNCH, Monte Alan (Ryden's S. Walton-on-Thames), b Georgetown, British Guiana 21 May 1958. 5'8". RHB, OB. Surrey 1977-94; cap 1982; benefit 1991. Gloucestershire 1995-97; cap 1996. Guyana 1982-83. **LOI**: 3 (1988; HS 6). Tours: SA 1983-84 (WI XI); P 1981-82 (Int). 1000 runs (9); most – 1714 (1985). HS 172* Sy v Kent (Oval) 1989. Gs HS 114 v Kent (Canterbury) 1995. BB 3-6 Sy v Glam (Swansea) 1981. Gs BB –. Awards: NWT 1; BHC 5. **NWT**: HS 129 Sy v Durham (Oval) 1982. BB 2-28 Sy v Glam (Swansea) 1992. **BHC**: HS 112* Sy v Kent (Oval) 1987. **SL**: HS 136 Sy v Yorks (Bradford) 1985. BB 2-2 Sy v Northants (Guildford) 1987 and Sy v Sussex (Hove) 1990.

READ, C.M.W. – *see NOTTINGHAMSHIRE*.

YOUNG, Shaun, b Burnie, Australia 13 Jun 1970. LHB, RFM. Tasmania 1991-92 to date. Gloucestershire 1997; cap 1997. **Tests** (A): 1 (1997); HS 4*; BB –. Tours: E 1995 (Young A), 1997 (*part*); Z 1995-96 (Tas). HS 237 v Derbys (Cheltenham) 1997. BB 7-64 Tasmania v P (Hobart) 1996-97. Gs BB 4-26 v Surrey (Oval) 1997. Award: BHC 1. **NWT**: HS 14* and BB 1-20 v Scot (Bristol) 1997. **BHC**: HS 67 v Surrey (Oval) 1997. BB 4-54 v Hants (Southampton) 1997. **SL**: HS 146* v Yorks (Leeds) 1997. BB 3-32 v Sussex (Hove) 1997.

GLOUCESTERSHIRE 1997

RESULTS SUMMARY

	Place	Won	Lost	Tied	Drew	No Result
Britannic Assurance Championship	7th	6	6	–	5	–
All First-Class Matches		6	6	–	7	–
NatWest Trophy	2nd Round					
Benson and Hedges Cup	3rd in Group C					
Sunday League	11th	7	6	–	–	4

BRITANNIC ASSURANCE CHAMPIONSHIP AVERAGES

BATTING AND FIELDING

Cap		M	I	NO	HS	Runs	Avge	100	50	Ct/St
1985	R.C.Russell	17	26	5	103*	999	47.57	1	8	44/4
1990	M.W.Alleyne	17	27	3	169	1017	42.37	1	8	13
1997	S.Young	16	27	3	237	980	40.83	2	5	9
–	T.H.C.Hancock	17	28	3	100*	787	31.48	1	4	9
–	R.I.Dawson	7	12	–	100	314	26.16	1	1	3
1995	M.A.Lynch	12	19	1	64	465	25.83	–	3	9
–	M.G.N.Windows	7	13	–	84	334	25.69	–	2	6
1996	M.C.J.Ball	16	25	3	41	512	23.27	–	–	24
1987	A.J.Wright	12	21	3	79	400	22.22	–	1	10
–	R.J.Cunliffe	8	13	1	49	212	17.66	–	–	4
–	J.Lewis	13	17	6	30	186	16.90	–	–	2
–	D.R.Hewson	3	4	–	42	56	14.00	–	–	3
–	N.J.Trainor	12	22	1	40	288	13.71	–	–	3
1995	A.M.Smith	15	22	8	41*	152	10.85	–	–	3
1985	D.V.Lawrence	4	6	3	23*	32	10.66	–	–	1
–	R.P.Davis	7	10	–	39	93	9.30	–	–	7

Also played: J.M.M.Averis (1 match) did not bat (1 ct); M.J.Church (1) 4, 16; K.P.Sheeraz (2) 12*, 3*.

BOWLING

	O	M	R	W	Avge	Best	5wI	10wM
A.M.Smith	450.2	111	1281	78	16.42	6-45	5	3
J.Lewis	365.5	86	1211	48	25.22	6-50	3	–
M.W.Alleyne	329.1	80	1051	40	26.27	6-64	3	–
R.P.Davis	201	67	486	16	30.37	4-35	–	–
S.Young	360.3	98	1000	30	33.33	4-26	–	–
M.C.J.Ball	418.5	114	1082	22	49.18	5-66	1	–

Also bowled: J.M.M.Averis 17-4-76-0; R.I.Dawson 3-0-22-0; T.H.C.Hancock 76.5-17-300-4; D.V.Lawrence 86-9-359-8; K.P.Sheeraz 7-0-40-0; N.J.Trainor 18-5-81-0; M.G.N.Windows 6-1-47-0.

The First-Class Averages (pp 118-133) give the records of Gloucestershire players in all first-class county matches (their other opponents being the Australians and Pakistan A), with the exception of J.M.Averis whose full county figures are as above, and:
A.M.Smith 17-24-8-41*-161-10.06-0-0-4ct. 489.2-123-1375-83-16.56-6/45-5-3.
S.Young 17-28-3-237-981-39.24-2-5-10ct. 362.3-98-1005-30-33.50-4/26.

GLOUCESTERSHIRE RECORDS

FIRST-CLASS CRICKET

Highest Total	For	653-6d	v	Glamorgan	Bristol	1928
	V	774-7d	by	Australians	Bristol	1948
Lowest Total	For	17	v	Australians	Cheltenham	1896
	V	12	by	Northants	Gloucester	1907
Highest Innings	For	318* W.G.Grace	v	Yorkshire	Cheltenham	1876
	V	296 A.O.Jones	for	Notts	Nottingham	1903

Highest Partnership for each Wicket

1st	395	D.M.Young/R.B.Nicholls	v	Oxford U	Oxford	1962
2nd	256	C.T.M.Pugh/T.W.Graveney	v	Derbyshire	Chesterfield	1960
3rd	336	W.R.Hammond/B.H.Lyon	v	Leics	Leicester	1933
4th	321	W.R.Hammond/W.L.Neale	v	Leics	Gloucester	1937
5th	261	W.G.Grace/W.O.Moberley	v	Yorkshire	Cheltenham	1876
6th	320	G.L.Jessop/J.H.Board	v	Sussex	Hove	1903
7th	248	W.G.Grace/E.L.Thomas	v	Sussex	Hove	1896
8th	239	W.R.Hammond/A.E.Wilson	v	Lancashire	Bristol	1938
9th	193	W.G.Grace/S.A.P.Kitcat	v	Sussex	Bristol	1896
10th	131	W.R.Gouldsworthy/J.G.Bessant	v	Somerset	Bristol	1923

Best Bowling	For	10-40	E.G.Dennett	v	Essex	Bristol	1906
(Innings)	V	10-66	A.A.Mailey	for	Australians	Cheltenham	1921
		10-66	K.Smales	for	Notts	Stroud	1956
Best Bowling	For	17-56	C.W.L.Parker	v	Essex	Gloucester	1925
(Match)	V	15-87	A.J.Conway	for	Worcs	Moreton-in-M	1914

Most Runs – Season	2860	W.R.Hammond	(av 69.75)		1933
Most Runs – Career	33664	W.R.Hammond	(av 57.05)		1920-51
Most 100s – Season	13	W.R.Hammond			1938
Most 100s – Career	113	W.R.Hammond			1920-51
Most Wkts – Season	222	T.W.J.Goddard	(av 16.80)		1937
	222	T.W.J.Goddard	(av 16.37)		1947
Most Wkts – Career	3170	C.W.L.Parker	(av 19.43)		1903-35

LIMITED-OVERS CRICKET

Highest Total	NWT	351-2		v	Scotland	Bristol	1997
	BHC	308-3		v	Ireland	Dublin	1996
	SL	284-4		v	Leics	Cheltenham	1996
Lowest Total	NWT	82		v	Notts	Bristol	1987
	BHC	62		v	Hampshire	Bristol	1975
	SL	49		v	Middlesex	Bristol	1978
Highest Innings	NWT	177	A.J.Wright	v	Scotland	Bristol	1997
	BHC	154*	M.J.Procter	v	Somerset	Taunton	1972
	SL	146*	S.Young	v	Yorkshire	Leeds	1997
Best Bowling	NWT	6-21	C.A.Walsh	v	Kent	Bristol	1990
		6-21	C.A.Walsh	v	Cheshire	Bristol	1992
	BHC	6-13	M.J.Procter	v	Hampshire	Southampton	1977
	SL	6-52	J.N.Shepherd	v	Kent	Bristol	1983

HAMPSHIRE

Formation of Present Club: 12 August 1863
Colours: Blue, Gold and White
Badge: Tudor Rose and Crown
Championships: (2) 1961, 1973
NatWest Trophy/Gillette Cup Winners: (1) 1991
Benson and Hedges Cup Winners: (2) 1988, 1992
Sunday League Champions: (3) 1975, 1978, 1986
Match Awards: NWT 54; BHC 63

Chief Executive: A.F.Baker
County Cricket Ground, Northlands Road, Southampton SO15 2UE
(Tel 01703 333788)
Captain: R.A.Smith. **Vice-Captain:** S.D.Udal. **Overseas Player:** M.S.Kasprowicz.
1998 Beneficiary: R.J.Maru. **Scorer:** V.H Isaacs

AYMES, Adrian Nigel (Bellemoor SM, Southampton), b Southampton 4 Jun 1964. 6'0". RHB, WK. Debut 1987; cap 1991. HS 113 v Essex (Southampton) 1996. BB 1-75. **NWT:** HS 34 v Kent (Southampton) 1994. **BHC:** HS 38 v Surrey (Oval) 1996. **SL:** HS 54 v Durham (Portsmouth) 1994.

CONNOR, Cardigan Adolphus (The Valley SS, Anguilla; Langley C, Berkshire), b The Valley, Anguilla 24 Mar 1961. 5'9". RHB, RFM. Debut 1984; cap 1988; benefit 1997. Buckinghamshire 1979-83. HS 59 v Surrey (Oval) 1993. 50 wkts (5); most – 72 (1994). BB 9-38 v Glos (Southampton) 1996. Award: NWT 1. **NWT:** HS 13 v Yorks (Southampton) 1990. BB 4-11 v Cambs (March) 1994. **BHC:** HS 11 v Glos (Southampton) 1995. BB 4-19 v Sussex (Hove) 1989. **SL:** HS 25 v Middx (Lord's) 1993. BB 5-25 v Northants (Basingstoke) 1996.

DIBDEN, Richard Rockley (Mountbatten S, Romsey; Barton Peveril C, Eastleigh; Loughborough U), b Southampton 29 Jan 1975. 6'0". RHB, OB. Debut 1995. British Us 1996. HS 1. H HS 0*. BB 2-36 v Yorks (Southampton) 1995.

FRANCIS, Simon Richard George (Yardley Court, Tonbridge; King Edward VI S, Southampton), b Bromley, Kent 15 Aug 1978. 6'2". RHB, RMF. Debut 1997. HS 4. **SL:** HS – and BB 2-31 v Sussex (Southampton) 1997.

GARAWAY, Mark (Sandown HS, IoW), b Swindon, Wilts 20 Jul 1973. 5'8". RHB, WK. Debut 1996. MCC YC. Awaiting BAC debut. HS 44 v CU (Cambridge) 1996.

HANSEN, Thomas Munkholt (Norregaard, Falkonergaarden), b Glostrup, Denmark 25 Mar 1976. 6'3". RHB, LFM. Debut 1997. Denmark 1996 to date. HS 19 v Worcs (Southampton) 1997.

JAMES, Kevan David (Edmonton County HS), b Lambeth, London 18 Mar 1961. 6'0". LHB, LMF. Middlesex 1980-84. Wellington 1982-83. Hampshire debut 1985; cap 1989. 1000 runs (2); most – 1274 (1991). HS 162 v Glam (Cardiff) 1989. BB 8-49 (13-93 match) v Somerset (Basingstoke) 1997. Achieved unique double of 4 wkts in 4 balls and a hundred (103) v I (Southampton) 1996. **NWT:** HS 42 v Glam (Cardiff) 1989. BB 4-42 v Worcs (Worcester) 1996. **BHC:** HS 56 v Glos (Bristol) 1996. BB 3-31 v Middx 1987 and v Glam 1988. **SL:** HS 66 v Glos (Trowbridge) 1989. BB 6-35 v Notts (Southampton) 1996.

KEECH, Matthew (Northumberland Park S), b Hampstead 21 Oct 1970. 6'0". RHB, RM. Middlesex 1991-93. Hampshire debut 1996. MCC YC. HS 127 v OU (Oxford) 1997. BAC HS 104 v Sussex (Arundel) 1996. BB 2-28 M v Glos (Bristol) 1993. H BB 1-12. Scored 251 (256 balls) v Glam II (Usk) – Hants II record. **NWT:** HS 34 v Glam (Southampton) 1997. **BHC:** HS 47 M v Warwks (Lord's) 1991. BB 1-37. **SL:** HS 98 v Worcs (Southampton) 1995. BB 2-22 M v Northants (Lord's) 1993.

KENDALL, William Salwey (Bradfield C; Keble C, Oxford), b Wimbledon, Surrey 18 Dec 1973. 5'10". RHB, RM. Oxford U 1994-96; blue 1995-96. Hampshire debut 1996. 1000 runs (1): 1045 (1996). HS 145* OU v CU (Lord's) 1996. H HS 103* and BB 2-46 v Notts (Southampton) 1996. BB 3-37 OU v Derbys (Oxford) 1995. **NWT:** HS 16 v Glam (Southampton) 1997. **BHC:** HS 26 v Kent (Canterbury) 1997. **SL:** HS 55 v Essex (Chelmsford) 1997.

KENWAY, Derek Anthony (St George's S, Southampton; Barton Peveril C, Eastleigh), b Fareham 12 Jun 1978. 5'11". RHB, WK. Debut 1997. HS 20* and BB 1-5 v Warwks (Southampton) 1997.

LANEY, Jason Scott (Pewsey Vale SS; St John's SFC, Marlborough; Leeds U), b Winchester 27 Apr 1973. 5'10". RHB, OB. Debut 1995; cap 1996. Matabeleland 1995-96. 1000 runs (1): 1163 (1996). HS 112 v OU (Oxford) 1996. BAC HS 105 v Kent (Canterbury) 1996. Award: NWT 1. **NWT:** HS 153 v Norfolk (Southampton) 1996. **BHC:** HS 41 v Surrey (Oval) 1996. **SL:** HS 69 v Notts (Nottingham) 1996.

MARU, Rajesh Jamandass (Rook's Heath HS, Harrow; Pinner SFC), b Nairobi, Kenya 28 Oct 1962. 5'6". RHB, SLA. Middlesex 1980-82. Hampshire debut 1984; cap 1986; benefit 1996. Tour: Z 1980-81 (Mx). HS 74 v Glos (Gloucester) 1988. 50 wkts (4); most – 73 (1985). BB 8-41 v Kent (Southampton) 1989. **NWT:** HS 22 v Yorks (Southampton) 1990. BB 3-46 v Leics (Leicester) 1990. **BHC:** HS 9*. BB 3-46 v Comb Us (Southampton) 1990. **SL:** HS 33* v Glam (Ebbw Vale) 1991. BB 4-29 v Yorks (Southampton) 1997.

MASCARENHAS, Adrian Dimitri (Trinity C, Perth, Australia), b Hammersmith, London 30 Oct 1977. Parents born in Ceylon. Resident in Perth 1979-96. RHB, RMF. Debut 1996, taking 6-88 v Glamorgan (Southampton); took 16 wickets in first two BAC matches. Dorset 1996. HS 21 v Glos (Bristol) 1997. BB 6-88 (*see above*). **BHC:** HS 20 v Glos (Southampton) 1997. **SL:** HS 10 v Yorks (Southampton) 1997. BB 2-34 v Kent (Canterbury) 1996.

RENSHAW, Simon John (Birkenhead S; Leeds U), b Bebington, Cheshire 6 Mar 1974. 6'3". RHB, RMF. Combined Us 1995. Hampshire debut 1996. Cheshire 1994-95. HS 56 v Surrey (Guildford) 1997. BB 5-110 v Derbys (Chesterfield) 1997. **NWT:** HS –. BB 2-71 v Glam (Southampton) 1997. **BHC:** HS 2*. BB 3-34 v Kent (Canterbury) 1997. **SL:** HS 25 v Surrey (Guildford) 1997. BB 3-45 v Somerset (Basingstoke) 1997.

SAVIDENT, Lee (Guernsey GS; Guernsey CFE), b Guernsey 22 Oct 1976. 6'5". RHB, RM. Debut 1997. HS 6 and BB 2-86 v Yorks (Portsmouth) 1997. **SL:** HS 7*. BB 3-41 v Middx (Lord's) 1997.

SMITH, Robin Arnold (Northlands BHS), b Durban, SA 13 Sep 1963. Brother of C.L. (Natal, Glam, Hants and England 1977-78 to 1992) and grandson of Dr V.L.Shearer (Natal). 5'11". RHB, LB. Natal 1980-81 to 1984-85. Hampshire debut 1982; cap 1985; benefit 1996; captain 1998. *Wisden* 1989. **Tests:** 62 (1988 to 1995-96); HS 175 v WI (St John's) 1993-94. **LOI:** 71 (1988 to 1995-96; HS 167* – Eng record). Tours: A 1990-91; SA 1995-96; WI 1989-90, 1993-94; NZ 1991-92; I/SL 1992-93. 1000 runs (10); most – 1577 (1989). HS 209* v Essex (Southend) 1987. BB 2-11 v Surrey (Southampton) 1985. Awards: NWT 8; BHC 5. **NWT:** HS 158 v Worcs (Worcester) 1996. BB 2-13 v Berks (Southampton) 1985. **BHC:** HS 155* v Glam (Southampton) 1989. **SL:** HS 131 v Notts (Nottingham) 1989. BB 1-0.

STEPHENSON, John Patrick (Felsted S; Durham U), b Stebbing, Essex 14 Mar 1965. 6'1". RHB, RM. Essex 1985-94 (cap 1989). Hampshire debut/cap 1995; captain 1996-97. Boland 1988-89. **Tests:** 1 (1989); HS 25 v A (Oval) 1989. Tours: WI 1991-92 (Eng A); Z 1989-90 (Eng A). 1000 runs (5); most – 1887 (1990). HS 202* Ex v Somerset (Bath) 1990. H HS 140 v OU (Oxford) 1997. BB 7-51 v Middx (Lord's) 1995. Awards: BHC 5. **NWT:** HS 107 v Norfolk (Southampton) 1996. BB 5-34 v Cambs (Wisbech) 1997. **BHC:** HS 142 Ex v Warwks (Birmingham) 1991. BB 3-22 Ex v Northants (Northampton) 1990. **SL:** HS 110* v Essex (Southampton) 1996. BB 6-33 v Worcs (Southampton) 1997.

UDAL, Shaun David (Cove CS), b Cove, Farnborough 18 Mar 1969. Grandson of G.F.U. (Middx 1932 and Leics 1946); great-great-grandson of J.S. (MCC 1871-75). 6'2". RHB, OB. Debut 1989; cap 1992. **LOI**: 10 (1994 to 1995); HS 11*; BB 2-37). Tours: A 1994-95; P 1995-96 (Eng A). HS 117* v Warwks (Southampton) 1997. 50 wkts; most – 74 (1993). BB 8-50 v Sussex (Southampton) 1992. Awards: NWT 1; BHC 1. **NWT**: HS 39* v Glam (Southampton) 1997. BB 3-13 v Cambs (Wisbech) 1997. **BHC**: HS 34 v Glos (Southampton) 1997. BB 4-40 v Middx (Southampton) 1992. **SL**: HS 78 v Surrey (Guildford) 1997. BB 4-51 v Northants (Bournemouth) 1997.

WHITAKER, Paul Robert (Whitcliffe Mount S), b Keighley, Yorks 28 Jun 1973. 5'9". LHB, OB. Debut 1994. Hampshire staff 1992-93. HS 119 v Worcs (Southampton) 1995. BB 3-36 v OU (Oxford) 1996. BAC BB 2-64 v Lancs (Manchester) 1996. Award: BHC 1. **NWT**: HS 13 v Leics (Leicester) 1995. BB 3-48 v Essex (Southampton) 1996. **BHC**: HS 53 v Sussex (Southampton) 1996. BB 2-33 v Surrey (Oval) 1996. **SL**: HS 97 v Worcs (Southampton) 1995. BB 3-44 v Surrey (Southampton) 1996.

WHITE, Giles William (Millfield S; Loughborough U), b Barnstaple, Devon 23 Mar 1972. 6'0". RHB, LB. Somerset 1991 (one match). Combined 1994. Hampshire debut 1994. Devon 1988-94. HS 145 v Yorks (Portsmouth) 1997. BB 1-30. **NWT**: HS 11 and BB 1-45 Devon v Kent (Canterbury) 1992. **BHC**: HS 56 v Brit Us (Oxford) 1997. **SL**: HS 67 v Warwks (Southampton) 1997.

NEWCOMERS

HARTLEY, Peter John (Greenhead GS; Bradford C), b Keighley, Yorks 18 Apr 1960. 6'0". RHB, RMF. Warwickshire 1982. Yorkshire 1985-97; cap 1987; benefit 1996. Tours (Y): SA 1991-92; WI 1986-87; Z 1995-96. HS 127* Y v Lancs (Manchester) 1988. 50 wkts (6); most – 81 (1995). BB 9-41 (inc hat-trick, 4 wkts in 5 balls and 5 in 9; 11-68 match) v Derbys (Chesterfield) 1995. Hat-trick 1995. Awards: NWT 1; BHC 2. **NWT**: HS 83 Y v Ire (Leeds) 1997. BB 5-46 Y v Hants (Southampton) 1990. **BHC**: HS 29* Y v Notts (Nottingham) 1986. BB 5-43 Y v Scot (Leeds) 1986. **SL**: HS 52 Y v Glos (Bristol) 1996. BB 5-36 Y v Sussex (Scarborough) 1993.

KASPROWICZ, Michael Scott (Brisbane State HS), b South Brisbane, Australia 10 Feb 1972. 6'4". RHB, RF. Queensland 1989-90 to date. Essex 1994; cap 1994. **Tests** (A): 5 (1996-97 to 1997); HS 21 v WI (Sydney) 1996-97; BB 7-36 v E (Oval) 1997. **LOI** (A): 5 (1995-96 to 1997; HS 28*; BB 1-27). Tours (A): E 1995 (Young A), 1997. HS 49 Q v WA (Perth) 1989-90. BAC HS 44 Ex v Middx (Uxbridge) 1994. 50 wkts (1+2); most – 64 (1995-96). BB 7-36 (see Tests). BAC BB 7-83 Ex v Somerset (Weston-s-M) 1994. **NWT**: HS 13 and BB 5-60 Ex v Glam (Cardiff) 1994. **BHC**: HS – . BB 2-52 Ex v Leics (Chelmsford) 1994. **SL**: HS 17 Ex v Glos (Chelmsford) 1994. BB 2-38 Ex v Glam (Southend) and Ex v Northants (Chelmsford) 1994.

LOUDON, Hugo John Hope (Eton C), b Westminster, London 11 Dec 1978. RHB, SLA.

MORRIS, Alexander Corfield (Holgate S; Barnsley C), b Barnsley, Yorks 4 Oct 1976. Elder brother of Z.C. 6'3". LHB, RMF. Yorkshire 1995-97. Yorks 2nd XI player when 16yr 332d. Tour: Z 1995-96 (Y). HS 60 Y v Lancs (Manchester) 1996 (not BAC). BAC HS 40 Y v Durham (Chester-le-St) 1996. BB 2-62 Y v Surrey (Oval) 1997. **NWT**: HS 1*. BB 1-43. **BHC**: – . **SL**: HS 48* Y v Durham (Chester-le-St) 1996. BB 4-49 Y v Leics (Leeds) 1997.

MORRIS, Zachary Clegg, b Barnsley, Yorks 4 Sep 1978. Younger brother of A.C. RHB, SLA.

DEPARTURES (who made first-class appearances in 1997)

BOVILL, James Noel Bruce (Charterhouse; Durham U), b High Wycombe, Bucks 2 Jun 1971. Son of M.E. (Dorset 1957-60). 6'1". RHB, RFM. Hampshire 1993-97. Combined Us 1994. Buckinghamshire 1990-92. HS 31 H v Worcs (Southampton) 1995. BB 6-29 (12-68 match) H v Durham (Stockton) 1995. **BHC**: HS 14* Comb Us v Glam (Cardiff) 1992. BB 2-21 Comb Us v Lancs (Oxford) 1994. **SL**: HS 7*. BB 4-44 v Warwks (Southampton) 1997.

continued on p 106

HAMPSHIRE 1997

RESULTS SUMMARY

	Place	Won	Lost	Tied	Drew	No Result
Britannic Assurance Championship	14th	3	5	–	8	1
All First-Class Matches		3	6	–	9	1
NatWest Trophy	2nd Round					
Benson and Hedges Cup	5th in Group C					
Sunday League	15th	5	11	–	–	1

BRITANNIC ASSURANCE CHAMPIONSHIP AVERAGES

BATTING AND FIELDING

Cap		M	I	NO	HS	Runs	Avge	100	50	Ct/St
1997	M.L.Hayden	16	28	3	235*	1438	57.52	4	7	12
–	G.W.White	9	16	2	145	667	47.64	1	4	6
1985	R.A.Smith	13	21	1	154	852	42.60	2	4	4
–	M.Keech	8	13	4	101*	368	40.88	1		9
1996	J.S.Laney	13	23	–	95	808	35.13	–	6	6
–	P.R.Whitaker	2	4	–	73	131	32.75	–	1	–
1995	J.P.Stephenson	15	23	3	114	644	32.20	1	1	6
1992	S.D.Udal	16	22	3	117*	577	30.36	1	4	2
–	W.S.Kendall	10	16	2	76	375	26.78	–	1	5
1989	K.D.James	9	14	2	85	306	25.50	–	4	5
–	S.J.Renshaw	12	17	6	56	252	22.90	–	1	3
1986	R.J.Maru	4	4	1	36*	67	22.33	–	–	6
1991	A.N.Aymes	16	21	3	96*	393	21.83	–	1	33/7
1988	C.A.Connor	4	4	2	12*	34	17.00	–	–	1
–	S.M.Milburn	9	6	2	19	64	16.00	–	–	1
–	J.N.B.Bovill	8	7	2	27	55	11.00	–	–	4
–	A.D.Mascarenhas	5	7	1	21	50	8.33	–	–	–
–	L.Savident	3	4	1	6	15	5.00	–	–	1

Also batted: (1 match each): S.R.G.Francis 4, 4; T.M.Hansen 12*, 19; D.A.Kenway 2, 20* (1 ct); C.M.Patel 6, 3*.

BOWLING

	O	M	R	W	Avge	Best	5wI	10wM
K.D.James	132.1	29	443	23	19.26	8- 49	2	1
C.A.Connor	102.5	15	364	11	33.09	7- 46	–	–
J.N.B.Bovill	207.4	30	815	23	35.43	4- 62	–	–
S.J.Renshaw	329.3	57	1171	33	35.48	5-110	1	–
J.P.Stephenson	386.5	62	1356	35	38.74	6- 54	1	–
S.D.Udal	564.1	131	1666	32	52.06	4- 17	–	–
S.M.Milburn	277	41	972	18	54.00	4- 38	–	–

Also bowled: A.N.Aymes 9-0-76-0; S.R.G.Francis 19-1-97-0; T.M.Hansen 26-10-75-0; M.L.Hayden 33-0-166-3; M.Keech 12-1-51-1; W.S.Kendall 5-0-46-0; D.A.Kenway 9-2-58-2; J.S.Laney 5-2-19-0; R.J.Maru 127-35-336-3; A.D.Mascarenhas 93.4-16-319-3; C.M.Patel 18-3-65-0; L.Savident 56-9-247-4; R.A.Smith 5.1-0-75-0; P.R.Whitaker 22-3-73-1; G.W.White 10.5-0-49-0.

The First-Class Averages (pp 118-133) give the records of Hampshire players in all first-class county matches (their other opponents being the Australians and Oxford University), with the exception of C.M.Patel whose full county figures are as above, M.Garaway who did not appear for the county, and:
  J.S.Laney 14-25-0-95-844-33.76-0-6-6ct. 5-2-19-0.

HAMPSHIRE RECORDS

FIRST-CLASS CRICKET

Highest Total	For	672-7d	v	Somerset	Taunton	1899
	V	742	by	Surrey	The Oval	1909
Lowest Total	For	15	v	Warwicks	Birmingham	1922
	V	23	by	Yorkshire	Middlesbrough	1965
Highest Innings	For	316	R.H.Moore	v	Warwicks	Bournemouth	1937
	V	303*	G.A.Hick	for	Worcs	Southampton	1997

Highest Partnership for each Wicket

1st	347	V.P.Terry/C.L.Smith	v	Warwicks	Birmingham	1987
2nd	321	G.Brown/E.I.M.Barrett	v	Glos	Southampton	1920
3rd	344	C.P.Mead/G.Brown	v	Yorkshire	Portsmouth	1927
4th	263	R.E.Marshall/D.A.Livingstone	v	Middlesex	Lord's	1970
5th	235	G.Hill/D.F.Walker	v	Sussex	Portsmouth	1937
6th	411	R.M.Poore/E.G.Wynyard	v	Somerset	Taunton	1899
7th	325	G.Brown/C.H.Abercrombie	v	Essex	Leyton	1913
8th	227	K.D.James/T.M.Tremlett	v	Somerset	Taunton	1985
9th	230	D.A.Livingstone/A.T.Castell	v	Surrey	Southampton	1962
10th	192	H.A.W.Bowell/W.H.Livsey	v	Worcs	Bournemouth	1921

Best Bowling	For	9- 25	R.M.H.Cottam	v	Lancashire	Manchester	1965
(Innings)	V	10- 46	W.Hickton	for	Lancashire	Manchester	1870
Best Bowling	For	16- 88	J.A.Newman	v	Somerset	Weston-s-Mare	1927
(Match)	V	17-119	W.Mead	for	Essex	Southampton	1895

Most Runs – Season	2854	C.P.Mead	(av 79.27)	1928
Most Runs – Career	48892	C.P.Mead	(av 48.84)	1905-36
Most 100s – Season	12	C.P.Mead		1928
Most 100s – Career	138	C.P.Mead		1905-36
Most Wkts – Season	190	A.S.Kennedy	(av 15.61)	1922
Most Wkts – Career	2669	D.Shackleton	(av 18.23)	1948-69

LIMITED-OVERS CRICKET

Highest Total	NWT	371-4		v	Glamorgan	Southampton	1975
	BHC	321-1		v	Minor C (S)	Amersham	1973
	SL	313-2		v	Sussex	Portsmouth	1993
Lowest Total	NWT	98		v	Lancashire	Manchester	1975
	BHC	50		v	Yorkshire	Leeds	1991
	SL	43		v	Essex	Basingstoke	1972
Highest Innings	NWT	177	C.G.Greenidge	v	Glamorgan	Southampton	1975
	BHC	173*	C.G.Greenidge	v	Minor C (S)	Amersham	1973
	SL	172	C.G.Greenidge	v	Surrey	Southampton	1987
Best Bowling	NWT	7-30	P.J.Sainsbury	v	Norfolk	Southampton	1965
	BHC	5-13	S.T.Jefferies	v	Derbyshire	Lord's	1988
	SL	6-20	T.E.Jesty	v	Glamorgan	Cardiff	1975

KENT

Formation of Present Club: 1 March 1859
Substantial Reorganisation: 6 December 1870
Colours: Maroon and White
Badge: White Horse on a Red Ground
Championships: (6) 1906, 1909, 1910, 1913, 1970, 1978
Joint Championship: (1) 1977
NatWest Trophy/Gillette Cup Winners: (2) 1967, 1974
Benson and Hedges Cup Winners: (3) 1973, 1976, 1978
Sunday League Champions: (4) 1972, 1973, 1976, 1995
Match Awards: NWT 47; BHC 87

Secretary: S.T.W.Anderson OBE, MC
  St Lawrence Ground, Canterbury, CT1 3NZ (Tel 01227 456886)
Captain: S.A.Marsh. **Vice-Captain:** No appointment. **Overseas Player:** C.L.Hooper.
1998 Beneficiary (testimonial): A.P.Igglesden. **Scorer:** J.C.Foley

COWDREY, Graham Robert (Tonbridge S; Durham U), b Farnborough 27 Jun 1964. Brother of C.S. (Kent, Glam and England 1977-92), son of M.C. (Kent and England 1950-76), grandson of E.A. (Europeans). 5'11". RHB, RM. Debut 1988; cap 1988; benefit 1997. 1000 runs (3); most – 1576 (1990). HS 147 v Glos (Bristol) 1992. BB 1-5. Award: BHC 1. **NWT:** HS 41 v Derbys (Derby) 1996. BB 2-4 v Devon (Canterbury) 1992. **BHC:** HS 77 v Glos (Bristol) 1997. BB 1-6. **SL:** HS 105* v Hants (Southampton) 1995. BB 4-15 v Essex (Ilford) 1987.

EALHAM, Mark Alan (Stour Valley SS, Chartham), b Willesborough, Ashford 27 Aug 1969. Son of A.G.E. (Kent 1966-82). 5'9". RHB, RMF. Debut 1989; cap 1992. **Tests:** 6 (1996 to 1997); HS 53* v A (Birmingham) 1997. BB 4-21 v I (Nottingham) 1996. **LOI:** 5 (1996 to 1997; HS 40; BB 2-21). Tours: A 1996-97 (Eng A); Z 1992-93 (K). 1000 runs (1): 1055 (1997). HS 139 v Leics (Canterbury) 1997. BB 8-36 (10-74 match) v Warwks (Birmingham) 1996. Awards: NWT 2; BHC 4. **NWT:** HS 58* v Warwks (Birmingham) 1993. BB 4-10 v Derbys (Derby) 1994. **BHC:** HS 75 v Brit Us (Oxford) 1996. BB 4-29 v Somerset (Canterbury) 1992. **SL:** HS 112 v Derbys (Maidstone) 1995 (off 44 balls – SL record). BB 6-53 v Hants (Basingstoke) 1993.

FLEMING, Matthew Valentine (St Aubyns S, Rottingdean; Eton C), b Macclesfield, Cheshire 12 Dec 1964. 5'11½". RHB, RM. Debut 1989; cap 1990. Tour: Z 1992-93 (K). HS 138 v Essex (Canterbury) 1997. BB 5-51 v Notts (Nottingham) 1997. Awards: NWT 1; BHC 6. **NWT:** HS 53 v Devon (Canterbury) 1992. BB 3-34 v Hants (Southampton) 1992. **BHC:** HS 72 v Brit Us (Oxford) 1996. BB 5-27 v Hants (Canterbury) 1997. **SL:** HS 112 v Essex (Canterbury) 1996. BB 4-13 v Yorks (Canterbury) 1996.

FORD, James Antony (Tonbridge S; Durham U), b Pembury 30 Mar 1976. 5'8". RHB, SLA. Debut 1996. Awaiting BAC debut. HS –. **BHC:** (Brit Us) HS 38 v Surrey (Oval) 1997. Hockey for Northern Us and Durham.

FULTON, David Paul (The Judd S; Kent U), b Lewisham 15 Nov 1971. 6'2". RHB, SLA. Debut 1992. HS 134* and BB 1-37 v OU (Canterbury) 1996. BAC HS 110 v Surrey (Canterbury) 1997. **NWT:** HS 19 v Staffs (Stone) 1995. **BHC:** HS 25 v Lancs (Lord's) 1995. **SL:** HS 29 v Lancs (Manchester) 1993.

HEADLEY, Dean Warren (Oldswinford Hospital S; Worcester RGS), b Norton, Stourbridge, Worcs 27 Jan 1970. Son of R.G.A. (Worcs, Jamaica and WI 1958-74); grandson of G.A. (Jamaica and WI 1927-28 to 1953-54). 6'4". RHB, RFM. Middlesex 1991-92; took 5-46 on BAC debut, including wicket of A.A.Metcalfe with his first ball. Kent debut 1992-93; cap 1993. **Tests:** 3 (1997); HS 22 v A (Leeds) 1997. BB 4-72 v A (Manchester) 1997 – on debut. **LOI:** 3 (1996 to 1997; HS 3*; BB 1-36). Tours (Eng A): A 1996-97; P 1995-96; Z 1992-93 (K). HS 91 M v Leics (Leicester) 1992. K HS 63* v Somerset (Canterbury) 1996. 50 wkts (1): 51 (1996). BB 8-98 (inc hat-trick; 11-165 match) v

46

HEADLEY, D.W. continued:
Derbys (Derby) 1996. 3 hat-tricks (v Derbys, Worcs and Hants) 1996. Awards: BHC 3. **NWT:** HS 24* v Warwks (Birmingham) 1995. BB 5-20 M v Salop (Telford) 1992. **BHC:** HS 26 M v Surrey (Lord's) 1991. BB 4-19 M v Sussex (Hove) 1992. **SL:** HS 29* v Glos (Moreton-in-M) 1996. BB 6-42 v Surrey (Canterbury) 1995.

HOOPER, Carl Llewellyn (Christchurch SS, Georgetown), b Georgetown, Guyana 15 Dec 1966. 6'1". RHB, OB. Demerara 1983-84. Guyana 1984-85 to date (captain 1996-97). Kent 1992-94, 1996; cap 1992. **Tests** (WI): 64 (1987-88 to 1996-97); HS 178* v P (St John's) 1992-93; BB 5-26 v SL (Kingstown) 1996-97. **LOI** (WI): 155 (1986-87 to 1996-97, 1 as captain; HS 113*; BB 4-34). Tours (WI): E 1988, 1991, 1995; A 1988-89, 1991-92, 1992-93, 1995-96, 1996-97; NZ 1986-87; I 1987-88, 1994-95; P 1990-91; SL 1993-94; Z 1986-87 (Young WI), 1989-90 (Young WI). 1000 runs (6+1); most – 1579 (1994). HS 236* v Glam (Canterbury) 1993. BB 5-52 v Durham (Canterbury) 1994. Awards: NWT 1; BHC 1. **NWT:** HS 136* v Berks (Finchampstead) 1994. BB 2-12 v Middx (Canterbury) 1993. **BHC:** HS 98 v Somerset (Maidstone) 1996. BB 3-28 v Yorks (Leeds) 1992. **SL:** HS 145 v Leics (Leicester) 1996. BB 5-41 v Essex (Maidstone) 1993.

HOUSE, William John (Sevenoaks S; Gonville & Caius C, Cambridge), b Sheffield, Yorks 16 Mar 1976. 5'11". LHB, RM. Debut (Cambridge U) 1996, scoring 136 v Derbys in his second innings; blue 1996-97. Kent debut 1997. HS 136 (*see above*). K HS 20 v A (Canterbury) 1997. BAC HS 2. BB 1-44 (CU). Award: BHC 1. **BHC:** (Brit Us) HS 93 v Surrey (Oval) 1997. **SL:** HS 19* v Derbys (Derby) 1996.

IGGLESDEN, Alan Paul (Churchill S, Westerham), b Farnborough 8 Oct 1964. 6'6". RHB, RFM. Debut 1986; cap 1989; testimonial 1998. W Province 1987-88. Boland 1992-93. **Tests:** 3 (1993 to 1993-94); HS 3*; BB 2-91 v A (Oval) 1989. **LOI:** 4 (1993-94; HS 18; BB 2-12). Tours: WI 1993-94; Z 1989-90 (Eng A), 1992-93 (K). HS 41 v Surrey (Canterbury) 1988. 50 wkts (4); most – 56 (1989). BB 7-28 (12-66 match) Boland v GW (Kimberley) 1992-93. K BB 6-34 v Surrey (Canterbury) 1988. **NWT:** HS 12* v Oxon (Oxford) 1990. BB 4-29 v Cambs (Canterbury) 1991. **BHC:** HS 26* v Worcs (Worcester) 1991. BB 3-24 v Scot (Glasgow) 1991 and v Notts (Nottingham) 1992. **SL:** HS 13* (twice). BB 5-13 v Sussex (Hove) 1989.

KEY, Robert William Trevor (Langley Park S), b East Dulwich, London 12 May 1979. 6'1". RHB, OB. His mother played for Kent Ladies. Staff 1997 – awaiting f-c debut.

LLONG, Nigel James (Ashford North S), b Ashford 11 Feb 1969. 6'0". LHB, OB. Debut 1990; cap 1993. Tour: Z 1992-93 (K). HS 130 v Hants (Canterbury) 1996. BB 5-21 v Middx (Canterbury) 1996. Awards: NWT 1; BHC 1. **NWT:** HS 115* and BB 3-36 v Cambs (March) 1996. **BHC:** HS 75 v Brit Us (Canterbury) 1997. BB 2-38 v Brit Us (Oxford) 1996. **SL:** HS 70 v Sussex (Tunbridge W) 1996. BB 4-24 v Sussex (Hove) 1993.

McCAGUE, Martin John (Hedland Sr HS; Carine Tafe C), b Larne, N Ireland 24 May 1969. 6'5". RHB, RF. W Australia 1990-91 to 1991-92. Kent debut 1991; cap 1992. **Tests:** 3 (1993 to 1994-95); HS 11 v A (Leeds) 1993; BB 4-121 v A (Nottingham) 1993. Tours: A 1994-95 (*part*); SA 1993-94 (Eng A). HS 63* v Surrey (Oval) 1996. 50 wkts (4); most – 76 (1996). BB 9-86 (15-147 match) v Derbys (Derby) 1994. Hat-trick 1996. Award: NWT 1. **NWT:** HS 31* v Staffs (Stone) 1995. BB 5-26 v Middx (Canterbury) 1993. **BHC:** HS 30 v Derbys (Canterbury) 1992. BB 5-43 v Somerset (Canterbury) 1992. **SL:** HS 22* v Glam (Swansea) 1992. BB 5-40 v Essex (Canterbury) 1995.

MARSH, Steven Andrew (Walderslade SS; Mid-Kent CFE), b Westminster, London 27 Jan 1961. 5'10". RHB, WK. Debut 1982; cap 1986; benefit 1995; captain 1996 to date. Tour: Z 1992-93 (K – captain). HS 142 v Sussex (Horsham) 1997. BB 2-20 v Warwks (Birmingham) 1990. Set world f-c record by holding eight catches in an innings AND scoring a hundred (v Middx at Lord's) 1991. **NWT:** HS 55 v Warwks (Birmingham) 1995. BB 1-3. **BHC:** HS 71 v Lancs (Manchester) 1991. **SL:** HS 59 v Leics (Canterbury) 1991.

PATEL, Minal Mahesh (Dartford GS; Erith TC), b Bombay, India 7 Jul 1970. 5'9". RHB, SLA. Debut 1989; cap 1994. **Tests:** 2 (1996); HS 27 and BB 1-101 v I (Nottingham) 1996. Tour: I 1994-95 (Eng A). HS 56 v Leics (Canterbury) 1995. 50 wkts (2); most – 90 (1994). BB 8-96 v Lancs (Canterbury) 1994. **NWT:** HS 5*. BB 2-29 v Oxon (Oxford) 1990. **BHC:** HS 18* v Glam (Canterbury) 1996. BB 2-29 v Somerset (Canterbury) 1995. **SL:** HS 5. BB 3-50 v Northants (Northampton) 1994.

PHILLIPS, Ben James (Langley Park S and SFC, Beckenham), b Lewisham 30 Sep 1974. 6'6". RHB, RFM. Debut 1996. HS 100* v Lancs (Manchester) 1997. BB 5-47 v Sussex (Horsham) 1997. **SL:** HS 29 v Glam (Cardiff) 1996. BB 2-42 v Somerset (Canterbury) 1996.

SMITH, Edward Thomas (Tonbridge S; Peterhouse C, Cambridge), b Pembury 19 Jul 1977. 6'2". RHB, RM. Debut (Cambridge U) 1996, scoring 101 v Glam (Cambridge); blue 1996-97. Kent debut 1996. 1000 runs (1): 1163 (1997). HS 190 CU v Leics (Cambridge) 1997. K HS 102 v Hants (Portsmouth) 1997. **BHC:** (Brit Us) HS 43 v Sussex (Cambridge) 1997. **SL:** HS 72* v Hants (Portsmouth) 1997.

STANFORD, Edward John (The Downs SS, Dartford), b Dartford 21 Jan 1971. 5'10". LHB, SLA. Debut 1995. HS 32 v CU (Canterbury) 1997. BAC HS 10* v Durham (Maidstone) 1996. BB 3-84 v Leics (Leicester) 1996.

THOMPSON, Dr Julian Barton deCourcy (The Judd S, Tonbridge; Guy's Hospital Medical S, London U), b Cape Town, SA 28 Oct 1968. 6'4". RHB, RFM. Debut 1994. HS 59* v Warwks (Tunbridge Wells) 1997. BB 5-72 v Surrey (Oval) 1996. Awards: BHC 2. **BHC:** HS 12* v Glam (Canterbury) 1996. BB 3-29 v Middx (Canterbury) 1996. **SL:** HS 30 v Glam (Cardiff) 1996. BB 3-17 v Somerset (Taunton) 1997.

WALKER, Matthew Jonathan (King's S, Rochester), b Gravesend 2 Jan 1974. Grandson of Jack (Kent 1949). 5'8". LHB, RM. Debut 1992-93 (Z tour). UK debut 1994. Tour: Z 1992-93 (K). HS 275* v Somerset (Canterbury) 1996. Awards: BHC 2. **NWT:** HS 51 v Derbys (Derby) 1996. **BHC:** HS 117 v Warwks (Canterbury) 1997. **SL:** HS 80 v Derbys (Canterbury) 1997.

WALSH, Christopher David (Tonbridge S; Exeter U), b Pembury 6 Nov 1975. Son of D.R. (Oxford U 1966-69). 6'1". RHB, LB. Debut 1996. Awaiting BAC debut. HS 56* v OU (Canterbury) 1996 – on debut.

WARD, Trevor Robert (Hextable CS, nr Swanley), b Farningham 18 Jan 1968. 5'11". RHB, OB. Debut 1986; cap 1989. Tour: Z 1992-93 (K). 1000 runs (6); most – 1648 (1992). HS 235* v Middx (Canterbury) 1991. BB 2-10 v Yorks (Canterbury) 1996. Awards: NWT 1; BHC 2. **NWT:** HS 120 v Berks (Finchampstead) 1994. BB 1-28. **BHC:** HS 125 v Surrey (Canterbury) 1995. **SL:** HS 131 v Notts (Nottingham) 1993. BB 3-20 v Glam (Canterbury) 1989.

WELLS, Alan Peter (Tideway CS, Newhaven), b Newhaven, Sussex 2 Oct 1961. Younger brother of C.M. (Sussex, Derbyshire, Border and WP 1979-96). 6'0". RHB, RM. Sussex 1981-96; cap 1986; captain 1992-96; benefit 1996. Border 1981-82. Kent debut/cap 1997. **Tests:** 1 (1995); HS 3*. **LOI:** 1 (1995; HS 15). Tours (Eng A): SA 1989-90 (Eng XI), 1993-94; I 1994-95 (captain). 1000 runs (11); most – 1784 (1991). HS 253* Sx v Yorks (Middlesbrough) 1991. K HS 109 v Essex (Canterbury) 1997. BB 3-67 Sx v Worcs (Worcester) 1987. Awards: NWT 3. **NWT:** HS 119 Sx v Bucks (Beaconsfield) 1992. **BHC:** HS 74 Sx v Middx (Hove) 1990. BB 1-17. **SL:** HS 127 Sx v Hants (Portsmouth) 1993. BB 1-10.

WILLIS, Simon Charles (Wilmington GS), b Greenwich, London 19 Mar 1974. 5'8". RHB, OB, WK. Debut 1993. HS 82 v CU (Folkestone) 1995. BAC HS 78 v Northants (Northampton) 1996. **NWT:** HS 19* v Staffs (Stone) 1995. **SL:** HS 31* v Worcs (Canterbury) 1996.

NEWCOMERS and DEPARTURES see p 106

KENT 1997

RESULTS SUMMARY

	Place	Won	Lost	Tied	Drew	No Result
Britannic Assurance Championship	2nd	8	4	–	5	–
All First-Class Matches		8	5	–	6	–
NatWest Trophy	1st Round					
Benson and Hedges Cup	Finalist					
Sunday League	2nd	12	4	–	–	1

BRITANNIC ASSURANCE CHAMPIONSHIP AVERAGES

BATTING AND FIELDING

Cap		M	I	NO	HS	Runs	Avge	100	50	Ct/St
1992	M.A.Ealham	12	20	6	139	809	57.78	3	4	9
1986	S.A.Marsh	17	25	5	142	797	39.85	1	3	54/2
1997	A.P.Wells	17	29	1	109	1055	37.67	1	8	16
–	D.P.Fulton	15	27	3	110	885	36.87	1	3	22
1989	T.R.Ward	16	28	2	161*	895	34.42	1	7	29
–	B.J.Phillips	11	15	4	100*	343	31.18	1	–	5
1988	G.R.Cowdrey	9	15	–	101	442	29.46	1	1	7
–	E.T.Smith	9	16	1	102	434	28.93	1	1	4
1990	M.V.Fleming	17	29	4	138	694	27.76	1	3	5
1997	P.A.Strang	16	24	2	82	588	26.72	–	5	17
–	J.B.D.Thompson	7	7	3	59*	103	25.75	–	1	3
–	M.J.Walker	9	17	–	51	298	17.52	–	1	4
1992	M.J.McCague	11	15	6	53*	190	17.27	–	1	3
1993	D.W.Headley	7	9	3	40	99	16.50	–	–	2
1993	N.J.Llong	7	12	–	57	140	11.66	–	1	9
1989	A.P.Igglesden	5	6	2	3	4	1.00	–	–	1

Also batted: (1 match each): W.J.House 2; M.M.Patel (cap 1994) 8, 30 (1 ct).

BOWLING

	O	M	R	W	Avge	Best	5wI	10wM
B.J.Phillips	254.1	67	773	41	18.85	5- 47	2	–
M.J.McCague	312.4	55	1125	48	23.43	7- 50	4	–
J.B.D.Thompson	186.2	24	713	24	29.70	5- 89	1	–
M.A.Ealham	317	62	928	31	29.93	4- 47	–	–
P.A.Strang	703	207	1843	61	30.21	7-118	4	1
A.P.Igglesden	131	21	454	15	30.26	4- 67	–	–
M.V.Fleming	382.2	95	1096	36	30.44	5- 51	2	–
D.W.Headley	253	44	841	26	32.34	5- 92	1	–

Also bowled: G.R.Cowdrey 5-0-31-0; N.J.Llong 52.3-11-200-4; M.M.Patel 3-0-12-0;
E.T.Smith 2-0-22-0; T.R.Ward 5-0-34-0; A.P.Wells 18-6-55-0.

The First-Class Averages (pp 118-133) give the records of Kent players in all first-class
county matches (their other opponents being the Australians and Cambridge University),
with the exception of:
  M.A.Ealham 13-22-6-139-924-57.75-3-5-9ct. 336-66-1010-32-31.56-4/47.
  D.W.Headley 8-10-3-40-104-14.85-0-0-2ct. 267-46-904-27-33.48-5/92-1-0.
  W.J.House 2-3-0-20-38-12.66-0-0-1ct. 2.5-0-24-0.
  E.T.Smith 10-18-1-102-480-28.23-1-1-5ct. 2-0-22-0.

KENT RECORDS

FIRST-CLASS CRICKET

Highest Total	For	803-4d	v	Essex	Brentwood	1934
	V	676	by	Australians	Canterbury	1921
Lowest Total	For	18	v	Sussex	Gravesend	1867
	V	16	by	Warwicks	Tonbridge	1913
Highest Innings	For	332	W.H.Ashdown	v	Essex	Brentwood	1934
	V	344	W.G.Grace	for	MCC	Canterbury	1876

Highest Partnership for each Wicket

1st	300	N.R.Taylor/M.R.Benson	v	Derbyshire	Canterbury	1991
2nd	366	S.G.Hinks/N.R.Taylor	v	Middlesex	Canterbury	1990
3rd	321*	A.Hearne/J.R.Mason	v	Notts	Nottingham	1899
4th	368	P.A.de Silva/G.R.Cowdrey	v	Derbyshire	Maidstone	1995
5th	277	F.E.Woolley/L.E.G.Ames	v	New Zealand	Canterbury	1931
6th	315	P.A.de Silva/M.A.Ealham	v	Notts	Nottingham	1995
7th	248	A.P.Day/E.Humphreys	v	Somerset	Taunton	1908
8th	157	A.L.Hilder/A.C.Wright	v	Essex	Gravesend	1924
9th	171	M.A.Ealham/P.A.Strang	v	Notts	Nottingham	1997
10th	235	F.E.Woolley/A.Fielder	v	Worcs	Stourbridge	1909

Best Bowling	For	10- 30	C.Blythe	v	Northants	Northampton	1907
(Innings)	V	10- 48	C.H.G.Bland	for	Sussex	Tonbridge	1899
Best Bowling	For	17- 48	C.Blythe	v	Northants	Northampton	1907
(Match)	V	17-106	T.W.J.Goddard	for	Glos	Bristol	1939

Most Runs – Season	2894	F.E.Woolley	(av 59.06)		1928
Most Runs – Career	47868	F.E.Woolley	(av 41.77)		1906-38
Most 100s – Season	10	F.E.Woolley			1928
	10	F.E.Woolley			1934
Most 100s – Career	122	F.E.Woolley			1906-38
Most Wkts – Season	262	A.P.Freeman	(av 14.74)		1933
Most Wkts – Career	3340	A.P.Freeman	(av 17.64)		1914-36

LIMITED-OVERS CRICKET

Highest Total	NWT	384-6	v	Berkshire	Finchampstead	1994
	BHC	338-6	v	Somerset	Maidstone	1996
	SL	327-6	v	Leics	Canterbury	1993
Lowest Total	NWT	60	v	Somerset	Taunton	1979
	BHC	73	v	Middlesex	Canterbury	1979
	SL	83	v	Middlesex	Lord's	1984
Highest Innings	NWT	136*	C.L.Hooper	v	Berkshire	Finchampstead	1994
	BHC	143	C.J.Tavaré	v	Somerset	Taunton	1985
	SL	145	C.L.Hooper	v	Leics	Leicester	1996
Best Bowling	NWT	8-31	D.L.Underwood	v	Scotland	Edinburgh	1987
	BHC	6-41	T.N.Wren	v	Somerset	Canterbury	1995
	SL	6- 9	R.A.Woolmer	v	Derbyshire	Chesterfield	1979

LANCASHIRE

Formation of Present Club: 12 January 1864
Colours: Red, Green and Blue
Badge: Red Rose
Championships (since 1890): (7) 1897, 1904, 1926, 1927, 1928, 1930, 1934
Joint Championship: (1) 1950
NatWest Trophy/Gillette Cup Winners: (6) 1970, 1971, 1972, 1975, 1990, 1996
Benson and Hedges Cup Winners: (4) 1984, 1990, 1995, 1996
Sunday League Champions: (3) 1969, 1970, 1989
Match Awards: NWT 63; BHC 73

Cricket Secretary: D.M.R.Edmundson
   Old Trafford, Manchester M16 0PX (Tel 0161 282 4021)
Captain/Overseas Player: Wasim Akram. **Vice-Captain:** J.P.Crawley.
1998 Beneficiary: Wasim Akram. **Scorer:** A.West

ATHERTON, Michael Andrew (Manchester GS; Downing C, Cambridge), b Failsworth, Manchester 23 Mar 1968. 5'11". RHB, LB. Cambridge U 1987-89; blue 1987-88-89; captain 1988-89. Lancashire debut 1987; cap 1989; benefit 1997. YC 1990. *Wisden* 1990. OBE 1997. **Tests:** 73 (1989 to 1997, 46 as captain – England record); HS 185* v SA (Jo'burg) 1995-96; BB 1-20. **LOI:** 53 (1990 to 1997, 43 as captain; HS 127). Tours (C=captain): A 1990-91, 1994-95C; SA 1995-96C; WI 1993-94C, 1995-96 (La); NZ 1996-97C; I/SL 1992-93; Z 1989-90 (Eng A), 1996-97C. 1000 runs (6); most – 1924 (1990). Scored 1193 in season of f-c debut. HS 199 v Durham (Gateshead) 1992. BB 6-78 v Notts (Nottingham) 1990. Awards: NWT 3; BHC 2. **NWT:** HS 115 v Derbys (Manchester) 1996. BB 2-15 v Glos (Manchester) 1990. **BHC:** HS 121* v Durham (Manchester) 1996. BB 4-42 Comb Us v Somerset (Taunton) 1989. **SL:** HS 111 v Essex (Colchester) 1990. BB 3-33 v Notts (Nottingham) 1990.

AUSTIN, Ian David (Haslingden HS), b Haslingden 30 May 1966. 5'10". LHB, RM. Debut 1987; cap 1990. Tours (La): WI 1995-96; Z 1988-89. HS 115* v Derbys (Blackpool) 1992. BB 5-23 (10-60 match) v Middx (Manchester) 1994. Awards: NWT 1; BHC 2. **NWT:** HS 97 v Sussex (Hove) 1991. BB 3-32 v Yorks (Leeds) 1995. **BHC:** HS 80 v Worcs (Worcester) 1987. BB 4-8 v Minor C (Leek) 1995. **SL:** HS 48 v Middx (Lord's) 1991. BB 5-56 v Derbys (Derby) 1991.

CHAPPLE, Glen (West Craven HS; Nelson & Colne C), b Skipton, Yorks 23 Jan 1974. 6'1". RHB, RFM. Debut 1992; cap 1994. Tours (Eng A): A 1996-97; WI 1995-96 (La); I 1994-95. HS 109* v Glam (Manchester) 1993 (100 off 27 balls in contrived circumstances). HS (authentic) 66 v Durham (Manchester) 1997. 50 wkts (2); most – 55 (1994). BB 6-48 v Durham (Stockton) 1994. Award: NWT 1. **NWT:** HS 4. BB 6-18 v Essex (Lord's) 1996. **BHC:** HS 8. BB 3-31 v Minor C (Manchester) 1996. **SL:** HS 43 v Worcs (Manchester) 1996. BB 3-22 v Kent (Manchester) 1997.

CHILTON, Mark James (Manchester GS; Durham U), b Sheffield, Yorks 2 Oct 1976. 6'3". RHB, RM. Debut 1997. HS 9. Award: BHC 1. **BHC:** (Brit Us) HS 43 v Kent (Canterbury) 1997. BB 5-26 v Sussex (Cambridge) 1997. **SL:** HS 22 v Middx (Uxbridge) 1997. BB 2-27 v Hants (Southampton) 1997.

CRAWLEY, John Paul (Manchester GS; Trinity C, Cambridge), b Maldon, Essex 21 Sep 1971. Brother of M.A. (Oxford U, Lancs and Notts 1987-94) and P.M. (Cambridge U 1992). 6'1". RHB, RM, occ WK. Debut 1990; cap 1994. Cambridge U 1991-93; blue 1991-92-93; captain 1992-93. YC 1994. **Tests:** 22 (1994 to 1997); HS 112 v Z (Bulawayo) 1996-97. **LOI:** 10 (1994-95 to 1997; HS 73). Tours: A 1994-95; SA 1993-94 (Eng A), 1995-96; WI 1995-96 (La); NZ 1996-97; Z 1996-97. 1000 runs (6); most – 1570 (1994). HS 286 England A v E Province (Pt Elizabeth) 1993-94. La HS 281* v Somerset (Southport) 1994. BB 1-90. Award: BHC 1. **NWT:** HS 113* v Sussex (Hove) 1997. **BHC:** HS 114 v Notts (Manchester) 1995. **SL:** HS 91 v Kent (Canterbury) 1994.

FAIRBROTHER, Neil Harvey (Lymm GS), b Warrington 9 Sep 1963. 5'8". LHB, LM. Debut 1982; cap 1985; captain 1992-93; benefit 1995. Transvaal 1994-95. **Tests:** 10 (1987 to 1992-93); HS 83 v I (Madras) 1992-93. **LOI:** 56 (1986-87 to 1995-96; HS 113). Tours: NZ 1987-88, 1991-92; I/SL 1992-93; P 1987-88, 1990-91 (Eng A); SL 1990-91 (Eng A). 1000 runs (10); most – 1740 (1990). HS 366 v Surrey (Oval) 1990 (ground record), including 311 in a day and 100 or more in each session. BB 2-91 v Notts (Manchester) 1987. Awards: NWT 5; BHC 9. **NWT:** HS 93* v Leics (Leicester) 1986. BB 1-28. **BHC:** HS 116* v Scot (Manchester) 1988. BB 1-17. **SL:** HS 116* v Notts (Nottingham) 1988. BB 1-33.

FLINTOFF, Andrew (Ribbleton Hall HS), b Preston 6 Dec 1977. 6'4". RHB, RM. Debut 1995. HS 117 v Hants (Southampton) 1997. BB 1-11. **NWT:** HS 2. **BHC:** HS 0. BB 1-10. **SL:** HS 31 v Middx (Uxbridge) 1997.

GREEN, Richard James (Bridgewater HS, Cheshire; Mid-Cheshire C), b Warrington 13 Mar 1976. 6'1". RHB, RM. Debut 1995. HS 51 v Essex (Manchester) 1997. BB 6-41 v Yorks (Manchester) 1996 (non-BAC match). BAC BB 4-78 v Northants (Northampton) 1996. **BHC:** HS 7. BB 2-33 v Minor C (Walsall) 1997. **SL:** HS 0*. BB 3-18 v Yorks (Manchester) 1997.

HARVEY, Mark Edward (Habergham HS; Loughborough U), b Burnley 26 Jun 1974. 5'9". RHB, RM/LB. Debut 1994. Combined Us 1995. HS 25 v Glos (Bristol) 1997. Award: NWT 1. **NWT:** HS 86 v Berks (Manchester) 1997. **BHC:** (Brit Us) HS 5. **SL:** HS 8.

HAYNES, Jamie Jonathan (St Edmunds C, Canberra; Canberra U), b Bristol 5 Jul 1974. 5'11". RHB, WK. Debut 1996. Represented Australian Capital Territory at cricket and Australian Rules football. HS 21 v Yorks (Leeds) 1997 (non-BAC match). BAC HS 18 v Kent (Manchester) 1997. **SL:** HS –.

HEGG, Warren Kevin (Unsworth HS, Bury; Stand C, Whitefield), b Whitefield 23 Feb 1968. 5'8". RHB, WK. Debut 1986; cap 1989. Tours: A 1996-97 (Eng A); WI 1986-87 (La), 1995-96 (La); SL 1990-91 (Eng A); Z 1988-89 (La). HS 134 v Leics (Manchester) 1996. Held 11 catches (equalling world f-c match record) v Derbys (Chesterfield) 1989. Award: BHC 1. **NWT:** HS 37 v Berks (Manchester) 1997. **BHC:** HS 81 v Yorks (Manchester) 1996. **SL:** HS 52 v Glam (Colwyn Bay) 1994.

KEEDY, Gary (Garforth CS), b Wakefield, Yorks 27 Nov 1974. 6'0". LHB, SLA. Yorkshire 1994 (one match). Lancashire debut 1995. Tour: WI 1995-96 (La). HS 26 v Essex (Chelmsford) 1996. BB 6-79 (10-173 match) v Surrey (Oval) 1997. **SL:** HS –. BB 1-40.

LLOYD, Graham David (Hollins County HS), b Accrington 1 Jul 1969. Son of D. (Lancs and England 1965-83). 5'9". RHB, RM. Debut 1988; cap 1992. **LOI:** 5 (1996 to 1997; HS 22). Tours: A 1992-93 (Eng A); WI 1995-96 (La). 1000 runs (4); most – 1389 (1992). HS 241 v Essex (Chelmsford) 1996. BB 1-4. Awards: BHC 2. **NWT:** HS 96 v Berks (Manchester) 1997. BB 1-23. **BHC:** HS 81* v Leics (Manchester) 1995. **SL:** HS 134 v Durham (Manchester) 1997.

McKEOWN, Patrick Christopher (Merchant Taylors S; Rossall S), b Liverpool 1 Jun 1976. 6'3". RHB, OB. Debut 1996. HS 64 v Warwks (Birmingham) 1996. **NWT:** HS 42 v Berks (Manchester) 1997. **BHC:** HS 10 v Minor C (Walsall) 1997. **SL:** HS 69 v Northants (Northampton) 1996.

MARTIN, Peter James (Danum S, Doncaster), b Accrington 15 Nov 1968. 6'4". RHB, RFM. Debut 1989; cap 1994. **Tests:** 8 (1995 to 1997); HS 29 v WI (Lord's) 1995; BB 4-60 v SA (Durban) 1995-96. **LOI:** 16 (1995 to 1996; HS 6; BB 4-44). Tour: SA 1995-96. HS 133 v Durham (Gateshead) 1992. 50 wkts (2); most – 58 (1997). BB 8-32 (13-79 match) v Middx (Uxbridge) 1997. Award: NWT 1. **NWT:** HS 16 v Surrey (Oval) 1994. BB 4-36 v Northants (Manchester) 1996. **BHC:** HS 10* (twice). BB 3-31 v Yorks (Manchester) 1997. **SL:** HS 35* v Worcs (Manchester) 1996. BB 5-21 v Northants (Manchester) 1997.

RIDGWAY, Paul Mathew (Settle HS), b Airedale, Yorks 13 Feb 1977. 6'4". RHB, RFM. Debut 1997. HS 0* and BB 2-46 v Kent (Manchester) 1997.

SHADFORD, Darren James (Breeze Hill HS; Oldham TC), b Oldham 4 Mar 1975. 6'3". RHB, RMF. Debut 1995. HS 30 v Hants (Southampton) 1997. BB 5-80 v Warwks (Blackpool) 1997. **NWT:** HS –. **SL:** HS 2. BB 3-30 v Middx (Uxbridge) 1997.

TITCHARD, Stephen Paul (Lymm County HS; Priestley C), b Warrington 17 Dec 1967. 6'3". RHB, RM. Debut 1990; cap 1995. HS 163 v Essex (Chelmsford) 1996. BB 1-11 (twice). Award: NWT 1. **NWT:** HS 92 v Worcs (Manchester) 1995. **BHC:** HS 82 v Surrey (Oval) 1992. **SL:** HS 96 v Essex (Chelmsford) 1994.

WASIM AKRAM (Islamia C), b Lahore, Pakistan 3 Jun 1966. 6'3". LHB, LF. PACO 1984-85 to 1985-86. Lahore 1985-86 to 1986-87. PIA 1987-88 to date. Lancashire debut 1988; cap 1989; captain 1998. *Wisden* 1992. **Tests** (P): 72 (1984-85 to 1996-97, 14 as captain); HS 257* v Z (Sheikhupura) 1996-97; BB 7-119 v NZ (Wellington) 1993-94. **LOI** (P): 232 (1984-85 to 1996-97, 66 as captain); HS 86; BB 5-15). Tours (P)(C=captain): E 1987, 1992, 1996C; A 1988-89, 1989-90, 1991-92, 1992-93, 1995-96C, 1996-97C; WI 1987-88, 1992-93C; NZ 1984-85, 1992-93, 1993-94, 1995-96C; I 1986-87; SL 1984-85 (P U-23), 1985-86, 1994-95. HS 257* (*see Tests*). La HS 122 v Hants (Basingstoke) 1991. 50 wkts (5+1); most – 82 (1992). BB 8-30 (13-147 match) v Somerset (Southport) 1994. Hat-trick 1988. Awards: BHC 3. **NWT:** HS 50 v Surrey (Oval) 1994. BB 4-27 v Lincs (Manchester) 1988. **BHC:** HS 64 v Worcs (Worcester) 1995. BB 5-10 v Leics (Leicester) 1993. **SL:** HS 51* v Yorks (Manchester) 1993. BB 5-41 v Northants (Northampton) 1994.

WATKINSON, Michael (Rivington and Blackrod HS, Horwich), b Westhoughton 1 Aug 1961. 6'1". RHB, RMF/OB. Debut 1982; cap 1987; captain 1994-97; benefit 1996. Cheshire 1982. **Tests:** 4 (1995 to 1995-96); HS 82* v WI (Nottingham) 1995; BB 3-64 v WI (Manchester) 1995 – on debut. **LOI:** 1 (1995-96; HS –). Tours: SA 1995-96; WI 1995-96 (La – captain). 1000 runs (1): 1016 (1993). HS 161 v Essex (Manchester) 1995. 50 wkts (7); most – 66 (1992). BB 8-30 (11-87 match) v Hants (Manchester) 1994 – completing match 'double' with 128 runs. Hat-trick 1992. Awards: NWT 2; BHC 3. **NWT:** HS 90 and BB 3-14 v Glos (Manchester) 1990. **BHC:** HS 76 v Northants (Northampton) 1992. BB 5-44 v Derbys (Chesterfield) 1996. **SL:** HS 121 v Notts (Nottingham) 1996. BB 5-46 v Warwks (Manchester) 1990.

WOOD, Nathan Theodore (Wm Hulme's GS), b Thornhill Edge, Yorks 4 Oct 1974. Son of B. (Yorks, Lancs, Derbys and England 1964-83). 5'8". LHB, OB. Debut 1996. HS 155 v Surrey (Oval) 1997.

YATES, Gary (Manchester GS), b Ashton-under-Lyne 20 Sep 1967. 6'0". RHB, OB. Debut 1990; cap 1994. HS 134* v Northants (Manchester) 1993. BB 5-34 v Hants (Manchester) 1994. **NWT:** HS 34* and BB 2-15 v Berks (Manchester) 1997. **BHC:** HS 26 v Yorks (Manchester) 1996. BB 3-42 v Warwks (Birmingham) 1995. **SL:** HS 38 v Essex (Chelmsford) 1996. BB 4-34 v Warwks (Birmingham) 1994.

NEWCOMER

SCHOFIELD, Christopher Paul, b Rochdale 6 Oct 1978. LHB, LB.

DEPARTURE (who made first-class appearances in 1997)

GALLIAN, J.E.R. – *see NOTTINGHAMSHIRE.*

LANCASHIRE 1997

RESULTS SUMMARY

	Place	Won	Lost	Tied	Drew	No Result
Britannic Assurance Championship	11th	5	6	–	6	–
All First-Class Matches		6	6	–	6	–
NatWest Trophy	2nd Round					
Benson and Hedges Cup	4th in Group A					
Sunday League	3rd	10	4	1	–	2

BRITANNIC ASSURANCE CHAMPIONSHIP AVERAGES

BATTING AND FIELDING

Cap		M	I	NO	HS	Runs	Avge	100	50	Ct/St
1994	J.P.Crawley	11	16	1	133	898	59.86	3	5	8
1992	G.D.Lloyd	15	22	2	122	831	41.55	3	5	16
1985	N.H.Fairbrother	15	22	1	132	855	40.71	2	4	17
1989	M.A.Atherton	10	16	1	149	596	39.73	2	3	6
1990	I.D.Austin	16	24	4	95	742	37.10	–	7	5
–	N.T.Wood	10	15	2	155	469	36.07	1	2	3
–	A.Flintoff	4	6	–	117	216	36.00	1	1	3
1987	M.Watkinson	11	17	–	135	473	27.82	1	2	5
–	R.J.Green	3	4	1	51	81	27.00	–	1	–
1989	W.K.Hegg	16	22	5	77*	455	26.76	–	5	36/2
1994	J.E.R.Gallian	10	17	2	99	394	26.26	–	3	11
1995	S.P.Titchard	5	7	–	79	155	22.14	–	1	2
1994	P.J.Martin	15	16	4	78*	258	21.50	–	1	3
1994	G.Chapple	10	13	3	66	214	21.40	–	2	2
1994	G.Yates	10	12	3	39	192	21.33	–	–	7
–	P.C.McKeown	3	4	–	46	68	17.00	–	–	2
–	D.J.Shadford	8	10	3	30	106	15.14	–	–	5
–	M.E.Harvey	2	4	–	25	49	12.25	–	–	1
–	G.Keedy	8	8	7	6*	11	11.00	–	–	1

Also batted: M.J.Chilton (1 match) 9; J.J.Haynes (1) 18, 2 (7 ct); P.M.Ridgway (2) 0, 0*; Wasim Akram (cap 1989)(1) 13, 3 (1 ct).

BOWLING

	O	M	R	W	Avge	Best	5wI	10wM
P.J.Martin	408	119	1180	52	22.69	8-32	3	1
I.D.Austin	409.1	119	1083	41	26.41	4-44	–	–
G.Chapple	255.2	39	816	25	32.64	4-80	–	–
G.Keedy	292.4	60	917	27	33.96	6-79	1	1
G.Yates	274.4	51	876	25	35.04	5-59	1	–
D.J.Shadford	149	8	786	19	41.36	5-80	1	–
M.Watkinson	204.4	35	735	17	43.23	3-35	–	–

Also bowled: M.A.Atherton 1-0-7-0; M.J.Chilton 4-0-23-0; J.E.R.Gallian 79.2-12-357-7; R.J.Green 60.2-15-172-4; G.D.Lloyd 11.5-0-101-0; P.M.Ridgway 39-6-163-2; S.P.Titchard 13-1-44-3; Wasim Akram 36-10-86-3; N.T.Wood 4.1-0-38-0.

The First-Class Averages (pp 118-133) give the records of Lancashire players in all first-class county matches (their other opponents being Yorkshire in a non-Championship match), with the exception of M.A.Atherton, G.Chapple, J.R.Crawley, J.E.R.Gallian and W.K.Hegg whose full county figures are as above, and:
  P.J.Martin 16-17-4-78*-258-19.84-0-1-3ct. 455.2-131-1291-58-22.25-8/32-3-1.

LANCASHIRE RECORDS

FIRST-CLASS CRICKET

Highest Total	For	863		v	Surrey	The Oval	1990
	V	707-9d		by	Surrey	The Oval	1990
Lowest Total	For	25		v	Derbyshire	Manchester	1871
	V	22		by	Glamorgan	Liverpool	1924
Highest Innings	For	424	A.C.MacLaren	v	Somerset	Taunton	1895
	V	315*	T.W.Hayward	for	Surrey	The Oval	1898

Highest Partnership for each Wicket

1st	368	A.C.MacLaren/R.H.Spooner	v	Glos	Liverpool	1903
2nd	371	F.B.Watson/G.E.Tyldesley	v	Surrey	Manchester	1928
3rd	364	M.A.Atherton/N.H.Fairbrother	v	Surrey	The Oval	1990
4th	358	S.P.Titchard/G.D.Lloyd	v	Essex	Chelmsford	1996
5th	249	B.Wood/A.Kennedy	v	Warwicks	Birmingham	1975
6th	278	J.Iddon/H.R.W.Butterworth	v	Sussex	Manchester	1932
7th	248	G.D.Lloyd/I.D.Austin	v	Yorks	Leeds	1997
8th	158	J.Lyon/R.M.Ratcliffe	v	Warwicks	Manchester	1979
9th	142	L.O.S.Poidevin/A.Kermode	v	Sussex	Eastbourne	1907
10th	173	J.Briggs/R.Pilling	v	Surrey	Liverpool	1885

Best Bowling	For	10-46	W.Hickton	v	Hampshire	Manchester	1870
(Innings)	V	10-40	G.O.B.Allen	for	Middlesex	Lord's	1929
Best Bowling	For	17-91	H.Dean	v	Yorkshire	Liverpool	1913
(Match)	V	16-65	G.Giffen	for	Australians	Manchester	1886

Most Runs – Season	2633	J.T.Tyldesley	(av 56.02)		1901
Most Runs – Career	34222	G.E.Tyldesley	(av 45.20)		1909-36
Most 100s – Season	11	C.Hallows			1928
Most 100s – Career	90	G.E.Tyldesley			1909-36
Most Wkts – Season	198	E.A.McDonald	(av 18.55)		1925
Most Wkts – Career	1816	J.B.Statham	(av 15.12)		1950-68

LIMITED-OVERS CRICKET

Highest Total	NWT	372-5		v	Glos	Manchester	1990
	BHC	353-7		v	Notts	Manchester	1995
	SL	300-7		v	Leics	Leicester	1993
Lowest Total	NWT	59		v	Worcs	Worcester	1963
	BHC	82		v	Yorkshire	Bradford	1972
	SL	71		v	Essex	Chelmsford	1987
Highest Innings	NWT	131	A.Kennedy	v	Middlesex	Manchester	1978
	BHC	136	G.Fowler	v	Sussex	Manchester	1991
	SL	134*	C.H.Lloyd	v	Somerset	Manchester	1970
Best Bowling	NWT	6-18	G.Chapple	v	Essex	Lord's	1996
	BHC	6-10	C.E.H.Croft	v	Scotland	Manchester	1982
	SL	6-29	D.P.Hughes	v	Somerset	Manchester	1977

LEICESTERSHIRE

Formation of Present Club: 25 March 1879
Colours: Dark Green and Scarlet
Badge: Gold Running Fox on Green Ground
Championships: (2) 1975, 1996
NatWest Trophy/Gillette Cup Winners: (0) Finalist 1992
Benson and Hedges Cup Winners: (3) 1972, 1975, 1985
Sunday League Champions: (2) 1974, 1977
Match Awards: NWT 38; BHC 66

Chief Executive: D.G.Collier. **Administrative Secretary:** K.P.Hill
County Ground, Grace Road, Leicester LE2 8AD (Tel 0116 283 2128)
Captain: J.J.Whitaker. **Vice-Captain:** C.C.Lewis. **Overseas Player:** P.V.Simmons.
1998 Beneficiary: None. **Scorer:** G.A.York

BRIMSON, Matthew Thomas (Chislehurst & Sidcup GS; Durham U), b Plumstead, London 1 Dec 1970. 6'0". RHB, SLA. Kent staff 1991. Debut 1993. Tour (Le): SA 1996-97. HS 30* v Durham (Leicester) 1997. BB 5-12 v Sussex (Leicester) 1996. **NWT:** HS 9 and BB 3-34 v Sussex (Leicester) 1996. **BHC:** HS 0 and BB 2-36 v Somerset (Leicester) 1997. **SL:** HS 12* v Glos (Leicester) 1997. BB 3-23 v Glam (Swansea) 1996.

CROWE, Carl Daniel (Lutterworth GS), b Leicester 25 Nov 1975. 6'0". RHB, OB. Debut 1995. HS 9. **SL:** HS –.

DAKIN, Jonathan Michael (King Edward VII S, Johannesburg) b Hitchin, Herts 28 Feb 1973. 6'4". LHB, RM. Debut 1993. Tour (Le): SA 1996-97. HS 190 v Northants (Northampton) 1997. BB 4-45 v CU (Cambridge) 1993 (on debut). BAC BB 2-12 v Durham (Leicester) 1997. Award: BHC 1. **NWT:** HS 26 v Hants (Leicester) 1995 and v Berks (Leicester) 1996. BB 1-63. **BHC:** HS 108* v Durham (Leicester) 1996. BB 2-35 v Notts (Leicester) 1997. **SL:** HS 45 v Notts (Leicester) 1995. BB 3-23 v Somerset (Weston-s-M) 1995.

HABIB, Aftab (Millfield S; Taunton S), b Reading, Berkshire 7 Feb 1972. 5'11". Cousin of Zahid Sadiq (Surrey and Derbys 1988-90). RHB, RMF. Middlesex 1992 (one match). Leicestershire debut 1995. HS 215 v Worcs (Leicester) 1996. Award: BHC 1. **NWT:** HS 35 v Berks (Leicester) 1996. **BHC:** HS 111 v Durham (Chester-le-St) 1997. **SL:** HS 99* v Glos (Cheltenham) 1996.

LEWIS, Clairmonte Christopher (Willesden HS, London), b Georgetown, Guyana 14 Feb 1968. 6'2½". RHB, RFM. Leicestershire 1987-91; cap 1990. Nottinghamshire 1992-94; cap 1994. Surrey 1996-97; cap 1996. **Tests:** 32 (1990 to 1996); HS 117 v I (Madras) 1992-93; BB 6-111 v WI (Birmingham) 1991. **LOI:** 51 (1989-90 to 1996; HS 33; BB 4-30). Tours: A 1990-91 (*part*), 1994-95 (*part*); WI 1989-90 (*part*), 1993-94; NZ 1991-92; I/SL 1992-93. HS 247 Nt v Durham (Chester-le-St) 1993. Le HS 189* v Essex (Chelmsford) 1990. 50 wkts (2); most – 56 (1996). BB 6-22 v OU (Oxford) 1988. BAC BB 6-55 v Glam (Cardiff) 1990. Award: NWT 1. **NWT:** HS 89 Nt v Northumb (Jesmond) 1994. BB 3-24 Nt v Somerset (Nottingham) 1993. **BHC:** HS 48* Nt v Minor C (Nottingham) 1994. BB 5-46 Nt v Kent (Nottingham) 1992. **SL:** HS 93* v Essex (Leicester) 1990. BB 4-13 v Essex (Leicester) 1988.

MADDY, Darren Lee (Wreake Valley C), b Leicester 23 May 1974. 5'9". RHB, RM/OB. Debut 1994; cap 1996. Tour (Le): SA 1996-97. 1000 runs (1): 1047 (1997). HS 131 v OU (Oxford) 1995. BAC HS 103 v Surrey (Leicester) 1997, v Middx (Lord's) 1997 and v Notts (Leicester) 1997. BB 2-21 v Lancs (Manchester) 1996. Awards: BHC 2. **NWT:** HS 34 and BB 2-38 v Hants (Leicester) 1996. **BHC:** HS 101 v Notts (Leicester) 1997. BB 3-32 v Leics (Leicester) 1996. **SL:** HS 106* v Durham (Chester-le-St) 1996. BB 3-11 v Durham (Leicester) 1997.

MASON, Timothy James (Denstone C), b Leicester 12 Apr 1975. 5'8". RHB, OB. Debut 1994. HS 4. BB 2-21 v A (Leicester) 1997. **BAC** BB 1-22. **NWT:** HS 36 v Yorks (Leicester) 1997. BB 3-29 v Devon (Exmouth) 1997. **BHC:** HS 30 v Surrey (Oval) 1997. BB 2-35 v Minor C (Jesmond) 1996. **SL:** HS 17* v Somerset (Weston-s-M) 1995 and v Kent (Canterbury) 1997. BB 2-15 v Durham (Leicester) 1997.

MILLNS, David James (Garibaldi CS), b Clipstone, Notts 27 Feb 1965. 6'3". LHB, RF. Nottinghamshire 1988-89. Leicestershire debut 1990; cap 1991. Boland 1996-97. Tours: A 1992-93 (Eng A); SA 1996-97 (Le). HS 121 v Northants (Northampton) 1997. 50 wkts (4); most – 76 (1994). BB 9-37 (12-91 match) v Derbys (Derby) 1991. Awards: NWT 1; BHC 1. **NWT:** HS 29* v Derbys (Derby) 1992. BB 3-22 v Norfolk (Leicester) 1992. **BHC:** HS 39* v Warwks (Birmingham) 1996. BB 4-26 v Durham (Stockton) 1995. **SL:** HS 20* v Notts (Leicester) 1991. BB 2-11 v Somerset (Leicester) 1994.

MULLALLY, Alan David (Cannington HS, Perth, Australia; Wembley TC), b Southend-on-Sea, Essex 12 Jul 1969. 6'5". RHB, LFM. W Australia 1987-88 to 1989-90. Victoria 1990-91. Hampshire (1 match) 1988. Leicestershire debut 1990; cap 1993. **Tests:** 9 (1996 to 1996-97); HS 24 v P (Oval) 1996; BB 3-44 v P (Lord's) 1996. **LOI:** 8 (1996 to 1996-97; HS 20; BB 3-29). Tours: NZ 1996-97; Z 1996-97. HS 75 v Middx (Leicester) 1996. 50 wkts (3); most – 70 (1996). BB 7-72 (10-170 match) v Glos (Leicester) 1993. **NWT:** HS 19* v Bucks (Marlow) 1993. BB 2-22 v Derbys (Derby) and v Northants (Lord's) 1992. **BHC:** HS 11 v Surrey (Leicester) 1992. BB 3-33 v Somerset (Leicester) 1997. **SL:** HS 38 v Kent (Leicester) 1994. BB 5-15 v Warwks (Birmingham) 1996.

NIXON, Paul Andrew (Ullswater HS, Penrith), b Carlisle, Cumberland 21 Oct 1970. 6'0". LHB, WK. Debut 1989; cap 1994. Cumberland 1987. MCC YC. Tours: I 1994-95 (Eng A); SA 1996-97 (Le). 1000 runs (1): 1046 (1994). HS 131 v Hants (Leicester) 1994. **NWT:** HS 39 v Sussex (Leicester) 1996. **BHC:** HS 53 v Surrey (Oval) 1997. **SL:** HS 84 v Sussex (Hove) 1995.

ORMOND, James (St Thomas More S, Nuneaton), b Walsgrave, Coventry, Warwks 20 Aug 1977. 6'3". RHB, RFM. Debut 1995. HS 35 v Glos (Leicester) 1997. BB 6-54 v A (Leicester) 1997. **BAC** BB 6-68 v Northants (Northampton) 1997. **SL:** HS 18 v Notts (Leicester) 1997. BB 3-30 v Essex (Colchester) 1997.

SIMMONS, Philip Verant (Holy Cross C, Arima), b Arima, Trinidad 18 Apr 1963. 6'3½". RHB, RM. Debut for N Trinidad 1982-83. Trinidad 1982-83 to date; captain 1988-89. Durham 1989-90 (NWT only). Leicestershire 1994-96; cap 1994. Eastern (SA) 1996-97. *Wisden* 1996. **Tests** (WI): 25 (1987-88 to 1996-97); HS 110 and BB 2-34 v A (Melbourne) 1992-93. **LOI** (WI): 119 (1987-88 to 1996-97; HS 122; BB 4-3). Tours (WI): E 1988 (*part*), 1991, 1992 (RW), 1993 (RW), 1995; A 1992-93, 1995-96; I 1987-88, 1994-95; SL 1993-94; Z 1983-84 (Young WI), 1986-87 (Young WI). 1000 runs (2); most – 1244 (1996). HS 261 v Northants (Leicester) 1994 – on Le debut (county record). BB 6-14 v Durham (Chester-le-St) 1996. Award: BHC 1. **NWT:** HS 82 v Berks (Leicester) 1996. BB 3-31 v Cumb (Netherfield) 1994. **BHC:** HS 64 and BB 1-29 v Ire (Leicester) 1994. **SL:** HS 140 v Middx (Leicester) 1994. BB 5-37 v Middx (Leicester) 1996.

SMITH, Benjamin Francis (Kibworth HS), b Corby, Northants 3 Apr 1972. 5'9". RHB, RM. Debut 1990; cap 1995. Tour (Le): SA 1996-97. 1000 runs (1): 1243 (1996). HS 190 v Glam (Swansea) 1996. BB 1-5. Award: NWT 1. **NWT:** HS 63* v Cumb (Netherfield) 1994. **BHC:** HS 61 v Warwks (Birmingham) 1996 and v Somerset (Leicester) 1997. **SL:** HS 115 v Somerset (Weston-s-M) 1995.

STEVENS, Darren Ian (Hinkley C), b Leicester 30 Apr 1976. 5'11". RHB, RM. Debut 1997. HS 27 v CU (Cambridge) 1997. BAC HS 8 and BB 1-5 v Sussex (Eastbourne) 1997. **SL:** HS 6.

SUTCLIFFE, Iain John (Leeds GS; Queen's C, Oxford), b Leeds, Yorks 20 Dec 1974. 6'2". LHB, occ OB. Oxford U 1994-96; blue 1995-96. Leicestershire debut 1995; cap 1997. Tour (Le): SA 1996-97. HS 163* OU v Hants (Oxford) 1995. Le HS 130 v Essex (Colchester) 1997. BB 2-21 OU v CU (Lord's) 1996. Award: NWT 1. **NWT:** HS 103* v Devon (Exmouth) 1997. **BHC:** HS 59 v Scot (Leicester) 1997. **SL:** HS 96 v Durham (Leicester) 1997. Boxing blue 1993-94.

WELLS, Vincent John (Sir William Nottidge S, Whitstable), b Dartford, Kent 6 Aug 1965. 6'0". RHB, RMF. Kent 1988-91. Leicestershire debut 1992; cap 1994. Tour (Le): SA 1996-97. 1000 runs (2); most – 1331 (1996). HS 224 v Middx (Lord's) 1997. BB 5-43 K v Leics (Leicester) 1990. Le BB 5-50 (inc hat-trick) v Durham (Durham) 1994. Hat-trick 1994. Awards: NWT 2; BHC 1. **NWT:** 201 v Berks (Leicester) 1996. BB 3-30 v Devon (Exmouth) 1997. **BHC:** HS 90 v Durham (Chester-le-St) 1997. BB 4-37 v Worcs (Leicester) 1993. **SL:** HS 101 v Middx (Leicester) 1994. BB 5-10 v Surrey (Oval) 1994.

WHITAKER, John James (Uppingham S), b Skipton, Yorks 5 May 1962. 5'10". RHB. OB. Debut 1983; cap 1986; benefit 1993; captain 1996 to date. *Wisden* 1986. YC 1986. **Tests:** 1 (1986-87); HS 11 v A (Adelaide) 1986-87. **LOI:** 2 (1986-87); HS 44*). Tours: A 1986-87; SA 1996-97 (Le); Z 1989-90 (Eng A). 1000 runs (10); most – 1767 (1990). HS 218 v Yorks (Bradford) 1996. BB 1-29. Awards: NWT 1; BHC 2. **NWT:** HS 155 v Wilts (Swindon) 1984. **BHC:** HS 100 v Kent (Canterbury) 1991. **SL:** HS 132 v Glam (Swansea) 1984.

WILLIAMSON, Dominic (St Leonard's CS, Durham; Durham SFC), b Durham City 15 Nov 1975. 5'8". RHB, RM. Debut 1996. MCC YC. HS 3 and BB 3-19 v Glam (Leicester) 1997 – on BAC debut. **BHC:** HS 6. BB 1-64. **SL:** HS 17 v Northants (Northampton) 1997. BB 5-32 v Sussex (Eastbourne) 1997.

NEWCOMERS

KIRBY, Steven P. (Bury C), b Bury, Lancs 4 Oct 1977. RHB, RFM.

WRIGHT, Ashley Spencer, b Grantham, Lincs 21 Oct 1980. RHB, RM.

DEPARTURES (who made first-class appearances in 1997)

JOHNSON, Neil Clarkson (Howick HS, Natal; Port Elizabeth U), b Salisbury, Rhodesia 24 Jan 1970. 6'2". LHB, RMF. Eastern Province B 1989-90 to 1991-92. Natal 1992-93 to date. Leicestershire 1997; cap 1997. Tour (SA A): Z 1994-95. HS 150 v Lancs (Leicester) 1997. BB 5-79 N v Boland (Stellenbosch) 1993-94. Le BB 3-61 v Worcs (Worcester) 1997. **NWT:** HS 15 v Yorks (Leicester) 1997. **BHC:** HS 58 v Northants (Northampton) 1997. BB 2-38 v Notts (Leicester) 1997. **SL:** HS 79* v Middx (Lord's) 1997. BB 3-37 v Notts (Leicester) 1997.

MACMILLAN, Gregor Innes (Guildford County S; Charterhouse; Southampton U; Keble C, Oxford), b Guildford, Surrey 7 Aug 1969. 6'5". RHB, OB. Oxford U 1993-95; blue 1994-95; captain 1995. Leicestershire 1995-97, scoring 103 v Sussex (Hove) on debut. HS 122 v Surrey (Leicester) 1995. BB 3-13 OU v CU (Lord's) 1993. Le BB 2-44 v Glam (Swansea) 1996. **NWT:** HS 9. BB 1-13. **BHC:** HS 77 Comb Us v Hants (Oxford) 1995. BB 1-18. **SL:** HS 58 v Glos (Cheltenham) 1996. BB 2-37 v Glam (Swansea) 1996.

PARSONS, Gordon James (Woodside County SS, Slough), b Slough, Bucks 17 Oct 1959. Brother-in-law of W.J.Cronje (OFS, Leics and South Africa). 6'1". LHB, RMF. Leicestershire 1978-85 and 1989-97; cap 1984; joint benefit 1994. Warwickshire 1986-88; cap 1987. Boland 1983-84 to 1984-85. GW 1985-86 to 1986-87. OFS 1988-89 to date. Buckinghamshire 1977. Tours: SA 1996-97 (Le); NZ 1979-80 (DHR); Z 1980-81 (Le). HS 76 Boland v W Province B (Cape Town) 1984-85. Le HS 73 v Durham (Leicester) 1995. 50 wkts (3); most – 67 (1984). BB 9-72 Boland v Transvaal B (Johannesburg) 1984-85. Le BB 6-11 v OU (Oxford) 1985. BAC BB 6-70 v Surrey (Oval) 1992. Awards: BHC 2. **NWT:** HS 25* v Glam (Leicester) 1995. BB 3-68 v Yorks (Leicester) 1997. **BHC:** HS 63* and BB 4-12 v Scot (Leicester) 1989. **SL:** HS 41* v Glos (Leicester) 1997. BB 4-19 v Essex (Harlow) 1982.

PIERSON, A.R.K. – *see* SOMERSET.

LEICESTERSHIRE 1997

RESULTS SUMMARY

	Place	Won	Lost	Tied	Drew	No Result
Britannic Assurance Championship	10th	4	1	–	11	1
All First-Class Matches		4	2	–	12	1
NatWest Trophy	2nd Round					
Benson and Hedges Cup	Semi-Finalist					
Sunday League	4th	9	5	1	–	2

BRITANNIC ASSURANCE CHAMPIONSHIP AVERAGES

BATTING AND FIELDING

Cap		M	I	NO	HS	Runs	Avge	100	50	Ct/St
1997	N.C.Johnson	12	18	5	150	819	63.00	2	5	13
–	J.M.Dakin	3	4	–	190	208	52.00	1	–	2
1994	P.A.Nixon	16	20	7	96	595	45.76	–	4	49/3
1995	B.F.Smith	13	19	5	131*	624	44.57	2	2	3
1994	V.J.Wells	16	24	–	224	1061	44.20	3	5	10
1986	J.J.Whitaker	14	20	1	133*	797	41.94	2	4	5
1996	D.L.Maddy	16	24	–	103	979	40.79	3	5	14
1997	I.J.Sutcliffe	11	16	1	130	582	38.80	2	2	3
1991	D.J.Millns	14	15	2	121	449	34.53	2	1	2
1984	G.J.Parsons	5	6	1	69*	113	22.60	–	1	4
–	A.Habib	7	11	2	77	198	22.00	–	1	4
1995	A.R.K.Pierson	15	15	–	59	266	17.73	–	1	8
–	M.T.Brimson	6	7	2	30*	59	11.80	–	–	3
–	G.I.Macmillan	4	5	1	19	40	10.00	–	–	2
–	J.Ormond	10	10	2	35	64	8.00	–	–	2
1993	A.D.Mullally	12	11	5	13*	41	6.83	–	–	2

Also batted (1 match each): D.I.Stevens 8 (1 ct); D.Williamson 3.

BOWLING

	O	M	R	W	Avge	Best	5wI	10wM
J.Ormond	269.3	58	906	35	25.88	6-68	2	–
D.J.Millns	395.4	84	1286	48	26.79	6-61	2	1
A.D.Mullally	369.1	88	1247	37	33.70	5-52	4	–
A.R.K.Pierson	485.1	101	1411	37	38.13	6-56	1	–
G.J.Parsons	161.2	43	425	11	38.63	4-22	–	–
V.J.Wells	187	43	621	16	38.81	2- 8	–	–

Also bowled: M.T.Brimson 131.5-34-357-9; J.M.Dakin 52-12-152-4; A.Habib 4-0-37-0; N.C.Johnson 116-18-420-8; G.I.Macmillan 11-1-41-0; D.L.Maddy 33.2-8-94-2; P.A.Nixon 2-0-4-0; B.F.Smith 1-0-4-0; D.I.Stevens 2-1-5-1; I.J.Sutcliffe 1-0-12-0; J.J.Whitaker 0.2-0-0-0; D.Williamson 17.5-5-40-4.

The First-Class Averages (pp 118-133) give the records of Leicestershire players in all first-class county matches (their other opponents being the Australians and Cambridge University), with the exception of:
D.L.Maddy 17-26-0-103-987-37.96-3-5-15ct. 47.2-10-122-2-61.00-1/2.
P.A.Nixon 18-23-8-96-656-43.73-0-4-50ct-3st. 2-0-4-0.
J.Ormond 12-11-2-35-65-7.22-0-0-2ct. 325.3-71-1061-44-24.11-6/54-3-0.

LEICESTERSHIRE RECORDS

FIRST-CLASS CRICKET

Highest Total	For	701-4d	v	Worcs	Worcester	1906
	V	761-6d	by	Essex	Chelmsford	1990
Lowest Total	For	25	v	Kent	Leicester	1912
	V	24	by	Glamorgan	Leicester	1971
		24	by	Oxford U	Oxford	1985
Highest Innings	For	261	P.V.Simmons	v	Northants	Leicester	1994
	V	341	G.H.Hirst	for	Yorkshire	Leicester	1905

Highest Partnership for each Wicket

1st	390	B.Dudleston/J.F.Steele	v	Derbyshire	Leicester	1979
2nd	289*	J.C.Balderstone/D.I.Gower	v	Essex	Leicester	1981
3rd	316*	W.Watson/A.Wharton	v	Somerset	Taunton	1961
4th	290*	P.Willey/T.J.Boon	v	Warwicks	Leicester	1984
5th	320	J.J.Whitaker/A.Habib	v	Worcs	Leicester	1996
6th	284	P.V.Simmons/P.A.Nixon	v	Durham	Chester-le-St	1996
7th	219*	J.D.R.Benson/P.Whitticase	v	Hampshire	Bournemouth	1991
8th	172	P.A.Nixon/D.J.Millns	v	Lancashire	Manchester	1996
9th	160	W.W.Odell/R.T.Crawford	v	Worcs	Leicester	1902
10th	228	R.Illingworth/K.Higgs	v	Northants	Leicester	1977

Best Bowling	For	10- 18	G.Geary	v	Glamorgan	Pontypridd	1929
(Innings)	V	10- 32	H.Pickett	for	Essex	Leyton	1895
Best Bowling	For	16- 96	G.Geary	v	Glamorgan	Pontypridd	1929
(Match)	V	16-102	C.Blythe	for	Kent	Leicester	1909

Most Runs – Season	2446	L.G.Berry	(av 52.04)		1937
Most Runs – Career	30143	L.G.Berry	(av 30.32)		1924-51
Most 100s – Season	7	L.G.Berry			1937
	7	W.Watson			1959
	7	B.F.Davison			1982
Most 100s – Career	45	L.G.Berry			1924-51
Most Wkts – Season	170	J.E.Walsh	(av 18.96)		1948
Most Wkts – Career	2130	W.E.Astill	(av 23.19)		1906-39

LIMITED-OVERS CRICKET

Highest Total	NWT	406-5	v	Berkshire	Leicester	1996
	BHC	371-6	v	Scotland	Leicester	1997
	SL	344-4	v	Durham	Chester-le-St	1996
Lowest Total	NWT	56	v	Northants	Leicester	1964
	BHC	56	v	Minor C	Wellington	1982
	SL	36	v	Sussex	Leicester	1973
Highest Innings	NWT	201	V.J.Wells	v	Berkshire	Leicester	1996
	BHC	158*	B.F.Davison	v	Warwicks	Coventry	1972
	SL	152	B.Dudleston	v	Lancashire	Manchester	1975
Best Bowling	NWT	6-20	K.Higgs	v	Staffs	Longton	1975
	BHC	6-35	L.B.Taylor	v	Worcs	Worcester	1982
	SL	6-17	K.Higgs	v	Glamorgan	Leicester	1973

MIDDLESEX

Formation of Present Club: 2 February 1864
Colours: Blue
Badge: Three Seaxes
Championships (since 1890): (10) 1903, 1920, 1921, 1947, 1976, 1980, 1982, 1985, 1990, 1993
Joint Championships: (2) 1949, 1977
NatWest Trophy/Gillette Cup Winners: (4) 1977, 1980, 1984, 1988
Benson and Hedges Cup Winners: (2) 1983, 1986
Sunday League Champions: (1) 1992
Match Awards: NWT 54; BHC 57

Secretary: V.J.Codrington
Lord's Cricket Ground, London NW8 8QN (Tel 0171 289 1300/286 1310)
Captain: M.R.Ramprakash. **Vice-Captain:** K.R.Brown. **Overseas Player:** J.L.Langer.
1998 Beneficiary: K.R.Brown. **Scorer:** M.J.Smith

BLANCHETT, Ian Neale (Downham Market SFC; Luton U), b Melbourne, Australia 2 Oct 1975. 6'4". RHB, RFM. Norfolk 1993-94. Staff 1996 – awaiting f-c debut. **BHC:** HS –. BB 1-44. **SL:** HS 1*. BB 1-51.

BLOOMFIELD, Timothy Francis, b Ashford 31 May 1973. RHB, RMF. Debut 1997. HS 4. BAC HS 0*. BB 5-77 v Essex (Chelmsford) 1997. **NWT:** HS –. BB 1-25. **SL:** HS 1. BB 2-8 v Surrey (Lord's) 1997.

BROWN, Keith Robert (Chace S, Enfield), b Edmonton 18 Mar 1963. Brother of G.K. (Middx 1986 and Durham 1992). 5'11". RHB, WK, RSM. Debut 1984; cap 1990; benefit 1998. MCC YC. 1000 runs – 1505 (1990). HS 200* v Notts (Lord's) 1990. BB 2-7 v Glos (Bristol) 1987. Awards: NWT 2; BHC 1. **NWT:** HS 103* v Surrey (Uxbridge) 1990. **BHC:** HS 75 v Comb U (Lord's) 1990. **SL:** HS 102 v Somerset (Lord's) 1988.

DUTCH, Keith Philip (Nower Hill HS; Weald C), b Harrow 21 Mar 1973. 5'10". RHB, OB. Debut 1993. MCC YC. HS 79 v Glos (Bristol) 1997. BB 3-25 v Somerset (Uxbridge) 1996. **NWT:** HS 6*. BB 1-24. **BHC:** HS 20 v Somerset (Lord's) 1997. BB 4-42 v Glam (Cardiff) 1997. **SL:** HS 58 v Kent (Lord's) 1997. BB 3-10 v Durham (Lord's) 1996.

FAY, Richard Anthony (Brondesbury & Kilburn HS; Queens Park Community S; City of Westminster C), b Kilburn, London 14 May 1974. Great-nephew of M.W.Tate (Sussex and England 1912-37). 6'4". RHB, RMF. MCC YC. Debut 1995. HS 26 and BB 4-53 v Glam (Cardiff) 1996. **NWT:** HS 0. BB 2-43 v Cumb (Carlisle) 1996. **BHC:** HS 3*. BB 1-13. **SL:** HS 12* v Sussex (Lord's) 1995. BB 4-33 v Warwks (Lord's) 1996.

FRASER, Angus Robert Charles (Gayton HS, Harrow; Orange Sr HS, Edgware), b Billinge, Lancs 8 Aug 1965. Brother of A.G.J. (Middx and Essex 1986-92). 6'5". RHB, RMF. Debut 1984; cap 1988; benefit 1997. *Wisden* 1995. **Tests:** 32 (1989 to 1995-96); HS 29 v A (Nottingham) 1989; BB 8-75 v WI (Bridgetown) 1993-94 – record England analysis v WI. **LOI:** 33 (1989-90 to 1995; HS 38*; BB 4-22). Tours: A 1990-91, 1994-95 (*part*); SA 1995-96; WI 1989-90, 1993-94. HS 92 v Surrey (Oval) 1990. 50 wkts (3); most – 92 (1989). BB 8-75 (*see Tests*). M BB 7-40 v Leics (Lord's) 1993. **NWT:** HS 19 v Durham (Darlington) 1989. BB 4-34 v Yorks (Leeds) 1988. **BHC:** HS 30* v Ire (Dublin) 1997. BB 4-49 v Kent (Canterbury) 1995. **SL:** HS 33 v Essex (Chelmsford) 1997. BB 5-32 v Derbys (Lord's) 1995.

GATTING, Michael William (John Kelly HS), b Kingsbury 6 Jun 1957. 5'10". RHB, RM. Debut 1975; cap 1977; captain 1983-97; benefit 1988; testimonial 1996. YC 1981. *Wisden* 1983. OBE 1987. **Tests:** 79 (1977-78 to 1994-95, 23 as captain); HS 207 v I (Madras) 1984-85; BB 1-14 (Bridgetown) 1993-94. **LOI:** 92 (1977-78 to 1992-93, 37 as captain; HS 115*; BB 3-32). Tours (C=captain): A 1986-87C, 1987-88C, 1994-95; SA 1989-90C (Eng XI); WI 1980-81, 1985-86; NZ 1977-78, 1983-84, 1987-88C; I/SL 1981-82, 1984-85, 1992-93; P

61

GATTING, M.W. continued:
1977-78, 1983-84, 1987-88C; Z 1980-81 (Mx). 1000 runs (18+1) inc 2000 (3); most –
2257 (1984). HS 258 v Somerset (Bath) 1984. BB 5-34 v Glam (Swansea) 1982. Awards:
NWT 7; BHC 11. **NWT:** HS 132* v Sussex (Lord's) 1989. BB 2-14 (twice). **BHC:** HS
143* v Sussex (Hove) 1985. BB 4-49 v Sussex (Lord's) 1984. **SL:** HS 124* v Leics
(Leicester) 1990. BB 4-30 v Glos (Bristol) 1989.

GOODCHILD, David John (Whitmore HS; Weald C; N London U), b Harrow 17 Sep
1976. 6'2". RHB, RM. Debut 1996. HS 4.

HEWITT, James Peter (Teddington S; Richmond C; City of Westminster C), b South-
wark, London 26 Feb 1976. 6'2½". LHB, RMF. Debut 1996. HS 75 v Essex (Chelmsford)
1997. 50 wkts (1): 60 (1997). BB 6-14 v Glam (Cardiff) 1997. Took wicket of R.I.Dawson
(Glos) with first ball in f-c cricket. **NWT:** HS 14* v Kent (Lord's) 1997. BB 1-37. **BHC:**
HS 14 v Ire (Dublin) 1997. BB 2-49 v Somerset (Lord's) 1997. **SL:** HS 32* v Glos
(Bristol) 1997. BB 3-26 v Hants (Portsmouth) 1996.

JOHNSON, Richard Leonard (Sunbury Manor S; S Pelthorne C), b Chertsey, Surrey 29
Dec 1974. 6'2". RHB, RMF. Debut 1992; cap 1995. Tour: I 1994-95 (Eng A – *part*). HS
50* v CU (Cambridge) 1994. BAC HS 47 v Hants (Southampton) 1994. 50 wkts (1): 50
(1997). BB 10-45 v Derbys (Derby) 1994 (second youngest to take all ten wickets in any
f-c match). **NWT:** HS 33 v Glam (Cardiff) 1995. BB 5-50 v Kent (Lord's) 1997. **BHC:**
HS 19 v Somerset (Lord's) 1997. BB 2-50 v Essex (Lord's) 1997. **SL:** HS 29 v Worcs
(Lord's) 1996 and v Essex (Chelmsford) 1997. BB 4-66 v Worcs (Worcester) 1993.

LARAMAN, Aaron William (Enfield GS), b Enfield 10 Jan 1979. RHB, RFM. Staff
1997 – awaiting f-c debut.

LYE, David Frank (Honiton Community C), b Exeter, Devon 11 Apr 1979. RHB, RM.
Staff 1997 – awaiting f-c debut.

MARTIN, Neil Donald (Verulam S), b Enfield 19 Aug 1979. RHB, RFM. Staff 1997 –
awaiting f-c debut. **SL:** HS –. BB 1-29.

NASH, David Charles (Sunbury Manor S; Malvern C), b Chertsey, Surrey 19 Jan 1978.
5'8". RHB, WK. Debut 1997. HS 100 and BB 1-8 v Essex (Chelmsford) 1997. **SL:** HS 23
v Derbys (Lord's) 1997.

POOLEY, Jason Calvin (Acton HS), b Hammersmith 8 Aug 1969. 6'0". LHB, occ OB.
Debut 1989; cap 1995. Tour: P 1995-96 (Eng A). 1000 runs (1): 1335 (1995). HS 138* v
CU (Cambridge) 1996. BAC HS 136 v Glos (Bristol) 1995. **NWT:** HS 79* v Glos
(Uxbridge) 1997. **BHC:** HS 50* v Essex (Lord's) 1997. **SL:** HS 109 v Derbys (Lord's)
1991.

RAMPRAKASH, Mark Ravin (Gayton HS; Harrow Weald SFC), b Bushey, Herts 5 Sep
1969. 5'9". RHB. Debut 1987; cap 1990; captain 1997 to date. YC 1991. **Tests:** 20
(1991 to 1997); HS 72 v A (Perth) 1994-95. **LOI:** 10 (1991 to 1995-96; YC 1991. Tours: A
1994-95 (*part*); SA 1995-96; WI 1991-92 (Eng A), 1993-94; NZ 1991-92; I 1994-95 (Eng
A); P 1990-91 (Eng A); SL 1990-91 (Eng A). 1000 runs (8) inc 2000 (1): 2258 (1995). HS
235 v Yorks (Leeds) 1995. BB 3-91 v Somerset (Taunton) 1995. Awards: NWT 2; BHC 3.
NWT: HS 104 v Surrey (Uxbridge) 1990. BB 2-15 v Ire (Dublin) 1991. **BHC:** HS 119*
v Northants (Lord's) 1994. BB 3-35 v Brit Us (Cambridge) 1996. **SL:** HS 147* v Worcs
(Lord's) 1990. BB 5-38 v Leics (Lord's) 1993.

RASHID, Umer Bin Abdul (Ealing Green HS; Ealing Tertiary C; Southbank U), b
Southampton, Hants 6 Feb 1976. 6'3". LHB, SLA. Debut 1996. HS 9. **BHC:** (Brit Us) HS
82 v Hants (Oxford) 1997. BB 2-57 v Essex (Chelmsford) 1996. **SL:** HS 8. BB 2-34 v
Yorks (Leeds) 1995.

SHAH, Owais Alam (Isleworth & Syon S), b Karachi, Pakistan 22 Oct 1978. 6'0". RHB,
OB. Debut 1996. Tour: A 1996-97 (Eng A). HS 104* v Notts (Lord's) 1997. BB 1-24.
NWT: HS 27* v Kent (Lord's) 1997. **BHC:** HS 42* v Kent (Canterbury) 1996. **SL:** HS
66* v Notts (Lord's) 1997. BB 1-4.

STRAUSS, Andrew John (Durham U), b Johannesburg, SA 2 Mar 1977. LHB. Staff 1997 – awaiting f-c debut. **BHC:** (Brit Uss) HS 1. **SL:** HS 4.

TUFNELL, Philip Clive Roderick (Highgate S), b Barnet, Herts 29 Apr 1966. 6'0". RHB, SLA. Debut 1986; cap 1990. MCC YC. **Tests:** 28 (1990-91 to 1997); HS 22* v I (Madras) 1992-93; BB 7-47 (11-147 match) v NZ (Christchurch) 1991-92, took 11-93 v A (Oval) 1997. **LOI:** 20 (1990-91 to 1996-97; HS 5*; BB 4-22). Tours: A 1990-91, 1994-95; WI 1993-94; NZ 1991-92, 1996-97; I/SL 1992-93, Z 1996-97. HS 67* v Worcs (Lord's) 1996. 50 wkts (7); most – 88 (1991). BB 8-29 v Glam (Cardiff) 1993. Award: NWT 1. **NWT:** HS 8. BB 3-29 v Herts (Lord's) 1988. **BHC:** HS 18 v Warwks (Lord's) 1991. BB 3-32 v Northants (Lord's) 1994. **SL:** HS 13* v Glam (Merthyr Tydfil) 1989. BB 5-28 v Leics (Lord's) 1993.

WEEKES, Paul Nicholas (Homerton House SS, Hackney), b Hackney, London 8 Jul 1969. 5'10". LHB, OB. Debut 1990; cap 1993. Tour: I 1994-95 (Eng A). MCC YC. 1000 runs (1): 1218 (1996). HS 171* v Somerset (Uxbridge) 1996. BB 8-39 v Glam (Lord's) 1996. Awards: NWT 2; BHC 3. **NWT:** HS 143* v Cornwall (St Austell) 1995. BB 3-35 v Cumb (Carlisle) 1996. **BHC:** HS 77 v Somerset (Lord's) 1997. BB 3-32 v Warwks (Lord's) 1994. **SL:** HS 119 v Glam (Lord's) 1996. BB 4-29 v Glos and v Essex (Lord's) 1996.

NEWCOMERS

COOK, Simon James, b Oxford 15 Jan 1977. RHB, RM. **BHC:** HS 6.

HUTTON, Benjamin Leonard (Radley C; Durham U), b Johannesburg, SA 29 Jan 1977. Elder son of R.A. (Yorks, Transvaal and England 1962 to 1975-76); grandson of Sir Leonard (Yorks and England 1934-60). RHB, RFM.

KETTLEBOROUGH, Richard Allan (Worksop C), b Sheffield, Yorks 15 Mar 1973. 6'0". LHB, RM. Yorkshire 1994-97. Tour: Z 1995-96 (Y). HS 108 Y v Essex (Leeds) 1996. BB 2-26 Y v Notts (Scarborough) 1996. **SL:** HS 28 Y v Somerset (Leeds) 1994. BB 2-43 Y v Surrey (Oval) 1995.

LANGER, Justin Lee (Aquinas C; U of WA), b Perth 21 Nov 1970. 5'8". LHB, RM. W Australia 1991-92 to date. **Tests** (A): 8 (1992-93 to 1996-97); HS 69 v P (Lahore) 1994-95. **LOI:** 8 (1993-94 to 1997; HS 36). Tours (A): E 1995 (Young A), 1997; SA 1996-97; WI 1994-95; NZ 1992-93; P 1994-95. 1000 runs (0+1): 1198 (1993-94). HS 274* WA v S Australia (Perth) 1996-97. UK HS 152* A v Glos (Bristol) 1997.

DEPARTURES (who made first-class appearances in 1997)

KALLIS, Jacques Henry (Wynberg HS), b Pinelands, SA 16 Oct 1975. RHB, RMF. Western Province 1993-94 to date. Middlesex 1997; cap 1997. **Tests** (SA): 5 (1996-97); HS 39 v A (Jo'burg) 1996-97; BB 3-29 v A (Pt Elizabeth) 1996-97. **LOI** (SA): 25 (1995-96 to 1996-97; HS 82; BB 3-21). Tours: E 1996 (SA A); A 1995-96 (WP); SL 1995-96 (SA U-24). 1000 runs (1): 1034 (1997). HS 186* WP v Queensland (Brisbane) 1995-96. M HS 172* v Worcs (Kidderminster) 1997. BB 5-54 v Kent (Lord's) 1997. Award: NWT 1. **NWT:** HS 100 and BB 4-47 v Glos (Uxbridge) 1997. **BHC:** HS 72 v Glam (Cardiff) 1997. BB 2-49 v Somerset (Lord's) 1997. **SL:** HS 24 v Leics (Lord's) 1997. BB 2-19 v Sussex (Lord's) 1997.

MOFFAT, Scott Park (Aldenham S, Elstree; Swansea U), b Germiston, SA 1 Feb 1973. 6'0". RHB, OB. Middlesex 1996-97. Hertfordshire 1993 to date. HS 47 v Warwks (Birmingham) 1997. **BHC:** HS 60 v Somerset (Lord's) 1997. **SL:** HS 29 v Essex (Chelmsford) 1997.

WELLINGS, Peter Edward (Smestow CS, Wolverhampton; Thames Valley U), b Wolverhampton, Staffs 5 Mar 1970. 6'1". RHB, RM. Debut 1996. HS 128* v CU (Cambridge) 1997. BAC HS 48 v Kent (Canterbury) 1996. **NWT:** HS 9*. BB 1-20. **BHC:** HS 23 v Ire (Dublin) 1997. BB 1-45. **SL:** HS 42 v Somerset (Uxbridge) 1996. BB 1-22.

MIDDLESEX 1997

RESULTS SUMMARY

	Place	Won	Lost	Tied	Drew	No Result
Britannic Assurance Championship	4th	7	4	–	6	–
All First-Class Matches		7	4	–	8	–
NatWest Trophy	Quarter-Finalist					
Benson and Hedges Cup	5th in Group D					
Sunday League	16th	3	10	1	–	3

BRITANNIC ASSURANCE CHAMPIONSHIP AVERAGES

BATTING AND FIELDING

Cap		M	I	NO	HS	Runs	Avge	100	50	Ct/St
–	D.C.Nash	5	7	2	100	311	62.20	1	1	3
1990	M.R.Ramprakash	16	25	3	190	1201	54.59	5	6	8
1997	J.H.Kallis	16	25	3	172*	1034	47.00	4	4	15
–	O.A.Shah	10	14	2	104*	520	43.33	1	2	13
1977	M.W.Gatting	17	26	1	108	761	30.44	1	3	22
1990	K.R.Brown	17	25	6	144*	515	27.10	1	2	46/2
–	K.P.Dutch	5	7	2	79	124	24.80	–	1	2
–	S.P.Moffat	4	6	1	47	122	24.40	–	–	2
1995	J.C.Pooley	16	24	–	98	549	22.87	–	3	16
–	J.P.Hewitt	17	21	4	75	264	15.52	–	1	5
1988	A.R.C.Fraser	17	22	6	35	229	14.31	–	–	4
1995	R.L.Johnson	16	22	–	39	292	13.27	–	–	6
1993	P.N.Weekes	13	20	–	44	261	13.05	–	–	18
1990	P.C.R.Tufnell	14	18	5	21	89	6.84	–	–	2

Also batted: T.F.Bloomfield (3 matches) 0*, 0* (2 ct); P.E.Wellings (1) 13 (1 ct).

BOWLING

	O	M	R	W	Avge	Best	5wI	10wM
T.F.Bloomfield	68	16	201	12	16.75	5-77	1	–
J.H.Kallis	234.3	61	655	32	20.46	5-54	1	–
J.P.Hewitt	424	90	1351	57	23.70	6-14	2	–
P.C.R.Tufnell	474.1	143	1000	41	24.39	5-61	2	–
R.L.Johnson	395.2	77	1277	47	27.17	4-26	–	–
A.R.C.Fraser	531.5	147	1308	47	27.82	6-77	2	–

Also bowled: K.P.Dutch 69-10-207-4; M.W.Gatting 7-1-46-1; D.C.Nash 3-0-19-1; M.R.Ramprakash 35.2-10-126-2; O.A.Shah 2-0-19-0; P.N.Weekes 128-16-397-4.

The First-Class Averages (pp 118-133) give the records of Middlesex players in all first-class county matches (their other opponents being the Australians and Cambridge University), with the exception of:
  M.R.Ramprakash 17-27-3-190-1293-53.87-5-7-8ct. 35.2-10-126-2-63.00-1/30.
  P.C.R.Tufnell 16-19-6-21-100-7,69-0-0-4ct. 514.1-152-1112-44-25.27-5/61-2-0.

MIDDLESEX RECORDS

FIRST-CLASS CRICKET

Highest Total	For	642-3d		v Hampshire	Southampton	1923
	V	665		by W Indies	Lord's	1939
Lowest Total	For	20		v MCC	Lord's	1864
	V	31		by Glos	Bristol	1924
Highest Innings	For	331*	J.D.B.Robertson	v Worcs	Worcester	1949
	V	316*	J.B.Hobbs	for Surrey	Lord's	1926

Highest Partnership for each Wicket

1st	367*	G.D.Barlow/W.N.Slack	v Kent	Lord's	1981
2nd	380	F.A.Tarrant/J.W.Hearne	v Lancashire	Lord's	1914
3rd	424*	W.J.Edrich/D.C.S.Compton	v Somerset	Lord's	1948
4th	325	J.W.Hearne/E.H.Hendren	v Hampshire	Lord's	1919
5th	338	R.S.Lucas/T.C.O'Brien	v Sussex	Hove	1895
6th	270	J.D.Carr/P.N.Weekes	v Glos	Lord's	1994
7th	271*	E.H.Hendren/F.T.Mann	v Notts	Nottingham	1925
8th	182*	M.H.C.Doll/H.R.Murrell	v Notts	Lord's	1913
9th	160*	E.H.Hendren/T.J.Durston	v Essex	Leyton	1927
10th	230	R.W.Nicholls/W.Roche	v Kent	Lord's	1899

Best Bowling	For	10- 40	G.O.B.Allen	v Lancashire	Lord's	1929
(Innings)	V	9- 38	R.C.R.Glasgow†	for Somerset	Lord's	1924
Best Bowling	For	16-114	G.Burton	v Yorkshire	Sheffield	1888
(Match)		16-114	J.T.Hearne	v Lancashire	Manchester	1898
	V	16-109	C.W.L.Parker	for Glos	Cheltenham	1930

Most Runs – Season	2669	E.H.Hendren	(av 83.41)		1923
Most Runs – Career	40302	E.H.Hendren	(av 48.81)		1907-37
Most 100s – Season	13	D.C.S.Compton			1947
Most 100s – Career	119	E.H.Hendren			1907-37
Most Wkts – Season	158	F.J.Titmus	(av 14.63)		1955
Most Wkts – Career	2361	F.J.Titmus	(av 21.27)		1949-82

LIMITED-OVERS CRICKET

Highest Total	NWT	304-7		v Surrey	The Oval	1995
		304-8		v Cornwall	St Austell	1995
	BHC	325-5		v Leics	Leicester	1992
	SL	290-6		v Worcs	Lord's	1990
Lowest Total	NWT	41		v Essex	Westcliff	1972
	BHC	73		v Essex	Lord's	1985
	SL	23		v Yorkshire	Leeds	1974
Highest Innings	NWT	158	G.D.Barlow	v Lancashire	Lord's	1984
	BHC	143*	M.W.Gatting	v Sussex	Hove	1985
	SL	147*	M.R.Ramprakash	v Worcs	Lord's	1990
Best Bowling	NWT	6-15	W.W.Daniel	v Sussex	Hove	1980
	BHC	7-12	W.W.Daniel	v Minor C (E)	Ipswich	1978
	SL	6- 6	R.W.Hooker	v Surrey	Lord's	1969

† R.C.Robertson-Glasgow

NORTHAMPTONSHIRE

Formation of Present Club: 31 July 1878
Colours: Maroon
Badge: Tudor Rose
Championships: (0) Second 1912, 1957, 1965, 1976
NatWest Trophy/Gillette Cup Winners: (2) 1976, 1992
Benson and Hedges Cup Winners: (1) 1980
Sunday League Champions: (0) Third 1991
Match Awards: NWT 50; BHC 54

Chief Executive: S.P.Coverdale
County Ground, Wantage Road, Northampton, NN1 4TJ (Tel 01604 32917)
Captain: K.M.Curran. **Vice-Captain:** no appointment. **Overseas Player:** P.R.Reiffel.
1998 Beneficiary (testimonial): A.Fordham. **Scorer:** A.C.Kingston

BAILEY, Robert John (Biddulph HS), b Biddulph, Staffs 28 Oct 1963. 6'3". RHB, OB. Debut 1982; cap 1985; benefit 1993; captain 1996-97. Staffordshire 1980. YC 1984. **Tests:** 4 (1988 to 1989-90); HS 43 v WI (Oval) 1988. **LOI:** 4 (1984-85 to 1989-90; HS 43*). Tours: SA 1991-92 (Nh); WI 1989-90; Z 1994-95 (Nh). 1000 runs (13); most – 1987 (1990). HS 224* v Glam (Swansea) 1986. BB 5-54 v Notts (Northampton) 1993. Awards: NWT 7; BHC 9. **NWT:** HS 145 v Staffs (Stone) 1991. BB 3-47 v Notts (Northampton) 1990. **BHC:** HS 134 v Glos (Northampton) 1987. BB 1-1. **SL:** HS 125* v Derbys (Derby) 1987. BB 3-23 v Leics (Leicester) 1987.

BAILEY, Tobin Michael Barnaby (Bedford S; Loughborough U), b Kettering 28 Aug 1976. 5'10". RHB, WK. Debut 1996. Bedfordshire 1994 to date. HS 31* v Lancs (Northampton) 1996. **BHC:** (Brit us) HS 52 v Glos (Bristol) 1997. **SL:** HS –.

BLAIN, John Angus Rae (Penicuik HS; Jewel & Esk Valley C), b Edinburgh, Scotland 4 Jan 1979. 6'1". RHB, RMF. Scotland 1996. Northamptonshire debut 1997. HS 0 and BB 1-18 v Worcs (Northampton) 1997. **SL:** HS –. BB 5-24 v Derbys (Derby) 1997.

BOSWELL, Scott Antony John (Pocklington S; Wolverhampton U), b Fulford, Yorks.11 Sep 1974. 6'5". RHB, RFM. Debut (British Us) 1996. Northamptonshire debut 1996. HS 35 v Leics (Northampton) 1997. BB 5-94 v Worcs (Northampton) 1997. **BHC:** (Brit us) HS 14 v Essex (Chelmsford) 1996. BB 3-39 v Kent (Canterbury) 1997. **SL:** HS 2. BB 1-20.

BROWN, Jason Fred (St Margaret Ward HS & SFC), b Newcastle-under-Lyme, Staffs 10 Oct 1974. 6'0". RHB, OB. Debut 1996. Staffordshire 1994 to date. HS 16* v Durham (Northampton) 1997. BB 4-50 v CU (Cambridge) 1997. BAC BB 3-23 v Derbys (Derby) 1997. **SL:** HS –. BB 4-26 v Leics (Northampton) 1997.

CAPEL, David (John (Roade CS), b Northampton 6 Feb 1963. 5'11". RHB, RMF. Debut 1981; cap 1986; benefit 1994. E Province 1985-86 to 1986-87. **Tests:** 15 (1987 to 1989-90); HS 98 v P (Karachi) 1987-88; BB 3-88 v WI (Bridgetown) 1989-90. **LOI:** 23 (1986-87 to 1989-90; HS 50*; BB 3-38). Tours: A 1987-88, 1992-93 (Eng A); WI 1989-90; NZ 1987-88; P 1987-88. 1000 runs (3); most – 1311 (1989). HS 175 v Leics (Northampton) 1995. 50 wkts (4); most – 63 (1986). BB 7-44 v Warwks (Birmingham) 1995. Awards: NWT 3; BHC 2. **NWT:** HS 101 v Notts (Northampton) 1990. BB 3-21 v Glam (Swansea) 1992. **BHC:** HS 97 v Yorks (Lord's) 1987. BB 5-51 v Yorks (Leeds) 1997. **SL:** HS 121 v Glam (Northampton) 1990. BB 4-30 v Yorks (Middlesbrough) 1982.

CURRAN, Kevin Malcolm (Marandellas HS), b Rusape, S Rhodesia 7 Sep 1959. Qualified for England 1994. Son of K.P. (Rhodesia 1947-48 to 1953-54). 6'1". RHB, RMF. Zimbabwe 1980-81 to 1987-88. Gloucestershire 1985-90; cap 1985. Natal 1988-89. Northamptonshire debut 1991; cap 1992; captain 1998. Boland 1994-95. **LOI** (Z): 11 (1983 to 1987-88; HS 73; BB 3-65). Tours (Z): E 1982; SL 1983-84. 1000 runs (7); most – 1353 (1986). HS 159 v Glam (Abergavenny) 1997. 50 wkts (5); most – 67 (1993). BB 7-47 Natal v Transvaal (Johannesburg) 1988-89 and v Yorks (Harrogate) 1993. Awards: NWT

CURRAN, K.M. continued:
2; BHC 2. **NWT:** HS 78* v Cambs (Northampton) 1992. BB 4-34 Gs v Northants (Bristol) 1985. **BHC:** HS 57 Gs v Derbys (Derby) 1987. BB 4-38 v Worcs (Northampton) 1995. **SL:** HS 119* v Kent (Canterbury) 1990. BB 5-15 Gs v Leics (Gloucester) 1988.

DAVIES, Michael Kenton, b Ashby-de-la-Zouch, Leics 17 Jul 1976. RHB, SLA. Debut 1997. HS 17 v Glam (Abergavenny) 1997. BB 5-46 v Derbys (Derby) 1997. **BHC:** (Brit Us) HS 1*. BB 1-69.

DOBSON, Andrew Michael (Frederick Gough CS, Scunthorpe; Oundle S), b Scunthorpe, Lincs 6 Apr 1980. 6'0". LHB, RFM. Staff 1997 – awaiting f-c debut.

FOLLETT, David (Moorland Road HS, Burslem; Stoke-on-Trent TC), b Newcastle-under-Lyme, Staffs 14 Oct 1968. 6'2". RHB, RFM. Middlesex 1995-96. Northamptonshire debut 1997. Staffordshire 1994. HS 17 M v Yorks (Lord's) 1996. Nh HS 3. BB 8-22 (10-87 match) M v Durham (Lord's) 1996. Nh BB 2-123 v Middx (Lord's) 1997. **BHC:** HS 4 (twice). BB 4-39 v Scot (Northampton) 1997. **SL:** HS 1*. BB 2-28 v Middx (Lord's) 1997.

INNES, Kevin John (Weston Favell Upper S), b Wellingborough 24 Sep 1975. 5'10", RHB, RM. 2nd XI debut 1990 (aged 14yr 8m – Northamptonshire record). Debut 1994. HS 63 and BB 4-61 v Lancs (Northampton) 1996. **NWT:** HS 25 v Cumb (Barrow) 1997. **BHC:** HS 1. BB 1-25. **SL:** HS 19* v Worcs (Northampton) 1997. BB 1-35.

LOGAN, Richard James, b Stone, Staffs 28 Jan 1980. RHB, RFM. Staff 1997 – awaiting f-c debut.

LOYE, Malachy Bernhard (Moulton S), b Northampton 27 Sep 1972. 6'2". RHB, OB. Debut 1991; cap 1994. Tours: SA 1993-94 (Eng A); Z 1994-95 (Nh). 1000 runs (1): 1048 (1996). HS 205 v Yorks (Northampton) 1996. Award: BHC 1. **NWT:** HS 65 v Essex (Chelmsford) 1993. **BHC:** HS 68* v Middx (Lord's) 1994. **SL:** HS 122 v Somerset (Luton) 1993.

MONTGOMERIE, Richard Robert (Rugby S; Worcester C, Oxford), b Rugby, Warwks 3 Jul 1971. 5'10½". RHB, OB. Oxford U 1991-94; blue 1991-92-93-94; captain 1994; half blues for rackets and real tennis. Northamptonshire debut 1991; cap 1995. Tour: Z 1994-95 (Nh). 1000 runs (2); most – 1178 (1996). HS 192 v Kent (Canterbury) 1995. **NWT:** HS 109 v Notts (Nottingham) 1995. **BHC:** HS 75 Comb Us v Worcs (Oxford) 1992. **SL:** HS 86 v Durham (Northampton) 1997.

PENBERTHY, Anthony Leonard (Camborne CS), b Troon, Cornwall 1 Sep 1969. 6'1". LHB, RM. Debut 1989; cap 1994. Tours (Nh): SA 1991-92; Z 1994-95. HS 101* v CU (Cambridge) 1990. BAC HS 96 v Surrey (Northampton) 1997. BB 5-37 v Glam (Swansea) 1993. Took wicket of M.A.Taylor (A) with his first ball in f-c cricket. Award: NWT 1. **NWT:** HS 79 v Lancs (Manchester) 1996. BB 5-56 v Cumb (Barrow) 1997. **BHC:** HS 41 v Warwks (Northampton) 1996. BB 3-38 v Notts (Northampton) 1996. **SL:** HS 81* v Surrey (Northampton) 1997. BB 5-36 v Glos (Northampton) 1993.

RIPLEY, David (Royds SS, Leeds), b Leeds, Yorks 13 Sep 1966. 5'9". RHB, WK. Debut 1984; cap 1987; benefit 1997. Tours (Nh): SA 1991-92; Z 1994-95. HS 134* v Yorks (Scarborough) 1986. BB 2-89 v Essex (Ilford) 1987. Award: BHC 1. **NWT:** HS 27* v Durham (Darlington) 1984. **BHC:** HS 36* v Glos (Bristol) 1991. **SL:** HS 52* v Surrey (Northampton) 1993.

ROBERTS, David James (Mullion CS), b Truro, Cornwall 29 Dec 1976. Cousin of C.K.Bullen (Surrey 1982-91). 5'11". RHB, RSM. Debut 1996. HS 117 v Essex (Northampton) 1997.

SALES, David John Grimwood (Caterham S; Cumnor House S), b Carshalton, Surrey 3 Dec 1977. 6'0". RHB, RM. Debut 1996 v Worcs (Kidderminster) scoring 0 and 210* – record Championship score on f-c debut; youngest (18yr 237d) to score 200 in a Championship match. HS 210* (*see above*). **NWT:** HS 53 v Cumb (Barrow) 1997. **BHC:** HS 15 v Kent (Canterbury) 1997. **SL:** HS 70* (off 56 balls) v Essex (Chelmsford) 1994, when 16yr 289d (youngest to score SL fifty). Soccer for Wimbledon and Crystal Palace.

67

SNAPE, Jeremy Nicholas (Denstone C; Durham U), b Stoke-on-Trent, Staffs 27 Apr 1973. 5'8½". RHB, OB. Debut 1992. Combined Us 1994. Tour: Z 1994-95 (Nh). HS 87 v Mashonaland Select XI (Harare) 1994-95. BAC HS 66 v Notts (Northampton) 1997. BB 5-65 v Durham (Northampton) 1995. Awards: BHC 2. **NWT:** HS 54 v Derbys (Derby) 1997. BB 2-44 v Glos (Bristol) 1995. **BHC:** HS 52 Comb Us v Hants (Southampton) 1993. BB 5-32 v Leics (Northampton) 1997. **SL:** HS 33 v Lancs (Manchester) 1997. BB 4-31 v Sussex (Hove) 1997.

SWANN, Alec James (Risade S; Sponne S, Towcester), b Northampton 26 Oct 1976. Elder brother of A.J. (*below*). 6'1". RHB, OB/RM. Debut 1996. Bedfordshire 1994. HS 136 v Warwks (Birmingham) 1997.

SWANN, Graeme Peter (Sponne S, Towcester), b Northampton 24 Mar 1979. 6'0". Younger brother of A.J. (*above*). RHB, OB. Staff 1997 – awaiting f-c debut. **SL:** HS 0*. BB 2-28 v Worcs (Northampton) 1997 – on 1st XI debut.

TAYLOR, Jonathan Paul (Pingle S, Swadlincote), b Ashby-de-la-Zouch, Leics 8 Aug 1964. 6'2". LHB, LFM. Derbyshire 1984-86. Northamptonshire debut 1991; cap 1992. Staffordshire 1989-90. **Tests:** 2 (1992-93 to 1994); HS 17* v I (Calcutta) 1992-93; BB 1-18. **LOI:** 1 (1992-93; HS 1). Tours: SA 1993-94 (A – *part*); I 1992-93; Z 1994-95 (Nh). HS 86 v Durham (Northampton) 1995. 50 wkts (5); most – 69 (1993). BB 7-23 v Hants (Bournemouth) 1992. Award: BHC 1. **NWT:** HS 9. BB 4-34 v Glos (Bristol) 1995. **BHC:** HS 7*. BB 5-45 v Notts (Northampton) 1996. **SL:** HS 24 v Worcs (Northampton) 1993. BB 3-14 De v Glos (Gloucester) 1986.

WALTON, Timothy Charles (Leeds GS; Newcastle upon Tyne Poly), b Low Head, Yorks 8 Nov 1972. 6'0½". RHB, RM. Debut 1994. HS 71 v Somerset (Northampton) 1995. BB 1-26. Award: BHC 1. **NWT:** HS 6. **BHC:** HS 70 v Warwks (Northampton) 1996. BB 1-27. **SL:** HS 72 v Glos (Bristol) 1994. BB 2-27 v Leics (Leicester) 1992.

WARREN, Russell John (Kingsthorpe Upper S), b Northampton 10 Sep 1971. 6'1". RHB, OB. Debut 1992; cap 1995. HS 201* v Glam (Northampton) 1996. Award: NWT 1. **NWT:** HS 100* v Ire (Northampton) 1994. **BHC:** HS 23 v Derbys (Derby) 1995. **SL:** HS 71* v Leics (Northampton) 1993.

NEWCOMERS

MALCOLM, Devon Eugene (St Elizabeth THS; Richmond C, Sheffield; Derby CHE), b Kingston, Jamaica 22 Feb 1963. Qualified for England 1987. 6'2". RHB, RF. Derbyshire 1984-97; cap 1989; benefit 1997. *Wisden* 1994. **Tests:** 40 (1989 to 1997); HS 29 v A (Sydney) 1994-95; BB 9-57 v SA (Oval) 1994 – sixth best analysis in Test cricket. **LOI:** 10 (1990 to 1993-94; HS 4; BB 3-40). Tours: A 1990-91, 1994-95; SA 1995-96; WI 1989-90, 1991-92 (Eng A), 1993-94; I 1992-93; SL 1992-93. HS 51 De v Surrey (Derby) 1989. 50 wkts (6); most – 82 (1996). BB 9-57 (*see Tests*). Awards: NWT 1; BHC 1. **NWT:** HS 10* De v Leics (Derby) 1992. BB 7-35 De v Northants (Derby) 1997. **BHC:** HS 15 De v Comb Us (Oxford) 1991. BB 5-27 De v Middx (Derby) 1988. **SL:** HS 42 De v Surrey (Oval) 1996. BB 4-21 De v Surrey (Derby) 1989 and De v Leics (Knypersley) 1990.

REIFFEL, Paul Ronald (Jordanville TS), b Box Hill, Victoria 19 Apr 1966. 6'2". RHB, RFM. Victoria 1987-88 to date. **Tests:** 29 (1991-92 to 1997); HS 56 v SL (Adelaide) 1995-96; BB 6-71 v E (Birmingham) 1993. **LOI** 19 (1991-92 to 1996-97; HS 58; BB 4-13). Tours (A): E 1993, 1997; SA 1993-94, 1996-97; WI 1994-95, I 1996-97; NZ 1992-93, Z 1991-92 (Aus B). HS 86 and BB 6-57 V v Tasmania (Melbourne) 1990-91. 50 wkts (0+1): 51 (1994-95). UK HS 56 A v Glam (Cardiff) 1997. UK BB 6-71 (*see Tests*).

DEPARTURES see p 106

NORTHAMPTONSHIRE 1997

RESULTS SUMMARY

	Place	Won	Lost	Tied	Drew	No Result
Britannic Assurance Championship	15th	5	5	–	9	–
All First-Class Matches		3	5	–	10	–
NatWest Trophy	2nd Round					
Benson and Hedges Cup	Semi-Finalist					
Sunday League	9th	8	6	–	–	3

BRITANNIC ASSURANCE CHAMPIONSHIP AVERAGES

BATTING AND FIELDING

Cap		M	I	NO	HS	Runs	Avge	100	50	Ct/St
1992	K.M.Curran	15	26	4	159	1032	46.90	2	6	8
1990	A.Fordham	8	16	2	85*	629	44.92	–	6	8
1995	R.J.Warren	9	16	2	174*	614	43.85	1	3	10/1
1987	D.Ripley	16	23	6	92	728	42.82	–	6	27/6
1985	R.J.Bailey	16	29	5	117*	973	40.54	2	5	19
1994	M.B.Loye	8	15	3	86	412	34.33	–	2	2
1995	R.R.Montgomerie	9	17	3	73	476	34.00	–	4	6
–	D.J.Roberts	6	12	–	117	367	30.58	1	–	–
–	D.J.G.Sales	12	18	1	103	510	30.00	1	2	4
–	T.C.Walton	7	10	1	60	231	25.66	–	2	1
1994	A.L.Penberthy	12	18	–	96	443	24.61	–	2	7
–	J.N.Snape	10	15	3	66	286	23.83	–	3	9
1986	D.J.Capel	4	7	–	57	140	20.00	–	1	1
–	S.A.J.Boswell	9	12	3	35	122	13.55	–	–	2
1992	J.P.Taylor	16	21	4	36	216	12.70	–	–	7
–	M.K.Davies	6	9	4	17	49	9.80	–	–	2
–	Mohammad Akram	11	14	2	28	116	9.66	–	–	1
–	J.F.Brown	5	8	4	16*	25	6.25	–	–	3

Also batted: J.A.R.Blain (1 match) 0 (1 ct); J.E.Emburey (3) 0, 0, 39 (1 ct); D.Follett (1) 0, 3; J.G.Hughes (1) 5*; A.J.Swann (2) 1, 25, 136.

BOWLING

	O	M	R	W	Avge	Best	5wI	10wM
J.P.Taylor	455.4	81	1532	54	28.37	7-87	3	1
M.K.Davies	234.2	71	674	23	29.30	5-46	1	–
K.M.Curran	215.2	57	715	24	29.79	4-32	–	–
J.F.Brown	178.2	32	583	16	36.43	3-23	–	–
R.J.Bailey	112.3	19	367	10	36.70	4-10	–	–
Mohammad Akram	287	43	1135	30	37.83	5-72	2	–
S.A.J.Boswell	185.5	26	769	15	51.26	5-94	1	–
J.N.Snape	225.1	47	681	11	61.90	4-46	–	–

Also bowled: J.A.R.Blain 30-8-105-2; D.J.Capel 39-4-180-2; J.E.Emburey 110.3-39-259-4; D.Follett 24.3-1-123-2; A.Fordham 2.3-0-7-0; J.G.Hughes 22-6-66-1; A.L.Penberthy 175-27-647-9; D.J.G.Sales 3-0-16-0; T.C.Walton 8-0-45-0.

The First-Class Averages (pp 118-133) give the records of Northamptonshire players in all first-class county matches (their other opponents being Cambridge University), with the exception of R.J.Warren whose full county figures are as above, and:
    D.J.G.Sales 13-19-1-103-520-28.88-1-2-4ct. 8-2-28-0.

NORTHAMPTONSHIRE RECORDS

FIRST-CLASS CRICKET

Highest Total	For 781-7d		v Notts	Northampton	1995
	V 670-9d		by Sussex	Hove	1921
Lowest Total	For 12		v Glos	Gloucester	1907
	V 33		by Lancashire	Northampton	1977
Highest Innings	For 300	R.Subba Row	v Surrey	The Oval	1958
	V 333	K.S.Duleepsinhji	for Sussex	Hove	1930

Highest Partnership for each Wicket

1st	372	R.R.Montgomerie/M.B.Loye	v Yorkshire	Northampton	1996
2nd	344	G.Cook/R.J.Boyd-Moss	v Lancashire	Northampton	1986
3rd	393	A.Fordham/A.J.Lamb	v Yorkshire	Leeds	1990
4th	370	R.T.Virgin/P.Willey	v Somerset	Northampton	1976
5th	347	D.Brookes/D.W.Barrick	v Essex	Northampton	1952
6th	376	R.Subba Row/A.Lightfoot	v Surrey	The Oval	1958
7th	229	W.W.Timms/F.A.Walden	v Warwicks	Northampton	1926
8th	164	D.Ripley/N.G.B.Cook	v Lancashire	Manchester	1987
9th	156	R.Subba Row/S.Starkie	v Lancashire	Northampton	1955
10th	148	B.W.Bellamy/J.V.Murdin	v Glamorgan	Northampton	1925

Best Bowling	For 10-127	V.W.C.Jupp	v Kent	Tunbridge W	1932
(Innings)	V 10- 30	C.Blythe	for Kent	Northampton	1907
Best Bowling	For 15- 31	G.E.Tribe	v Yorkshire	Northampton	1958
(Match)	V 17- 48	C.Blythe	for Kent	Northampton	1907

Most Runs – Season	2198	D.Brookes	(av 51.11)		1952
Most Runs – Career	28980	D.Brookes	(av 36.13)		1934-59
Most 100s – Season	8	R.A.Haywood			1921
Most 100s – Career	67	D.Brookes			1934-59
Most Wkts – Season	175	G.E.Tribe	(av 18.70)		1955
Most Wkts – Career	1097	E.W.Clark	(av 21.31)		1922-47

LIMITED-OVERS CRICKET

Highest Total	NWT 360-2		v Staffs	Northampton	1990
	BHC 304-6		v Scotland	Northampton	1995
	SL 306-2		v Surrey	Guildford	1985
Lowest Total	NWT 62		v Leics	Leicester	1974
	BHC 85		v Sussex	Northampton	1978
	SL 41		v Middlesex	Northampton	1972
Highest Innings	NWT 145	R.J.Bailey	v Staffs	Stone	1991
	BHC 134	R.J.Bailey	v Glos	Northampton	1987
	SL 172*	W.Larkins	v Warwicks	Luton	1983
Best Bowling	NWT 7-37	N.A.Mallender	v Worcs	Northampton	1984
	BHC 5-21	Sarfraz Nawaz	v Middlesex	Lord's	1980
	SL 7-39	A.Hodgson	v Somerset	Northampton	1976

NOTTINGHAMSHIRE

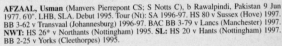

Formation of Present Club: March/April 1841
Substantial Reorganisation: 11 December 1866
Colours: Green and Gold
Badge: Badge of City of Nottingham
Championships (since 1890): (4) 1907, 1929, 1981, 1987
NatWest Trophy/Gillette Cup Winners: (1) 1987
Benson and Hedges Cup Winners: (1) 1989
Sunday League Champions: (1) 1991
Match Awards: NWT 39; BHC 64

Secretary/General Manager: B.Robson
   Trent Bridge, Nottingham NG2 6AG (Tel 0115 982 1525)
Captain: P.Johnson. **Vice-Captain:** no appointment. **Overseas Player:** P.A.Strang.
1998 Beneficiary: K.P.Evans. **Scorer:** G.Stringfellow

AFZAAL, Usman (Manvers Pierrepont CS; S Notts C), b Rawalpindi, Pakistan 9 Jun 1977. 6'0". LHB, SLA. Debut 1995. Tour (Nt): SA 1996-97. HS 80 v Sussex (Hove) 1997. BB 3-62 v Transvaal (Johannesburg) 1996-97. BAC BB 3-79 v Lancs (Manchester) 1997. **NWT:** HS 26* v Northants (Nottingham) 1995. **SL:** HS 20 v Hants (Nottingham) 1997. BB 2-25 v Yorks (Cleethorpes) 1995.

ARCHER, Graeme Francis (Heron Brook Middle S; King Edward VI HS, Stafford), b Carlisle, Cumberland 26 Sep 1970. 6'1". RHB, OB. Debut 1992; cap 1995. Staffordshire 1990. Tour (Nt): SA 1996-97. 1000 runs (1): 1171 (1995). HS 168 v Glam (Worksop) 1994. BB 3-18 v Hants (Southampton) 1996. Award: BHC 1. **NWT:** HS 39 v Cheshire (Warrington) 1993. BB 1-17. **BHC:** HS 111* v Durham (Nottingham) 1997. BB 1-34. **SL:** HS 104* v Derbys (Nottingham) 1997. BB 2-16 v Surrey (Guildford) 1995.

BATES, Richard Terry (Bourne GS; Stamford CFE), b Stamford, Lincs 17 Jun 1972. 6'1". RHB, OB. Debut 1993. Lincolnshire 1990-91. HS 34 v Worcs (Worcester) 1996. BB 5-88 v Durham (Chester-le-St) 1995. Award: BHC 1. **NWT:** HS 11 v Surrey (Oval) 1997. **BHC:** HS 27 v Yorks (Leeds) 1996. BB 3-21 v Scot (Nottingham) 1996. **SL:** HS 16 v Worcs (Worcester) 1994 and v Hants (Southampton) 1996. BB 3-33 v Kent (Nottingham) 1997.

BOWEN, Mark Nicholas (Sacred Heart, Redcar; St Mary's C; Teesside Poly), b Redcar, Yorks 6 Dec 1967. 6'2". RHB, RM. Nottinghamshire 1991-92/1994. Nottinghamshire debut 1996; cap 1997. Tours: SA 1991-92 (Nh), 1996-97 (Nt). HS 32 v Northants (Northampton) 1997. **NWT:** BB 7-75 (11-109 match) v Derbys (Nottingham) 1997. **NWT:** HS 8* and BB 3-38 v Surrey (Oval) 1997. **BHC:** HS 0. BB 1-39. **SL:** HS 27* Nh v Kent (Northampton) 1994. BB 4-29 v Warwks (Nottingham) 1997.

DOWMAN, Mathew Peter (St Hugh's CS; Grantham C), b Grantham, Lincs 10 May 1974. 5'10". LHB, RMF. Debut 1994. Scored 267 for England YC v WI YC (Hove) 1993 – record score in youth 'Tests'. 1000 runs (1): 1091 (1997). HS 149 v Leics (Leicester) 1997. BB 3-10 v Pak A (Nottingham) 1997. BAC BB 2-43 v Leics (Nottingham) 1996. **NWT:** HS 14 v Essex (Nottingham) 1997. **BHC:** HS 92 v Northants (Nottingham) 1997. BB 3-21 v Worcs (Nottingham) 1996. **SL:** HS 74* v Glam (Nottingham) 1996. BB 2-31 v Lancs (Manchester) 1997.

EVANS, Kevin Paul (Colonel Frank Seely S) b Calverton 10 Sep 1963. Elder brother of R.J. (Notts 1987-90). 6'2". RHB, RMF. Debut 1984; cap 1990; benefit 1998. HS 104 v Surrey (Nottingham) 1992 and v Sussex (Nottingham) 1994. BB 6-40 v Lancs (Manchester) 1997. Awards: BHC 2. **NWT:** HS 21 v Worcs (Worcester) 1994. BB 6-10 v Northumb (Jesmond) 1994. **BHC:** HS 47 v Lancs (Manchester) 1995. BB 4-19 v Minor C (Leek) 1995. **SL:** HS 30 v Kent (Canterbury) 1990 and v Hants (Southampton) 1992. BB 4-26 v Kent (Canterbury) 1994 and v Sussex (Hove) 1997.

FRANKS, Paul John (Southwell Minster CS), b Mansfield 3 Feb 1979. 6'2". LHB, RMF. Debut 1996. HS 50 v Derbys (Nottingham) 1997. BB 4-47 v Surrey (Oval) 1997. Hat-trick 1997. **NWT:** HS 4. BB 3-80 v Essex (Nottingham) 1997. **SL:** HS 8. BB 2-46 v Middx (Lord's) 1997.

GIE, Noel Addison (Trent C), b Pretoria, SA 12 Apr 1977. UK resident since 1984. Son of C.A. (WP and SAU 1970-71 to 1980-81). 6'0". RHB, RM. Debut 1995. HS 50 v OU (Oxford) 1997. BAC HS 34 v Glam (Cardiff) 1995. **BHC:** HS 47 v Leics (Leicester) 1997. **SL:** HS 75* v Kent (Nottingham) 1997.

HART, Jamie Paul (Millfield S), b Blackpool, Lancs 31 Dec 1975. Son of P. (Nottingham Forest footballer). 6'3". RHB, RM. Debut 1996. HS 18* v Yorks (Scarborough) 1996 (on debut). **SL:** HS –. BB 1-48.

HINDSON, James Edward (Toot Hill CS, Bingham), b Huddersfield, Yorks 13 Sep 1973. 6'1". RHB, SLA. Debut 1992. HS 53* v OU (Oxford) 1995. BAC HS 47 v Kent (Nottingham) 1995. 50 wkts (1): 65 (1995). BB 5-42 v CU (Nottingham) 1992. BAC BB 5-53 v Glam (Worksop) 1994. **NWT:** HS 16* and BB 2-57 v Northants (Nottingham) 1995. **BHC:** HS 41* and BB 1-69 v Lancs (Manchester) 1995. **SL:** HS 21 v Middx (Nottingham) 1994. BB 4-19 v Worcs (Worcester) 1994.

JOHNSON, Paul (Grove CS, Balderton), b Newark 24 Apr 1965. 5'7". RHB, RM. Debut 1982; cap 1986; benefit 1995; captain 1996 to date. Tours: SA 1996-97 (Nt); WI 1991-92 (Eng A). 1000 runs (8): most – 1518 (1990). HS 187 v Lancs (Manchester) 1993. BB 1-9. BAC BB 1-14. Awards: NWT 2; BHC 3. **NWT:** HS 146 v Northumb (Jesmond) 1994. **BHC:** HS 104* v Essex (Chelmsford) 1990. **SL:** HS 167* v Kent (Nottingham) 1993.

NEWELL, Michael (West Bridgford CS), b Blackburn, Lancs 25 Feb 1965. 5'8". RHB, LB. Debut 1984; cap 1987. 1000 runs (1): 1054 (1987). HS 203* v Derbys (Derby) 1987. BB 2-38 v SL (Nottingham) 1988. BAC BB 1-0. **NWT:** HS 60 v Derbys (Derby) 1987. **BHC:** HS 39 v Somerset (Taunton) 1989. **SL:** HS 109* v Essex (Southend) 1990.

NOON, Wayne Michael (Caistor S), b Grimsby, Lincs 5 Feb 1971. 5'9". RHB, WK. Northamptonshire 1989-93. Nottinghamshire debut 1994; cap 1995. Canterbury 1994-95. Worcs 2nd XI debut when aged 15yr 199d. Tours: SA 1991-92 (Nh), 1996-97 (Nt). HS 83 v Northants (Northampton) 1997. **NWT:** HS 34 v Worcs (Worcester) 1994. **BHC:** HS 24 v Leics (Leicester) 1997. **SL:** HS 38 v Durham (Chester-le-St) 1995.

ORAM, Andrew Richard (Roade CS), b Northampton 7 Mar 1975. 6'2". RHB, RM. Debut 1997. HS 5*. BB 4-53 v Somerset (Nottingham) 1997. **NWT:** HS –. BB 1-51. **SL:** HS 0*. BB 4-45 v Glam (Colwyn Bay) 1997.

POLLARD, Paul Raymond (Gedling CS), b Carlton, Nottingham 24 Sep 1968. 5'11". LHB, RM. Debut 1987; cap 1992. Tour (Nt): SA 1996-97. 1000 runs (3): most – 1463 (1993). HS 180 v Derbys (Nottingham) 1993. BB 2-79 v Glos (Bristol) 1993. **NWT:** HS 96 v Northants (Nottingham) 1995. **BHC:** HS 104 v Surrey (Nottingham) 1994. **SL:** HS 132* v Somerset (Nottingham) 1995.

ROBINSON, Robert Timothy (Dunstable GS; High Pavement SFC; Sheffield U), b Sutton in Ashfield 21 Nov 1958. 6'0". RHB, RM. Debut 1978; cap 1983; captain 1988-95; benefit 1992. *Wisden* 1985. Tests: 29 (1984-85 to 1989); HS 175 v A (Leeds) 1985. **LOI:** 26 (1984-85 to 1988; HS 83). Tours: A 1987-88; SA 1989-90 (Eng XI), 1996-97 (Nt); NZ 1987-88; WI 1985-86; I/SL 1984-85; P 1987-88. 1000 runs (14) inc 2000 (1): 2032 (1984). HS 220* v Yorks (Nottingham) 1990. BB 1-22. Awards: NWT 4; BHC 7. **NWT:** HS 139 v Worcs (Worcester) 1985. **BHC:** HS 120 v Scot (Glasgow) 1985. **SL:** HS 119* v Lancs (Nottingham) 1994.

TOLLEY, Christopher Mark (King Edward VI C, Stourbridge; Loughborough U), b Kidderminster, Worcs 30 Dec 1967. 5'9". RHB, LMF. Worcestershire 1989-95; cap 1993. Nottinghamshire debut 1996; cap 1997. Tours (Wo): SA 1996-97 (Nt); Z 1990-91, 1993-94. HS 84 Wo v Derbys (Derby) 1994. Nt HS 73* v Glam (Colwyn Bay) 1997. BB 6-61 (inc hat-trick) v Leics (Leicester) 1997. Hat-trick 1997. Award: BHC 1. **NWT:** HS 18 and BB 3-21 v Surrey (Oval) 1997. **BHC:** HS 77 Comb Us v Lancs (Cambridge) 1990. BB 1-12. **SL:** HS 43 v Warwks (Nottingham) 1997. BB 5-16 v Hants (Southampton) 1996.

WALKER, Lyndsay Nicholas Paton (Cardiff HS, NSW), b Armidale, NSW, Australia 22 Jun 1974. 6'0". RHB, WK. Debut 1994. HS 42* v OU (Oxford) 1997. BAC HS 36 v Northants (Nottingham) 1996. **NWT:** HS 1. **SL:** HS 22 v Glam (Colwyn Bay) 1997.

WELTON, Guy Edward (Healing CS; Grimsby C), b Grimsby, Lincs 4 May 1978. 6'1". RHB, OB. Debut 1997. MCC YC. HS 95 v Sussex (Hove) 1997. **SL:** HS 68 v Middx (Lord's) 1997. Soccer for Grimsby Town (reserves; sub in one 1st team match).

NEWCOMERS

GALLIAN, Jason Edward Riche (Pittwater House S, Sydney; Keble C, Oxford), b Manly, Sydney, Australia 25 Jun 1971. Qualified for England 1994. 6'0". RHB, RM. Lancashire 1990-97, taking wicket of D.A.Hagan (OU) with his first ball; cap 1994. Oxford U 1992-93; blue 1992-93; captain 1993. Captained Australia YC v England YC 1989-90, scoring 158* in 1st 'Test'. **Tests:** 3 (1995 to 1995-96); HS 28 v SA (Pt Elizabeth) 1995-96. Tours: A 1996-97 (Eng A); I 1995-96 (La); SA 1995-96 (*part*); I 1994-95 (Eng A); P 1995-96 (Eng A). 1000 runs (2); most – 1156 (1996). HS 312 La v Derbys (Manchester) 1996 (record score at Old Trafford). BB 6-115 La v Surrey (Southport) 1996. Awards: NWT 1; BHC 1. **NWT:** HS 101* La v Norfolk (Manchester) 1995. BB 1-11. **BHC:** HS 134 La v Notts (Manchester) 1995. BB 5-15 La v Minor C (Leek) 1995. **SL:** HS 104 La v Leics (Leicester) 1997. BB 2-10 La v Somerset (Manchester) 1994.

READ, Christopher Mark Wells (Torquay GS), b Paignton, Devon 10 Aug 1978. RHB, WK. Gloucestershire (Sunday League) 1997. **SL:** HS 1.

STRANG, Paul Andrew (Falcon C; Cape Town U), b Bulawayo, Rhodesia 28 Jul 1970. Elder brother of B.C. (Mashonaland and Zimbabwe 1994-95 to date). RHB, LBG. Debut (Zimbabwe B) 1992-93. Mashonaland Country Dists 1993-94 to 1995-96. Mashonaland 1996-97. Kent 1997; cap 1997. **Tests** (Z): 13 (1994-95 to 1996-97); HS 106* v P (Sheikhupura) 1996-97; BB 5-106 v SL (Colombo) 1996-97. **LOI** (Z): 38 (1994-95 to 1996-97; HS 47; BB 5-21). Tours (Z): E 1996 (MCC); A 1994-95; SA 1993-94 (Z Board), 1994-95 (Z Board), 1995-96 (Z A); NZ 1995-96; P 1996-97; SL 1996-97. HS 106* (*see Tests*). BAC HS 82 K v Leics (Canterbury) 1997. 50 wkts (1): 63 (1997). BB 7-75 Mashonaland CD v Mashonaland U-24 (Harare South) 1994-95. BAC BB 7-118 K v Lancs (Manchester) 1997. **NWT:** HS 6. **BHC:** HS 38* K v Glos (Bristol) 1997. BB 4-27 K v Sussex (Canterbury) 1997. **SL:** HS 40 and BB 3-31 K v Warwks (Tunbridge Wells) 1997.

WHARF, Alexander George (Buttershaw Upper S), b Bradford, Yorks 4 Jun 1975. 6'5". RHB, RMF. Yorkshire 1994-97. HS 62 Y v Glam (Cardiff) 1996. BB 4-29 Y v Lancs (Manchester) 1996 (not BAC). BAC BB 1-23. **BHC:** HS –. BB 4-29 Y v Notts (Leeds) 1996. **SL:** HS 2*. BB 3-39 Y v Warwks (Scarborough) 1994.

DEPARTURES (who made first-class appearances in 1996-97 or 1997)

AFFORD, John Andrew (Spalding GS; Stamford CFE), b Crowland, Lincs 12 May 1964. 6'1½". RHB, SLA. Nottinghamshire 1984 to 1996-97; cap 1990. Tours: SA 1996-97 (Nt); Z 1989-90 (Eng A). HS 22* v Leics (Nottingham) 1989. 50 wkts (5); most – 57 (1991, 1993). BB 6-51 v Lancs (Nottingham) 1996. Awards: BHC 2. **NWT:** HS 2*. BB 3-32 v Herts (Hitchin) 1989. **BHC:** HS 1*. BB 4-38 v Kent (Nottingham) 1989. **SL:** HS 1. BB 3-33 v Northants (Northampton) 1993.

ASTLE, Nathan John, b Christchurch, NZ 15 Sep 1971. RHB, RM. Canterbury 1991-92 to date. **Tests** (NZ): 11 (1995-96 to 1996-97); HS 125 v WI (Bridgetown) 1995-96; BB 2-26 v E (Christchurch) 1996-97. **LOI** (NZ): 46 (1994-95 to 1996-97; HS 120; BB 4-43). Tours (NZ): W 1995-96; P 1996-97. HS 191 C v Wellington (Christchurch) 1994-95. Nt HS 100 v Warwks (Nottingham) 1997 and v Essex (Worksop) 1997. BB 6-22 C v Otago (Christchurch) 1996-97. Nt BB 5-46 v Glos (Bristol) 1997. Awards: NWT 2. **NWT:** HS 56 v Surrey (Oval) 1997. BB 3-20 v Staffs (Nottingham) 1997. **SL:** HS 75 v Northants (Milton Keynes) 1997. BB 3-22 v Warwks (Nottingham) 1997.

continued on p 107

NOTTINGHAMSHIRE 1997

RESULTS SUMMARY

	Place	Won	Lost	Tied	Drew	No Result
Britannic Assurance Championship	13th	4	3	–	10	–
All First-Class Matches		4	3	–	13	–
NatWest Trophy	Quarter-Finalist
Benson and Hedges Cup	4th in Group B
Sunday League	12th	7	7	–		3

BRITANNIC ASSURANCE CHAMPIONSHIP AVERAGES

BATTING AND FIELDING

Cap		M	I	NO	HS	Runs	Avge	100	50	Ct/St
1986	P.Johnson	15	26	5	96*	936	44.57	–	8	12
–	M.P.Dowman	16	28	1	149	1046	38.74	3	5	11
–	N.J.Astle	9	15	–	100	545	36.33	2	2	10
1992	P.R.Pollard	8	14	4	81	340	34.00	–	1	8
1983	R.T.Robinson	15	25	3	143*	737	33.50	1	4	5
1997	C.M.Tolley	11	20	4	73*	458	28.62	–	3	6
–	G.E.Welton	5	10	–	95	279	27.90	–	1	1
1995	W.M.Noon	17	24	4	83	542	27.10	–	3	34/4
–	U.Afzaal	15	26	2	80	638	26.58	–	5	7
–	P.J.Franks	11	16	5	50	245	22.27	–	1	7
–	A.A.Metcalfe	7	10	1	79	145	16.11	–	1	3
1995	G.F.Archer	10	18	1	49	242	14.23	–	–	15
–	R.T.Bates	6	9	5	21	51	12.75	–	–	6
1990	K.P.Evans	14	17	1	47	187	11.68	–	–	6
1997	M.N.Bowen	14	17	4	32	145	11.15	–	–	6
–	N.A.Gie	2	4	–	9	28	7.00	–	–	1
–	A.R.Oram	7	8	4	5*	14	3.50	–	–	6

Also batted: J.E.Hindson (2 matches) 6, 0, 42* (2 ct); R.A.Pick (cap 1987)(2) 8*; L.N.P.Walker (1) 4.

BOWLING

	O	M	R	W	Avge	Best	5wI	10wM
N.J.Astle	196	43	488	22	22.18	5-46	1	–
A.R.Oram	221.4	54	670	26	25.76	4-53	–	–
K.P.Evans	442.5	102	1226	44	27.86	6-40	2	–
C.M.Tolley	347	81	973	32	30.40	6-61	1	–
M.N.Bowen	451.2	104	1345	41	32.80	7-75	3	1
P.J.Franks	315.4	48	1038	26	39.92	4-47	–	–
U.Afzaal	183.5	39	593	13	45.61	3-79	–	–

Also bowled: G.F.Archer 50-9-173-4; R.T.Bates 167.4-36-442-8; M.P.Dowman 48-9-159-0; J.E.Hindson 44.2-9-162-3; P.Johnson 14-5-34-0; W.M.Noon 1-0-12-0; R.A.Pick 62.2-13-193-2.

The First-Class Averages (pp 118-133) give the records of Nottinghamshire players in all first-class county matches (their other opponents being the Australians, Pakistan A and Oxford University).

NOTTINGHAMSHIRE RECORDS

FIRST-CLASS CRICKET

Highest Total	For	739-7d	v Leics	Nottingham	1903
	V	781-7d	by Northants	Northampton	1995
Lowest Total	For	13	v Yorkshire	Nottingham	1901
	V	16	by Derbyshire	Nottingham	1879
		16	by Surrey	The Oval	1880
Highest Innings	For	312* W.W.Keeton	v Middlesex	The Oval	1939
	V	345 C.G.Macartney	for Australians	Nottingham	1921

Highest Partnership for each Wicket

1st	391	A.O.Jones/A.Shrewsbury	v Glos	Bristol	1899
2nd	398	A.Shrewsbury/W.Gunn	v Sussex	Nottingham	1890
3rd	369	W.Gunn/J.R.Gunn	v Leics	Nottingham	1903
4th	361	A.O.Jones/J.R.Gunn	v Essex	Leyton	1905
5th	266	A.Shrewsbury/W.Gunn	v Sussex	Hove	1884
6th	303*	F.H.Winrow/P.F.Harvey	v Derbyshire	Nottingham	1947
7th	301	C.C.Lewis/B.N.French	v Durham	Chester-le-St	1993
8th	220	G.F.H.Heane/R.Winrow	v Somerset	Nottingham	1935
9th	170	J.C.Adams/K.P.Evans	v Somerset	Taunton	1994
10th	152	E.B.Alletson/W.Riley	v Sussex	Hove	1911

Best Bowling	For	10-66 K.Smales	v Glos	Stroud	1956
(Innings)	V	10-10 H.Verity	for Yorkshire	Leeds	1932
Best Bowling	For	17-89 F.C.Matthews	v Northants	Nottingham	1923
(Match)	V	17-89 W.G.Grace	for Glos	Cheltenham	1877

Most Runs – Season	2620	W.W.Whysall	(av 53.46)	1929
Most Runs – Career	31592	G.Gunn	(av 35.69)	1902-32
Most 100s – Season	9	W.W.Whysall		1928
	9	M.J.Harris		1971
	9	B.C.Broad		1990
Most 100s – Career	65	J.Hardstaff jr		1930-55
Most Wkts – Season	181	B.Dooland	(av 14.96)	1954
Most Wkts – Career	1653	T.G.Wass	(av 20.34)	1896-1920

LIMITED-OVERS CRICKET

Highest Total	NWT	344-6	v Northumb	Jesmond	1994
	BHC	296-6	v Kent	Nottingham	1989
	SL	329-6	v Derbyshire	Nottingham	1993
Lowest Total	NWT	123	v Yorkshire	Scarborough	1969
	BHC	74	v Leics	Leicester	1987
	SL	66	v Yorkshire	Bradford	1969
Highest Innings	NWT	149* D.W.Randall	v Devon	Torquay	1988
	BHC	130* C.E.B.Rice	v Scotland	Glasgow	1982
	SL	167* P.Johnson	v Kent	Nottingham	1993
Best Bowling	NWT	6-10 K.P.Evans	v Northumb	Jesmond	1994
	BHC	6-22 M.K.Bore	v Leics	Leicester	1980
		6-22 C.E.B.Rice	v Northants	Northampton	1981
	SL	6-12 R.J.Hadlee	v Lancashire	Nottingham	1980

SOMERSET

Formation of Present Club: 18 August 1875
Colours: Black, White and Maroon
Badge: Somerset Dragon
Championships: (0) Third 1892, 1958, 1963, 1966, 1981
NatWest Trophy/Gillette Cup Winners: (2) 1979, 1983
Benson and Hedges Cup Winners: (2) 1981, 1982
Sunday League Champions: (1) 1979
Match Awards: NWT 50; BHC 63

Chief Executive: P.W.Anderson
    The County Ground, Taunton TA1 1JT (Tel 01823 272946)
Captain: P.D.Bowler. **Vice-Captain:** S.C.Ecclestone. **Overseas Player:** Mushtaq Ahmed.
1998 Beneficiary: Somerset CCC. **Scorer:** D.A.Oldam

BOULTON, Nicholas Ross (King's C, Taunton), b Johannesburg, SA 22 Mar 1979. 6'1½". LHB, RM. Debut 1997 – awaiting BAC debut. HS 14 v Pak A (Taunton) 1997.

BOWLER, Peter Duncan (Educated at Canberra, Australia), b Plymouth, Devon 30 Jul 1963. 6'1". RHB, OB, occ WK. Leicestershire 1986 – first to score hundred on f-c debut for Leics (100* and 62 v Hants). Tasmania 1986-87. Derbyshire 1988-94; cap 1989; scored 155* v CU (Cambridge) on debut – first instance of hundreds on debut for two counties. Somerset debut/cap 1995; captain 1997 to date. 1000 runs (8) inc 2000 (1): 2047 (1992). HS 241* De v Hants (Portsmouth) 1992. Sm HS 207 v Surrey (Taunton) 1996. BB 3-41 De v Leics (Leicester) 1991 and De v Yorks (Chesterfield) 1991. Sm BB 2-48 v Yorks (Taunton) 1997. Awards: BHC 4. **NWT:** HS 111 De v Berks (Derby) 1992. **BHC:** HS 109 De v Somerset (Taunton) 1990. BB 1-15. **SL:** HS 138* De v Somerset (Derby) 1993. BB 3-31 De v Glos (Cheltenham) 1991.

BURNS, Michael (Walney CS), b Barrow-in-Furness, Lancs 6 Jun 1969. 6'0". RHB, RM, WK. Warwickshire 1992-96. Somerset debut 1997. Cumberland 1988-90. HS 82 v Northants (Northampton) 1997. BB 2-18 v Kent (Taunton) 1997. **NWT:** HS 37* v Cornwall (St Austell) 1996. **BHC:** HS 91 v Essex (Chelmsford) 1997. BB 3-18 v Glam (Taunton) 1997. **SL:** HS 115* v Middx (Taunton) 1997. BB 4-39 v Glos (Taunton) 1997.

CADDICK, Andrew Richard (Papanui HS), b Christchurch, NZ 21 Nov 1968. Son of English emigrants – qualified for England 1992. 6'5". RHB, RFM. Debut 1991; cap 1992. Represented NZ in 1987-88 Youth World Cup. **Tests:** 16 (1993 to 1997); HS 29* v WI (Kingston) 1993-94; BB 6-65 v WI (P-o-S) 1993-94. **LOI:** 9 (1993 to 1996-97; HS 20*; BB 3-35). Tours: A 1992-93 (Eng A); WI 1993-94; NZ 1996-97; Z 1996-97. HS 92 v Worcs (Worcester) 1995. 50 wkts (5); most – 81 (1997). BB 9-32 (12-120 match) v Lancs (Taunton) 1993. Award: NWT 1. **NWT:** HS 8. BB 6-30 v Glos (Taunton) 1992. **BHC:** HS 38 v Leics (Leicester) 1997. BB 5-41 v Brit Us (Taunton) 1996. **SL:** HS 39 v Hants (Taunton) 1996. BB 4-18 v Lancs (Manchester) 1992.

ECCLESTONE, Simon Charles (Bryanston S; Durham U; Keble C, Oxford), b Great Dunmow, Essex 16 Jul 1971. 6'3". LHB, RM. Oxford U 1994; blue 1994. Somerset debut 1994; cap 1997. Cambridgeshire 1990-94. HS 133 v OU (Oxford) 1997. BAC HS 123 v Kent (Taunton) 1997. BB 4-66 OU v Surrey (Oval) 1994. BAC BB 2-48 v Notts (Nottingham) 1995. Awards: NWT 2; BHC 1. **NWT:** HS 101 v Herefords (Taunton) 1997. **BHC:** HS 112* v Middx (Lord's) 1996. BB 2-41 v Kent (Canterbury) 1995. **SL:** HS 130 v Surrey (Taunton) 1996. BB 4-31 v Essex (Weston-s-M) 1994.

HARDEN, Richard John (King's C, Taunton), b Bridgwater 16 Aug 1965. 5'11". RHB, SLA. Debut 1985; cap 1989; benefit 1996. C Districts 1987-88. 1000 runs (7); most – 1460 (1990). HS 187 v Notts (Taunton) 1992. BB 2-7 CD v Canterbury (Blenheim) 1987-88. Sm BB 2-24 v Hants (Taunton) 1986. Award: NWT 1. **NWT:** HS 108* v Scot (Taunton) 1992. **BHC:** HS 76 v Kent (Canterbury) 1992. **SL:** HS 100* v Durham (Chester-le-St) 1995.

HOLLOWAY, Piran Christopher Laity (Millfield S; Taunton S; Loughborough U), b Helston, Cornwall 1 Oct 1970. 5'8". LHB, WK. Warwickshire 1988-93. Somerset debut 1994; cap 1997. HS 168 v Middx (Uxbridge) 1996. **NWT:** HS 90 v Herefords (Taunton) 1997. **BHC:** HS 27 Comb Us v Derbys (Oxford) 1991. **SL:** HS 117 v Glos (Taunton) 1997.

JONES, Philip Steffan (Stradey CS, Llanelli; Neath TC; Loughborough U; Homerton C, Cambridge), b Llanelli, Wales 9 Feb 1974. 6'2". RHB, RMF. Debut (Cambridge U) 1997; blue 1997. Somerset debut 1997. Wales MC 1992-96. HS 36 CU v Essex (Cambridge) 1997. BB 6-67 CU v OU (Lord's) 1997. Sm HS 13 and Sm BB 3-30 v Glos (Taunton) 1997. **BHC:** (Brit Us) HS 12 v Surrey (Oval) 1997. BB 2-51 v Hants (Oxford) 1997. **SL:** HS –. Rugby Union for Swansea and Wales U-18, U-19, U-20 and U-21.

KERR, Jason Ian Douglas (Withins HS; Bolton C), b Bolton, Lancs 7 Apr 1974. 6'2". RHB, RMF. Debut 1993. HS 80 and BB 5-82 v WI (Taunton) 1995. BAC HS 68* v Derbys (Taunton) 1996. BAC BB 4-68 v Sussex (Bath) 1995. **NWT:** HS 3. BB 3-32 v Herefords (Taunton) 1997. **BHC:** HS 17 v Essex (Chelmsford) 1997. BB 3-34 v Middx (Lord's) 1997. **SL:** HS 33 v Warwks (Birmingham) 1997. BB 4-28 v Hants (Basingstoke) 1997.

LATHWELL, Mark Nicholas (Braunton S, Devon), b Bletchley, Bucks 26 Dec 1971. 5'8". RHB, RM. Debut 1991; cap 1992. YC 1993. MCC YC. **Tests:** 2 (1993); HS 33 v A (Nottingham) 1993. Tours (Eng A): A 1992-93; SA 1993-94. 1000 runs (5); most – 1230 (1994). HS 206 v Surrey (Bath) 1994. BB 2-21 v Sussex (Hove) 1994. Awards: NWT 1; BHC 2. **NWT:** HS 103 and BB 1-23 v Salop (Telford) 1993. **BHC:** HS 121 v Middx (Lord's) 1996. **SL:** HS 117 v Notts (Taunton) 1992.

MUSHTAQ AHMED, b Sahiwal, Pakistan 28 Jun 1970. 5'5". RHB, LBG. Multan 1986-87 to 1990-91. United Bank 1986-87 to date. Somerset debut 1993; cap 1993. *Wisden* 1996. **Tests** (P): 28 (1989-90 to 1996-97); HS 42 v NZ (Rawalpindi) 1996-97; BB 7-56 (10-171 match) v NZ (Christchurch) 1995-96. **LOI** (P): 124 (1988-89 to 1996-97); HS 26; BB 5-36). Tours (P): E 1992, 1996; A 1989-90, 1991-92, 1992-93, 1995-96, 1996-97; WI 1992-93; NZ 1992-93, 1993-94, 1995-96; SL 1994-95, 1996-97. HS 90 and Sm BB 7-91 (12-175 match) v Sussex (Taunton) 1993. 50 wkts (4+1); most – 95 (1995). BB 9-93 Multan v Peshawar (Sahiwal) 1990-91. Awards: NWT 1; BHC 2. **NWT:** HS 35 v Surrey (Taunton) 1993. BB 4-27 v Herefords (Taunton) 1997. **BHC:** HS 31 v Essex (Chelmsford) 1997. BB 7-24 v Ire (Taunton) 1997. **SL:** HS 32 v Middx (Bath) 1993. BB 3-17 v Glos (Taunton) 1993.

PARSONS, Keith Alan (The Castle S, Taunton; Richard Huish SFC), b Taunton 2 May 1973. Identical twin brother of K.J. (Somerset staff 1992-94). 6'1". RHB, RM. Debut 1992. HS 105 v Young A (Taunton) 1996. BAC HS 83* v Middx (Uxbridge) 1996. BB 2-4 v OU (Taunton) 1997. BAC BB 2-11 v Derbys (Derby) 1996. **NWT:** HS 51 v Suffolk (Taunton) 1996. BB 3-34 v Warwks (Birmingham) 1997. **BHC:** HS 33* v Brit Us (Taunton) 1996. BB 2-60 v Kent (Maidstone) 1996. **SL:** HS 56 v Sussex (Hove) 1996. BB 3-36 v Leics (Taunton) 1996.

REEVE, Dermot Alexander (King George V S, Kowloon), b Kowloon, Hong Kong 2 Apr 1963. 6'0". RHB, RMF. Sussex 1983-87; cap 1986. Warwickshire 1988-96; cap 1989; captain 1993-96; benefit 1996. *Wisden* 1995. OBE 1996. Hong Kong 1982 (ICC Trophy). MCC YC. Somerset 1st XI coach 1997 to date. Available for limited-overs matches 1998. **Tests:** 3 (1991-92); HS 59 v NZ (Christchurch) 1991-92 (on debut); BB 1-4. **LOI:** 29 (1991 to 1995-96; HS 35; BB 3-20). Tours (C=captain): SA 1992-93C (Wa), 1994-95C (Wa); NZ 1991-92; I 1992-93; Z 1993-94C (Wa). 1000 runs (2); most – 1412 (1990). HS 202* Wa v Northants (Northampton) 1990. 50 wkts (2); most – 55 (1984). BB 7-37 Sx v Lancs (Lytham) 1987. Awards: NWT 5; BHC 2. **NWT:** HS 81* Wa v Sussex (Lord's) 1993. BB 4-20 Sx v Lancs (Lord's) 1986. **BHC:** HS 80 Wa v Essex (Birmingham) 1991. BB 4-23 Wa v Minor C (Jesmond) 1996. **SL:** HS Wa 100 v Lancs (Birmingham) 1991. BB 5-23 Wa v Essex (Birmingham) 1988.

ROSE, Graham David (Northumberland Park S, Tottenham), b Tottenham, London 12 Apr 1964. 6'4". RHB, RM. Middlesex 1985-86. Somerset debut 1987; cap 1988; benefit 1997. 1000 runs (1): 1000 (1990). HS 191 v Sussex (Taunton) 1997. 50 wkts (4); most – 63 (1997). BB 7-47 (13-88 match) v Notts (Taunton) 1996. Awards: BHC 3. **NWT:** HS 110 v Devon (Torquay) 1990. BB 3-11 v Salop (Telford) 1993. **BHC:** HS 79 v Surrey (Taunton) 1995. BB 4-21 v Ire (Erlington) 1995. **SL:** HS 148 v Glam (Neath) 1990. BB 4-26 v Kent (Taunton) 1993.

SHINE, Kevin James (Maiden Erlegh CS), b Bracknell, Berks 22 Feb 1969. 6'2½". RHB, RFM. Hampshire 1989-93. Middlesex 1994-95. Somerset debut 1996; cap 1997. Berkshire 1986. HS 40 v Surrey (Taunton) 1996 (on Sm debut). 50 wkts (1): 55 (1997). BB 8-47 (8 wkts in 38 balls inc hat-trick and 4 in 5; 13-105 match) H v Lancs (Manchester) 1992. Sm BB 7-43 (11-97 match) v Lancs (Taunton) 1997. Hat-trick 1992. **NWT:** HS –. BB 3-31 M v Wales MC (Northop Hall) 1994. **BHC:** HS 38* v Kent (Maidstone) 1996. BB 4-68 H v Surrey (Oval) 1990. **SL:** HS 3. BB 4-31 v Northants (Taunton) 1996.

SUTTON, Luke David (Millfield S; Durham U), b Keynsham 4 Oct 1976. 5'11". RHB, WK. Debut 1997 – awaiting BAC debut. HS 11* v OU (Taunton) 1997.

TRESCOTHICK, Marcus Edward (Sir Bernard Lovell S), b Keynsham 25 Dec 1975. 6'2". LHB, RM. Debut 1993. HS 178 v Hants (Taunton) 1996. BB 4-36 (inc hat-trick) v Young A (Taunton) 1995. BAC BB 1-18. Hat-trick 1995. Award: NWT 1. **NWT:** HS 116 v Oxon (Aston Rowant) 1994. **BHC:** HS 122 v Ire (Erlington) 1995. **SL:** HS 74 v Yorks (Leeds) 1994. BB 1-13.

TROTT, Benjamin James (Court Fields Community S; Richard Huish C, Taunton; Plymouth U), b Wellington 14 Mar 1975. 6'5". RHB, RFM. Debut 1997. HS 1* and BB 3-74 v Glam (Taunton) 1997. **SL:** HS –. BB 1-29.

TURNER, Robert Julian (Millfield S; Magdalene C, Cambridge), b Malvern, Worcs 25 Nov 1967. 6'1½". RHB, WK. Brother of S.J. (Somerset 1984-85). Cambridge U 1988-91; blue 1988-89-90-91; captain 1991. Somerset debut 1991; cap 1994. 1000 runs (1): 1069 (1997). HS 144 v Kent (Taunton) 1997. Award: BHC 1. **NWT:** HS 40 v Suffolk (Taunton) 1996. **BHC:** HS 70 v Glam (Cardiff) 1996. **SL:** HS 39 v Northants (Taunton) 1996.

Van TROOST, Adrianus Pelrus ('Andre') (Spieringshoek C, Schiedam), b Schiedam, Holland Oct 1972. 6'7". RHB, RF. Debut 1991; cap 1997. Qualified for England 1998. Holland 1990 (inc ICC Trophy final v Zimbabwe). HS 35 v Lancs (Taunton) 1993. BB 6-48 v Essex (Taunton) 1992. **NWT:** HS 17* v Surrey (Taunton) 1993. BB 5-22 v Oxon (Aston Rowant) 1994. **BHC:** HS 42 v Ire (Taunton) 1997. BB 2-38 v Notts (Nottingham) 1993. **SL:** HS 67 v Worcs (Worcester) 1994. BB 4-23 v Notts (Taunton) 1994.

NEWCOMERS

BULBECK, Matthew Paul L., b Taunton 8 Nov 1979. LHB, LMF.

PIERSON, Adrian Roger Kirshaw (Kent C, Canterbury; Hatfield Poly), b Enfield, Middx 21 Jul 1963. 6'4". RHB, OB. Warwickshire 1985-91. Leicestershire 1993-97; cap 1995. Cambridgeshire 1992. MCC YC. Tour (Le): SA 1996-97. HS 59 Le v Durham (Leicester) 1997. 50 wkts (1): 69 (1995). BB 8-42 Le v Warwks (Birmingham) 1994. Awards: NWT 1; BHC 1. **NWT:** HS 20* Le v Hants (Leicester) 1995. BB 3-20 Wa v Wilts (Birmingham) 1989. **BHC:** HS 11 Wa v Minor C (Walsall) 1986. BB 3-34 Wa v Lancs (Birmingham) 1988. **SL:** HS 29* Le v Kent (Leicester) 1994. BB 5-36 Le v Derbys (Leicester) 1995.

TUCKER, Joseph Peter (Colson Collegiate S), b Bath 14 Sep 1979. RHB, RMF.

DEPARTURES (who made first-class appearances in 1997)

DIMOND, Matthew (Castle S; Richard Huish C), b Taunton 24 Sep 1975. 6'1". RHB, RMF. Somerset 1994-97. HS 26 v Derbys (Derby) 1995. BB 4-73 v Yorks (Bradford) 1994. **BHC:** HS –. **SL:** HS –.

continued on p 107

SOMERSET 1997

RESULTS SUMMARY

	Place	Won	Lost	Tied	Drew	No Result
Britannic Assurance Championship	12th	3	3	–	11	–
All First-Class Matches		4	4	–	12	–
NatWest Trophy	2nd Round					
Benson and Hedges Cup	Quarter-Finalist					
Sunday League	6th	9	6	–	–	2

BRITANNIC ASSURANCE CHAMPIONSHIP AVERAGES

BATTING AND FIELDING

Cap		M	I	NO	HS	Runs	Avge	100	50	Ct/St
1988	G.D.Rose	17	25	9	191	848	53.00	2	3	6
1994	R.J.Turner	16	26	6	144	946	47.30	1	5	47/2
1989	R.J.Harden	7	11	2	136*	395	43.88	2	1	3
–	S.Herzberg	5	6	2	56	167	41.75	–	1	2
1997	S.C.Ecclestone	10	18	2	123	608	38.00	1	4	11
–	K.A.Parsons	7	11	3	74	281	35.12	–	2	9
1997	P.C.L.Holloway	16	29	4	106	855	34.20	1	5	9
1992	M.N.Lathwell	17	29	1	95	802	28.64	–	5	8
–	M.Burns	13	20	1	82	454	23.89	–	3	7/1
–	M.E.Trescothick	11	17	1	83*	379	23.68	–	4	5
1992	A.R.Caddick	12	13	2	56*	246	22.36	–	1	4
1995	P.D.Bowler	14	23	1	73	487	22.13	–	5	17
1993	Mushtaq Ahmed	14	16	2	33	174	12.42	–	–	3
1997	K.J.Shine	17	18	4	18	92	6.57	–	–	5
1997	A.P.van Troost	5	7	2	5	8	1.60	–	–	1

Also batted: M.Dimond (1 match) 4; P.S.Jones (1) 13 (1 ct); J.I.D.Kerr (3) 0, 26, 26 (1 ct); B.J.Trott (1) 1*, 0.

BOWLING

	O	M	R	W	Avge	Best	5wI	10wM
G.D.Rose	474.5	121	1513	62	24.40	5-53	1	–
Mushtaq Ahmed	513	146	1407	50	28.14	6-70	3	–
A.R.Caddick	506.5	110	1468	52	28.23	6-65	3	–
K.J.Shine	399.3	81	1547	47	32.91	7-43	2	1

Also bowled: P.D.Bowler 41.3-18-129-3; M.Burns 56-12-236-4; M.Dimond 11-3-30-0; S.C.Ecclestone 1-1-0-0; S.Herzberg 47-11-136-6; P.S.Jones 9-0-49-3; J.I.D.Kerr 59-12-217-7; M.N.Lathwell 5-0-60-1; K.A.Parsons 55-14-139-3; M.E.Trescothick 13-3-56-1; B.J.Trott 11-0-74-3; A.P.van Troost 63.2-5-364-5.

The First-Class Averages (pp 118-133) give the records of Somerset players in all first-class county matches (their other opponents being the Australians, Pakistan A and Oxford University), with the exception of:
A.R.Caddick 13-14-2-56*-262-21.83-0-1-4ct. 522.5-112-1522-57-26.70-6/65-4-0.
P.S.Jones 3-5-1-13-26-6.50-0-0-3ct. 31-3-165-6-27.50-3/30.

SOMERSET RECORDS

FIRST-CLASS CRICKET

Highest Total	For	675-9d		v Hampshire	Bath	1924
	V	811		by Surrey	The Oval	1899
Lowest Total	For	25		v Glos	Bristol	1947
	V	22		by Glos	Bristol	1920
Highest Innings	For	322	I.V.A.Richards	v Warwicks	Taunton	1985
	V	424	A.C.MacLaren	for Lancashire	Taunton	1895

Highest Partnership for each Wicket

1st	346	H.T.Hewett/L.C.H.Palairet	v Yorkshire	Taunton	1892
2nd	290	J.C.W.MacBryan/M.D.Lyon	v Derbyshire	Buxton	1924
3rd	319	P.M.Roebuck/M.D.Crowe	v Leics	Taunton	1984
4th	310	P.W.Denning/I.T.Botham	v Glos	Taunton	1980
5th	235	J.C.White/C.C.C.Case	v Glos	Taunton	1927
6th	265	W.E.Alley/K.E.Palmer	v Northants	Northampton	1961
7th	279	R.J.Harden/G.D.Rose	v Sussex	Taunton	1997
8th	172	I.V.A.Richards/I.T.Botham	v Leics	Leicester	1983
9th	183	C.H.M.Greetham/H.W.Stephenson	v Leics	Weston-s-Mare	1963
	183	C.J.Tavaré/N.A.Mallender	v Sussex	Hove	1990
10th	143	J.J.Bridges/A.H.D.Gibbs	v Essex	Weston-s-Mare	1919

Best Bowling	For	10- 49	E.J.Tyler	v Surrey	Taunton	1895
(Innings)	V	10- 35	A.Drake	for Yorkshire	Weston-s-Mare	1914
Best Bowling	For	16- 83	J.C.White	v Worcs	Bath	1919
(Match)	V	17-137	W.Brearley	for Lancashire	Manchester	1905

Most Runs – Season	2761	W.E.Alley	(av 58.74)	1961
Most Runs – Career	21142	H.Gimblett	(av 36.96)	1935-54
Most 100s – Season	11	S.J.Cook		1991
Most 100s – Career	49	H.Gimblett		1935-54
Most Wkts – Season	169	A.W.Wellard	(av 19.24)	1938
Most Wkts – Career	2166	J.C.White	(av 18.02)	1909-37

LIMITED-OVERS CRICKET

Highest Total	NWT	413-4		v Devon	Torquay	1990
	BHC	349-7		v Ireland	Taunton	1997
	SL	360-3		v Glamorgan	Neath	1990
Lowest Total	NWT	59		v Middlesex	Lord's	1977
	BHC	98		v Middlesex	Lord's	1982
	SL	58		v Essex	Chelmsford	1977
Highest Innings	NWT	162*	C.J.Tavaré	v Devon	Torquay	1990
	BHC	177	S.J.Cook	v Sussex	Hove	1990
	SL	175*	I.T.Botham	v Northants	Wellingborough	1986
Best Bowling	NWT	7-15	R.P.Lefebvre	v Devon	Torquay	1990
	BHC	7-24	Mushtaq Ahmed	v Ireland	Taunton	1997
	SL	6-24	I.V.A.Richards	v Lancashire	Manchester	1983

SURREY

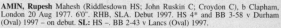

Formation of Present Club: 22 August 1845
Colours: Chocolate
Badge: Prince of Wales' Feathers
Championships (since 1890): (15) 1890, 1891, 1892, 1894, 1895, 1899, 1914, 1952, 1953, 1954, 1955, 1956, 1957, 1958, 1971. Joint: (1) 1950
NatWest Trophy/Gillette Cup Winners: (1) 1982
Benson and Hedges Cup Winners: (2) 1974, 1997
Sunday League Champions: (1) 1996
Match Awards: NWT 45; BHC 63

Chief Executive: P.C.J.Sheldon
Kennington Oval, London, SE11 5SS (Tel 0171 582 6660)
Captain: A.J.Hollioake. **Vice-Captain:** no appointment. **Overseas Player:** Saqlain Mushtaq.
1998 Beneficiary: None. **Scorer:** K.R.Booth.

AMIN, Rupesh Mahesh (Riddlesdown HS; John Ruskin C; Croydon C), b Clapham, London 20 Aug 1977. 6'0". RHB, SLA. Debut 1997. HS 4* and BB 3-58 v Durham (Oval) 1997 – on debut. **SL:** HS –. BB 2-43 v Lancs (Oval) 1997.

BATTY, Jonathan Neil (Wheatley Park S, Oxon; Repton S; Durham U; Keble C, Oxford), b Chesterfield, Derbys 18 Apr 1974. 5'10". RHB, WK. Minor C 1994. Comb Us 1995. Oxford U 1996; blue 1996. Surrey debut 1997. Oxfordshire 1993 to date. HS 56 OU v Northants (Oxford) 1996. Sy HS 23* v Middx (Lord's) 1997. **NWT:** (Oxon) HS 1. **BHC:** (Minor C) HS 26* v Warwks (Jesmond) 1996. **SL:** HS 8.

BENJAMIN, Joseph Emmanuel (Cayon HS, St Kitts; Mount Pleasant S, Highgate, Birmingham), b Christ Church, St Kitts 2 Feb 1961. 6'2". RHB, RMF. Warwickshire 1988-91. Surrey debut 1992; cap 1993. Staffordshire 1986-88. **Tests:** 1 (1994); HS 0 and BB 4-42 v SA (Oval) 1994. **LOI:** 2 (1994-95; HS 0; BB 1-22). Tour: A 1994-95. HS 49 v Essex (Oval) 1995. 50 wkts (3); most – 80 (1994). BB 6-19 v Notts (Oval) 1993. Awards: NWT 2; BHC 1. **NWT:** HS 25 v Worcs (Oval) 1994. BB 4-20 v Berks (Oval) 1995. **BHC:** HS 20 Wa v Worcs (Birmingham) 1990. BB 4-27 v Somerset (Taunton) 1995. **SL:** HS 24 Wa v Lancs (Manchester) 1990. BB 4-44 v Middx (Oval) 1992.

BICKNELL, Darren John (Robert Haining SS; Guildford TC), b Guildford 24 Jun 1967. Elder brother of M.P. 6'4". LHB, SLA. Debut 1987; cap 1990. Tours (Eng A): WI 1991-92; P 1990-91; SL 1990-91; Z 1989-90. 1000 runs (6); most – 1888 (1991). HS 235* v Notts (Nottingham) 1994. BB 3-7 v Sussex (Guildford) 1996. Awards: NWT 1; BHC 3. **NWT:** HS 135* v Yorks (Oval) 1989. **BHC:** HS 119 v Hants (Oval) 1990. **SL:** HS 125 v Durham (Durham) 1992. BB 1-11.

BICKNELL, Martin Paul (Robert Haining SS), b Guildford 14 Jan 1969. Younger brother of D.J. 6'3". RHB, RFM. Debut 1986; cap 1989; benefit 1997. **Tests:** 2 (1993); HS 14 and BB 3-99 v A (Birmingham) 1993. **LOI:** 7 (1990-91; HS 31*; BB 3-55). Tours: A 1990-91; SA 1993-94 (Eng A); Z 1989-90 (Eng A). HS 88 v Hants (Southampton) 1992. 50 wkts (6); most – 71 (1992). BB 9-45 v CU (Oval) 1988. BAC BB 7-52 v Sussex (Oval) 1991. Awards: BHC 3. **NWT:** HS 66* v Northants (Oval) 1991. BB 4-35 v Somerset (Taunton) 1993. **BHC:** HS 43 v Kent (Canterbury) 1995. BB 4-41 v Leics (Oval) 1997. **SL:** HS 57* v Worcs (Worcester) 1997. BB 5-12 v Northants (Oval) 1994.

BROWN, Alistair Duncan (Caterham S), b Beckenham, Kent 11 Feb 1970. 5'10". RHB, occ LB. Debut 1992; cap 1994. **LOI:** 3 (1996; HS 118). 1000 runs (3); most – 1382 (1993). HS 187 v Glos (Oval) 1995. Award: BHC 1. **NWT:** HS 72 v Holland (Oval) 1996. **BHC:** HS 117* v Sussex (Hove) 1996. **SL:** HS 203 v Hants (Guildford) 1997.

BUTCHER, Mark Alan (Trinity S; Archbishop Tenison's S, Croydon), b Croydon 23 Aug 1972. Son of A.R. (Surrey, Glam and England 1972-92); brother of G.P. (*see GLAMORGAN*). 5'11". LHB, RM. Debut 1992; cap 1996. **Tests**: 5 (1997); HS 87 v A (Lord's) 1997. Tour: A 1996-97 (Eng A). 1000 runs (3); most – 1604 (1996). HS 167 v Durham (Oval) 1995. BB 4-31 v Worcs (Oval) 1994. Award: NWT 1. **NWT:** HS 91 v Somerset (Oval) 1996. BB 2-57 v Somerset (Taunton) 1993. **BHC:** HS 48 v Sussex (Oval) 1997. BB 3-37 v Somerset (Oval) 1994. **SL:** HS 81 v Durham (Oval) 1997. BB 3-23 v Sussex (Oval) 1992.

HOLLIOAKE, Adam John (St George's C, Weybridge), b Melbourne, Australia 5 Sep 1971. Brother of B.C. 5'11". RHB, RMF. Debut 1993, scoring 13 and 123 v Derbys (Ilkeston); cap 1995; captain 1998. Qualified for England 1992. **Tests**: 2 (1997); HS 45 and BB 2-31 v A (Nottingham) 1997 – on debut. **LOI:** 5 (1996 to 1997; HS 66*; BB 4-23). Tour: A 1996-97 (Eng A – captain). 1000 runs (2); most – 1522 (1996). HS 182 v Middx (Lord's) 1997. BB 4-22 v Yorks (Oval) 1995. Award: BHC 1. **NWT:** HS 60 v Worcs (Oval) 1994. BB 4-53 v Middx (Oval) 1995. **BHC:** HS 63 v Leics (Oval) 1997. BB 4-34 v Hants (Oval) 1996. **SL:** HS 93 v Kent (Canterbury) 1997. BB 5-38 v Kent (Canterbury) 1997.

HOLLIOAKE, Benjamin Caine (Millfield S), b Melbourne, Australia 11 Nov 1977. Brother of A.J. 6'2". RHB, RMF. Debut 1996. YC 1997. **Tests**: 1 (1997); HS 28 and BB 1-26 v A (Nottingham) 1997. **LOI:** 1 (1997; HS 63). HS 76 v Middx (Lord's) 1997. BB 4-54 v Kent (Canterbury) 1997. Award: BHC 1. **NWT:** HS 0. BB 1-39. **BHC:** HS 98 v Kent (Lord's) 1997. BB 2-51 v Brit Us (Oval) 1997. **SL:** HS 61 v Lancs (Oval) 1997. BB 5-10 v Derbys (Oval) 1996. Rugby for Somerset. Hockey for West of England.

KNOTT, James Alan (City of Westminster C), b Canterbury, Kent 14 Jun 1975. Son of A.P.E. (Kent, Tasmania and England 1964-85). 5'6". RHB, WK. Debut 1995. MCC YC. HS 49* v SA A (Oval) 1996. BAC HS 27* v Essex (Oval) 1997. **BHC:** HS –. **SL:** HS 22 v Kent (Canterbury) 1997.

PATTERSON, Mark William (Belfast Royal Academy; Ulster U), b Belfast, N Ireland 2 Feb 1974. Elder brother of A.D. (Ireland 1996). 6'1". RHB, RFM. Debut 1996, taking 6-80 v SA A (Oval). Awaiting BAC debut. Soccer (goalkeeper) for N Ireland, Irish Us and Coleraine. HS 4 and BB 6-80 (*see above*).

RATCLIFFE, Jason David (Sharman's Cross SS; Solihull SFC), b Solihull, Warwks 19 Jun 1969. Son of D.P. (Warwks 1957-68). 6'4". RHB, RM. Warwickshire 1988-94. Surrey debut 1995. Tours (Wa): SA 1991-92, 1992-93; Z 1993-94. HS 135 v Worcs (Worcester) 1997. BB 2-26 v Yorks (Middlesbrough) 1996. Awards: NWT 2. **NWT:** HS 105 Wa v Yorks (Leeds) 1993. **BHC:** HS 29 Wa v Surrey (Oval) 1991. BB 2-42 v Sussex (Oval) 1997. **SL:** HS 82 v Northants (Northampton) 1997. BB 2-11 Wa v Glam (Neath) 1993.

SALISBURY, Ian David Kenneth (Moulton CS), b Northampton 21 Jan 1970. 5'11". RHB, LBG. Sussex 1989-96; cap 1991. Surrey debut 1997. MCC YC. YC 1992. *Wisden* 1992. **Tests**: 9 (1992 to 1996); HS 50 v P (Manchester) 1992; BB 4-163 v WI (Georgetown) 1993-94. **LOI:** 4 (1992-93 to 1993-94); HS 5; BB 3-41). Tours: WI 1991-92 (Eng A), 1993-94; Z 1992-93; 1994-95 (Eng A); P 1990-91 (Eng A), 1995-96 (Eng A); SL 1990-91 (Eng A). HS 86 Eng A v Pak A (Rawalpindi) 1995-96. BAC HS 83 Sx v Glam (Hove) 1996. Sy HS 30* v Somerset (Oval) 1997 – on Surrey debut. 50 wkts (4); most – 87 (1992). BB 8-75 (11-169 match) Sx v Essex (Chelmsford) 1996. Sy BB 6-19 v Notts (Oval) 1992. Awards: NWT 1, BHC 2. **NWT:** HS 33 Sx v Ire (Belfast) 1996. BB 3-28 Sx v Bucks (Beaconsfield) 1992. **BHC:** HS 19 Sx v Hants (Southampton) 1996. BB 4-53 v Sussex (Oval) 1997. **SL:** HS 48* Sx v Glam (Swansea) 1995. BB 5-30 Sx v Leics (Leicester) 1992.

SAQLAIN MUSHTAQ (Govt Muslim League HS, M.A.O. College, Lahore), b Lahore, Pakistan 29 Dec 1976. Brother of Sibtain Mushtaq (Lahore 1988-89). 5'11". RHB, OB. Islamabad 1994-95. PIA 1994-95 to date. Surrey debut 1997. **Tests** (P): 9 (1995-96 to 1996-97); HS 79 v Z (Sheikhupura) 1996-97; BB 5-89 v SL (Colombo) 1996-97. **LOI** (P): 65 (1995-96 to 1997-98; HS 30*; BB 5-29). Tours: P: E 1996; A 1995-96, 1996-97; SL 1996-97. HS 79 (*see Tests*). 50 wkts (0+1): 52 (1994-95 – on debut). BB 7-66 PIA v Pakistan Railways (Lahore) 1994-95. Sy HS 41* and Sy BB 5-17 v Durham (Oval) 1997.

SAQLAIN MUSHTAQ continued:
Hat-trick 1997. **NWT:** HS 6* and BB 3-30 v Notts (Oval) 1997. **BHC:** HS –. BB 2-33 v Kent (Lord's) 1997. **SL:** HS 29* v Warwks (Birmingham) 1997. BB 3-31 v Northants (Northampton) 1997.

SHAHID, Nadeem (Ipswich S), b Karachi, Pakistan 23 Apr 1969. 6'0". RHB, LB. Essex 1989-94. Surrey debut 1995. Suffolk 1988. 1000 runs (1): 1003 (1990). HS 139 v Yorks (Oval) 1995. BB 3-91 Ex v Surrey (Oval) 1990. Sy BB 3-93 v SA A (Oval) 1996. **NWT:** HS 85* Ex v Glam (Cardiff) 1994. BB 1-0. **BHC:** HS 65* and BB 1-59 v Kent (Canterbury) 1995. **SL:** HS 101 v Derbys (Derby) 1995.

STEWART, Alec James (Tiffin S), b Merton 8 Apr 1963. Son of M.J. (Surrey and England 1954-72). 5'11". RHB, WK. Debut 1981; cap 1985; benefit 1992-97; benefit 1994. *Wisden* 1992. **Tests:** 69 (1989-90 to 1997, 2 as captain); HS 190 v P (Birmingham) 1992. **LOI:** 90 (1989-90 to 1997, 7 as captain; HS 103). Tours: A 1990-91, 1994-95; SA 1995-96; WI 1989-90, 1993-94; NZ 1991-92, 1996-97; I 1992-93; SL 1992-93 (captain); Z 1996-97. 1000 runs (8); most – 1665 (1986). HS 206* v Essex (Oval) 1989. BB 1-7. Held 11 catches (equalling world f-c match record) v Leics (Leicester) 1989. Awards: NWT 4; BHC 5. **NWT:** HS 125* v Essex (Oval) 1996. **BHC:** HS 167* v Somerset (Oval) 1994. **SL:** HS 125 v Lancs (Oval) 1990.

THORPE, Graham Paul (Weydon CS; Farnham SFC), b Farnham 1 Aug 1969. 5'11". LHB, RM. Debut 1988; cap 1991. **Tests:** 43 (1993 to 1997); HS 138 v A (Birmingham) 1997; scored 114* v A (Nottingham) 1993 on debut. **LOI:** 39 (1993 to 1997; HS 89 – twice; BB 2-15). Tours: A 1992-93 (Eng A), 1994-95; SA 1995-96; WI 1991-92 (Eng A), 1993-94; NZ 1996-97; P 1990-91 (Eng A); SL 1990-91 (Eng A); Z 1989-90 (Eng A). 1996-97. 1000 runs (8); most – 1895 (1992). HS 222 v Glam (Oval) 1997. BB 4-40 v A (Oval) 1993. BAC BB 2-14 v Derbys (Oval) 1996. Awards: NWT 2. **NWT:** HS 145* v Lancs (Oval) 1994. **BHC:** HS 103 v Lancs (Oval) 1993. BB 3-35 v Middx (Lord's) 1989. **SL:** HS 115* v Lancs (Manchester) 1991. BB 3-21 v Somerset (Oval) 1991.

TUDOR, Alex Jeremy (St Mark's S, Hammersmith; City of Westminster C), b West Brompton, London 23 Oct 1977. 6'5". RHB, RF. Debut 1995. HS 56 v Leics (Leicester) 1995. BB 6-101 v Glos (Oval) 1997. **NWT:** HS –. BB 1-27. **SL:** HS 29* v Essex (Oval) 1995. BB 1-19.

WARD, Ian James (Millfield S), b Plymouth, Devon 30 Sep 1972. 5'8½". LHB, RM. Debut 1992. HS 56 v Durham (Oval) 1997. **NWT:** HS 14 v Holland (Oval) 1996. **SL:** HS 31 v Essex (Oval) 1997.

NEWCOMER

BELL, Michael Anthony Vincent (Bishop Milner CS; Dudley TC), b Birmingham 19 Dec 1966. 6'2". RHB, LMF. Warwickshire 1992-97. MCC YC. Tour (Wa): Z 1993-94. HS 30 Wa v Notts (Nottingham) 1997. BB 7-48 Wa v Glos (Birmingham) 1993. **NWT:** HS –. BB 2-41 Wa v Northants (Lord's) 1995. **BHC:** HS –. BB 2-34 Wa v Middx (Lord's) 1994. **SL:** HS 8*. BB 5-19 Wa v Leics (Birmingham) 1994.

DEPARTURES (who made first-class appearances in 1997)

KENNIS, Gregor John (Tiffin S), b Yokohama, Japan 9 Mar 1974. 6'1". RHB, OB. MCC YC. Debut 1994. Scored 258 (395 balls, 41 fours) v Leics II (Kibworth) 1995 – Surrey II record. HS 29 v Kent (Canterbury) 1995. **SL:** HS 5.

LEWIS, C.C. – *see LEICESTERSHIRE.*

PEARSON, Richard Michael (Batley GS; St John's C, Cambridge), b Batley, Yorks 27 Jan 1972. 6'3". RHB, OB. Cambridge U 1991-92; blue 1991-92. Northamptonshire 1992. Essex 1994-95. Surrey 1996-97. HS 37 v Sussex (Guildford) 1996. BB 5-108 CU v Warwks (Cambridge) 1992. BAC BB 5-142 v Essex (Southend) 1996. **NWT:** HS 11 v Holland (Oval) 1996. BB 1-39. **BHC:** HS 12* v Yorks (Oval) 1996. BB 3-46 Ex v Glos (Chelmsford) 1995. **SL:** HS 9*. BB 3-33 Ex v Leics (Leicester) 1994 and v Warwks (Oval) 1996.

SURREY 1997

RESULTS SUMMARY

	Place	Won	Lost	Tied	Drew	No Result
Britannic Assurance Championship	8th	5	5	–	7	–
All First-Class Matches		5	5	–	7	–
NatWest Trophy	2nd Round					
Benson and Hedges Cup	Winners					
Sunday League	5th	9	5	–	–	3

BRITANNIC ASSURANCE CHAMPIONSHIP AVERAGES

BATTING AND FIELDING

Cap		M	I	NO	HS	Runs	Avge	100	50	Ct/St
1991	G.P.Thorpe	8	12	2	222	707	70.70	2	3	9
1985	A.J.Stewart	9	14	1	271*	726	55.84	2	2	16
1994	A.D.Brown	14	21	1	170*	848	42.40	3	2	11
1990	D.J.Bicknell	9	15	–	162	594	39.60	2	1	1
1995	A.J.Hollioake	13	19	–	182	731	38.47	1	5	10
–	J.D.Ratcliffe	15	26	2	135	759	31.62	1	4	3
1996	M.A.Butcher	13	22	1	79	659	31.38	–	5	19
–	I.J.Ward	3	4	–	56	102	25.50	–	1	6
–	B.C.Hollioake	12	19	–	76	483	25.42	–	3	10
–	Saqlain Mushtaq	8	10	4	41*	149	24.83	–	–	1
1996	C.C.Lewis	13	19	2	76	389	22.88	–	1	10
–	A.J.Tudor	8	11	6	35*	109	21.80	–	–	–
1989	M.P.Bicknell	15	20	5	74	305	20.33	–	2	8
–	J.A.Knott	5	9	3	27*	118	19.66	–	–	8/1
–	N.Shahid	7	11	–	34	198	18.00	–	–	4
1993	J.E.Benjamin	11	15	6	35	152	16.88	–	–	–
–	I.D.K.Salisbury	13	17	2	30*	159	10.60	–	–	7
–	G.J.Kennis	3	5	–	24	49	9.80	–	–	3
–	R.M.Amin	4	6	3	4	11	3.66	–	–	2

Also batted: J.N.Batty (3 matches) 23, 8, 23* (7 ct, 1 st); R.M.Pearson (1) 1 (1 ct).

BOWLING

	O	M	R	W	Avge	Best	5wI	10wM
Saqlain Mushtaq	254.5	75	617	32	19.28	5- 17	4	2
M.P.Bicknell	385.2	94	1174	44	26.68	5- 34	1	–
C.C.Lewis	291.4	66	970	33	29.39	5- 42	1	–
A.J.Hollioake	108.4	19	388	13	29.84	4- 22	–	–
I.D.K.Salisbury	314.1	65	936	30	31.20	6- 19	2	–
A.J.Tudor	127.3	17	526	16	32.87	6-101	1	–
B.C.Hollioake	169.2	34	594	17	34.94	4- 54	–	–
J.E.Benjamin	211	39	759	13	58.38	3- 52	–	–

Also bowled: R.M.Amin 134.3-35-348-8; J.N.Batty 4-0-9-0; D.J.Bicknell 12-1-38-1; A.D.Brown 16-4-37-0; M.A.Butcher 39-8-83-7; G.J.Kennis 1-0-4-0; R.M.Pearson 26-4-90-2; J.D.Ratcliffe 58-10-177-1; N.Shahid 5-0-14-0; G.P.Thorpe 4-0-13-0.

These averages give the records of Surrey players in all first-class county matches, no fixtures being undertaken outside the County Championship.

SURREY RECORDS

FIRST-CLASS CRICKET

Highest Total	For	811		v	Somerset	The Oval	1899
	V	863		by	Lancashire	The Oval	1990
Lowest Total	For	14		v	Essex	Chelmsford	1983
	V	16		by	MCC	Lord's	1872
Highest Innings	For	357*	R.Abel	v	Somerset	The Oval	1899
	V	366	N.H.Fairbrother	for	Lancashire	The Oval	1990

Highest Partnership for each Wicket

1st	428	J.B.Hobbs/A.Sandham	v	Oxford U	The Oval	1926
2nd	371	J.B.Hobbs/E.G.Hayes	v	Hampshire	The Oval	1909
3rd	413	D.J.Bicknell/D.M.Ward	v	Kent	Canterbury	1990
4th	448	R.Abel/T.W.Hayward	v	Yorkshire	The Oval	1899
5th	308	J.N.Crawford/F.C.Holland	v	Somerset	The Oval	1908
6th	298	A.Sandham/H.S.Harrison	v	Sussex	The Oval	1913
7th	262	C.J.Richards/K.T.Medlycott	v	Kent	The Oval	1987
8th	205	I.A.Greig/M.P.Bicknell	v	Lancashire	The Oval	1990
9th	168	E.R.T.Holmes/E.W.J.Brooks	v	Hampshire	The Oval	1936
10th	173	A.Ducat/A.Sandham	v	Essex	Leyton	1921

Best Bowling	For	10-43	T.Rushby	v	Somerset	Taunton	1921
(Innings)	V	10-28	W.P.Howell	for	Australians	The Oval	1899
Best Bowling	For	16-83	G.A.R.Lock	v	Kent	Blackheath	1956
(Match)	V	15-57	W.P.Howell	for	Australians	The Oval	1899

Most Runs – Season	3246	T.W.Hayward	(av 72.13)	1906
Most Runs – Career	43554	J.B.Hobbs	(av 49.72)	1905-34
Most 100s – Season	13	T.W.Hayward		1906
	13	J.B.Hobbs		1925
Most 100s – Career	144	J.B.Hobbs		1905-34
Most Wkts – Season	252	T.Richardson	(av 13.94)	1895
Most Wkts – Career	1775	T.Richardson	(av 17.87)	1892-1904

LIMITED-OVERS CRICKET

Highest Total	NWT	350		v	Worcs	The Oval	1994
	BHC	333-6		v	Hampshire	The Oval	1996
	SL	375-4		v	Yorkshire	Scarborough	1994
Lowest Total	NWT	74		v	Kent	The Oval	1967
	BHC	89		v	Notts	Nottingham	1984
	SL	64		v	Worcs	Worcester	1978
Highest Innings	NWT	146	G.S.Clinton	v	Kent	Canterbury	1985
	BHC	167*	A.J.Stewart	v	Somerset	The Oval	1994
	SL	203	A.D.Brown	v	Hampshire	Guildford	1997
Best Bowling	NWT	7-33	R.D.Jackman	v	Yorkshire	Harrogate	1970
	BHC	5-15	S.G.Kenlock	v	Ireland	The Oval	1995
	SL	6-25	Intikhab Alam	v	Derbyshire	The Oval	1974

SUSSEX

Formation of Present Club: 1 March 1839
Substantial Reorganisation: August 1857
Colours: Dark Blue, Light Blue and Gold
Badge: County Arms of Six Martlets
Championships: (0) Second 1902, 1903, 1932, 1933, 1934, 1953, 1981
NatWest Trophy/Gillette Cup Winners: (4) 1963, 1964, 1978, 1986
Benson and Hedges Cup Winners: (0) Semi-Finalists 1982
Sunday League Champions: (1) 1982
Match Awards: NWT 55; BHC 53

Chief Executive: A.C.S.Pigott. **Deputy Chief Executive/Director of Cricket:** D.R.Gilbert
County Ground, Eaton Road, Hove BN3 3AN (Tel 01273 827100)
Captain: C.J.Adams. **Vice-Captain:** M.G.Bevan. **Overseas Player:** M.G.Bevan.
1998 Beneficiary: P.Moores. **Scorer:** L.V.Chandler

BATES, Justin Jonathan (Hurstpierpoint C), b Farnborough, Hants 9 Apr 1976. 5'11". RHB, OB. Debut 1997. HS 47 v Glos (Hove) 1997. BB 5-89 v Notts (Hove) 1997. **SL:** HS 8. BB 1-24.

CARPENTER, James Robert (Birkenhead S), b Birkenhead, Cheshire 20 Oct 1975. 6'1½". LHB, SLA. MCC YC. Debut 1997. HS 63 v Hants (Southampton) 1997. BB 1-50. **SL:** HS 18 v Hants (Southampton) 1997.

EDWARDS, Alexander David (Imberhorne CS, E Grinstead; Loughborough U), b Cuckfield 2 Aug 1975. 6'0". RHB, RFM. Combined Us 1995. Sussex debut 1995. HS 22 v Young A (Hove) 1995. BAC HS 20 and BAC BB 4-94 v Surrey (Hove) 1997. BB 5-34 v Pak A (Hove) 1997. **BHC:** HS 9. BB 2-51 v Middx (Lord's) 1995. **SL:** HS 9*. BB 2-44 v Leics (Eastbourne) 1997.

GREENFIELD, Keith (Falmer HS), b Brighton 6 Dec 1968. 6'0". RHB, RM. Debut 1987; cap 1996. This is 154* v Glam (Hove) 1996. BB 2-40 v Essex (Hove) 1993. Awards: NWT 2. **NWT:** HS 129 v Lancs (Hove) 1997. BB 2-35 v Glam (Hove) 1993. **BHC:** HS 62 v Leics (Leicester) 1992. BB 1-17. **SL:** HS 102 v Notts (Arundel) 1995. BB 3-34 v Northants (Hove) 1995.

HAYWOOD, Giles Ronald (Lancing C), b Chichester 8 Sep 1979. 6'1". LHB, RM. Awaiting f-c debut. **SL:** HS 4.

HUMPHRIES, Shaun (The Weald, Billingshurst; Kingston C, London), b Horsham 11 Jan 1973. 5'9". RHB, WK. Debut 1993. Awaiting BAC debut. HS 41* v OU (Oxford) 1997.

JARVIS, Paul William (Bydales CS, Marske), b Redcar, Yorks 29 Jun 1965. 5'10". RHB, RFM. Yorkshire 1981-93; cap 1986; youngest Yorkshire debutant at 16yr 75d. Sussex debut/cap 1994. **Tests:** 9 (1987-88 to 1992-93); HS 29* and BB 4-107 v WI (Lord's) 1988. **LOI:** 16 (1987-88 to 1993; HS 16*; BB 5-35). Tours: SA 1989-90 (Eng XI); WI 1986-87 (Y); NZ 1987-88; I/SL 1992-93; P 1987-88. HS 80 Y v Northants (Scarborough) 1992. Sx HS 70* v SA (Hove) 1994. 50 wkts (4); most – 81 (1987). BB 7-55 Y v Surrey (Leeds) 1986. Sx BB 7-58 v Somerset (Hove) 1994. Hat-trick 1985 (Y). Award: BHC 1. **NWT:** HS 34* v Yorks (Hove) 1996. BB 4-41 Y v Leics (Leeds) 1987. **BHC:** HS 63 v Kent (Canterbury) 1997. BB 4-34 Y v Warwks (Birmingham) 1992. **SL:** HS 43 v Surrey (Guildford) 1996. BB 6-27 Y v Somerset (Taunton) 1989.

KHAN, Amer Ali (Muslim Modle HS, Lahore; MAO C, Lahore), b Lahore, Pakistan 5 Nov 1969. 5'9½". RHB, LB. Rawalpindi 1987-88 (one match as AAMER ALI). Middlesex 1995. Sussex debut 1997. HS 52 v Hants (Southampton) 1997. BB 5-137 v Middx (Lord's) 1997. **NWT:** HS 4. BB 1-13. **BHC:** HS 8. BB 3-31 v Hants (Hove) 1997. **SL:** HS 22* v Middx (Lord's) 1997. BB 5-40 v Kent (Horsham) 1997.

KIRTLEY, Robert James (Clifton C), b Eastbourne 10 Jan 1975. 6'0". RHB, RFM. Debut 1995. Mashonaland 1996-97. HS 15* v Surrey (Hove) 1997. BB 6-60 v Glam (Swansea) 1997. Took 5-53 (7-88 match) for Mashonaland v Eng XI (Harare) 1996-97. Award: NWT 1. **NWT:** HS – . BB 5-39 v Salop (Hove) 1997. **SL:** HS 7. BB 2-36 v Glos (Hove) 1997.

LEWRY, Jason David (Durrington HS, Worthing), b Worthing 2 Apr 1971. 6'2". LHB, LMF. Debut 1994; cap 1996. HS 34 v Kent (Hove) 1995. BB 6-43 v Worcs (Eastbourne) 1995. **NWT:** HS 5*. BB 3-45 V Leics (Leicester) 1996. **BHC:** HS 14* v Ire (Hove) 1995. **SL:** HS 7*. BB 4-29 v Somerset (Bath) 1995.

MARTIN-JENKINS, Robin Simon Christopher (Radley C; Durham U), b Guildford, Surrey 28 Oct 1975. Son of C.D.A. (*Daily Telegraph* Cricket Correspondent). 6'5". RHB, RFM. Debut 1995. British Us 1996. HS 50 v Northants (Hove) 1995. BB 3-26 v Pak A (Hove) 1997. BAC BB 2-51 v Worcs (Arundel) 1997. **BHC** (Brit Us): HS 12 v Glam (Cambridge) 1996. BB 4-57 v Glos (Bristol) 1997. **SL:** HS 10 v Northants (Hove) 1995. BB 2-41 v Middx (Lord's) 1995.

MOORES, Peter (King Edward VI S, Macclesfield), b Macclesfield, Cheshire 18 Dec 1962. 6'0". RHB, WK. Worcestershire 1983-84. Sussex debut 1985; cap 1989; captain 1997; benefit 1998. OFS 1988-89. HS 185 v CU (Hove) 1996. BAC HS 119* v Surrey (Guildford) 1996. **NWT:** HS 45 v Warwks (Birmingham) 1997. **BHC:** HS 76 v Middx (Hove) 1990. **SL:** HS 89* v Leics (Hove) 1995.

NEWELL, Keith (Ifield Community C), b Crawley 25 Mar 1972. Brother of M. 6'0". RHB, RM. Debut 1995. Matabeleland 1995-96. HS 135 v WI (Hove) 1995. BAC HS 112 and BB 4-61 v Kent (Horsham) 1997. **NWT:** HS 52 v Derbys (Hove) 1995. BB 1-61. **BHC:** HS 46 v Glos (Bristol) 1996. BB 1-25. **SL:** HS 76* v Kent (Hove) 1995. BB 2-22 v Glos (Hove) 1997.

NEWELL, Mark (Hazelwick SS; City of Westminster C), b Crawley 19 Dec 1973. Brother of K. 6'1½". RHB, OB. Debut 1996. MCC YC: HS 100 v Notts (Hove) 1997. **NWT:** HS 79 v Warwks (Birmingham) 1997. **BHC:** HS 87 v Glos (Hove) 1997. **SL:** HS 69 v Northants (Northampton) 1996.

PEIRCE, Michael Toby Edward (Ardingly C; Durham U), b Maidenhead, Berks 14 Jun 1973. 5'10". LHB, SLA. Combined Us 1994. Sussex 1995, 1997. HS 104 v Hants (Southampton) 1997. **BHC:** HS 44 Comb Us v Middx (Lord's) 1995. **SL:** HS 7 (twice).

PYEMONT, James Patrick (Tonbridge S; Trinity C, Cambridge), b Eastbourne 10 Apr 1978. Son of C.P. (Cambridge U 1967; cricket and hockey blue). 6'0". RHB, OB. Debut 1997 – awaiting BAC debut. HS 22 v OU (Oxford) 1997. **SL:** HS 18* v Notts (Hove) 1997.

RAO, Rajesh Krishnakant (Alperton HS; Brighton U), b Park Royal, Middlesex 9 Dec 1974. 5'10". RHB, LBG. Debut 1996. MCC YC: HS 89 v Essex (Hove) 1997. BB 1-14. Award: NWT 1. **NWT:** HS 158 v Derbys (Derby) 1997. **BHC:** HS 61 v Surrey (Oval) 1997. **SL:** HS 91 v Glos (Bristol) 1996. BB 3-31 v Worcs (Worcester) 1996.

ROBINSON, Mark Andrew (Hull GS), b Hull, Yorkshire 23 Nov 1966. 6'3". RHB, RFM. Northamptonshire 1987-90; cap 1990. Canterbury 1988-89. Yorkshire 1991-95; cap 1992. Sussex debut/cap 1997. Tours (Y): SA 1991-92, 1992-93. Failed to score in 12 successive f-c innings 1990 – world record. HS 27 v Lancs (Manchester) 1997. 50 wkts (1): 50 (1992). BB 9-37 (12-124 match) Y v Northants (Harrogate) 1993. Sx BB 6-78 v Northants (Hove) 1997 on Sussex debut. Award: BHC 1. **NWT:** HS 3*. BB 4-32 Nh v Somerset (Taunton) 1989. **BHC:** HS 3*. BB 3-20 Nh v Scot (Glasgow) 1989. **SL:** HS 9* (twice). BB 4-23 Y v Northants (Leeds) 1993.

STRONG, Michael Richard (Brighton C; Brunel UC), b Cuckfield 28 Jun 1974. 6'1". LHB, RMF. Summer contract – awaiting f-c debut. **SL:** HS 2*.

TAYLOR, Neil Royston (Cray Valley THS), b Orpington, Kent 21 Jul 1959. 6'1". RHB, OB. Kent 1979-95, scoring 110 and 11 on debut v SL (Canterbury); cap 1982; benefit 1992. Sussex debut/cap 1997. 1000 runs (11); most – 1979 (1990). HS 204 K v Surrey (Canterbury) 1990. Sx HS 127 v Northants (Hove) 1997 on Sussex debut. BB 2-20 K v Somerset (Canterbury) 1985. Sx BB – . Awards: BHC 9. **NWT:** HS 86 K v Staffs (Stone) 1995. BB 3-29 K v Dorset (Canterbury) 1989. **BHC:** HS 137 K v Surrey (Oval) 1988. **SL:** HS 95 K v Hants (Canterbury) 1990.

WILTON, Nicholas James (Beacon Community C), b Pembury, Kent 23 Sep 1978. RHB, WK. Staff 1997 – awaiting f-c debut.

NEWCOMERS

ADAMS, Christopher John (Repton S), b Whitwell, Derbys 6 May 1970. 6'0". RHB, OB. Derbyshire 1988-97; cap 1992. Sussex captain 1998. 1000 runs (3); most – 1742 (1996). HS 239 De v Hants (Southampton) 1996. BB 4-29 De v Lancs (Derby) 1991. Awards: NWT 2; BHC 4. **NWT:** HS 129* De v Sussex (Derby) 1997. BB 1-15 De v Berks (Derby) 1992. **BHC:** HS 138 De v Minor C (Lakenham) 1997. **SL:** HS 141* De v Kent (Chesterfield) 1992. BB 2-15 De v Essex (Chelmsford) 1993.

BEVAN, Michael Gwyl (Western Creek HS, Canberra), b Belconnen, ACT, Australia 8 May 1970. 5'11½". LHB, SLC. S Australia 1989-90. NSW 1990-91 to date. Yorkshire 1995-96; cap 1995. **Tests** (A): 17 (1994-95 to 1997); HS 91 v P (Lahore) 1994-95; BB 6-82 (10-113 match) v WI (Adelaide) 1996-97. **LOI** (A): 59 (1993-94 to 1997; HS 108*; BB 3-36). Tours (A): E 1997; SA 1996-97; I 1996-97; P 1994-95; Z 1991-92 (Aus B). 1000 runs (2+2); most – 1598 (1995). HS 203* NSW v WA (Sydney) 1993-94. UK HS 160* Y v Surrey (Middlesbrough) 1996. BB 6-82 (see Tests). BB 3-36 Y v Warwks (Leeds) 1996. Awards: NWT 2; BHC 3. **NWT:** HS 91* v Essex (Chelmsford) 1995. BB 2-47 v Lancs (Manchester) 1996. **BHC:** HS 95* v Lancs (Manchester) 1996. BB 1-25. **SL:** HS 103* v Glos (Middlesbrough) 1995. BB 5-29 v Sussex (Eastbourne) 1996.

CAMPBELL, George Richard Angus, b Hammersmith, London 9 Feb 1979. LHB, occ WK.

DAVIS, Richard Peter (King Ethelbert's S, Birchington; Thanet TC), b Westbrook, Margate, Kent 18 Mar 1966. 6'3". RHB, SLA. Kent 1986-93; cap 1990. Warwickshire 1993-94 to 1995; cap 1994. Gloucestershire 1996-97. Tours: SA 1994-95 (Wa); Z 1992-93 (K), 1993-94 (Wa). HS 67 K v Hants (Southampton) 1989. 50 wkts (2); most – 74 (1992). BB 7-64 K v Durham (Gateshead) 1992. Award: BHC 1. **NWT:** HS 22 K v Warwks (Birmingham) 1992. BB 3-19 K v Bucks (Canterbury) 1988. **BHC:** HS 18* K v Glam (Canterbury) 1993. BB 2-25 Gs v Sussex (Bristol) 1996. **SL:** HS 40* K v Northants (Canterbury) 1991. BB 5-52 K v Somerset (Bath) 1989.

KHAN, Wasim Gulzar (Small Heath CS; Josiah Mason SFC, Erdington), b Birmingham 26 Feb 1971. 6'1". LHB, LB. Warwickshire 1995-97. HS 181 Wa v Hants (Southampton) 1995. **BHC:** HS 0*. **SL:** HS 27 Wa v Surrey (Birmingham) 1997.

DEPARTURES (who made first-class appearances in 1997)

ATHEY, Charles William Jeffrey (Stainsby S; Acklam Hall HS), b Middlesbrough, Yorks 27 Sep 1957. 5'9½". RHB, RM. Yorkshire 1976-83; cap 1980. Gloucestershire 1984-92; cap 1985; captain 1989; benefit 1990. Sussex 1993-97; cap 1993. **Tests:** 23 (1980 to 1988); HS 123 v P (Lord's) 1987. **LOI:** 31 (1980 to 1987-88; HS 142*). Tours: A 1986-87, 1987-88; SA 1989-90 (Eng A); WI 1980-81; NZ 1979-80 (DHR), 1987-88; P 1987-88; SL 1985-86 (Eng B). 1000 runs (13); most – 1812 (1984). HS 184 Eng B v Sri Lanka (Galle) 1985-86. BAC HS 181 Gs v Sussex (Cheltenham) 1992. Sx HS 169* v Kent (Tunbridge W) 1994. BB 3-3 Gs v Hants (Bristol) 1985. Sx BB 2-40 v Notts (Eastbourne) 1993. Awards: NWT 4; BHC 6. **NWT:** HS 115 v Kent (Leeds) 1980. BB 1-18. **BHC:** HS 118 v Kent (Hove) 1995. BB 4-48 Gs v Comb Us (Bristol) 1984. **SL:** HS 121* Gs v Worcs (Moreton-in-M) 1985. BB 5-35 Y v Derbys (Chesterfield) 1981.

BATT, Christopher James (Cox Green CS), b Taplow, Bucks 22 Sep 1976. 6'4". LHB, LMF. Debut 1997 – no BAC appearances. Berkshire 1997. HS – and BB 4-56 v OU (Oxford) 1997.

DRAKES, Vasbert Conneil (St Lucy SS), b St James, Barbados 5 Aug 1969. 6'2". RHB, RFM. Barbados 1991-92 to date. Sussex 1996-97; cap 1996. Border 1996-97. **LOI** (WI): 5 (1994-95; HS 16; BB 1-36). Tour (WI): E 1995. HS 180* Barbados v Leeward Is (Anguilla) 1994-95. Sx HS 145* v Essex (Chelmsford) 1996. 50 wkts (1): 50 (1996). BB 8-59 Border v Natal (Durban) 1996-97. UK BB 5-20 WI v Kent (Canterbury) 1995. Sx BB 5-47 v Derbys (Hove) 1996. **NWT:** HS 35 v Yorks (Hove) 1996. BB 4-62 v Derbys (Derby) 1997. **BHC:** HS 58 v Brit Us (Cambridge) 1997. BB 5-19 v Ire (Hove) 1996. **SL:** HS 37 v Hants (Arundel) 1996. BB 4-50 v Surrey (Guildford) 1996.

continued on p 108

SUSSEX 1997

RESULTS SUMMARY

	Place	Won	Lost	Tied	Drew	No Result
Britannic Assurance Championship	18th	1	10	–	6	–
All First-Class Matches		2	10	–	7	–
NatWest Trophy	Semi-Finalist					
Benson and Hedges Cup	4th in Group C					
Sunday League	18th	2	13	–	–	2

BRITANNIC ASSURANCE CHAMPIONSHIP AVERAGES

BATTING AND FIELDING

Cap		M	I	NO	HS	Runs	Avge	100	50	Ct/St
1997	N.R.Taylor	15	27	1	127	996	38.30	3	5	2
1993	C.W.J.Athey	12	21	2	138*	682	35.89	1	5	9
–	K.Newell	17	31	2	112	827	28.51	2	3	2
–	M.T.E.Peirce	11	21	–	104	539	25.66	1	3	8
–	J.R.Carpenter	3	6	–	63	153	25.50	–	1	2
1990	N.J.Lenham	6	10	–	93	245	24.50	–	2	1
–	M.Newell	10	19	1	100	435	24.16	1	3	8
1994	P.W.Jarvis	11	18	2	64	374	23.37	–	4	5
–	R.S.C.Martin-Jenkins	2	4	1	36*	68	22.66	–	–	1
1989	P.Moores	17	31	4	102*	571	21.14	1	2	36
–	J.J.Bates	5	7	1	47	95	15.83	–	–	3
1996	K.Greenfield	10	19	–	37	248	13.05	–	–	9
1996	V.C.Drakes	10	18	1	48	221	13.00	–	–	7
–	R.K.Rao	9	16	–	89	207	12.93	–	1	2
–	A.A.Khan	14	22	3	52	241	12.68	–	1	3
–	A.D.Edwards	5	8	2	20	49	8.16	–	–	4
1997	M.A.Robinson	17	25	9	27	114	7.12	–	–	4
–	R.J.Kirtley	9	15	7	15*	49	6.12	–	–	4

Also batted: N.C.Phillips (2 matches) 1*, 6; T.A.Radford (1) 4, 0 (2 ct); M.J.Thursfield (1) 32*.

BOWLING

	O	M	R	W	Avge	Best	5wI	10wM
A.D.Edwards	75.2	13	284	10	28.40	4- 94	–	–
M.A.Robinson	448.2	87	1426	48	29.70	6- 78	2	–
V.C.Drakes	300	60	1043	31	33.64	4- 55	–	–
R.J.Kirtley	227.3	41	881	26	33.88	6- 60	1	–
P.W.Jarvis	318.5	46	1091	30	36.36	5- 44	2	–
J.J.Bates	152	42	373	10	37.30	5- 89	1	–
K.Newell	138.1	35	436	11	39.63	4- 61	–	–
A.A.Khan	398.1	85	1244	30	41.46	5-137	1	–

Also bowled: C.W.J.Athey 7-0-21-0; J.R.Carpenter 21.3-5-81-1; K.Greenfield 10-2-45-0; R.S.C.Martin-Jenkins 36-7-127-2; M.T.E.Peirce 20.1-2-76-0; N.C.Phillips 13-2-52-0; R.K.Rao 14-2-46-1; M.J.Thursfield 3.3-0-38-0.

The First-Class Averages (pp 118-133) give the records of Sussex players in all first-class county matches (their other opponents being Pakistan A and Oxford University).

SUSSEX RECORDS

FIRST-CLASS CRICKET

Highest Total	For	705-8d		v Surrey	Hastings	1902
	V	726		by Notts	Nottingham	1895
Lowest Total	For	19		v Surrey	Godalming	1830
		19		v Notts	Hove	1873
	V	18		by Kent	Gravesend	1867
Highest Innings	For	333	K.S.Duleepsinhji	v Northants	Hove	1930
	V	322	E.Paynter	for Lancashire	Hove	1937

Highest Partnership for each Wicket

1st	490	E.H.Bowley/J.G.Langridge	v Middlesex	Hove	1933
2nd	385	E.H.Bowley/M.W.Tate	v Northants	Hove	1921
3rd	298	K.S.Ranjitsinhji/E.H.Killick	v Lancashire	Hove	1901
4th	326*	J.Langridge/G.Cox	v Yorkshire	Leeds	1949
5th	297	J.H.Parks/H.W.Parks	v Hampshire	Portsmouth	1937
6th	255	K.S.Duleepsinhji/M.W.Tate	v Northants	Hove	1930
7th	344	K.S.Ranjitsinhji/W.Newham	v Essex	Leyton	1902
8th	229*	C.L.A.Smith/G.Brann	v Kent	Hove	1902
9th	178	H.W.Parks/A.F.Wensley	v Derbyshire	Horsham	1930
10th	156	G.R.Cox/H.R.Butt	v Cambridge U	Cambridge	1908

Best Bowling	For	10- 48	C.H.G.Bland	v Kent	Tonbridge	1899
(Innings)	V	9- 11	A.P.Freeman	for Kent	Hove	1922
Best Bowling	For	17-106	G.R.Cox	v Warwicks	Horsham	1926
(Match)	V	17- 67	A.P.Freeman	for Kent	Hove	1922

Most Runs – Season	2850	J.G.Langridge	(av 64.77)		1949
Most Runs – Career	34152	J.G.Langridge	(av 37.69)		1928-55
Most 100s – Season	12	J.G.Langridge			1949
Most 100s – Career	76	J.G.Langridge			1928-55
Most Wkts – Season	198	M.W.Tate	(av 13.47)		1925
Most Wkts – Career	2211	M.W.Tate	(av 17.41)		1912-37

LIMITED-OVERS CRICKET

Highest Total	NWT	384-9		v Ireland	Belfast	1996
	BHC	305-6		v Kent	Hove	1982
	SL	312-8		v Hampshire	Portsmouth	1993
Lowest Total	NWT	49		v Derbyshire	Chesterfield	1969
	BHC	61		v Middlesex	Hove	1978
	SL	59		v Glamorgan	Hove	1996
Highest Innings	NWT	158	R.K.Rao	v Derbyshire	Derby	1997
	BHC	118	C.W.J.Athey	v Kent	Hove	1995
	SL	129	A.W.Greig	v Yorkshire	Scarborough	1976
Best Bowling	NWT	6- 9	A.I.C.Dodemaide	v Ireland	Downpatrick	1990
	BHC	5- 8	Imran Khan	v Northants	Northampton	1978
	SL	7-41	A.N.Jones	v Notts	Nottingham	1986

WARWICKSHIRE

Formation of Present Club: 8 April 1882
Substantial Reorganisation: 19 January 1884
Colours: Dark Blue, Gold and Silver
Badge: Bear and Ragged Staff
Championships: (5) 1911, 1951, 1972, 1994, 1995
NatWest Trophy/Gillette Cup Winners: (5) 1966, 1968, 1989, 1993, 1995
Benson and Hedges Cup Winners: (1) 1994
Sunday League Champions: (3) 1980, 1994, 1997
Match Awards: NWT 61; BHC 56

Chief Executive: D.L.Amiss MBE
  County Ground, Edgbaston, Birmingham, B5 7QU (Tel 0121 446 4422)
Captain/Overseas Player: B.C.Lara. **Vice-Captain:** N.V.Knight.
1998 Beneficiary: T.A.Munton. **Scorer:** A.E.Davis

ALTREE, Darren Anthony (Ashlawn S, Rugby, b Rugby 30 Sep 1974. 5'11". RHB, LMF. Debut 1996. HS 0*. BB 3-41 v P (Birmingham) 1996. BAC BB 2-108 v Hants (Southampton) 1997.

BROWN, Douglas Robert (Alloa Academy; W London IHE), b Stirling, Scotland 29 Oct 1969. 6'2". RHB, RFM. Scotland 1989. Warwickshire debut 1991-92 (SA tour); cap 1995. Wellington 1995-96. Tours (Wa): SA 1991-92, 1994-95. HS 85 v Essex (Ilford) 1995. 50 wkts (1): 81 (1997). BB 8-89 (11-154 match) ECB Select XI v Pak A (Chelmsford) 1997. Wa BB 6-52 (11-120 match) v Kent (Birmingham) 1996. Award: BHC 1. **NWT:** HS 67 v Cornwall (St Austell) 1996. BB 2-34 v Middx (Lord's) 1997. **BHC:** HS 62 v Minor C (Birmingham) 1997. BB 5-31 v Worcs (Worcester) 1997. **SL:** HS 78* v Notts (Nottingham) 1995. BB 4-42 v Kent (Tunbridge W) 1997.

EDMOND, Michael Denis (Airds HS, Cambelltown, NSW, Australia), b Barrow-in-Furness, Lancs 30 Jul 1969. 6'1". RHB, RMF. Debut 1996. Indoor Cricket for Australia. Scored 100 off 48 balls for Warwks II v Somerset II (Taunton) 1997. HS 21 v Kent (Tunbridge Wells) 1997. BB 2-26 v OU (Oxford) 1997. BAC BB 1-6. **NWT:** HS 0. BB 1-24. **SL:** HS 19 v Kent (Tunbridge W) 1997. BB 2-4 v Derbys (Birmingham) 1997.

FROST, Tony (James Brinkley HS; Stoke-on-Trent C), b Stoke-on-Trent, Staffs 17 Nov 1975. 5'11". RHB, WK. Debut 1997. HS 56 v Somerset (Birmingham) 1997. **NWT:** HS 0. **BHC:** HS 10* v Minor C (Birmingham) 1997. **SL:** HS 2*.

GILES, Ashley Fraser (George Abbot S, Guildford) b Chertsey, Surrey 19 Mar 1973. 6'3". RHB, SLA. Debut 1993; cap 1996. Tour: A 1996-97 (Eng A). HS 106* v Lancs (Birmingham) 1996. **LOI:** 1 (1997; HS –). 50 wkts (1): 64 (1996). BB 6-45 v Durham (Birmingham) 1996. Award: NWT 1. **NWT:** HS 69 and BB 5-21 v Norfolk (Birmingham) 1997. **BHC:** HS 29 and BB 2-26 v Minor C (Birmingham) 1997. **SL:** HS 57 v Hants (Southampton) 1997. BB 5-36 v Worcs (Birmingham) 1996.

HEMP, David Lloyd (Olchfa CS; Millfield S; W Glamorgan C), b Bermuda 15 Nov 1970. UK resident since 1976. 6'0". LHB, RM. Glamorgan 1991-96; cap 1994. Warwickshire debut/cap 1997. Wales (MC) 1992-94. Tours: SA 1995-96 (Gm); I 1994-95 (Eng A); Z 1994-95 (Gm). 1000 runs (2): most – 1452 (1994). HS 157 Gm v Glos (Abergavenny) 1995. Wa HS 138 v Hants (Southampton) 1997. BB 3-23 Gm v SA A (Cardiff) 1996. BAC BB 1-9. Wa BB – . Awards: NWT 3; BHC 1. **NWT:** HS 112 v Middx (Lord's) 1997. **BHC:** HS 121 Gm v Comb Us (Cardiff) 1995. **SL:** HS 74 Gm v Leics (Leicester) 1995. BB 1-14 (Gm).

91

KNIGHT, Nicholas Verity (Felsted S; Loughborough U), b Watford, Herts 28 Nov 1969. 6'0". LHB, occ RM. Essex 1991-94; cap 1994. Warwickshire debut 1994-95 (SA tour); cap 1995. **Tests:** 11 (1995 to 1996-97); HS 113 v P (Leeds) 1996. **LOI:** 12 (1996 to 1997; HS 125*). Tours: SA 1994-95 (Wa); NZ 1996-97; I 1994-95 (Eng A); P 1995-96 (Eng A); Z 1996-97. 1000 runs (1): 1196 (1996). HS 174 v Kent (Canterbury) 1995. BB 1-61. Awards: NWT 1; BHC 2. **NWT:** HS 51 v Somerset (Birmingham) 1995. **BHC:** HS 104 v Minor C (Jesmond) 1996. **SL:** HS 134 v Hants (Birmingham) 1996. BB 1-14.

LARA, Brian Charles, b Santa Cruz, Trinidad 2 May 1969. 5'8". LHB, LB. Trinidad 1987-88 to date (captain 1995-96 to date). Warwickshire 1994; cap 1994; captain 1998. *Wisden* 1994. **Tests:** (WI) 45 (1990-91 to 1996-97, 1 as captain); HS 375 (world Test record) v E (St John's) 1993-94. **LOI** (WI): 118 (1990-91 to 1996-97, 2 as captain; HS 169; BB 2-5). Tours (WI): E 1991, 1995; A 1991-92, 1992-93, 1996-97; NZ 1994-95; I 1994-95; P 1990-91; SL 1993-94; Z 1989-90 (Young WI). 1000 runs (2+2) including 2000 (1): 2066 off 2262 balls in 1994. HS 501* (world f-c record) v Durham (Birmingham) 1994. Scored 6 hundreds in his first 7 innings for Warwks (147, 106, 120*, 136, 26, 140, 501*). BB 1-14. Wa BB –. **NWT:** HS 81 v Worcs (Lord's) 1994. **BHC:** HS 70 v Surrey (Oval) 1994. **SL:** HS 75 v Notts (Birmingham) 1994.

MOLES, Andrew James (Finham Park CS; Butts CHE), b Solihull 12 Feb 1961. 5'10". RHB, RM. Debut 1986; cap 1987; benefit 1997. GW 1986-87 to 1988-89. Tours (Wa): SA 1991-92, 1992-93, 1994-95. 1000 runs (6); most – 1854 (1990). Wa HS 230* GW v N Transvaal B (Verwoerdburg) 1988-89. Wa HS 224* v Glam (Swansea) 1990. BB 3-21 v OU (Oxford) 1987. BAC BB 3-50 v Essex (Chelmsford) 1987. Awards: NWT 2; BHC 2. **NWT:** HS 127 v Bucks (Birmingham) 1987. **BHC:** HS 89 v Lancs (Birmingham) 1995. BB 1-11. **SL:** HS 96* v Glam (Birmingham) 1992. BB 2-24 v Worcs (Worcester) 1987.

MUNTON, Timothy Alan (Sarson HS; King Edward VII Upper S), b Melton Mowbray, Leics 30 Jul 1965. 6'5". RHB, RMF. Debut 1985; cap 1989; captain 1997 (no appearances – back injury); benefit 1998. *Wisden* 1994. **Tests:** 2 (1992); HS 25* v P (Manchester) 1992; BB 2-22 v P (Leeds) 1992. Tours: SA 1992-93 (Wa); WI 1991-92 (Eng A); P 1990-91 (Eng A), 1995-96 (Eng A – *part*); SL 1990-91 (Eng A); Z 1993-94 (Wa). HS 54* v Worcs (Worcester) 1996. 50 wkts (5); most – 81 (1994). BB 8-89 (11-128 match) v Middx (Birmingham) 1991. Awards: NWT 2; BHC 1. **NWT:** HS 5. BB 3-36 v Kent (Canterbury) 1989. **BHC:** HS 13 v Leics (Leicester) 1989. BB 4-35 v Surrey (Oval) 1991. **SL:** HS 15* v Yorks (Scarborough) 1994. BB 5-23 v Glos (Moreton-in-M) 1990.

OSTLER, Dominic Piers (Princethorpe C; Solihull TC), b Solihull 15 Jul 1970. 6'3". RHB, occ RM. Debut 1990; cap 1991. Tours: SA 1992-93 (Wa); P 1995-96 (Eng A). 1000 runs (4); most – 1284 (1991). HS 208 v Surrey (Birmingham) 1995. Awards: NWT 2; BHC 1. **NWT:** HS 104 and BB 1-4 v Norfolk (Lakenham) 1993. **BHC:** HS 87 v Notts (Nottingham) 1995. **SL:** HS 91* v Sussex (Hove) 1996.

PENNEY, Trevor Lionel (Prince Edward S, Salisbury), b Salisbury, Rhodesia 12 Jun 1968. 6'0". RHB, RM. Qualified for England 1992. Boland 1991-92. Warwickshire debut 1991-92 (SA tour); UK debut v CU (Cambridge) 1992, scoring 102*; cap 1994. Mashonaland 1993-94. Tours (Wa): SA 1991-92, 1992-93, 1994-95; Z 1993-94. 1000 runs (2); most – 1295 (1996). HS 151 v Middx (Lord's) 1992. BB 3-18 Mashonaland v Mashonaland U-24 (Harare) 1993-94. Wa BB 1-40 (Z tour). BAC BB –. Award: NWT 1. **NWT:** HS 90 v Cornwall (St Austell) 1996. BB 1-8. **BHC:** HS 55 v Lancs (Birmingham) 1997. **SL:** HS 83* v Kent (Canterbury) 1993.

PIPER, Keith John (Haringey Cricket C), b Leicester 18 Dec 1969. 5'6". RHB, WK. Debut 1989; cap 1992. Tours (Wa): SA 1991-92, 1992-93, 1994-95; I 1994-95 (Eng A); P 1995-96 (Eng A); Z 1993-94. HS 116* v Durham (Birmingham) 1994. BB 1-57. **NWT:** HS 16* v Worcs (Lord's) 1994. **BHC:** HS 11* v Surrey (Oval) 1991. **SL:** HS 30 v Lancs (Manchester) 1990.

POWELL, Michael James (Lawrence Sheriff S, Rugby), b Bolton, Lancs 5 Apr 1975. 5'11". RHB, RM. Debut 1996. HS 39 v Glam (Birmingham) 1996. BB 1-18.

SHEIKH, Mohamed Avez (Broadway S), b Birmingham 2 Jul 1973. LHB, LM. Debut 1997. HS 24 and BB 2-14 v Middx (Birmingham) 1997. **SL:** HS 1.

SINGH, Anurag (King Edward's S, Birmingham; Gonville & Caius C, Cambridge), b Kanpur, India 9 Sep 1975. 5'11½". RHB, OB. Debut 1995. Cambridge U 1996; blue 1996-97; captain 1997. HS 157 CU v Sussex (Hove) 1996. Wa HS 23* v Worcs (Worcester) 1996. Award: BHC 1. **BHC:** (Brit Us) HS 123 v Somerset (Taunton) 1996. **SL:** HS 86 v Somerset (Birmingham) 1997.

SMALL, Gladstone Cleophas (Moseley S; Hall Green TC), b St George, Barbados 18 Oct 1961. 5'11". RHB, RFM. Debut 1979-80 (DHR XI in NZ). Warwickshire debut 1980; cap 1982; benefit 1992. S Australia 1985-86. **Tests:** 17 (1986 to 1990); HS 59 v A (Oval) 1989; BB 5-48 v A (Melbourne) 1986-87. **LOI:** 53 (1986-87 to 1992; HS 18*; BB 4-31). Tours: A 1986-87, 1990-91; SA 1992-93 (Wa), 1994-95 (Wa); WI 1989-90; NZ 1979-80 (DHR); P 1981-82 (Int); Z 1993-94 (Wa). HS 70 v Lancs (Manchester) 1988. 50 wkts (6); most – 80 (1988). BB 7-15 v Notts (Birmingham) 1988. Awards: NWT 1; BHC 2. **NWT:** HS 33 v Surrey (Lord's) 1982. BB 3-22 v Glam (Cardiff) 1982 and v Somerset (Birmingham) 1997. **BHC:** HS 22 v Kent (Canterbury) 1990. BB 5-23 v Minor C (Birmingham) 1997. **SL:** HS 40* v Essex (Ilford) 1984. BB 5-26 v Middx (Birmingham) 1997.

SMITH, Neil Michael Knight (Warwick S), b Birmingham 27 Jul 1967. Son of M.J.K. (Leics, Warwks and England 1951-75). 6'0". RHB, OB. Debut 1987; cap 1993. MCC YC. **LOI:** 7 (1995-96 to 1996; HS 31; BB 3-29). Tours (Wa): SA 1991-92, 1994-95; Z 1993-94. HS 161 v Yorks (Leeds) 1989. BB 7-42 v Lancs (Birmingham) 1994. Awards: NWT 1; BHC 2. **NWT:** HS 72 v Sussex (Birmingham) 1997. BB 5-17 v Norfolk (Lakenham) 1993. **BHC:** HS 125 v Kent (Canterbury) 1997. BB 3-29 v Middx (Lord's) 1994. **SL:** HS 111* v Sussex (Hove) 1996. BB 6-33 v Sussex (Birmingham) 1995.

VESTERGAARD, Soren (Fredericksberg C; Haslev Laerer Seminarium), b Copenhagen, Denmark 1 Mar 1972. 6'2". RHB, RFM. Represented Denmark in 1994 ICC Trophy. Awaiting f-c debut.

WAGH, Mark Anant (King Edward's S, Birmingham; Keble C, Oxford), b Birmingham 20 Oct 1976. 6'2". RHB, OB. Oxford U 1996-97; blue 1996-97; captain 1997. Warwickshire debut 1996. 1000 runs (1): 1156 (1997). HS 125* OU v Somerset (Taunton) 1997. Wa HS 124 v Durham (Chester-le-St) 1997. BB 3-82 OU v Glam (Oxford) 1996. Wa BB –. **BHC:** (Brit Us) HS 23 v Middx (Cambridge) 1996. BB 1-39 (twice).

WELCH, Graeme (Hetton CS), b Durham 21 Mar 1972. 5'11½". RHB, RM. Debut 1994; cap 1997. Tour: SA 1994-95 (Wa). HS 84* v Notts (Birmingham) 1994. 50 wkts (1): 65 (1997). BB 6-115 (11-140 match) v Lancs (Blackpool) 1997. **NWT:** HS 20 v Somerset (Birmingham) 1997. BB 1-11. **BHC:** HS 55* v Lancs (Birmingham) 1997. BB 2-43 v Lancs (Manchester) 1996. **SL:** HS 54 v Northants (Northampton) 1996. BB 3-37 v Yorks (Leeds) 1996.

NEWCOMER

GIDDINS, Edward Simon Hunter (Eastbourne C), b Eastbourne, Sussex 20 Jul 1971. 6'4½". RHB, RMF. Sussex 1991-96; cap 1994. MCC YC. Tour: P 1995-96 (Eng A). HS 34 Sx v Essex (Hove) 1995. 50 wkts (2); most – 68 (1995). BB 6-47 Sx v Yorks (Eastbourne) 1996. **NWT:** HS 13 Sx v Essex (Hove) 1994. BB 3-24 Sx v Ire (Belfast) 1996. **BHC:** HS 0*. BB 3-28 Sx v Surrey (Oval) 1995. **SL:** HS 9*. BB 4-23 Sx v Kent (Tunbridge W) 1994.

DEPARTURES (who made first-class appearances in 1997)

BELL, M.A.V. – *see SURREY.*

continued on p 108

WARWICKSHIRE 1997

RESULTS SUMMARY

	Place	Won	Lost	Tied	Drew	No Result
Britannic Assurance Championship	4th	7	2	–	7	1
All First-Class Matches		8	2	–	7	1
NatWest Trophy	Finalist					
Benson and Hedges Cup	Quarter-Finalist					
Sunday League	1st	13	4	–	–	–

BRITANNIC ASSURANCE CHAMPIONSHIP AVERAGES

BATTING AND FIELDING

Cap		M	I	NO	HS	Runs	Avge	100	50	Ct/St
1995	N.V.Knight	10	16	3	119*	677	52.07	2	3	7
1997	D.L.Hemp	16	28	4	138	1008	42.00	3	4	7
1994	T.L.Penney	16	24	5	99	784	41.26	–	6	11
–	M.A.Wagh	8	13	1	124	472	39.33	1	3	7
1987	A.J.Moles	12	22	3	168	635	33.42	1	2	10
1996	A.F.Giles	14	18	3	97	474	31.60	–	3	2
1993	N.M.K.Smith	14	21	2	148	587	30.89	1	2	7
1195	D.R.Brown	15	21	2	79	448	23.57	–	4	8
1197	G.Welch	16	24	6	75	393	21.83	–	1	3
1989	A.A.Donald	11	13	6	29	140	20.00	–	–	5
1991	D.P.Ostler	14	21	1	65	368	18.40	–	2	27
–	T.Frost	8	11	2	56	158	17.55	–	1	25/1
–	W.G.Khan	2	4	–	29	59	14.75	–	–	1
1992	K.J.Piper	8	11	3	34*	111	13.87	–	–	24/1
1982	G.C.Small	3	4	1	11	13	4.33	–	–	1

Also played: D.A.Altree (1 match) did not bat; M.A.V.Bell (3) 30, 0 (1 ct); M.D.Edmond (2) 21, 9, 5* (1 ct); M.A.Sheikh (1) 24; A.Singh (2) 0, 1, 0 (2 ct).

BOWLING

	O	M	R	W	Avge	Best	5wI	10wM
A.A.Donald	387.5	123	938	60	15.63	6- 55	3	1
D.R.Brown	462.1	123	1382	64	21.59	5- 62	3	–
G.Welch	487.2	133	1501	56	26.80	6-115	3	1
A.F.Giles	436.1	126	1086	32	33.93	4- 54	–	–
N.M.K.Smith	307.2	74	907	23	39.43	4- 32	–	–

Also bowled: D.A.Altree 25-3-119-2; M.A.V.Bell 79.3-14-232-3; M.D.Edmond 43-9-135-2; D.L.Hemp 23-4-120-0; N.V.Knight 6-0-71-0; D.P.Ostler 6-0-66-0; M.A.Sheikh 14.3-7-24-3; G.C.Small 50-12-158-3; M.A.Wagh 3-3-0-0.

The First-Class Averages (pp 118-133) give the records of Warwickshire players in all first-class county matches (their other opponents being Oxford University), with the exception of M.A.Wagh and A.Singh whose full county figures are as above, and:

D.R.Brown 16-22-2-79-448-22.40-0-4-9ct. 484.4-131-1415-70-20.21-5/62-3-0.
A.F.Giles 15-19-4-97-543-36.20-0-4-2ct. 478.1-145-1157-37-31.27-4/54.
D.L.Hemp 17-29-4-138-1013-40.52-3-4-9ct. 23-4-120-0.
G.Welch 17-25-6075-393-20.68-0-1-3ct. 511.5-140-1555-63-24.68-6/115-3-1.

WARWICKSHIRE RECORDS

FIRST-CLASS CRICKET

Highest Total	For	810-4d		v Durham	Birmingham	1994
	V	887		by Yorkshire	Birmingham	1896
Lowest Total	For	16		v Kent	Tonbridge	1913
	V	15		by Hampshire	Birmingham	1922
Highest Innings	For	501*	B.C.Lara	v Durham	Birmingham	1994
	V	322	I.V.A.Richards	for Somerset	Taunton	1985

Highest Partnership for each Wicket

1st	377*	N.F.Horner/K.Ibadulla	v Surrey	The Oval	1960
2nd	465*	J.A.Jameson/R.B.Kanhai	v Glos	Birmingham	1974
3rd	327	S.P.Kinneir/W.G.Quaife	v Lancashire	Birmingham	1901
4th	470	A.I.Kallicharran/G.W.Humpage	v Lancashire	Southport	1982
5th	322*	B.C.Lara/K.J.Piper	v Durham	Birmingham	1994
6th	220	H.E.Dollery/J.Buckingham	v Derbyshire	Derby	1938
7th	250	H.E.Dollery/J.S.Ord	v Kent	Maidstone	1953
8th	228	A.J.W.Croom/R.E.S.Wyatt	v Worcs	Dudley	1925
9th	154	G.W.Stephens/A.J.W.Croom	v Derbyshire	Birmingham	1925
10th	141	A.F.Giles/T.A.Munton	v Worcs	Worcester	1996

Best Bowling	For	10-41	J.D.Bannister	v Comb Servs	Birmingham	1959
(Innings)	V	10-36	H.Verity	for Yorkshire	Leeds	1931
Best Bowling	For	15-76	S.Hargreave	v Surrey	The Oval	1903
(Match)	V	17-92	A.P.Freeman	for Kent	Folkestone	1932

Most Runs – Season	2417	M.J.K.Smith	(av 60.42)	1959
Most Runs – Career	35146	D.L.Amiss	(av 41.64)	1960-87
Most 100s – Season	9	A.I.Kallicharran		1984
	9	B.C.Lara		1994
Most 100s – Career	78	D.L.Amiss		1960-87
Most Wkts – Season	180	W.E.Hollies	(av 15.13)	1946
Most Wkts – Career	2201	W.E.Hollies	(av 20.45)	1932-57

LIMITED-OVERS CRICKET

Highest Total	NWT	392-5		v Oxfordshire	Birmingham	1984
	BHC	369-8		v Minor C	Jesmond	1996
	SL	301-6		v Essex	Colchester	1982
Lowest Total	NWT	109		v Kent	Canterbury	1971
	BHC	96		v Leics	Leicester	1972
	SL	65		v Kent	Maidstone	1979
Highest Innings	NWT	206	A.I.Kallicharran	v Oxfordshire	Birmingham	1984
	BHC	137*	T.A.Lloyd	v Lancashire	Birmingham	1985
	SL	134	N.V.Knight	v Hampshire	Birmingham	1996
Best Bowling	NWT	6-32	K.Ibadulla	v Hampshire	Birmingham	1965
		6-32	A.I.Kallicharran	v Oxfordshire	Birmingham	1984
	BHC	7-32	R.G.D.Willis	v Yorkshire	Birmingham	1981
	SL	6-15	A.A.Donald	v Yorkshire	Birmingham	1995

WORCESTERSHIRE

Formation of Present Club: 11 March 1865
Colours: Dark Green and Black
Badge: Shield Argent a Fess between three Pears Sable
Championships: (5) 1964, 1965, 1974, 1988, 1989
NatWest Trophy/Gillette Cup Winners: (1) 1994
Benson and Hedges Cup Winners: (1) 1991
Sunday League Champions: (3) 1971, 1987, 1988
Match Awards: NWT 44; BHC 65

Secretary: Revd M.D.Vockins OBE
County Ground, New Road, Worcester, WR2 4QQ (Tel 01905 748474)
Captain/Overseas Player: T.M.Moody. **Vice-Captain:** G.A.Hick.
1998 Beneficiary: P.J.Newport. **Scorer:** S.S.Hale.

CHAPMAN, Robert James (Farnborough CS; S Notts CFE), b Nottingham 28 Jul 1972. Son of footballer R.O. ('Sammy') (Nottingham Forest, Notts County and Shrewsbury Town). 6'1". RHB, RFM. Nottinghamshire 1992-96. Worcestershire debut 1996-97 (on Zimbabwe tour). Tour (Wo): Z 1996-97. HS 25 Nt v Lancs (Nottingham) 1994. Wo HS 7*. BB 4-109 Nt v SA A (Nottingham) 1996. Wo BB 3-26 v OU (Oxford) 1997. BAC BB 3-67 v Glos (Bristol) 1997. **NWT:** HS –. **BHC:** HS 0. **SL:** HS 4*. BB 3-27 v Hants (Southampton) 1997.

ELLIS, Scott William Kenneth (Shrewsbury S; Warwick U), b Newcastle-under-Lyme, Staffs 3 Oct 1975. 6'3". RHB, RMF. Debut (Combined Us) v WI (Oxford) 1995 taking 5-59. Worcestershire debut 1996. HS 15 v Middx (Lord's) 1996. BB (*see above*). Wo BB 3-29 v Durham (Worcester) 1996. **NWT:** HS 0* and BB 2-34 v Glam (Cardiff) 1996. **BHC:** (Brit Us) HS 4. BB 1-50. **SL:** HS 1. BB 2-35 v Kent (Canterbury) 1996.

HAYNES, Gavin Richard (High Park S; King Edward VI S, Stourbridge), b Stourbridge 29 Sep 1969. 5'10". RHB, RM. Debut 1991; cap 1994. Tours (Wo): Z 1993-94, 1996-97. 1000 runs (1): 1021 (1994). HS 158 v Kent (Worcester) 1993. BB 4-33 v Kent (Worcester) 1995. Awards: NWT 2; BHC 1. **NWT:** HS 116* v Cumberland (Worcester) 1995. BB 1-9. **BHC:** HS 65 v Hants (Worcester) 1994. BB 3-17 v Derbys (Worcester) 1995. **SL:** HS 83 v Hants (Worcester) 1994. BB 4-13 v Surrey (Worcester) 1997.

HICK, Graeme Ashley (Prince Edward HS, Salisbury), b Salisbury, Rhodesia 23 May 1966. 6'3". RHB, OB. Zimbabwe 1983-84 to 1985-86. Worcestershire debut 1984; cap 1986. N Districts 1987-88 to 1988-89. Queensland 1990-91. *Wisden* 1986. **Tests:** 58 (1991 to 1996); HS 178 v I (Bombay) 1992-93; BB 4-126 v NZ (Wellington) 1991-92. **LOI:** 62 (1991 to 1996); HS 105*; BB 3-41). Tours: E 1985 (Z); A 1994-95; SA 1995-96; WI 1993-94; NZ 1991-92; I 1992-93; SL 1983-84 (Z), 1990-93 (Z); Z 1990-91 (Wo), 1996-97 (Wo). 1000 runs (13+1) inc 2000 (3); most – 2713 (1988); youngest to score 2000 (1986). Scored 1019 runs before June 1988, including a record 410 runs in April. Fewest innings for 10,000 runs in county cricket (179). Youngest (24) to score 50 first-class hundreds. Scored 645 runs without being dismissed (UK record) in 1990. HS 405* (Worcs record and then second highest in UK f-c matches) v Somerset (Taunton) 1988. BB 5-18 v Leics (Worcester) 1995. Awards: NWT 4; BHC 11. **NWT:** HS 172* v Devon (Worcester) 1987. BB 4-54 v Hants (Worcester) 1988 and v Surrey (Oval) 1994. **BHC:** HS 127* v Derbys (Worcester) 1995. BB 3-36 v Warwks (Birmingham) 1990. **SL:** HS 130 v Durham (Darlington) 1995. BB 4-21 v Somerset (Worcester) 1995.

ILLINGWORTH, Richard Keith (Salts GS), b Bradford, Yorks 23 Aug 1963. 5'11". RHB, SLA. Debut 1982; cap 1986; benefit 1997. Natal 1988-89. **Tests:** 9 (1991 to 1995-96); HS 28 v SA (Pt Elizabeth) 1995-96; BB 4-96 v WI (Nottingham) 1995. Took wicket of P.V.Simmons with his first ball in Tests – v WI (Nottingham) 1991. **LOI:** 25 (1991 to 1995-96; HS 14 (SL 1991-92; P 1990-91 (Eng A); SL 1990-91 (Eng A); Z 1989-90 (Eng A), 1990-91 (Wo), 1993-94 (Wo), 1996-97 (Wo). HS 120* v Warwks (Worcester) 1987 – as night-watchman. Scored 106 for England

ILLINGWORTH, R.K. continued:

A v Z (Harare) 1989-90 – also as night-watchman. 50 wkts (5); most – 75 (1990). BB 7-50 v OU (Oxford) 1985. BAC BB 7-79 v Hants (Southampton) 1997. **NWT:** HS 29* v Hants (Worcester) 1996. BB 4-20 v Devon (Worcester) 1987. **BHC:** HS 36* v Kent (Worcester) 1990. BB 4-36 v Yorks (Bradford) 1985. **SL:** HS 31 v Yorks (Worcester) 1994. BB 5-24 v Somerset (Worcester) 1983.

LAMPITT, Stuart Richard (Kingswinford S; Dudley TC), b Wolverhampton, Staffs 29 Jul 1966. 5'11". RHB, RMF. Debut 1985; cap 1989. Tours (Wo): Z 1990-91, 1993-94, 1996-97. HS 122 v Middx (Lord's) 1994. 50 wkts (5); most – 64 (1994). BB 5-32 v Kent (Worcester) 1989. Awards: NWT 1; BHC 4. **NWT:** HS 29 v Lancs (Manchester) 1995. BB 5-22 v Suffolk (Bury St E) 1990. **BHC:** HS 41 v Glam (Worcester) 1990. BB 6-26 v Derbys (Derby) 1994. **SL:** HS 41* v Leics (Worcester) 1993. BB 5-67 v Middx (Lord's) 1990.

LEATHERDALE, David Anthony (Pudsey Grangefield S), b Bradford, Yorks 26 Nov 1967. 5'10½". RHB, RM. Debut 1988; cap 1994. Tours (Wo): Z 1993-94, 1996-97. HS 157 v Somerset (Worcester) 1991. BB 5-56 v Somerset (Worcester) 1997. **NWT:** HS 43 v Hants (Worcester) 1988. BB 3-14 v Norfolk (Lakenham) 1994. **BHC:** HS 66 v Northants (Worcester) 1996. BB 4-13 v Minor C (Worcester) 1997. **SL:** HS 62* v Kent (Folkestone) 1988. BB 4-31 v Middx (Lord's) 1996.

MIRZA, Maneer Mohamed (*registered as 'Mohamed MANEER'*), b Birmingham 1 Apr 1978. Younger brother of the late Parvaz (Worcestershire 1994-95). RHB, RFM. Debut 1997. HS 10* and BB 4-51 v Warwks (Birmingham) 1997. **SL:** HS –. BB 1-31.

MOODY, Thomas Masson (Guildford GS, WA), b Adelaide, Australia 2 Oct 1965. 6'6½". RHB, RM. W Australia 1985-86 to date; captain 1995-96 to date. Warwickshire 1990; cap 1990. Worcestershire debut/cap 1991; captain 1995 to date. **Tests** (A): 8 (1989-90 to 1992-93); HS 106 v SL (Brisbane) 1989-90; BB 1-17. **LOI** (A): 40 (1987-88 to 1996-97; HS 89; BB 3-56). Tours (A): E 1989; I 1989-90 (WA); SL 1992-93; Z 1991-92 (Aus B). 1000 runs (5+1); most – 1887 (1991). HS 272 WA v Tasmania (Hobart) 1994-95. Wo HS 212 v Notts (Worcester) 1996. BB 7-38 WA v Tasmania (Hobart) 1995-96. Wo BB 7-92 (13-159 match) v Glos (Worcester) 1996. Awards: NWT 3; BHC 6. **NWT:** HS 180* v Surrey (Oval) 1994. BB 2-33 v Norfolk (Lakenham) 1994. **BHC:** HS 110* v Derbys (Worcester) 1991. BB 4-59 v Somerset (Worcester) 1992. **SL:** HS 160 v Kent (Worcester) 1991 (on Wo debut). BB 4-46 v Lancs (Manchester) 1996.

NEWPORT, Philip John (High Wycombe RGS; Portsmouth Poly), b High Wycombe, Bucks 11 Oct 1962. 6'3". RHB, RFM. Debut 1982; cap 1986; benefit 1998. Boland 1987-88. N Transvaal 1992-93. Buckinghamshire 1981-82. **Tests:** 3 (1988 to 1990-91); HS 40* v A (Perth) 1990-91; BB 4-87 v SL (Lord's) 1988 – on debut. Tours: A 1990-91 (*part*); P 1990-91 (Eng A); SL 1990-91 (Eng A); Z 1993-94 (Wo), 1996-97 (Wo). HS 98 v NZ (Worcester) 1990. BAC HS 96 v Essex (Worcester) 1990. 50 wkts (8); most – 93 (1988). BB 8-52 v Middx (Lord's) 1988. Awards: BHC 2. **NWT:** HS 25 v Northants (Northampton) 1984. BB 4-30 v Northants (Worcester) 1994. **BHC:** HS 28 v Kent (Worcester) 1990. BB 5-22 v Warwks (Birmingham) 1987. **SL:** HS 26* v Leics (Leicester) 1987 and v Surrey (Worcester) 1993. BB 5-32 v Essex (Chelmsford) 1995.

RAWNSLEY, Matthew James (Shenley Court CS, Birmingham), b Birmingham 8 Jun 1976. 6'2". RHB, SLA. Debut 1996. HS 26 and BAC BB 2-45 v Essex (Chelmsford) 1997. BB 3-67 v Pak A (Worcester) 1997. **NWT:** HS –. BB 2-50 v Holland (Worcester) 1997. **SL:** HS 7. BB 2-29 v Essex (Chelmsford) 1997.

RHODES, Steven John (Lapage Middle S; Carlton-Bolling S, Bradford), b Bradford, Yorks 17 Jun 1964. Son of W.E. (Notts 1961-64). 5'7". RHB, WK. Yorkshire 1981-84. Worcestershire debut 1985; cap 1986; benefit 1998. *Wisden* 1994. **Tests:** 11 (1994 to 1994-95); HS 65* v SA (Leeds) 1994. **LOI:** 9 (1989 to 1994-95; HS 56). Tours: A 1994-95; SA 1993-94 (Eng A); WI 1991-92 (Eng A); SL 1985-86 (Eng B), 1990-91 (Eng A); Z 1989-90 (Eng A), 1990-91 (Wo), 1993-94 (Wo), 1996-97 (Wo – captain). 1000 runs (1): 1018 (1995). HS 122* v Young A (Worcester) 1995. BAC HS 116* v Warwks (Worcester) 1992. Awards: NWT 1; BHC 1. **NWT:** HS 61 v Derbys (Worcester) 1989. **BHC:** HS 51* v Warwks (Birmingham) 1987. **SL:** HS 48* v Kent (Worcester) 1989.

SHERIYAR, Alamgir (George Dixon S; Joseph Chamberlain SFC; Oxford Poly), b Birmingham 15 Nov 1973. 6'1". RHB, LFM. Leicestershire 1994-95. Worcestershire debut 1996; cap 1997. HS 21 v Notts (Nottingham) 1997 and v Pak A (Worcester) 1997. 50 wkts (1): 62 (1997). BB 6-19 (10-63 match) v Sussex (Arundel) 1997. Hat-trick Le v Durham (Durham) 1994 (his second match). **NWT:** HS 10 v Hants (Worcester) 1996. BB 1-35. **BHC:** HS 1*. BB 3-40 v Northants (Worcester) 1996. BB 1-65. **SL:** HS 19 v Derbys (Chesterfield) 1996. BB 4-18 v Yorks (Leeds) 1997.

SOLANKI, Vikram Singh (Regis S, Wolverhampton), b Udaipur, India 1 Apr 1976. 6'0". RHB, OB. Debut 1995. Tour (Wo): Z 1996-97. HS 128* v OU (Oxford) 1997. BAC HS 90 v Surrey (Oval) 1996. BB 5-69 v Middx (Lord's) 1996. **NWT:** HS 50 v Glam (Cardiff) 1996. BB 1-48. **BHC:** HS 21 v Yorks (Leeds) 1997. BB 1-17. **SL:** HS 58 v Lancs (Worcester) 1997. BB 1-9.

SPIRING, Karl Reuben (Monmouth S; Durham U), b Southport, Lancs 13 Nov 1974. 5'11". RHB, OB. Debut 1994; cap 1997. 1000 runs (1): 1084 (1996). HS 150 v Essex (Chelmsford) 1997. **NWT:** HS 53 v Holland (Worcester) 1997. **BHC:** HS 35 Comb Us v Essex (Cambridge) 1995. **SL:** HS 58* v Sussex (Arundel) 1997.

WESTON, William Philip Christopher (Durham S), b Durham 16 Jun 1973. Son of M.P. (Durham; England RFU); brother of R.M.S. (see DURHAM). 6'3". RHB, LM. Debut 1991; cap 1995. Tours (Wo): Z 1993-94, 1996-97. 1000 runs (3); most – 1389 (1996). HS 205 v Northants (Northampton) 1997. BB 2-39 v P (Worcester) 1992. BAC BB –. **NWT:** HS 31 v Scot (Edinburgh) 1993. **BHC:** HS 32* v Essex (Worcester) 1993. **SL:** HS 80* v Durham (Worcester) 1996.

WILSON, Elliott James (Felsted S), b St Pancras, London 3 Nov 1976. RHB. Summer contract – awaiting f-c debut.

WYLIE, Alex (Bromsgrove S; Warwick C of Ag), b Tamworth, Staffs 20 Feb 1973. 6'2½". LHB, RF. Worcestershire 1993-95. HS 7. BB 1-50.

NEWCOMERS

CATTERALL, Duncan Neil, b Preston, Lancs 17 Sep 1978. RHB, RFM.

DRIVER, Ryan Craig (Redruth Community C; Durham U), b Truro, Cornwall 30 Apr 1979. LHB. Cornwall 1996 to date.

PATEL, Depesh, b Wolverhampton, Staffs 23 Sep 1981. RHB, RFM.

DEPARTURES (who made first-class appearances in 1997)

CURTIS, Timothy Stephen (Worcester RGS; Durham U; Magdalene C, Cambridge), b Chislehurst, Kent 15 Jan 1960. 5'11". RHB, LB. Worcestershire 1979-97; cap 1984; captain 1992-95; benefit 1994. Cambridge U 1983; blue 1983. **Tests:** 5 (1988 to 1989); HS 41 v A (Birmingham) 1989. Tours (Wo): Z 1990-91, 1993-94 (captain), 1996-97. 1000 runs (11); most – 1829 (1992). HS 248 v Somerset (Worcester) 1991. BB 2-17 v OU (Oxford) 1991. BAC BB 2-72 v Warwks (Worcester) 1987 and v Derbys (Worcester) 1992. Awards: NWT 6; BHC 2. **NWT:** HS 136* v Surrey (Oval) 1994. BB 1-6. **BHC:** HS 97 v Warwks (Birmingham) 1990. **SL:** HS 124 v Somerset (Taunton) 1990.

DAWOOD, I. – see GLAMORGAN.

THOMAS, Paul Anthony (Brodway S; Sutton C; Sandwell C), b Perry Barr, Birmingham 3 Jun 1971. 5'11". RHB, RFM. Worcestershire 1995-97. Shropshire 1992-94. HS 25 v Warwks (Birmingham) 1995. BB 5-70 v WI (Worcester) 1995 – on debut. BAC BB 4-78 v Sussex (Eastbourne) 1995. **NWT:** HS –. BB 2-30 v Cumberland (Worcester) 1995. **BHC:** HS 3. BB 1-34.

WORCESTERSHIRE 1997

RESULTS SUMMARY

	Place	Won	Lost	Tied	Drew	No Result
Britannic Assurance Championship	3rd	6	3	–	8	–
All First-Class Matches		6	3	–	10	–
NatWest Trophy	2nd Round					
Benson and Hedges Cup	5th in Group A					
Sunday League	8th	8	6	1	–	2

BRITANNIC ASSURANCE CHAMPIONSHIP AVERAGES

BATTING AND FIELDING

Cap		M	I	NO	HS	Runs	Avge	100	50	Ct/St
1986	R.K.Illingworth	5	4	2	112	157	78.50	1	–	3
1986	G.A.Hick	16	25	5	303*	1161	58.05	4	3	18
1994	D.A.Leatherdale	15	22	7	129	863	57.53	2	5	14
1995	W.P.C.Weston	15	25	4	205	1029	49.00	3	3	6
1991	T.M.Moody	14	21	1	180*	973	48.65	3	4	14
1984	T.S.Curtis	13	21	1	160	742	37.10	4	1	9
1997	K.R.Spiring	15	24	2	150	800	36.36	1	4	7
1986	S.J.Rhodes	17	22	6	78	581	36.31	–	4	39/3
1994	G.R.Haynes	15	22	3	70	657	34.57	–	5	3
1989	S.R.Lampitt	15	17	7	52	277	27.70	–	1	16
–	V.S.Solanki	11	13	–	61	279	21.46	–	2	8
1986	P.J.Newport	8	6	–	45	91	15.16	–	–	–
1997	A.Sheriyar	16	12	4	21	73	9.12	–	–	4
–	M.M.Mirza	5	6	4	10*	11	5.50	–	–	–

Also batted: M.J.Rawnsley (2 matches) 9, 26; R.J.Chapman (5) 3, 0, 0 (2 ct).

BOWLING

	O	M	R	W	Avge	Best	5wI	10wM
P.J.Newport	177.2	56	444	19	23.36	7- 37	1	–
R.K.Illingworth	206	75	442	18	24.55	7- 79	1	1
A.Sheriyar	404.1	87	1438	56	25.67	6- 19	3	1
D.A.Leatherdale	195.3	43	674	25	26.96	5- 56	1	–
G.R.Haynes	270.1	63	826	29	28.48	3- 46	–	–
M.M.Mirza	125.4	23	484	16	30.25	4- 51	–	–
S.R.Lampitt	334.4	70	1302	35	37.20	5- 39	1	–
T.M.Moody	213.4	42	829	19	43.63	5-148	1	–

Also bowled: R.J.Chapman 78.4-13-388-8; T.S.Curtis 12-1-65-1; G.A.Hick 187-45-603-9; M.J.Rawnsley 32-9-85-3; V.S.Solanki 44-8-152-1; K.R.Spiring 2-0-10-0; W.P.C.Weston 7-0-57-0.

The First-Class Averages (pp 118-133) give the records of Worcestershire players in all first-class county matches (their other opponents being Pakistan A and Oxford University), with the exception of:
  V.S.Solanki 13-17-1-128*-473-29.56-1-2-9ct. 65-13-238-1-238.00-1/98.

WORCESTERSHIRE RECORDS

FIRST-CLASS CRICKET

Highest Total	For	670-7d		v	Somerset	Worcester	1995
	V	701-4d		by	Leics	Worcester	1906
Lowest Total	For	24		v	Yorkshire	Huddersfield	1903
	V	30		by	Hampshire	Worcester	1903
Highest Innings	For	405*	G.A.Hick	v	Somerset	Taunton	1988
	V	331*	J.D.B.Robertson	for	Middlesex	Worcester	1949

Highest Partnership for each Wicket

1st	309	F.L.Bowley/H.K.Foster	v	Derbyshire	Derby	1901
2nd	300	W.P.C.Weston/G.A.Hick	v	Indians	Worcester	1996
3rd	438*	G.A.Hick/T.M.Moody	v	Hampshire	Southampton	1997
4th	281	J.A.Ormrod/Younis Ahmed	v	Notts	Nottingham	1979
5th	393	E.G.Arnold/W.B.Burns	v	Warwicks	Birmingham	1909
6th	265	G.A.Hick/S.J.Rhodes	v	Somerset	Taunton	1988
7th	205	G.A.Hick/P.J.Newport	v	Yorkshire	Worcester	1988
8th	184	S.J.Rhodes/S.R.Lampitt	v	Derbyshire	Kidderminster	1991
9th	181	J.A.Cuffe/R.D.Burrows	v	Glos	Worcester	1907
10th	119	W.B.Burns/G.A.Wilson	v	Somerset	Worcester	1906

Best Bowling	For	9- 23	C.F.Root	v	Lancashire	Worcester	1931
(Innings)	V	10- 51	J.Mercer	for	Glamorgan	Worcester	1936
Best Bowling	For	15- 87	A.J.Conway	v	Glos	Moreton-in-M	1914
(Match)	V	17-212	J.C.Clay	for	Glamorgan	Swansea	1937

Most Runs – Season	2654	H.H.I.Gibbons	(av 52.03)	1934
Most Runs – Career	34490	D.Kenyon	(av 34.18)	1946-67
Most 100s – Season	10	G.M.Turner		1970
	10	G.A.Hick		1988
Most 100s – Career	72†	G.M.Turner		1967-82
Most Wkts – Season	207	C.F.Root	(av 17.52)	1925
Most Wkts – Career	2143	R.T.D.Perks	(av 23.73)	1930-55

† G.A.Hick has scored 69 hundreds

LIMITED-OVERS CRICKET

Highest Total	NWT	404-3		v	Devon	Worcester	1987
	BHC	314-5		v	Lancashire	Manchester	1980
	SL	307-4		v	Derbyshire	Worcester	1975
Lowest Total	NWT	98		v	Durham	Chester-le-St	1968
	BHC	81		v	Leics	Worcester	1983
	SL	86		v	Yorkshire	Leeds	1969
Highest Innings	NWT	180*	T.M.Moody	v	Surrey	The Oval	1994
	BHC	143*	G.M.Turner	v	Warwicks	Birmingham	1976
	SL	160	T.M.Moody	v	Kent	Worcester	1991
Best Bowling	NWT	7-19	N.V.Radford	v	Beds	Bedford	1991
	BHC	6- 8	N.Gifford	v	Minor C (S)	High Wycombe	1979
	SL	6-26	A.P.Pridgeon	v	Surrey	Worcester	1978

YORKSHIRE

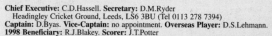

Formation of Present Club: 8 January 1863
Substantial Reorganisation: 10 December 1891
Colours: Dark Blue, Light Blue and Gold
Badge: White Rose
Championships (since 1890): (29) 1893, 1896, 1898, 1900, 1901, 1902, 1905, 1908, 1912, 1919, 1922, 1923, 1924, 1925, 1931, 1932, 1933, 1935, 1937, 1938, 1939, 1946, 1959, 1960, 1962, 1963, 1966, 1967, 1968. Joint: (1) 1949
NatWest Trophy/Gillette Cup Winners: (2) 1965, 1969
Benson and Hedges Cup Winners: (1) 1987
Sunday League Champions: (1) 1983
Match Awards: NWT 33; BHC 66

Chief Executive: C.D.Hassell. **Secretary:** D.M.Ryder
   Headingley Cricket Ground, Leeds, LS6 3BU (Tel 0113 278 7394)
Captain: D.Byas. **Vice-Captain:** no appointment. **Overseas Player:** D.S.Lehmann.
1998 Beneficiary: R.J.Blakey. **Scorer:** J.T.Potter

BLAKEY, Richard John (Rastrick GS), b Huddersfield 15 Jan 1967. 5'9". RHB, WK. Debut 1985; cap 1987; benefit 1998. YC 1987. **Tests:** 2 (1992-93); HS 6. **LOI:** 3 (1992-93); HS 25). Tours: SA 1991-92 (Y); WI 1986-87 (Y); I 1992-93; P 1990-91 (Eng A); SL 1990-91 (Eng A); Z 1989-90 (Eng A), 1995-96 (Y). 1000 runs (5); most – 1361 (1987). HS 221 Eng A v Z (Bulawayo) 1989-90. Y HS 204* v Glos (Leeds) 1987. BB 1-68. Awards: BHC 2. **NWT:** HS 75 v Warwks (Leeds) 1993. **BHC:** HS 80* v Lancs (Manchester) 1996. **SL:** HS 130* v Kent (Scarborough) 1991.

BYAS, David (Scarborough C), b Kilham 26 Aug 1963. 6'4". LHB, RM. Debut 1986; cap 1991; captain 1996 to date. Tours (Y): SA 1991-92, 1992-93; Z 1995-96. 1000 runs (5); most – 1913 (1995). HS 213 v Worcs (Scarborough) 1995. BB 3-55 v Derbys (Chester-field) 1990. Award: BHC 1. **NWT:** HS 117* v Middx (Leeds) 1996. BB 1-23. **BHC:** HS 116* v Surrey (Oval) 1996. BB 2-38 v Somerset (Leeds) 1989. **SL:** HS 111* v Lancs (Leeds) 1996. BB 3-19 v Notts (Leeds) 1989.

CHAPMAN, Colin Anthony (Beckfoot GS, Bingley; Bradford & Ilkley Art C), b Bradford 8 Jun 1971. 5'8½". RHB, WK. Debut 1990. Tour: SA 1992-93 (Y). HS 80 v Lancs (Leeds) 1997 (non-BAC match). BAC HS 20 v Middx (Uxbridge) 1990. **NWT:** BAC HS –. **SL:** HS 36* v Middx (Scarborough) 1990.

FISHER, Ian Douglas (Beckfoot GS, Bingley; Thomas Danby C, Leeds), b Bradford 31 Mar 1976. 5'10½". LHB, SLA. Debut 1995-96 (Y tour). UK debut 1996. Tour: Z 1995-96 (Y). HS 37 v Derbys (Derby) 1997. BB 5-35 v Mashonaland Inv XI (Harare) 1995-96 (on debut). UK BB 1-26. BAC BB –. **SL:** HS –. BB 2-23 v Kent (Leeds) 1997.

GOUGH, Darren (Priory CS, Lundwood), b Barnsley 18 Sep 1970. 5'11". RHB, RFM. Debut 1989; cap 1993. **Tests:** 21 (1994 to 1997); HS 65 v NZ (Manchester) 1994 – on debut; BB 6-49 v A (Sydney) 1994-95. **LOI:** 38 (1994 to 1997; HS 45; BB 5-44 – twice). Took wickets with his sixth balls in both Tests and LOIs. Tours: A 1994-95; SA 1991-92 (Y), 1992-93 (Y), 1993-94 (Eng A), 1995-96; NZ 1996-97; Z 1996-97. HS 121 v Warwks (Leeds) 1996. 50 wkts (4); most – 67 (1996). BB 7-28 (10-80 match) v Lancs (Leeds) 1995 (not BAC). BAC BB 7-42 (10-96 match) v Somerset (Taunton) 1993. Hat-trick (and 4 wkts in 5 balls) v Kent (Leeds) 1995. Awards: NWT 2. **NWT:** HS 46 and BB 7-27 v Ire (Leeds) 1997. **BHC:** HS 48* v Scot (Leeds) 1996. BB 3-38 v Worcs (Birmingham) 1997. **SL:** HS 72* v Leics (Leicester) 1991. BB 5-13 v Sussex (Hove) 1994.

HAMILTON, Gavin Mark (Hurstmere SS, Kent), b Broxburn, Scotland 16 Sep 1974. 6'1". RHB, RFM. Scotland 1993-94. Yorkshire debut 1994. Tour: Z 1995-96 (Y). HS 61 v Essex (Leeds) 1996. BB 5-65 Scot v Ire (Eglinton) 1993. Y BB 5-89 v Hants (Portsmouth) 1997. **SL:** HS 18* v Glos (Leeds) 1997. BB 4-27 v Warwks (Birmingham) 1995.

HOGGARD, Matthew James (Grangefield S, Pudsey), b Leeds 31 Dec 1976. 6'2". RHB, RFM. Debut 1996. Awaiting BAC debut. HS 10 and BB 1-41 v SA A (Leeds) 1996.

HUTCHISON, Paul Michael (Crawshaw HS, Pudsey), b Leeds 9 Jun 1977. 6'3". LHB, LFM. Debut 1995-96 (Y tour). Rest 1996. Awaiting Yorks f-c debut in UK. Tour: Z 1995-96 (Y). HS 15* v Derbys (Derby) 1997. BB 7-38 (11-102 match) v Pak A (Leeds) 1997. BAC BB 7-50 v Hants (Portsmouth) 1997.

LEHMANN, Darren Scott (Gawler HS), b Gawler, South Australia 5 Feb 1970. 5'10". LHB, SLA. South Australia 1987-88 to 1989-90, 1993-94 to date. Victoria 1990-91 to 1992-93. Yorkshire debut/cap 1997. **LOI** (A): 3 (1996-97; HS 15; BB 1-29). Tour: E 1991 (Vic). 1000 runs (1+4); – most 1575 (1997). HS 255 S Aus v Queensland (Adelaide) 1996-97. Y HS 182 v Hants (Portsmouth) 1997. BB 2-15 Victoria v WA (Melbourne) 1990-91. Y BB 1-0. **NWT:** HS 105 v Glam (Cardiff) 1997. **BHC:** HS 67 v Warwks (Birmingham) 1997. **SL:** HS 78* v Kent (Leeds) 1997. BB 3-43 v Northants (Leeds) 1997.

McGRATH, Anthony (Yorkshire Martyrs Collegiate S), b Bradford 6 Oct 1975. 6'2". RHB, OB. Debut 1995. Tours (Eng A): A 1996-97; P 1995-96; Z 1995-96 (Y). HS 141 v Worcs (Leeds) 1997. BB 1-6 (Eng A). Y BB 1-19. Award: BHC 1. **NWT:** HS 34 v Lancs (Manchester) 1995. **BHC:** HS 109* v Minor C (Leeds) 1997. BB 2-10 v Scot (Leeds) 1996. **SL:** HS 72 v Sussex (Scarborough) 1995.

PARKER, Bradley (Bingley GS), b Mirfield 23 Jun 1970. 5'11". RHB, RM. Debut 1992. Tour: Z 1995-96 (Y). HS 138* v OU (Oxford) 1994. BAC HS 127 v Surrey (Scarborough) 1994. **NWT:** HS 69 v Leics (Leicester) 1997. **BHC:** HS 58 v Northants (Leeds) 1997. **SL:** HS 42 v Warwks (Birmingham) 1997.

SIDEBOTTOM, Ryan Jay (King James's GS, Almondbury), b Huddersfield 15 Jan 1978. Son of A. (Yorks, OFS and England 1973-91). 6'3". LHB, LFM. Debut 1997. HS 2* and BB 3-71 v Leics (Leicester) 1997 – on debut. **SL:** HS –. BB 1-41.

SILVERWOOD, Christopher Eric Wilfred (Garforth CS), b Pontefract 5 Mar 1975. 6'1". RHB, RFM. Debut 1993; cap 1996. YC 1996. **Tests:** 1 (1996-97); HS 0 and BB 3-63 v Z (Bulawayo) 1996-97. **LOI:** 6 (1996-97 to 1997; HS 12; BB 2-27). Tours: NZ 1996-97; Z 1995-96 (Y), 1996-97. HS 58 v Lancs (Manchester) 1997. 50 wkts (1): 58 (1997). BB 7-93 (12-148 match) v Kent (Leeds) 1997. Awards: BHC 2. **NWT:** HS 8*. BB 3-24 v Ire (Leeds) 1997. **BHC:** HS 8. BB 5-28 v Scot (Leeds) 1997. **SL:** HS 14* v Northants (Northampton) 1996. BB 4-26 v Durham (Chester-le-St) 1996.

STEMP, Richard David (Britannia HS, Rowley Regis), b Erdington, Birmingham 11 Dec 1967. 6'0". RHB, SLA. Worcestershire 1990-92. Yorkshire debut 1993; cap 1996. Tours (Eng A): SA 1992-93 (Y); I 1994-95; P 1995-96. HS 65 v Durham (Chester-le-St) 1996. BB 6-37 v Durham (Durham) 1994. Award: BHC 1. **NWT:** HS 1*. BB 4-45 v Notts (Leeds) 1996. **BHC:** HS 2. BB 3-22 v Minor C (Leeds) 1997. **SL:** HS 23* v Warwks (Birmingham) 1993. BB 4-25 v Glos (Bristol) 1996.

VAUGHAN, Michael Paul (Silverdale CS, Sheffield), b Manchester, Lancs 29 Oct 1974. 6'2". RHB, OB. Debut 1993; cap 1995. Tours (Eng A): A 1996-97; I 1994-95; Z 1995-96 (Y). 1000 runs (3); most – 1244 (1995). HS 183 v Glam (Cardiff) 1996. BB 4-39 v OU (Oxford) 1994. BAC 4-62 v Surrey (Middlesbrough) 1996. Award: BHC 1. **NWT:** HS 64 v Notts (Leeds) 1996. BB 1-17. **BHC:** HS 88 v Warwks (Birmingham) 1997. BB 1-15. **SL:** HS 71* v Sussex (Eastbourne) 1996. BB 3-48 v Essex (Ilford) 1997.

WHITE, Craig (Flora Hill HS, Bendigo, Australia; Bendigo HS), b Morley 16 Dec 1969. 6'0". RHB, RFM. Debut 1990; cap 1993. Victoria 1990-91 (2 matches). **Tests:** 8 (1994 to 1996-97); HS 51 v NZ (Lord's) 1994; BB 3-18 v NZ (Manchester) 1994. **LOI:** 15 (1994-95 to 1996-97; HS 38; BB 4-37). Tours: A 1994-95, 1996-97 (Eng A); SA 1991-92 (Y), 1992-93 (Y); NZ 1996-97; P 1995-96 (Eng A); Z 1996-97 (*part*). HS 181 v Lancs (Leeds) 1996. BB 6-66 Eng A v Queensland (Brisbane) 1996-97. Y BB 5-31 v Northants (Leeds) 1997. Awards: NWT 1; BHC 1. **NWT:** HS 113 and BB 3-38 v Ire (Leeds) 1995. **BHC:** HS 57* v Notts (Leeds) 1996. BB 3-22 v Minor C (Leeds) 1997. **SL:** HS 148 v Leics (Leicester) 1997. BB 4-18 v Durham (Scarborough) 1997.

WOOD, Matthew James (Shelley HS & SFC), b Huddersfield 6 Apr 1977. 5'9". RHB, OB. Debut 1997 – awaiting BAC debut. HS 81 v Lancs (Leeds) 1997 (non-BAC match) – on debut.

DEPARTURES (who made first-class appearances in 1997)

BATTY, Gareth Jon (Bingley GS), b Bradford 13 Oct 1977. Younger brother of J.D. (Yorkshire and Somerset 1989-96). 5'11". RHB, OB. Yorkshire 1997 – no BAC appearances. HS 18 and BB 1-11 v Lancs (Leeds) 1997 (non-BAC match).

HARTLEY, P.J. – *see HAMPSHIRE*.

KETTLEBOROUGH, R.A. – *see MIDDLESEX*.

MORRIS, A.C. – *see HAMPSHIRE*.

MOXON, Martyn Douglas (Holgate GS, Barnsley), b Barnsley 4 May 1960. 6'0". RHB, RM. Yorkshire 1981-97, scoring 5 and 116 v Essex (Leeds) on debut; cap 1984; captain 1990-95; benefit 1993. GW 1982-83 to 1983-84. *Wisden* 1992. **Tests:** 10 (1986 to 1989); HS 99 v NZ (Auckland) 1987-88. **LOI:** 8 (1984-85 to 1987-88; HS 70). Tours (C=captain): A 1987-88, 1992-93C (Eng A); SA 1992-93C (Y); WI 1986-87 (Y); NZ 1987-88; I 1984-85; SL 1984-85, 1985-86 (Eng B); Z 1995-96 (Y). 1000 runs (11); most – 1669 (1991). HS 274* v Worcs (Worcester) 1994. BB 3-24 v Hants (Southampton) 1989. Awards: NWT 5; BHC 7. **NWT:** HS 137 v Notts (Leeds) 1996. BB 2-19 v Norfolk (Leeds) 1990. **BHC:** HS 141* v Glam (Cardiff) 1991. BB 5-31 v Warwks (Leeds) 1991. **SL:** HS 129* v Surrey (Oval) 1991. BB 3-29 v Sussex (Hove) 1990. Appointed Yorkshire's Director of Coaching 1998.

WHARF, A.G. – *see NOTTINGHAMSHIRE*.

YORKSHIRE 1997

RESULTS SUMMARY

	Place	Won	Lost	Tied	Drew	No Result
Britannic Assurance Championship	6th	6	3	–	8	–
All First-Class Matches		7	4	–	9	–
NatWest Trophy	Quarter-Finalist					
Benson and Hedges Cup	Quarter-Finalist					
Sunday League	10th	8	7	1	–	1

BRITANNIC ASSURANCE CHAMPIONSHIP AVERAGES

BATTING AND FIELDING

Cap		M	I	NO	HS	Runs	Avge	100	50	Ct/St
1997	D.S.Lehmann	17	27	2	182	1575	63.00	4	10	9
1991	D.Byas	17	28	3	128	1044	41.76	2	8	20
1987	R.J.Blakey	17	23	5	92	670	37.22	–	6	48/4
1995	M.P.Vaughan	12	21	2	161	667	35.10	2	2	2
1993	C.White	16	23	2	172*	633	30.14	1	2	17
–	A.McGrath	12	20	–	141	575	28.75	1	2	4
–	P.M.Hutchison	6	6	5	15*	27	27.00	–	–	1
1984	M.D.Moxon	9	13	–	63	342	26.30	–	4	2
–	B.Parker	16	25	3	74*	496	22.54	–	3	3
1996	C.E.W.Silverwood	15	20	6	58	300	21.42	–	1	2
1993	D.Gough	7	10	1	58	179	19.88	–	1	–
–	G.M.Hamilton	9	12	2	45	159	15.90	–	–	2
1987	P.J.Hartley	8	10	–	39	121	12.10	–	–	2
1996	R.D.Stemp	15	18	6	33*	120	10.00	–	–	6
–	A.C.Morris	6	7	–	35	67	9.57	–	–	3

Also batted: I.D.Fisher (1 match) 25, 37; R.A.Kettleborough (2) 10, 8, 3 (1 ct); R.J.Sidebottom (1) 2*; A.G.Wharf (1) 0.

BOWLING

	O	M	R	W	Avge	Best	5wI	10wM
P.J.Hartley	163	38	511	23	22.21	5-34	1	–
D.Gough	181.4	42	598	25	23.92	5-56	2	–
C.E.W.Silverwood	394.3	87	1272	53	24.00	7-93	4	1
P.M.Hutchison	197.2	47	639	26	24.57	7-50	2	–
C.White	349.4	57	1222	40	30.55	5-31	1	–
G.M.Hamilton	180.2	36	654	18	36.33	5-89	1	–
R.D.Stemp	456	109	1309	36	36.36	6-77	1	–

Also bowled: I.D.Fisher 21-5-39-0; D.S.Lehmann 20.3-3-71-2; A.McGrath 8.5-0-44-1; A.C.Morris 69-15-260-4; B.Parker 1-0-3-0; R.J.Sidebottom 16.4-4-71-3; M.P.Vaughan 118-11-522-3; A.G.Wharf 18-2-57-1.

The First-Class Averages (pp 118-133) give the records of Yorkshire players in all first-class county matches (their other opponents being Lancashire in a non-Championship match, Pakistan A and Oxford University), with the exception of:
D.Gough 8-10-1-58-179-19.88-0-1-0ct. 192.4-43-638-27-23.62-5/56-2-0.
A.McGrath 14-23-1-141-724-32.90-2-2-4ct. 8.5-0-44-1-44.00-1/19.
C.E.W.Silverwood 17-22-6-58-321-20.06-0-1-0ct. 440.3-102-1393-57-24.43-7/93-4-1.
M.P.Vaughan 14-25-2-161-828-36.00-3-2-3ct. 147.1-17-619-5-123.80-2/3.

YORKSHIRE RECORDS

FIRST-CLASS CRICKET

Highest Total	For	887		v Warwicks	Birmingham	1896
	V	681-7d		by Leics	Bradford	1996
Lowest Total	For	23		v Hampshire	Middlesbrough	1965
	V	13		by Notts	Nottingham	1901
Highest Innings	For	341	G.H.Hirst	v Leics	Leicester	1905
	V	318*	W.G.Grace	for Glos	Cheltenham	1876

Highest Partnership for each Wicket

1st	555	P.Holmes/H.Sutcliffe	v Essex	Leyton	1932
2nd	346	W.Barber/M.Leyland	v Middlesex	Sheffield	1932
3rd	323*	H.Sutcliffe/M.Leyland	v Glamorgan	Huddersfield	1928
4th	312	D.Denton/G.H.Hirst	v Hampshire	Southampton	1914
5th	340	E.Wainwright/G.H.Hirst	v Surrey	The Oval	1899
6th	276	M.Leyland/E.Robinson	v Glamorgan	Swansea	1926
7th	254	W.Rhodes/D.C.F.Burton	v Hampshire	Dewsbury	1919
8th	292	R.Peel/Lord Hawke	v Warwicks	Birmingham	1896
9th	192	G.H.Hirst/S.Haigh	v Surrey	Bradford	1898
10th	149	G.Boycott/G.B.Stevenson	v Warwicks	Birmingham	1982

Best Bowling	For	10-10	H.Verity	v Notts	Leeds	1932
(Innings)	V	10-37	C.V.Grimmett	for Australians	Sheffield	1930
Best Bowling	For	17-91	H.Verity	v Essex	Leyton	1933
(Match)	V	17-91	H.Dean	for Lancashire	Liverpool	1913

Most Runs – Season	2883	H.Sutcliffe	(av 80.08)	1932
Most Runs – Career	38561	H.Sutcliffe	(av 50.20)	1919-45
Most 100s – Season	12	H.Sutcliffe		1932
Most 100s – Career	112	H.Sutcliffe		1919-45
Most Wkts – Season	240	W.Rhodes	(av 12.72)	1900
Most Wkts – Career	3608	W.Rhodes	(av 16.00)	1898-1930

LIMITED-OVERS CRICKET

Highest Total	NWT	345-5		v Notts	Leeds	1996
	BHC	317-5		v Scotland	Leeds	1986
	SL	318-7		v Leics	Leicester	1993
Lowest Total	NWT	76		v Surrey	Harrogate	1970
	BHC	88		v Worcs	Leeds	1995
	SL	56		v Warwicks	Birmingham	1995
Highest Innings	NWT	146	G.Boycott	v Surrey	Lord's	1965
	BHC	142	G.Boycott	v Worcs	Worcester	1980
	SL	148	C.White	v Leics	Leicester	1997
Best Bowling	NWT	7-27	D.Gough	v Ireland	Leeds	1997
	BHC	6-27	A.G.Nicholson	v Minor C (N)	Middlesbrough	1972
	SL	7-15	R.A.Hutton	v Worcs	Leeds	1969

HAYDEN, Matthew Lawrence (Marist C, Ashgrove; Queensland U of Tech), b Kingaroy 29 Oct 1971. 6'2". LHB, RM. Queensland 1991-92 to date. Hampshire 1997; cap 1997. **Tests:** 7 (1993-94 to 1996-97); HS 125 v WI (Adelaide) 1996-97. **LOI:** 13 (1993 to 1993-94; HS 67). Tours (A): E 1993, 1995 (Young A); SA 1993-94, 1996-97. 1000 runs (2+3); most – 1446 (1997). HS 235* v Warwks (Southampton) 1997. BB 2-17 v Sussex (Southampton) 1997. Award: BHC 1. **NWT:** HS 90 v Cambs (Wisbech) 1997. **BHC:** HS 120* and BB 2-45 v Brit Us (Oxford) 1997. **SL:** HS 118 v Warwks (Southampton) 1997. BB 2-38 v Leics (Southampton) 1997.

MILBURN, Stuart Mark (Upper Nidderdale HS), b Harrogate, Yorks 29 Sep 1972. 6'1". RHB, RMF. Yorkshire 1992-95. Hampshire 1996-97. HS 54* v I (Southampton) 1996. BAC HS 25 v Yorks (Harrogate) 1996. BB 4-38 v Sussex (Southampton) 1997. **NWT:** HS 27 v Essex (Southampton) 1996. **BHC:** HS 2. BB 2-7 v Ire (Southampton) 1996. **SL:** HS 13* Y v Surrey (Oval) 1995. BB 2-18 v Sussex (Arundel) 1996.

PATEL, Chetan Morar (Fortismere S; Loughborough U; Keble C, Oxford), b Islington, London 12 Apr 1972. 6'2". LHB, RM. Debut (Oxford U) 1997; blue 1997. Hampshire 1997. HS 63* OU v Glam (Oxford) 1997. H HS 6. BB 6-110 OU v CU (Lord's) 1997. Hat-trick (OU) 1997. **SL:** HS –.

KENT – NEWCOMERS

HOCKLEY, James Bernard (Kelsey Park S, Beckenham), b Beckenham 16 Apr 1979. RHB, OB.

MASTERS, David D., b Chatham 22 Apr 1978. RHB, RMF.

KENT – DEPARTURES (who made first-class appearances in 1997)

PRESTON, Nicholas William (Meopham SS; Gravesend GS; Exeter U), b Dartford 22 Jan 1972. 6'1". RHB, RFM. Kent 1996-97. HS 17* v Derbys (Derby) 1996. BB 4-68 v Yorks (Canterbury) 1996. **NWT:** HS –. **SL:** HS 7*.

STRANG, P.A. – see NOTTINGHAMSHIRE.

WREN, Timothy Neil (Harvey GS, Folkestone), b Folkestone 26 Mar 1970. 6'3". RHB, LM. Kent 1990-97. Tour: Z 1992-93 (K). HS 23 v Sussex (Hove) 1995. BB 6-48 v Somerset (Canterbury) 1994. Award: BHC 1. **NWT:** HS 1*. BB 1-51. **BHC:** HS 7. BB 6-41 v Somerset (Canterbury) 1995. **SL:** HS 7*. BB 3-20 v Yorks (Leeds) 1995.

NORTHAMPTONSHIRE – DEPARTURES
(who made first-class appearances in 1997)

EMBUREY, John Ernest (Peckham Manor S), b Peckham, London 20 Aug 1952. 6'2". RHB, OB. Middlesex 1973-95; cap 1977; benefit 1986; testimonial 1995. Northamptonshire 1996-97; chief coach 1996 to date. *Wisden* 1983. W Province 1982-83/1983-84. **Tests:** 64 (1978 to 1995, 2 as captain); HS 75 v NZ (Nottingham) 1986; BB 7-78 v A (Sydney) 1986-87. **LOI:** 61 (1979-80 to 1992-93, 4 as captain; HS 34; BB 4-37). Tours: A 1978-79, 1979-80, 1986-87, 1987-88; SA 1981-82 (SAB), 1989-90 (Eng XI); WI 1980-81, 1985-86; NZ 1987-88; I 1979-80, 1981-82, 1992-93; P 1987-88; SL 1977-78 (DHR), 1981-82, 1991-92; Z 1980-81 (Mx). HS 133 M v Essex (Chelmsford) 1983. Nh HS 67* v Notts (Nottingham) 1996. 50 wkts (17) inc 100 (1): 103 (1983). BB 8-40 (12-115 match) M v Hants (Lord's) 1994. Nh BB 4-48 v Essex (Chelmsford) 1996. Awards: NWT 2; BHC 7. **NWT:** HS 46 v Lancs (Manchester) 1996. BB 3-11 M v Sussex (Lord's) 1989. **BHC:** HS 50 M v Kent (Lord's) 1984. BB 5-37 M v Somerset (Taunton) 1991. **SL:** HS 50 M v Lancs (Blackpool) 1988. BB 5-23 M v Somerset (Taunton) 1991.

FORDHAM, Alan (Bedford Modern S; Durham U), b Bedford 9 Nov 1964. 6'1". RHB, RM. Northamptonshire 1986-97; cap 1990; testimonial 1998. Bedfordshire 1982-85. Tours (Nh): SA 1991-92; Z 1994-95. 1000 runs (5); most – 1840 (1991). HS 206* v Yorks (Leeds) 1990. BB 1-0. Awards: NWT 4; BHC 3. **NWT:** HS 132* v Leics (Northampton) 1991. BB 1-3. **BHC:** HS 108 v Scot (Northampton) 1995. **SL:** HS 111 v Durham (Hartlepool) 1994. Appointed ECB Cricket Operations Manager (First-Class) 1997.

HUGHES, John Gareth (Sir Christopher Hatton SS, Wellingborough; Sheffield City Poly), b Wellingborough 3 May 1971. 6'1". RHB, RM. Debut 1990. Tours (Nh): SA 1991-92; Z 1994-95. HS 17 and BB 5-69 v Hants (Southampton) 1994. **BHC:** HS 9. BB 2-47 v Derbys (Derby) 1995. **SL:** HS 21 v Kent (Canterbury) 1993. BB 2-39 v Derbys (Northampton) 1995.

MOHAMMAD AKRAM, b Islamabad, Pakistan 10 Sep 1972. RHB, RFM. Rawalpindi 1992-93 to date. Northamptonshire 1997. **Tests:** 6 (1995-96 to 1996-97); HS 5 and BB 3-39 v SL (Sialkot) 1995-96. **LOI:** 12 (1995-96 to 1997; HS 7*; BB 2-28). Tours (P): E 1996; A 1995-96. HS 28 v Durham (Northampton) 1997. BB 7-51 P v Leics (Leicester) 1996. Nh BB 5-72 v Somerset (Northampton) 1997. **NWT:** HS 0*. BB 1-42. **BHC:** HS 4. BB 4-47 v Notts (Nottingham) 1997. **SL:** HS 2*. BB 4-19 v Surrey (Northampton) 1997.

NOTTINGHAMSHIRE – DEPARTURES (continued from p 73)

METCALFE, Ashley Anthony (Bradford GS; University C, London), b Horsforth, Yorks 25 Dec 1963. 5'8". RHB, OB. Yorkshire 1983-95 (scoring 122 v Notts (Bradford) on debut; cap 1986; benefit 1995. Nottinghamshire 1996-97. YC 1986. OFS 1988-89. Tours (Y): SA 1991-92, 1992-93, 1996-97 (Nt); WI 1986-87. 1000 runs (6) inc 2000 (1): 2047 (1990). HS 216* Y v Middx (Leeds) 1988. Nt HS 128 v Glam (Worksop) 1996. BB 2-18 Y v Warwks (Scarborough) 1987. Awards: NWT 2; BHC 5. **NWT:** HS 127* Y v Warwks (Leeds) 1990. BB 2-44 Y v Wilts (Trowbridge) 1987. **BHC:** HS 114 Y v Lancs (Manchester) 1991. **SL:** HS 116 Y v Middx (Lord's) 1991. Registered by Cumberland for 1998.

PICK, Robert Andrew (Alderman Derbyshire CS; High Pavement SFC), b Nottingham 19 Nov 1963. 5'10". LHB, RFM. Nottinghamshire 1983-97; cap 1987; benefit 1996. Wellington 1989-90. Tours: SA 1996-97 (Nt); WI 1991-92 (Eng A); SL 1990-91 (Eng A). HS 65* v Northants (Nottingham) 1994. 50 wkts (5); most – 67 (1991). BB 7-128 v Leics (Leicester) 1990. Awards: NWT 2; BHC 1. **NWT:** HS 34* v Sussex (Hove) 1983. BB 5-22 v Glos (Bristol) 1987. **BHC:** HS 25* v Hants (Southampton) 1991. BB 4-42 v Northants (Nottingham) 1987. **SL:** HS 58* v Essex (Nottingham) 1995. BB 4-32 v Glos (Moreton-in-M) 1987.

SOMERSET – DEPARTURES (continued from p 78)

HERZBERG, Steven, b Carshalton, Surrey 25 May 1967. Emigrated to Australia when aged 9. 6'4". RHB, OB. W Australia 1991-92 and 1992-93. Tasmania 1993-94. Kent 1995. Somerset 1997. HS 57* WA v NSW (Sydney) 1992-93. Sm HS 56 v Surrey (Oval) 1997 – on Sm debut. BB 5-33 K v Leics (Canterbury) 1995. Sm BB 3-100 v Kent (Taunton) 1997. **BHC:** HS –. **SL:** HS –. BB 1-37.

MacGILL, Stuart Charles Glyndwr, b Mount Lawley, Australia 25 Feb 1971. RHB, LBG. Western Australia 1993-94. New South Wales 1996-97. Somerset 1997 (unregistered). HS 25 and Sm BB 2-49 v Pak A (Taunton) 1997. BB 4-72 NSW v Victoria (Sydney) 1996-97.

SLADDIN, Richard William (Sowerby Bridge HS), b Halifax, Yorks 8 Jan 1969. 6'0". RHB, SLA. Derbyshire 1991-94. Somerset 1997. HS 51* De v Durham (Durham) 1993. Sm HS – . BB 6-58 De v CU (Cambridge) 1992. BAC BB 5-186 De v Essex (Chelmsford) 1991. Sm BB 5-60 v OU (Taunton) 1997. **SL:** HS 26 De v Durham (Durham) 1993. BB 2-26 De v Glos (Cheltenham) 1993.

LENHAM, Neil John (Brighton C), b Worthing 17 Dec 1965. Son of L.J. (Sussex 1956-70). 5'11". RHB, RM. Sussex 1984-97; cap 1990. 1000 runs (3); most – 1663 (1990). HS 222* v Kent (Hove) 1992. BB 4-13 v Durham (Durham) 1993. Awards: NWT 2; BHC 1. **NWT:** HS 129* v Devon (Hove) 1995. BB 2-12 v Ire (Downpatrick) 1990. **BHC:** HS 82 v Somerset (Hove) 1986. BB 1-3. **SL:** HS 86 v Kent (Hove) 1991. BB 5-28 v Durham (Durham) 1993.

PHILLIPS, Nicholas Charles (Wm Parker S, Hastings), b Pembury, Kent 10 May 1974. 5'10½". RHB, OB. Sussex 1993-97. HS 53 v Young A (Hove) 1995. BB 3-39 v CU (Hove) 1993. BAC HS 52 and BB 3-78 v Lancs (Lytham) 1995. **BHC:** HS 11 v Kent (Canterbury) 1997. BB 3-48 v Glos (Hove) 1997. **SL:** HS 38* v Essex (Chelmsford) 1996. BB 2-19 v Somerset (Hove) 1994.

RADFORD, Toby Alexander (St Bartholomew's S, Newbury; Loughborough U), b Caerphilly, Glam 3 Dec 1971. 5'10". RHB, OB. Middlesex 1994-95. Sussex 1996-97. HS 69* v OU (Oxford) 1997. BAC HS 69 M v Essex (Chelmsford) 1995 – on BAC debut. BB (M) 1-0. **NWT:** HS 82 M v Surrey (Oval) 1995. **SL:** HS 38 M v Worcs (Worcester) 1993.

THURSFIELD, Martin John (Boldon CS), b South Shields, Co Durham 14 Dec 1971. 6'3". RHB, RM. Middlesex 1990. Hampshire 1992-96. Sussex 1997. MCC YC. HS 47 H v Glam (Southampton) 1994. Sx HS 32* v Somerset (Taunton) 1997 – on Sussex debut. BB 6-130 H v Middx (Southampton) 1994. Sx BB 2-36 v OU (Oxford) 1997. **NWT:** HS –. BB 1-34. **BHC:** HS 19 H v Surrey (Oval) 1996. BB 2-33 H v Sussex (Southampton) 1996. **SL:** HS 9. BB 3-31 H v Leics (Leicester) 1994.

DONALD, Allan Anthony (Grey College HS), b Bloemfontein, SA 20 Oct 1966. 6'2". RHB, RF. OFS 1985-86 to date. Warwickshire 1987-93, 1995, 1997; cap 1989; benefit 1999. *Wisden* 1991. **Tests** (SA): 33 (1991-92 to 1996-97); HS 33 and BB 8-71 (11-113 match) v Z (Harare) 1995-96. **LOI** (SA): 87 (1991-92 to 1996-97); HS 7*; BB 6-23). Tours (SA): E 1994; A 1993-94; WI 1991-92; NZ 1994-95; I 1996-97; SL 1993-94; Z 1995-96. HS 46* OFS v W Province (Cape Town) 1990-91. Wa HS 44 v Essex (Ilford) 1995. 50 wkts (5+1); most – 89 (1995). BB 8-37 OFS v Transvaal (Johannesburg) 1986-87. Wa BB 7-37 v Durham (Birmingham) 1992. Awards: NWT 3. **NWT:** HS 14* v Northants (Birmingham) 1992. BB 5-12 v Wilts (Birmingham) 1989. **BHC:** HS 23* v Leics (Leicester) 1989. BB 5-25 v Lancs (Birmingham) 1997. **SL:** HS 18* v Middx (Lord's) 1988. BB 6-15 v Yorks (Birmingham) 1995.

KHAN, W.G. – *see SUSSEX*.

BALDERSTONE, John Christopher (Paddock Council S, Huddersfield), b Longwood, Huddersfield, Yorks 16 Nov 1940. RHB, SLA. Yorkshire 1961-69. Leicestershire 1971-86 (cap 1973; testimonial 1984). **Tests:** 2 (1976); HS 35 v WI (Leeds) 1976; BB 1-80. Tour: Z 1980-81 (Le). 1000 runs (11); most – 1482 (1982). HS 181* Le v Glos (Leicester) 1984. BB 6-25 Le v Hants (Southampton) 1978. Hat-trick 1976 (Le). F-c career: 390 matches; 19034 runs @ 34.11, 32 hundreds; 310 wickets @ 26.32; 210 ct. Soccer for Huddersfield Town, Carlisle United, Doncaster Rovers and Queen of the South. Appointed 1988. Umpired 1 LOI (1994).

BIRD, Harold Dennis ('Dickie') (Raley SM, Barnsley), b Barnsley, Yorks 19 Apr 1933. RHB, RM. Yorkshire 1956-59. Leicestershire 1960-64 (cap 1960). MBE 1986. 1000 runs (1): 1028 (1960). HS 181* Y v Glam (Bradford) 1959. F-c career: 93 matches; 3314 runs @ 20.71, 2 hundreds. Appointed 1970. Umpired 66 Tests (world record – 1973 to 1996) and 69 LOI (1973 to 1995), including 1975, 1979, 1983 and 1987-88 World Cups (first 3 finals), 1985-86 Asia Cup and 7 Sharjah tournaments. International Panel 1994 to 1995-96.

BURGESS, Graham Iefvion (Millfield S), b Glastonbury, Somerset 5 May 1943. RHB, RM. Somerset 1966-79 (cap 1968; testimonial 1977). HS 129 v Glos (Taunton) 1973. BB 7-43 (13-75 match) v OU (Oxford) 1975. F-c career: 252 matches; 7129 runs @ 18.90, 2 hundreds; 474 wickets @ 28.57. Appointed 1991.

CLARKSON, Anthony (Harrogate GS), b Killinghall, Harrogate, Yorks 5 Sep 1939. RHB, OB. Yorkshire 1963. Somerset 1966-71 (cap 1968). Devon. 1000 runs (2); most – 1246 (1970). HS 131 Sm v Northants (Northampton) 1969. BB 3-51 Sm v Essex (Yeovil) 1967. F-c career: 110 matches; 4458 runs @ 25.18, 2 hundreds; 13 wickets @ 28.23. Appointed 1996.

CONSTANT, David John, b Bradford-on-Avon, Wilts 9 Nov 1941. LHB, SLA. Kent 1961-63. Leicestershire 1965-68. HS 80 Le v Glos (Bristol) 1966. F-c career: 61 matches; 1517 runs @ 19.20; 1 wicket @ 36.00. Appointed 1969. Umpired 36 Tests (1971 to 1988) and 30 LOI (1972 to 1996). Represented Gloucestershire at bowls 1984-86.

DUDLESTON, Barry (Stockport S), b Bebington, Cheshire 16 Jul 1945. RHB, SLA. Leicestershire 1966-80 (cap 1969; benefit 1980). Gloucestershire 1981-83. Rhodesia 1976-80. 1000 runs (8); most – 1374 (1970). HS 202 Le v Derbys (Leicester) 1979. BB 4-6 Le v Surrey (Leicester) 1972. F-c career: 295 matches; 14747 runs @ 32.48, 32 hundreds; 47 wickets @ 29.04. Appointed 1984. Umpired 2 Tests (1991 to 1992) and 1 LOI (1992).

HAMPSHIRE, John Harry (Oakwood THS, Rotherham), b Thurnscoe, Yorks 10 Feb 1941. RHB, LB. Son of J. (Yorks 1937); brother of A.W. (Yorks 1975). Yorkshire 1961-81 (cap 1963; benefit 1976; captain 1979-80). Derbyshire 1982-84 (cap 1982). Tasmania 1967-69, 1977-79. **Tests:** 8 (1969 to 1975); 403 runs @ 26.86, HS 107 v WI (Lord's) 1969 on debut (only English player to score hundred at Lord's on Test debut). Tours: A 1970-71; SA 1972-73 (DHR), 1974-75 (DHR); WI 1964-65 (Cav); NZ 1970-71; P 1967-68 (Cwlth XI); SL 1969-70; Z 1980-81 (Le XI). 1000 runs (15); most – 1596 (1978). HS 183* Y v Sussex (Hove) 1971. BB 7-52 Y v Glam (Cardiff) 1963. F-c career: 577 matches; 28059 runs @ 34.55, 43 hundreds; 30 wickets @ 54.56; 445 ct. Appointed 1985. Umpired 11 Tests (1989 to 1993) and 7 LOI (1989 to 1997).

HARRIS, John Henry, b Taunton, Somerset 13 Feb 1936. LHB, RFM. Somerset 1952-59. Suffolk 1960-62. Devon 1965. HS 41 v Worcs (Taunton) 1957. BB 3-29 v Worcs (Bristol) 1959. F-c career: 15 matches; 154 runs @ 11.00; 19 wickets @ 32.57. Appointed 1983.

HARRIS, Michael John ('Pasty') (Gerrans S, nr Truro), b St Just-in-Roseland, Cornwall 25 May 1944. RHB, LB, WK. Middlesex 1964-68 (cap 1967). Nottinghamshire 1969-82 (cap 1970; benefit 1977). Eastern Province 1971-72. Wellington 1975-76. 1000 runs (11); most – 2238 (1971). Scored 9 hundreds in 1971 to equal Notts record. HS 201* Nt v Glam (Nottingham) 1973. BB 4-16 Nt v Warwks (Nottingham) 1969. F-c career: 344 matches; 19,196 runs @ 36.70, 41 hundreds; 79 wickets @ 43.78; 302 dismissals (288 ct, 14 st). Appointed 1998.

HOLDER, John Wakefield (Combermere S, Barbados), b St George, Barbados 19 Mar 1945. RHB, RFM. Hampshire 1968-72. Hat-trick 1972. HS 33 v Sussex (Hove) 1971. BB 7-79 v Glos (Gloucester) 1972. F-c career: 47 matches; 374 runs @ 10.68; 139 wickets @ 24.56. Appointed 1983. Umpired 10 Tests (1988 to 1991) and 14 LOI (1988 to 1996) including 1989-90 Nehru Cup and one Sharjah tournament.

HOLDER, Vanburn Alonza (Richmond SM, Barbados), b Bridgetown, Barbados 8 Oct 1945. RHB, RFM. Barbados 1966-78. Worcestershire 1968-80 (cap 1970; benefit 1979). Shropshire 1981. **Tests** (WI): 40 (1969 to 1978-79); 682 runs @ 14.20, HS 42 v NZ (P-o-S) 1971-72; 109 wkts @ 33.27, BB 6-28 v A (P-o-S) 1977-78. **LOI** (WI): 12. Tours (WI): E 1969, 1973, 1976; A 1975-76; I 1974-75, 1978-79; P 1973-74 (RW), 1974-75; SL 1974-75, 1978-79. HS 122 Barbados v Trinidad (Bridgetown) 1973-74. BB 7-40 Wo v Glam (Cardiff) 1974. F-c career: 311 matches; 3559 runs @ 13.03, 1 hundred; 947 wickets @ 24.48. Appointed 1992.

JESTY, Trevor Edward (Privet County SS, Gosport), b Gosport, Hants 2 Jun 1948. RHB, RM. Hampshire 1966-84 (cap 1971; benefit 1982). Surrey 1985-87 (cap 1985; captain 1985). Lancashire 1988-91 (cap 1989). Border 1973-74. GW 1974-76, 1980-81. Canterbury 1979-80. *Wisden* 1982. **LOI**: 10. Tours: WI 1982-83 (Int); Z 1988-89 (La). 1000 runs (10); most – 1645 (1982). HS 248 H v CU (Cambridge) 1984. Scored 122* La v OU (Oxford) 1991 in his final f-c innings. 50 wkts (2); most – 52 (1981). BB 7-75 H v Worcs (Southampton) 1976. F-c career: 490 matches; 21916 runs @ 32.71, 35 hundreds; 585 wickets @ 27.47. Appointed 1994.

JONES, Allan (St John's C, Horsham), b Horley, Surrey 9 Dec 1947. RHB, RFM. Sussex 1966-69. Somerset 1970-75 (cap 1972). Middlesex 1976-79 (cap 1976). Glamorgan 1980-81. Northern Transvaal 1972-73. Orange Free State 1976-77. HS 33 M v Kent (Canterbury) 1978. BB 9-51 Sm v Sussex (Hove) 1972. F-c career: 214 matches; 799 runs @ 5.39; 549 wickets @ 28.07. Appointed 1985. Umpired 1 LOI (1996).

JULIAN, Raymond (Wigston SM), b Cosby, Leics 23 Aug 1936. RHB, WK. Leicestershire 1953-71 (cap 1961). HS 51 v Worcs (Worcester) 1962. F-c career: 192 matches; 2581 runs @ 9.73; 421 dismissals (382 ct, 39 st). Appointed 1972. Umpired 2 LOI (1996 to 1997).

KITCHEN, Mervyn John (Backwell SM, Nailsea), b Nailsea, Somerset 1 Aug 1940. LHB, RM. Somerset 1960-79 (cap 1966; testimonial 1973). Tour: Rhodesia 1972-73 (Int W). 1000 runs (7); most – 1730 (1968). HS 189 v Pakistanis (Taunton) 1967. BB 1-4. F-c career: 354 matches; 15230 runs @ 26.25, 17 hundreds; 2 wickets @ 54.50. Appointed 1982. Umpired 15 Tests (1990 to 1997) and 20 LOI (1983 to 1997), including one Sharjah tournament. **Appointed to International Panel 1995.**

LEADBEATER, Barrie (Harehills SS), b Harehills, Leeds, Yorks 14 Aug 1943. RHB, RM. Yorkshire 1966-79 (cap 1969; joint benefit with G.A.Cope 1980). Tour: WI 1969-70 (DN). HS 140* v Hants (Portsmouth) 1976. F-c career: 147 matches; 5373 runs @ 25.34, 1 hundred; 1 wicket @ 5.00. Appointed 1981. Umpired 4 LOI (1983).

LLOYDS, Jeremy William (Blundells S), b Penang, Malaya 17 Nov 1954. LHB, OB. Somerset 1979-84 (cap 1982). Gloucestershire 1985-91 (cap 1985). Orange Free State 1983-88. Tour (Glos): SL 1986-87. 1000 runs (3); most – 1295 (1986). HS 132* Sm v Northants (Northampton) 1982. BB 7-88 Sm v Essex (Chelmsford) 1982. F-c career: 267 matches; 10,679 runs @ 31.04, 10 hundreds; 333 wickets @ 38.86. Appointed 1998.

PALMER, Kenneth Ernest (Southbroom SM, Devizes), b Winchester, Hants 22 Apr 1937. RHB, RFM. Brother of R. (below) and father of G.V. (Somerset 1982-88). Somerset 1955-69 (cap 1958; testimonial 1968). Tours: WI 1963-64 (Cav); P 1963-64 (Cwlth XI). **Tests**: 1 (1964-65; while coaching in South Africa); 10 runs; 1 wicket. 1000 runs (1): 1036 (1961). 100 wickets (4); most – 139 (1963). HS 125* v Northants (Northampton) 1961. BB 9-57 v Notts (Nottingham) 1963. F-c career: 314 matches; 7761 runs @ 20.64, 2 hundreds; 866 wickets @ 21.34. Appointed 1972. Umpired 22 Tests (1978 to 1994) and 19 LOI (1977 to 1994). International Panel 1994.

PALMER, Roy (Southbroom SM, Devizes), b Devizes, Wilts 12 Jul 1942. RHB, RFM. Brother of K.E. (above). Somerset 1965-70. HS 84 v Leics (Taunton) 1967. BB 6-45 v Middx (Lord's) 1967. F-c career: 74 matches; 1037 runs @ 13.29; 172 wickets @ 31.62. Appointed 1980. Umpired 2 Tests (1992 to 1993) and 8 LOI (1983 to 1995).

PLEWS, Nigel Trevor (Mundella GS, Nottingham), b Nottingham 5 Sep 1934. Former policeman (Fraud Squad). No first-class appearances. Appointed 1982. Umpired 11 Tests (1988 to 1995-96) and 16 LOI (1986 to 1996), including 2 Sharjah tournaments. International Panel 1994 to 1995-96.

SHARP, George (Elwick Road SS, Hartlepool), b West Hartlepool, Co Durham 12 Mar 1950. RHB, WK, occ LM. Northamptonshire 1968-85 (cap 1973; benefit 1982). HS 98 v Yorks (Northampton) 1983. BB 1-47. F-c career: 306 matches; 6254 runs @ 19.85; 1 wicket @ 70.00; 655 dismissals (565 ct, 90 st). Appointed 1992. Umpired 4 Tests (1996 to 1997) and 10 LOI (1995-96 to 1997), including tournaments in Sharjah (1) and Singapore (1). **Appointed to International Panel 1996.**

SHEPHERD, David Robert (Barnstaple GS; St Luke's C, Exeter), b Bideford, Devon 27 Dec 1940. RHB, RM. Gloucestershire 1965-79 (cap 1969; joint benefit with J.Davey 1978). Scored 108 on debut (v OU). Devon 1959-64. 1000 runs (2); most – 1079 (1970). HS 153 v Middx (Bristol) 1968. F-c career: 282 matches; 10672 runs @ 24.47, 12 hundreds; 2 wickets @ 53.00. Appointed 1981. Umpired 36 Tests (1985 to 1997) and 69 LOI (1983 to 1997), including 1987-88, 1991-92 and 1995-96 World Cups (1 final), 1985-86 Asia Cup and tournaments in Sharjah (5) and Canada (1). **Appointed to International Panel 1994.**

STEELE, John Frederick (Endon SS), b Brown Edge, Staffs 23 Jul 1946. RHB, SLA. Brother of D.S. (Northants, Derbys and England 1963-84). Leicestershire 1970-83 (cap 1971; benefit 1983). Glamorgan 1984-86 (cap 1984). Natal 1973-78. Staffordshire 1965-69. Tour: SA 1974-75 (DHR). 1000 runs (6); most – 1347 (1972). HS 195 Le v Derbys (Leicester) 1971. BB 7-29 Natal B v GW (Umzinto) 1973-74, and Le v Glos (Leicester) 1980. F-c career: 379 matches; 15054 runs @ 28.95, 21 hundreds; 584 wickets @ 27.04. Appointed 1997.

WHITE, Robert Arthur (Chiswick GS), b Fulham, London 6 Oct 1936. LHB, OB. Middlesex 1958-65 (cap 1963). Nottinghamshire 1966-80 (cap 1966; benefit 1974). 1000 runs (1): 1355 (1963). HS 116* Nt v Surrey (Oval) 1967. BB 7-41 Nt v Derbys (Ilkeston) 1971. F-c career: 413 matches; 12452 runs @ 23.18, 5 hundreds; 693 wickets @ 30.50. Appointed 1983.

WHITEHEAD, Alan Geoffrey Thomas, b Butleigh, Somerset 28 Oct 1940. LHB, SLA. Somerset 1957-61. HS 15 v Hants (Southampton) 1959 and v Leics (Leicester) 1960. BB 6-74 v Sussex (Eastbourne) 1959. F-c career: 38 matches; 137 runs @ 5.70; 67 wickets @ 34.41. Appointed 1970. Umpired 5 Tests (1982 to 1987) and 13 LOI (1979 to 1996).

WILLEY, Peter (Seaham SS), b Sedgefield, Co Durham 6 Dec 1949. RHB, OB. Northamptonshire 1966-83 (cap 1971; benefit 1981). Leicestershire 1984-91 (cap 1984; captain 1987). E Province 1982-85. Northumberland 1992. **Tests:** 26 (1976 to 1986); 1184 runs @ 26.90, HS 102* v WI (St John's) 1980-81; 7 wkts @ 65.14, BB 2-73 v WI (Lord's) 1980. **LOI:** 26. Tours: A 1979-80; SA 1972-73 (DHR), 1981-82 (SAB); WI 1980-81, 1985-86; I 1979-80; SL 1977-78 (DHR). 1000 runs (10); most – 1783 (1982). HS 227 Nh v Somerset (Northampton) 1976. 50 wkts (3); most – 52 (1979). BB 7-37 Nh v OU (Oxford) 1975. F-c career: 559 matches; 24361 runs @ 30.56, 44 hundreds; 756 wickets @ 30.95. Appointed 1993. Umpired 7 Tests (1995-96 to 1997) and 3 LOI (1996 to 1997). **Appointed to International Panel 1996.**

RESERVE FIRST-CLASS LIST: P.Adams, M.R.Benson, P.Carrick, N.G.Cowley, K.J.Lyons, N.A.Mallender, M.K.Reed, K.Shuttleworth.

CURRENT INTERNATIONAL PANEL: M.J.Kitchen, G.Sharp, D.R.Shepherd, P.Willey (England); D.B.Hair, S.G.Randell (Australia); V.K.Ramaswamy, S.Venkataraghavan (India); D.B.Cowie, R.S.Dunne (New Zealand); Javed Akhtar, Salim Badar (Pakistan); R.E.Koertzen, C.J.Mitchley (South Africa); B.C.Cooray, K.T.Francis (Sri Lanka); S.A.Bucknor (West Indies); I.D.Robinson, R.B.Tiffin (Zimbabwe).

1998 TEXACO TROPHY and TRIANGULAR TOURNAMENT PANEL: D.J.Constant, B.Dudleston, J.H.Hampshire, J.W.Holder, R.Julian, M.J.Kitchen, K.E.Palmer, G.Sharp, D.R.Shepherd, P.Willey.

Test Match and LOI statistics to 17 September 1997. See page 15 for key to abbreviations.

IRELAND REGISTER 1997

Full Names	Birthdate	Birthplace	Bat/Bowl	F-C Debut
BENSON, Justin David Ramsay	1. 3.67	Dublin	RHB/RM	1988
BYRNE, John Edward	17. 1.72	Dublin	RHB	1997
COOKE, Gordon	24. 7.75	Derry	RHB/RMF	1994
CURRY, Desmond John	20.12.66	Strabane	LHB/OB	1993
DAVY, John Oliver	1. 7.74	Dublin	RHB/LFM	1997
JOYCE, Edmund Christopher	22. 9.78	Dublin	LHB/RM	1997
McCALLAN, William Kyle	27. 8.75	Carrickfergus	RHB/OB	1996
McCRUM, Paul	11. 8.62	Waringston	RHB/RFM	1990
MOLINS, Gregory Leo	19. 3.75	Dublin	RHB/SLA	1996
PATTERSON, Andrew David	4. 9.75	Belfast	RHB/WK	1996
RUTHERFORD, Alan Thomas	2. 6.67	Strabane	RHB/WK	1996

SCOTLAND REGISTER 1997

Full Names	Birthdate	Birthplace	Bat/Bowl	F-C Debut
ALLINGHAM, Michael James de Grey	6. 1.65	Inverness	RHB/RM	1996
DAVIES, Andrew George	15. 5.62	Altrincham	RHB/WK	1982
DYER, Nicholas Rayner	10. 6.69	Edinburgh	RHB/OB	1997
LOCKHART, Douglas Ross	19. 1.76	Glasgow	RHB	1996
PATTERSON, Bruce Mathew Winston	29. 1.65	Ayr	RHB	1988
SALMOND, George	1.12.69	Dundee	RHB	1991
SHERIDAN, Keith Lamont Paton	26. 3.71	Glasgow	RHB/SLA	1992
STANGER, Ian Michael	5.10.71	Glasgow	RHB/RFM	1997
THOMSON, Kevin	24. 2.71	Dundee	RHB/RMF	1992
WILLIAMSON, John Greig	20.12.68	Glasgow	RHB/RM	1994
WRIGHT, Craig McIntyre	28. 4.74	Paisley	RHB/RM	1997

UNIVERSITY REGISTER 1997

CAMBRIDGE

Full Names	Birthdate	Birthplace	College	Bat/Bowl	F-C Debut
BAILEY, Matthew Richard Kelland	6.10.77	Cambridge	Magdalene	RHB/WK	1997
CHURTON, David Richard Harding	29. 3.75	Salisbury	St Catharine's	RHB/WK	1995
DAWSON, Mark William	28. 3.74	Clifton	Christ's	LHB/LM	1997
FREETH, James William Owen	9. 4.74	Bournemouth	Pembroke	RHB/OB	1995
HOUSE, William John	16. 3.76	Sheffield	Gonville & Caius	LHB/RM	1996
HOW, Edward Joseph	16. 5.74	Amersham	Gonville & Caius	RHB/LMF	1995
HUGHES, Quentin John	17.10.74	Durham City	St Edmund's	LHB/OB	1997
JANISCH, Adam Nicholas	21.10.75	Hammersmith	Trinity	RHB/RM	1995
JONES, Philip Steffan	9. 2.74	Llanelli	Homerton	RHB/RMF	1997
JONES, Robin Owen	4.10.73	Crewe	Homerton	RHB/OB	1996
MOHAMMED, Imraan	31.12.76	Solihull	St Catharine's	RHB/OB	1997
RATLEDGE, John	8. 8.74	Preston	St John's	RHB/RM	1994
SCHAFFTER, Prakash Anand	19. 6.67	Colombo	King's	RHB/RFM	1997
SINGH, Anurag	9. 9.75	Kanpur	Gonville & Caius	RHB/OB	1995
SMITH, Edward Thomas	19. 7.77	Pembury	Peterhouse	RHB/RM	1996

Full Names	Birthdate	Birthplace	College	Bat/Bowl	F-C Debut
AVERIS, James Maxwell Michael	28. 5.74	Bristol	St Cross	RHB/RMF	1997
BATTARBEE, Christopher Mark	11. 4.75	Sidcup	Keble	RHB/RM	1997
BUCHANAN, Laurence George	9. 3.76	Perivale	Keble	RHB	1997
BULL, James Jonathan	22.12.76	Leicester	Keble	RHB/OB	1996
BYRNE, Byron Walter	15. 2.72	Sydney	Balliol	RHB/OB	1997
COCKCROFT, Jonathan Richard	28. 5.77	Bradford	Oriel	RHB/LB	1997
FULTON, James Anthony Gervase	21. 9.77	Plymouth	Brasenose	LHB/RM	1997
HAYNES, James Edward	29. 9.72	Nottingham	Linacre	RHB/OB	1997
HUDSON, Roger Douglas	8. 6.67	Birmingham	Keble	RHB/RM	1997
LAUGHTON, Nigel Ewan Felix	12.10.65	Aldershot	Harris Manchester	RHB/OB	1997
LIGHTFOOT, Charles Gordon Rufus	25. 2.76	Amersham	Keble	LHB/SLA	1996
MATHER, David Peter	20.11.75	Bebington	St Hugh's	LHB/LM	1995
MORGAN, Peter Gregory	29. 9.72	Johannesburg	Keble	RHB	1997
PATEL, Chetan Morar	12. 4.72	Islington	Keble	LHB/RM	1997
PIRIHI, Nicholas Gordon	19. 4.97	Whangarei	Merton	RHB	1997
SCRINI, Alex Philip	18.11.76	Sheffield	Hertford	RHB/WK	1997
WAGH, Mark Anant	20.10.76	Birmingham	Keble	RHB/OB	1996
WRIGHT, Gavin James	15.12.73	Holmfirth	Balliol	RHB/RM	1996

YOUNG CRICKETER OF THE YEAR

This annual award, made by The Cricket Writers' Club (founded in 1946), is currently restricted to players qualified for England, Symonds meeting that requirement at the time of his award, and under the age of 23 on 1 May. In 1986 their ballot resulted in a dead heat. Only seven of their selections (marked †) have failed to win an England cap.

1950	R.Tattersall	1975	†A.Kennedy
1951	P.B.H.May	1976	G.Miller
1952	F.S.Trueman	1977	I.T.Botham
1953	M.C.Cowdrey	1978	D.I.Gower
1954	P.J.Loader	1979	P.W.G.Parker
1955	K.F.Barrington	1980	G.R.Dilley
1956	†B.Taylor	1981	M.W.Gatting
1957	M.J.Stewart	1982	N.G.Cowans
1958	†A.C.D.Ingleby-Mackenzie	1983	N.A.Foster
1959	G.Pullar	1984	R.J.Bailey
1960	D.A.Allen	1985	D.V.Lawrence
1961	P.H.Parfitt	1986	†A.A.Metcalfe
1962	P.J.Sharpe		J.J.Whitaker
1963	G.Boycott	1987	R.J.Blakey
1964	J.M.Brearley	1988	M.P.Maynard
1965	A.P.E.Knott	1989	N.Hussain
1966	D.L.Underwood	1990	M.A.Atherton
1967	A.W.Greig	1991	M.R.Ramprakash
1968	R.M.H.Cottam	1992	I.D.K.Salisbury
1969	A.Ward	1993	M.N.Lathwell
1970	C.M.Old	1994	J.P.Crawley
1971	†J.Whitehouse	1995	†A.Symonds
1972	†D.R.Owen-Thomas	1996	C.E.W.Silverwood
1973	M.Hendrick	1997	B.C.Hollioake
1974	P.H.Edmonds		

THE 1997 FIRST-CLASS SEASON
STATISTICAL HIGHLIGHTS

HIGHEST INNINGS TOTALS († *County record*)

631-7d	Warwickshire v Hampshire	Southampton
597-8d†	Glamorgan v Durham	Cardiff
592-4d	Lancashire v Surrey	The Oval
581-7d	Surrey v Northamptonshire	Northampton
569-8d	Lancashire v Hampshire	Southampton
561-8d	Lancashire v Sussex	Manchester
557	Leicestershire v Northamptonshire	Northampton
554-8d	Worcestershire v Derbyshire	Worcester
551-3d	Glamorgan v Warwickshire	Cardiff
551	Worcestershire v Northamptonshire	Northampton
549-6d	Hampshire v Warwickshire	Southampton
549	Surrey v Yorkshire	The Oval
538-2d	Worcestershire v Hampshire	Southampton
533-8d	Essex v Leicestershire	Colchester
531-9d	Surrey v Middlesex	Lord's
531	Middlesex v Northamptonshire	Lord's
527	Glamorgan v Somerset	Taunton
525-9d	Kent v Essex	Canterbury
523	Derbyshire v Hampshire	Chesterfield
515-9d	Leicestershire v Essex	Colchester
513-6d	Derbyshire v Glamorgan	Chesterfield
506	Lancashire v Durham	Manchester
501-7d	Yorkshire v Worcestershire	Leeds
501-8d	Yorkshire v Hampshire	Portsmouth
501-9d	Australia v England (*4th Test*)	Leeds

LOWEST INNINGS TOTALS († *One batsman absent/retired hurt*)

31	Glamorgan v Middlesex	Cardiff
51	Lancashire v Glamorgan	Liverpool
54	Sussex v Glamorgan (*1st innings*)	Swansea
63	Sussex v Warwickshire	Birmingham
67	Sussex v Glamorgan (*2nd innings*)	Swansea
69	Leicestershire v Worcestershire	Worcester
71	Sussex v Worcestershire	Arundel
77	England v Australia (*2nd Test*)	Lord's
86	Derbyshire v Essex	Southend
86	Durham v Gloucestershire	Cheltenham
88	Lancashire v Somerset	Taunton
97	Hampshire v Middlesex	Lord's
99†	Derbyshire v Middlesex	Lord's
99†	Gloucestershire v Middlesex	Bristol

MATCH AGGREGATES OF 1500 RUNS

Runs-Wkts

1706-23	Hampshire v Warwickshire	Southampton
1545-32	Northamptonshire v Worcestershire	Northampton
1513-30	Leicestershire v Lancashire	Leicester

BATSMEN'S MATCH (*Qualification: 1200 runs, average 70 per wicket*)
74.17 Hampshire (549-6d, 274-9) v Warwickshire (631-7d, 252-1d)   Southampton

FIRST TO INDIVIDUAL TARGETS

1000 RUNS	S.P.James	Glamorgan	July 18
2000 RUNS	No instance – most: 1,775 runs – S.P.James (Glamorgan)		
100 WICKETS	No instance – most: 83 wickets – A.M.Smith (Gloucestershire)		

DOUBLE HUNDREDS

K.L.T.Arthurton	200*	MCC v Pakistan A	Shenley
K.J.Barnett	210*	Derbyshire v Yorkshire	Derby
M.L.Hayden	235*	Hampshire v Warwickshire	Southampton
G.A.Hick	303*	Worcestershire v Hampshire	Southampton
N.Hussain	207	England v Australia (*1st Test*)	Birmingham
J.J.B.Lewis	210*	Durham v Oxford U	Oxford
G.D.Lloyd	225	Lancashire v Yorkshire	Leeds
H.Morris	233*	Glamorgan v Warwickshire	Cardiff
M.J.Powell	200*	Glamorgan v Oxford U	Oxford
P.J.Prichard	224	Essex v Kent	Canterbury
A.S.Rollins	210	Derbyshire v Hampshire	Chesterfield
Salim Elahi	229	Pakistan A v Worcestershire	Worcester
A.J.Stewart	271*	Surrey v Yorkshire	The Oval
G.P.Thorpe	222	Surrey v Glamorgan	The Oval
V.J.Wells	224	Leicestershire v Middlesex	Lord's
W.P.C.Weston	205	Worcestershire v Northamptonshire	Northampton
S.Young	237	Gloucestershire v Derbyshire	Cheltenham

HUNDREDS IN THREE CONSECUTIVE INNINGS
S.P.James (Glamorgan) 130 v Worcs (Worcester), 103 and 113 v Northants (Abergavenny)

HUNDRED IN EACH INNINGS OF A MATCH

M.L.Hayden	235*	119	Hampshire v Warwickshire	Southampton
D.L.Hemp	138	114*†	Warwickshire v Hampshire	Southampton
S.P.James	103	113	Glamorgan v Northamptonshire	Abergavenny
M.A.Wagh	116	101	Oxford U v Glamorgan	Oxford
S.R.Waugh	108	116	Australia v England (*3rd Test*)	Manchester

† *In contrived circumstances*

FASTEST AUTHENTIC HUNDRED (SIR WALTER LAWRENCE TROPHY)
G.D.Lloyd	73 balls	Lancashire v Leicestershire	Leicester

HUNDRED BEFORE LUNCH

		Day		
C.J.Adams	0-107*	1	Derbyshire v Durham	Chester-le-Street
K.J.Barnett	0-105*	3	Derbyshire v Leicestershire	Leicester
D.L.Hemp	0-114*†	4	Warwickshire v Hampshire	Southampton
S.P.James	0-109*	1	Glamorgan v Durham	Cardiff
N.V.Knight	0-119*†	4	Warwickshire v Hampshire	Southampton
G.D.Lloyd	0-100*	4	Lancashire v Leicestershire	Leicester
A.S.Rollins	0-108*	1	Derbyshire v Glamorgan	Chesterfield

† *In contrived circumstances*

HUNDRED ON FIRST-CLASS DEBUT
M.J.Powell	200*	Glamorgan v Oxford U	Oxford

CARRYING BAT THROUGH COMPLETED INNINGS
J.J.B.Lewis	158*	Durham (251) v Kent	Darlington
M.R.Ramprakash	113*	Middlesex (256) v Kent	Lord's

FIRST-WICKET PARTNERSHIP OF 100 IN EACH INNINGS
110	213	J.S.Laney/M.L.Hayden	Hampshire v Derbyshire	Chesterfield
144	153	V.J.Wells/D.L.Maddy	Leicestershire v Derbyshire	Leicester

OTHER NOTABLE PARTNERSHIPS († *County record*)

First Wicket
290	J.J.B.Lewis/P.D.Collingwood	Durham v Oxford U	Oxford
259	N.T.Wood/M.A.Atherton	Lancashire v Surrey	The Oval

Second Wicket
417†	K.J.Barnett/T.A.Tweats	Derbyshire v Yorkshire	Derby
317*	J.H.Kallis/M.R.Ramprakash	Middlesex v Worcestershire	Kidderminster
257*	P.E.Wellings/M.W.Gatting	Middlesex v Cambridge U	Cambridge

Third Wicket
438*†	G.A.Hick/T.M.Moody	Worcestershire v Hampshire	Southampton
317	N.Hussain/S.G.Law	Essex v Leicestershire	Colchester
316*†	A.S.Rollins/K.J.Barnett	Derbyshire v Leicestershire	Leicester

Fourth Wicket
288	N.Hussain/G.P.Thorpe	England v Australia (*1st Test*)	Birmingham
204†	J.J.B.Lewis/J.Boiling	Durham v Derbyshire	Chester-le-Street

Fifth Wicket
268	M.T.G.Elliott/R.T.Ponting	Australia v England (*4th Test*)	Leeds
244	S.Young/M.W.Alleyne	Gloucestershire v Derbyshire	Cheltenham
241	W.P.C.Weston/D.A.Leatherdale	Worcestershire v Northamptonshire	Northampton
225*	N.C.Johnson/B.F.Smith	Leicestershire v Kent	Canterbury

Seventh Wicket
279†	R.J.Harden/G.D.Rose	Somerset v Sussex	Taunton
248†	G.D.Lloyd/I.D.Austin	Lancashire v Yorkshire	Leeds
205*	M.L.Hayden/S.D.Udal	Hampshire v Warwickshire	Southampton
205	J.M.Dakin/D.J.Millns	Leicestershire v Northamptonshire	Northampton

Eighth Wicket
186	N.M.K.Smith/D.R.Brown	Warwickshire v Gloucestershire	Birmingham

Ninth Wicket
171†	M.A.Ealham/P.A.Strang	Kent v Nottinghamshire	Nottingham

Tenth Wicket
183	S.A.Marsh/B.J.Phillips	Kent v Sussex	Horsham
146	G.Chapple/P.J.Martin	Lancashire v Durham	Manchester
101	P.A.Nixon/J.Ormond	Leicestershire v Gloucestershire	Leicester
100*	J.O.Davy/P.McCrum	Ireland v Scotland	Dublin

EIGHT OR MORE WICKETS IN AN INNINGS
M.M.Betts	9-64	Durham v Northamptonshire	Northampton
D.R.Brown	8-89	ECB Select XI v Pakistan A	Chelmsford
K.D.James	8-49	Hampshire v Somerset	Basingstoke
G.D.McGrath	8-38	Australia v England (*2nd Test*)	Lord's
P.J.Martin	8-32	Lancashire v Middlesex	Uxbridge
Waqar Younis	8-17	Glamorgan v Sussex	Swansea

TEN OR MORE WICKETS IN A MATCH
H.A.G.Anthony	10-113	MCC v Pakistan A	Shenley
M.M.Betts	13-143	Durham v Northamptonshire	Northampton
M.N.Bowen	11-109	Nottinghamshire v Derbyshire	Nottingham
D.R.Brown	11-154	ECB Select XI v Pakistan A	Chelmsford
S.J.E.Brown	10-141	Durham v Leicestershire	Leicester
P.A.J.DeFreitas	(2) 10- 99	Derbyshire v Kent	Canterbury
	10-172	Derbyshire v Yorkshire	Derby
A.A.Donald	10-119	Warwickshire v Surrey	Birmingham
P.M.Hutchison	11-102	Yorkshire v Pakistan A	Leeds
R.K.Illingworth	10-147	Worcestershire v Hampshire	Southampton
K.D.James	13- 93	Hampshire v Somerset	Basingstoke
G.Keedy	10-173	Lancashire v Surrey	The Oval
D.E.Malcolm	(2) 11-125	Derbyshire v Middlesex	Lord's
	10- 65	Derbyshire v Lancashire	Derby

P.J.Martin	13- 79	Lancashire v Middlesex	Uxbridge
D.J.Millns	10-130	Leicestershire v Durham	Leicester
Saqlain Mushtaq (2)	10-128	Surrey v Durham	The Oval
	10-116	Surrey v Middlesex	Lord's
A.Sheriyar	10- 63	Worcestershire v Sussex	Arundel
K.J.Shine	11- 97	Somerset v Lancashire	Taunton
C.E.W.Silverwood	12-148	Yorkshire v Kent	Leeds
A.M.Smith (3)	10-106	Gloucestershire v Hampshire	Bristol
	10-132	Gloucestershire v Yorkshire	Leeds
	10-106	Gloucestershire v Derbyshire	Cheltenham
P.A.Strang	11-186	Kent v Lancashire	Manchester
P.M.Such	11-215	Essex v Yorkshire	Ilford
J.P.Taylor	10-141	Northamptonshire v Nottinghamshire	Northampton
P.C.R.Tufnell	11- 93	England v Australia (6th Test)	The Oval
Waqar Younis	10-134	Glamorgan v Northamptonshire	Abergavenny
G.Welch	11-140	Warwickshire v Lancashire	Blackpool

HAT-TRICKS

P.J.Franks		Nottinghamshire v Warwickshire	Nottingham
C.M.Patel		Oxford U v Warwickshire	Oxford
Saqlain Mushtaq		Surrey v Middlesex	Lord's
C.M.Tolley		Nottinghamshire v Leicestershire	Leicester
Waqar Younis		Glamorgan v Lancashire	Liverpool

60 OVERS IN AN INNINGS

| P.M.Such | 86-49-94-4 | Essex v Leicestershire | Colchester |

SIX OR MORE WICKET-KEEPING DISMISSALS IN AN INNINGS

I.A.Healy	6 ct	Australia v England (1st Test)	Birmingham
S.A.Marsh	6 ct	Kent v Nottinghamshire	Nottingham
W.M.Noon	6 ct	Nottinghamshire v Derbyshire	Nottingham
A.J.Stewart	6 ct	England v Australia (3rd Test)	Manchester

NINE OR MORE WICKET-KEEPING DISMISSALS IN A MATCH

| Javed Qadir | 9 ct | Pakistan A v Nottinghamshire | Nottingham |
| P.A.Nixon | 9 ct | Leicestershire v Nottinghamshire | Leicester |

NO BYES CONCEDED IN TOTAL OF 500 OR MORE

561-8d	P.Moores	Sussex v Lancashire	Manchester
531	D.Ripley	Northamptonshire v Middlesex	Lord's
527	R.J.Turner	Somerset v Glamorgan	Taunton
523	A.N.Aymes	Hampshire v Derbyshire	Chesterfield
501-7d	S.J.Rhodes	Worcestershire v Yorkshire	Leeds
501-8d	A.N.Aymes	Hampshire v Yorkshire	Portsmouth

SIXTY EXTRAS IN AN INNINGS

Ext	B	LB	W	NB		
86	10	16	8	52	Somerset (463) v Surrey	The Oval
72	17	13	–	42	Yorkshire (378) v Pakistan A	Leeds
71	6	27	2	36	Glamorgan (551-3d) v Warwickshire	Cardiff
71	1	26	28	16	Nottinghamshire (263) v Lancashire	Manchester
64	6	6	14	38	Hampshire (549-6d) v Warwickshire	Southampton
60	16	8	16	20	Hampshire (415-5d) v Oxford U	Oxford

Under ECB regulations (Test matches excluded), two extras were scored for each no-ball, in addition to any runs scored off that ball, and, for the first time, two extras were also scored for each wide. There were a further 16 instances of 50-59 extras in an innings.

1997 FIRST-CLASS AVERAGES

These averages involve the 478 cricketers who played in the 196 first-class matches staged in the British Isles during the 1997 season.

'Cap' denotes the season in which the player was awarded a 1st XI cap by the county he represented in 1997. Durham award caps upon joining the playing staff and not on merit.

Team abbreviations: A – Australia(ns); CU – Cambridge University; De – Derbyshire; Du – Durham; E – England; EA – England A; ECB – England & Wales Cricket Board Select XI; Ex – Essex; Gm – Glamorgan; Gs – Gloucestershire; H – Hampshire; Ire – Ireland; K – Kent; La – Lancashire; Le – Leicestershire; M – Middlesex; MCC – Marylebone Cricket Club; Nh – Northamptonshire; Nt – Nottinghamshire; OU – Oxford University; PA – Pakistan A; R – The Rest; Sc – Scotland; Sm – Somerset; Sx – Surrey; Sx – Sussex; Wa – Warwickshire; Wo – Worcestershire; Y – Yorkshire.

† Left-handed batsman

BATTING AND FIELDING

	Cap	M	I	NO	HS	Runs	Avge	100	50	Ct/St
Abdul Razzak (PA)	–	6	9	2	62	216	30.85	–	2	–
Adams, C.J.(De/R)	1992	15	25	1	108	767	31.95	2	3	18
†Afzaal, U.(Nt)	–	17	29	2	80	720	26.66	–	5	9
Aldred, P.(De)	–	8	8	2	83	133	22.16	–	1	7
Ali Naqvi (PA)	–	8	13	–	114	362	27.84	1	1	4
Ali Rizvi (PA)	–	8	13	1	28	77	6.41	–	–	5
Alleyne, M.W.(Gs)	1990	19	30	4	169	1059	40.73	1	8	14
Allingham, M.J.D.(Sc)	–	2	2	–	13	13	6.50	–	–	1
Altree, D.A.(Wa)	–	1	–	–						
Amin, R.M.(Sy)	–	4	6	3	4*	11	3.66	–	–	2
Andrew, S.J.W.(Ex)	–	3	3	–	24	27	9.00	–	–	–
Anthony, H.A.G.(MCC)	–	1	1	–	0	0	0.00	–	–	1
Archer, G.F.(Nt)	1995	12	22	2	81	375	18.75	–	2	15
†Arthurton, K.L.T.(MCC)	–	1	1	1	200*	200	–	1	–	1
Asif Din (MCC)	–	1	2	1	12*	16	16.00	–	–	–
Astle, N.J.(Nt)	–	10	16	–	100	644	40.25	2	3	11
Atherton, M.A.(La/E)	1989	16	28	2	149	853	32.80	2	5	8
Athey, C.W.J.(Sx)	1993	12	21	2	138*	682	35.89	1	5	9
†Austin, I.D.(La)	1990	17	25	4	95	825	39.28	–	8	6
Averis, J.M.M.(Gs/OU)	–	10	15	4	42	276	25.09	–	–	2
Aymes, A.N.(H)	1991	18	23	4	96*	442	23.26	–	1	35/7
Azhar Mahmood (PA)	–	8	13	1	92	379	31.58	–	3	2
Badenhorst, A.(MCC)	–	1	1	–	0	0	0.00	–	–	–
Bailey, M.R.K.(CU)	–	1	1	1	6*	6	–	–	–	1/1
Bailey, R.J.(Nh)	1985	17	30	5	117*	1078	43.12	3	5	19
Ball, M.C.J.(Gs)	1996	18	27	3	50	587	24.45	–	1	24
Barnett, K.J.(De)	1982	15	24	3	210*	1055	50.23	3	5	3
Bates, J.J.(Sx)	–	7	9	2	47	113	16.14	–	–	6
Bates, R.T.(Nt)	–	8	12	5	21	69	9.85	–	–	6
†Batt, C.J.(Sx)	–	1	–	–						1
Battarbee, C.M.(OU)	–	7	8	6	10*	29	14.50	–	–	1
Batty, G.J.(Y)	–	1	2	–	18	18	9.00	–	–	–
Batty, J.N.(Sy)	–	3	3	1	23*	54	27.00	–	–	7/1
Bell, M.A.V.(Wa)	–	3	2	–	30	30	15.00	–	–	1
Benjamin, J.E.(Sy)	1993	11	15	6	35	152	16.88	–	–	–
Benson, J.D.R.(Ire)	–	1	2	1	61*	61	61.00	–	1	1
Berry, D.S.(A)	–	2	2	–	12	21	10.50	–	–	9/1

118

	Cap	M	I	NO	HS	Runs	Avge	100	50	Ct/St
Betts, M.M.(Du)	1994	13	19	1	35	207	11.50	–	–	1
†Bevan, M.G.(A)	–	11	16	3	104*	463	35.61	1	3	6
Bichel, A.J.(A)	–	1	–	–	–	–	–	–	–	–
†Bicknell, D.J.(Sy)	1990	9	15	–	162	594	39.60	2	1	1
Bicknell, M.P.(Sy)	1989	15	20	5	74	305	20.33	–	2	8
†Blackwell, I.D.(De)	–	4	5	–	42	51	10.20	–	–	–
Blain, J.A.R.(Nh)	–	1	1	–	0	0	0.00	–	–	1
Blakey, R.J.(Y)	1987	18	24	6	92	680	37.77	–	6	49/4
Blewett, G.S.(A)	–	12	18	1	125	686	40.35	2	4	17
Bloomfield, T.F.(M)	–	4	3	2	4	4	4.00	–	–	1
Boiling, J.(Du)	1995	17	26	4	62	334	15.18	–	1	13
Boon, D.C.(Du)	1997	18	30	3	117	1144	42.37	3	8	19
Boswell, S.A.J.(Nh)	–	9	12	3	35	122	13.55	–	–	2
†Boulton, N.R.(Sm)	–	1	2	–	14	15	7.50	–	–	–
Bovill, J.N.B.(H)	–	9	9	2	27	65	9.28	–	–	5
Bowen, M.N.(Nt)	1997	15	19	6	32	145	11.15	–	–	5
Bowler, P.D.(Sm)	1995	16	26	1	123	666	26.64	1	5	20
Brimson, M.T.(Le)	–	7	7	2	30*	59	11.80	–	–	3
Brown, A.D.(Sy)	1994	14	21	1	170*	848	42.40	3	2	11
Brown, D.R.(Wa/ECB)	1995	17	24	3	79	504	24.00	–	4	9
Brown, J.F.(Nh)	–	6	8	4	16*	25	6.25	–	–	2
Brown, K.R.(M)	1990	19	29	9	144*	601	30.05	1	–	47/3
Brown, S.J.E.(Du/R)	1992	17	24	5	30	121	6.36	–	–	2
Buchanan, L.G.(OU)	–	8	14	4	43*	168	16.80	–	–	1
Bull, J.J.(OU)	–	3	5	1	30	49	12.25	–	–	–
Burns, M.(Sm)	–	14	21	1	82	510	25.50	–	4	8/1
Butcher, G.P.(Gm)	–	11	11	2	101*	296	32.88	1	1	1
†Butcher, M.A.(Sy/E/EA)	1996	19	34	1	153	1068	32.36	1	7	28
†Byas, D.(Y)	1991	20	33	4	128	1319	45.48	3	9	24
Byrne, B.W.(OU)	–	11	20	–	49	354	17.70	–	–	2
Byrne, J.E.(Ire)	–	1	2	1	12*	19	19.00	–	–	1
Caddick, A.R.(Sm/E)	1992	18	22	4	56*	321	17.83	–	1	5
Campbell, C.L.(Du)	1996	1	–	–	–	–	–	–	–	–
Capel, D.J.(Nh)	1986	4	7	–	57	140	20.00	–	1	1
†Carpenter, J.R.(Sx)	–	3	6	–	63	153	25.50	–	1	2
Cassar, M.E.(De)	–	7	8	1	78	227	32.42	–	2	2
Chapman, C.A.(Y)	–	2	4	–	80	139	34.75	–	1	3/1
Chapman, R.J.(Wo)	–	6	4	1	7*	10	3.33	–	–	2
Chapple, G.(La/EA)	1994	11	14	4	66	237	23.70	–	2	2
Chilton, M.J.(La)	–	1	1	–	9	9	9.00	–	–	1
Church, M.J.(Gs)	–	2	4	–	53	73	18.25	–	1	–
Churton, D.R.H.(CU)	–	7	7	1	44	177	29.50	–	–	9/1
Clarke, V.P.(De)	–	19	30	4	99	847	35.29	–	5	9
Cockcroft, J.R.(OU)	–	1	1	–	1	1	1.00	–	–	–
Collingwood, P.D.(Du)	1996	8	13	1	107	316	26.33	1	1	11
Connor, C.A.(H)	1988	5	4	2	12*	34	17.00	–	–	–
Cooke, G.(Ire)	–	1	1	–	0	0	0.00	–	–	1
Cork, D.G.(De)	1993	6	9	1	55*	192	24.00	–	2	4
Cosker, D.A.(Gm/R)	–	16	9	5	7	16	4.00	–	–	4
Cottey, P.A.(Gm)	1992	17	21	4	83	475	27.94	–	2	15
Cowan, A.P.(Ex)	1997	16	26	6	77	447	22.35	–	1	7
Cowdrey, G.R.(K)	1988	9	15	–	101	442	29.46	1	1	7
†Cox, D.M.(Du)	1993	4	3	–	24	46	15.33	–	–	1
Crawley, J.P.(La/E)	1994	16	25	2	133	1141	49.60	3	7	11
Croft, R.D.B.(Gm/E)	1992	18	26	1	86	652	26.08	–	4	14
Cunliffe, R.J.(Gs)	–	9	14	1	61	273	21.00	–	1	4

	Cap	M	I	NO	HS	Runs	Avge	100	50	Ct/St
Curran, K.M.(Nh)	1992	15	26	4	159	1032	46.90	2	6	8
†Curry, D.J.(Ire)	–	1	2	–	6	9	4.50	–	–	–
Curtis, T.S.(Wo)	1984	13	21	1	160	742	37.10	4	1	9
†Dakin, J.M.(Le)	–	4	5	1	190	311	77.75	2	–	2
Dale, A.(Gm)	1992	19	27	4	142*	860	37.39	2	5	6
Daley, J.A.(Du)	1992	2	2	–	39	46	23.00	–	–	2
Davies, A.G.(Sc)	–	1	1	–	10	10	10.00	–	–	2
Davies, M.K.(Nh)	–	6	9	4	17	49	9.80	–	–	2
Davis, R.P.(Gs)	–	9	12	–	39	135	11.25	–	–	9
Davy, J.O.(Ire)	–	1	2	1	51*	53	53.00	–	1	–
Dawood, I.(Wo)	–	1	2	1	10*	10	10.00	–	–	1/2
†Dawson, M.W.(CU)	–	4	7	–	23	35	5.00	–	–	1
Dawson, R.I.(Gs)	–	8	14	–	100	329	23.50	1	1	3
†Dean, K.J.(De)	–	10	12	5	21*	79	11.28	–	–	2
DeFreitas, P.A.J.(De)	1994	19	24	1	96	484	21.04	–	2	5
Dimond, M.(Sm)	–	1	1	–	4	4	4.00	–	–	–
Donald, A.A.(Wa)	1989	11	13	6	29	140	20.00	–	–	5
†Dowman, M.P.(Nt)	–	19	33	1	149	1091	34.09	3	5	11
Drakes, V.C.(Sx)	1996	10	18	1	48	221	13.00	–	–	7
Dutch, K.P.(M)	–	7	9	2	79	138	19.71	–	1	2
Dyer, N.R.(Sc)	–	1	1	1	0*	–	–	–	–	1
Ealham, M.A.(K/E/EA)	1992	18	30	10	139	1055	52.75	3	6	12
†Ecclestone, S.C.(Sm)	1997	13	23	2	133	951	45.28	3	4	12
Edmond, M.D.(Wa)	–	3	3	1	21	35	17.50	–	–	1
Edwards, A.D.(Sx)	–	6	10	2	20	66	8.25	–	–	5
Edwards, G.J.M.(Gm)	–	1	–	–	–	–	–	–	–	–
†Elliott, M.T.G.(A)	–	12	19	–	199	1091	57.42	4	5	7
Emburey, J.E.(Nh)	–	3	3	–	39	39	13.00	–	–	1
Evans, A.W.(Gm)	–	2	3	–	31	61	20.33	–	–	1
Evans, K.P.(Nt)	1990	15	18	1	47	208	12.23	–	–	6
†Fairbrother, N.H.(La)	1985	16	24	2	132	887	40.31	2	4	19
Farhan Adil (PA)	–	5	9	–	50	198	22.00	–	1	3
Fazal-e-Akber (PA)	–	2	3	1	6	11	5.50	–	–	–
†Fisher, I.D.(Y)	–	2	4	–	37	75	18.75	–	–	1
†Flanagan, I.N.(Ex)	–	2	3	1	40	72	36.00	–	–	–
Fleming, M.V.(K)	1990	18	31	4	138	790	29.25	1	4	5
Flintoff, A.(La)	–	5	8	–	117	243	30.37	1	1	4
†Flower, A.(MCC)	–	1	1	–	14	14	14.00	–	–	1
Flower, G.W.(MCC)	–	1	1	–	78	78	78.00	–	1	1
†Foley, G.I.(MCC)	–	1	1	–	4	4	4.00	–	–	1
Follett, D.(Nh)	–	1	2	–	3	3	1.50	–	–	–
Fordham, A.(Nh)	1990	9	17	2	85*	673	44.86	–	6	10
Foster, M.J.(Du)	1996	14	24	–	129	575	23.95	1	3	2
Francis, N.B.(MCC)	–	1	1	–	1	1	1.00	–	–	1
Francis, S.R.G.(H)	–	1	2	–	4	8	4.00	–	–	–
†Franks, P.J.(Nt)	–	14	19	6	50	280	21.53	–	1	7
Fraser, A.R.C.(M)	1988	19	23	6	35	244	14.35	–	–	4
Freeth, J.W.O.(CU)	–	7	5	2	7*	9	3.00	–	–	1
†Frost, T.(Wa)	–	9	11	2	56	158	17.55	–	1	27/2
Fulton, D.P.(K)	–	16	29	3	110	953	36.65	1	4	23
†Fulton, J.A.G.(OU)	–	10	19	–	78	451	23.73	–	4	6
Gallian, J.E.R.(La/EA)	1994	11	19	2	106	506	29.76	1	3	12
Garaway, M.(MCC)	–	1	1	–	5	5	5.00	–	–	1
Gatting, M.W.(M)	1977	19	29	2	160*	1053	39.00	2	4	23
Gie, N.A.(Nt)	–	3	6	–	50	85	14.16	–	1	4
†Gilchrist, A.C.(A)	–	1	1	1	9*	9	–	–	–	3

120

	Cap	M	I	NO	HS	Runs	Avge	100	50	Ct/St
Giles, A.F.(Wa/ECB)	–	16	20	4	97	624	39.00	–	5	4
Gillespie, J.N.(A)	–	8	9	2	28*	67	9.57	–	–	5
Gooch, G.A.(Ex)	1975	10	17	1	56	369	23.06	–	2	12
Gough, D.(Y/E)	1993	12	16	1	58	196	13.06	–	1	–
Grayson, A.P.(Ex/ECB)	1996	19	28	3	105	1022	40.88	1	6	20
Green, R.J.(La)	–	4	5	2	51	93	31.00	–	1	1
Greenfield, K.(Sx)	1996	11	21	–	108	372	17.71	1	–	12
Griffiths, S.P.(De)	–	1	1	–	1	1	1.00	–	–	3
Habib, A.(Le)	–	9	14	4	175*	397	39.70	1	1	4
Hamilton, G.M.(Y)	–	11	16	2	49	240	17.14	–	–	3
Hancock, T.H.C.(Gs)	–	19	31	3	100*	854	30.50	1	5	10
Hansen, T.M.(H)	–	1	2	1	19	31	31.00	–	–	–
Harden, R.J.(Sm)	1989	7	11	2	136*	395	43.88	2	1	3
Harris, A.J.(De/EA)	1996	18	24	4	36	171	8.55	–	–	9
Hartley, P.J.(Y)	1987	9	10	–	39	121	12.10	–	–	3
Harvey, M.E.(La)	–	2	4	–	25	49	12.25	–	–	1
Hasan Raza (PA)	–	6	10	–	96	349	34.90	–	4	3
†Hayden, M.L.(H)	1997	17	30	3	235*	1446	53.55	4	7	13
Hayhurst, A.N.(De)	–	2	2	–	6	6	3.00	–	–	3
Haynes, G.R.(Wo)	1994	17	25	3	70	794	36.09	–	6	5
Haynes, J.E.(OU)	–	2	4	–	9	13	3.25	–	–	–
Haynes, J.J.(La)	–	2	3	–	21	41	13.66	–	–	12
Headley, D.W.(K/E/EA)	1993	12	17	5	40	166	13.83	–	–	3
Healy, I.A.(A)	–	12	16	4	63	407	33.91	–	1	39/4
Hegg, W.K.(La/EA)	1989	17	23	5	77*	456	25.33	–	5	37/2
†Hemp, D.L.(Wa/ECB)	1997	18	31	4	138	1107	41.00	3	5	9
Herzberg, S.(Sm)	–	7	8	3	56	207	41.40	–	1	2
†Hewitt, J.P.(M)	–	18	21	4	75	264	15.52	–	1	6
Hewson, D.R.(Gs)	–	3	4	–	42	56	14.00	–	–	3
Hibbert, A.J.E.(Ex)	–	1	1	–	17	17	17.00	–	–	3
Hick, G.A.(Wo)	1986	18	28	6	303*	1524	69.27	6	4	20
Hindson, J.E.(Nt)	–	3	4	2	42*	54	27.00	–	–	2
†Hodgson, T.P.(Ex)	–	3	6	–	44	101	16.83	–	–	–
Hoggard, M.J.(Y)	–	1	2	1	1*	2	2.00	–	–	–
Hollioake, A.J.(Sy/E/EA)	1995	16	25	1	182	891	37.12	1	6	15
Hollioake, B.C.(Sy/E/R)	–	14	22	1	76	559	26.61	–	3	13
†Holloway, P.C.L.(Sm)	1997	19	34	4	106	905	30.16	1	5	12
†House, W.J.(K/CU)	–	10	14	1	94	331	25.46	–	2	11
How, E.J.(CU)	–	8	4	1	0*	0	0.00	–	–	1
Hudson, R.D.(OU)	–	11	20	2	62	202	11.22	–	1	2
Hughes, J.G.(Nh)	–	2	1	1	5*	5	–	–	–	–
†Hughes, Q.J.(CU)	–	8	12	3	47*	197	21.88	–	1	1
Humphries, S.(Sx)	–	2	3	1	41*	52	26.00	–	–	6
Hussain, N.(Ex/E)	1989	16	28	–	207	1081	38.60	4	3	17
†Hutchison, P.M.(Y)	–	7	8	7	15*	29	29.00	–	–	1
†Hutton, S.(Du)	1992	7	13	1	95	258	21.50	–	1	1
Hyam, B.J.(Ex)	–	7	10	2	26	79	9.87	–	–	15
Igglesden, A.P.(K)	1989	6	8	3	3	6	1.20	–	–	1
Illingworth, R.K.(Wo)	1986	5	4	2	112	157	78.50	1	–	3
†Ilott, M.C.(Ex)	1993	13	20	5	47	290	19.33	–	1	2
Innes, K.J.(Nh)	–	1	1	1	8*	8	–	–	–	–
Irani, R.C.(Ex)	1994	16	24	1	123*	793	34.47	3	3	5
Irfan Fazil (PA)	–	3	5	2	19	43	14.33	–	–	–
†James, K.D.(H)	1989	10	15	2	85	359	27.61	–	5	5
James, S.P.(Gm)	1992	18	30	4	162	1775	68.26	7	8	14
Janisch, A.N.(CU)	–	4	3	–	11	18	6.00	–	–	–

	Cap	M	I	NO	HS	Runs	Avge	100	50	Ct/St
Jarvis, P.W.(Sx)	1994	11	18	2	64	374	23.37	–	4	5
Javed Qadir (PA)	–	9	15	4	61	277	25.18	–	2	26/1
Jeh, M.P.W.(MCC)	–	1	1	–	30	30	30.00	–	–	–
†Johnson, N.C.(Le)	1997	12	18	5	150	819	63.00	2	5	13
Johnson, P.(Nt)	1986	16	27	4	96*	942	42.81	–	8	12
Johnson, R.L.(M)	1995	18	24	1	39	320	13.91	–	–	6
Jones, D.M.(De)	1996	7	12	1	99*	458	41.63	–	5	8
Jones, P.S.(Sm/CU)	–	10	13	3	36	142	14.20	–	–	4
Jones, R.O.(CU)	–	8	11	2	60	325	36.11	–	3	4
†Joyce, E.C.(Ire)	–	1	2	–	43	56	28.00	–	–	1
Julian, B.P.(A)	–	5	5	1	71	162	40.50	–	2	4
Kallis, J.H.(M)	1997	16	25	3	172*	1034	47.00	4	4	15
Kasprowicz, M.S.(A)	–	10	8	3	17	56	11.20	–	–	8
Keech, M.(H)	–	10	16	4	127	518	43.16	2	1	10
†Keedy, G.(La)	–	8	8	7	6*	11	11.00	–	–	1
Kendall, W.S.(H)	–	12	19	2	76	413	24.29	–	1	6
Kennis, G.J.(Sy)	–	3	5	–	24	49	9.80	–	–	3
Kenway, D.A.(H)	–	1	2	1	20*	22	22.00	–	–	1
Kerr, J.I.D.(Sm)	–	5	6	1	35	133	26.60	–	–	1
†Kettleborough, R.A.(Y)	–	3	5	–	10	22	4.40	–	–	2
Khan, A.A.(Sx)	–	15	24	5	52	291	15.31	–	1	4
Khan, G.A.(De)	–	3	5	1	62*	95	23.75	–	1	–
†Khan, W.G.(Wa)	–	3	5	–	43	102	20.40	–	–	2
Killeen, N.(Du)	1995	3	3	2	15	24	24.00	–	–	2
Kirtley, R.J.(Sx)	–	11	16	7	15*	49	5.44	–	–	4
†Knight, N.V.(Wa)	1995	11	17	3	119*	689	49.21	2	3	8
Knott, J.A.(Sy)	–	5	9	3	27*	118	19.66	–	–	8/1
Krikken, K.M.(De)	1992	19	27	4	72	558	24.26	–	3	53/2
Lacey, S.J.(De)	–	6	8	4	50	129	32.25	–	1	1
Lampitt, S.R.(Wo)	1989	15	17	7	52	277	27.70	–	1	16
Laney, J.S.(H/R)	1996	15	27	1	95	848	32.61	–	6	6
†Langer, J.L.(A)	–	6	10	3	152*	312	44.57	1	1	5
Lathwell, M.N.(Sm)	1992	20	34	1	95	912	27.63	–	6	11
Laughton, N.E.F.(OU)	–	1	2	–	5	6	3.00	–	–	1
Lavender, M.P.(MCC)	–	1	2	1	6*	6	6.00	–	–	3
Law, D.R.(Ex)	1996	19	29	–	81	492	16.96	–	2	11
Law, S.G.(Ex)	1996	17	28	2	175	1482	57.00	5	8	19
Law, W.L.(Gm)	–	1	1	1	38*	38	–	–	–	–
Lawrence, D.V.(Gs)	1985	4	6	3	23*	32	10.66	–	–	1
Leatherdale, D.A.(Wo)	1994	17	25	8	129	886	52.11	2	5	15
Lee, S.(A)	–	1	1	–	1	1	1.00	–	–	1
†Lehmann, D.S.(Y)	1997	17	27	2	182	1575	63.00	4	10	9
Lenham, N.J.(Sx)	1990	7	12	–	93	290	24.16	–	2	2
Lewis, C.C.(Sy)	1996	13	19	2	76	389	22.88	–	1	10
Lewis, J.(Gs)	–	15	19	8	30	193	17.54	–	–	2
Lewis, J.J.B.(Du/ECB)	1997	18	32	4	210*	1252	44.71	3	5	10
†Lightfoot, C.G.R.(OU)	–	9	16	–	61	289	18.06	–	1	2
†Llong, N.J.(K)	1993	8	14	–	99	256	18.28	–	2	9
Lloyd, G.D.(La)	1992	16	24	2	225	1073	48.77	4	5	17
Lockhart, D.R.(Sc)	–	1	2	1	77*	96	96.00	–	1	1
Loye, M.B.(Nh)	1994	8	15	3	86	412	34.33	–	2	2
Lugsden, S.(Du)	1994	1	2	1	4	4	4.00	–	–	–
Lynch, M.A.(Gs)	1995	12	19	1	64	465	25.83	–	3	9
McCague, M.J.(K)	1992	11	17	6	53*	190	17.27	–	1	3
McCallan, W.K.(Ire)	–	1	2	–	65	112	56.00	–	1	1
McCrum, P.(Ire)	–	1	1	1	44*	44	–	–	–	1

	Cap	M	I	NO	HS	Runs	Avge	100	50	Ct/St
MacGill, S.C.G.(Sm)	–	1	2	–	25	32	16.00	–	–	–
McGrath, A.(Y/EA)	–	15	25	1	141	832	34.66	2	3	5
McGrath, G.D.(A)	–	11	10	6	20*	25	6.25	–	–	4
McKeown, P.C.(La)	–	4	6	–	46	135	22.50	–	–	2
Macmillan, G.I.(Le)	–	5	7	1	34	99	16.50	–	–	3
Maddy, D.L.(Le/R/ECB)	1996	19	30	1	103	1047	36.10	3	5	18
Malcolm, D.E.(De/E)	1989	19	24	9	21*	92	6.13	–	–	2
Marsh, S.A.(K)	1986	18	27	6	142	837	39.85	1	3	61/2
Martin, P.J.(La/E)	1994	17	19	4	78*	281	18.73	–	1	4
Martin-Jenkins, R.S.C.(Sx)	–	3	6	1	36*	77	15.40	–	–	2
Maru, R.J.(H)	1986	4	4	1	36*	67	22.33	–	–	6
Mascarenhas, A.D.(H)	–	6	7	1	21	50	8.33	–	–	–
Mason, T.J.(Le)	–	1	1	–	4	4	4.00	–	–	1
†Mather, D.P.(OU)	–	2	3	1	5*	10	5.00	–	–	–
May, M.R.(De)	–	9	17	2	116	588	39.20	2	3	2
Maynard, M.P.(Gm)	1987	18	25	7	161*	1170	65.00	3	7	21
Metcalfe, A.A.(Nt)	–	9	12	1	79	262	23.81	–	2	4
Metson, C.P.(Gm)	1987	1	1	–	0	0	0.00	–	–	3/1
Milburn, S.M.(H)	–	11	8	2	23	90	15.00	–	–	1
†Millns, D.J.(Le)	1991	15	15	2	121	449	34.53	2	1	2
Mirza, M.M.(Wo)	–	6	7	4	10*	17	5.66	–	–	1
Moffat, S.P.(M)	–	4	6	1	47	122	24.40	–	–	2
Mohammad Akram (Nh)	–	11	14	2	28	116	9.66	–	–	1
Mohammad Wasim (PA)	–	9	15	–	155	390	26.00	1	1	17
Mohammed, I.(CU)	–	1	1	–	12	12	12.00	–	–	–
Moles, A.J.(Wa)	1987	12	22	3	168	635	33.42	1	2	10
Molins, G.L.(Ire)	–	1	1	–	1	1	1.00	–	–	–
Montgomerie, R.R.(Nh)	1995	10	18	3	73	504	33.60	–	4	7
Moody, T.M.(Wo)	1991	14	21	1	180*	973	48.65	3	4	14
Moores, P.(Sx)	1989	17	31	4	102*	571	21.14	1	2	36
Morgan, P.G.(OU)	–	10	18	1	63	444	26.11	–	2	4
†Morris, A.C.(Y)	–	7	9	–	37	117	13.00	–	–	3
†Morris, H.(Gm)	1986	17	28	4	233*	1262	52.58	4	3	14
Morris, J.E.(Du)	1994	17	30	1	149	1009	34.79	2	4	7
Moxon, M.D.(Y)	1984	12	18	–	155	589	32.72	1	5	3
Mujahid Jamshed (PA)	–	9	15	–	59	230	15.33	–	1	3
Mullally, A.D.(Le)	1993	13	12	6	13*	43	7.16	–	–	2
Mushtaq Ahmed (Sm)	1993	14	16	2	33	174	12.42	–	–	1
Napier, G.R.(Ex)	–	2	2	2	35*	39		–	–	1
Nash, D.C.(M)	–	6	8	2	100	332	55.33	1	1	4
Newell, K.(Sx)	–	17	31	2	112	827	28.51	2	3	2
Newell, M.(Sx)	–	12	22	1	100	471	22.42	1	3	9
Newport, P.J.(Wo)	1986	8	6	–	45	91	15.16	–	–	–
†Nixon, P.A.(Le/ECB)	1994	19	25	9	96	708	44.25	–	4	57/4
Noon, W.M.(Nt)	1995	18	25	4	83	542	25.80	–	3	34/4
Oram, A.R.(Nt)	–	8	9	5	5*	14	3.50	–	–	6
Ormond, J.(Le/ECB)	–	13	12	2	35	69	6.90	–	–	1
Ostler, D.P.(Wa/EA)	1991	15	22	1	65	419	19.95	–	3	29
Owen, J.E.H.(De)	–	4	6	–	22	83	13.83	–	–	1
Parker, B.(Y)	–	19	30	5	138*	806	32.24	1	4	6
Parkin, O.T.(Gm)	–	1	1	1	0*	0		–	–	1
†Parsons, G.J.(Le)	1984	6	6	1	69*	113	22.60	–	1	1
Parsons, K.A.(Sm)	–	10	15	3	74	437	36.41	–	3	12
†Patel, C.M.(H/OU)	–	12	22	5	63*	420	24.70	–	3	2
Patel, M.M.(K)	1994	1	2	–	30	38	19.00	–	–	1
Patterson, A.D.(Ire)	–	1	2	–	31	43	21.50	–	–	1

	Cap	M	I	NO	HS	Runs	Avge	100	50	Ct/St
Patterson, B.M.W.(Sc)	–	1	2	–	83	115	57.50	–	1	1
Pearson, R.M.(Sy)	–	1	1	–	1	1	1.00	–	–	1
†Peirce, M.T.E.(Sx)	–	12	23	–	104	576	25.04	1	3	10
†Penberthy, A.L.(Nh)	1994	13	19	–	96	499	26.26	–	3	8
Penney, T.L.(Wa)	1994	16	24	5	99	784	41.26	–	6	11
Peters, S.D.(Ex)	–	3	3	1	102*	135	67.50	1	–	3
Phillips, B.J.(K)	–	13	19	4	100*	376	25.06	1	1	6
Phillips, N.C.(Sx)	–	3	2	1	6	7	7.00	–	–	–
†Pick, R.A.(Nt)	1987	4	2	1	8*	15	15.00	–	–	–
Pierson, A.R.K.(Le)	1995	16	16	–	59	266	16.62	–	1	8
Piper, K.J.(Wa)	1992	8	11	3	34*	111	13.87	–	–	24/1
Pirihi, N.G.(OU)	–	2	3	–	15	15	5.00	–	–	–
†Pollard, P.R.(Nt)	1992	10	17	5	115*	480	40.00	1	1	8
Ponting, R.T.(A)	–	8	12	3	127	571	63.44	2	2	7
†Pooley, J.C.(M)	1995	18	28	1	98	619	22.92	–	3	21
Powell, J.C.(Ex)	–	1	1	1	4*	4	–	–	–	–
Powell, M.J.(Gm)	–	5	8	3	200*	286	57.20	1	–	1
Powell, M.J.(Wa)	–	1	1	–	20	20	20.00	–	–	2
†Pratt, A.(Du)	–	1	–	–	–	–	–	–	–	–
Preston, N.W.(K)	–	1	1	–	8	8	8.00	–	–	–
Prichard, P.J.(Ex)	1986	17	27	2	224	1184	47.36	3	9	10
Pyemont, J.P.(Sx)	–	1	1	–	22	22	22.00	–	–	1
Radford, T.A.(Sx)	–	8	12	3	69*	131	65.50	–	2	3
Ramprakash, M.R.(M/E/R)	1990	19	30	4	190	1453	55.88	6	7	9
Rana Qayyum (PA)	–	8	13	1	97	320	26.66	–	2	2
Rao, R.K.(Sx)	–	11	20	1	89	375	19.73	–	3	6
Ratcliffe, J.D.(Sy)	–	15	26	2	135	759	31.62	1	4	3
Ratledge, J.(CU)	–	8	12	1	100*	268	24.36	1	–	–
Rawnsley, M.J.(Wo)	–	4	4	1	26	64	21.33	–	–	1
Reiffel, P.R.(A)	–	8	9	4	56	242	48.40	–	2	2
Renshaw, S.J.(H)	–	13	19	7	56	269	22.41	–	1	3
Rhodes, S.J.(Wo)	1986	18	23	6	78	584	34.35	–	4	44/3
Ridgway, P.M.(La)	–	2	2	1	0*	0	0.00	–	–	–
Ripley, D.(Nh)	1987	17	24	6	92	772	42.88	–	6	29/7
Roberts, D.J.(Nh)	–	7	13	–	117	385	29.61	1	–	1
†Roberts, G.M.(De)	–	2	3	–	30*	45	22.50	–	–	–
Robinson, D.D.J.(Ex)	1997	14	22	1	148	735	35.00	2	3	13
Robinson, M.A.(Sx)	1997	17	25	9	27	114	7.12	–	–	4
Robinson, R.T.(Nt)	1983	17	29	4	143*	812	32.48	1	5	7
Rollins, A.S.(De)	1995	17	29	3	210	1142	43.92	3	6	11
Rollins, R.J.(Ex)	1995	13	19	1	82	452	25.11	–	4	24/2
Rose, G.D.(Sm)	1988	18	26	9	191	852	50.11	2	3	7
Roseberry, M.A.(Du)	1995	4	8	1	45	97	13.85	–	–	3
†Russell, R.C.(Gs)	1985	19	29	6	103*	1049	45.60	1	8	52/5
Rutherford, A.T.(Ire)	–	1	1	–	19	19	19.00	–	–	1
Saggers, M.J.(Du)	1996	3	4	2	10*	14	7.00	–	–	2
Sales, D.J.G.(Nh/ECB)	–	14	21	1	103	548	27.40	1	3	6
Salim Elahi (PA)	–	8	13	–	229	625	48.07	1	3	6
Salisbury, I.D.K.(Sy)	1991	13	17	2	30*	159	10.60	–	–	7
†Salmond, G.(Sc)	–	1	2	–	89	135	67.50	–	1	2
Saqlain Mushtaq (Sy)	–	8	10	4	41*	149	24.83	–	1	1
Savident, L.(H)	–	3	4	1	6	15	5.00	–	–	1
Schaffter, P.A.(CU)	–	1	1	–	0	0	0.00	–	–	–
Scrini, A.P.(OU)	–	11	18	6	58*	253	21.08	–	1	13
Shadford, D.J.(La)	–	8	10	3	30	106	15.14	–	–	5
Shah, O.A.(M)	–	11	16	2	104*	548	39.14	1	2	14

	Cap	M	I	NO	HS	Runs	Avge	100	50	Ct/St
Shahid, N.(Sy)	–	7	11	–	34	198	18.00	–	–	4
Shaw, A.D.(Gm)	–	18	21	5	53*	389	24.31	–	1	52/2
Sheeraz, K.P.(Gs)	–	2	2	2	12*	15	–	–	–	–
†Sheikh, M.A.(Wa)	–	1	1	–	24	24	24.00	–	–	–
Sheridan, K.L.P.(Sc)	–	1	1	–	0	0	0.00	–	–	2
Sheriyar, A.(Wo)	1997	18	13	4	21	94	10.44	–	–	4
Shine, K.J.(Sm)	1997	18	20	5	18	96	6.40	–	–	5
Shoaib Akhtar (PA)	–	7	10	4	10	32	5.33	–	–	6
Shoaib Malik (PA)	–	3	4	–	9	18	4.50	–	–	–
†Sidebottom, R.J.(Y)	–	1	1	–	2*	2	–	–	–	–
Silverwood, C.E.W.(Y/R)	1996	18	23	6	58	365	21.47	–	1	–
Singh, A.(Wa/CU)	–	10	14	1	134	355	27.30	1	1	5
Sladdin, R.W.(Sm)	–	1	–	–	–	–	–	–	–	1
Slater, M.J.(A)	–	5	8	–	47	159	19.87	–	–	3
Small, G.C.(Wa)	1982	3	4	1	11	13	4.33	–	–	1
Smith, A.M.(Gs/E)	1995	18	26	9	41*	165	9.70	–	–	4
Smith, B.F.(Le)	1995	13	19	5	131*	624	44.57	2	3	3
Smith, E.T.(K/CU)	–	18	30	3	190	1163	43.07	2	6	7
Smith, N.M.K.(Wa)	1993	15	22	3	148	642	33.78	1	3	7
Smith, R.A.(H)	1985	14	23	1	154	918	41.72	2	4	4
†Smith, T.M.(De)	–	1	–	–	–	–	–	–	–	1
Snape, J.N.(Nh)	–	11	16	3	66	306	23.53	–	3	9
Solanki, V.S.(Wo/R)	–	14	18	1	128*	478	28.11	1	2	10
Speak, N.J.(Du)	1997	12	21	3	124*	426	23.66	1	1	6
Speight, M.P.(Du)	1997	17	28	3	73*	573	22.92	–	3	54
Spendlove, B.L.(De)	–	2	3	1	15*	27	13.50	–	–	2
Spiring, K.R.(Wo)	1997	17	28	3	150	876	35.04	1	4	7
†Stanford, E.J.(K)	–	1	1	–	32	32	32.00	–	–	–
Stanger, I.M.(Sc)	–	1	1	–	8	8	8.00	–	–	–
Stemp, R.D.(Y)	1996	17	20	6	33*	154	11.00	–	–	7
Stephenson, J.P.(H)	1995	17	26	3	140	784	34.08	2	1	7
Stevens, D.I.(Le)	–	2	2	–	27	35	17.50	–	–	1
Stewart, A.J.(Sy/E)	1985	15	26	2	271*	994	41.41	2	3	39
Strang, P.A.(K)	1997	17	26	2	82	590	24.58	–	5	17
†Stubbings, S.D.(De)	–	1	2	–	22	27	13.50	–	–	–
Such, P.M.(Ex/EA/ECB)	1991	21	22	11	14	63	5.72	–	–	5
†Sutcliffe, I.J.(Le)	1997	13	20	2	130	727	40.38	2	3	6
Sutton, L.D.(Sm)	–	1	2	1	11*	17	17.00	–	–	5
Swann, A.J.(Nh)	–	2	3	–	136	162	54.00	1	–	3
†Taylor, J.P.(Nh)	1992	16	21	4	36	216	12.70	–	–	7
†Taylor, M.A.(A)	–	12	19	–	129	680	35.78	2	4	8
Taylor, N.R.(Sx)	1997	16	28	1	127	1033	38.25	3	5	3
Thomas, P.A.(Wo)	–	2	2	1	16*	16	16.00	–	–	–
†Thomas, S.D.(Gm)	1997	18	19	5	75*	301	21.50	–	1	8
Thompson, J.B.D.(K)	–	9	10	3	59*	106	15.14	–	1	3
Thomson, K.(Sc)	–	1	1	1	9*	9	–	–	–	–
†Thorpe, G.P.(Sy/E)	1991	14	23	4	222	1160	61.05	3	6	17
Thursfield, M.J.(Sx)	–	2	2	1	32*	32	32.00	–	–	1
Titchard, S.P.(La)	1995	6	9	–	79	180	20.00	–	1	2
Tolley, C.M.(Nt)	1997	12	22	4	73*	479	26.61	–	3	6
Trainor, N.J.(Gs)	–	14	25	1	121	484	20.16	1	1	3
†Trescothick, M.E.(Sm)	–	13	19	1	83*	390	21.66	–	4	6
Trott, B.J.(Sm)	–	2	2	1	1*	1	1.00	–	–	1
Tudor, A.J.(Sy/R)	–	9	11	6	35*	109	21.80	–	–	–
Tufnell, P.C.R.(M/E)	1990	17	21	6	21	101	6.73	–	–	4
Turner, R.J.(Sm)	1994	17	28	7	144	1069	50.90	1	7	51/2

	Cap	M	I	NO	HS	Runs	Avge	100	50	Ct/St
Tweats, T.A.(De)	–	7	13	2	189	590	53.63	1	1	7
Udal, S.D.(H)	1992	18	24	3	117*	600	28.57	1	4	3
Vandrau, M.J.(De)	–	5	8	1	54	186	26.57	–	1	1
Van Troost, A.P.(Sm)	1997	6	8	3	12*	20	4.00	–	–	1
Vaughan, M.P.(Y/EA)	1995	15	27	2	161	839	33.56	3	2	3
Wagh, M.A.(Wa/OU)	–	18	31	2	125*	1156	39.86	4	5	14
†Walker, A.(Du)	1994	12	20	8	16	92	7.66	–	–	–
Walker, L.N.P.(Nt)	–	4	5	2	42*	97	32.33	–	–	1
†Walker, M.J.(K)	–	10	19	–	62	369	19.42	–	2	4
Walton, T.C.(Nh)	–	7	10	1	60	231	25.66	–	2	1
Waqar Younis (Gm)	1997	16	17	1	47	289	18.06	–	–	3
†Ward, I.J.(Sy)	–	3	4	–	56	102	25.50	–	1	6
Ward, T.R.(K)	1989	18	32	2	161*	1018	33.93	1	8	30
Warne, S.K.(A)	–	12	17	1	53	293	18.31	–	1	5
Warren, P.M.(Gm)	–	1	–	–	–	–	–	–	–	1
Warren, R.J.(Nh/R)	1995	10	17	2	174*	664	44.26	1	4	12/1
†Wasim Akram (La)	1989	1	2	–	13	16	8.00	–	–	1
Watkin, S.L.(Gm)	1989	17	16	3	39	138	10.61	–	–	3
Watkinson, M.(La)	1987	12	19	1	135	520	28.88	1	2	5
Waugh, M.E.(A)	–	13	20	3	173	746	43.88	2	3	11
Waugh, S.R.(A)	–	13	17	–	154	924	54.35	4	4	9
†Weekes, P.N.(M)	1993	15	24	–	101	439	18.29	1	–	18
Welch, G.(Wa/ECB)	1997	18	26	6	75	455	22.75	–	2	3
Wellings, P.E.(M)	–	2	2	1	128*	141	141.00	1	–	1
Wells, A.P.(K)	1997	18	31	1	109	1120	37.33	1	9	16
Wells, V.J.(Le)	1994	18	27	–	224	1200	44.44	3	6	10
Welton, G.E.(Nt)	–	6	11	–	95	295	26.81	–	1	1
Weston, R.M.S.(Du)	1994	5	8	–	36	137	17.12	–	–	5
†Weston, W.P.C.(Wo)	1995	17	29	5	205	1190	49.58	4	3	7
Wharf, A.G.(Y)	–	2	3	–	14	19	6.33	–	–	1
Whitaker, J.J.(Le)	1986	16	23	2	133*	919	43.76	3	4	5
†Whitaker, P.R.(H)	–	3	5	1	73	132	33.00	–	1	1
White, C.(Y)	1993	17	24	2	172*	639	29.04	1	2	17
White, G.W.(H)	–	10	17	2	145	681	45.40	1	4	8
Williams, N.F.(Ex)	1996	4	5	1	23	66	16.50	–	–	3
Williamson, D.(Le)	–	1	1	–	3	3	3.00	–	–	–
Williamson, J.G.(Sc)	–	1	1	–	5	5	5.00	–	–	–
Willis, S.C.(K)	–	1	2	1	19	37	37.00	–	–	1
Wilson, D.G.(Ex)	–	1	–	–	–	–	–	–	–	1
Windows, M.G.N.(Gs)	–	8	15	–	84	369	24.60	–	2	7
Wood, J.(Du)	1992	6	8	4	21*	72	18.00	–	–	4
Wood, M.J.(Y)	–	1	2	–	81	102	51.00	–	1	1
†Wood, N.T.(La)	–	10	15	2	155	469	36.07	1	2	3
Wren, T.N.(K)	–	1	1	1	11*	11	–	–	–	–
Wright, A.J.(Gs)	1987	13	22	3	79	416	21.89	–	1	11
Wright, C.M.(Sc)	–	1	1	–	0	0	0.00	–	–	–
Wright, G.J.(OU)	–	3	2	1	0*	0	0.00	–	–	–
Yates, G.(La)	1994	11	13	3	39	194	19.40	–	–	7
†Young, S.(Gs/A)	1997	19	31	4	237	985	36.48	2	5	10

BOWLING

See BATTING and FIELDING section for details of caps and teams

	Cat	O	M	R	W	Avge	Best	5wI	10wM
Abdul Razzak	RFM	187.2	29	753	23	32.73	5-106	1	–
Adams, C.J.	OB	2.5	0	16	0				
Afzaal, U.	SLA	199.1	40	689	14	49.21	3- 79	–	–
Aldred, P.	RM	181	52	454	12	37.83	3- 28	–	–
Ali Naqvi	RM	6	1	20	1	20.00	1- 11	–	–
Ali Rizvi	LB	306	70	822	24	34.25	5- 68	1	–
Alleyne, M.W.	RM	360.1	89	1148	44	26.09	6- 64	3	–
Allingham, M.J.D.	RM	1	0	3	0				
Altree, D.A.	LMF	25	3	119	2	59.50	2-108	–	–
Amin, R.M.	SLA	134.3	35	348	8	43.50	3- 58	–	–
Andrew, S.J.W.	RMF	68	17	223	4	55.75	1- 16	–	–
Anthony, H.A.G.	RFM	42	11	113	10	11.30	6- 34	1	1
Archer, G.F.	OB	53	9	188	4	47.00	1- 24	–	–
Arthurton, K.L.T.	SLA	3	1	5	0				
Astle, N.J.	RM	209	44	525	22	23.86	5- 46	1	–
Atherton, M.A.	LB	1	0	7	0				
Athey, C.W.J.	RM	7	0	21	0				
Austin, I.D.	RM	448.4	130	1218	45	27.06	4- 44	–	–
Averis, J.M.M.	RMF	272.3	40	1104	16	69.00	5- 98	1	–
Aymes, A.N.	(WK)	9	0	76	0				
Azhar Mahmood	RFM	290.5	66	829	40	20.72	5- 66	1	–
Badenhorst, A.	RF	31	10	72	5	14.40	3- 48	–	–
Bailey, R.J.	OB	112.3	19	367	10	36.70	4- 10	–	–
Ball, M.C.J.	OB	479.2	129	1271	29	43.82	5- 66	1	–
Bates, J.J.	OB	227.2	71	525	19	27.63	5- 89	1	–
Bates, R.T.	OB	225.4	51	576	11	52.36	3- 89	–	–
Batt, C.J.	LMF	40	11	100	6	16.66	4- 56	–	–
Battarbee, C.M.	RM	150.4	21	627	11	57.00	2- 56	–	–
Batty, G.J.	OB	11	0	70	2	35.00	1- 11	–	–
Batty, J.N.	(WK)	4	0	9	0				
Bell, M.A.V.	LMF	79.3	14	232	3	77.33	1- 12	–	–
Benjamin, J.E.	RMF	211	39	759	13	58.38	3- 52	–	–
Benson, J.D.R.	RM	9.1	2	44	3	14.66	2- 38	–	–
Betts, M.M.	RMF	329	77	1085	49	22.14	9- 64	3	1
Bevan, M.G.	SLC	152.4	23	606	11	55.09	3- 73	–	–
Bichel, A.J.	RFM	5	1	28	0				
Bicknell, D.J.	SLA	12	1	38	1	38.00	1- 12	–	–
Bicknell, M.P.	RFM	385.2	94	1174	44	26.68	5- 34	1	–
Blackwell, I.D.	SLA	52	10	227	2	113.50	1- 27	–	–
Blain, J.A.R.	RMF	30	8	105	2	52.50	1- 18	–	–
Blewett, G.S.	RM	20	4	93	0				
Bloomfield, T.F.	RMF	85	17	258	13	19.84	5- 77	1	–
Boiling, J.	OB	336	98	925	21	44.04	3- 21	–	–
Boon, D.C.	OB	12.2	3	39	2	19.50	2- 18	–	–
Boswell, S.A.J.	RFM	185.5	26	769	15	51.26	5- 94	1	–
Bovill, J.N.B.	RFM	233.4	37	902	23	39.21	4- 62	–	–
Bowen, M.N.	RM	467.2	107	1394	41	34.00	7- 75	3	1
Bowler, P.D.	OB	44.2	18	145	3	48.33	2- 48	–	–
Brimson, M.T.	SLA	170.5	48	451	11	41.00	3- 49	–	–
Brown, A.D.	LB	16	0	37	0				
Brown, D.R.	RFM	522.3	135	1569	81	19.37	8- 89	4	1
Brown, J.F.	OB	203.4	39	651	20	32.55	4- 50	–	–

	Cat	O	M	R	W	Avge	Best	5wI	10wM
Brown, S.J.E.	LFM	590.3	126	1855	67	27.68	5- 58	4	1
Burns, M.	RM	62	13	266	5	53.20	2- 18	–	–
Butcher, G.P.	RM	114.1	21	466	12	38.83	3- 87	–	–
Butcher, M.A.	RM	41	8	97	7	13.85	3- 24	–	–
Byrne, B.W.	OB	98	11	439	3	146.33	1- 19	–	–
Caddick, A.R.	RFM	702.4	139	2156	81	26.61	6- 65	6	–
Campbell, C.L.	RFM	12	0	92	1	92.00	1- 92	–	–
Capel, D.J.	RMF	39	4	180	2	90.00	1- 22	–	–
Carpenter, J.R.	SLA	21.3	5	81	1	81.00	1- 50	–	–
Cassar, M.E.	RFM	52.1	6	224	8	28.00	3- 31	–	–
Chapman, R.J.	RMF	103.3	18	468	13	36.00	3- 26	–	–
Chapple, G.	RMF	275.5	45	900	27	33.33	4- 80	–	–
Chilton, M.J.	RM	4	0	23	0				
Clarke, V.P.	RM/LB	223.5	48	835	13	64.23	3- 47	–	–
Collingwood, P.D.	RMF	48	4	203	6	33.83	3- 46	–	–
Connor, C.A.	RFM	122.5	18	430	13	33.07	7- 46	1	–
Cooke, G.	RMF	17	5	63	2	31.50	1- 31	–	–
Cork, D.G.	RFM	132	28	457	11	41.54	4- 48	–	–
Cosker, D.A.	SLA	375.2	92	1100	29	37.93	4- 64	–	–
Cottey, P.A.	OB	3.3	1	19	0				
Cowan, A.P.	RFM	420	106	1334	52	25.65	5- 45	3	–
Cowdrey, G.R.	RM	5	0	31	0				
Cox, D.M.	SLA	69.3	18	202	7	28.85	3- 72	–	–
Croft, R.D.B.	OB	666.1	159	1698	62	27.38	5- 33	1	–
Curran, K.M.	RMF	215.2	57	715	24	29.79	4- 32	–	–
Curtis, T.S.	LB	12	1	65	1	65.00	1- 55	–	–
Dakin, J.M.	RM	68	17	204	5	40.80	2- 12	–	–
Dale, A.	RM	71.1	24	261	0				
Davies, M.K.	SLA	234.2	71	674	23	29.30	5- 46	1	–
Davis, R.P.	SLA	241	76	607	17	35.70	4- 35	–	–
Davy, J.O.	LFM	19	2	93	0				
Dawson, M.W.	LM	59.2	6	240	0				
Dawson, R.I.	RM	3	0	22	0				
Dean, K.J.	LMF	234.4	47	811	28	28.96	4- 39	–	–
DeFreitas, P.A.J.	RFM	574.1	132	1810	67	27.01	7- 64	5	2
Dimond, M.	RMF	11	3	30	0				
Donald, A.A.	RF	387.5	123	938	60	15.63	6- 55	3	1
Dowman, M.P.	RMF	81	15	260	6	43.33	3- 10	–	–
Drakes, V.C.	RFM	300	60	1043	31	33.64	4- 55	–	–
Dutch, K.P.	OB	88.1	15	289	9	32.11	3- 79	–	–
Dyer, N.R.	OB	21	4	59	2	29.50	1- 29	–	–
Ealham, M.A.	RMF	407.4	80	1238	40	30.95	4- 47	–	–
Ecclestone, S.C.	RM	1	1	0	0				
Edmond, M.D.	RMF	58	14	175	4	43.75	2- 26	–	–
Edwards, A.D.	RFM	103.2	19	389	17	22.88	5- 34	1	–
Edwards, G.J.M.	OB	9	2	49	0				
Elliott, M.T.G.	SLA	9	0	43	0				
Emburey, J.E.	OB	110.3	39	259	4	64.75	2- 36	–	–
Evans, K.P.	RMF	457.5	103	1277	45	28.37	6- 40	2	–
Fazal-e-Akber	RMF	45	10	181	4	45.25	2- 47	–	–
Fisher, I.D.	SLA	39	7	103	1	103.00	1- 26	–	–
Fleming, M.V.	RM	398.2	97	1145	37	30.94	5- 51	2	–
Flintoff, A.	RM	10	6	11	1	11.00	1- 11	–	–
Flower, G.W.	SLA	5	1	10	0				
Foley, G.I.	RM	19	5	53	0				
Follett, D.	RFM	24.3	1	123	2	61.50	2-123	–	–

	Cat	O	M	R	W	Avge	Best	5wI	10wM
Fordham, A.	RM	4.3	1	8	0			–	–
Foster, M.J.	RFM	275.4	55	1027	30	34.23	4- 58	–	–
Francis, N.B.	RF	18	2	56	0			–	–
Francis, S.R.G.	RMF	19	1	97	0				
Franks, P.J.	RMF	372.4	63	1158	30	38.60	4- 47	–	–
Fraser, A.R.C.	RMF	571.5	155	1460	47	31.06	6- 77	2	–
Freeth, J.W.O.	OB	149	16	609	11	55.36	4-101	–	–
Fulton, J.A.G.	RM	5	0	18	0			–	–
Gallian, J.E.R.	RM	83.2	12	375	8	46.87	3- 51	–	–
Gatting, M.W.	RM	7	1	46	1	46.00	1- 46	–	–
Giles, A.F.	SLA	506.1	155	1225	38	32.23	4- 54	–	–
Gillespie, J.N.	RF	198.4	43	692	29	23.86	7- 37	2	–
Gooch, G.A.	RM	2	1	3	0			–	–
Gough, D.	RFM	334.4	70	1149	43	26.72	5- 56	3	–
Grayson, A.P.	SLA	394.5	112	1009	28	36.03	4- 53	–	–
Green, R.J.	RM	102.2	25	320	5	64.00	3- 66	–	–
Greenfield, K.	RM	10	1	45	0			–	–
Habib, A.	RMF	4	0	37	0				
Hamilton, G.M.	RFM	241	53	907	27	33.59	5- 89	1	–
Hancock, T.H.C.	RM	99.5	22	386	5	77.20	1- 24	–	–
Hansen, T.M.	LMF	26	10	75	0				
Harris, A.J.	RM	481.3	98	1694	35	48.40	3- 66	–	–
Hartley, P.J.	RMF	170	39	532	23	23.13	5- 34	1	–
Hasan Raza	LB	19	4	50	1	50.00	1- 36	–	–
Hayden, M.L.	RM	33	0	166	3	55.33	2- 17	–	–
Hayhurst, A.N.	RM	9	2	30	1	30.00	1- 12	–	–
Haynes, G.R.	RM	287.1	68	875	31	28.22	3- 46	–	–
Headley, D.W.	RFM	425.2	75	1419	46	30.84	5- 92	1	–
Hemp, D.L.	RM	23	4	120	0			–	–
Herzberg, S.	OB	102	25	281	10	28.10	3-100	–	–
Hewitt, J.P.	RMF	437	96	1389	60	23.15	6- 14	2	–
Hibbert, A.J.E.	RM	1	0	1	0			–	–
Hick, G.A.	OB	193	46	629	9	69.88	4- 70	–	–
Hindson, J.E	SLA	96.4	24	287	11	26.09	4- 22	–	–
Hoggard, M.J.	RFM	27	4	155	2	77.50	1- 45	–	–
Hollioake, A.J.	RM	132.4	23	458	15	30.53	4- 22	–	–
Hollioake, B.C.	RFM	214.2	42	782	23	34.00	4- 54	–	–
House, W.J.	RM	68.5	9	284	0			–	–
How, E.J.	LMF	193.4	41	685	12	57.08	5- 59	1	–
Hudson, R.D.	RM	41	5	184	0			–	–
Hughes, J.G.	RM	46	11	141	4	35.25	2- 15	–	–
Hughes, Q.J.	OB	33	6	128	3	42.66	2- 73	–	–
Hutchison, P.M.	LFM	233.1	56	741	37	20.02	7- 38	3	1
Igglesden, A.P.	RFM	152	23	538	18	29.88	4- 67	–	–
Illingworth, R.K.	SLA	206	75	442	18	24.55	7- 79	1	1
Ilott, M.C.	LFM	332	91	946	43	22.00	7- 59	1	–
Innes, K.J.	RM	20	6	49	0				
Irani, R.C.	RMF	261.5	73	695	18	38.61	3- 51	–	–
Irfan Fazil	RFM	56	12	234	7	33.42	3- 51	–	–
James, K.D.	LMF	161.1	37	504	27	18.66	8- 49	2	1
Janisch, A.N.	RM	79.5	10	299	9	33.22	4- 71	–	–
Jarvis, P.W.	RFM	318.5	46	1091	30	36.36	5- 44	2	–
Jeh, M.P.W.	RMF	18.5	4	61	5	12.20	3- 37	–	–
Johnson, N.C.	RMF	116	18	420	8	52.50	3- 61	–	–
Johnson, P.	RM	14	5	34	0				
Johnson, R.L.	RMF	429.2	80	1429	50	28.58	4- 26	–	–

	Cat	O	M	R	W	Avge	Best	5wI	10wM
Jones, D.M.	OB	6	2	20	0			–	–
Jones, P.S.	RFM	207.5	37	739	23	32.13	6- 67	1	–
Jones, R.O.	OB	148.4	17	580	9	64.44	3-116	–	–
Joyce, E.C.	RM	2	0	20	0			–	–
Julian, B.P.	LFM	108	17	455	9	50.55	3- 88	–	–
Kallis, J.H.	RM	234.3	61	655	32	20.46	5- 54	1	–
Kasprowicz, M.S.	RF	267.2	50	1010	39	25.89	7- 36	1	–
Keech, M.	RM	12	1	51	1	51.00	1- 12	–	–
Keedy, G.	SLA	292.4	60	917	27	33.96	6- 79	1	1
Kendall, W.S.	RM	5	0	46	0			–	–
Kennis, G.J.	OB	1	0	4	0			–	–
Kenway, D.A.	RM	9	2	58	2	29.00	1- 5	–	–
Kerr, J.I.D.	RMF	103	20	374	10	37.40	4- 83	–	–
Kettleborough, R.A.	RM	13	3	74	1	74.00	1- 74	–	–
Khan, A.A.	LB	444.3	100	1397	33	42.33	5-137	1	–
Khan, W.G.	LB	1	1	0	0			–	–
Killeen, N.	RFM	64	13	205	7	29.28	4- 50	–	–
Kirtley, R.J.	RFM	276.3	48	1094	31	35.29	6- 60	1	–
Knight, N.V.	RM	6	0	71	0			–	–
Lacey, S.J.	OB	94	19	291	7	41.57	3- 97	–	–
Lampitt, S.R.	RMF	334.4	70	1302	35	37.20	5- 39	1	–
Laney, J.S.	OB	5	2	19	0			–	–
Lathwell, M.N.	RM	5	0	60	1	60.00	1- 60	–	–
Law, D.R.	RFM	270.3	51	969	31	31.25	5- 93	1	–
Law, S.G.	RM/LB	116	30	356	5	71.20	3- 27	–	–
Lawrence, D.V.	RF	86	9	359	8	44.87	2- 28	–	–
Leatherdale, D.A.	RM	219.3	46	742	26	28.53	5- 56	1	–
Lee, S.	RFM	35.3	11	113	8	14.12	4- 27	–	–
Lehman, D.S.	SLA	20.3	3	71	2	35.50	1- 0	–	–
Lewis, C.C.	RFM	291.4	66	970	33	29.39	5- 42	1	–
Lewis, J.	RMF	418.5	98	1401	54	25.94	6- 50	3	–
Lightfoot, C.G.R.	SLA	21	2	126	0			–	–
Llong, N.J.	OB	52.3	11	200	4	50.00	2- 33	–	–
Lloyd, G.D.	RM	11.5	0	101	0			–	–
Lugsden, S.	RFM	16.5	2	88	1	88.00	1- 88	–	–
McCague, M.J.	RF	312.4	55	1125	48	23.43	7- 50	4	–
McCallan, W.K.	OB	20	2	59	1	59.00	1- 10	–	–
McCrum, P.	RFM	24	2	88	1	88.00	1- 27	–	–
MacGill, S.C.G.	LBG	36	11	123	4	30.75	2- 49	–	–
McGrath, A.	OB	12.5	0	59	1	59.00	1- 19	–	–
McGrath, G.D.	RF	363.4	104	1012	49	20.65	8- 38	2	–
Macmillan, G.I.	OB	11	1	41	0			–	–
Maddy, D.L.	RM/OB	47.2	10	122	2	61.00	1- 2	–	–
Malcolm, D.E.	RF	526.1	81	1761	75	23.48	6- 23	5	2
Martin, P.J.	RFM	474.2	136	1342	58	23.13	8- 32	3	1
Martin-Jenkins, R.S.C.	RFM	57	10	184	5	36.80	3- 26	–	–
Maru, R.J.	SLA	127	35	336	3	112.00	2- 60	–	–
Mascarenhas, A.D.	RMF	126.4	22	417	8	52.12	5- 63	1	–
Mason, T.J.	OB	5.4	0	22	2	11.00	2- 21	–	–
Mather, D.P.	LM	45	7	190	2	95.00	2- 38	–	–
May, M.R.	OB	4.1	0	50	0				
Maynard, M.P.	RM	13.5	0	66	0				
Milburn, S.M.	RMF	332	56	1127	22	51.22	4- 38	–	–
Millns, D.J.	RF	408.4	87	1341	49	27.36	6- 61	2	1
Mirza, M.M.	RFM	152.4	25	620	19	32.63	4- 51	–	–
Mohammad Akram	RFM	287	43	1135	30	37.83	5- 72	2	–

	Cat	O	M	R	W	Avge	Best	5wI	10wM
Mohammad Wasim	LB	7	2	21	0			–	–
Molins, G.L.	SLA	17	2	55	2	27.50	2- 55	–	–
Montgomerie, R.R.	OB	1	0	1	0				
Moody, T.M.	RM	213.4	42	829	19	43.63	5-148	1	–
Morris, A.C.	RMF	78	17	289	4	72.25	2- 62	–	–
Morris, J.E.	RM	1	0	1	0				
Mujahid Jamshed	RM	3.1	0	18	0				
Mullally, A.D.	LFM	383.1	89	1302	37	35.18	5- 52	4	–
Mushtaq Ahmed	LBG	513	146	1407	50	28.14	6- 70	3	–
Napier, G.R.	RM	17	6	65	3	21.66	2- 25	–	–
Nash, D.C.	LB	3	0	19	1	19.00	1- 8	–	–
Newell, K.	RM	138.1	35	436	11	39.63	4- 61	–	–
Newport, P.J.	RFM	177.2	56	444	19	23.36	7- 37	1	–
Nixon, P.A.	(WK)	2	0	4	0				
Noon, W.M.	(WK)	1	0	12	0				
Oram, A.R.	RM	226.4	55	684	26	26.30	4- 53	–	–
Ormond, J.	RFM	345.3	72	1162	44	26.40	6- 54	3	–
Ostler, D.P.	RM	6	0	66	0				
Parker, B.	RM	1	0	3	0				
Parkin, O.T.	RFM	34	7	116	3	38.66	3- 38	–	–
Parsons, G.J.	RMF	182.2	48	500	13	38.46	4- 22	–	–
Parsons, K.A.	RM	78.5	18	204	7	29.14	2- 4	–	–
Patel, C.M.	RM	327	51	1326	27	49.11	6-110	1	–
Patel, M.M.	SLA	3	0	12	0				
Pearson, R.M.	OB	26	4	90	2	45.00	2- 90	–	–
Peirce, M.T.E.	SLA	20.1	2	76	0				
Penberthy, A.L.	RM	190	29	722	9	80.22	2- 52	–	–
Phillips, B.J.	RFM	282.1	73	877	44	19.93	5- 47	2	–
Phillips, N.C.	OB	26	3	114	1	114.00	1- 47	–	–
Pick, R.A.	RFM	97.2	22	307	5	61.40	2- 23	–	–
Pierson, A.R.K.	OB	499.1	104	1478	38	38.89	6- 56	1	–
Ponting, R.T.	OB	3	0	9	0				
Powell, J.C.	OB	39	5	109	1	109.00	1-109		
Powell, M.J.	RM	1	0	3	0				
Preston, N.W.	RFM	8	2	21	1	21.00	1- 21	–	–
Ramprakash, M.R.	RM	35.2	10	126	2	63.00	1- 30	–	–
Rao, R.K.	LBG	28	3	100	2	50.00	1- 14	–	–
Ratcliffe, J.D.	RM	58	10	177	1	177.00	1- 14	–	–
Rawnsley, M.J.	SLA	86.3	23	218	6	36.33	3- 67	–	–
Reiffel, P.R.	RFM	188.4	49	520	28	18.57	5- 49	2	–
Renshaw, S.J.	RMF	356.3	62	1278	37	34.54	5-110	1	–
Ridgway, P.M.	RFM	39	6	163	2	81.50	2- 46	–	–
Roberts, G.M.	SLA	6	1	8	0				
Robinson, M.A.	RFM	448.2	87	1426	48	29.70	6- 78	2	–
Rollins, A.S.	RM	3	0	21	0				
Rose, G.D.	RM	488.5	124	1563	63	24.80	5- 53	1	–
Russell, R.C.	(WK)	3	0	15	0				
Saggers, M.J.	RMF	64	15	177	7	25.28	5- 57	1	–
Sales, D.J.G.	RM	8	2	28	0				
Salisbury, I.D.K.	LBG	314.1	65	936	30	31.20	6- 19	2	–
Saqlain Mushtaq	OB	254.5	75	617	32	19.28	5- 17	4	2
Savident, L.	RM	56	9	247	4	61.75	2- 86	–	–
Schaffter, P.A.	RFM	28	8	77	1	77.00	1- 58	–	–
Shadford, D.J.	RMF	149	8	786	19	41.36	5- 80	1	–
Shah, O.A.	OB	2	0	19	0				
Shahid, N.	LB	5	0	14	0				

	Cat	O	M	R	W	Avge	Best	5wI	10wM
Sheeraz, K.P.	RMF	7	0	40	0			–	–
Sheikh, M.A.	LM	14.3	7	24	3	8.00	2- 14	–	–
Sheridan, K.L.P.	SLA	38	16	59	4	14.75	4- 43	–	–
Sheriyar, A.	LFM	446.1	94	1575	62	25.40	6- 19	3	1
Shine, K.J.	RFM	443.3	89	1678	55	30.50	7- 43	3	1
Shoaib Akhtar	RFM	194.3	29	747	25	29.88	5- 62	2	–
Shoaib Malik	OB	123	24	333	12	27.75	3- 49	–	–
Sidebottom, R.J.	LFM	16.4	4	71	3	23.66	3- 71	–	–
Silverwood, C.E.W.	RFM	478.4	108	1531	58	26.39	7- 93	4	1
Singh, A.	OB	3	1	10	0			–	–
Sladdin, R.W.	SLA	38	10	105	6	17.50	5- 60	1	–
Small, G.C.	RFM	50	12	158	3	52.66	3- 51	–	–
Smith, A.M.	LMF	512.2	125	1464	83	17.63	6- 45	5	3
Smith, B.F.	RM	1	0	4	0			–	–
Smith, E.T.	RM	2	0	22	0			–	–
Smith, N.M.K.	OB	318.2	77	930	23	40.43	4- 32	–	–
Smith, R.A.	LB	5.1	0	75	0			–	–
Smith, T.M.	RFM	18	6	51	1	51.00	1- 27	–	–
Snape, J.N.	OB	253.1	60	724	15	48.26	4- 46	–	–
Solanki, V.S.	OB	89	21	309	2	154.50	1- 33	–	–
Speak, N.J.	RM/OB	4	0	14	0			–	–
Spiring, K.R.	OB	2	0	10	0			–	–
Stanford, E.J.	SLA	5	2	10	1	10.00	1- 10	–	–
Stanger, I.M.	RFM	13	2	61	1	61.00	1- 38	–	–
Stemp, R.D.	SLA	473	111	1379	42	32.83	6- 77	1	–
Stephenson, J.P.	RM	428.5	68	1480	37	40.00	6- 54	1	–
Stevens, D.I.	RM	2	1	5	1	5.00	1- 5	–	–
Strang, P.A.	LBG	733.1	211	1929	63	30.61	7-118	4	1
Such, P.M.	OB	725.1	219	1739	66	26.34	6- 55	6	1
Sutcliffe, I.J.	OB	1	0	12	0			–	–
Taylor, J.P.	LFM	455.4	81	1532	54	28.37	7- 87	3	1
Thomas, P.A.	RFM	43	6	166	4	41.50	3- 43	–	–
Thomas, S.D.	RFM	405.3	58	1444	53	27.24	5- 24	3	–
Thompson, J.B.D.	RFM	223.2	30	890	31	28.70	5- 89	1	–
Thomson, K.	RM	34	10	93	2	46.50	2- 41	–	–
Thorpe, G.P.	RM	4	0	13	0			–	–
Thursfield, M.J.	RM	29.3	5	108	3	36.00	2- 36	–	–
Titchard, S.P.	RM	15	1	47	3	15.66	1- 11	–	–
Tolley, C.M.	LMF	363	87	1005	35	28.71	6- 61	1	–
Trainor, N.J.	OB	21	7	89	0			–	–
Trescothick, M.E.	RM	15	3	69	1	69.00	1- 18	–	–
Trott, B.J.	RFM	27	3	128	5	25.60	3- 74	–	–
Tudor, A.J.	RF	160.3	27	607	17	35.70	6-101	1	–
Tufnell, P.C.R.	SLA	561.5	174	1205	55	21.90	7- 66	3	1
Udal, S.D.	OB	627.1	153	1810	34	53.23	4- 17	–	–
Vandrau, M.J.	OB	45	7	182	4	45.50	3- 78	–	–
Van Troost, A.P.	RF	78.5	5	496	7	70.85	3- 79	–	–
Vaughan, M.P.	OB	147.1	17	619	5	123.80	2- 3	–	–
Wagh, M.A.	OB	197	39	669	6	111.50	2- 45	–	–
Walker, A.	RFM	341.1	87	1063	33	32.21	7- 56	2	–
Walton, T.C.	RM	8	0	45	0			–	–
Waqar Younis	RF	441.4	83	1551	68	22.80	8- 17	3	1
Ward, T.R.	OB	5	0	34	0			–	–
Warne, S.K.	LBG	433.4	112	1154	57	20.24	7-103	4	–
Warren, P.M.	RM	19	7	60	0			–	–
Wasim Akram	LF	36	10	86	3	28.66	3- 74	–	–

	Cat	O	M	R	W	Avge	Best	5wI	10wM
Watkin, S.L.	RMF	508.2	143	1393	61	22.83	7- 41	2	–
Watkinson, M.	RMF/OB	231.4	41	805	20	40.25	3- 35	–	–
Waugh, M.E.	OB	47	10	150	4	37.50	1- 16	–	–
Waugh, S.R.	RM	26	5	97	1	97.00	1- 13	–	–
Weekes, P.N.	OB	143	21	432	6	72.00	2- 35	–	–
Welch, G.	RM	540.5	151	1625	65	25.00	6-115	3	1
Wellings, P.E.	RM	3	0	18	0				
Wells, A.P.	RM	18	6	55	0				
Wells, V.J.	RMF	204	47	671	17	39.47	2- 8	–	–
Weston, R.M.S.	LB	1	0	5	0				
Weston, W.P.C.	LM	9	0	63	0				
Wharf, A.G.	RMF	43	5	155	4	38.75	2- 37	–	–
Whitaker, J.J.	OB	0.2	0	0	0				
Whitaker, P.R.	OB	24.4	4	89	1	89.00	1- 31	–	–
White, C.	RFM	353.4	58	1236	41	30.14	5- 31	1	–
White, G.W.	LB	10.5	0	49	0				
Williams, N.F.	RFM	101	16	336	13	25.84	5- 55	1	–
Williamson, D.	RM	17.5	5	40	4	10.00	3- 19	–	–
Williamson, J.G.	RM	21	3	84	2	42.00	1- 40	–	–
Wilson, D.G.	RM	15.3	2	67	2	33.50	1- 31	–	–
Windows, M.G.N.	RSM	7	1	51	0				
Wood, J.	RFM	112	14	541	11	49.18	4- 73	–	–
Wood, N.T.	OB	4.1	0	38	0				
Wren, T.N.	LM	8.4	1	22	2	11.00	2- 22	–	–
Wright, C.M.	RM	31.2	9	89	3	29.66	3- 66	–	–
Wright, G.J.	RM	46	7	246	1	246.00	1- 60	–	–
Yates, G.	OB	302.4	57	963	29	33.20	5- 59	1	–
Young, S.	RFM	396.3	111	1104	32	34.50	4- 26	–	–

BRITANNIC ASSURANCE
COUNTY CHAMPIONSHIP 1997 FINAL TABLE

	P	W	L	D	Bonus Points Bat	Bowl	Total Points
1 GLAMORGAN (10)	17	8	2	7	50	57	256
2 Kent (4)	17	8	4	5	44	60	252
3 Worcestershire (7)	17	6	3	8	49	54	228
4=Warwickshire(8)	16†	7	2	7	32	51	219
4=Middlesex (9)	17	7	4	6	33	56	219
6 Yorkshire (6)	17	6	3	8	41	54	215
7 Gloucestershire (13)	17	6	6	5	35	60	206
8=Surrey (3)	17	5	5	7	39	52	192
8=Essex (5)	17	5	6	6	39	55	192
10 Leicestershire (1)	16†	4	1	11	37	54	191
11 Lancashire (15)	17	5	6	6	34	54	186
12 Somerset (11)	17	3	3	11	38	64	183
13 Nottinghamshire (17)	17	4	3	10	26	55	175
14 Hampshire (14)	16†	3	5	8	42	41	158
15 Northamptonshire (16)	17	3	5	9	33	48	156
16 Derbyshire (2)	17	2	9	6	32	59	141
17 Durham (18)	16†	2	8	6	22	56	131
18 Sussex (12)	17	1	10	6	24	57	115

† The matches between Leicestershire and Warwickshire at Leicester on 26-30 June and between Durham and Hampshire at Chester-le-Street on 2-5 July were abandoned without a ball bowled, each side receiving three points – see note (g) below.

1996 final positions are shown in brackets.

SCORING OF POINTS 1996

(a) For a win, 16 points, plus any points scored in the first innings.

(b) In a tie, each side to score eight points, plus any points scored in the first innings.

(c) In a drawn match, each side to score three points, plus any points scored in the first innings (see also paragraph (f) below).

(d) If the scores are equal in a drawn match, the side batting in the fourth innings to score eight points plus any points scored in the first innings, and the opposing side to score three points plus any points scored in the first innings.

(e) First Innings Points (awarded only for the performances **in the first 120 overs** of each first innings and retained whatever the result of the match).

    (i) A maximum of four batting points to be available as under:-
      200 to 249 runs – 1 point
      250 to 299 runs – 2 points
      300 to 349 runs – 3 points
      350 runs or over – 4 points

    (ii) A maximum of four bowling points to be available as under:-
      3 to 4 wickets taken – 1 point
      5 to 6 wickets taken – 2 points
      7 to 8 wickets taken – 3 points
      9 to 10 wickets taken – 4 points

(f) If play starts when less than eight hours playing time remains (in which event a one innings match shall be played as provided for in First Class Playing Condition 20), no first innings points shall be scored. The side winning on the one innings to score 12 points. In a tie, each side to score six points. In a drawn match, each side to score three points. If the scores are equal in a drawn match, the side batting in the second innings to score six points and the opposing side to score three points.

(g) If a match is abandoned without a ball being bowled, each side to score three points.

(h) A County which is adjudged to have prepared a pitch which is 'unsuitable for four day First-Class Cricket' shall be liable to have 25 points deducted from its aggregate of points under the procedure agreed by the Board in December 1988 and revised in December 1993. In addition, a penalty of 10 or 15 points may in certain circumstances be imposed on a County in respect of a 'Poor' pitch under the procedure agreed by the Board in March 1995. There shall be no right of appeal against any points penalty provided for in this Clause.

(i) The side which has the highest aggregate of points gained at the end of the season shall be the Champion County. Should any sides in the Championship table be equal on points, the side with most wins will have priority.

COUNTY CHAMPIONS

The English County Championship was not officially constituted until December 1889. Prior to that date there was no generally accepted method of awarding the title; although the 'least matches lost' method existed, it was not consistently applied. Rules governing playing qualifications were not agreed until 1873, and the first unofficial points system was not introduced until 1888.

Research has produced a list of champions dating back to 1826, but at least seven different versions exist for the period from 1864 to 1889 (see *The Wisden Book of Cricket Records*). Only from 1890 can any authorised list of county champions commence.

That first official Championship was contested between eight counties: Gloucestershire, Kent, Lancashire, Middlesex, Nottinghamshire, Surrey, Sussex and Yorkshire. The remaining counties were admitted in the following seasons: 1891 – Somerset, 1895 – Derbyshire, Essex, Hampshire, Leicestershire and Warwickshire, 1899 – Worcestershire, 1905 – Northamptonshire, 1921 – Glamorgan, and 1992 – Durham.

The Championship pennant was introduced by the 1951 champions, Warwickshire, and the Lord's Taverners' Trophy was first presented in 1973. The first sponsors, Schweppes (1977 to 1983), were succeeded by BRITANNIC ASSURANCE in 1984.

1890	Surrey	1928	Lancashire	1966	Yorkshire
1891	Surrey	1929	Nottinghamshire	1967	Yorkshire
1892	Surrey	1930	Lancashire	1968	Yorkshire
1893	Yorkshire	1931	Yorkshire	1969	Glamorgan
1894	Surrey	1932	Yorkshire	1970	Kent
1895	Surrey	1933	Yorkshire	1971	Surrey
1896	Yorkshire	1934	Lancashire	1972	Warwickshire
1897	Lancashire	1935	Yorkshire	1973	Hampshire
1898	Yorkshire	1936	Derbyshire	1974	Worcestershire
1899	Surrey	1937	Yorkshire	1975	Leicestershire
1900	Yorkshire	1938	Yorkshire	1976	Middlesex
1901	Yorkshire	1939	Yorkshire	1977	{ Kent
1902	Yorkshire	1946	Yorkshire		{ Middlesex
1903	Middlesex	1947	Middlesex	1978	Kent
1904	Lancashire	1948	Glamorgan	1979	Essex
1905	Yorkshire	1949	{ Middlesex	1980	Middlesex
1906	Kent		{ Yorkshire	1981	Nottinghamshire
1907	Nottinghamshire	1950	{ Lancashire	1982	Middlesex
1908	Yorkshire		{ Surrey	1983	Essex
1909	Kent	1951	Warwickshire	1984	Essex
1910	Kent	1952	Surrey	1985	Middlesex
1911	Warwickshire	1953	Surrey	1986	Essex
1912	Yorkshire	1954	Surrey	1987	Nottinghamshire
1913	Kent	1955	Surrey	1988	Worcestershire
1914	Surrey	1956	Surrey	1989	Worcestershire
1919	Yorkshire	1957	Surrey	1990	Middlesex
1920	Middlesex	1958	Surrey	1991	Essex
1921	Middlesex	1959	Yorkshire	1992	Essex
1922	Yorkshire	1960	Yorkshire	1993	Middlesex
1923	Yorkshire	1961	Hampshire	1994	Warwickshire
1924	Yorkshire	1962	Yorkshire	1995	Warwickshire
1925	Yorkshire	1963	Yorkshire	1996	Leicestershire
1926	Lancashire	1964	Worcestershire	1997	Glamorgan
1927	Lancashire	1965	Worcestershire		

ANOTHER EARLY DINNER

Victims of rogue conditions a year earlier when they had been despatched by Lancashire for the lowest total in any domestic Lord's final, Essex turned their wheel of fortune full circle to inflict upon Warwickshire a nine-wicket defeat with 55% of their overs unused.

Delayed a day by the funeral of Diana, Princess of Wales, the first Lord's final to be started on a Sunday was played before an audience subdued both by the sombre events of the previous week and by yet another final which failed to develop into a genuine contest.

Essex were again very much the underdogs. They had reached the summit only after their number eleven had snatched an evil-tempered semi-final from Glamorgan with his only scoring stroke of the competition. As in 1996, they won the toss, chose to bowl and, taking full advantage of the autumnal early-morning conditions, restricted their opponents to a modest total. This time they managed totally to rewrite the script. Dismissed for 57 by Lancashire, their opening pair savaged that tally off just six overs. The captains of Queensland and Essex flayed the Warwickshire attack, Allan Donald *et al*, in a partnership of 109 runs from 82 balls, reaching their fifties from 40 and 39 balls respectively.

Stuart Law's tenth four ended proceedings at 5.20pm, six minutes earlier than the 1996 fiasco, with a monumental 33.3 overs still unbowled. Involving a mere 86.3 overs, it was the shortest final in the 35 seasons of this, the oldest of all limited-overs competitions.

For those with deadlines to meet before a two-hour drive home to dinner, these brief encounters are eminently preferable to frenetic last-over finishes in near darkness. Purchasers of expensive tickets are unlikely to share such sentiments, however, nor do the sponsors. Nothing will change in 1998 but the following season will bring a vastly expanded tournament culminating in a final staged at Lord's on the last Saturday of August. It is unlikely that a mere week will solve the problems imposed by making a 10.30am start on an overused square.

The duration of innings in that revised competition has yet to be agreed. Many, including the sponsors, favour the retention of a 60-over format. Others want a 50-over uniformity for limited-overs matches so that all the domestic competitions provide a proper training ground for the abbreviated international game. The 60-over supporters argue that even the replacement of the Benson and Hedges Cup and Sunday League with a solitary 50-over competition will provide ample training in that format and the longer version provides a contest closer to 'real' cricket – unless it is staged in St John's Wood in early autumn.

GILLETTE CUP WINNERS

1963	Sussex	1969	Yorkshire	1975	Lancashire
1964	Sussex	1970	Lancashire	1976	Northamptonshire
1965	Yorkshire	1971	Lancashire	1977	Middlesex
1966	Warwickshire	1972	Lancashire	1978	Sussex
1967	Kent	1973	Gloucestershire	1979	Somerset
1968	Warwickshire	1974	Kent	1980	Middlesex

NATWEST TROPHY WINNERS

1981	Derbyshire	1987	Nottinghamshire	1993	Warwickshire
1982	Surrey	1988	Middlesex	1994	Worcestershire
1983	Somerset	1989	Warwickshire	1995	Warwickshire
1984	Middlesex	1990	Lancashire	1996	Lancashire
1985	Essex	1991	Hampshire	1997	Essex
1986	Sussex	1992	Northamptonshire		

The Essex boys can grin, but Warwickshire can't bear it!

Congratulations to Essex
on winning
the 1997 NatWest Trophy.

1997 NATWEST TROPHY FINAL
ESSEX v WARWICKSHIRE

At Lord's, London on 7 September 1997.
Toss: Essex. Result: ESSEX won by 9 wickets.
Award: S.G.Law.

WARWICKSHIRE		Runs	Balls	4/6	Fall
N.V.Knight	lbw b Cowan	0	3	–	1- 1
*N.M.K.Smith	c S.G.Law b Cowan	5	18	1	2- 12
D.L.Hemp	run out (*Grayson*)	21	68	3	3- 45
D.P.Ostler	c D.R.Law b Irani	34	108	3	5- 90
T.L.Penney	c Rollins b Cowan	5	35	–	4- 75
D.R.Brown	c D.R.Law b Ilott	37	65	1	8-156
G.Welch	c and b Such	2	12	–	6- 96
A.F.Giles	run out (*Grayson/Rollins*)	21	28	2	7-147
†K.J.Piper	not out	15	17	1	
A.A.Donald	not out	3	7	–	
G.C.Small					
Extras	(B 5, LB 15, W 5, NB 2)	27			
Total	(60 overs; 8 wickets)	**170**			

ESSEX		Runs	Balls	4/6	Fall
*P.J.Prichard	lbw b Donald	57	45	7/1	1-109
S.G.Law	not out	80	71	10/1	
N.Hussain	not out	25	43	4/1	
R.C.Irani					
D.D.J.Robinson					
A.P.Grayson					
D.R.Law					
†R.J.Rollins					
A.P.Cowan					
M.C.Ilott					
P.M.Such					
Extras	(B 1, LB 4, W 4)	9			
Total	(26.3 overs; 1 wicket)	**171**			

ESSEX	O	M	R	W	WARWICKSHIRE	O	M	R	W
Cowan	12	3	29	3	Welch	5	0	34	0
Ilott	12	3	29	1	Brown	4	0	29	0
Irani	12	4	22	1	Small	7	0	43	0
S.G.Law	12	4	38	0	Donald	6	0	36	1
Such	12	1	32	1	Giles	4	1	20	0
					Penney	0.3	0	4	0

Umpires: M.J.Kitchen and P.Willey.

Dates to work from home.

First Round
Wednesday 24th June

Second Round
Wednesday 8th July

Quarter Finals
Tuesday 28th July

Semi Finals
Tuesday 11th August
Wednesday 12th August

Final
Saturday 5th September

NatWest

T R●P H Y

National Westminster Bank Plc, 41 Lothbury, London EC2P 2BP

THE NATWEST TROPHY 1997 RESULTS CHART

First Round 24 June	Second Round 9 July	Quarter-finals 29 July	Semi-finals 12-14 August	Final 7 September
ESSEX	ESSEX†	ESSEX	ESSEX†	ESSEX (£45,000)
Buckinghamshire†				
WORCESTERSHIRE†	Worcestershire			
Holland				
NOTTINGHAMSHIRE†	NOTTINGHAMSHIRE	Nottinghamshire (£5,500)		
Staffordshire				
SURREY†	Surrey†			
Durham				
GLAMORGAN†	GLAMORGAN	GLAMORGAN†	Glamorgan (£11,250)	
Bedfordshire				
HAMPSHIRE	Hampshire†			
Cambridgeshire†				
YORKSHIRE†	YORKSHIRE†	Yorkshire (£5,500)		
Ireland				
LEICESTERSHIRE	Leicestershire†			
Devon†				
DERBYSHIRE†	DERBYSHIRE†	Derbyshire† (£5,500)	Sussex (£11,250)	
Lincolnshire†				
NORTHAMPTONSHIRE	Northamptonshire			
Cumberland†				
SUSSEX†	SUSSEX†	SUSSEX		
Shropshire				
LANCASHIRE†	Lancashire			
Berkshire				
GLOUCESTERSHIRE†	Gloucestershire	Middlesex† (£5,500)	WARWICKSHIRE†	Warwickshire (£22,500)
Scotland				
MIDDLESEX†	MIDDLESEX†			
Kent				
SOMERSET†	Somerset	WARWICKSHIRE		
Herefordshire				
WARWICKSHIRE†	WARWICKSHIRE†			
Norfolk				

† Home team. Winning teams are in capitals. Prize-money shown in brackets.

NATWEST TROPHY
PRINCIPAL RECORDS 1963-97
(Including The Gillette Cup)

Highest Total	413-4	Somerset v Devon	Torquay	1990
Highest Total in a Final	322-5	Warwicks v Sussex	Lord's	1993
Highest Total by a Minor County	305-9	Durham v Glam	Darlington	1991
Highest Total Batting Second	350	Surrey v Worcs	The Oval	1994
Highest Total to Win Batting Second	329-5	Sussex v Derbyshire	Derby	1997
Lowest Total	39	Ireland v Sussex	Hove	1985
Lowest Total in a Final	57	Essex v Lancashire	Lord's	1996
Lowest Total to Win Batting First	98	Worcs v Durham	Chester-le-St	1968

Highest Score	206	A.I.Kallicharran	Warwicks v Oxon	Birmingham	1984
HS (Minor County)	132	G.Robinson	Lincs v Northumb	Jesmond	1971
Hundreds	309	(Gillette Cup 93; NatWest Trophy 216)			1963-97
Fastest Hundred	36 balls	G.D.Rose	Somerset v Devon	Torquay	1990
Most Hundreds	7	C.L.Smith	Hampshire		1980-91
	7	R.A.Smith	Hampshire		1985-97
Most Runs	2547	(av 48.98)	G.A.Gooch	Essex	1973-96

Highest Partnership for each Wicket

1st	311	A.J.Wright/N.J.Trainor	Glos v Scotland	Bristol	1997
2nd	286	I.S.Anderson/A.Hill	Derbys v Cornwall	Derby	1986
3rd	309*	T.S.Curtis/T.M.Moody	Worcs v Surrey	The Oval	1994
4th	234*	D.Lloyd/C.H.Lloyd	Lancashire v Glos	Manchester	1978
5th	166	M.A.Lynch/G.R.J.Roope	Surrey v Durham	The Oval	1982
6th	178	J.P.Crawley/I.D.Austin	Lancashire v Sussex	Hove	1997
7th	160*	C.J.Richards/I.R.Payne	Surrey v Lincs	Sleaford	1983
8th	112	A.L.Penberthy/J.E.Emburey	Northants v Lancs	Manchester	1996
9th	87	M.A.Nash/A.E.Cordle	Glamorgan v Lincs	Swansea	1974
10th	81	S.Turner/R.E.East	Essex v Yorkshire	Leeds	1982

Best Bowling	8-21	M.A.Holding	Derbys v Sussex	Hove	1988
	8-31	D.L.Underwood	Kent v Scotland	Edinburgh	1987
Most Wickets	81	(av 14.85)	G.G.Arnold	Surrey	1963-80

Hat-Tricks (11): J.D.F.Larter (Northamptonshire 1963), D.A.D.Sydenham (Surrey 1964), R.N.S.Hobbs (Essex 1968), N.M.McVicker (Warwickshire 1971), G.S.Le Roux (Sussex 1985), M.Jean-Jacques (Derbyshire 1987), J.F.M.O'Brien (Cheshire 1988), R.A.Pick (Nottinghamshire 1995), J.E.Emburey (Northamptonshire 1996), A.R.Caddick (Somerset 1996), D.Gough (Yorkshire 1997).

Most Wicket-Keeping Dismissals in an Innings

7	(7ct)	A.J.Stewart	Surrey v Glamorgan	Swansea	1994

Most Catches in an Innings
4 – A.S.Brown (Gloucestershire 1963), G.Cook (Northamptonshire 1972), C.G.Greenidge (Hampshire 1981), D.C.Jackson (Durham 1984), T.S.Smith (Hertfordshire 1984), H.Morris (Glamorgan 1988), C.C.Lewis (Nottinghamshire 1992).

Most Appearances	64	M.W.Gatting	Middlesex	1975-97
Most Match Awards	9	G.A.Gooch	Essex	1973-96

Most Match Wins   71 – Warwickshire   **Most Cup/Trophy Wins**   6 – Lancashire.

1997 BENSON AND HEDGES CUP FINAL
KENT v SURREY

At Lord's, London on 12 July 1997.
Toss: Kent. Result: SURREY won by 8 wickets.
Award: B.C.Hollioake.

KENT		Runs	Balls	4/6	Fall
M.V.Fleming	lbw b Lewis	7	7	1	2- 15
M.J.Walker	b Bicknell	6	12	1	1- 15
T.R.Ward	lbw b A.J.Hollioake	15	40	2	4- 68
A.P.Wells	lbw b Bicknell	5	15	1	3- 23
N.J.Llong	c Butcher b Saqlain	42	65	5	5-106
M.A.Ealham	c Brown b Lewis	52	88	4	8-194
G.R.Cowdrey	b Lewis	8	20	1	6-135
P.A.Strang	b Salisbury	23	25	2	7-170
*†S.A.Marsh	not out	24	23	2	
M.J.McCague	c Thorpe b Saqlain	0	3	–	9-198
D.W.Headley	not out	3	3	–	
Extras	(B 1, LB 7, W 17, NB 2)	27			
Total	(50 overs; 9 wickets)	**212**			

SURREY		Runs	Balls	4/6	Fall
A.D.Brown	c Fleming b McCague	2	4	–	1- 2
†A.J.Stewart	not out	75	125	7	
B.C.Hollioake	c Strang b Ealham	98	112	15	2-161
G.P.Thorpe	not out	17	32	–	
*A.J.Hollioake					
M.A.Butcher					
C.C.Lewis					
J.D.Ratcliffe					
M.P.Bicknell					
I.D.K.Salisbury					
Saqlain Mushtaq					
Extras	(LB 11, W 6, NB 6)	23			
Total	(45 overs; 2 wickets)	**215**			

SURREY	O	M	R	W	KENT	O	M	R	W
Bicknell	8	0	33	2	McCague	8	0	45	1
Lewis	10	3	39	3	Headley	10	0	53	0
A.J.Hollioake	7	0	31	1	Fleming	7	1	29	0
B.C.Hollioake	6	0	28	0	Ealham	6	0	31	1
Saqlain Mushtaq	9	1	33	2	Strang	10	1	31	0
Salisbury	10	0	40	1	Llong	4	0	15	0

Scores after 15 overs: Kent 56-3; Surrey 80-1

Umpires: G.Sharp and D.R.Shepherd.

1997 BENSON AND HEDGES CUP

FINAL GROUP TABLES

GROUP A	P	W	L	NR	Pts	Net Run Rate
YORKSHIRE	5	4	1	–	8	16.13
WARWICKSHIRE	5	3	2	–	6	15.21
Derbyshire	5	3	2	–	6	2.68
Lancashire	5	3	2	–	6	−1.50
Worcestershire	5	2	3	–	4	−3.90
Minor Counties	5	–	5	–	–	−28.56

GROUP B	P	W	L	NR	Pts	Net Run Rate
LEICESTERSHIRE	4	3	1	–	6	18.15
NORTHAMPTONSHIRE	4	3	1	–	6	9.20
Durham	4	2	2	–	4	14.74
Nottinghamshire	4	1	2	1	3	−13.07
Scotland	4	–	3	1	1	−51.27

GROUP C	P	W	L	NR	Pts	Net Run Rate
KENT	5	4	–	1	9	9.84
SURREY	5	4	1	–	8	21.19
Gloucestershire	5	2	2	1	5	7.06
Sussex	5	2	3	–	4	−0.51
Hampshire	5	1	4	–	2	−15.50
British Universities	5	1	4	–	2	−18.57

GROUP D	P	W	L	NR	Pts	Net Run Rate
ESSEX	4	3	–	1	7	8.54
SOMERSET	4	3	1	–	6	29.88
Glamorgan	4	2	2	–	4	−6.83
Ireland	4	1	2	1	3	−32.62
Middlesex	4	–	4	–	–	−6.75

FINAL ROUNDS

QUARTER-FINALS 27 May	SEMI-FINALS 10 June	FINAL 12 July
KENT†		
Warwickshire (£5,250)	KENT†	
		Kent (£21,000)
NORTHAMPTONSHIRE		
Yorkshire† (£5,250)	Northamptonshire (£10,500)	
LEICESTERSHIRE†		
Somerset (£5,250)	Leicestershire (£10,500)	
		SURREY (£42,000)
SURREY		
Essex† (£5,250)	SURREY†	

† Home team. Winning teams are in capitals. Prize-money in brackets.

BENSON AND HEDGES CUP
PRINCIPAL RECORDS 1972-97

Highest Total		388-7	Essex v Scotland	Chelmsford	1992
Highest Total Batting Second		318-5	Lancashire v Leics	Manchester	1995
Highest Total to Lose Batting 2nd		303-7	Derbys v Somerset	Taunton	1990
Lowest Total		50	Hampshire v Yorks	Leeds	1991
Highest Score	198*	G.A.Gooch	Essex v Sussex	Hove	1982
Hundreds	298				1972-97
Fastest Hundred	62 min	M.A.Nash	Glamorgan v Hants	Swansea	1976

Highest Partnership for each Wicket

1st	252*	V.P.Terry/C.L.Smith	Hants v Comb Us	Southampton	1990
2nd	285*	C.G.Greenidge/D.R.Turner	Hants v Minor C (S)	Amersham	1973
3rd	269*	P.M.Roebuck/M.D.Crowe	Somerset v Hants	Southampton	1987
4th	184*	D.Lloyd/B.W.Reidy	Lancashire v Derbys	Chesterfield	1980
5th	160	A.J.Lamb/D.J.Capel	Northants v Leics	Northampton	1986
6th	167*	M.G.Bevan/R.J.Blakey	Yorkshire v Lancs	Manchester	1996
7th	149*	J.D.Love/C.M.Old	Yorks v Scotland	Bradford	1981
8th	109	R.E.East/N.Smith	Essex v Northants	Chelmsford	1977
9th	83	P.G.Newman/M.A.Holding	Derbyshire v Notts	Nottingham	1985
10th	80*	D.L.Bairstow/M.Johnson	Yorkshire v Derbys	Derby	1981

Best Bowling	7-12	W.W.Daniel	Middx v Minor C (E)	Ipswich	1978
	7-22	J.R.Thomson	Middx v Hampshire	Lord's	1981
	7-24	Mushtaq Ahmed	Somerset v Ireland	Taunton	1997
	7-32	R.G.D.Willis	Warwicks v Yorks	Birmingham	1981
Four wickets in Four Balls		S.M. Pollock	Warwicks v Leics	Birmingham	1996
Hat-Tricks		G.D.McKenzie	Leics v Worcs	Worcester	1972
		K.Higgs	Leics v Surrey	Lord's	1974
		A.A.Jones	Middlesex v Essex	Lord's	1977
		M.J.Procter	Glos v Hampshire	Southampton	1977
		W.Larkins	Northants v Comb Us	Northampton	1980
		E.A.Moseley	Glamorgan v Kent	Cardiff	1981
		G.C.Small	Warwickshire v Leics	Leicester	1984
		N.A.Mallender	Somerset v Comb Us	Taunton	1987
		W.K.M.Benjamin	Leics v Notts	Leicester	1987
		A.R.C.Fraser	Middlesex v Sussex	Lord's	1988

Most Wicket-Keeping Dismissals in an Innings

8	(8ct)	D.J.S.Taylor	Somerset v Comb Us	Taunton	1982

Most Catches in an Innings

5		V.J.Marks	Comb Us v Kent	Oxford	1976

Most Match Awards	22		G.A.Gooch	Essex	1973-97

BENSON AND HEDGES CUP WINNERS

1972	Leicestershire	1981	Somerset	1990	Lancashire
1973	Kent	1982	Somerset	1991	Worcestershire
1974	Surrey	1983	Middlesex	1992	Hampshire
1975	Leicestershire	1984	Lancashire	1993	Derbyshire
1976	Kent	1985	Leicestershire	1994	Warwickshire
1977	Gloucestershire	1986	Middlesex	1995	Lancashire
1978	Kent	1987	Yorkshire	1996	Lancashire
1979	Essex	1988	Hampshire	1997	Surrey
1980	Northamptonshire	1989	Nottinghamshire		

SUNDAY LEAGUE
FINAL TABLE 1997

	P	W	L	T	NR	Pts	NRR
1 WARWICKSHIRE (4)	17	13	4	–	–	52	14.14
2 Kent (10)	17	12	4	–	1	50	7.70
3 Lancashire (9)	17	10	4	1	2	46	1.89
4 Leicestershire (12)	17	9	5	1	2	42	7.11
5 Surrey (1)	17	9	5	–	3	42	1.06
6 Somerset (5)	17	9	6	–	2	40	4.31
7 Essex (17)	17	9	6	1	1	40	–2.38
8 Worcestershire (8)	17	8	6	1	2	38	6.87
9 Northamptonshire (6)	17	8	6	–	3	38	2.78
10 Yorkshire (3)	17	8	7	1	1	36	5.24
11 Gloucestershire (16)	17	7	6	–	4	36	1.01
12 Nottinghamshire (2)	17	7	7	–	3	34	–0.19
13 Glamorgan (13)	17	5	9	–	3	26	–4.01
14 Derbyshire (11)	17	4	9	–	4	24	–3.04
15 Hampshire (15)	17	5	11	–	1	22	–4.73
16 Middlesex (7)	17	3	10	1	3	20	–8.28
17 Durham (18)	17	3	13	–	1	14	–12.27
18 Sussex (14)	17	2	13	–	2	12	–16.72

Win = 4 points. Tie (T)/No Result (NR) = 2 points. Positions of counties finishing equal on points are decided by most wins or, if equal, by higher net run-rate (NRR – overall run-rate in all matches, i.e. total runs scored x 100 divided by balls received, minus the run-rate of its opponents in those same matches).

1996 final positions are shown in brackets.

The Sunday League's sponsors have been John Player & Sons (1969-1986), Refuge Assurance (1987-1991), TCCB (1992) and AXA Equity & Law Insurance (1993 to date). The competition has been limited to 40 overs per innings, apart from 1993 when it was experimentally extended to 50.

WINNERS

1969 Lancashire	1979 Somerset	1989 Lancashire
1970 Lancashire	1980 Warwickshire	1990 Derbyshire
1971 Worcestershire	1981 Essex	1991 Nottinghamshire
1972 Kent	1982 Sussex	1992 Middlesex
1973 Kent	1983 Yorkshire	1993 Glamorgan
1974 Leicestershire	1984 Essex	1994 Warwickshire
1975 Hampshire	1985 Essex	1995 Kent
1976 Kent	1986 Hampshire	1996 Surrey
1977 Leicestershire	1987 Worcestershire	1997 Warwickshire
1978 Hampshire	1988 Worcestershire	

SUNDAY LEAGUE
PRINCIPAL RECORDS 1969-97

Highest Total		375-4	Surrey v Yorkshire	Scarborough	1994
Highest Total Batting Second		317-6	Surrey v Notts	The Oval	1993
Lowest Total		23	Middlesex v Yorks	Leeds	1974

Highest Score	203	A.D.Brown	Surrey v Hampshire	Guildford	1997
Total Hundreds	578				1969-97
Fastest Hundred	44 balls	M.A.Ealham	Kent v Derbyshire	Maidstone	1995

Highest Partnership for each Wicket

1st	239	G.A.Gooch/B.R.Hardie	Essex v Notts	Nottingham	1985
2nd	273	G.A.Gooch/K.S.McEwan	Essex v Notts	Nottingham	1983
3rd	223	S.J.Cook/G.D.Rose	Somerset v Glam	Neath	1990
4th	219	C.G.Greenidge/C.L.Smith	Hampshire v Surrey	Southampton	1987
5th	190	R.J.Blakey/M.J.Foster	Yorkshire v Leics	Leicester	1993
6th	137	M.P.Speight/I.D.K.Salisbury	Sussex v Surrey	Guildford	1996
7th	132	K.R.Brown/N.F.Williams	Middx v Somerset	Lord's	1988
8th	110*	C.L.Cairns/B.N.French	Notts v Surrey	The Oval	1993
9th	105	D.G.Moir/R.W.Taylor	Derbyshire v Kent	Derby	1984
10th	82	G.Chapple/P.J.Martin	Lancashire v Worcs	Manchester	1996

Best Bowling	8-26	K.D.Boyce	Essex v Lancashire	Manchester	1971
	7-15	R.A.Hutton	Yorkshire v Worcs	Leeds	1969
	7-39	A.Hodgson	Northants v Somerset	Northampton	1976
	7-41	A.N.Jones	Sussex v Notts	Nottingham	1986

Four Wkts in Four Balls	A.Ward		Derbyshire v Sussex	Derby	1970

Hat-Tricks (24): Derbyshire – A.Ward (1970), C.J.Tunnicliffe (1979); Essex – K.D.Boyce (1971); Glamorgan – M.A.Nash (1975), A.E.Cordle (1979), G.C.Holmes (1987), A.Dale (1993); Gloucestershire – K.M.Curran (1989); Hampshire – J.M.Rice (1975), M.D.Marshall (1981); Kent – R.M.Ellison (1983), M.J.McCague (1992); Leicestershire – G.D.McKenzie (1972); Northamptonshire – A.Hodgson (1976); Nottinghamshire – K.Saxelby (1987), K.P.Evans (1994); Somerset – R.Palmer (1970), I.V.A.Richards (1982); Surrey – M.P.Bicknell (1992); Sussex – A.Buss (1974); Warwickshire – R.G.D.Willis (1973), W.Blenkiron (1974); Worcestershire – R.K.Illingworth (1993); Yorkshire – P.W.Jarvis (1982).

Most Wicket-Keeping Dismissals in an Innings

7	(6ct, 1st)	R.W.Taylor	Derbyshire v Lancs	Manchester	1975

Most Catches in an Innings

5	J.M.Rice		Hampshire v Warwicks	Southampton	1978

COUNTY CAPS AWARDED IN 1997

Derbyshire	–
Durham	D.C.Boon, J.J.B.Lewis, N.J.Speak, M.P.Speight
Essex	A.P.Cowan, D.D.J.Robinson
Glamorgan	S.D.Thomas, Waqar Younis
Gloucestershire	S.Young
Hampshire	M.L.Hayden
Kent	P.A.Strang, A.P.Wells
Lancashire	–
Leicestershire	N.C.Johnson, I.J.Sutcliffe
Middlesex	J.H.Kallis
Northamptonshire	–
Nottinghamshire	M.N.Bowen, C.M.Tolley
Somerset	S.C.Ecclestone, P.C.L.Holloway, K.J.Shine, A.P.van Troost
Surrey	–
Sussex	M.A.Robinson, N.R.Taylor
Warwickshire	D.L.Hemp, G.Welch
Worcestershire	A.Sheriyar, K.R.Spiring
Yorkshire	D.S.Lehmann

MINOR COUNTIES CHAMPIONSHIP

FINAL TABLE 1997

							Bonus Points		Total
		P	W	L	D	NR	Bat	Bowl	Points
EASTERN DIVISION									
Bedfordshire	NW	9	4	1	3	1	25	22	116
Staffordshire	NW	9	3	1	2	3	15	20	98
Norfolk	NW	9	3	2	4	0	23	26	97
Cumberland	NW	9	3	0	5	1	15	19	87
Buckinghamshire	NW	9	2	2	5	0	26	25	83
Cambridgeshire	NW	9	2	0	6	1	20	23	80
Hertfordshire		9	2	3	4	0	22	15	69
Lincolnshire		9	1	5	3	0	21	15	52
Northumberland		9	1	4	3	1	9	21	51
Suffolk		9	0	3	5	1	9	19	33
WESTERN DIVISION									
Devon	NW	9	4	3	1	1	22	27	118
Wales	NW	9	4	1	3	1	12	17	98
Cheshire	NW	9	3	2	3	1	17	20	90
Dorset	NW	9	3	2	3	1	11	21	85
Hertfordshire	NW	9	2	2	4	1	16	22	75
Shropshire		9	2	0	6	1	13	15	65
Oxfordshire		9	2	3	3	1	12	15	64
Berkshire		9	2	2	5	0	9	21	62
Wiltshire		9	1	2	5	1	16	14	51
Cornwall		9	0	6	3	0	8	21	29

NW   Qualified for 1998 NatWest Trophy

1997 CHAMPIONSHIP FINAL
BEDFORDSHIRE v DEVON

At Wardown Park, Luton on 7, 8 September. Toss: Bedfordshire.
Result: **MATCH DRAWN; DEVON** awarded Championship on run rate.

DEVON

N.R.Gaywood	run out	32		lbw b Sher	34
K.A.O.Barrett	b Dalton	27		b Bullen	10
N.A.Folland	c Bullen b Roberts	58		c Bullen b Dalton	5
*P.M.Roebuck	not out	56	(5)	c and b Dalton	4
G.T.J.Townsend	c Roberts b Bullen	4	(4)	b Roberts	28
A.J.Pugh	st Sandford b Roberts	23		lbw b Dalton	7
†C.M.W.Read				not out	30
K.Donohue				b Dalton	45
P.Warren				b Dalton	0
J.Rhodes				not out	4
R.J.Coupe					
Extras	(B 1, LB 3, W 6, NB 6)	16		(B 5, LB 4, NB 4)	13
Total	(5 wickets; 50 overs)	**216**		(8 wickets declared)	**180**

BEDFORDSHIRE

W.Larkins	c Read b Warren	11	(2)	c Pugh b Rhodes	51
R.N.Dalton	c Roebuck b Donohue	6	(6)	c Gaywood b Roebuck	0
A.R.Roberts	c Read b Roebuck	12	(1)	lbw b Roberts	62
D.R.Clarke	c Read b Donohue	0	(3)	c Gaywood b Coupe	36
D.J.M.Mercer	lbw b Rhodes	9	(4)	c Warren b Rhodes	38
C.K.Bullen	c Barrett b Coupe	36	(5)	c Pugh b Roebuck	19
*P.D.B.Hoare	c Coupe	18		not out	8
Z.A.Sher	lbw b Roebuck	3		not out	16
K.J.Wright	lbw b Roebuck	2			
†G.D.Sandford	not out	5			
M.R.White	not out	9			
Extras	(LB 4, NB 4)	8		(B 9, LB 10, NB 2)	21
Total	(9 wickets; 50 overs)	**119**		(6 wickets)	**251**

BEDFORDSHIRE	O	M	R	W	O	M	R	W	FALL OF WICKETS				
White	3	0	21	0	4	1	10	0		D	B	D	B
Sher	5	1	30	0	10	4	27	1	Wkt	1st	1st	2nd	2nd
Dalton	13	4	39	1	20	6	43	5	1st	39	17	48	92
Roberts	20	2	83	2	17	7	40	1	2nd	111	17	48	159
Bullen	9	0	39	1	16	4	51	1	3rd	163	17	79	163
									4th	173	30	87	220
DEVON									5th	216	65	99	223
Donohue	8	2	17	3	9	1	38	0	6th	–	97	99	223
Warren	4	1	13	1	4	0	21	0	7th	–	101	176	–
Roebuck	16	4	27	2	27	4	67	3	8th	–	101	176	–
Rhodes	6	1	20	1	8	0	30	2	9th	–	104	–	–
Coupe	16	2	38	2	17	1	69	1	10th	–	–	–	–
Pugh					2	0	7	0					

Umpires: P.Adams and M.P.Moran.

MINOR COUNTIES CHAMPIONS

1895	Norfolk / Durham / Worcestershire	1929	Oxfordshire	1968	Yorkshire II
1896	Worcestershire	1930	Durham	1969	Buckinghamshire
1897	Worcestershire	1931	Leicestershire II	1970	Bedfordshire
1898	Worcestershire	1932	Buckinghamshire	1971	Yorkshire II
1899	Northamptonshire / Buckinghamshire	1933	*Undecided*	1972	Bedfordshire
		1934	Lancashire II	1973	Shropshire
1900	Glamorgan / Durham / Northamptonshire	1935	Middlesex II	1974	Oxfordshire
		1936	Hertfordshire	1975	Hertfordshire
		1937	Lancashire II	1976	Durham
1901	Durham	1938	Buckinghamshire	1977	Suffolk
1902	Wiltshire	1939	Surrey II	1978	Devon
1903	Northamptonshire	1946	Suffolk	1979	Suffolk
1904	Northamptonshire	1947	Yorkshire II	1980	Durham
1905	Norfolk	1948	Lancashire II	1981	Durham
1906	Staffordshire	1949	Lancashire II	1982	Oxfordshire
1907	Lancashire II	1950	Surrey II	1983	Hertfordshire
1908	Staffordshire	1951	Kent II	1984	Durham
1909	Wiltshire	1952	Buckinghamshire	1985	Cheshire
1910	Norfolk	1953	Berkshire	1986	Cumberland
1911	Staffordshire	1954	Surrey II	1987	Buckinghamshire
1912	*In abeyance*	1955	Surrey II	1988	Cheshire
1913	Norfolk	1956	Kent II	1989	Oxfordshire
1920	Staffordshire	1957	Yorkshire II	1990	Hertfordshire
1921	Staffordshire	1958	Yorkshire II	1991	Staffordshire
1922	Buckinghamshire	1959	Warwickshire II	1992	Staffordshire
1923	Buckinghamshire	1960	Lancashire II	1993	Staffordshire
1924	Berkshire	1961	Somerset II	1994	Devon
1925	Buckinghamshire	1962	Warwickshire II	1995	Devon
1926	Durham	1963	Cambridgeshire	1996	Devon
1927	Staffordshire	1964	Lancashire II	1997	Devon
1928	Berkshire	1965	Somerset II		
		1966	Lincolnshire		
		1967	Cheshire		

MINOR COUNTIES RECORDS

Highest Total	621		Surrey II v Devon	The Oval	1928
Lowest Total	14		Cheshire v Staffs	Stoke	1909
Highest Score	282	E.Garnett	Berkshire v Wiltshire	Reading	1908
Most Runs – Season	1212	A.F.Brazier	Surrey II		1949
Record Partnership					
2nd 388*		T.H.Clark and A.F.Brazier	Surrey II v Sussex II	The Oval	1949
Best Bowling – Innings	10- 11	S.Turner	Cambs v Cumberland	Penrith	1987
— **Match**	18-100	N.W.Harding	Kent II v Wiltshire	Swindon	1937
Most Wickets – Season	119	S.F.Barnes	Staffordshire		1906

1997 MINOR COUNTIES CHAMPIONSHIP

LEADING BATTING AVERAGES
(Qualification: 8 completed innings (or 500 runs) average 41.00)

		I	NO	HS	Runs	Avge
N.A.Folland	Devon	15	4	116*	862	78.36
I.Cockbain	Cheshire	13	5	103*	540	67.50
D.M.Ward	Hertfordshire	12	2	123*	648	64.80
J.R.Wileman	Lincolnshire	10	2	123*	478	59.75
S.V.Laudat	Oxfordshire	10	2	133*	473	59.12
S.A.Kellett	Cambridgeshire	14	3	121	626	56.90
J.C.Harrison	Buckinghamshire	15	5	107*	565	56.50
D.A.Winter	Wiltshire	15	1	136	788	56.28
I.R.Payne	Shropshire	11	3	107*	412	51.50
W.Larkins	Bedfordshire	18	1	125	865	50.88
S.J.Dean	Staffordshire	12	1	131	553	50.27
J.S.G.Norman	Cambridgeshire	11	1	107*	494	49.40
B.C.A.Ellison	Oxfordshire	16	5	77*	543	49.36
S.C.Goldsmith	Norfolk	17	4	99*	614	47.23
D.W.Randall	Suffolk	14	1	148	614	47.23
A.D.Griffin	Hertfordshire	16	5	138*	519	47.18
P.J.Caley	Suffolk	13	2	126	498	45.27
D.R.Clarke	Bedfordshire	12	1	114*	479	43.54
T.W.Adcock	Northumberland	15	1	108*	603	43.07
J.J.E.Hardy	Dorset	13	2	102	471	42.81
R.G.Hignett	Cheshire	16	1	112	637	42.46
D.J.M.Mercer	Bedfordshire	13	4	89	378	42.00
M.R.Davies	Shropshire	13	3	80	417	41.70
R.J.Scott	Dorset	14	2	108*	492	41.00

LEADING BOWLING AVERAGES
(Qualification: 20 wickets, average 30.00)

		O	M	R	W	Avge
J.H.Shackleton	Dorset	220.3	72	497	37	13.43
K.E.Cooper	Herefordshire	310.3	101	652	43	15.16
M.W.Thomas	Norfolk	160.1	28	535	35	15.28
S.C.Goldsmith	Norfolk	144.2	41	398	24	16.58
S.Barwick	Wales	214.1	73	514	29	17.72
P.M.Roebuck	Devon	347.1	106	709	40	17.72
N.V.Radford	Herefordshire	253.5	65	715	39	18.33
Ajaz Akhtar	Cambridgeshire	170.4	47	429	23	18.65
K.Donohue	Devon	186.5	46	487	26	18.73
N.M.Kendrick	Berkshire	260.3	65	817	41	19.92
A.Jones	Oxfordshire	153.5	39	458	22	20.81
A.K.Golding	Northumberland	228.2	68	633	29	21.82
A.R.Clarke	Buckinghamshire	287	73	913	41	22.26
C.E.Shreck	Cornwall	135.2	19	672	29	23.17
A.M.Simmons	Shropshire	136	28	469	20	23.45
P.D.North	Wales	174	40	587	25	23.48
A.Richardson	Staffordshire	162.3	32	485	20	24.25
I.J.Curtis	Oxfordshire	171.5	26	622	25	24.88
L.J.Crozier	Northumberland	153	39	512	20	25.60
D.B.Pennett	Cumberland	159.2	37	569	22	25.86
M.A.Sharp	Cumberland	161	42	524	20	26.20
A.R.Roberts	Bedfordshire	255	89	944	35	26.97
K.A.Arnold	Oxfordshire	268.1	59	778	28	27.78
C.K.Bullen	Bedfordshire	194.4	47	650	23	28.26
A.B.Byram	Shropshire	145.3	20	660	23	28.69

SECOND XI CHAMPIONSHIP 1997
FINAL TABLE

	P	W	L	D	Bonus Points Bat	Bowl	Total Points
1 LANCASHIRE (5)	17	10	1	6	37	52	225†
2 Yorkshire (4)	17	8	5	4	41	45	214
3 Derbyshire (9)	17	7	2	8	43	47	202
4 Warwickshire (1)	17	7	3	7	44	38	194
5 Hampshire (15)	17	6	5	6	39	50	185
6 Surrey (17)	17	5	3	9	44	53	177
7 Northamptonshire (2)	17	5	5	7	40	54	174
8 Leicestershire (7)	17	6	3	8	39	38	173
9 Sussex (16)	17	5	4	8	37	42	155‡
10 Glamorgan (13)	17	5	6	6	36	33	149
11 Middlesex (3)	17	4	4	9	35	50	149
12 Gloucestershire (12)	17	4	4	9	38	42	144
13 Somerset (14)	17	3	7	7	37	50	135
14 Durham (8)	17	2	4	11	38	42	112
15 Worcestershire (10)	17	2	7	8	36	43	111
16 Kent (6)	17	2	5	10	34	39	105
17 Essex (18)	17	1	10	6	29	45	90
18 Nottinghamshire (11)	17	–	4	13	42	41	83

Win = 16 points. 1996 final positions are shown in brackets.
† Forfeited their total points (24) v Yorkshire for fielding a second overseas player.
‡ Includes 12 points for winning a match begun with fewer than 8 hours of play remaining.

ECB SECOND XI AWARDS 1997

Player of the Season   M.J.Powell   Glamorgan
   Powell, who made 200* on first-class debut, scored 1210 runs (avge 75) with five hundreds in the Second XI Championship.
Player of the Month
April/May   M.J.Powell   Glamorgan
June   M.Garaway   Hampshire
July   M.E.Trescothick   Somerset
August/September   M.D.Edmond   Warwickshire

SECOND XI CHAMPIONS

1959 Gloucestershire	1973 Essex	1987 Kent/Yorkshire
1960 Northamptonshire	1974 Middlesex	1988 Surrey
1961 Kent	1975 Surrey	1989 Middlesex
1962 Worcestershire	1976 Kent	1990 Sussex
1963 Worcestershire	1977 Yorkshire	1991 Yorkshire
1964 Lancashire	1978 Sussex	1992 Surrey
1965 Glamorgan	1979 Warwickshire	1993 Middlesex
1966 Surrey	1980 Glamorgan	1994 Somerset
1967 Hampshire	1981 Hampshire	1995 Hampshire
1968 Surrey	1982 Worcestershire	1996 Warwickshire
1969 Kent	1983 Leicestershire	1997 Lancashire
1970 Kent	1984 Yorkshire	
1971 Hampshire	1985 Nottinghamshire	
1972 Nottinghamshire	1986 Lancashire	

FIRST-CLASS CAREER RECORDS

Compiled by Philip Bailey

The following career records are for all players who appeared in first-class or limited-overs cricket during the 1997 season, and are complete to the end of that season. Some players who did not appear in 1997 but may do so in 1998, are also included.

BATTING AND FIELDING

'1000' denotes instances of scoring 1000 runs in a season. Where these have been achieved outside the UK, they are shown after a plus sign.

	M	I	NO	HS	Runs	Avge	100	1000	Ct/St
Abdul Razzak	7	11	3	62	224	28.00	–	–	1
Adams, C.J.	155	253	20	239	8431	36.18	21	3	172
Afford, J.A.	170	167	72	22*	398	4.18	–	–	57
Afzaal, U.	31	53	5	80	1159	24.14	–	–	15
Aldred, P.	20	25	4	83	280	13.33	–	–	13
Ali Naqvi	8	13	–	114	362	25.85	1	–	4
Ali Rizvi	31	44	8	28	243	6.75	–	–	19
Alleyne, M.W.	219	359	37	256	10239	31.79	13	5	169/2
Allingham, M.J.D.	2	4	2	50*	99	49.50	–	–	2
Altree, D.A.	4	5	2	0*	0	0.00	–	–	1
Amin, R.M.	4	6	3	4*	11	3.66	–	–	2
Andrew, S.J.W.	132	112	42	35	499	7.12	–	–	26
Anthony, H.A.G.	74	108	9	91	1707	17.24	–	–	28
Archer, G.F.	72	128	13	168	4072	35.40	8	1	77
Arthurton, K.L.T.	115	180	25	200*	7171	46.26	19	1	61
Asif Din	211	343	46	217	9074	30.55	9	2	114
Astle, N.J.	48	77	7	191	2635	37.64	8	–	33
Atherton, M.A.	249	431	39	199	16725	42.66	44	6	196
Athey, C.W.J.	467	784	71	184	25453	35.69	55	13	429/2
Austin, I.D.	105	146	31	115*	3349	29.12	2	–	26
Averis, J.M.M.	10	15	4	42	276	25.09	–	–	2
Aymes, A.N.	145	212	56	113	4771	30.58	3	–	321/31
Azhar Mahmood	43	67	11	92	1321	23.58	–	–	33
Badenhorst, A.	24	27	10	21*	86	5.05	–	–	7
Bailey, M.R.K.	1	1	–	6*	6	–	–	–	1/1
Bailey, R.J.	317	537	80	224*	19099	41.79	42	13	241
Bailey, T.M.B.	2	2	1	31*	33	33.00	–	–	4
Ball, M.C.J.	103	158	28	71	2231	17.16	–	–	122
Barnett, K.J.	414	670	62	239*	24327	40.01	52	14	242
Bates, J.J.	7	9	2	47	113	16.14	–	–	6
Bates, R.T.	30	43	10	34	433	13.12	–	–	18
Batt, C.J.	1								1
Battarbee, C.M.	7	8	6	10*	29	14.50	–	–	1
Batty, G.J.	1	2	–	18	18	9.00	–	–	–
Batty, J.N.	15	19	5	56	396	28.28	–	–	18/3
Bell, M.A.V.	20	23	10	30	109	8.38	–	–	8
Benjamin, J.E.	116	134	40	49	1095	11.64	–	–	23
Benson, J.D.R.	57	85	9	153	2158	28.39	4	–	66
Berry, D.S.	86	126	17	148	2212	20.29	1	–	305/31
Betts, M.M.	37	57	10	57*	574	12.21	–	–	7
Bevan, M.G.	134	226	38	203*	9750	51.86	31	2+2	77
Bichel, A.J.	25	31	3	61*	561	20.03	–	–	15
Bicknell, D.J.	200	352	34	235*	12696	39.92	30	6	75
Bicknell, M.P.	181	215	58	88	2979	18.97	–	–	63

152

	M	I	NO	HS	Runs	Avge	100	1000	Ct/St
Blackwell, I.D.	4	5	–	42	51	10.20	–	–	–
Blain, J.A.R.	2	1	–	0	0	0.00	–	–	2
Blakey, R.J.	258	413	65	221	11364	32.65	10	5	517/46
Blewett, G.S.	87	149	11	268	6438	46.55	18	0+3	62
Bloomfield, T.F.	4	3	2	4	4	4.00	–	–	2
Boiling, J.	88	125	38	69	1160	13.33	–	–	70
Boon, D.C.	296	496	44	227	20583	45.53	63	3+7	251
Boswell, S.A.J.	12	16	5	35	127	11.54	–	–	4
Boulton, N.R.	1	2	–	14	15	7.50	–	–	–
Bovill, J.N.B.	38	49	16	31	324	9.81	–	–	7
Bowen, M.N.	42	52	13	32	462	11.84	–	–	11
Bowler, P.D.	212	368	33	241*	13438	40.11	29	8	140/1
Brimson, M.T.	34	36	15	30*	217	10.33	–	–	6
Brown, A.D.	93	150	14	187	5628	41.38	14	3	92
Brown, D.R.	64	97	11	85	2143	24.91	–	–	34
Brown, J.F.	7	9	5	16*	25	6.25	–	–	3
Brown, K.R.	230	348	69	200*	9911	35.52	13	2	425/28
Brown, S.J.E.	124	172	50	69	1490	12.21	–	–	36
Buchanan, L.G.	8	14	4	43*	168	16.80	–	–	1
Bull, J.J.	5	6	1	30	53	10.60	–	–	–
Burns, M.	34	55	3	82	1150	22.11	–	–	49/6
Butcher, G.P.	31	44	8	101*	1046	29.05	1	–	11
Butcher, M.A.	78	139	11	167	5029	39.28	7	3	91
Byas, E.	200	337	32	213	11232	36.82	20	5	247
Byrne, B.W.	11	20	–	49	354	17.70	–	–	2
Byrne, J.E.	1	2	1	12*	19	19.00	–	–	–
Caddick, A.R.	103	132	23	92	1797	16.48	–	–	37
Campbell, C.L.	2	1	–	7	7	7.00	–	–	–
Capel, D.J.	311	477	66	175	12202	29.68	16	3	156
Carpenter, J.R.	3	6	–	63	153	25.50	–	–	2
Cassar, M.E.	10	12	1	78	361	32.81	–	–	4
Chapman, A.J.	6	11	1	80	211	21.10	–	–	8/3
Chapman, R.J.	21	21	5	25	131	8.18	–	–	5
Chapple, G.	74	102	38	109*	1386	21.65	1	–	24
Chilton, M.J.	1	1	–	9	9	9.00	–	–	–
Church, M.J.	16	29	1	152	544	19.42	1	–	8
Churton, D.R.H.	20	24	1	44	329	14.30	–	–	23/7
Clarke, V.P.	26	43	7	99	991	27.52	–	–	11
Cockroft, J.R.	1	1	–	1	1	1.00	–	–	–
Collingwood, P.D.	19	33	1	107	780	24.37	1	–	17
Connor, C.A.	217	205	53	59	1814	11.93	–	–	61
Cooke, G.	2	1	–	0	0	0.00	–	–	1
Cork, D.G.	137	201	30	104	4216	24.65	2	–	86
Cosker, D.A.	21	15	6	24	61	6.77	–	–	7
Cottey, P.A.	184	297	46	203	9607	38.27	19	6	122
Cousins, D.M.	14	23	5	18*	145	8.05	–	–	5
Cowan, A.P.	33	50	13	77	682	18.43	–	–	14
Cowdrey, G.R.	179	284	29	147	8858	34.73	17	3	97
Cox, D.M.	17	25	5	95*	535	26.75	–	–	4
Crawley, J.P.	154	252	26	286	11111	49.16	22	6	126
Croft, R.D.B.	185	269	49	143	5621	25.55	2	–	93
Crowe, C.D.	1	2	–	9	10	5.00	–	–	1
Cunliffe, R.J.	29	46	5	190*	1291	31.48	2	–	15
Curran, K.M.	297	467	78	159	14722	37.84	25	7	179
Curry, D.J.	2	4	–	41	54	13.50	–	–	–
Curtis, T.S.	339	579	67	248	20832	40.68	43	11	192
Dakin, J.M.	16	24	3	190	706	33.61	3	–	9

153

	M	I	NO	HS	Runs	Avge	100	1000	Ct/St
Dale, A.	146	240	23	214*	7129	32.85	14	2	57
Daley, J.A.	46	79	8	159*	2224	31.32	1	–	26
Davies, A.G.	3	4	2	26*	65	32.50	–	–	8/2
Davies, A.P.	3	2	1	11*	19	19.00	–	–	–
Davies, M.K.	6	9	4	17	49	9.80	–	–	2
Davis, R.P.	169	208	46	67	2452	15.13	–	–	155
Davy, J.O.	1	2	1	51*	53	53.00	–	–	–
Dawood, I.	3	4	2	10*	13	6.50	–	–	4/2
Dawson, M.W.	4	7	–	23	35	5.00	–	–	1
Dawson, R.I.	55	98	7	127*	2375	26.09	3	1	27
Dean, K.J.	18	20	6	21*	112	8.00	–	–	3
DeFreitas, P.A.J.	273	385	35	113	7624	21.78	6	–	96
Dibden, R.R.	5	8	2	1	1	0.16	–	–	–
Dimond, M.	5	5	1	26	71	17.75	–	–	4
Donald, M.A.	241	279	107	46*	2126	12.36	–	–	92
Dowman, M.P.	40	70	3	149	2087	31.14	6	1	22
Drakes, V.C.	63	100	15	180*	2048	24.09	4	–	17
Dutch, K.P.	12	13	2	79	177	16.09	–	–	8
Dyer, N.J.	1	1	1	0*	0	–	–	–	1
Ealham, M.A.	106	171	28	139	4689	32.79	4	1	44
Ecclestone, S.C.	41	67	9	133	2091	36.05	3	–	18
Edmond, M.D.	4	4	2	21	43	21.50	–	–	1
Edwards, A.D.	9	13	2	22	104	9.45	–	–	7
Edwards, G.J.M.	1	–	–	–	–	–	–	–	–
Elliott, M.T.G.	62	115	10	203	5512	52.49	16	1+2	67
Ellis, S.W.K.	10	11	4	15	63	9.00	–	–	7
Emburey, J.E.	513	644	130	133	12021	23.38	7	–	459
Evans, A.W.	9	16	3	71*	437	33.61	–	–	6
Evans, K.P.	151	207	44	104	4069	24.96	3	–	108
Fairbrother, N.H.	303	483	68	366	17182	41.40	37	10	220
Farhan Adil	6	11	–	50	214	19.45	–	–	8
Fay, R.A.	16	25	3	26	164	7.45	–	–	5
Fazal-e-Akber	4	7	3	6	19	4.75	–	–	1
Fisher, I.D.	5	5	1	37	75	18.75	–	–	–
Flanagan, I.N.	2	3	1	40	72	36.00	–	–	–
Fleming, M.V.	149	244	27	138	6689	30.82	9	–	60
Flintoff, A.	7	11	–	117	252	22.90	1	–	7
Flower, A.	63	103	19	156	3912	46.57	10	–	111/10
Flower, G.W.	65	116	9	243*	4501	42.06	8	–	57
Foley, G.I.	29	48	5	155	1322	30.74	1	–	27
Follett, D.	8	10	6	17	30	7.50	–	–	3
Ford, J.A.	1	–	–	–	–	–	–	–	1
Fordham, A.	167	297	24	206*	10939	40.06	25	5	117
Foster, M.J.	22	37	1	129	807	22.41	1	–	8
Francis, N.B.	25	34	3	26	251	8.09	–	–	12
Francis, S.R.G.	1	2	–	4	8	4.00	–	–	–
Franks, P.J.	15	19	6	50	280	21.53	–	–	7
Fraser, A.R.C.	220	258	63	92	2175	11.15	–	–	42
Freeth, J.W.O.	14	11	3	18	44	5.50	–	–	4
Frost, T.	9	11	2	56	158	17.55	–	–	27/2
Fulton, D.P.	59	106	8	134*	3105	31.68	4	–	90
Fulton, J.A.G.	10	19	–	78	451	23.73	–	–	6
Gallian, J.E.R.	91	159	13	312	5728	39.23	12	2	62
Garaway, M.	2	2	–	44	49	24.50	–	–	9/1
Gatting, M.W.	534	832	120	258	35410	49.73	92	18+1	474
Giddins, E.S.H.	80	96	39	34	321	5.63	–	–	12
Gie, N.A.	7	12	–	50	183	15.25	–	–	4

154

	M	I	NO	HS	Runs	Avge	100	1000	Ct/St
Gilchrist, A.C.	55	84	15	189*	2669	38.68	5	–	220/11
Giles, A.F.	44	60	14	106*	1427	31.02	1	–	15
Gillespie, J.N.	33	45	10	58	412	11.77	–	–	15
Gooch, G.A.	580	988	75	333	44841	49.11	128	20+1	555
Goodchild, D.J.	1	2	–	4	4	2.00	–	–	–
Gough, D.	136	182	31	121	2475	16.39	1	–	34
Grayson, A.P.	88	138	16	140	3919	32.12	4	2	75
Green, R.J.	12	16	5	51	185	16.81	–	–	3
Greenfield, K.	78	135	15	154*	3550	29.58	9	–	65
Griffiths, S.P.	6	10	–	20	76	7.60	–	–	17
Habib, A.	29	45	9	215	1438	39.94	3	–	14
Hamilton, G.M.	25	32	7	61	476	19.04	–	–	10
Hancock, T.H.C.	94	165	13	123	4015	26.41	4	–	58
Hansen, T.M.	1	2	1	19	31	31.00	–	–	–
Harden, R.J.	229	374	58	187	12596	39.86	28	7	172
Harmison, S.J.	1	2	–	6	10	5.00	–	–	–
Harris, A.J.	37	51	11	36	335	8.37	–	–	12
Hart, J.P.	1	2	2	18*	18	–	–	–	–
Hartley, P.J.	198	241	52	127*	3875	20.50	2	–	62
Harvey, M.E.	5	8	–	25	116	14.50	–	–	2
Hasan Raza	9	15	–	96	566	37.73	–	–	3
Hayden, M.L.	108	194	23	235*	9280	54.26	28	2+3	92
Hayhurst, A.N.	166	265	34	172*	7825	33.87	14	3	56
Haynes, G.R.	80	122	9	158	3464	30.65	3	1	37
Haynes, J.E.	2	4	–	9	13	3.25	–	–	–
Haynes, J.J.	3	5	–	21	67	13.40	–	–	12/1
Headley, D.W.	98	127	33	91	1655	17.60	–	–	38
Healy, I.A.	183	266	56	161*	6717	31.98	3	–	566/49
Hegg, W.K.	223	325	63	134	6745	25.74	4	–	536/63
Hemp, D.L.	94	164	16	157	4984	33.67	9	2	59
Herzberg, S.	21	26	8	57*	394	21.88	–	–	6
Hewitt, J.P.	28	36	8	75	576	20.57	–	–	11
Hewson, D.R.	9	16	1	87	317	21.13	–	–	5
Hibbert, A.J.E.	4	7	1	85	151	25.16	–	–	3
Hick, G.A.	346	565	59	405*	28473	56.27	96	13+1	417
Hindson, J.E.	28	36	7	53*	384	13.24	–	–	14
Hodgson, T.P.	3	6	–	44	101	16.83	–	–	–
Hoggard, M.J.	2	3	1	10	12	6.00	–	–	–
Hollioake, A.J.	76	123	12	182	4691	42.26	11	2	63
Hollioake, B.C.	17	26	1	76	622	24.88	–	–	16
Holloway, P.C.L.	59	99	18	168	2921	36.06	5	–	54/1
Hooper, C.L.	229	363	35	236*	14689	44.78	37	6+1	260
House, W.J.	18	29	6	136	857	37.26	2	–	13
How, E.J.	14	10	5	7*	7	1.40	–	–	2
Hudson, R.D.	11	20	2	62	202	11.22	–	–	2
Hughes, J.G.	20	26	2	17	128	5.33	–	–	5
Hughes, Q.J.	8	12	3	47*	197	21.88	–	–	1
Humphries, S.	4	3	1	41*	52	26.00	–	–	9
Hussain, N.	210	331	34	207	13107	44.13	35	5	261
Hutchison, P.M.	10	10	7	15*	29	9.66	–	–	2
Hutton, S.	65	118	6	172*	3241	28.93	3	–	34
Hyam, B.J.	10	16	2	49	153	10.92	–	–	20/1
Igglesden, A.P.	151	166	62	41	868	8.34	–	–	38
Illingworth, R.K.	330	368	108	120*	5818	22.37	4	–	146
Ilott, M.C.	137	168	39	60	1883	14.59	–	–	32
Innes, K.J.	6	8	1	63	116	16.57	–	–	3
Irani, R.C.	86	139	16	123*	4334	35.23	7	2	37

155

	M	I	NO	HS	Runs	Avge	100	1000	Ct/St
Irfan Fazil	3	5	2	19	43	14.33	–	–	–
James, K.D.	205	307	48	162	7928	30.61	10	2	70
James, S.P.	168	296	25	235	10485	38.69	31	5	133
Janisch, A.N.	14	14	5	25	85	9.44	–	–	2
Jarvis, P.W.	201	252	66	80	3189	17.14	–	–	59
Javed Qadir	27	38	10	66*	578	20.64	–	–	77/9
Jeh, M.P.W.	20	22	6	30	137	8.56	–	–	5
Johnson, N.C.	64	97	14	150	2777	33.45	4	–	73
Johnson, P.	301	501	49	187	16755	37.06	34	8	188/1
Johnson, R.L.	56	77	8	50*	1005	14.56	–	–	23
Jones, D.M.	234	394	41	324*	18292	51.81	52	3+5	182
Jones, P.S.	10	13	3	36	142	14.20	–	–	4
Jones, R.O.	16	24	3	61	530	25.23	–	–	8
Joyce, E.C.	1	2	–	43	56	28.00	–	–	1
Julian, B.P.	105	143	24	119	2785	23.40	2	–	65
Kallis, J.H.	54	80	8	186*	3271	45.43	8	1	36
Kasprowicz, M.S.	88	113	19	49	1343	14.28	–	–	36
Keech, M.	49	84	11	127	2136	29.26	3	–	36
Keedy, G.	38	40	27	26	158	12.15	–	–	10
Kendall, W.S.	44	68	11	145*	2168	38.03	4	1	32
Kennis, G.J.	6	11	1	29	140	14.00	–	–	6
Kenway, D.A.	1	2	1	20*	22	22.00	–	–	1
Kerr, J.I.D.	32	47	9	80	730	19.21	–	–	10
Kettleborough, R.A.	13	19	2	108	446	26.23	1	–	9
Khan, A.A.	19	24	5	52	291	15.31	–	–	5
Khan, G.A.	16	23	3	101*	703	35.15	1	–	7
Khan, W.G.	31	56	7	181	1687	34.42	4	–	30
Killeen, N.	15	23	6	48	201	11.82	–	–	7
Kirtley, R.J.	23	31	13	15*	76	4.22	–	–	11
Knight, N.V.	107	180	21	174	6412	40.32	16	1	148
Knott, J.A.	7	11	4	49*	170	24.28	–	–	11/2
Krikken, K.M.	151	221	46	104	4057	23.18	1	–	382/25
Lacey, S.J.	6	8	4	50	129	32.25	–	–	1
Lampitt, S.R.	176	224	49	122	4219	24.10	1	–	117
Laney, J.S.	43	78	2	112	2584	34.00	4	1	28
Langer, J.L.	77	134	16	274*	5920	50.16	17	0+1	59
Lara, B.C.	128	209	6	501*	10978	54.07	31	2+2	161
Lathwell, M.N.	122	218	9	206	7194	34.42	11	5	85
Laughton, N.E.F.	1	2	–	5	6	3.00	–	–	1
Lavender, M.P.	52	98	8	173*	3079	34.21	6	–	47
Law, D.R.	47	72	–	115	1370	19.02	1	–	24
Law, S.G.	133	224	23	179.	9522	47.37	27	2+1	135
Law, W.L.	1	1	1	38*	38	–	–	–	–
Lawrence, D.V.	185	211	38	66	1851	10.69	–	–	45
Leatherdale, D.A.	125	193	24	157	5777	34.18	8	–	111
Lee, S.	51	83	16	167*	2968	44.29	9	1	41
Lehmann, D.S.	115	200	11	255	9792	51.80	29	1+4	67
Lenham, N.J.	192	332	29	222*	10135	33.44	20	3	73
Lewis, C.C.	161	241	29	247	6439	30.37	7	–	131
Lewis, J.	28	30	10	30	315	11.25	–	–	6
Lewis, J.J.B.	76	133	18	210*	4211	36.61	7	1	59
Lewry, J.D.	26	40	11	34	302	10.41	–	–	2
Lightfoot, C.G.R.	13	20	1	61	304	16.00	–	–	2
Llong, N.J.	66	104	10	130	2992	31.82	6	–	57
Lloyd, G.D.	145	236	24	241	8306	39.17	18	4	95
Lockhart, D.R.	2	4	1	77*	136	45.33	–	–	2
Loye, M.B.	82	133	15	205	4107	34.80	7	1	48

	M	I	NO	HS	Runs	Avge	100	1000	Ct/St
Lugsden, S.	10	13	5	9	30	3.75	–	–	1
Lynch, M.A.	359	585	64	172*	18325	35.17	39	9	367
McCague, M.J.	106	146	36	63*	1691	15.37	–	–	58
McCallan, W.K.	2	4	–	65	174	43.50	–	–	1
McCrum, P.	4	5	2	44*	49	16.33	–	–	–
MacGill, S.C.G.	9	14	6	25	90	11.25	–	–	3
McGrath, A.	49	84	4	141	2436	30.45	5	–	29
McGrath, G.D.	65	64	22	24	181	4.30	–	–	13
McKeown, P.C.	6	8	–	64	208	26.00	–	–	3
Macmillan, G.I.	48	76	9	122	1848	27.58	3	–	51
Maddy, D.L.	52	85	4	131	2401	29.64	5	1	53
Malcolm, D.E.	232	277	86	51	1524	7.97	–	–	33
Marsh, S.A.	260	379	63	142	9012	28.51	9	–	618/50
Martin, P.J.	134	154	38	133	2316	19.96	1	–	34
Martin-Jenkins, R.S.C.	7	9	2	50	147	21.00	–	–	2
Maru, R.J.	227	229	57	74	2938	17.08	–	–	252
Mascarenhas, A.D.	8	10	1	21	74	8.22	–	–	–
Mason, T.J.	3	2	–	4	7	3.50	–	–	4
Mather, D.P.	18	11	4	8*	31	4.42	–	–	2
May, M.R.	12	21	4	116	748	44.00	2	–	3
Maynard, M.P.	288	473	52	243	18516	43.98	43	11	274/5
Metcalfe, A.A.	216	369	21	216*	11938	34.30	26	6	82
Metson, C.P.	231	302	71	96	4059	17.57	–	–	560/51
Milburn, S.M.	27	28	6	54*	292	13.27	–	–	1
Millns, D.J.	145	171	51	121	2455	20.45	3	–	64
Mirza, M.M.	6	7	4	10*	17	5.66	–	–	1
Moffat, S.P.	5	7	1	47	122	20.33	–	–	2
Mohammad Akram	37	47	12	28	258	7.37	–	–	13
Mohammad Wasim	27	45	4	155	1276	31.12	4	–	33
Mohammad, I.	1	1	–	12	12	12.00	–	–	–
Moles, A.J.	230	416	40	230*	15305	40.70	29	6	146
Molins, G.L.	2	1	–	1	1	1.00	–	–	–
Montgomerie, R.R.	88	154	16	192	4675	33.87	9	2	80
Moody, T.M.	258	429	35	272	18555	47.09	56	5+1	258
Moores, P.	228	342	41	185	7295	24.23	7	–	500/44
Morgan, P.G.	10	18	1	63	444	26.11	–	–	4
Morris, A.C.	16	23	2	60	362	17.23	–	–	12
Morris, H.	314	544	53	233*	19785	40.29	53	10	197
Morris, J.E.	313	527	31	229	18739	37.78	44	11	134
Moxon, M.D.	317	541	47	274*	21161	42.83	45	11	218
Mujahid Jamshed	77	124	4	196	4103	34.19	11	–	33
Mullally, A.D.	142	159	42	75	1034	8.83	–	–	28
Munton, T.A.	205	206	85	54*	1339	11.06	–	–	68
Mushtaq Ahmed	150	189	22	90	2345	14.04	–	–	73
Napier, G.R.	2	2	2	35*	39		–	–	–
Nash, D.C.	6	8	2	100	332	55.33	1	–	4
Newell, K.	33	61	5	135	1625	29.01	4	–	6
Newell, M. (Sx)	13	24	1	100	471	20.47	1	–	10
Newell, M. (Nt)	102	178	26	203*	4636	30.50	6	1	93/1
Newport, P.J.	266	307	87	98	5442	24.75	–	–	72
Nixon, P.A.	144	206	48	131	4803	30.39	8	1	382/31
Noon, W.M.	81	128	21	83	2423	22.64	–	–	168/20
Oram, A.R.	8	9	5	5*	14	3.50	–	–	6
Ormond, J.	14	12	2	35	69	6.90	–	–	3
Ostler, D.P.	147	246	20	208	7659	33.88	9	4	179
Owen, J.E.H.	17	29	–	105	782	26.96	2	–	6
Parker, B.	36	61	8	138*	1659	31.30	2	–	16

157

	M	I	NO	HS	Runs	Avge	100	1000	Ct/St
Parkin, O.T.	13	15	10	14	67	13.40	–	–	5
Parsons, G.J.	338	449	100	76	6763	19.37	–	–	147
Parsons, K.A.	43	74	8	105	1839	27.86	1	–	32
Patel, C.M.	12	22	5	63*	420	24.70	–	–	2
Patel, M.M.	80	114	25	56	1231	13.83	–	–	43
Patterson, A.D.	2	4	–	31	88	22.00	–	–	1
Patterson, B.M.W.	8	14	–	114	756	54.00	3	–	10
Patterson, M.W.	1	2	–	4	6	3.00	–	–	–
Pearson, R.M.	51	56	16	37	475	11.87	–	–	15
Peirce, M.T.E.	19	35	–	104	819	23.40	1	–	15
Penberthy, A.L.	101	151	19	101*	3010	22.80	1	–	58
Penney, T.L.	114	180	34	151	6268	42.93	13	2	67
Peters, S.D.	7	10	2	110	277	34.62	2	–	8
Phillips, B.J.	16	22	4	100*	381	21.16	1	–	7
Phillips, N.C.	19	26	10	53	450	28.12	–	–	9
Pick, R.A.	195	206	55	65*	2259	14.96	–	–	50
Pierson, A.R.K.	147	180	60	59	1948	16.23	–	–	72
Piper, K.J.	138	191	29	116*	3197	19.73	2	–	372/24
Pirihi, N.G.	2	3	–	15	15	5.00	–	–	–
Pollard, P.R.	153	268	20	180	8226	33.16	13	3	145
Ponting, R.T.	67	114	14	211	5366	53.66	18	0+2	58
Pooley, J.C.	81	137	12	138*	3811	30.48	8	1	81
Powell, J.C.	1	1	1	4*	4	–	–	–	–
Powell, M.J. (Gm)	5	8	3	200*	286	57.20	1	–	1
Powell, M.J. (Wa)	5	9	–	39	202	22.44	–	–	4
Pratt, A.	1	–	–	–	–	–	–	–	–
Preston, N.W.	9	12	4	17*	71	8.87	–	–	3
Prichard, P.J.	280	454	46	245	14769	36.19	29	8	178
Pyemont, J.P.	1	1	–	22	22	22.00	–	–	2
Radford, T.A.	14	24	6	69*	476	26.44	–	–	13
Ramprakash, M.R.	224	364	47	235	14596	46.04	39	8	120
Rana Qayyum	33	55	3	150*	1205	23.17	2	–	24
Rao, R.K.	13	23	2	89	462	22.00	–	–	6
Rashid, U.B.A.	1	2	–	9	15	7.50	–	–	–
Ratcliffe, J.D.	111	203	11	135	5666	29.51	4	–	58
Ratledge, J.	27	48	1	100*	942	20.04	1	–	5
Rawnsley, M.J.	8	5	2	26	68	22.66	–	–	1
Reiffel, P.R.	115	137	42	86	2137	22.49	–	–	58
Renshaw, S.J.	21	27	12	56	279	18.60	–	–	6
Rhodes, S.J.	328	450	126	122*	10837	33.44	9	1	821/108
Ridgway, P.M.	2	2	1	0*	0	0.00	–	–	–
Ripley, D.	247	323	87	134*	6249	26.47	6	–	525/74
Roberts, D.J.	11	20	–	117	639	31.95	1	–	1
Roberts, G.M.	3	4	1	52	97	32.33	–	–	1
Robinson, D.D.J.	46	82	3	148	2335	29.55	4	–	47
Robinson, M.A.	172	186	77	27	426	3.90	–	–	35
Robinson, R.T.	402	699	82	220*	26493	42.93	62	14	241
Rollins, A.S.	76	140	15	210	4438	35.50	8	3	61/1
Rollins, R.J.	58	95	9	133*	2022	23.51	1	–	139/20
Rose, G.D.	204	284	54	191	7170	31.17	8	1	107
Roseberry, M.A.	196	332	37	185	10203	34.58	19	4	144
Russell, R.C.	367	536	118	129*	12934	30.94	7	1	893/109
Rutherford, A.T.	2	1	–	19	19	19.00	–	–	4
Saggers, M.J.	8	13	3	18	103	10.30	–	–	2
Salim Elahi	28	49	2	229	1446	30.76	1	–	33/1
Sales, D.J.G.	18	29	2	210*	828	30.66	2	–	8
Salisbury, I.D.K.	178	234	50	86	3335	18.12	–	–	131

	M	I	NO	HS	Runs	Avge	100	1000	Ct/St
Salmond, G.	6	10	1	181	668	74.22	2	–	4
Saqlain Mushtaq	41	61	17	79	716	16.27	–	–	21
Savident, L.	3	4	1	6	15	5.00	–	–	1
Schaffter, P.A.	1	1	–	0	0	0.00	–	–	–
Schofield, C.J.	1	1	–	25	25	25.00	–	–	–
Scrini, A.P.	11	18	6	58*	253	21.08	–	–	13
Searle, J.P.	2	4	3	5*	7	7.00	–	–	–
Shadford, D.J.	10	12	4	30	107	13.37	–	–	5
Shah, O.A.	18	28	3	104*	813	32.52	1	–	16
Shahid, N.	98	154	21	139	4195	31.54	5	1	89
Shaw, A.D.	36	46	8	74	708	18.63	–	–	89/9
Sheeraz, K.P.	13	16	9	12*	27	3.85	–	–	4
Sheikh, M.A.	1	1	–	24	24	24.00	–	–	–
Sheridan, K.L.P.	3	1	–	0	0	0.00	–	–	2
Sheriyar, A.	46	43	16	21	219	8.11	–	–	11
Shine, K.J.	99	91	35	40	520	9.28	–	–	21
Shoaib Akhtar	35	42	15	23	217	8.03	–	–	14
Shoaib Malik	3	4	–	9	18	4.50	–	–	–
Sidebottom, R.J.	1	1	–	2*	2	–	–	–	–
Silverwood, C.E.W.	55	77	18	58	829	14.05	–	–	14
Simmons, P.V.	169	289	13	261	10297	37.30	22	2	197
Singh, A.	23	38	3	157	1085	31.00	3	–	12
Sladdin, R.W.	34	42	9	51*	372	11.27	–	–	15
Slater, M.J.	95	167	10	219	7110	45.28	17	1+3	47
Small, G.C.	315	404	97	70	4409	14.36	–	–	95
Smith, A.M.	92	115	24	55*	1044	11.47	–	–	15
Smith, B.F.	109	167	25	190	4726	33.28	7	1	41
Smith, E.T.	25	42	3	190	1739	44.58	4	1	8
Smith, N.M.K.	127	182	25	161	4084	26.01	2	–	44
Smith, R.A.	333	568	78	209*	21645	44.11	53	10	192
Smith, T.M.	1								1
Snape, J.N.	39	56	11	87	1139	25.31	–	–	34
Solanki, V.S.	35	53	5	128*	1517	31.60	1	–	29
Speak, N.J.	135	235	24	232	7826	37.09	13	3	90
Speight, M.P.	140	234	18	184	7387	34.19	13	3	154
Spendlove, B.L.	2	3	1	15*	27	13.50	–	–	2
Spiring, K.R.	37	64	9	150	2072	37.67	4	1	19
Stanford, E.J.	5	6	4	32	48	24.00	–	–	2
Stanger, I.M.	1	1	–	8	8	8.00	–	–	–
Stemp, R.D.	124	145	44	65	1292	12.79	–	–	53
Stephenson, J.P.	237	405	41	202*	12517	34.38	21	5	135
Stevens, D.I.	2	2	–	27	35	17.50	–	–	1
Stewart, A.J.	333	551	62	271*	19965	40.82	41	8	456/17
Strang, P.A.	61	91	19	106*	2050	28.47	2	–	50
Stubbings, S.D.	1	2	–	22	27	13.50	–	–	–
Such, P.M.	239	240	81	54	1206	7.58	–	–	98
Sutcliffe, I.J.	41	62	7	163*	2036	37.01	3	–	18
Sutton, L.D.	1	2	1	11*	17	17.00	–	–	5
Swann, A.J.	5	8	1	136	262	37.42	1	–	1
Taylor, J.P.	132	145	56	86	1197	13.44	–	–	45
Taylor, M.A.	219	377	15	219	15194	41.97	36	1+5	300
Taylor, N.R.	319	543	69	204	18804	39.67	45	11	154
Thomas, P.A.	21	24	5	25	119	6.26	–	–	1
Thomas, S.D.	53	69	20	78*	929	18.95	–	–	17
Thompson, J.B.D.	18	23	6	59*	281	16.52	–	–	4
Thomson, K.	2	1	1	9*	9	–	–	–	–
Thorpe, G.P.	215	362	49	222	14048	44.88	30	8	167

159

	M	I	NO	HS	Runs	Avge	100	1000	Ct/St
Thursfield, M.J.	24	26	6	47	309	15.45	–	–	2
Titchard, S.P.	75	131	8	163	3945	32.07	4	–	52
Tolley, C.M.	85	112	28	84	1963	23.36	–	–	35
Trainor, N.J.	22	39	2	121	745	20.13	1	–	8
Trescothick, M.E.	54	93	2	121	2465	27.08	4	–	48
Trott, B.J.	2	2	1	1*	1	1.00	–	–	1
Tudor, A.J.	14	20	6	56	232	16.57	–	–	1
Tufnell, P.C.R.	222	235	95	67*	1445	10.32	–	–	93
Turner, R.J.	119	186	40	144	4431	30.34	5	1	272/36
Tweats, T.A.	20	37	5	189	1052	32.87	1	–	19
Udal, S.D.	126	180	30	117*	3352	22.34	1	–	60
Vandrau, M.J.	59	94	18	66	1567	20.61	–	–	29
Van Troost, A.P.	66	78	26	35	400	7.69	–	–	10
Vaughan, M.P.	80	146	6	183	4679	33.42	10	3	31
Wagh, M.A.	29	44	5	125*	1354	34.71	4	1	18
Walker, A.	127	140	61	41*	917	11.60	–	–	43
Walker, L.N.P.	12	15	3	42*	233	19.41	–	–	19/3
Walker, M.J.	33	55	5	275*	1415	28.30	2	–	16
Walsh, C.A.	357	452	115	66	4148	12.30	–	–	98
Walsh, C.D.	1	1	1	56*	56	–	–	–	2
Walton, T.C.	19	29	3	71	653	25.11	–	–	5
Waqar Younis	151	168	41	55	1683	13.25	–	–	37
Ward, I.J.	5	7	–	56	121	17.28	–	–	7
Ward, T.R.	186	320	19	235*	11241	37.34	23	6	180
Warne, S.K.	109	140	20	74*	1874	15.61	–	–	67
Warren, P.M.	1	–	–	–	–	–	–	–	1
Warren, R.J.	56	92	12	201*	2713	33.91	3	–	75/3
Wasim Akram	197	271	31	257*	5380	22.41	5	–	67
Watkin, S.L.	210	232	74	41	1531	9.68	–	–	54
Watkinson, M.	290	434	47	161	10276	26.55	10	1	146
Waugh, M.E.	262	419	52	229*	19846	54.07	64	5+5	304
Waugh, S.R.	237	361	61	216*	15568	51.89	45	2+3	202
Weekes, P.N.	103	157	15	171*	4425	31.16	8	1	84
Welch, G.	45	62	10	84*	1121	21.55	–	–	18
Wellings, P.E.	6	10	2	128*	378	47.25	1	–	4
Wells, A.P.	339	568	78	253*	19628	40.04	44	11	220
Wells, V.J.	115	182	14	224	5735	34.13	9	2	75
Welton, G.E.	6	11	–	95	295	26.81	–	–	1
Weston, R.M.S.	11	19	–	36	181	9.52	–	–	11
Weston, W.P.C.	106	182	20	205	6033	37.24	13	3	58
Wharf, A.G.	7	9	1	62	186	23.25	–	–	2
Whitaker, J.J.	309	490	51	218	17068	38.87	38	10	171
Whitaker, P.R.	30	51	4	119	1425	30.31	1	–	8
White, C.	135	204	30	181	5582	32.08	7	–	87
White, G.W.	50	86	8	145	2396	30.71	2	–	47
Williams, N.F.	246	286	57	77	4286	18.71	–	–	65
Williams, R.C.J.	35	44	8	90	640	17.77	–	–	94/14
Williamson, D.	2	1	–	3	3	3.00	–	–	–
Williamson, J.G.	3	3	–	55	109	36.33	–	–	–
Willis, S.C.	10	13	3	82	331	33.10	–	–	24
Wilson, D.G.	1	–	–	–	–	–	–	–	1
Windows, M.G.N.	40	75	4	184	2064	29.07	2	–	35
Wood, J.	51	76	15	63*	779	12.77	–	–	14
Wood, M.J.	1	2	–	81	102	51.00	–	–	1
Wood, N.T.	11	16	2	155	470	33.57	1	–	3
Wren, T.N.	30	34	13	23	141	6.71	–	–	12
Wright, A.J.	276	484	38	193	13095	29.36	18	6	213

	M	I	NO	HS	Runs	Avge	100	1000	Ct/St
Wright, C.M.	1	1	–	0	0	0.00	–	–	–
Wright, G.J.	4	2	1	0*	0	0.00	–	–	–
Wylie, A.	3	5	1	7	14	3.50	–	–	–
Yates, G.	66	87	34	134*	1496	28.22	3	–	26
Young, S.	90	147	25	237	4951	40.58	10	–	56

BOWLING

'50wS' denotes instances of taking 50 or more wickets in a season. Where these have been achieved outside the UK, they are shown after a plus sign.

	Runs	Wkts	Avge	Best	5wI	10wM	50wS
Abdul Razzak	872	32	27.25	7- 51	2	–	–
Adams, C.J.	1088	18	60.44	4- 29	–	–	–
Afford, J.A.	15436	468	32.98	6- 51	16	2	5
Afzaal, U.	1537	25	61.48	3- 62	–	–	–
Aldred, P.	1366	35	39.02	3- 28	–	–	–
Ali Naqvi	20	1	20.00	1- 11	–	–	–
Ali Rizvi	2519	101	24.94	6- 77	6	1	0+1
Alleyne, M.W.	8007	256	31.27	6- 64	6	–	1
Allingham, M.J.D.	101	4	25.25	3- 53	–	–	–
Altree, D.A.	386	8	48.25	3- 41	–	–	–
Amin, R.M.	348	8	43.50	3- 58	–	–	–
Andrew, S.J.W.	10679	317	33.68	7- 47	7	–	–
Anthony, H.A.G.	6303	222	28.39	6- 22	6	1	–
Archer, G.F.	648	14	46.28	3- 18	–	–	–
Arthurton, K.L.T.	926	27	34.29	3- 14	–	–	–
Asif Din	4393	79	55.60	5- 61	2	–	–
Astle, N.J.	1869	61	30.63	6- 22	2	–	–
Atherton, M.A.	4733	108	43.82	6- 78	3	–	–
Athey, C.W.J.	2673	48	55.68	3- 3	–	–	–
Austin, I.D.	6501	215	30.23	5- 23	5	1	–
Averis, J.M.M.	1104	16	69.00	5- 98	1	–	–
Aymes, A.N.	151	1	151.00	1- 75	–	–	–
Azhar Mahmood	3682	179	20.56	7- 55	8	2	0+1
Badenhorst, A.	2134	76	28.07	5- 49	2	–	–
Bailey, R.J.	4561	105	43.43	5- 54	2	–	–
Ball, M.C.J.	7337	195	37.62	8- 46	8	1	–
Barnett, K.J.	6717	180	37.31	6- 28	3	–	–
Bates, J.J.	525	19	27.63	5- 89	1	–	–
Bates, R.T.	2339	50	46.78	5- 88	1	–	–
Batt, C.J.	100	6	16.66	4- 56	–	–	–
Battarbee, C.M.	627	11	57.00	2- 56	–	–	–
Batty, G.J.	70	2	35.00	1- 11	–	–	–
Batty, J.N.	9	0					
Bell, M.A.V.	1565	49	31.93	7- 48	3	–	–
Benjamin, J.E.	10884	364	29.90	6- 19	16	1	3
Benson, J.D.R.	532	11	48.36	2- 24	–	–	–
Betts, M.M.	3710	111	33.42	9- 64	5	1	–
Bevan, M.G.	3003	68	44.16	6- 82	1	1	–
Bichel, A.J.	2614	103	25.37	6- 56	7	1	–
Bicknell, D.J.	789	23	34.20	3- 7	–	–	–
Bicknell, M.P.	16405	630	26.03	9- 45	27	2	6
Blackwell, I.D.	227	2	113.50	1- 27	–	–	–
Blain, J.A.R.	208	2	104.00	1- 18	–	–	–
Blakey, R.J.	68	1	68.00	1- 68	–	–	–
Blewett, G.S.	2263	55	41.14	5- 29	1	–	–

	Runs	Wkts	Avge	Best	5wI	10wM	50wS
Bloomfield, T.F.	258	13	19.84	5- 77	1	–	–
Boiling, J.	6633	140	47.37	6- 84	4	1	–
Boon, D.C.	569	12	47.41	2- 18	–	–	–
Boswell, S.A.J.	1012	22	46.00	5- 94	1	–	–
Bovill, J.N.B.	3384	104	32.53	6- 29	4	1	–
Bowen, M.N.	3970	111	35.76	7- 75	5	1	–
Bowler, P.D.	1901	27	70.40	3- 41	–	–	–
Brimson, M.T.	2384	67	35.58	5- 12	2	–	–
Brown, A.D.	176	0					
Brown, D.R.	4813	201	23.94	8- 89	8	3	1
Brown, J.F.	715	20	35.75	4- 50	–	–	–
Brown, K.R.	276	6	46.00	2- 7	–	–	–
Brown, S.J.E.	12692	408	31.10	7- 70	25	2	5
Burns, M.	287	5	57.40	2- 18	–	–	–
Butcher, G.P.	1559	35	44.54	7- 77	1	–	–
Butcher, M.A.	2494	68	36.67	4- 31	–	–	–
Byas, D.	719	12	59.91	3- 55	–	–	–
Byrne, B.W.	439	3	146.33	1- 19	–	–	–
Caddick, A.R.	11187	415	26.95	9- 32	26	8	5
Campbell, C.L.	136	2	68.00	1- 29	–	–	–
Capel, D.J.	17507	545	32.12	7- 44	14	–	4
Carpenter, J.R.	81	1	81.00	1- 50	–	–	–
Cassar, M.E.	409	16	25.56	4- 54	–	–	–
Chapman, R.J.	1759	38	46.28	4-109	–	–	–
Chapple, G.	6470	214	30.23	6- 48	8	–	2
Chilton, M.J.	23	0					
Church, M.J.	163	9	18.11	4- 50	–	–	–
Clarke, V.P.	1276	20	63.80	3- 47	–	–	–
Collingwood, P.D.	384	9	42.66	3- 46	–	–	–
Connor, C.A.	19338	612	31.59	9- 38	18	4	5
Cooke, G.	128	4	32.00	1- 26	–	–	–
Cork, D.G.	11468	429	26.73	9- 43	12	2	3
Cosker, D.A.	1722	45	38.26	4- 60	–	–	–
Cottey, P.A.	767	13	59.00	4- 49	–	–	–
Cousins, D.M.	1086	26	41.76	6- 35	1	–	–
Cowan, A.P.	2911	93	31.30	5- 45	4	–	1
Cowdrey, G.R.	872	12	72.66	1- 5	–	–	–
Cox, D.M.	1852	45	41.15	5- 97	2	1	–
Crawley, J.P.	108	1	108.00	1- 90	–	–	–
Croft, R.D.B.	18172	497	36.56	8- 66	20	2	5
Crowe, C.D.	4	0					
Curran, K.M.	16234	586	27.70	7- 47	15	4	5
Curry, D.J.	16	1	16.00	1- 12	–	–	–
Curtis, T.S.	813	14	58.07	2- 17	–	–	–
Dakin, J.M.	733	17	43.11	4- 45	–	–	–
Dale, A.	5358	132	40.59	6- 18	1	–	–
Daley, J.A.	9	0					
Davies, A.P.	135	1	135.00	1- 25	–	–	–
Davies, M.K.	674	23	29.30	5- 46	1	–	–
Davis, R.P.	14543	414	35.12	7- 64	16	2	2
Davy, J.O.	93	0					
Dawson, M.W.	240	0					
Dawson, R.I.	132	3	44.00	2- 38	–	–	–
Dean, K.J.	1282	44	29.13	4- 39	–	–	–
DeFreitas, P.A.J.	25616	916	27.96	7- 21	47	5	10
Dibden, R.R.	592	8	74.00	2- 36	–	–	–
Dimond, M.	316	6	52.66	4- 73	–	–	–

	Runs	Wkts	Avge	Best	5wI	10wM	50wS
Donald, A.A.	21160	945	22.39	8- 37	51	8	5+1
Dowman, M.P.	457	8	57.12	3- 10	–	–	–
Drakes, V.C.	6027	198	30.43	8- 59	6	1	1
Dutch, K.P.	416	12	34.66	3- 25	–	–	–
Dyer, N.J.	59	2	29.50	1- 29	–	–	–
Ealham, M.A.	7037	236	29.81	8- 36	8	1	–
Ecclestone, S.C.	1208	33	36.60	4- 66	–	–	–
Edmond, M.D.	254	5	50.80	2- 26	–	–	–
Edwards, A.D.	699	20	34.95	5- 34	1	–	–
Edwards, G.J.M.	49	0					
Elliott, M.T.G.	170	3	56.66	1- 13	–	–	–
Ellis, S.W.K.	832	19	43.78	5- 59	1	–	–
Emburey, J.E.	41958	1608	26.09	8- 40	72	12	17
Evans, K.P.	11292	334	33.80	6- 40	8	–	–
Fairbrother, N.H.	440	5	88.00	2- 91	–	–	–
Fazal-e-Akber	429	10	42.90	3- 97	–	–	–
Fay, R.A.	1146	31	36.96	4- 53	–	–	–
Fisher, I.D.	285	12	23.75	5- 35	1	–	–
Fleming, M.V.	6726	173	38.87	5- 51	2	–	–
Flintoff, A.	50	1	50.00	1- 11	–	–	–
Flower, A.	163	4	40.75	1- 1	–	–	–
Flower, G.W.	1834	43	42.65	3- 20	–	–	–
Foley, G.I.	1566	29	54.00	3- 64	–	–	–
Follett, D.	807	26	31.03	8- 22	3	1	–
Ford, J.A.	54	0					
Fordham, A.	297	4	74.25	1- 0	–	–	–
Foster, M.J.	1488	44	33.81	4- 21	–	–	–
Francis, N.B.	1863	50	37.26	4- 32	–	–	–
Francis, S.R.G.	97	0					
Franks, P.J.	1260	33	38.18	4- 47	–	–	–
Fraser, A.R.C.	18208	660	27.58	8- 75	26	3	6
Freeth, J.W.O.	1330	19	70.00	4-101	–	–	–
Fulton, D.P.	65	1	65.00	1- 37	–	–	–
Fulton, J.A.G.	18	0					
Gallian, J.E.R.	3332	82	40.63	6-115	1	–	–
Gatting, M.W.	4694	157	29.89	5- 34	2	–	–
Giddins, E.S.H.	7427	248	29.94	6- 47	13	1	2
Giles, A.F.	3521	127	27.72	6- 45	4	–	1
Gillespie, J.N.	2986	128	23.32	7- 34	6	–	0+1
Gooch, G.A.	8457	246	34.37	7- 14	3	–	–
Goodchild, D.J.	26	0					
Gough, D.	12625	463	27.36	7- 28	19	3	4
Grayson, A.P.	2614	59	44.30	4- 53	–	–	–
Green, R.J.	1006	30	33.53	6- 41	1	–	–
Greenfield, K.	524	5	104.80	2- 40	–	–	–
Habib, A.	37	0					
Hamilton, G.M.	2033	59	34.45	5- 65	2	–	–
Hancock, T.H.C.	945	18	52.50	3- 10	–	–	–
Hansen, T.M.	75	0					
Harden, R.J.	1011	20	50.55	2- 7	–	–	–
Harmison, S.J.	77	0					
Harris, A.J.	3647	107	34.08	6- 40	2	1	1
Hart, J.P.	51	0					
Hartley, P.J.	17653	581	30.38	9- 41	21	2	6
Hasan Raza	50	1	50.00	1- 36	–	–	–
Hayden, M.L.	282	4	70.50	2- 17	–	–	–
Hayhurst, A.N.	4991	110	45.37	4- 27	–	–	–

	Runs	Wkts	Avge	Best	5wI	10wM	50wS
Haynes, G.R.	2558	67	38.17	4- 33	–	–	–
Headley, D.W.	9419	318	29.61	8- 98	18	2	1
Healy, I.A.	2	0					
Hegg, W.K.	7	0					
Hemp, D.L.	450	10	45.00	3- 23	–	–	–
Herzberg, S.	1813	47	38.57	5- 33	1	–	–
Hewitt, J.P.	2070	84	24.64	6- 14	2	–	1
Hibbert, A.J.E.	1	0					
Hick, G.A.	9218	210	43.89	5- 18	5	1	–
Hindson, J.E.	3045	93	32.74	5- 42	7	2	1
Hoggard, M.J.	196	3	65.33	1- 41	–	–	–
Hollioake, A.J.	3324	82	40.53	4- 22	–	–	–
Hollioake, B.C.	1034	33	31.33	4- 54	–	–	–
Holloway, P.C.L.	46	0					
Hooper, C.L.	13179	367	35.91	5- 26	12	–	–
House, W.J.	696	2	348.00	1- 44	–	–	–
How, E.J.	1145	13	88.07	5- 59	1	–	–
Hudson, R.D.	184	0					
Hughes, J.G.	1622	37	43.83	5- 69	1	–	–
Hughes, Q.J.	128	3	42.66	2- 73	–	–	–
Hussain, N.	307	2	153.50	1- 38	–	–	–
Hutchison, P.M.	1028	49	20.97	7- 38	3	1	–
Hutton, S.	18	0					
Igglesden, A.P.	13286	501	26.51	7- 28	23	4	4
Illingworth, R.K.	23794	780	30.50	7- 50	27	6	5
Ilott, M.C.	13008	468	27.79	9- 19	23	3	5
Innes, K.J.	275	8	34.37	4- 61	–	–	–
Irani, R.C.	4547	135	33.68	5- 19	3	–	–
Irfan Fazil	234	7	33.42	3- 51	–	–	–
James, K.D.	11323	357	31.71	8- 49	11	1	–
James, S.P.	3	0					
Janisch, A.N.	1285	23	55.86	4- 71	–	–	–
Jarvis, P.W.	17786	621	28.64	7- 55	22	3	4
Jeh, M.P.W.	2047	46	44.50	5- 63	1	–	–
Johnson, N.C.	3308	110	30.07	5- 79	2	–	–
Johnson, P.	595	6	99.16	1- 9	–	–	–
Johnson, R.L.	4417	158	27.95	10- 45	4	2	1
Jones, D.M.	1533	27	56.77	5-112	1	–	–
Jones, P.S.	739	23	32.13	6- 67	1	–	–
Jones, R.O.	1240	18	68.88	3-116	–	–	–
Joyce, E.C.	20	0					
Julian, B.P.	10080	330	30.54	7- 48	19	2	1
Kallis, J.H.	2079	76	27.35	5- 54	2	–	–
Kasprowicz, M.S.	9459	344	27.49	7- 36	22	2	1+2
Keech, M.	383	8	47.87	2- 28	–	–	–
Keedy, G.	3703	89	41.60	6- 79	1	1	–
Kendall, W.S.	383	10	38.30	3- 37	–	–	–
Kennis, G.J.	4	0					
Kenway, D.A.	58	2	29.00	1- 5	–	–	–
Kerr, J.I.D.	2590	64	40.46	5- 82	1	–	–
Kettleborough, R.A.	153	3	51.00	2- 26	–	–	–
Khan, A.A.	1557	41	37.97	5-137	1	–	–
Khan, G.A.	190	3	63.33	2- 48	–	–	–
Khan, W.G.	24	0					
Killeen, N.	1406	36	39.05	5-118	1	–	–
Kirtley, R.J.	2125	74	28.71	6- 60	4	–	–
Knight, N.V.	176	1	176.00	1- 61	–	–	–

	Runs	Wkts	Avge	Best	5wI	10wM	50wS
Krikken, K.M.	40	0					
Lacey, S.J.	291	7	41.57	3- 97	–	–	–
Lampitt, S.R.	13164	432	30.47	5- 32	13	–	5
Laney, J.S.	83	0					
Langer, J.L.	30	0					
Lara, B.C.	307	2	153.50	1- 14	–	–	–
Lathwell, M.N.	684	13	52.61	2- 21	–	–	–
Lavender, M.P.	15	0					
Law, D.R.	2709	84	32.25	5- 33	3	–	–
Law, S.G.	2963	64	46.29	5- 39	1	–	–
Lawrence, D.V.	16521	515	32.07	7- 47	21	1	5
Leatherdale, D.A.	1647	47	35.04	5- 56	1	–	–
Lee, S.	3838	92	41.71	4- 20	–	–	–
Lehmann, D.S.	730	12	60.83	2- 15	–	–	–
Lenham, N.J.	1847	42	43.97	4- 13	–	–	–
Lewis, C.C.	14366	481	29.86	6- 22	18	3	2
Lewis, J.	2456	84	29.23	6- 50	3	–	1
Lewis, J.J.B.	48	0					
Lewry, J.D.	2504	95	26.35	6- 43	7	1	–
Lightfoot, C.G.R.	255	2	127.50	2- 65	–	–	–
Llong, N.J.	1259	35	35.97	5- 21	2	–	–
Lloyd, G.D.	291	2	145.50	1- 4	–	–	–
Loye, M.B.	1	0					
Lugsden, S.	847	17	49.82	3- 45	–	–	–
Lynch, M.A.	1398	26	53.76	3- 6	–	–	–
McCague, M.J.	10369	392	26.45	9- 86	24	2	4
McCallan, W.K.	123	1	123.00	1- 10	–	–	–
McCrum, P.	343	5	68.60	3- 56	–	–	–
MacGill, S.C.G.	806	20	40.30	4- 72	–	–	–
McGrath, A.	129	2	64.50	1- 6	–	–	–
McGrath, G.D.	6353	273	23.27	8- 38	13	1	0+1
Macmillan, G.I.	1203	23	52.30	3- 13	–	–	–
Maddy, D.L.	298	6	49.66	2- 21	–	–	–
Malcolm, D.E.	24247	793	30.57	9- 57	31	7	6
Marsh, S.A.	240	2	120.00	2- 20	–	–	–
Martin, P.J.	10414	341	30.53	8- 32	7	1	2
Martin-Jenkins, R.S.C.	353	6	58.83	3- 26	–	–	–
Maru, R.J.	17547	525	33.42	8- 41	15	1	4
Mascarenhas, A.D.	714	24	29.75	6- 88	2	–	–
Mason, T.J.	123	3	41.00	2- 21	–	–	–
Mather, D.P.	1436	29	49.51	4- 65	–	–	–
May, M.R.	69	0					
Maynard, M.P.	783	6	130.50	3- 21	–	–	–
Metcalfe, A.A.	362	4	90.50	2- 18	–	–	–
Metson, C.P.	0	0					
Milburn, S.M.	2497	53	47.11	4- 38	–	–	–
Millns, D.J.	12973	465	27.90	9- 37	21	4	4
Mirza, M.M.	620	19	32.63	4- 51	–	–	–
Mohammad Akram	3294	113	29.15	7- 51	7	–	–
Mohammad Wasim	35	2	17.50	2- 12	–	–	–
Moles, A.J.	1882	40	47.05	3- 21	–	–	–
Molins, G.L.	174	6	29.00	3- 62	–	–	–
Montgomerie, R.R.	66	0					
Moody, T.M.	8424	269	31.31	7- 38	7	2	–
Moores, P.	16	0					
Morris, A.C.	508	9	56.44	2- 62	–	–	–
Morris, H.	380	2	190.00	1- 6	–	–	–

	Runs	Wkts	Avge	Best	5wI	10wM	50wS
Morris, J.E.	913	7	130.42	1- 6	–	–	–
Moxon, M.D.	1481	28	52.89	3- 24	–	–	–
Mujahid Jamshed	239	3	79.66	3- 68	–	–	–
Mullally, A.D.	12608	393	32.08	7- 72	13	2	3
Munton, T.A.	15577	594	26.22	8- 89	26	6	5
Mushtaq Ahmed	17052	671	25.41	9- 93	47	13	4+1
Napier, G.R.	65	3	21.66	2- 25	–	–	–
Nash, D.C.	19	1	19.00	1- 8	–	–	–
Newell, K.	647	12	53.91	4- 61	–	–	–
Newell, M. (Nt)	282	7	40.28	2- 38	–	–	–
Newport, P.J.	22097	813	27.17	8- 52	35	3	8
Nixon, P.A.	4	0					
Noon, W.M.	34	0					
Oram, A.R.	684	26	26.30	4- 53	–	–	–
Ormond, J.	1227	46	26.67	6- 54	3	–	–
Ostler, D.P.	188	0					
Parker, B.	3	0					
Parkin, O.T.	1030	24	42.91	3- 22	–	–	–
Parsons, G.J.	24509	809	30.29	9- 72	19	1	3
Parsons, K.A.	851	15	56.73	2- 4	–	–	–
Patel, C.M.	1326	27	49.11	6-110	1	–	–
Patel, M.M.	8118	250	32.47	8- 96	15	7	2
Patterson, M.W.	124	7	17.71	6- 80	1	–	–
Pearson, R.M.	5516	100	55.16	5-108	2	–	–
Peirce, M.T.E.	106	0					
Penberthy, A.L.	5848	154	37.97	5- 37	3	–	–
Penney, T.L.	183	6	30.50	3- 18	–	–	–
Phillips, B.J.	986	48	20.54	5- 47	2	–	–
Phillips, N.C.	1643	27	60.85	3- 39	–	–	–
Pick, R.A.	16454	495	33.24	7-128	16	3	5
Pierson, A.R.K.	11815	322	36.69	8- 42	13	–	1
Piper, K.J.	57	1	57.00	1- 57	–	–	–
Pollard, P.R.	268	4	67.00	2- 79	–	–	–
Ponting, R.T.	345	5	69.00	1- 0	–	–	–
Pooley, J.C.	68	0					
Powell, J.C.	109	1	109.00	1-109	–	–	–
Powell, M.J. (Gm)	3	0					
Powell, M.J. (Wa)	18	1	18.00	1- 18	–	–	–
Preston, N.W.	373	12	31.08	4- 68	–	–	–
Prichard, P.J.	497	2	248.50	1- 28	–	–	–
Radford, T.A.	0	1	0.00	1- 0	–	–	–
Ramprakash, M.R.	1151	18	63.94	3- 91	–	–	–
Rao, R.K.	107	2	53.50	1- 14	–	–	–
Rashid, U.B.A.	17	0					
Ratcliffe, J.D.	578	10	57.80	2- 26	–	–	–
Ratledge, J.	108	1	108.00	1- 16	–	–	–
Rawnsley, M.J.	437	11	39.72	3- 67	–	–	–
Reiffel, P.R.	10349	374	27.67	6- 57	14	2	0+1
Renshaw, S.J.	2212	54	40.96	5-110	1	–	–
Rhodes, S.J.	30	0					
Ridgway, P.M.	163	2	81.50	2- 46	–	–	–
Ripley, D.	103	2	51.50	2- 89	–	–	–
Roberts, G.M.	81	1	81.00	1- 55	–	–	–
Robinson, D.D.J.	31	0					
Robinson, M.A.	13485	417	32.33	9- 37	9	2	1
Robinson, R.T.	289	4	72.25	1- 22	–	–	–
Rollins, A.W.	122	1	122.00	1- 19	–	–	–

	Runs	Wkts	Avge	Best	5wI	10wM	50wS
Rose, G.D.	14749	503	29.32	7- 47	12	1	4
Roseberry, M.A.	406	4	101.50	1- 1	–	–	–
Russell, R.C.	68	1	68.00	1- 4	–	–	–
Saggers, M.J.	620	20	31.00	6- 65	2	–	–
Sales, D.J.G.	28	0					
Salisbury, I.D.K.	17285	509	33.95	8- 75	26	4	4
Saqlain Mushtaq	4011	172	23.31	7- 66	13	3	0+1
Savident, L.	247	4	61.75	2- 86	–	–	–
Schaffter, P.A.	77	1	77.00	1- 58	–	–	–
Searle, J.P.	133	2	66.50	2-126	–	–	–
Shadford, D.J.	383	22	40.59	5- 80	1	–	–
Shah, O.A.	43	1	43.00	1- 24	–	–	–
Shadid, N.	1927	41	47.00	3- 91	–	–	–
Sheeraz, K.P.	1104	27	40.88	6- 67	2	1	–
Sheikh, M.A.	24	3	8.00	2- 14	–	–	–
Sheridan, K.L.P.	259	7	37.00	4- 43	–	–	–
Sheriyar, A.	4435	139	31.90	6- 19	6	2	1
Shine, K.J.	8772	245	35.80	8- 47	12	2	1
Shoaib Akhtar	3409	127	26.84	6- 69	10	–	0+1
Shoaib Malik	333	12	27.75	3- 49	–	–	–
Sidebottom, R.J.	71	3	23.66	3- 71	–	–	–
Silverwood, C.E.W.	4849	168	28.86	7- 93	8	1	1
Simmons, P.V.	4779	161	29.68	6- 14	4	–	1
Singh, A.	24	0					
Sladdin, R.W.	3910	99	39.49	6- 58	3	–	–
Slater, M.J.	26	1	26.00	1- 4	–	–	–
Small, G.C.	24392	852	28.62	7- 15	29	2	6
Smith, A.M.	7916	299	26.47	8- 73	13	5	3
Smith, B.F.	194	2	97.00	1- 5	–	–	–
Smith, E.T.	22	0					
Smith, N.M.K.	9964	265	37.60	7- 42	15	–	–
Smith, R.A.	768	12	64.00	2- 11	–	–	–
Smith, T.M.	51	1	51.00	1- 27	–	–	–
Snape, J.N.	2931	65	45.09	5- 65	1	–	–
Solanki, V.S.	1550	32	48.43	5- 69	3	1	–
Speak, N.J.	178	2	89.00	1- 0	–	–	–
Speight, M.P.	32	2	16.00	1- 2	–	–	–
Spiring, K.R.	10	0					
Stanford, E.J.	388	9	43.11	3- 84	–	–	–
Stanger, I.M.	61	1	61.00	1- 38	–	–	–
Stemp, R.D.	9867	292	33.79	6- 37	12	1	–
Stephenson, J.P.	8771	254	34.53	7- 51	9	–	–
Stevens, D.I.	5	1	5.00	1- 5	–	–	–
Stewart, A.J.	417	3	139.00	1- 7	–	–	–
Strang, P.A.	6424	200	32.12	7- 75	15	2	1
Such, P.M.	19800	684	28.94	8- 93	39	7	5
Sutcliffe, I.J.	149	4	37.25	2- 21	–	–	–
Swann, A.J.	15	0					
Taylor, J.P.	11969	404	29.62	7- 23	16	3	5
Taylor, M.A.	68	2	34.00	1- 4	–	–	–
Taylor, N.R.	891	16	55.68	2- 20	–	–	–
Thomas, P.A.	2295	49	46.83	5- 70	1	–	–
Thomas, S.D.	5252	149	35.24	5- 24	8	–	1
Thompson, J.B.D.	1503	47	31.97	5- 72	2	–	–
Thomson, K.	175	4	43.75	2- 41	–	–	–
Thorpe, G.P.	1235	25	49.40	4- 40	–	–	–
Thursfield, M.J.	1539	38	40.50	6-130	1	–	–

	Runs	Wkts	Avge	Best	5wI	10wM	50wS
Titchard, S.P.	171	4	42.75	1- 11	–	–	–
Tolley, C.M.	5357	146	36.69	6- 61	2	–	–
Trainor, N.J.	93	0					
Trescothick, M.E.	309	6	51.50	4- 36	–	–	–
Trott, B.J.	128	5	25.60	3- 74	–	–	–
Tudor, A.J.	927	31	29.90	6-101	2	–	–
Tufnell, P.C.R.	22265	767	29.02	8- 29	40	5	7
Turner, R.J.	29	0					
Tweats, T.A.	208	4	52.00	1- 23	–	–	–
Udal, S.D.	12934	356	36.33	8- 50	20	4	4
Vandrau, M.J.	4440	132	33.63	6- 34	7	2	–
Van Troost, A.P.	5199	131	39.68	6- 48	4	–	–
Vaughan, M.P.	3121	61	51.16	4- 39	–	–	–
Wagh, M.A.	1301	16	81.31	3- 82	–	–	–
Walker, A.	9616	298	32.26	8-118	6	1	1
Walker, M.J.	19	0					
Walsh, C.A.	32593	1465	22.24	9- 72	86	16	9+3
Walsh, C.D.	64	0					
Walton, T.C.	282	4	70.50	1- 26	–	–	–
Waqar Younis	14501	688	21.07	8- 17	54	13	4+3
Ward, I.J.	84	0					
Ward, T.R.	643	8	80.37	2- 10	–	–	–
Warne, S.K.	11513	471	24.44	8- 71	21	3	2+2
Warren, P.M.	60	0					
Wasim Akram	17731	829	21.39	8- 30	63	15	5+1
Watkin, S.L.	20720	726	28.53	8- 59	24	4	9
Watkinson, M.	23940	709	33.76	8- 30	26	3	7
Waugh, M.E.	6971	184	37.88	6- 68	3	–	–
Waugh, S.R.	7405	234	31.64	6- 51	5	–	–
Weekes, P.N.	4905	120	40.87	8- 39	3	–	–
Welch, G.	3749	125	29.99	6-115	3	1	1
Wellings, P.E.	18	0					
Wells, A.P.	820	10	82.00	3- 67	–	–	–
Wells, V.J.	4851	174	27.87	5- 43	2	–	–
Weston, R.M.S.	81	1	81.00	1- 41	–	–	–
Weston, W.P.C.	579	4	144.75	2- 39	–	–	–
Wharf, A.G.	454	11	41.27	4- 29	–	–	–
Whitaker, J.J.	268	2	134.00	1- 29	–	–	–
Whitaker, P.R.	546	12	45.50	3- 36	–	–	–
White, C.	5902	205	28.79	6- 66	5	–	–
White, G.W.	189	1	189.00	1- 30	–	–	–
Williams, N.F.	19599	649	30.19	8- 75	22	2	3
Williamson, D.	135	5	27.00	3- 19	–	–	–
Williamson, J.G.	284	4	71.00	2- 51	–	–	–
Wilson, D.G.	67	2	33.50	1- 31	–	–	–
Windows, M.G.N.	90	2	45.00	1- 6	–	–	–
Wood, J.	4880	129	37.82	6-110	4	–	–
Wood, N.T.	38	0					
Wren, T.N.	2416	66	36.60	6- 48	3	–	–
Wright, A.J.	68	1	68.00	1- 16	–	–	–
Wright, C.M.	89	3	29.66	3- 66	–	–	–
Wright, G.J.	279	1	279.00	1- 60	–	–	–
Wylie, A.	216	2	108.00	1- 50	–	–	–
Yates, G.	5821	137	42.48	5- 34	3	–	–
Young, S.	7300	214	34.11	7- 64	8	1	–

LEADING CURRENT PLAYERS

The leading career records of players currently registered for first-class county cricket. All figures are to the end of the 1997 English season.

BATTING
(Qualification: 100 innings)

	Runs	Avge
G.A.Hick	28473	56.27
B.C.Lara	10978	54.07
M.G.Bevan	9750	51.86
D.S.Lehmann	9792	51.80
J.L.Langer	5920	50.16
M.W.Gatting	35410	49.73
J.P.Crawley	11111	49.16
S.G.Law	9522	47.37
T.M.Moody	18555	47.09
Saeed Anwar	6961	46.71
M.R.Ramprakash	14596	46.04
D.C.Boon	20583	45.53
G.P.Thorpe	14048	44.88
C.L.Hooper	14689	44.78
R.A.Smith	21645	44.17
N.Hussain	13107	44.13
M.P.Maynard	18516	43.98
R.T.Robinson	26493	42.938
T.L.Penney	6268	42.931
M.A.Atherton	16725	42.66
A.J.Hollioake	4691	42.26
R.J.Bailey	19099	41.79
N.H.Fairbrother	17182	41.40
A.D.Brown	5628	41.38
A.J.Stewart	19965	40.82
A.J.Moles	15305	40.70
N.V.Knight	6412	40.32
P.D.Bowler	13438	40.11
A.P.Wells	19628	40.04
K.J.Barnett	24327	40.01
D.J.Bicknell	12696	39.92
R.J.Harden	12596	39.86
N.R.Taylor	18804	39.67
M.A.Butcher	5029	39.28
J.E.R.Gallian	5728	39.23
J.D.Lloyd	8306	39.17

BOWLING
(Qualification: 100 wickets)

	Wkts	Avge
Waqar Younis	688	21.07
Wasim Akram	829	21.39
C.A.Walsh	1465	22.24
Saqlain Mushtaq	172	23.31
D.R.Brown	201	23.94
Mushtaq Ahmed	671	25.41
M.P.Bicknell	630	26.03
T.A.Munton	594	26.22
M.J.McCague	392	26.45
A.M.Smith	299	26.47
A.P.Igglesden	501	26.51
D.G.Cork	429	26.73
A.R.Caddick	415	26.95
P.J.Newport	813	27.17
D.Gough	463	27.26
M.S.Kasprowicz	344	27.49
A.R.C.Fraser	660	27.58
P.R.Reiffel	374	27.67
K.M.Curran	586	27.70
A.F.Giles	127	27.72
M.C.Ilott	468	27.79
V.J.Wells	174	27.87
D.J.Millns	465	27.90
R.L.Johnson	158	27.95
P.A.J.DeFreitas	916	27.96
S.L.Watkin	726	28.53
G.C.Small	852	28.62
P.W.Jarvis	621	28.64
C.White	205	28.79
C.E.W.Silverwood	168	28.86
P.M.Such	684	28.94
P.C.R.Tufnell	767	29.02
G.D.Rose	503	29.32
D.W.Headley	318	29.61
J.P.Taylor	404	29.62
P.V.Simmons	161	29.68
M.A.Ealham	236	29.81
C.C.Lewis	481	29.86

FIELDING

	Ct
M.W.Gatting	474
G.A.Hick	417
M.P.Maynard	274
N.Hussain	261
C.L.Hooper	260
T.M.Moody	258
R.J.Maru	252
D.C.Boon	251

WICKET-KEEPING

	Total	Ct	St
R.C.Russell	1002	893	109
S.J.Rhodes	929	821	108
S.A.Marsh	668	618	50
W.K.Hegg	599	536	63
D.Ripley	599	525	74
R.J.Blakey	563	517	46
P.Moores	544	500	44

TEST CAREER RECORDS

These records, complete to 17 September 1997 prior to the start of Test No. 1378, include all players registered for county cricket in 1998 at the time of going to press, plus those who have appeared in Test matches since 1 September 1996 (No. 1333 onwards).

ENGLAND – BATTING AND FIELDING

	M	I	NO	HS	Runs	Avge	100	50	Ct/St
M.A.Atherton	73	134	5	185*	5243	40.64	11	33	49
R.J.Bailey	4	8	–	43	119	14.87	–	–	–
K.J.Barnett	4	7	–	80	207	29.57	–	2	1
J.E.Benjamin	1	1	–	0	0	0.00	–	–	–
M.P.Bicknell	2	4	–	14	26	6.50	–	–	–
R.J.Blakey	2	4	–	6	7	1.75	–	–	2
S.J.E.Brown	1	2	1	10*	11	11.00	–	–	1
M.A.Butcher	5	10	–	87	254	25.40	–	2	8
A.R.Caddick	16	26	4	29*	272	12.36	–	–	6
D.J.Capel	15	25	1	98	374	15.58	–	2	6
D.G.Cork	19	27	4	59	482	20.95	–	2	10
J.P.Crawley	22	35	4	112	1028	33.16	2	7	21
R.D.B.Croft	10	14	1	31	138	10.61	–	–	6
P.A.J.DeFreitas	44	68	5	88	934	14.82	–	4	14
M.A.Ealham	6	9	3	53*	186	31.00	–	2	4
N.H.Fairbrother	10	15	1	83	219	15.64	–	1	4
A.R.C.Fraser	32	46	10	29	265	7.36	–	–	7
J.E.R.Gallian	3	6	–	28	74	12.33	–	–	1
M.W.Gatting	79	138	14	207	4409	35.55	10	21	59
D.Gough	21	30	4	65	363	13.96	–	2	8
D.W.Headley	3	6	2	22	39	9.75	–	–	1
G.A.Hick	46	80	6	178	2672	36.10	4	15	62
A.J.Hollioake	2	4	–	45	51	12.75	–	–	1
B.C.Hollioake	1	2	–	28	30	15.00	–	–	1
N.Hussain	23	40	3	207	1391	37.59	5	3	23
A.P.Igglesden	3	5	3	3*	6	3.00	–	–	1
R.K.Illingworth	9	14	7	28	128	18.28	–	–	5
M.C.Ilott	5	6	2	15	28	7.00	–	–	–
R.C.Irani	2	3	–	41	76	25.33	–	–	–
P.W.Jarvis	9	15	2	29*	132	10.15	–	–	2
N.V.Knight	11	19	–	113	573	30.15	1	4	21
D.V.Lawrence	5	6	–	34	60	10.00	–	–	–
M.N.Lathwell	2	4	–	33	78	19.50	–	–	–
C.C.Lewis	32	51	3	117	1105	23.02	1	4	25
M.J.McCague	3	5	–	11	21	4.20	–	–	–
D.E.Malcolm	40	58	19	29	236	6.05	–	–	7
P.J.Martin	8	13	–	29	115	8.84	–	–	6
M.P.Maynard	4	8	–	35	87	10.87	–	–	3
J.E.Morris	3	5	2	32	71	23.66	–	–	3
A.D.Mullally	9	12	4	24	79	9.87	–	–	1
T.A.Munton	2	2	1	25*	25	25.00	–	–	1
P.J.Newport	3	5	1	40*	110	27.50	–	–	1
M.M.Patel	2	2	–	27	45	22.50	–	–	2
M.R.Ramprakash	20	35	1	72	585	17.20	–	2	13
D.A.Reeve	3	5	–	59	124	24.80	–	1	1
S.J.Rhodes	11	17	5	65*	294	24.50	–	1	46/3

	M	I	NO	HS	Runs	Avge	100	50	Ct/St
R.T.Robinson	29	49	5	175	1601	36.38	4	6	8
R.C.Russell	49	77	15	128*	1807	29.14	2	6	141/11
I.D.K.Salisbury	9	17	2	50	255	17.00	–	1	3
C.E.W.Silverwood	1	1	–	0	0	0.00	–	–	1
G.C.Small	17	24	7	59	263	15.47	–	1	9
A.M.Smith	1	2	1	4*	4	4.00	–	–	–
R.A.Smith	62	112	15	175	4236	43.67	9	28	39
J.P.Stephenson	1	2	–	25	36	18.00	–	–	–
A.J.Stewart	69	123	8	190	4701	40.87	10	23	112/7
P.M.Such	8	11	4	14*	65	9.28	–	–	2
J.P.Taylor	2	4	2	17*	34	17.00	–	–	–
G.P.Thorpe	43	78	8	138	2964	42.34	5	22	39
P.C.R.Tufnell	28	39	20	22*	112	5.89	–	–	11
S.L.Watkin	3	5	–	13	25	5.00	–	–	1
M.Watkinson	4	6	1	82*	167	33.40	–	1	1
A.P.Wells	1	2	1	3*	3	3.00	–	–	–
J.J.Whitaker	1	1	–	11	11	11.00	–	–	1
C.White	8	12	–	51	166	13.83	–	1	3
N.F.Williams	1	1	–	38	38	38.00	–	–	–

ENGLAND – BOWLING

	O	R	W	Avge	Best	5wI	10wM
M.A.Atherton	68	302	2	151.00	1- 20	–	–
K.J.Barnett	6	32	0				
J.E.Benjamin	28	80	4	20.00	4- 42	–	–
M.P.Bicknell	87	263	4	65.75	3- 99	–	–
S.J.E.Brown	33	138	2	69.00	1- 60	–	–
M.A.Butcher	2	14	0				
A.R.Caddick	648.2	2006	61	32.88	6- 65	4	–
D.J.Capel	333.2	1064	21	50.66	3- 88	–	–
D.G.Cork	724.1	2249	74	30.39	7- 43	3	–
R.D.B.Croft	391.4	904	28	32.28	5- 95	1	–
P.A.J.DeFreitas	1639.4	4700	140	33.57	7- 70	4	–
M.A.Ealham	138.4	383	15	25.53	4- 21	–	–
N.H.Fairbrother	2	9	0				
A.R.C.Fraser	1327.5	3509	119	29.48	8- 75	8	–
J.E.R.Gallian	14	62	0				
M.W.Gatting	125.2	317	4	79.25	1- 14	–	–
D.Gough	753.4	2401	85	28.24	6- 49	3	–
D.W.Headley	131.2	444	16	27.75	4- 72	–	–
G.A.Hick	495.3	1247	22	56.68	4-126	–	–
A.J.Hollioake	19	55	2	27.50	2- 31	–	–
B.C.Hollioake	15	83	2	41.50	1- 26	–	–
A.P.Igglesden	92.3	329	6	54.83	2- 91	–	–
R.K.Illingworth	247.3	615	19	32.36	4- 96	–	–
M.C.Ilott	173.4	542	12	45.16	3- 48	–	–
R.C.Irani	21	74	2	37.00	1- 22	–	–
P.W.Jarvis	318.4	965	21	45.95	4-107	–	–
D.V.Lawrence	181.3	676	18	37.55	5-106	1	–
C.C.Lewis	1142	3490	93	37.52	6-111	3	–
M.J.McCague	98.5	390	6	65.00	4-121	–	–
D.E.Malcolm	1413.2	4748	128	37.09	9- 57	5	2
P.J.Martin	242	580	17	34.11	4- 60	–	–

ENGLAND – BOWLING (continued)

	O	R	W	Avge	Best	5wI	10wM
A.D.Mullally	396.3	927	28	33.10	3- 44	–	–
T.A.Munton	67.3	200	4	50.00	2- 22	–	–
P.J.Newport	111.3	417	10	41.70	4- 87	–	–
M.M.Patel	46	180	1	180.00	1-101	–	–
M.R.Ramprakash	44.1	149	0				
D.A.Reeve	24.5	60	2	30.00	1- 4	–	–
R.T.Robinson	1	0	0				
I.D.K.Salisbury	295.3	1154	18	64.11	4-163	–	–
C.E.W.Silverwood	25	71	4	17.75	3- 63	–	–
G.C.Small	654.3	1871	55	34.01	5- 48	2	–
A.M.Smith	23	89	0				
R.A.Smith	4	6	0				
A.J.Stewart	3.2	13	0				
P.M.Such	362.5	805	22	36.59	6- 67	1	–
J.P.Taylor	48	156	3	52.00	1- 18	–	–
G.P.Thorpe	23	37	0				
P.C.R.Tufnell	1325.3	3198	93	34.38	7- 47	5	2
S.L.Watkin	89	305	11	27.72	4- 65	–	–
M.Watkinson	112	348	10	34.80	3- 64	–	–
C.White	135.1	452	11	41.09	3- 18	–	–
N.F.Williams	41	148	2	74.00	2-148	–	–

AUSTRALIA – BATTING AND FIELDING

	M	I	NO	HS	Runs	Avge	100	50	Ct/St
M.G.Bevan	17	29	3	91	773	29.73	–	6	8
A.J.Bichel	2	3	–	18	40	13.33	–	–	–
G.S.Blewett	22	37	2	214	1421	40.60	4	7	26
D.C.Boon	107	190	20	200	7422	43.65	21	32	99
M.T.G.Elliott	11	19	1	199	866	48.11	2	4	7
J.N.Gillespie	9	14	7	28*	86	12.28	–	–	3
M.L.Hayden	7	12	–	125	261	21.75	1	–	8
I.A.Healy	94	143	19	161*	3470	27.98	3	18	307/22
G.B.Hogg	1	2	–	4	5	2.50	–	–	–
M.S.Kasprowicz	5	6	–	21	48	8.00	–	–	2
J.L.Langer	8	12	–	69	272	22.66	–	3	2
S.G.Law	1	1	1	54*	54	–	–	1	1
G.D.McGrath	34	40	13	24	106	3.92	–	–	8
P.E.McIntyre	2	4	1	16	22	7.33	–	–	–
T.M.Moody	8	14	–	106	456	32.57	2	3	9
R.T.Ponting	9	15	–	127	571	38.06	1	3	10
P.R.Reiffel	29	41	12	56	648	22.34	–	3	14
M.J.Slater	34	59	3	219	2655	47.41	7	10	11
M.A.Taylor	87	155	9	219	6116	41.89	15	34	123
S.K.Warne	58	80	9	74*	1027	14.46	–	2	41
M.E.Waugh	69	112	4	140	4464	41.33	11	28	87
S.R.Waugh	95	148	28	200	5960	49.66	14	34	70
S.Young	1	2	1	4*	4	4.00	–	–	–

AUSTRALIA – BOWLING

	O	R	W	Avge	Best	5wI	10wM
M.G.Bevan	188.1	629	27	23.29	6- 82	1	1
A.J.Bichel	37.2	143	1	143.00	1- 31	–	–
G.S.Blewett	90.2	277	4	69.25	2- 25	–	–
D.C.Boon	6	14	0				

AUSTRALIA – BOWLING (continued)

	O	R	W	Avge	Best	5wI	10wM
J.N.Gillespie	228.2	713	32	22.28	7- 37	2	–
G.B.Hogg	17	69	1	69.00	1- 69	–	–
M.S.Kasprowicz	141.3	436	14	31.14	7- 36	1	–
S.G.Law	3	9	0				
G.D.McGrath	1355.3	3636	155	23.45	8- 38	8	–
P.E.McIntyre	65.3	194	5	38.80	3-103	–	–
T.M.Moody	72	147	2	73.50	1- 17	–	–
R.T.Ponting	5.5	8	2	4.00	1- 0	–	–
P.R.Reiffel	882.1	2401	91	26.38	6- 71	5	–
M.J.Slater	1.1	4	1	4.00	1- 4	–	–
M.A.Taylor	7	26	1	26.00	1- 11	–	–
S.K.Warne	2773.4	6323	264	23.95	8- 71	11	3
M.E.Waugh	529	1489	41	36.31	5- 40	1	–
S.R.Waugh	1085.5	2894	80	36.17	5- 28	3	–
S.Young	8	13	0				

SOUTH AFRICA – BATTING AND FIELDING

	M	I	NO	HS	Runs	Avge	100	50	Ct/St
P.R.Adams	9	13	2	29	66	6.00	–	–	8
A.M.Bacher	5	10	–	96	302	30.20	–	2	4
W.J.Cronje	36	63	7	135	2012	35.92	5	7	12
D.J.Cullinan	28	49	5	153*	1778	40.40	3	11	21
P.S.de Villiers	16	23	6	67*	305	17.94	–	2	10
A.A.Donald	33	44	18	33	334	12.84	–	–	7
H.H.Gibbs	4	8	–	31	125	15.62	–	–	1
A.C.Hudson	32	58	3	163	1920	34.90	4	13	33
J.H.Kallis	5	7	–	39	57	8.14	–	–	1
G.Kirsten	29	53	2	133	1806	35.41	4	9	22
L.Klusener	7	12	3	102*	282	31.33	1	–	6
B.M.McMillan	31	51	11	113	1702	42.55	3	11	41
S.M.Pollock	10	16	4	79	344	28.66	–	1	3
J.N.Rhodes	29	47	5	101*	1267	30.16	1	7	16
D.J.Richardson	37	56	7	109	1273	25.97	1	8	134/1
B.N.Schultz	8	7	2	6	8	1.60	–	–	2
P.L.Symcox	10	13	1	50	259	21.58	–	1	–

SOUTH AFRICA – BOWLING

	O	R	W	Avge	Best	5wI	10wM
P.R.Adams	342	1011	35	28.88	6-55	1	–
A.M.Bacher	1	4	0				
W.J.Cronje	401.5	768	17	45.17	2-11	–	–
P.S.de Villiers	742.1	1909	75	25.45	6-43	4	2
A.A.Donald	1268.1	3621	155	23.36	8-71	8	2
J.H.Kallis	62.4	136	5	27.20	3-29	–	–
G.Kirsten	54.1	135	2	67.50	1- 0	–	–
L.Klusener	221.1	684	21	32.57	8-64	1	–
B.M.McMillan	890	2238	73	30.65	4-65	–	–
S.M.Pollock	283.5	719	30	23.96	5-32	1	–
J.N.Rhodes	2	5	0				
B.N.Schultz	273.5	691	36	19.19	5-48	2	–
P.L.Symcox	313.5	861	18	47.83	3-75	–	–

WEST INDIES – BATTING AND FIELDING

	M	I	NO	HS	Runs	Avge	100	50	Ct/St
J.C.Adams	29	46	11	208*	1991	56.88	5	9	30
C.E.L.Ambrose	72	102	22	53	1064	13.30	–	1	14
K.C.G.Benjamin	24	32	7	43*	215	8.60	–	–	2
I.R.Bishop	37	54	9	48	509	11.31	–	–	7
C.O.Browne	13	20	6	39*	250	17.85	–	–	59/1
S.L.Campbell	23	39	2	208	1487	40.18	2	9	17
S.Chanderpaul	21	33	6	137*	1454	53.85	1	14	9
C.E.Cuffy	3	5	2	3*	6	2.00	–	–	1
M.V.Dillon	2	3	1	21	21	10.50	–	–	–
A.F.G.Griffith	1	2	–	13	14	7.00	–	–	–
R.I.C.Holder	7	11	2	91	290	32.22	–	2	7
C.L.Hooper	64	108	10	178*	3303	33.70	7	15	72
B.C.Lara	45	76	2	375	4004	54.10	10	20	59
J.R.Murray	28	37	4	101*	848	25.69	1	3	92/3
F.L.Reifer	2	4	–	29	48	12.00	–	–	1
F.A.Rose	7	7	2	34	64	12.80	–	–	1
R.G.Samuels	6	12	2	125	372	37.20	1	1	8
P.V.Simmons	25	45	2	110	1000	23.25	1	4	26
P.I.C.Thompson	2	3	1	10*	17	8.50	–	–	–
C.A.Walsh	93	122	37	30*	769	9.04	–	–	18
D.Williams	3	6	–	15	21	3.50	–	–	15/1
S.C.Williams	19	31	2	128	799	27.55	1	2	19

WEST INDIES – BOWLING

	O	R	W	Avge	Best	5wI	10wM
J.C.Adams	199.3	654	15	43.60	5- 17	1	–
C.E.L.Ambrose	2748.1	6566	306	21.45	8- 45	18	3
K.C.G.Benjamin	792.2	2619	89	29.42	6- 66	4	1
I.R.Bishop	1283.1	3522	154	22.87	6- 40	6	–
S.Chanderpaul	171	490	4	122.50	1- 2	–	–
C.E.Cuffy	85.2	306	7	43.71	3- 80	–	–
M.V.Dillon	54	148	4	37.00	3- 92	–	–
C.L.Hooper	1273.4	3307	63	52.49	5- 26	3	–
B.C.Lara	10	28	0				
F.A.Rose	178.1	545	23	23.69	6-100	1	–
P.V.Simmons	102	248	4	62.00	2- 34	–	–
P.I.C.Thompson	38	215	5	43.00	2- 58	–	–
C.A.Walsh	3308.3	8798	339	25.95	7- 37	13	2
S.C.Williams	3	19	0				

NEW ZEALAND – BATTING AND FIELDING

	M	I	NO	HS	Runs	Avge	100	50	Ct/St
G.I.Allott	4	6	2	8*	12	3.00	–	–	1
N.J.Astle	11	21	1	125	633	31.65	3	2	8
C.L.Cairns	23	39	–	120	1084	27.79	1	9	11
H.T.Davis	4	6	4	8*	19	9.50	–	–	1
S.B.Doull	18	30	5	31*	338	13.52	–	–	14
S.P.Fleming	27	47	2	129	1649	36.64	1	13	32
L.K.Germon	12	21	3	55	382	21.22	–	1	27/2
M.J.Greatbatch	41	71	5	146*	2021	30.62	3	10	27
C.Z.Harris	9	18	1	56	191	11.23	–	1	4
M.J.Horne	3	5	–	66	158	31.60	–	1	2

	M	I	NO	HS	Runs	Avge	100	50	Ct/St
D.K.Morrison	48	71	26	42	379	8.42	–	–	14
A.C.Parore	34	59	6	100*	1304	24.60	1	7	69/2
D.N.Patel	37	66	8	99	1200	20.68	–	5	15
B.A.Pocock	11	21	–	85	427	20.33	–	3	3
R.G.Twose	7	11	1	94	314	31.40	–	3	1
J.T.C.Vaughan	6	12	1	44	201	18.27	–	–	4
D.L.Vettori	4	7	3	29*	70	17.50	–	–	2
B.A.Young	25	49	2	267*	1700	36.17	2	11	39

NEW ZEALAND – BOWLING

	O	R	W	Avge	Best	5wI	10wM
G.I.Allott	127.4	406	9	45.11	4-74	–	–
N.J.Astle	109	264	8	33.00	2-26	–	–
C.L.Cairns	655.5	2206	60	36.76	6-52	3	–
H.T.Davis	135.2	397	12	33.08	5-63	1	–
S.B.Doull	573.5	1740	64	27.18	5-46	5	–
M.J.Greatbatch	1	0	0				
C.Z.Harris	126	375	7	53.57	2-57	–	–
M.J.Horne	10	22	0				
D.K.Morrison	1677.2	5549	160	34.68	7-89	10	–
D.N.Patel	1099	3154	75	42.05	6-50	3	–
B.A.Pocock	4	20	0				
R.G.Twose	26	80	3	26.66	2-36	–	–
J.T.C.Vaughan	173.2	450	11	40.90	4-27	–	–
D.L.Vettori	185.5	429	18	23.83	5-84	1	–

INDIA – BATTING AND FIELDING

	M	I	NO	HS	Runs	Avge	100	50	Ct/St
M.Azharuddin	85	123	7	199	5267	45.40	19	16	92
R.K.Chauhan	16	12	3	23	88	9.77	–	–	8
R.Dravid	16	26	3	148	1116	48.52	1	9	16
D.Ganesh	4	7	3	8	25	6.25	–	–	–
S.C.Ganguly	14	22	1	147	960	45.71	3	3	3
N.D.Hirwani	17	22	12	17	54	5.40	–	–	5
A.Jadeja	11	16	1	96	473	31.53	–	4	3
D.Johnson	2	3	1	5	8	4.00	–	–	–
S.B.Joshi	9	13	1	43	181	15.08	–	1	3
A.R.Kapoor	4	6	1	42	97	19.40	–	–	1
N.M.Kulkarni	1	–	–	–	–	–	–	–	1
A.Kumble	40	48	10	88	645	16.97	–	2	15
A.Kuruvilla	7	7	–	9	25	3.57	–	–	–
V.V.S.Laxman	8	13	2	64	289	26.27	–	3	5
S.V.Manjrekar	37	61	6	218	2043	37.14	4	9	25/1
D.S.Mohanty	1	1	1	0*	0	–	–	–	–
N.R.Mongia	27	40	3	152	1021	27.59	1	3	66/5
B.K.V.Prasad	17	23	9	15	69	4.92	–	–	3
W.V.Raman	11	19	1	96	448	24.88	–	4	6
V.Rathore	6	10	–	44	131	13.10	–	–	12
N.S.Sidhu	42	63	2	201	2519	41.29	8	10	9
J.Srinath	27	38	12	60	432	16.61	–	3	11
S.R.Tendulkar	55	83	8	179	3907	52.09	13	18	43

INDIA – BOWLING

	O	R	W	Avge	Best	5wI	10wM
M.Azharuddin	1.1	12	0				
R.K.Chauhan	620.5	1465	35	41.85	3- 8	–	–
R.Dravid	3	6	0				
D.Ganesh	76.5	287	5	57.40	2- 28	–	–
S.C.Ganguly	112.5	373	13	28.69	3- 71	–	–
N.D.Hirwani	716.2	1987	66	30.10	8- 61	4	1
D.Johnson	40	143	3	47.66	2- 52	–	–
S.B.Joshi	254.4	673	21	32.04	4- 43	–	–
A.R.Kapoor	107	255	6	42.50	2- 19	–	–
N.M.Kulkarni	70	195	1	195.00	1-195	–	–
A.Kumble	2017.4	4903	168	29.18	7- 59	9	1
A.Kuruvilla	230	712	17	41.88	5- 68	1	–
V.V.S.Laxman	15	49	0				
S.V.Manjrekar	2.5	15	0				
D.S.Mohanty	36.4	150	4	37.50	4- 78	–	–
B.K.V.Prasad	616.4	1840	57	32.28	6-104	5	1
W.V.Raman	58	129	2	64.50	1- 7	–	–
N.S.Sidhu	1	9	0				
J.Srinath	1051.3	2932	92	31.86	6- 21	2	–
S.R.Tendulkar	89.4	249	4	62.25	2- 10	–	–

PAKISTAN – BATTING AND FIELDING

	M	I	NO	HS	Runs	Avge	100	50	Ct/St
Aamir Sohail	34	62	3	205	2103	35.64	2	13	31
Asif Mujtaba	25	41	3	65*	928	24.42	–	8	19
Azam Khan	1	1	–	14	14	14.00	–	–	–
Hasan Raza	1	1	–	27	27	27.00	–	–	–
Ijaz Ahmed	36	54	2	141	2034	39.11	7	9	22
Inzamam-ul-Haq	37	63	8	148	2491	45.29	5	17	35
Mohammad Akram	6	9	3	5	8	1.33	–	–	4
Mohammad Hussain	1	1	–	0	0	0.00	–	–	1
Mohammad Wasim	2	3	1	109*	114	57.00	1	–	3
Mohammad Zahid	3	3	1	6*	6	3.00	–	–	–
Moin Khan	26	38	5	117*	1055	31.96	3	5	55/7
Mushtaq Ahmed	28	42	7	42	355	10.14	–	–	10
Ramiz Raja	57	94	5	122	2833	31.83	2	22	34
Rashid Latif	19	29	4	68*	623	24.92	–	3	58/8
Saeed Anwar	21	37	1	176	1739	48.30	4	13	12
Salim Elahi	4	7	–	17	57	8.14	–	–	8/1
Salim Malik	96	142	21	237	5528	45.68	15	28	62
Saqlain Mushtaq	9	14	4	79	256	25.60	–	2	4
Shadab Kabir	3	5	–	35	89	17.80	–	–	4
Shahid Nazir	6	7	2	13*	27	5.40	–	2	2
Waqar Younis	44	57	11	34	429	9.32	–	–	6
Wasim Akram	72	100	13	257*	1944	22.34	2	4	27
Zahoor Elahi	2	3	–	22	30	10.00	–	–	1

TESTS **PAKISTAN – BOWLING**

	O	R	W	Avge	Best	5wI	10wM
Aamir Sohail	268.5	710	17	41.76	4- 54	–	–
Asif Mujtaba	111	303	4	75.75	1- 0	–	–
Ijaz Ahmed	14	36	1	36.00	1- 9	–	–
Mohammad Akram	172.1	522	10	52.20	3- 39	–	–
Mohammad Hussain	10	21	1	21.00	1- 7	–	–
Mohammad Zahid	81	278	13	21.38	7- 66	1	1
Mushtaq Ahmed	1195.2	3309	117	28.28	7- 56	7	2
Rashid Latif	2	10	0				
Saeed Anwar	3	4	0				
Salim Malik	91.2	322	5	64.40	1- 3	–	–
Saqlain Mushtaq	507.3	1386	38	36.47	5- 89	1	–
Shadab Kabir	1	9	0				
Shahid Nazir	136.3	435	14	31.07	5- 53	1	–
Waqar Younis	1511.5	4844	227	21.33	7- 76	19	4
Wasim Akram	2744	7054	311	22.68	7-119	21	4

SRI LANKA – BATTING AND FIELDING

	M	I	NO	HS	Runs	Avge	100	50	Ct/St
S.D.Anurasiri	17	21	4	24	88	5.17	–	–	3
R.P.Arnold	3	6	–	50	138	23.00	–	1	4
M.S.Atapattu	9	17	–	29	182	10.70	–	–	7
K.S.C.de Silva	5	8	5	6	13	4.33	–	–	2
P.A.de Silva	63	110	6	267	4220	40.57	14	14	27
H.D.P.K.Dharmasena	15	27	4	62*	503	21.86	–	2	8
A.P.Gurusinha	41	70	7	143	2452	38.92	7	8	33
S.T.Jayasuriya	27	45	6	340	1944	49.84	4	9	23
D.R.M.Jayawardene	2	3	–	66	89	29.66	–	1	4
R.S.Kalpage	9	15	1	63	270	19.28	–	2	6
R.S.Kaluwitharana	16	26	2	132*	785	32.70	2	4	31/3
R.S.Mahanama	45	77	1	225	2383	31.35	4	10	46
M.Muralitharan	32	44	20	39	301	12.54	–	–	17
K.R.Pushpakumara	12	17	6	23	77	7.00	–	–	4
A.Ranatunga	71	121	7	135*	4034	35.38	4	28	32
S.Ranatunga	9	17	1	118	531	33.18	2	2	2
K.J.Silva	5	4	1	6*	6	2.00	–	–	1
H.P.Tillekeratne	43	72	12	126*	2579	42.98	6	14	72
W.P.U.C.J.Vaas	20	33	4	57	518	17.86	–	2	9
G.P.Wickremasinghe	24	39	4	43	323	9.22	–	–	9
D.N.T.Zoysa	3	5	1	16*	43	10.75	–	–	1

SRI LANKA – BOWLING

	O	R	W	Avge	Best	5wI	10wM
S.D.Anurasiri	616.1	1442	37	38.97	4- 71	–	–
R.P.Arnold	13	31	0				
M.S.Atapattu	5	12	1	12.00	1- 9	–	–
K.S.C.de Silva	167.3	555	12	46.25	5- 85	1	–
P.A.de Silva	209.3	646	17	38.00	3- 39	–	–
H.D.P.K.Dharmasena	601.1	1423	34	41.85	6- 99	1	–
A.P.Gurusinha	234.4	681	20	34.05	2- 7	–	–
S.T.Jayasuriya	174	566	9	62.88	3- 45	–	–
D.R.M.Jayawardene	11	35	0				
R.S.Kalpage	195.5	507	6	84.50	2- 27	–	–
R.S.Mahanama	6	30	0				

TESTS   **SRI LANKA – BOWLING (continued)**

	O	R	W	Avge	Best	5wI	10wM
M.Muralitharan	1502	3895	132	29.50	6- 98	9	–
K.R.Pushpakumara	305.5	1197	33	36.27	7-116	2	–
A.Ranatunga	372.3	984	15	65.60	2- 17	–	–
K.J.Silva	196.4	504	17	29.64	4- 16	–	–
H.P.Tillekeratne	5.4	14	0				
W.P.U.C.J.Vaas	742	1865	71	26.26	6- 87	4	1
G.P.Wickremasinghe	750.5	2337	47	49.72	5- 73	1	–
D.N.T.Zoysa	90.4	267	7	38.14	3- 47	–	–

ZIMBABWE – BATTING AND FIELDING

	M	I	NO	HS	Runs	Avge	100	50	Ct/St
E.A.Brandes	9	13	2	39	111	10.09	–	–	4
A.D.R.Campbell	22	38	1	99	1115	30.13	–	9	17
S.V.Carlisle	6	10	1	58	175	19.44	–	1	10
M.H.Dekker	14	22	1	68*	333	15.85	–	2	12
C.N.Evans	1	2	–	9	10	5.00	–	–	1
A.Flower	22	37	5	156	1330	41.56	3	9	50/4
G.W.Flower	22	38	1	201*	1175	31.75	2	6	11
D.L.Houghton	20	32	2	266	1396	46.53	4	4	15
E.Matambanadzo	1	2	1	7	7	7.00	–	–	–
M.Mbangwa	1	2	–	2	2	1.00	–	–	–
H.K.Olonga	7	9	1	7	14	1.75	–	–	4
A.H.Shah	3	5	–	62	122	24.40	–	1	–
B.C.Strang	9	15	5	42	117	11.70	–	–	6
P.A.Strang	13	21	5	106*	505	31.56	1	1	6
H.H.Streak	15	22	5	53	225	13.23	–	1	5
A.C.Waller	2	3	–	50	69	23.00	–	1	1
A.R.Whittall	3	6	1	12	27	5.40	–	–	2
G.J.Whittall	18	30	2	113*	642	22.92	1	3	7
C.B.Wishart	6	12	1	51	154	14.00	–	1	3

ZIMBABWE – BOWLING

	O	R	W	Avge	Best	5wI	10wM
E.A.Brandes	311.4	886	22	40.27	3- 45	–	–
A.D.R.Campbell	5	7	0				
M.H.Dekker	10	15	0				
C.N.Evans	6	27	0				
A.Flower	0.1	0	0				
G.W.Flower	112	322	3	107.33	1- 4	–	–
D.L.Houghton	0.5	0	0				
E.Matambanadzo	16	89	2	44.50	2- 62	–	–
M.Mbangwa	24	81	2	40.50	2- 67	–	–
H.K.Olonga	133.4	487	10	48.70	3- 90	–	–
A.H.Shah	31	125	1	125.00	1- 46	–	–
B.C.Strang	296	661	24	27.54	5-101	1	–
P.A.Strang	482.2	1278	32	39.93	5-106	3	–
H.H.Streak	606.5	1551	69	22.47	6- 90	3	–
A.R.Whittall	89.2	261	2	130.50	2-146	–	–
G.J.Whittall	369	919	27	34.03	4- 18	–	–

178

LIMITED-OVERS INTERNATIONALS CAREER RECORDS

These records, complete to 27 September 1997, include all players registered for county cricket in 1998 at the time of going to press, plus those who have appeared in LOI matches since 27 September 1996.

ENGLAND – BATTING AND FIELDING

	M	I	NO	HS	Runs	Avge	100	50	Ct/St
M.A.Atherton	53	53	3	127	1727	34.54	2	11	15
R.J.Bailey	4	4	2	43*	137	68.50	–	–	1
K.J.Barnett	1	1	–	84	84	84.00	–	1	–
J.E.Benjamin	2	1	–	–	–	–	–	–	–
M.P.Bicknell	7	6	2	31*	96	24.00	–	–	2
R.J.Blakey	3	2	–	25	25	12.50	–	–	2/1
A.D.Brown	3	3	–	118	155	51.66	1	–	1
A.R.Caddick	9	5	4	20*	35	35.00	–	–	2
D.J.Capel	23	19	2	50*	327	19.23	–	1	6
D.G.Cork	25	15	2	31*	132	10.15	–	–	6
J.P.Crawley	10	9	–	73	180	20.00	–	2	1
R.D.B.Croft	14	9	3	30*	89	14.83	–	–	4
P.A.J.DeFreitas	103	66	23	67	690	16.04	–	1	26
M.A.Ealham	5	1	–	40	40	40.00	–	–	1
N.H.Fairbrother	56	54	13	113	1539	37.53	1	11	24
A.R.C.Fraser	33	14	6	38*	80	10.00	–	–	1
M.W.Gatting	92	88	17	115*	2095	29.50	1	9	22
A.F.Giles	1	–	–	–	–	–	–	–	–
D.Gough	38	24	7	45	203	11.94	–	–	4
D.W.Headley	3	1	1	3*	3	–	–	–	–
G.A.Hick	62	61	7	105*	2105	38.98	2	16	32
A.J.Hollioake	5	5	3	66*	151	75.50	–	2	1
B.C.Hollioake	1	1	–	63	63	63.00	–	1	–
N.Hussain	12	12	4	49*	155	19.37	–	–	5
A.P.Igglesden	4	3	1	18	20	10.00	–	–	1
R.K.Illingworth	25	11	5	14	68	11.33	–	–	8
R.C.Irani	10	10	2	45*	78	9.75	–	–	2
P.W.Jarvis	16	8	2	16*	31	5.16	–	–	1
N.V.Knight	12	12	3	125*	428	47.55	2	1	3
D.V.Lawrence	1	–	–	–	–	–	–	–	–
C.C.Lewis	51	38	13	33	348	13.92	–	–	20
G.D.Lloyd	5	4	1	22	39	13.00	–	–	1
D.E.Malcolm	10	5	2	4	9	3.00	–	–	1
P.J.Martin	16	10	6	6	33	8.25	–	–	1
M.P.Maynard	10	10	1	41	153	17.00	–	–	3
J.E.Morris	8	8	1	63*	167	23.85	–	1	2
A.D.Mullally	8	3	–	20	22	7.33	–	–	3
M.R.Ramprakash	10	10	3	32	184	26.28	–	–	5
S.J.Rhodes	9	8	2	56	107	17.83	–	1	9/2
R.T.Robinson	26	26	–	83	597	22.96	–	3	6
R.C.Russell	38	29	7	50	383	17.40	–	1	41/6
I.D.K.Salisbury	4	2	1	5	7	7.00	–	–	1
C.E.W.Silverwood	6	4	–	12	17	4.25	–	–	–
G.C.Small	53	24	9	18*	98	6.53	–	–	7
N.M.K.Smith	7	6	1	31	100	20.00	–	–	1

	M	I	NO	HS	Runs	Avge	100	50	Ct/St
R.A.Smith	71	70	8	167*	2419	39.01	4	15	26
A.J.Stewart	90	85	7	103	2452	31.43	1	14	77/8
J.P.Taylor	1	1	–	1	1	1.00	–	–	–
G.P.Thorpe	39	39	6	89	1349	40.87	–	12	21
P.C.R.Tufnell	20	10	9	5*	15	15.00	–	–	4
S.D.Udal	10	6	4	11*	35	17.50	–	–	4
S.L.Watkin	4	2	–	4	4	2.00	–	–	–
M.Watkinson	1	–	–	–	–	–	–	–	–
A.P.Wells	1	1	–	15	15	15.00	–	–	–
J.J.Whitaker	2	2	1	44*	48	48.00	–	–	1
C.White	15	13	–	38	187	14.38	–	–	2

ENGLAND – BOWLING

	O	R	W	Avge	Best	4wI
R.J.Bailey	6	25	0			
J.E.Benjamin	12	47	1	47.00	1-22	–
M.P.Bicknell	68.5	347	13	26.69	3-55	–
A.R.Caddick	87	398	15	26.53	3-35	–
D.J.Capel	173	805	17	47.35	3-38	–
D.G.Cork	240	1071	35	30.60	3-27	–
R.D.B.Croft	130	516	15	34.40	2-26	–
P.A.J.DeFreitas	952	3775	115	32.82	4-35	1
M.A.Ealham	33	131	4	32.75	2-21	–
N.H.Fairbrother	1	9	0			
A.R.C.Fraser	312.4	1132	38	29.78	4-22	1
M.W.Gatting	65.2	336	10	33.60	3-32	–
A.F.Giles	9	48	0			
D.Gough	353.2	1438	58	24.79	5-44	4
D.W.Headley	25	120	1	120.00	1-36	–
G.A.Hick	140	696	18	38.66	3-41	–
A.J.Hollioake	30.5	150	12	12.50	4-23	2
B.C.Hollioake	7	36	0			
A.P.Igglesden	28	122	2	61.00	2-12	–
R.K.Illingworth	250.1	1059	30	35.30	3-33	–
R.C.Irani	54.5	246	4	61.50	1-23	–
P.W.Jarvis	146.3	672	24	28.00	5-35	2
D.V.Lawrence	11	67	4	16.75	4-67	1
C.C.Lewis	418.5	1854	65	28.52	4-30	4
D.E.Malcolm	87.4	404	16	25.25	3-40	–
P.J.Martin	139.4	610	25	24.40	4-44	1
A.D.Mullally	66	276	10	27.60	3-29	–
M.R.Ramprakash	2	14	0			
D.A.Reeve	191.1	820	20	41.00	3-20	–
I.D.K.Salisbury	31	177	5	35.40	3-41	–
C.E.W.Silverwood	42	201	3	67.00	2-27	–
G.C.Small	465.3	1942	58	33.48	4-31	1
N.M.K.Smith	43.3	190	6	31.66	3-29	–
J.P.Taylor	3	20	0			
G.P.Thorpe	20	97	2	48.50	2-15	–
P.C.R.Tufnell	170	699	19	36.78	4-22	1
S.D.Udal	95	371	8	46.37	2-37	–
S.L.Watkin	36.5	193	7	27.57	4-49	1
M.Watkinson	9	43	0			
C.White	101.2	445	15	29.66	4-37	1

AUSTRALIA – BATTING AND FIELDING

	M	I	NO	HS	Runs	Avge	100	50	Ct/St
M.G.Bevan	59	53	19	108*	1912	56.23	2	11	20
A.J.Bichel	8	4	1	17	35	11.66	–	–	1
G.S.Blewett	24	23	3	57*	458	22.90	–	2	7
D.C.Boon	181	177	16	122	5964	37.04	5	37	45
A.C.Dale	7	4	4	15*	38	–	–	–	3
M.J.Di Venuto	5	5	–	89	150	30.00	–	1	1
M.T.G.Elliott	1	1	1	1	1	1.00	–	–	–
D.W.Fleming	27	9	6	5*	19	6.33	–	–	5
A.C.Gilchrist	10	9	1	77	231	28.87	–	2	4/1
J.N.Gillespie	14	8	2	26	65	10.83	–	–	–
I.A.Healy	168	120	36	56	1764	21.00	–	4	195/39
G.B.Hogg	7	7	4	11*	38	12.66	–	–	2
B.P.Julian	3	2	–	11	11	5.50	–	–	–
M.S.Kasprowicz	5	2	2	28*	45	–	–	–	–
J.L.Langer	8	7	2	36	160	32.00	–	–	2/1
S.G.Law	44	42	3	110	1145	29.35	1	7	10
D.S.Lehmann	3	3	–	15	27	9.00	–	–	2
G.D.McGrath	69	23	12	10	45	4.09	–	–	8
T.M.Moody	40	36	4	89	766	23.93	–	7	11
R.T.Ponting	33	33	3	123	929	30.96	2	5	4
P.R.Reiffel	75	48	19	58	444	15.31	–	1	23
G.R.Robertson	4	3	2	5*	7	7.00	–	–	–
M.J.Slater	42	42	1	73	987	24.07	–	9	8
A.M.Stuart	3	1	–	1	1	1.00	–	–	2
M.A.Taylor	113	110	1	105	3514	32.23	1	28	56
S.K.Warne	76	43	13	55	375	12.50	–	1	25
M.E.Waugh	135	130	11	130	4542	38.16	10	28	52
S.R.Waugh	221	201	43	102*	5092	32.22	1	30	80

AUSTRALIA – BOWLING

	O	R	W	Avge	Best	4wI
M.G.Bevan	167.3	810	18	45.00	3-36	–
A.J.Bichel	74.2	355	12	29.58	3-17	–
G.S.Blewett	109.4	551	12	45.91	2-34	–
D.C.Boon	13.4	86	0			
A.C.Dale	65	275	8	34.37	3-18	–
D.W.Fleming	226	995	40	24.87	5-36	3
J.N.Gillespie	126.1	607	13	46.69	2-39	–
G.B.Hogg	49.1	218	3	72.66	1-23	–
B.P.Julian	29	169	5	33.80	3-50	–
M.S.Kasprowicz	40.2	208	5	41.60	1-27	–
S.G.Law	124.3	572	12	47.66	2-22	–
D.S.Lehmann	13	65	1	65.00	1-29	–
G.D.McGrath	618.3	2442	85	28.72	5-52	4
T.M.Moody	193.5	854	21	40.66	3-56	–
P.R.Reiffel	649.4	2526	90	28.06	4-13	5
G.R.Robertson	24	127	0			
M.J.Slater	2	11	0			
A.M.Stuart	30	109	8	13.62	5-26	1
S.K.Warne	710	2859	129	22.16	5-33	10
M.E.Waugh	440.3	2123	71	29.90	5-24	2
S.R.Waugh	1310	5877	172	34.16	4-33	2

SOUTH AFRICA – BATTING AND FIELDING

	M	I	NO	HS	Runs	Avge	100	50	Ct/St
P.R.Adams	9	4	1	10	10	3.33	–	–	1
A.M.Bacher	7	7	–	45	123	17.57	–	–	1
N.Boje	7	5	2	13*	27	9.00	–	–	2
R.E.Bryson	7	4	3	17*	32	32.00	–	–	1
W.J.Cronje	115	107	20	112	3473	39.91	2	22	46
D.N.Crookes	18	14	2	54	190	15.83	–	1	13
D.J.Cullinan	77	75	11	124	2529	39.51	3	17	35
P.S.de Villiers	79	34	15	20*	163	8.57	–	–	13
A.A.Donald	87	21	10	7*	40	3.63	–	–	12
H.H.Gibbs	9	9	–	35	205	22.77	–	–	3
A.C.Hudson	85	84	1	161	2530	30.48	2	18	16
J.H.Kallis	25	24	6	82	700	38.88	–	6	5
G.Kirsten	66	66	8	188*	2723	46.94	7	14	21/1
L.Klusener	15	11	2	92	270	30.00	–	2	3
L.J.Koen	2	2	–	22	22	11.00	–	–	–
B.M.McMillan	68	46	16	127	787	26.23	1	–	38
C.R.Matthews	56	22	9	26	141	10.84	–	–	10
S.M.Pollock	33	21	10	75	433	39.36	–	2	6
J.N.Rhodes	110	102	19	121	2639	31.79	1	11	42
D.J.Richardson	108	69	28	53	793	19.34	–	1	131/15
P.L.Symcox	47	30	4	61	382	14.69	–	1	10

SOUTH AFRICA – BOWLING

	O	R	W	Avge	Best	4wI
P.R.Adams	70	296	13	22.76	3-26	–
N.Boje	63	263	9	29.22	2-38	–
R.E.Bryson	63	323	7	46.14	2-34	–
W.J.Cronje	592.2	2559	69	37.08	5-32	2
D.N.Crookes	112.1	527	10	52.70	3-30	–
D.J.Cullinan	4	22	1	22.00	1- 7	–
P.S.de Villiers	700	2480	90	27.55	4-27	2
A.A.Donald	785	3211	147	21.84	6-23	7
J.H.Kallis	95	459	8	57.37	3-21	–
G.Kirsten	5	23	0			
L.Klusener	115.4	592	20	29.60	5-42	1
B.M.McMillan	529.5	2269	62	36.59	4-32	1
C.R.Matthews	500.3	1975	79	25.00	4-10	3
S.M.Pollock	302.1	1209	47	25.72	4-33	2
P.L.Symcox	404	1635	46	35.54	3-20	–

WEST INDIES – BATTING AND FIELDING

	M	I	NO	HS	Runs	Avge	100	50	Ct/St
J.C.Adams	74	57	20	81*	1038	28.05	–	7	48/5
C.E.L.Ambrose	146	77	32	31*	513	11.40	–	–	36
K.C.G.Benjamin	26	13	7	17	65	10.83	–	–	4
I.R.Bishop	83	43	18	33*	390	15.60	–	–	12
C.O.Browne	24	18	4	26	172	12.28	–	–	30/5
S.L.Campbell	36	36	–	86	835	23.19	–	3	10
S.Chanderpaul	42	39	2	109*	1210	32.70	1	9	10
C.E.Cuffy	11	7	3	17*	25	6.25	–	–	3
O.D.Gibson	15	11	1	52	141	14.10	–	1	3
A.F.G.Griffith	5	4	1	47	50	16.66	–	–	4
R.I.C.Holder	35	29	6	65	597	25.95	–	2	8
C.L.Hooper	155	139	33	113*	3600	33.96	3	20	76

WEST INDIES – BATTING AND FIELDING (continued)

	M	I	NO	HS	Runs	Avge	100	50	Ct/St
B.C.Lara	118	116	12	169	4881	46.93	11	31	59
N.A.M.McLean	6	3	–	7	8	2.66	–	–	2
J.R.Murray	49	30	6	86	557	23.20	–	4	44/7
D.Ramnarine	1	–	–	–	–	–	–	–	–
F.L.Reifer	1	1	–	9	9	9.00	–	–	1
F.A.Rose	5	3	–	9	21	7.00	–	–	1
R.G.Samuels	8	5	2	36*	54	18.00	–	–	–
P.V.Simmons	119	117	7	122	3242	29.47	5	17	51
P.I.C.Thompson	2	1	–	2	2	2.00	–	–	–
C.A.Walsh	176	66	28	30	291	7.65	–	–	26
L.R.Williams	5	3	–	14	20	6.66	–	–	3
S.C.Williams	33	33	3	90	999	33.30	–	8	7

WEST INDIES – BOWLING

	O	R	W	Avge	Best	4wI
J.C.Adams	139	669	22	30.40	5-37	1
C.E.L.Ambrose	1300.5	4518	200	22.59	5-17	10
K.C.G.Benjamin	219.5	923	33	27.96	3-34	–
I.R.Bishop	717	3085	117	26.36	5-25	9
S.Chanderpaul	77.4	414	8	51.75	2-16	–
C.E.Cuffy	91.1	352	9	39.11	2-19	–
O.D.Gibson	123.1	621	34	18.26	5-40	4
C.L.Hooper	1043.5	4536	134	33.85	4-34	1
B.C.Lara	4	22	2	11.00	2- 5	–
N.A.M.McLean	34	145	3	48.33	2-33	–
D.Ramnarine	10	52	2	26.00	2-52	–
F.A.Rose	41	175	5	35.00	3-25	–
P.V.Simmons	505.4	2185	62	35.24	4- 3	2
P.I.C.Thompson	19	110	2	55.00	1-46	–
C.A.Walsh	1548	5936	196	30.28	5- 1	6
L.R.Williams	25.5	141	8	17.62	3-16	–

NEW ZEALAND – BATTING AND FIELDING

	M	I	NO	HS	Runs	Avge	100	50	Ct/St
G.I.Allott	3	2	1	3	4	4.00	–	–	2
N.J.Astle	46	46	1	120	1460	32.44	4	8	13
C.L.Cairns	67	63	5	103	1521	26.22	1	7	25
H.T.Davis	9	6	4	7*	13	6.50	–	–	1
S.B.Doull	22	18	8	22	136	13.60	–	–	5
S.P.Fleming	65	64	5	106*	1798	30.47	1	11	28
L.K.Germon	37	31	5	89	519	19.96	–	3	21/9
M.J.Greatbatch	84	83	5	111	2206	28.28	2	13	35
C.Z.Harris	85	76	19	130	1402	24.59	1	3	26
M.N.Hart	11	6	–	16	49	8.16	–	–	7
M.J.Horne	5	5	–	45	136	27.20	–	–	–
R.J.Kennedy	7	4	3	8*	17	17.00	–	–	1
G.R.Larsen	94	58	22	37	541	15.02	–	–	15
C.D.McMillan	1	1	–	10	10	10.00	–	–	1
D.K.Morrison	96	43	24	20*	171	9.00	–	–	19
D.J.Murray	1	1	–	3	3	3.00	–	–	–
D.J.Nash	28	18	5	40*	128	9.84	–	–	6
S.B.O'Connor	1	1	–	0	0	0.00	–	–	–
A.C.Parore	72	68	10	108	1936	33.37	1	10	37/10
D.N.Patel	75	63	10	71	623	11.75	–	1	23
A.J.Penn	3	2	1	7*	8	8.00	–	–	–
C.M.Spearman	24	24	–	78	485	20.20	–	2	6
R.G.Twose	21	20	–	92	612	30.60	–	4	5

NEW ZEALAND – BATTING AND FIELDING (continued)

	M	I	NO	HS	Runs	Avge	100	50	Ct/St
J.T.C.Vaughan	18	16	7	33	162	18.00	–	–	4
D.L.Vettori	1	1	–	4	4	4.00	–	–	–
B.A.Young	62	61	4	74	1360	23.85	–	6	26

NEW ZEALAND – BOWLING

	O	R	W	Avge	Best	4wI
G.I.Allott	22	110	5	22.00	2-21	–
N.J.Astle	253.5	1130	37	30.54	4-43	1
C.L.Cairns	412	1883	58	32.46	4-55	1
H.T.Davis	66	385	11	35.00	4-35	1
S.B.Doull	159.5	865	19	45.52	3-42	–
S.P.Fleming	4.5	28	1	28.00	1- 8	–
M.J.Greatbatch	1	5	0			
C.Z.Harris	637.2	2738	86	31.83	5-42	1
M.N.Hart	91.2	347	13	26.69	5-22	1
R.J.Kennedy	52	283	5	56.60	2-36	–
G.R.Larsen	836.4	3096	88	35.18	4-24	1
D.K.Morrison	764.2	3470	126	27.53	5-34	3
D.J.Nash	214	1024	26	39.38	3-26	–
S.B.O'Connor	9	44	3	14.66	3-44	–
D.N.Patel	541.5	2260	45	50.22	3-22	–
A.J.Penn	16.3	123	1	123.00	1-50	–
C.M.Spearman	0.3	6	0			
R.G.Twose	45.2	237	4	59.25	2-31	–
J.T.C.Vaughan	116	524	15	34.93	4-33	1
D.L.Vettori	2	21	0			

INDIA – BATTING AND FIELDING

	M	I	NO	HS	Runs	Avge	100	50	Ct/St
S.A.Ankola	20	13	4	9	34	3.77	–	–	2
M.Azharuddin	259	239	46	111*	7294	37.79	4	45	117
R.K.Chauhan	26	13	3	26*	80	8.00	–	–	7
N.David	4	2	2	8*	9	–	–	–	–
P.Dharmani	1	1	–	8	8	8.00	–	–	–
R.Dravid	49	43	4	107	1345	34.48	1	10	23
D.Ganesh	1	1	–	4	4	4.00	–	–	–
S.C.Ganguly	40	37	4	113	1233	37.36	1	8	11
Harvinder Singh	6	1	–	1	1	1.00	–	–	1
A.Jadeja	104	92	13	119	2644	33.46	2	14	30
S.B.Joshi	22	13	3	48	127	12.70	–	–	10
V.G.Kambli	81	74	19	106	2077	37.76	2	12	12
A.R.Kapoor	15	6	–	19	43	7,16	–	–	1
S.S.Karim	19	13	2	55	168	15.27	–	1	17/2
N.M.Kulkarni	6	2	1	4*	7	–	–	–	1
A.Kumble	126	65	21	24	422	9.59	–	–	46
A.Kuruvilla	20	8	3	7	19	3.80	–	–	2
S.V.Manjrekar	74	70	10	105	1994	33.23	1	15	23
D.S.Mohanty	6	1	1	0*	0	–	–	–	2
N.R.Mongia	78	52	17	69	693	19.80	–	1	61/23
B.K.V.Prasad	75	30	17	19	74	5.69	–	–	23
W.V.Raman	27	27	1	114	617	23.73	1	3	2
V.Rathore	7	7	–	54	193	27.57	–	2	4
N.S.Sidhu	114	107	8	134*	3964	40.04	6	31	17
R.R.Singh	34	29	4	100	640	25.60	1	1	7
S.Somasunder	2	2	–	10	17	8.50	–	–	–
J.Srinath	123	64	19	53	500	11.11	–	1	17
S.R.Tendulkar	164	159	15	137	5621	39.03	12	34	53

INDIA – BOWLING

	O	R	W	Avge	Best	4wI
S.A.Ankola	134.3	615	13	47.30	3-33	–
M.Azharuddin	92	479	12	39.91	3-19	–
R.K.Chauhan	202	912	22	41.45	3-29	–
N.David	32	133	4	33.25	3-21	–
R.Dravid	2	6	0			
D.Ganesh	5	20	1	20.00	1-20	–
S.C.Ganguly	90.5	378	16	23.62	5-16	1
Harvinder Singh	37.2	184	9	20.44	3-44	–
A.Jadeja	196.5	1030	14	73.57	2-16	–
S.B.Joshi	179.4	812	21	38.66	3-40	–
V.G.Kambli	0.4	7	1	7.00	1- 7	–
A.R.Kapoor	136	547	8	68.37	2-33	–
N.M.Kulkarni	29	147	5	29.40	3-73	–
A.Kumble	1123.1	4601	169	27.22	6-12	7
A.Kuruvilla	149.1	682	22	31.00	4-43	1
S.V.Manjrekar	1.2	10	1	10.00	1- 2	–
D.S.Mohanty	44	225	8	28.12	3-15	–
B.K.V.Prasad	624.5	3005	88	34.14	4-17	2
W.V.Raman	27	170	2	85.00	1-23	–
N.S.Sidhu	0.4	3	0			
R.R.Singh	190.4	914	26	35.15	3-13	–
J.Srinath	1064.3	4576	158	28.96	5-24	4
S.R.Tendulkar	584.2	2847	49	58.10	4-34	1

PAKISTAN – BATTING AND FIELDING

	M	I	NO	HS	Runs	Avge	100	50	Ct/St
Aamir Sohail	125	124	2	134	3926	32.18	5	26	41
Abdul Razzak	4	2	1	8	8	8.00	–	–	–
Aqib Javed	148	49	25	45*	265	11.04	–	–	21
Arshad Khan	9	6	4	9*	21	10.50	–	–	3
Azam Khan	5	4	–	72	113	28.25	–	1	1
Azhar Mahmood	15	11	2	33*	97	10.77	–	–	5
Hasan Raja	8	7	–	41	71	10.14	–	–	–
Ijaz Ahmed	181	165	23	124*	4418	31.11	5	26	70
Ijaz Ahmed II	2	1	1	3*	3		–	–	–
Inzamam-ul-Haq	143	137	18	137*	4446	37.36	4	31	34
Kabir Khan	6	2	2	1*	2	–	–	–	1
Mohammad Akram	12	7	5	7*	13	6.50	–	–	5
Mohammad Hussain	6	6	3	20	71	23.66	–	–	1
Mohammad Wasim	14	14	1	54	338	26.00	–	2	4
Mohammad Zahid	4	2	1	1	2	1.00	–	–	–
Moin Khan	91	73	19	61	1127	20.87	–	3	86/36
Mujahid Jamshed	4	3	1	23	27	13.50	–	–	–
Mushtaq Ahmed	124	64	27	26	332	8.97	–	–	27
Ramiz Raja	198	197	15	119*	5841	32.09	9	31	33
Rashid Latif	85	57	16	50	664	16.19	–	1	81/22
Saeed Anwar	131	130	12	194	4659	39.48	12	19	27
Saeed Azad	4	4	–	31	65	16.25	–	–	2
Sajid Ali	3	3	–	28	47	15.66	–	–	–
Salim Elahi	14	14	1	102*	437	33.61	1	3	4
Salim Malik	268	242	37	102	6884	33.58	5	46	77
Saqlain Mushtaq	65	42	11	30*	321	10.35	–	–	20
Shahid Afridi	42	39	2	102	842	22.75	1	5	13
Shahid Nazir	14	6	1	8	25	25.00	–	–	2
Waqar Younis	156	78	29	37	463	9.44	–	–	18

PAKISTAN – BATTING AND FIELDING (continued)

	M	I	NO	HS	Runs	Avge	100	50	Ct/St
Wasim Akram	232	181	33	86	2180	14.72	–	4	56
Zahoor Elahi	14	14	1	86	297	22.84	–	3	2

PAKISTAN – BOWLING

	O	R	W	Avge	Best	4wI
Aamir Sohail	687.4	3083	71	43.42	4-22	1
Abdul Razzak	24.3	139	4	34.75	2-29	–
Aqib Javed	1216.4	5148	164	31.39	7-37	5
Arshad Khan	65.5	285	5	57.00	2-54	–
Azhar Mahmood	94.3	443	7	63.28	2-27	–
Ijaz Ahmed	88.5	373	4	93.25	2-31	–
Ijaz Ahmed II	5	25	1	25.00	1- 9	–
Inzamam-ul-Haq	6.4	52	2	26.00	1- 4	–
Kabir Khan	32.5	138	7	19.71	2-23	–
Mohammad Akram	81	403	12	33.58	2-28	–
Mohammad Hussain	41	221	3	73.66	2-56	–
Mohammad Zahid	36	164	3	54.66	2-53	–
Mujahid Jamshed	4	6	1	6.00	1- 6	–
Mushtaq Ahmed	1072.3	4638	141	32.89	5-36	3
Ramiz Raja	1	10	0			
Saeed Anwar	29.4	156	3	52.00	1- 9	–
Salim Malik	550.3	2753	80	34.41	5-35	1
Saqlain Mushtaq	557.4	2392	123	19.44	5-29	9
Shahid Afridi	303.5	1370	30	45.66	3-33	–
Shahid Nazir	105	498	15	33.20	3-14	–
Waqar Younis	1284.3	5762	265	21.74	6-26	20
Wasim Akram	1992.2	7517	333	22.57	5-15	18

SRI LANKA – BATTING AND FIELDING

	M	I	NO	HS	Runs	Avge	100	50	Ct/St
M.S.Atapattu	30	29	5	118	913	38.04	1	7	7
U.D.U.Chandana	21	14	3	26	119	10.81	–	–	13
P.A.de Silva	218	212	22	145	6874	36.17	9	46	67
K.S.C.de Silva	24	12	6	13*	27	4.50	–	–	8
S.K.L.de Silva	7	4	3	50	103	103.00	–	1	4/5
H.D.P.K.Dharmasena	64	37	15	51*	531	24.13	–	3	17
A.P.Gurusinha	147	143	5	117*	3902	28.27	2	22	49
S.T.Jayasuriya	141	133	4	151*	3592	27.84	5	22	54
R.S.Kalpage	81	64	27	51	773	20.89	–	1	30
R.S.Kaluwitharana	76	72	5	100*	1090	16.26	1	5	51/33
D.K.Liyanage	14	9	2	43	120	17.14	–	–	5
R.S.Mahanama	176	163	19	119*	4360	30.27	4	30	93
M.Muralitharan	77	33	16	9*	94	5.52	–	–	39
K.R.Pushpakumara	24	7	5	14*	36	18.00	–	–	5
A.Ranatunga	221	209	41	131*	6074	36.15	3	40	47
H.P.Tillekeratne	159	136	32	104	2935	28.22	2	9	70/5
W.P.U.C.J.Vaas	77	41	15	33	328	12.61	–	–	12
D.N.T.Zoysa	3	1	1	3*	3	–	–	–	–

SRI LANKA – BOWLING

	O	R	W	Avge	Best	4wI
M.S.Atapattu	9.3	45	0			
U.D.U.Chandana	112	512	16	32.00	4-35	1
P.A.de Silva	555.2	2695	69	39.05	3-36	–
K.S.C.de Silva	181.5	865	37	23.37	3-18	–
H.D.P.K.Dharmasena	526.4	2333	64	36.45	4-37	1

LOIs — **SRI LANKA – BOWLING (continued)**

	O	R	W	Avge	Best	4wI
A.P.Gurusinha	264.1	1354	26	52.07	2-25	–
S.T.Jayasuriya	831	4036	121	33.35	6-29	5
R.S.Kalpage	616	2746	70	39.22	4-36	1
D.K.Liyanage	92	430	8	53.75	3-49	–
R.S.Mahanama	0.2	7	0			
M.Muralitharan	702	2927	101	28.98	4-18	3
K.R.Pushpakumara	185.2	918	19	48.31	3-25	–
A.Ranatunga	785	3757	79	47.55	4-14	1
H.P.Tillekeratne	20.4	92	4	23.00	1- 3	–
W.P.U.C.J.Vaas	615.2	2457	98	25.07	4-20	3
D.N.T.Zoysa	27	122	5	24.40	2-29	–

ZIMBABWE – BATTING AND FIELDING

	M	I	NO	HS	Runs	Avge	100	50	Ct/St
E.A.Brandes	44	31	8	55	245	10.65	–	1	8
G.B.Brent	1	1	–	1	1	1.00	–	–	–
A.D.R.Campbell	57	54	4	131*	1205	24.10	1	7	24
S.V.Carlisle	8	8	1	28	79	11.28	–	–	4
M.H.Dekker	23	22	2	79	379	18.95	–	2	5
C.N.Evans	24	22	4	96*	406	22.55	–	1	3
A.Flower	65	63	4	115*	1711	29.00	1	12	52/10
G.W.Flower	55	53	3	91	1526	30.52	–	11	27
D.L.Houghton	60	57	2	142	1485	27.00	1	12	29/2
E.Matambanadzo	6	5	3	5*	8	4.00	–	–	1
M.Mbangwa	1	1	–	11	11	11.00	–	–	–
G.J.Rennie	2	2	–	6	6	3.00	–	–	2
J.A.Rennie	21	11	6	27	81	16.20	–	–	6
B.C.Strang	12	8	4	6	17	4.25	–	–	7
P.A.Strang	38	34	10	47	603	25.12	–	–	12
H.H.Streak	44	35	10	43*	423	16.92	–	–	9
D.P.Viljoen	3	3	–	25	64	21.33	–	–	1
A.C.Waller	39	38	3	83*	818	23.37	–	4	10
A.R.Whittall	8	7	2	4*	12	2.40	–	–	2
G.J.Whittall	45	45	5	70	694	17.35	–	2	12
C.B.Wishart	10	10	–	53	160	16.00	–	1	3

ZIMBABWE – BOWLING

	O	R	W	Avge	Best	4wI
E.A.Brandes	365	1755	59	29.74	5-28	3
G.B.Brent	5	29	0			
A.D.R.Campbell	27.3	116	3	38.66	2-22	–
M.H.Dekker	57.5	290	9	32.22	2-16	–
C.N.Evans	41	171	5	34.20	1- 6	–
A.Flower	5	23	0			
G.W.Flower	143.5	719	16	44.93	3-15	–
D.L.Houghton	2	19	1	19.00	1-19	–
E.Matambanadzo	44.3	193	10	19.30	4-32	1
M.Mbangwa	5.4	48	0			
J.A.Rennie	148.4	732	18	40.66	3-27	–
B.C.Strang	81.2	347	10	34.70	4-36	1
P.A.Strang	301.5	1313	37	35.48	5-21	2
H.H.Streak	391.2	1646	58	28.37	5-32	4
A.R.Whittall	61	261	6	43.50	3-36	–
G.J.Whittall	261.3	1286	34	37.82	3-46	–

BANGLADESH – BATTING AND FIELDING

	M	I	NO	HS	Runs	Avge	100	50	Ct/St
Amin-ul-Islam	13	13	3	42	257	25.70	–	–	3
Athar Ali Khan	11	11	1	82	368	36.80	–	2	1
Inam-ul-Haq	9	9	2	18	67	9.57	–	–	–
Habib-ul-Bashar	4	4	–	16	22	5.50	–	–	3
Hasib-ul-Hassan	5	4	1	10	13	4.33	–	–	–
Khalid Masud	6	6	2	27*	67	16.75	–	–	5
Mafiz-ur-Rehman	2	2	1	15*	21	21.00	–	–	1
Minhaz-ul-Abedin	15	14	–	40	200	14.28	–	–	2
Naim-ur-Rehman	4	4	–	47	58	14.50	–	–	3
Saif-ul-Islam	6	4	2	22*	37	18.50	–	–	–
Sheikh Salahuddin	3	2	2	3*	3	–	–	–	–
Zakir Hassan	1	–	–	–	–	–	–	–	–

BANGLADESH – BOWLING

	O	R	W	Avge	Best	4wI
Amin-ul-Islam	18.2	125	0			
Athar Ali Khan	42	217	3	72.33	1-10	–
Inam-ul-Haq	47	284	2	142.00	1-34	–
Hasib-ul-Hassan	29	194	3	64.66	1-29	–
Mafiz-ur-Rehman	8	53	0			
Minhaz-ul-Abedin	63	355	9	39.44	2-39	–
Naim-ur-Rehman	21.4	124	1	124.00	1-29	–
Saif-ul-Islam	44	221	6	36.83	4-36	1
Sheikh Salahuddin	21	120	3	40.00	2-48	–
Zakir Hassan	2	17	0			

KENYA – BATTING AND FIELDING

	M	I	NO	HS	Runs	Avge	100	50	Ct/St
R.Ali	7	3	3	6*	7	–	–	–	1
Asif Karim	9	6	1	24	42	8.40	–	–	–
D.Chudasama	9	8	–	51	183	22.87	–	1	2
S.Gupta	3	3	–	41	43	14.33	–	–	–
H.Modi	9	8	1	78*	179	25.57	–	1	3
T.Odoyo	8	7	–	32	83	11.85	–	–	1
E.T.Odumbe	8	7	1	20	61	10.16	–	–	4
M.Odumbe	9	8	–	50	135	16.87	–	1	1
L.Onyango	2	2	–	23	27	13.50	–	–	1
K.Otieno	9	8	–	85	174	21.75	–	1	2/1
A.Suji	2	2	–	10	14	7.00	–	–	–
M.Suji	9	7	4	15	24	8.00	–	–	3
S.O.Tikolo	9	8	–	96	216	27.00	–	2	3

KENYA – BOWLING

	O	R	W	Avge	Best	4wI
R.Ali	45.2	213	10	21.30	3-17	–
Asif Karim	75	289	6	48.16	2-44	–
T.Odoyo	44	225	4	56.25	3-25	–
E.T.Odumbe	22.5	137	6	22.83	2- 8	–
M.Odumbe	60.5	265	8	33.12	3-15	–
L.Onyango	7	76	1	76.00	1-45	–
A.Suji	10.2	54	1	54.00	1-16	–
M.Suji	70	361	6	60.16	2-42	–
S.O.Tikolo	13	102	1	102.00	1-26	–

WISDEN CRICKET MONTHLY

THE ONLY MAGAZINE YOU NEED.

FIRST-CLASS CRICKET RECORDS

To 21 September 1997

TEAM RECORDS

HIGHEST INNINGS TOTALS

1107	Victoria v New South Wales	Melbourne	1926-27
1059	Victoria v Tasmania	Melbourne	1922-23
952-6d	Sri Lanka v India	Colombo	1997-98
951-7d	Sind v Baluchistan	Karachi	1973-74
944-6d	Hyderabad v Andhra	Secunderabad	1993-94
918	New South Wales v South Australia	Sydney	1900-01
912-8d	Holkar v Mysore	Indore	1945-46
910-6d	Railways v Dera Ismail Khan	Lahore	1964-65
903-7d	England v Australia	The Oval	1938
887	Yorkshire v Warwickshire	Birmingham	1896
863	Lancashire v Surrey	The Oval	1990
860-6d	Tamil Nadu v Goa	Panjim	1988-89

Excluding penalty runs in India, there have been 30 innings totals of 800 runs or more in first-class cricket. Tamil Nadu's total of 860-6d was boosted to 912 by 52 penalty runs.

HIGHEST SECOND INNINGS TOTAL

770	New South Wales v South Australia	Adelaide	1920-21

HIGHEST FOURTH INNINGS TOTAL

654-5	England v South Africa	Durban	1938-39

HIGHEST MATCH AGGREGATE

2376	Maharashtra v Bombay	Poona	1948-49

RECORD MARGIN OF VICTORY

Innings and 851 runs: Railways v Dera Ismail Khan	Lahore	1964-65

MOST RUNS IN A DAY

721	Australians v Essex	Southend	1948

MOST HUNDREDS IN AN INNINGS

6	Holkar v Mysore	Indore	1945-46

LOWEST INNINGS TOTALS

12	†Oxford University v MCC and Ground	Oxford	1877
12	Northamptonshire v Gloucestershire	Gloucester	1907
13	Auckland v Canterbury	Auckland	1877-78
13	Nottinghamshire v Yorkshire	Nottingham	1901
14	Surrey v Essex	Chelmsford	1983
15	MCC v Surrey	Lord's	1839
15	†Victoria v MCC	Melbourne	1903-04
15	†Northamptonshire v Yorkshire	Northampton	1908
15	Hampshire v Warwickshire	Birmingham	1922

† Batted one man short

There have been 26 instances of a team being dismissed for under 20.

LOWEST MATCH AGGREGATE BY ONE TEAM

34 (16 and 18)   Border v Natal   East London   1959-60

LOWEST COMPLETED MATCH AGGREGATE BY BOTH TEAMS

105   MCC v Australians   Lord's   1878

FEWEST RUNS IN AN UNINTERRUPTED DAY'S PLAY

95   Australia (80) v Pakistan (15-2)   Karachi   1956-57

TIED MATCHES

Before 1949 a match was considered to be tied if the scores were level after the fourth innings, even if the side batting last had wickets in hand when play ended. Law 22 was amended in 1948 and since then a match has been tied only when the scores are level after the fourth innings have been completed. There have been 53 tied first-class matches, five of which would not have qualified under the current law. The most recent is:

Worcestershire (203/325-8d) v Nottinghamshire (233/295)   Nottingham   1993

BATTING RECORDS
HIGHEST INDIVIDUAL INNINGS

501*	B.C.Lara	Warwickshire v Durham	Birmingham	1994
499	Hanif Mohammad	Karachi v Bahawalpur	Karachi	1958-59
452*	D.G.Bradman	New South Wales v Queensland	Sydney	1929-30
443*	B.B.Nimbalkar	Maharashtra v Kathiawar	Poona	1948-49
437	W.H.Ponsford	Victoria v Queensland	Melbourne	1927-28
429	W.H.Ponsford	Victoria v Tasmania	Melbourne	1922-23
428	Aftab Baloch	Sind v Baluchistan	Karachi	1973-74
424	A.C.MacLaren	Lancashire v Somerset	Taunton	1895
405*	G.A.Hick	Worcestershire v Somerset	Taunton	1988
385	B.Sutcliffe	Otago v Canterbury	Christchurch	1952-53
383	C.W.Gregory	New South Wales v Queensland	Brisbane	1906-07
377	S.V.Manjrekar	Bombay v Hyderabad	Bombay	1990-91
375	B.C.Lara	West Indies v England	St John's	1993-94
369	D.G.Bradman	South Australia v Tasmania	Adelaide	1935-36
366	N.H.Fairbrother	Lancashire v Surrey	The Oval	1990
366	M.V.Sridhar	Hyderabad v Andhra	Secunderabad	1993-94
365*	C.Hill	South Australia v NSW	Adelaide	1900-01
365*	G.St A.Sobers	West Indies v Pakistan	Kingston	1957-58
364	L.Hutton	England v Australia	The Oval	1938
359*	V.M.Merchant	Bombay v Maharashtra	Bombay	1943-44
359	R.B.Simpson	New South Wales v Queensland	Brisbane	1963-64
357*	R.Abel	Surrey v Somerset	The Oval	1899
357	D.G.Bradman	South Australia v Victoria	Melbourne	1935-36
356	B.A.Richards	South Australia v W Australia	Perth	1970-71
355*	G.R.Marsh	W Australia v S Australia	Perth	1989-90
355	B.Sutcliffe	Otago v Auckland	Dunedin	1949-50
352	W.H.Ponsford	Victoria v New South Wales	Melbourne	1926-27
350	Rashid Israr	Habib Bank v National Bank	Lahore	1976-77

There have been 119 triple hundreds in first-class cricket, W.V.Raman (313) and Arjan Kripal Singh (302*) for Tamil Nadu v Goa at Panjim in 1988-89 providing the only instance of two batsmen scoring 300 in the same innings.

MOST HUNDREDS IN SUCCESSIVE INNINGS

6	C.B.Fry	Sussex and Rest of England	1901
6	D.G.Bradman	South Australia and D.G.Bradman's XI	1938-39
6	M.J.Procter	Rhodesia	1970-71

TWO DOUBLE HUNDREDS IN A MATCH

244	202*	A.E.Fagg	Kent v Essex	Colchester	1938

TRIPLE HUNDRED AND HUNDRED IN A MATCH

333	123	G.A.Gooch	England v India	Lord's	1990

DOUBLE HUNDRED AND HUNDRED IN A MATCH MOST TIMES

4	Zaheer Abbas	Gloucestershire	1976-81

TWO HUNDREDS IN A MATCH MOST TIMES

8	Zaheer Abbas	Gloucestershire and PIA	1976-82
7	W.R.Hammond	Gloucestershire, England and MCC	1927-45

MOST HUNDREDS IN A SEASON

18	D.C.S.Compton	1947	16	J.B.Hobbs	1925

100 HUNDREDS IN A CAREER

	Total Hundreds	Inns	100th Hundred Season	Inns
J.B.Hobbs	197	1315	1923	821
E.H.Hendren	170	1300	1928-29	740
W.R.Hammond	167	1005	1935	679
C.P.Mead	153	1340	1927	892
G.Boycott	151	1014	1977	645
H.Sutcliffe	149	1088	1932	700
F.E.Woolley	145	1532	1929	1031
L.Hutton	129	814	1951	619
G.A.Gooch	128	988	1992-93	820
W.G Grace	126	1493	1895	1113
D.C.S.Compton	123	839	1952	552
T.W.Graveney	122	1223	1964	940
D.G.Bradman	117	338	1947-48	295
I.V.A.Richards	114	796	1988-89	658
Zaheer Abbas	108	768	1982-83	658
A.Sandham	107	1000	1935	871
M.C.Cowdrey	107	1130	1973	1035
T.W.Hayward	104	1138	1913	1076
G.M.Turner	103	792	1982	779
J.H.Edrich	103	979	1977	945
L.E.G.Ames	102	951	1950	915
G.E.Tyldesley	102	961	1934	919
D.L.Amiss	102	1139	1986	1081

MOST 400s: 2 – W.H.Ponsford
MOST 300s or more: 6 – D.G.Bradman; 4 – W.R.Hammond
MOST 200s or more: 37 – D.G.Bradman; 36 – W.R.Hammond; 22 – E.H.Hendren

MOST RUNS IN A MONTH

1294 (avge 92.42)	L.Hutton	Yorkshire	June 1949

MOST RUNS IN A SEASON

Runs			I	NO	HS	Avge	100	Season
3816	D.C.S.Compton	Middlesex	50	8	246	90.85	18	1947
3539	W.J.Edrich	Middlesex	52	8	267*	80.43	12	1947
3518	T.W.Hayward	Surrey	61	8	219	66.37	13	1906

The feat of scoring 3000 runs in a season has been achieved 28 times, the most recent instance being by W.E.Alley (3019) in 1961. The highest aggregate in a season since 1969 is 2755 by S.J.Cook in 1991.

1000 RUNS IN A SEASON MOST TIMES

28   W.G.Grace (Gloucestershire), F.E.Woolley (Kent)

HIGHEST BATTING AVERAGE IN A SEASON
(Qualification: 12 innings)

Avge			I	NO	HS	Runs	100	Season
115.66	D.G.Bradman	Australians	26	5	278	2429	13	1938
102.53	G.Boycott	Yorkshire	20	5	175*	1538	6	1979
102.00	W.A.Johnston	Australians	17	16	28*	102	–	1953
101.70	G.A.Gooch	Essex	30	3	333	2746	12	1990
100.12	G.Boycott	Yorkshire	30	5	233	2503	13	1971

FASTEST HUNDRED AGAINST AUTHENTIC BOWLING

35 min   P.G.H.Fender   Surrey v Northamptonshire   Northampton   1920

FASTEST DOUBLE HUNDRED

113 min   R.J.Shastri   Bombay v Baroda   Bombay   1984-85

FASTEST TRIPLE HUNDRED

181 min   D.C.S.Compton   MCC v NE Transvaal   Benoni   1948-49

MOST SIXES IN AN INNINGS

16   A.Symonds   Gloucestershire v Glamorgan   Abergavenny   1995

MOST SIXES IN A MATCH

20   A.Symonds   Gloucestershire v Glamorgan   Abergavenny   1995

MOST SIXES IN A SEASON

80   I.T.Botham   Somerset and England   1985

MOST BOUNDARIES IN AN INNINGS

71   B.C.Lara   Warwickshire v Durham   Birmingham   1994
Plus one four all run.

MOST RUNS OFF ONE OVER

36	G.St A.Sobers	Nottinghamshire v Glamorgan	Swansea	1968
36	R.J.Shastri	Bombay v Baroda	Bombay	1984-85

Both batsmen hit for six all six balls of overs bowled by M.A.Nash and Tilak Raj respectively.

MOST RUNS IN A DAY

390*   B.C.Lara   Warwickshire v Durham   Birmingham   1994
There have been 19 instances of a batsman scoring 300 or more runs in a day.

HIGHEST PARTNERSHIPS FOR EACH WICKET

First Wicket

561	Waheed Mirza/Mansoor Akhtar	Karachi W v Quetta	Karachi	1976-77
555	P.Holmes/H.Sutcliffe	Yorkshire v Essex	Leyton	1932
554	J.T.Brown/J.Tunnicliffe	Yorkshire v Derbys	Chesterfield	1898

Second Wicket

576	S.T.Jayasuriya/R.S.Mahanama	Sri Lanka v India	Colombo (RPS)	1997-98
475	Zahir Alam/L.S.Rajput	Assam v Tripura	Gauhati	1991-92
465*	J.A.Jameson/R.B.Kanhai	Warwickshire v Glos	Birmingham	1974

Third Wicket

467	A.H.Jones/M.D.Crowe	N Zealand v Sri Lanka	Wellington	1990-91
456	Khalid Irtiza/Aslam Ali	United Bank v Multan	Karachi	1975-76
451	Mudassar Nazar/Javed Miandad	Pakistan v India	Hyderabad	1982-83
445	P.E.Whitelaw/W.N.Carson	Auckland v Otago	Dunedin	1936-37
438	G.A.Hick/T.M.Moody	Worcestershire v Hants	Southampton	1997

Fourth Wicket

577	V.S.Hazare/Gul Mahomed	Baroda v Holkar	Baroda	1946-47
574*	C.L.Walcott/F.M.M.Worrell	Barbados v Trinidad	Port-of-Spain	1945-46
502*	F.M.M.Worrell/J.D.C.Goddard	Barbados v Trinidad	Bridgetown	1943-44
470	A.I.Kallicharran/G.W.Humpage	Warwickshire v Lancs	Southport	1982

Fifth Wicket

464*	M.E.Waugh/S.R.Waugh	NSW v W Australia	Perth	1990-91
405	S.G.Barnes/D.G.Bradman	Australia v England	Sydney	1946-47
397	W.Bardsley/C.Kelleway	NSW v S Australia	Sydney	1920-21
393	E.G.Arnold/W.B.Burns	Worcs v Warwickshire	Birmingham	1909

Sixth Wicket

487*	G.A.Headley/C.C.Passailaigue	Jamaica v Tennyson's	Kingston	1931-32
428	W.W.Armstrong/M.A.Noble	Australians v Sussex	Hove	1902
411	R.M.Poore/E.G.Wynyard	Hampshire v Somerset	Taunton	1899

Seventh Wicket

460	Bhupinder Singh jr/P.Dharmani	Punjab v Delhi	Delhi	1994-95
347	D.St E.Atkinson/C.C.Depeiza	W Indies v Australia	Bridgetown	1954-55
344	K.S.Ranjitsinhji/W.Newham	Sussex v Essex	Leyton	1902

Eighth Wicket

433	V.T.Trumper/A.Sims	Australians v C'bury	Christchurch	1913-14
313	Wasim Akram/Saqlain Mushtaq	Pakistan v Zimbabwe	Sheikhupura	1996-97
292	R.Peel/Lord Hawke	Yorkshire v Warwicks	Birmingham	1896

Ninth Wicket

283	J.Chapman/A.Warren	Derbys v Warwicks	Blackwell	1910
268	J.B.Commins/N.Boje	SA 'A' v Mashonaland	Harare	1994-95
251	J.W.H.T.Douglas/S.N.Hare	Essex v Derbyshire	Leyton	1921

Tenth Wicket

307	A.F.Kippax/J.E.H.Hooker	NSW v Victoria	Melbourne	1928-29
249	C.T.Sarwate/S.N.Banerjee	Indians v Surrey	The Oval	1946
235	F.E.Woolley/A.Fielder	Kent v Worcs	Stourbridge	1909

35000 RUNS IN A CAREER

	Career	I	NO	HS	Runs	Avge	100
J.B.Hobbs	1905-34	1315	106	316*	**61237**	50.65	197
F.E.Woolley	1906-38	1532	85	305*	**58969**	40.75	145
E.H.Hendren	1907-38	1300	166	301*	**57611**	50.80	170
C.P.Mead	1905-36	1340	185	280*	**55061**	47.67	153
W.G.Grace	1865-1908	1493	105	344	**54896**	39.55	126
W.R.Hammond	1920-51	1005	104	336*	**50551**	56.10	167
H.Sutcliffe	1919-45	1088	123	313	**50138**	51.95	149
G.Boycott	1962-86	1014	162	261*	**48426**	56.83	151
T.W.Graveney	1948-71/72	1223	159	258	**47793**	44.91	122
G.A.Gooch	1973-97	988	75	333	**44841**	49.11	128
T.W.Hayward	1893-1914	1138	96	315*	**43551**	41.79	104
D.L.Amiss	1960-87	1139	126	262*	**43423**	42.86	102
M.C.Cowdrey	1950-76	1130	134	307	**42719**	42.89	107
A.Sandham	1911-37/38	1000	79	325	**41284**	44.82	107
L.Hutton	1934-60	814	91	364	**40140**	55.51	129
M.J.K.Smith	1951-75	1091	139	204	**39832**	41.84	69
W.Rhodes	1898-1930	1528	237	267*	**39802**	30.83	58
J.H.Edrich	1956-78	979	104	310*	**39790**	45.47	103
R.E.S.Wyatt	1923-57	1141	157	232	**39405**	40.04	85
D.C.S.Compton	1936-64	839	88	300	**38942**	51.85	123
G.E.Tyldesley	1909-36	961	106	256*	**38874**	45.46	102
J.T.Tyldesley	1895-1923	994	62	295*	**37897**	40.60	86
K.W.R.Fletcher	1962-88	1167	170	228*	**37665**	37.77	63
C.G.Greenidge	1970-92	889	75	273*	**37354**	45.88	92
J.W.Hearne	1909-36	1025	116	285*	**37252**	40.98	96
L.E.G.Ames	1926-51	951	95	295	**37248**	43.51	102
D.Kenyon	1946-67	1159	59	259	**37002**	33.63	74
W.J.Edrich	1934-58	964	92	267*	**36965**	42.39	86
J.M.Parks	1949-76	1227	172	205*	**36673**	34.76	51
D.Denton	1894-1920	1163	70	221	**36479**	33.37	69
G.H.Hirst	1891-1929	1215	151	341	**36323**	34.13	60
I.V.A.Richards	1971/72-93	796	63	322	**36212**	49.40	114
A.Jones	1957-83	1168	72	204*	**36049**	32.89	56
W.G.Quaife	1894-1928	1203	185	255*	**36012**	35.37	72
R.E.Marshall	1945/46-72	1053	59	228*	**35725**	35.94	68
M.W.Gatting	1975-97	832	120	258	**35410**	49.73	92
G.Gunn	1902-32	1061	82	220	**35208**	35.96	62

BOWLING RECORDS

ALL TEN WICKETS IN AN INNINGS

This feat has been achieved 76 times in first-class matches (excluding 12-a-side fixtures).
Three Times: A.P.Freeman (1929, 1930, 1931)
Twice: V.E.Walker (1859, 1865); H.Verity (1931, 1932); J.C.Laker (1956)

Instances since 1945:

W.E.Hollies	Warwickshire v Notts	Birmingham	1946
J.M.Sims	East v West	Kingston on Thames	1948
J.K.R.Graveney	Gloucestershire v Derbyshire	Chesterfield	1949
T.E.Bailey	Essex v Lancashire	Clacton	1949
R.Berry	Lancashire v Worcestershire	Blackpool	1953
S.P.Gupte	President's XI v Combined XI	Bombay	1954-55
J.C.Laker	Surrey v Australians	The Oval	1956

K.Smales	Nottinghamshire v Glos	Stroud	1956
G.A.R.Lock	Surrey v Kent	Blackheath	1956
J.C.Laker	England v Australia	Manchester	1956
P.M.Chatterjee	Bengal v Assam	Jorhat	1956-57
J.D.Bannister	Warwicks v Combined Services	Birmingham (M & B)	1959
A.J.G.Pearson	Cambridge U v Leicestershire	Loughborough	1961
N.I.Thomson	Sussex v Warwickshire	Worthing	1964
P.J.Allan	Queensland v Victoria	Melbourne	1965-66
I.J.Brayshaw	Western Australia v Victoria	Perth	1967-68
Shahid Mahmood	Karachi Whites v Khairpur	Karachi	1969-70
E.E.Hemmings	International XI v W Indians	Kingston	1982-83
P.Sunderam	Rajasthan v Vidarbha	Jodhpur	1985-86
S.T.Jefferies	Western Province v OFS	Cape Town	1987-88
Imran Adil	Bahawalpur v Faisalabad	Faisalabad	1989-90
G.P.Wickremasinghe	Sinhalese v Kalutara	Colombo	1991-92
R.L.Johnson	Middlesex v Derbyshire	Derby	1994
Naeem Akhtar	Rawalpindi B v Peshawar	Peshawar	1995-96

MOST WICKETS IN A MATCH

| 19 | J.C.Laker | England v Australia | Manchester | 1956 |

MOST WICKETS IN A SEASON

Wkts		Career	Matches	Overs	Mdns	Runs	Avge
304	A.P.Freeman	1928	37	1976.1	423	5489	18.05
298	A.P.Freeman	1933	33	2039	651	4549	15.26

The feat of taking 250 wickets in a season has been achieved on 12 occasions, the last instance being by A.P.Freeman in 1933. 200 or more wickets in a season have been taken on 59 occasions, the last being by G.A.R.Lock (212 wickets, average 12.02) in 1957.

The highest aggregates of wickets taken in a season since the reduction of County Championship matches in 1969 are as follows:

Wkts		Season	Matches	Overs	Mdns	Runs	Avge
134	M.D.Marshall	1982	22	822	225	2108	15.73
131	L.R.Gibbs	1971	23	1024.1	295	2475	18.89
125	F.D.Stephenson	1988	22	819.1	196	2289	18.31
121	R.D.Jackman	1980	23	746.2	220	1864	15.40

Since 1969 there have been 47 instances of bowlers taking 100 wickets in a season.

MOST HAT-TRICKS IN A CAREER

7	D.V.P.Wright
6	T.W.J.Goddard, C.W.L.Parker
5	S.Haigh, V.W.C.Jupp, A.E.G.Rhodes, F.A.Tarrant

2000 WICKETS IN A CAREER

	Career	Runs	Wkts	Avge	100w
W.Rhodes	1898-1930	69993	4187	16.71	23
A.P.Freeman	1914-36	69577	3776	18.42	17
C.W.L.Parker	1903-35	63817	3278	19.46	16
J.T.Hearne	1888-1923	54352	3061	17.75	15
T.W.J.Goddard	1922-52	59116	2979	19.84	16
W.G.Grace	1865-1908	51545	2876	17.92	10
A.S.Kennedy	1907-36	61034	2874	21.23	15
D.Shackleton	1948-69	53303	2857	18.65	20
G.A.R.Lock	1946-70/71	54709	2844	19.23	14
F.J.Titmus	1949-82	63313	2830	22.37	16
M.W.Tate	1912-37	50571	2784	18.16	13+1

	Career	Runs	Wkts	Avge	100w
G.H.Hirst	1891-1929	51282	**2739**	18.72	15
C.Blythe	1899-1914	42136	**2506**	16.81	14
D.L.Underwood	1963-87	49993	**2465**	20.28	10
W.E.Astill	1906-39	57783	**2431**	23.76	9
J.C.White	1909-37	43759	**2356**	18.57	14
W.E.Hollies	1932-57	48656	**2323**	20.94	14
F.S.Trueman	1949-69	42154	**2304**	18.29	12
J.B.Statham	1950-68	36999	**2260**	16.37	13
R.T.D.Perks	1930-55	53771	**2233**	24.07	16
J.Briggs	1879-1900	35431	**2221**	15.95	12
D.J.Shepherd	1950-72	47302	**2218**	21.32	12
E.G.Dennett	1903-26	42571	**2147**	19.82	12
T.Richardson	1892-1905	38794	**2104**	18.43	10
T.E.Bailey	1945-67	48170	**2082**	23.13	9
R.Illingworth	1951-83	42023	**2072**	20.28	10
F.E.Woolley	1906-38	41066	**2068**	19.85	8
N.Gifford	1960-88	48731	**2068**	23.56	4
G.Geary	1912-38	41339	**2063**	20.03	11
D.V.P.Wright	1932-57	49307	**2056**	23.98	10
J.A.Newman	1906-30	51111	**2032**	25.15	9
A.Shaw	1864-97	24580	**2026+1**	12.12	9
S.Haigh	1895-1913	32091	**2012**	15.94	11

ALL-ROUND RECORDS

THE 'DOUBLE'

3000 runs and 100 wickets: J.H.Parks (1937)
2000 runs and 200 wickets: G.H.Hirst (1906)
2000 runs and 100 wickets: F.E.Woolley (4), J.W.Hearne (3), W.G.Grace (2), G.H.Hirst (2), W.Rhodes (2), T.E.Bailey, D.E.Davies, G.L.Jessop, V.W.C.Jupp, J.Langridge, F.A.Tarrant, C.L.Townsend, L.F.Townsend
1000 runs and 200 wickets: M.W.Tate (3), A.E.Trott (2), A.S.Kennedy

Most Doubles: 16 – W.Rhodes; 14 – G.H.Hirst; 10 – V.W.C.Jupp

Double in Debut Season: D.B.Close (1949) – the youngest (18) to achieve this feat.
   The feat of scoring 1000 runs and taking 100 wickets in a season has been achieved on 305 occasions, R.J.Hadlee (1984) and F.D.Stephenson (1988) being the only players to complete the 'double' since the reduction of County Championship matches in 1969.

WICKET-KEEPING RECORDS

EIGHT DISMISSALS IN AN INNINGS

9	(8ct, 1st)	Tahir Rashid	Habib Bank v PACO	Gujranwala	1992-93
9	(7ct, 2st)	W.R.James	Matabeleland v Mashonaland CD	Bulawayo	1995-96
8	(8ct)	A.T.W.Grout	Queensland v W Australia	Brisbane	1959-60
8	(8ct)	D.E.East	Essex v Somerset	Taunton	1985
8	(8ct)	S.A.Marsh	Kent v Middlesex	Lord's	1991
8	(6ct, 2st)	T.J.Zoehrer	Australians v Surrey	The Oval	1993
8	(7ct, 1st)	D.S.Berry	Victoria v South Australia	Melbourne	1996-97

TWELVE DISMISSALS IN A MATCH

13	(11ct, 2st)	W.R.James	Matabeleland v Mashonaland CD	Bulawayo	1995-96
12	(8ct, 4st)	E.Pooley	Surrey v Sussex	The Oval	1868

| 12 | (9ct, 3st) | D.Tallon | Queensland v NSW | Sydney | 1938-39 |
| 12 | (9ct, 3st) | H.B.Taber | NSW v South Australia | Adelaide | 1968-69 |

MOST DISMISSALS IN A SEASON

128 (79ct, 49st) L.E.G.Ames   1929

1000 DISMISSALS IN A CAREER

	Career	Dismissals	Ct	St
R.W.Taylor	1960-88	**1649**	1473	176
J.T.Murray	1952-75	**1527**	1270	257
H.Strudwick	1902-27	**1497**	1242	255
A.P.E.Knott	1964-85	**1344**	1211	133
F.H.Huish	1895-1914	**1310**	933	377
B.Taylor	1949-73	**1294**	1083	211
D.Hunter	1889-1909	**1253**	906	347
H.R.Butt	1890-1912	**1228**	953	275
J.H.Board	1891-1914/15	**1207**	852	355
H.Elliott	1920-47	**1206**	904	302
J.M.Parks	1949-76	**1181**	1088	93
R.Booth	1951-70	**1126**	948	178
L.E.G.Ames	1926-51	**1121**	703	418
D.L.Bairstow	1970-90	**1099**	961	138
G.Duckworth	1923-47	**1096**	753	343
H.W.Stephenson	1948-64	**1082**	748	334
J.G.Binks	1955-75	**1071**	895	176
T.G.Evans	1939-69	**1066**	816	250
A.Long	1960-80	**1046**	922	124
G.O.Dawkes	1937-61	**1042**	895	147
R.W.Tolchard	1965-83	**1037**	912	125
W.L.Cornford	1921-47	**1017**	675	342
R.C.Russell	1981-97	**1002**	893	109

FIELDING RECORDS

MOST CATCHES IN AN INNINGS

| 7 | M.J.Stewart | Surrey v Northamptonshire | Northampton | 1957 |
| 7 | A.S.Brown | Gloucestershire v Nottinghamshire | Nottingham | 1966 |

MOST CATCHES IN A MATCH

| 10 | W.R.Hammond | Gloucestershire v Surrey | Cheltenham | 1928 |

MOST CATCHES IN A SEASON

| 78 | W.R.Hammond | 1928 | 77 | M.J.Stewart | 1957 |

750 CATCHES IN A CAREER

1018	F.E.Woolley	1906-38	784	J.G.Langridge	1928-55
887	W.G.Grace	1865-1908	764	W.Rhodes	1898-1930
830	G.A.R.Lock	1946-70/71	758	C.A.Milton	1948-74
819	W.R.Hammond	1920-51	754	E.H.Hendren	1907-38
813	D.B.Close	1949-86			

LIMITED-OVERS INTERNATIONALS RESULTS SUMMARY

1970-71 to 27 September 1997

	Opponents	Matches	E	A	SA	WI	NZ	I	P	SL	Z	B	C	EA	H	K	UAE	Tied	NR
England	Australia	60	29	29	–	–	–	–	–	–	–	–	–	–	–	–	–	1	1
	South Africa	12	5	–	7	–	–	–	–	–	–	–	–	–	–	–	–	–	–
	West Indies	51	22	–	–	27	–	–	–	–	–	–	–	–	–	–	–	–	2
	New Zealand	47	23	–	–	–	20	–	–	–	–	–	–	–	–	–	–	1	3
	India	32	18	–	–	–	–	13	–	–	–	–	–	–	–	–	–	–	1
	Pakistan	40	25	–	–	–	–	–	14	–	–	–	–	–	–	–	–	–	1
	Sri Lanka	12	8	–	–	–	–	–	–	4	–	–	–	–	–	–	–	–	–
	Zimbabwe	6	1	–	–	–	–	–	–	–	5	–	–	–	–	–	–	–	–
	Canada	1	1	–	–	–	–	–	–	–	–	–	0	–	–	–	–	–	–
	East Africa	1	1	–	–	–	–	–	–	–	–	–	–	0	–	–	–	–	–
	Holland	1	1	–	–	–	–	–	–	–	–	–	–	–	0	–	–	–	–
	U A Emirates	1	1	–	–	–	–	–	–	–	–	–	–	–	–	–	0	–	–
Australia	South Africa	30	–	16	14	–	–	–	–	–	–	–	–	–	–	–	–	–	–
	West Indies	84	–	33	–	49	–	–	–	–	–	–	–	–	–	–	–	1	1
	New Zealand	63	–	44	–	–	17	–	–	–	–	–	–	–	–	–	–	–	–
	India	47	–	26	–	–	–	18	–	–	–	–	–	–	–	–	–	–	3
	Pakistan	46	–	22	–	–	–	–	21	–	–	–	–	–	–	–	–	1	2
	Sri Lanka	35	–	22	–	–	–	–	–	11	–	–	–	–	–	–	–	–	2
	Zimbabwe	9	–	8	–	–	–	–	–	–	1	–	–	–	–	–	–	–	–
	Bangladesh	1	–	1	–	–	–	–	–	–	–	0	–	–	–	–	–	–	–
	Canada	1	–	1	–	–	–	–	–	–	–	–	0	–	–	–	–	–	–
	Kenya	1	–	1	–	–	–	–	–	–	–	–	–	–	–	0	–	–	–
S Africa	West Indies	9	–	–	4	5	–	–	–	–	–	–	–	–	–	–	–	–	–
	New Zealand	8	–	–	4	–	4	–	–	–	–	–	–	–	–	–	–	–	–
	India	27	–	–	18	–	–	8	–	–	–	–	–	–	–	–	–	–	1
	Pakistan	16	–	–	9	–	–	–	7	–	–	–	–	–	–	–	–	–	–
	Sri Lanka	8	–	–	3	–	–	–	–	4	–	–	–	–	–	–	–	–	1
	Zimbabwe	7	–	–	6	–	–	–	–	–	0	–	–	–	–	–	–	–	1
	Holland	1	–	–	1	–	–	–	–	–	–	–	–	–	0	–	–	–	–
	Kenya	1	–	–	1	–	–	–	–	–	–	–	–	–	–	0	–	–	–
	U A Emirates	1	–	–	1	–	–	–	–	–	–	–	–	–	–	–	0	–	–
W Indies	New Zealand	24	–	–	–	18	4	–	–	–	–	–	–	–	–	–	–	–	2
	India	55	–	–	35	–	19	–	–	–	–	–	–	–	–	–	–	1	–
	Pakistan	81	–	–	54	–	–	25	–	–	–	–	–	–	–	–	–	2	–
	Sri Lanka	28	–	–	20	–	–	–	7	–	–	–	–	–	–	–	–	–	1
	Zimbabwe	5	–	–	5	–	–	–	–	0	–	–	–	–	–	–	–	–	–
	Kenya	1	–	–	0	–	–	–	–	–	–	–	–	–	1	–	–	–	–
N Zealand	India	42	–	–	–	18	24	–	–	–	–	–	–	–	–	–	–	–	–
	Pakistan	48	–	–	–	18	–	28	–	–	–	–	–	–	–	–	–	1	1
	Sri Lanka	37	–	–	–	24	–	–	10	–	–	–	–	–	–	–	–	1	2
	Zimbabwe	8	–	–	–	7	–	–	–	1	–	–	–	–	–	–	–	–	–
	Bangladesh	1	–	–	–	1	–	–	–	–	0	–	–	–	–	–	–	–	–
	East Africa	1	–	–	–	1	–	–	–	–	–	–	0	–	–	–	–	–	–
	Holland	1	–	–	–	1	–	–	–	–	–	–	–	0	–	–	–	–	–
	U A Emirates	1	–	–	–	1	–	–	–	–	–	–	–	–	–	0	–	–	–
India	Pakistan	58	–	–	–	–	20	34	–	–	–	–	–	–	–	–	–	–	4
	Sri Lanka	49	–	–	–	–	25	–	20	–	–	–	–	–	–	–	–	–	–
	Zimbabwe	16	–	–	–	–	12	–	–	2	–	–	–	–	–	–	–	2	–
	Bangladesh	4	–	–	–	–	4	–	–	–	0	–	–	–	–	–	–	–	–
	East Africa	1	–	–	–	–	1	–	–	–	–	–	0	–	–	–	–	–	–

Opponents	Matches	E	A	SA	WI	NZ	I	P	SL	Z	B	C	EA	H	K	UAE	Tied	NR
India Kenya	1	–	–	–	–	–	1	–	–	–	–	–	–	–	0	–	–	–
U A Emirates	1	–	–	–	–	–	1	–	–	–	–	–	–	–	0	–	–	–
Pakistan Sri Lanka	67	–	–	–	–	–	–	44	21	–	–	–	–	–	–	–	–	2
Zimbabwe	14	–	–	–	–	–	–	12	–	1	–	–	–	–	1	–	–	–
Bangladesh	4	–	–	–	–	–	–	4	–	–	0	–	–	–	–	–	–	–
Canada	1	–	–	–	–	–	–	1	–	–	–	0	–	–	–	–	–	–
Holland	1	–	–	–	–	–	–	1	–	–	–	–	–	0	–	–	–	–
Kenya	1	–	–	–	–	–	–	1	–	–	–	–	–	–	0	–	–	–
U A Emirates	2	–	–	–	–	–	–	2	–	–	–	–	–	–	0	–	–	–
Sri Lanka Zimbabwe	10	–	–	–	–	–	–	–	8	2	–	–	–	–	–	–	–	–
Bangladesh	5	–	–	–	–	–	–	–	5	–	0	–	–	–	–	–	–	–
Kenya	2	–	–	–	–	–	–	–	2	–	–	–	–	–	0	–	–	–
Zimbabwe Kenya	2	–	–	–	–	–	–	–	–	1	–	–	–	–	0	–	–	1
Holland U A Emirates	1	–	–	–	–	–	–	–	–	–	–	–	–	0	–	1	–	–
	1232	135	203	68	213	116	146	194	92	13	0	0	0	0	1	1	12	38

MERIT TABLE OF ALL L-O INTERNATIONALS

1970-71 to 27 September 1997 (1232 matches)

	Matches	Won	Lost	Tied	No Result	% Won (exc NR)
West Indies	338	213	115	4	6	64.15
South Africa	120	68	49	–	3	58.11
Australia	377	203	160	3	11	55.46
England	264	135	119	2	8	52.73
Pakistan	379	194	170	5	10	52.57
India	333	146	171	3	13	45.62
New Zealand	281	116	152	3	10	42.80
Sri Lanka	253	92	148	1	12	38.17
Zimbabwe	77	13	59	3	2	17.33
United Arab Emirates	7	1	6	–	–	14.28
Kenya	9	1	7	–	1	12.50
Canada	3	–	3	–	–	–
East Africa	3	–	3	–	–	–
Holland	5	–	5	–	–	–
Bangladesh	15	–	15	–	–	–

RECORDS

To 27 September 1997

TEAM RECORDS

HIGHEST TOTALS

398-5	(50 overs)	Sri Lanka v Kenya	Kandy	1995-96
371-9	(50 overs)	Pakistan v Sri Lanka	Nairobi	1996-97
363-7	(55 overs)	England v Pakistan	Nottingham	1992
360-4	(50 overs)	West Indies v Sri Lanka	Karachi	1987-88

349-9	(50 overs)	Sri Lanka v Pakistan	Singapore	1995-96
348-8	(50 overs)	New Zealand v India	Nagpur	1995-96
339-4	(50 overs)	Sri Lanka v Pakistan	Chandigarh	1996-97
338-4	(50 overs)	New Zealand v Bangladesh	Sharjah	1989-90
338-5	(60 overs)	Pakistan v Sri Lanka	Swansea	1983
334-4	(60 overs)	England v India	Lord's	1975
333-7	(50 overs)	West Indies v Sri Lanka	Sharjah	1995-96
333-8	(45 overs)	West Indies v India	Jamshedpur	1983-84
333-9	(60 overs)	England v Sri Lanka	Taunton	1983
332-3	(50 overs)	Australia v Sri Lanka	Sharjah	1989-90
330-6	(60 overs)	Pakistan v Sri Lanka	Nottingham	1975

Highest Totals by other ICC Full Members:

328-3	(50 overs)	South Africa v Holland	Rawalpindi	1995-96
312-4	(50 overs)	Zimbabwe v Sri Lanka	New Plymouth	1991-92
305-5	(50 overs)	India v Pakistan	Sharjah	1995-96

HIGHEST TOTALS BATTING SECOND

WINNING:

313-7	(49.2 overs)	Sri Lanka v Zimbabwe	New Plymouth	1991-92

LOSING:

329	(49.3 overs)	Sri Lanka v West Indies	Sharjah	1995-96

HIGHEST MATCH AGGREGATES

664-19	(99.4 overs)	Pakistan v Sri Lanka	Singapore	1995-96
662-17	(99.3 overs)	West Indies v Sri Lanka	Sharjah	1995-96
652-12	(100 overs)	Sri Lanka v Kenya	Kandy	1995-96

LARGEST MARGINS OF VICTORY

232 runs		Australia beat Sri Lanka	Adelaide	1984-85
206 runs		New Zealand beat Australia	Adelaide	1985-86
202 runs		England beat India	Lord's	1975

LOWEST TOTALS†

43	(19.5 overs)	Pakistan v West Indies	Cape Town	1992-93
45	(40.3 overs)	Canada v England	Manchester	1979
55	(28.3 overs)	Sri Lanka v West Indies	Sharjah	1986-87
63	(25.5 overs)	India v Australia	Sydney	1980-81
64	(35.5 overs)	New Zealand v Pakistan	Sharjah	1985-86
69	(28 overs)	South Africa v Australia	Sydney	1993-94
70	(25.2 overs)	Australia v England	Birmingham	1977
70	(26.3 overs)	Australia v New Zealand	Adelaide	1985-86

Lowest Totals by other ICC Full Members:

87	(29.3 overs)	West Indies v Australia	Sydney	1992-93
93	(36.2 overs)	England v Australia	Leeds	1975
94	(31.4 overs)	Zimbabwe v Pakistan	Sharjah	1996-97

† *Excluding instances when the number of overs was reduced after play began*

LOWEST MATCH AGGREGATE

88-13	(32.2 overs)	West Indies v Pakistan	Cape Town	1992-93

TIED MATCHES

Australia	222-9	(50)	West Indies	222-5	(50)	Melbourne	1983-84
England	226-5	(55)	Australia	226-8	(55)	Nottingham	1989
West Indies	186-5	(39)	Pakistan	186-9	(39)	Lahore	1991-92
India	126	(47.4)	West Indies	126	(41)	Perth	1991-92
Australia	228-7	(50)	Pakistan	228-9	(50)	Hobart	1992-93
Pakistan	244-6	(50)	West Indies	244-5	(50)	Georgetown	1992-93
India	248-5	(50)	Zimbabwe	248	(50)	Indore	1993-94
Pakistan	161-9	(50)	New Zealand	161	(49.4)	Auckland	1993-94
Zimbabwe	219-9	(50)	Pakistan	219	(49.5)	Harare	1994-95
New Zealand	169-8	(50)	Sri Lanka	169	(48)	Sharjah	1996-97
Zimbabwe	236-5	(50)	India	236	(49.5)	Paarl	1996-97
New Zealand	237	(49.4)	England	237-8	(50)	Napier	1996-97

200 APPEARANCES

	LOI	E	A	SA	WI	NZ	I	P	SL	Z	Ass
A.R.Border (A)	273	43	–	15	61	52	38	34	23	5	2
Salim Malik (P)	268	24	24	16	45	42	45	–	53	13	6
M.Azharuddin (I)	259	21	35	26	41	29	–	44	43	14	6
D.L.Haynes (WI)	238	35	64	8	–	13	36	65	14	3	–
Javed Miandad (P)	233	27	35	3	64	24	35	–	35	6	4
Wasim Akram (P)	232	24	29	11	52	26	33	–	37	14	6
Kapil Dev (I)	225	23	41	13	42	29	–	32	34	9	2
R.B.Richardson (WI)	224	35	51	9	–	11	32	61	21	3	1
A.Ranatunga (SL)	221	10	28	8	21	32	45	61	–	10	6
S.R.Waugh (A)	221	26	–	28	39	40	33	28	20	5	2
P.A.de Silva (SL)	218	8	29	8	24	28	43	61	–	10	7

Most Appearances for other ICC Full Members:

	LOI	E	A	SA	WI	NZ	I	P	SL	Z	Ass
J.G.Wright (NZ)	149	30	42	–	11	–	21	18	24	2	1
G.A.Gooch (E)	125	–	32	1	32	16	18	16	6	3	1
W.J.Cronje (SA)	115	12	30	–	8	8	24	15	7	7	4
A.Flower (Z)	65	6	5	7	3	6	12	14	10	–	2

BATTING RECORDS

HIGHEST INDIVIDUAL INNINGS

194	Saeed Anwar	Pakistan v India	Madras	1996-97
189*	I.V.A.Richards	West Indies v England	Manchester	1984
188*	G.Kirsten	South Africa v UAE	Rawalpindi	1995-96
181	I.V.A.Richards	West Indies v Sri Lanka	Karachi	1987-88
175*	Kapil Dev	India v Zimbabwe	Tunbridge Wells	1983
171*	G.M.Turner	New Zealand v East Africa	Birmingham	1975
169*	D.J.Callaghan	South Africa v New Zealand	Pretoria	1994-95
169	B.C.Lara	West Indies v Sri Lanka	Sharjah	1995-96
167*	R.A.Smith	England v Australia	Birmingham	1993
161	A.C.Hudson	South Africa v Holland	Rawalpindi	1995-96
158	D.I.Gower	England v New Zealand	Brisbane	1982-83
153*	I.V.A.Richards	West Indies v Australia	Melbourne	1979-80
153	B.C.Lara	West Indies v Pakistan	Sharjah	1993-94
152*	D.L.Haynes	West Indies v India	Georgetown	1988-89
151*	S.T.Jayasuriya	Sri Lanka v India	Bombay	1996-97

Highest individual scores for other ICC Full Members:

145	D.M.Jones	Australia v England	Brisbane	1990-91
142	D.L.Houghton	Zimbabwe v New Zealand	Hyderabad, India	1987-88

HIGHEST PARTNERSHIP FOR EACH WICKET

1st	212	G.R.Marsh/D.C.Boon	Australia v India	Jaipur	1986-87
2nd	263	Aamir Sohail/Inzamam-ul-Haq	Pakistan v New Zealand	Sharjah	1993-94
3rd	224*	D.M.Jones/A.R.Border	Australia v Sri Lanka	Adelaide	1984-85
4th	232	D.J.Cullinan/J.N.Rhodes	South Africa v Pakistan	Nairobi	1996-97
5th	223	M.Azharuddin/A.Jadeja	India v Sri Lanka	Colombo (RPS)	1997-98
6th	154	R.B.Richardson/P.J.L.Dujon	West Indies v Pakistan	Sharjah	1991-92
7th	115	P.J.L.Dujon/M.D.Marshall	West Indies v Pakistan	Gujranwala	1986-87
	115	A.C.Parore/L.K.Germon	New Zealand v Pakistan	Sharjah	1996-97
8th	119	P.R.Reiffel/S.K.Warne	Australia v South Africa	Port Elizabeth	1993-94
9th	126*	Kapil Dev/S.M.H.Kirmani	India v Zimbabwe	Tunbridge Wells	1983
10th	106*	I.V.A.Richards/M.A.Holding	West Indies v England	Manchester	1984

4000 RUNS IN A CAREER

		LOI	I	NO	HS	Runs	Avge	100	50
D.L.Haynes	WI	238	237	28	152*	8648	41.37	17	57
Javed Miandad	P	233	218	41	119*	7381	41.70	8	50
M.Azharuddin	I	259	239	46	111*	7294	37.79	4	45
Salim Malik	P	268	242	37	102	6884	33.58	5	46
P.A.de Silva	SL	218	212	22	145	6874	36.17	9	46
I.V.A.Richards	WI	187	167	24	189*	6721	47.00	11	45
A.R.Border	A	273	252	39	127*	6524	30.62	3	39
R.B.Richardson	WI	224	217	30	122	6248	33.41	5	44
A.Ranatunga	SL	221	209	41	131*	6074	36.15	3	40
D.M.Jones	A	164	161	25	145	6068	44.61	7	46
D.C.Boon	A	181	177	16	122	5964	37.04	5	37
Ramiz Raja	P	198	197	15	119*	5841	32.09	9	31
S.R.Tendulkar	I	164	159	15	137	5621	39.03	12	34
C.G.Greenidge	WI	128	127	13	133*	5134	45.03	11	31
S.R.Waugh	A	221	201	43	102*	5092	32.22	1	30
B.C.Lara	WI	118	116	12	169	4881	46.93	11	31
M.D.Crowe	NZ	143	141	19	107*	4704	38.55	4	34
Saeed Anwar	P	131	130	12	194	4659	39.48	12	19
M.E.Waugh	A	135	130	11	130	4542	38.16	10	28
Inzamam-ul-Haq	P	143	137	18	137*	4446	37.36	4	31
Ijaz Ahmed	P	181	165	23	124*	4418	31.11	5	26
R.S.Mahanama	SL	176	163	19	119*	4360	30.27	4	30
G.R.Marsh	A	117	115	6	126*	4357	39.97	9	22
G.A.Gooch	E	125	122	6	142	4290	36.98	8	23
K.Srikkanth	I	146	145	4	123	4092	29.02	4	27
A.J.Lamb	E	122	118	16	118	4010	39.31	4	26
Highest aggregates for other ICC Full Members:									
W.J.Cronje	SA	115	107	20	112	3473	39.91	2	22
A.Flower	Z	65	63	4	115*	1711	29.00	1	12

EIGHT HUNDREDS IN A CAREER

		E	A	SA	WI	NZ	I	P	SL	Z	Ass
17	D.L.Haynes (WI)	2	6	–	–	2	2	4	1	–	–
12	Saeed Anwar (P)	–	1	–	1	2	1	–	6	1	–
12	S.R.Tendulkar (I)	–	1	1	1	2	–	2	3	1	1
11	C.G.Greenidge (WI)	–	1	–	–	3	3	2	1	1	–
11	B.C.Lara (WI)	–	2	–	–	2	–	4	1	–	–
11	I.V.A.Richards (WI)	3	3	–	1	1	3	–	1	–	–
10	M.E.Waugh (A)	1	–	2	1	2	1	1	1	–	1

		E	A	SA	WI	NZ	I	P	SL	Z	Ass
9	P.A.de Silva (SL)	–	1	–	–	–	3	2	–	2	1
9	G.R.Marsh (A)	1	–	–	2	2	3	1	–	–	–
9	Ramiz Raja (P)	1	–	–	2	3	–	–	3	–	–
8	G.A.Gooch (E)	–	4	–	1	1	1	1	–	–	–
8	Javed Miandad (P)	1	–	1	1	–	3	–	2	–	–

BOWLING RECORDS

BEST ANALYSES

7-37	Aqib Javed	Pakistan v India	Sharjah	1991-92
7-51	W.W.Davis	West Indies v Australia	Leeds	1983
6-12	A.Kumble	India v West Indies	Calcutta	1993-94
6-14	G.J.Gilmour	Australia v England	Leeds	1975
6-14	Imran Khan	Pakistan v India	Sharjah	1984-85
6-15	C.E.H.Croft	West Indies v England	Kingstown	1980-81
6-23	A.A.Donald	South Africa v Kenya	Nairobi	1996-97
6-26	Waqar Younis	Pakistan v Sri Lanka	Sharjah	1989-90
6-29	B.P.Patterson	West Indies v India	Nagpur	1987-88
6-29	S.T.Jayasuriya	Sri Lanka v England	Moratuwa	1992-93
6-30	Waqar Younis	Pakistan v New Zealand	Auckland	1993-94
6-39	K.H.Macleay	Australia v India	Nottingham	1983
6-41	I.V.A.Richards	West Indies v India	Delhi	1989-90
6-50	A.H.Gray	West Indies v Australia	Port-of-Spain	1990-91

Best analyses for other ICC Full Members:

5-20	V.J.Marks	England v New Zealand	Wellington	1983-84
5-21	P.A.Strang	Zimbabwe v Kenya	Patna	1995-96
5-22	M.N.Hart	New Zealand v West Indies	Margao	1994-95

HAT-TRICKS

Jalaluddin	Pakistan v Australia	Hyderabad	1982-83
B.A.Reid	Australia v New Zealand	Sydney	1985-86
C.Sharma	India v New Zealand	Nagpur	1987-88
Wasim Akram	Pakistan v West Indies	Sharjah	1989-90
Wasim Akram	Pakistan v Australia	Sharjah	1989-90
Kapil Dev	India v Sri Lanka	Calcutta	1990-91
Aqib Javed	Pakistan v India	Sharjah	1991-92
D.K.Morrison	New Zealand v India	Napier	1993-94
Waqar Younis	Pakistan v New Zealand	East London	1994-95
Saqlain Mushtaq	Pakistan v Zimbabwe	Peshawar	1996-97
E.A.Brandes	Zimbabwe v England	Harare	1996-97
A.M.Stuart	Australia v Pakistan	Melbourne	1996-97

100 WICKETS IN A CAREER

		LOI	O	R	W	Avge	Best	4w
Wasim Akram	P	232	1992.2	7517	**333**	22.57	5-15	18
Waqar Younis	P	156	1284.3	5762	**265**	21.74	6-26	20
Kapil Dev	I	225	1867	6945	**253**	27.45	5-43	4
C.J.McDermott	A	138	1243.3	5018	**203**	24.71	5-44	5
C.E.L.Ambrose	WI	146	1300.5	4518	**200**	22.59	5-17	10
C.A.Walsh	WI	176	1548	5936	**196**	30.28	5- 1	6
Imran Khan	P	175	1243.3	4845	**182**	26.62	6-14	4
S.R.Waugh	A	221	1310	5877	**172**	34.16	4-33	2
A.Kumble	I	126	1123.1	4601	**169**	27.22	6-12	7
Aqib Javed	P	148	1216.4	5148	**164**	31.39	7-37	5

		LOI	O	R	W	Avge	Best	4w
R.J.Hadlee	NZ	115	1030.2	3407	**158**	21.56	5-25	6
J.Srinath	I	123	1064.3	4576	**158**	28.96	5-24	4
M.D.Marshall	WI	136	1195.5	4233	**157**	26.96	4-18	6
M.Prabhakar	I	130	1060	4534	**157**	28.87	5-33	6
A.A.Donald	SA	87	785	3211	**147**	21.84	6-23	7
J.Garner	WI	98	888.2	2752	**146**	18.84	5-31	5
I.T.Botham	E	116	1045.1	4139	**145**	28.54	4-31	3
M.A.Holding	WI	102	912.1	3034	**142**	21.36	5-26	6
Mushtaq Ahmed	P	124	1072.3	4630	**141**	32.89	5-36	3
E.J.Chatfield	NZ	114	1010.5	3618	**140**	25.84	5-34	4
C.L.Hooper	WI	155	1043.5	4536	**134**	33.85	4-34	1
Abdul Qadir	P	104	850	3453	**132**	26.15	5-44	6
S.K.Warne	A	76	710	2859	**129**	22.16	5-33	10
R.J.Shastri	I	150	1102.1	4650	**129**	36.04	5-15	3
D.K.Morrison	NZ	96	764.2	3470	**126**	27.53	5-34	3
Saqlain Mushtaq	P	65	557.4	2392	**123**	19.44	5-29	9
S.T.Jayasuriya	SL	141	831	4036	**121**	33.35	6-29	5
I.V.A.Richards	WI	187	940.4	4228	**118**	35.83	6-41	3
I.R.Bishop	WI	83	717	3085	**117**	26.36	5-25	9
P.A.J.DeFreitas	E	103	952	3775	**115**	32.82	4-35	1
M.C.Snedden	NZ	93	754.1	3237	**114**	28.39	4-34	1
Mudassar Nazar	P	122	809.1	3432	**111**	30.91	5-28	2
S.P.O'Donnell	A	87	725	3102	**108**	28.72	5-13	6
D.K.Lillee	A	63	598.5	2145	**103**	20.82	5-34	6
C.Pringle	NZ	64	552.2	2455	**103**	23.83	5-45	3
M.Muralitharan	SL	77	702	2927	**101**	28.98	4-18	3
W.K.M.Benjamin	WI	85	740.2	3079	**100**	30.79	5-22	1
R.A.Harper	WI	105	862.3	3431	**100**	34.31	4-40	3
Highest aggregate for Zimbabwe:								
E.A.Brandes		44	365	1755	**59**	29.74	5-28	3

WICKET-KEEPING RECORDS

FIVE DISMISSALS IN AN INNINGS

5 (5ct)	R.W.Marsh	Australia v England	Leeds	1981
5 (5ct)	R.G.de Alwis	Sri Lanka v Australia	Colombo (PSS)	1982-83
5 (5ct)	S.M.H.Kirmani	India v Zimbabwe	Leicester	1983
5 (3ct, 2st)	S.Viswanath	India v England	Sydney	1984-85
5 (5ct)	K.S.More	India v New Zealand	Sharjah	1987-88
5 (5ct)	H.P.Tillekeratne	Sri Lanka v Pakistan	Sharjah	1990-91
5 (3ct, 2st)	N.R.Mongia	India v New Zealand	Auckland	1993-94
5 (3ct, 2st)	A.C.Parore	New Zealand v West Indies	Margao	1994-95
5 (5ct)	D.J.Richardson	South Africa v Pakistan	Johannesburg	1994-95
5 (5ct)	Moin Khan	Pakistan v Zimbabwe	Harare	1994-95
5 (4ct, 1st)	R.S.Kaluwitharana	Sri Lanka v Pakistan	Sharjah	1994-95
5 (5ct)	D.J.Richardson	South Africa v Zimbabwe	Harare	1995-96
5 (5ct)	A.Flower	Zimbabwe v South Africa	Harare	1995-96
5 (5ct)	C.O.Browne	West Indies v Sri Lanka	Brisbane	1995-96
5 (5ct)	J.C.Adams	West Indies v Kenya	Poona	1995-96
5 (4ct, 1st)	Rashid Latif	Pakistan v New Zealand	Lahore	1995-96
5 (3ct, 2st)	N.R.Mongia	India v Pakistan	Toronto	1996
5 (5ct)	A.Flower	Zimbabwe v England	Harare	1996-97

100 DISMISSALS IN A CAREER

		LOI	Ct	St	Dis
I.A.Healy	Australia	168	195	39	234
P.J.L.Dujon	West Indies	169	183	21	204
D.J.Richardson	South Africa	108	131	15	146
R.W.Marsh	Australia	92	120	4	124
Moin Khan	Pakistan	91	86	36	122
Rashid Latif	Pakistan	85	81	22	103
Salim Yousuf	Pakistan	86	80	22	102

FIELDING RECORDS

FIVE CATCHES IN AN INNINGS

5	J.N.Rhodes	South Africa v West Indies	Bombay	1993-94

70 CATCHES IN A CAREER†

		LOI	Ct
A.R.Border	Australia	273	127
M.Azharuddin	India	259	117
I.V.A.Richards	West Indies	187	101
R.S.Mahanama	Sri Lanka	176	93
S.R.Waugh	Australia	221	80
Salim Malik	Pakistan	268	77
C.L.Hooper	West Indies	155	76
R.B.Richardson	West Indies	224	74
Kapil Dev	India	225	71
Ijaz Ahmed	Pakistan	181	70

† Excluding catches taken as wicket-keeper

ALL-ROUND RECORDS

1000 RUNS AND 100 WICKETS

		LOI	Runs	Wkts
I.T.Botham	England	116	2113	145
R.J.Hadlee	New Zealand	115	1751	158
C.L.Hooper	West Indies	155	3600	134
Imran Khan	Pakistan	175	3709	182
S.T.Jayasuriya	Sri Lanka	141	3592	121
Kapil Dev	India	225	3783	253
Mudassar Nazar	Pakistan	122	2653	111
S.P.O'Donnell	Australia	87	1242	108
M.Prabhakar	India	130	1858	157
I.V.A.Richards	West Indies	187	6721	118
R.J.Shastri	India	150	3108	129
Wasim Akram	Pakistan	232	2180	333
S.R.Waugh	Australia	221	5092	172

1000 RUNS AND 100 DISMISSALS

		LOI	Runs	Dis
P.J.L.Dujon	West Indies	169	1945	204
I.A.Healy	Australia	168	1764	234
R.W.Marsh	Australia	92	1225	124
Moin Khan	Pakistan	91	1127	122

SUMMARY OF ALL TEST MATCHES

To 17 September 1997

	Opponents	Tests	Won by									Tied	Drawn
			E	A	SA	WI	NZ	I	P	SL	Z		
England	Australia	291	92	114	–	–	–	–	–	–	–	–	85
	South Africa	110	47	–	20	–	–	–	–	–	–	–	43
	West Indies	115	27	–	–	48	–	–	–	–	–	–	40
	New Zealand	78	36	–	–	–	4	–	–	–	–	–	38
	India	84	32	–	–	–	–	14	–	–	–	–	38
	Pakistan	55	14	–	–	–	–	–	9	–	–	–	32
	Sri Lanka	5	3	–	–	–	–	–	–	1	–	–	1
	Zimbabwe	2	0	–	–	–	–	–	–	–	0	–	2
Australia	South Africa	62	–	33	14	–	–	–	–	–	–	–	15
	West Indies	86	–	35	–	29	–	–	–	–	–	1	21
	New Zealand	32	–	13	–	–	7	–	–	–	–	–	12
	India	51	–	24	–	–	–	9	–	–	–	1	17
	Pakistan	40	–	14	–	–	–	–	11	–	–	–	15
	Sri Lanka	10	–	7	–	–	–	–	–	0	–	–	3
South Africa	West Indies	1	–	–	0	1	–	–	–	–	–	–	–
	New Zealand	21	–	–	12	–	3	–	–	–	–	–	6
	India	10	–	–	4	–	–	2	–	–	–	–	4
	Pakistan	1	–	–	1	–	–	–	0	–	–	–	–
	Sri Lanka	3	–	–	1	–	–	–	–	0	–	–	2
	Zimbabwe	1	–	–	1	–	–	–	–	–	0	–	–
West Indies	New Zealand	28	–	–	–	10	4	–	–	–	–	–	14
	India	70	–	–	–	28	–	7	–	–	–	–	35
	Pakistan	31	–	–	–	12	–	–	7	–	–	–	12
	Sri Lanka	3	–	–	–	1	–	–	–	0	–	–	2
New Zealand	India	35	–	–	–	–	6	13	–	–	–	–	16
	Pakistan	39	–	–	–	–	5	–	18	–	–	–	16
	Sri Lanka	15	–	–	–	–	6	–	–	2	–	–	7
	Zimbabwe	4	–	–	–	–	1	–	–	–	0	–	3
India	Pakistan	44	–	–	–	–	–	4	7	–	–	–	33
	Sri Lanka	16	–	–	–	–	–	7	–	1	–	–	8
	Zimbabwe	2	–	–	–	–	–	1	–	–	0	–	1
Pakistan	Sri Lanka	19	–	–	–	–	–	–	9	3	–	–	7
	Zimbabwe	8	–	–	–	–	–	–	5	–	1	–	2
Sri Lanka	Zimbabwe	5	–	–	–	–	–	–	–	2	0	–	3
		1377	251	240	53	129	36	57	66	9	1	2	533

	Tests	Won	Lost	Drawn	Tied	Toss Won
England	740	251	210	279	–	362
Australia	572	240	162	168	2	287
South Africa	209	53	86	70	–	100
West Indies	334	129	80	124	1	174
New Zealand	252	36	104	112	–	128
India	312	57	102	152	1	159
Pakistan	237	66	54	117	–	116
Sri Lanka	76	9	34	33	–	38
Zimbabwe	22	1	10	11	–	13

TEST CRICKET RECORDS

To 17 September 1997

TEAM RECORDS

HIGHEST INNINGS TOTALS

952-6d	Sri Lanka v India	Colombo (RPS)	1997-98
903-7d	England v Australia	The Oval	1938
849	England v West Indies	Kingston	1929-30
790-3d	West Indies v Pakistan	Kingston	1957-58
758-8d	Australia v West Indies	Kingston	1954-55
729-6d	Australia v England	Lord's	1930
708	Pakistan v England	The Oval	1987
701	Australia v England	The Oval	1934
699-5	Pakistan v India	Lahore	1989-90
695	Australia v England	The Oval	1930
692-8d	West Indies v England	The Oval	1995
687-8d	West Indies v England	The Oval	1976
681-8d	West Indies v England	Port-of-Spain	1953-54
676-7	India v Sri Lanka	Kanpur	1986-87
674-6	Pakistan v India	Faisalabad	1984-85
674	Australia v India	Adelaide	1947-48
671-4	New Zealand v Sri Lanka	Wellington	1990-91
668	Australia v West Indies	Bridgetown	1954-55
660-5d	West Indies v New Zealand	Wellington	1994-95
659-8d	Australia v England	Sydney	1946-47
658-8d	England v Australia	Nottingham	1938
657-8d	Pakistan v West Indies	Bridgetown	1957-58
656-8d	Australia v England	Manchester	1964
654-5	England v South Africa	Durban	1938-39
653-4d	England v India	Lord's	1990
653-4d	Australia v England	Leeds	1993
652-7d	England v India	Madras	1984-85
652-8d	West Indies v England	Lord's	1973
652	Pakistan v India	Faisalabad	1982-83
650-6d	Australia v West Indies	Bridgetown	1964-65

The highest innings for other countries are:

622-9d	South Africa v Australia	Durban	1969-70
544-4d	Zimbabwe v Pakistan	Harare	1994-95

LOWEST INNINGS TOTALS

26	New Zealand v England	Auckland	1954-55
30	South Africa v England	Port Elizabeth	1895-96
30	South Africa v England	Birmingham	1924
35	South Africa v England	Cape Town	1898-99
36	Australia v England	Birmingham	1902
36	South Africa v Australia	Melbourne	1931-32
42	Australia v England	Sydney	1887-88
42	New Zealand v Australia	Wellington	1945-46
42	India v England	Lord's	1974
43	South Africa v England	Cape Town	1888-89
44	Australia v England	The Oval	1896
45	England v Australia	Sydney	1886-87
45	South Africa v Australia	Melbourne	1931-32

208

46	England v West Indies	Port-of-Spain	1993-94
47	South Africa v England	Cape Town	1888-89
47	New Zealand v England	Lord's	1958

The lowest innings for other countries are:

53	West Indies v Pakistan	Faisalabad	1986-87
62	Pakistan v Australia	Perth	1981-82
71	Sri Lanka v Pakistan	Kandy	1994-95
127	Zimbabwe v Sri Lanka	Colombo (RPS)	1996-97

BATTING RECORDS

HIGHEST INDIVIDUAL INNINGS

375	B.C.Lara	WI v E	St John's	1993-94
365*	G.St A.Sobers	WI v P	Kingston	1957-58
364	L.Hutton	E v A	The Oval	1938
340	S.T.Jayasuriya	SL v I	Colombo (RPS)	1997-98
337	Hanif Mohammed	P v WI	Bridgetown	1957-58
336*	W.R.Hammond	E v NZ	Auckland	1932-33
334	D.G.Bradman	A v E	Leeds	1930
333	G.A.Gooch	E v I	Lord's	1990
325	A.Sandham	E v WI	Kingston	1929-30
311	R.B.Simpson	A v E	Manchester	1964
310*	J.H.Edrich	E v NZ	Leeds	1965
307	R.M.Cowper	A v E	Melbourne	1965-66
304	D.G.Bradman	A v E	Leeds	1934
302	L.G.Rowe	WI v E	Bridgetown	1973-74
299*	D.G.Bradman	A v SA	Adelaide	1931-32
299	M.D.Crowe	NZ v SL	Wellington	1990-91
291	I.V.A.Richards	WI v E	The Oval	1976
287	R.E.Foster	E v A	Sydney	1903-04
285*	P.B.H.May	E v WI	Birmingham	1957
280*	Javed Miandad	P v I	Hyderabad	1982-83
278	D.C.S.Compton	E v P	Nottingham	1954
277	B.C.Lara	WI v A	Sydney	1992-93
274	R.G.Pollock	SA v A	Durban	1969-70
274	Zaheer Abbas	P v E	Birmingham	1971
271	Javed Miandad	P v NZ	Auckland	1988-89
270*	G.A.Headley	WI v E	Kingston	1934-35
270	D.G.Bradman	A v E	Melbourne	1936-37
268	G.N.Yallop	A v P	Melbourne	1983-84
267*	B.A.Young	NZ v SL	Dunedin	1996-97
267	P.A.de Silva	SL v NZ	Wellington	1990-91
266	W.H.Ponsford	A v E	The Oval	1934
266	D.L.Houghton	Z v SL	Bulawayo	1994-95
262*	D.L.Amiss	E v WI	Kingston	1973-74
261	F.M.M.Worrell	WI v E	Nottingham	1950
260	C.C.Hunte	WI v P	Kingston	1957-58
260	Javed Miandad	P v E	The Oval	1987
259	G.M.Turner	NZ v WI	Georgetown	1971-72
258	T.W.Graveney	E v WI	Nottingham	1957
258	S.M.Nurse	WI v NZ	Christchurch	1968-69
257*	Wasim Akram	P v Z	Sheikhupura	1996-97
256	R.B.Kanhai	WI v I	Calcutta	1958-59
256	K.F.Barrington	E v A	Manchester	1964
255*	D.J.McGlew	SA v NZ	Wellington	1952-53
254	D.G.Bradman	A v E	Lord's	1930

251	W.R.Hammond	E v A	Sydney	1928-29
250	K.D.Walters	A v NZ	Christchurch	1976-77
250	S.F.A.F.Bacchus	WI v I	Kanpur	1978-79

The highest individual innings for India is:

| 236* | S.M.Gavaskar | I v WI | Madras | 1983-84 |

750 RUNS IN A SERIES

Runs			Series	M	I	NO	HS	Avge	100	50
974	D.G.Bradman	A v E	1930	5	7	–	334	139.14	4	–
905	W.R.Hammond	E v A	1928-29	5	9	1	251	113.12	4	–
839	M.A.Taylor	A v E	1989	6	11	1	219	83.90	2	5
834	R.N.Harvey	A v SA	1952-53	5	9	–	205	92.66	4	3
829	I.V.A.Richards	WI v E	1976	4	7	–	291	118.42	3	2
827	C.L.Walcott	WI v A	1954-55	5	10	–	155	82.70	5	2
824	G.St A.Sobers	WI v P	1957-58	5	8	2	365*	137.33	3	3
810	D.G.Bradman	A v E	1936-37	5	9	–	270	90.00	3	1
806	D.G.Bradman	A v SA	1931-32	5	5	1	299*	201.50	4	–
798	B.C.Lara	WI v E	1993-94	5	8	–	375	99.75	2	2
779	E.de C.Weekes	WI v I	1948-49	5	7	–	194	111.28	4	2
774	S.M.Gavaskar	I v WI	1970-71	4	8	3	220	154.80	4	3
765	B.C.Lara	WI v E	1995	6	10	1	179	85.00	3	3
761	Mudassar Nazar	P v I	1982-83	6	8	2	231	126.83	4	1
758	D.G.Bradman	A v E	1934	5	8	–	304	94.75	2	1
753	D.C.S.Compton	E v SA	1947	5	8	–	208	94.12	4	2
752	G.A.Gooch	E v I	1990	3	6	–	333	125.33	3	2

HIGHEST PARTNERSHIP FOR EACH WICKET

1st	413	V.Mankad/Pankaj Roy	I v NZ	Madras	1955-56
2nd	576	S.T.Jayasuriya/R.S.Mahanama	SL v I	Colombo (RPS)	1997-98
3rd	467	A.H.Jones/M.D.Crowe	NZ v SL	Wellington	1990-91
4th	411	P.B.H.May/M.C.Cowdrey	E v WI	Birmingham	1957
5th	405	S.G.Barnes/D.G.Bradman	A v E	Sydney	1946-47
6th	346	J.H.W.Fingleton/D.G.Bradman	A v E	Melbourne	1936-37
7th	347	D.St E.Atkinson/C.C.Depeiza	WI v A	Bridgetown	1954-55
8th	313	Wasim Akram/Saqlain Mushtaq	P v Z	Sheikhupura	1996-97
9th	190	Asif Iqbal/Intikhab Alam	P v E	The Oval	1967
10th	151	B.F.Hastings/R.O.Collinge	NZ v P	Auckland	1972-73

WICKET PARTNERSHIPS OF OVER 350

576	2nd	S.T.Jayasuriya/R.S.Mahanama	SL v I	Colombo (RPS)	1997-98
467	3rd	A.H.Jones/M.D.Crowe	NZ v SL	Wellington	1990-91
451	2nd	W.H.Ponsford/D.G.Bradman	A v E	The Oval	1934
451	3rd	Mudassar Nazar/Javed Miandad	P v I	Hyderabad	1982-83
446	2nd	C.C.Hunte/G.St A.Sobers	WI v P	Kingston	1957-58
413	1st	V.Mankad/Pankaj Roy	I v NZ	Madras	1955-56
411	4th	P.B.H.May/M.C.Cowdrey	E v WI	Birmingham	1957
405	5th	S.G.Barnes/D.G.Bradman	A v E	Sydney	1946-47
399	4th	G.St A.Sobers/F.M.M.Worrell	WI v E	Bridgetown	1959-60
397	3rd	Qasim Omar/Javed Miandad	P v SL	Faisalabad	1985-86
388	4th	W.H.Ponsford/D.G.Bradman	A v E	Leeds	1934
387	1st	G.M.Turner/T.W.Jarvis	NZ v WI	Georgetown	1971-72
385	5th	S.R.Waugh/G.S.Blewett	A v SA	Johannesburg	1996-97
382	2nd	L.Hutton/M.Leyland	E v A	The Oval	1938
382	1st	W.M.Lawry/R.B.Simpson	A v WI	Bridgetown	1964-65
370	3rd	W.J.Edrich/D.C.S.Compton	SA v A	Lord's	1947

369	2nd	J.H.Edrich/K.F.Barrington	E v NZ	Leeds	1965
359	1st	L.Hutton/C.Washbrook	E v SA	Johannesburg	1948-49
351	2nd	G.A.Gooch/D.I.Gower	E v A	The Oval	1985
350	4th	Mushtaq Mohammed/Asif Iqbal	P v NZ	Dunedin	1972-73

4000 RUNS IN A TEST CAREER

Runs			M	I	NO	HS	Avge	100	50
11174	A.R.Border	A	156	265	44	205	50.56	27	63
10122	S.M.Gavaskar	I	125	214	16	236*	51.12	34	45
8900	G.A.Gooch	E	118	215	6	333	42.58	20	46
8832	Javed Miandad	P	124	189	21	280*	52.57	23	43
8540	I.V.A.Richards	WI	121	182	12	291	50.23	24	45
8231	D.I.Gower	E	117	204	18	215	44.25	18	39
8114	G.Boycott	E	108	193	23	246*	47.72	22	42
8032	G.St.A.Sobers	WI	93	160	21	365*	57.78	26	30
7624	M.C.Cowdrey	E	114	188	15	182	44.06	22	38
7558	C.G.Greenidge	WI	108	185	16	226	44.72	19	34
7515	C.H.Lloyd	WI	110	175	14	242*	46.67	19	39
7487	D.L.Haynes	WI	116	202	25	184	42.29	18	39
7422	D.C.Boon	A	107	190	20	200	43.65	21	32
7249	W.R.Hammond	E	85	140	16	336*	58.45	22	24
7110	G.S.Chappell	A	87	151	19	247*	53.86	24	31
6996	D.G.Bradman	A	52	80	10	334	99.94	29	13
6971	L.Hutton	E	79	138	15	364	56.67	19	33
6868	D.B.Vengsarkar	I	116	185	22	166	42.13	17	35
6806	K.F.Barrington	E	82	131	15	256	58.67	20	35
6227	R.B.Kanhai	WI	79	137	6	256	47.53	15	28
6149	R.N.Harvey	A	79	137	10	205	48.41	21	24
6116	M.A.Taylor	A	87	155	9	219	41.89	15	34
6080	G.R.Viswanath	I	91	155	10	222	41.93	14	35
5960	S.R.Waugh	A	95	148	28	200	49.66	14	34
5949	R.B.Richardson	WI	86	146	12	194	44.39	16	27
5807	D.C.S.Compton	E	78	131	15	278	50.06	17	28
5528	Salim Malik	P	96	142	21	237	45.68	15	28
5444	M.D.Crowe	NZ	77	131	11	299	45.36	17	18
5410	J.B.Hobbs	E	61	102	7	211	56.94	15	28
5357	K.D.Walters	A	74	125	14	250	48.26	15	33
5345	I.M.Chappell	A	75	136	10	196	42.42	14	26
5334	J.G.Wright	NZ	82	148	7	185	37.82	12	23
5267	M.Azharuddin	I	85	123	7	199	45.40	19	16
5248	Kapil Dev	I	131	184	15	163	31.05	8	27
5243	M.A.Atherton	E	73	134	5	185*	40.64	11	33
5234	W.M.Lawry	A	67	123	12	210	47.15	13	27
5200	I.T.Botham	E	102	161	6	208	33.54	14	22
5138	J.H.Edrich	E	77	127	9	310*	43.54	12	24
5062	Zaheer Abbas	P	78	124	11	274	44.79	12	20
4882	T.W.Graveney	E	79	123	13	258	44.38	11	20
4869	R.B.Simpson	A	62	111	7	311	46.81	10	27
4737	I.R.Redpath	A	66	120	11	171	43.45	8	31
4701	A.J.Stewart	E	69	123	8	190	40.87	10	23
4656	A.J.Lamb	E	79	139	10	142	36.09	14	18
4555	H.Sutcliffe	E	54	84	9	194	60.73	16	23
4537	P.B.H.May	E	66	106	9	285*	46.77	13	22
4502	E.R.Dexter	E	62	102	8	205	47.89	9	27
4464	M.E.Waugh	A	69	112	4	140	41.33	11	28
4455	E.de C.Weekes	WI	48	81	5	207	58.61	15	19

Runs			M	I	NO	HS	Avge	100	50
4415	K.J.Hughes	A	70	124	6	213	37.41	9	22
4409	M.W.Gatting	E	79	138	14	207	35.55	10	21
4399	A.I.Kallicharran	WI	66	109	10	187	44.43	12	21
4389	A.P.E.Knott	E	95	149	15	135	32.75	5	30
4378	M.Amarnath	I	69	113	10	138	42.50	11	24
4334	R.C.Fredericks	WI	59	109	7	169	42.49	8	26
4236	R.A.Smith	E	62	112	15	175	43.67	9	28
4220	P.A.de Silva	SL	63	110	6	267	40.57	14	14
4114	Mudassar Nazar	P	76	116	8	231	38.09	10	17
4034	A.Ranatunga	SL	71	121	7	135*	35.38	4	28
4004	B.C.Lara	WI	45	76	2	375	54.10	10	20

The highest aggregates for other countries are:

Runs			M	I	NO	HS	Avge	100	50
3471	B.Mitchell	SA	42	80	9	189*	48.88	8	21
1396	D.L.Houghton	Z	20	32	2	266	46.53	4	4

18 HUNDREDS

					Opponents							
			200	I	E	A	SA	WI	NZ	I	P	SL	Z
34	S.M.Gavaskar	I	4	214	4	8	–	13	2	–	5	2	–
29	D.G.Bradman	A	12	80	19	–	4	2	–	4	–	–	–
27	A.R.Border	A	2	265	8	–		3	5	4	6	1	–
26	G.St A.Sobers	WI	2	160	10	4	–		1	8	3	–	–
24	G.S.Chappell	A	4	151	9		–	5	3	1	6	–	–
24	I.V.A.Richards	WI	3	182	8	5	–		1	8	2	–	–
23	Javed Miandad	P	6	189	2	6	–	2	7	5	–	1	–
22	W.R.Hammond	E	7	140		9	6	1	4	2	–	–	–
22	M.C.Cowdrey	E	–	188		5	3	6	2	3	3	–	
22	G.Boycott	E	1	193		7	1	5	2	4	3	–	
21	R.N.Harvey	A	2	137	6		8	3	–	4	–	–	
21	D.C.Boon	A	1	190	7		3	3	6	1	1	–	
21	K.F.Barrington	E	1	131		5	2	3	3	3	4	–	
20	G.A.Gooch	E	2	215		5	–	5	4	5	1	1	
19	M.Azharuddin	I	–	123	6	1	3	–	1		3	5	–
19	C.G.Greenidge	WI	4	185	7	4	–		2	5	1	–	
19	L.Hutton	E	4	138		5	4	5	3	2	–	–	
19	C.H.Lloyd	WI	1	175	5	6	–		7	1	–	–	
18	D.I.Gower	E	2	204		9	–	1	4	2	2	–	
18	D.L.Haynes	WI	–	202	5	5	–		3	2	3	–	

The most hundreds for countries not included above is: South Africa – 9 in 62 innings by A.D.Nourse; New Zealand – 17 in 131 innings by M.D.Crowe; Sri Lanka – 14 in 110 innings by P.A.de Silva; Zimbabwe – 4 in 32 innings by D.L.Houghton. The most double hundreds by batsmen not qualifying for the above list is four by Zaheer Abbas (12 hundreds for Pakistan) and three by R.B.Simpson (10 hundreds for Australia).

BOWLING RECORDS

NINE WICKETS IN AN INNINGS

10- 53	J.C.Laker	E v A	Manchester	1956
9- 28	G.A.Lohmann	E v SA	Johannesburg	1895-96
9- 37	J.C.Laker	E v A	Manchester	1956
9- 52	R.J.Hadlee	NZ v A	Brisbane	1985-86
9- 56	Abdul Qadir	P v E	Lahore	1987-88
9- 57	D.E.Malcolm	E v SA	The Oval	1994
9- 69	J.M.Patel	I v A	Kanpur	1959-60
9- 83	Kapil Dev	I v WI	Ahmedabad	1983-84

9- 86	Sarfraz Nawaz	P v A	Melbourne	1978-79
9- 95	J.M.Noreiga	WI v I	Port-of-Spain	1970-71
9-102	S.P.Gupte	I v WI	Kanpur	1958-59
9-103	S.F.Barnes	E v SA	Johannesburg	1913-14
9-113	H.J.Tayfield	SA v E	Johannesburg	1956-57
9-121	A.A.Mailey	A v E	Melbourne	1920-21

The best innings analyses for other countries are:

| 8- 83 | J.R.Ratnayeke | SL v P | Sialkot | 1985-86 |
| 6- 90 | H.H.Streak | Z v P | Harare | 1994-95 |

15 WICKETS IN A TEST († *On debut*)

19- 90	J.C.Laker	E v A	Manchester	1956
17-159	S.F.Barnes	E v SA	Johannesburg	1913-14
16-136†	N.D.Hirwani	I v WI	Madras	1987-88
16-137†	R.A.L.Massie	A v E	Lord's	1972
15- 28	J.Briggs	E v SA	Cape Town	1888-89
15- 45	G.A.Lohmann	E v SA	Port Elizabeth	1895-96
15- 99	C.Blythe	E v SA	Leeds	1907
15-104	H.Verity	E v A	Lord's	1934
15-123	R.J.Hadlee	NZ v A	Brisbane	1985-86
15-124	W.Rhodes	E v A	Melbourne	1903-04

35 WICKETS IN A SERIES

Wkts			Series	M	Balls	Runs	Avge	5 wI	10 wM
49	S.F.Barnes	E v SA	1913-14	4	1356	536	10.93	7	3
46	J.C.Laker	E v A	1956	5	1703	442	9.60	4	2
44	C.V.Grimmett	A v SA	1935-36	5	2077	642	14.59	5	3
42	T.M.Alderman	A v E	1981	6	1950	893	21.26	4	–
41	R.M.Hogg	A v E	1978-79	6	1740	527	12.85	5	2
41	T.M.Alderman	A v E	1989	6	1616	712	17.36	6	1
40	Imran Khan	P v I	1982-83	6	1339	558	13.95	4	2
39	A.V.Bedser	E v A	1953	5	1591	682	17.48	5	1
39	D.K.Lillee	A v E	1981	6	1870	870	22.30	2	1
38	M.W.Tate	E v A	1924-25	5	2528	881	23.18	5	1
37	W.J.Whitty	A v SA	1910-11	5	1395	632	17.08	2	–
37	H.J.Tayfield	SA v E	1956-57	5	2280	636	17.18	4	1
36	A.E.E.Vogler	SA v E	1909-10	5	1349	783	21.75	4	1
36	A.A.Mailey	A v E	1920-21	5	1465	946	26.27	4	2
36	G.D.McGrath	A v E	1997	6	1499	701	19.47	2	–
35	G.A.Lohmann	E v SA	1895-96	3	520	203	5.80	4	2
35	B.S.Chandrasekhar	I v E	1972-73	5	1747	662	18.91	4	–
35	M.D.Marshall	WI v E	1988	5	1219	443	12.65	3	1

200 WICKETS IN TESTS

Wkts			M	Balls	Runs	Avge	5 wI	10 wM
434	Kapil Dev	I	131	27740	12867	29.64	23	2
431	R.J.Hadlee	NZ	86	21918	9611	22.29	36	9
383	I.T.Botham	E	102	21815	10878	28.40	27	4
376	M.D.Marshall	WI	81	17584	7876	20.94	22	4
362	Imran Khan	P	88	19458	8258	22.81	23	6
355	D.K.Lillee	A	70	18467	8493	23.92	23	7
339	C.A.Walsh	WI	93	19851	8798	25.95	13	2
325	R.G.D.Willis	E	90	17357	8190	25.20	16	–

Wkts			M	Balls	Runs	Avge	5 wI	10 wM
311	Wasim Akram	P	72	16464	7054	22.68	21	4
309	L.R.Gibbs	WI	79	27115	8989	29.09	18	2
307	F.S.Trueman	E	67	15178	6625	21.57	17	3
306	C.E.L.Ambrose	WI	72	16489	6566	21.45	18	3
297	D.L.Underwood	E	86	21862	7674	25.83	17	6
291	C.J.McDermott	A	71	16586	8332	28.63	14	2
266	B.S.Bedi	I	67	21364	7637	28.71	14	1
264	S.K.Warne	A	58	16642	6323	23.95	11	3
259	J.Garner	WI	58	13169	5433	20.97	7	—
252	J.B.Statham	E	70	16056	6261	24.84	9	1
249	M.A.Holding	WI	60	12680	5898	23.68	13	2
248	R.Benaud	A	63	19108	6704	27.03	16	1
246	G.D.McKenzie	A	60	17681	7328	29.78	16	3
242	B.S.Chandrasekhar	I	58	15963	7199	29.74	16	2
236	A.V.Bedser	E	51	15918	5876	24.89	15	5
236	Abdul Qadir	P	67	17126	7742	32.80	15	5
235	G.St A.Sobers	WI	93	21599	7999	34.03	6	—
228	R.R.Lindwall	A	61	13650	5251	23.03	12	—
227	Waqar Younis	P	44	9071	4844	21.33	19	4
216	C.V.Grimmett	A	37	14513	5231	24.21	21	7
212	M.G.Hughes	A	53	12285	6017	28.38	7	1
202	A.M.E.Roberts	WI	47	11136	5174	25.61	11	2
202	J.A.Snow	E	49	12021	5387	26.66	8	1
200	J.R.Thomson	A	51	10535	5601	28.00	8	—

The highest aggregates for other countries are:

170	H.J.Tayfield	SA	37	13568	4405	25.91	14	2
132	M.Muralitharan	SL	29	9012	3895	29.50	9	—
69	H.H.Streak	Z	15	3641	1551	22.47	3	—

HAT-TRICKS

F.R.Spofforth	Australia v England	Melbourne	1878-79
W.Bates	England v Australia	Melbourne	1882-83
J.Briggs	England v Australia	Sydney	1891-92
G.A.Lohmann	England v South Africa	Port Elizabeth	1895-96
J.T.Hearne	England v Australia	Leeds	1899
H.Trumble	Australia v England	Melbourne	1901-02
H.Trumble	Australia v England	Melbourne	1903-04
T.J.Matthews (2)**	Australia v South Africa	Manchester	1912
M.J.C.Allom*†	England v New Zealand	Christchurch	1929-30
T.W.J.Goddard	England v South Africa	Johannesburg	1938-39
P.J.Loader	England v West Indies	Leeds	1957
L.F.Kline	Australia v South Africa	Cape Town	1957-58
W.W.Hall	West Indies v Pakistan	Lahore	1958-59
G.M.Griffin	South Africa v England	Lord's	1960
L.R.Gibbs	West Indies v Australia	Adelaide	1960-61
P.J.Petherick*	New Zealand v Pakistan	Lahore	1976-77
C.A.Walsh‡	West Indies v Australia	Brisbane	1988-89
M.G.Hughes‡	Australia v West Indies	Perth	1988-89
D.W.Fleming*	Australia v Pakistan	Rawalpindi	1994-95
S.K.Warne	Australia v England	Melbourne	1994-95
D.G.Cork	England v West Indies	Manchester	1995

*On debut ** Hat-trick in each innings † Four wickets in five balls ‡ Involving both innings

WICKET-KEEPING RECORDS

SIX DISMISSALS IN AN INNINGS

7	Wasim Bari	Pakistan v New Zealand	Auckland	1978-79
7	R.W.Taylor	England v India	Bombay	1979-80
7	I.D.S.Smith	New Zealand v Sri Lanka	Hamilton	1990-91
6	A.T.W.Grout	Australia v South Africa	Johannesburg	1957-58
6	D.T.Lindsay	South Africa v Australia	Johannesburg	1966-67
6	J.T.Murray	England v India	Lord's	1967
6†	S.M.H.Kirmani	India v New Zealand	Christchurch	1975-76
6	R.W.Marsh	Australia v England	Brisbane	1982-83
6	S.A.R.Silva	Sri Lanka v India	Colombo (SSC)	1985-86
6	R.C.Russell	England v Australia	Melbourne	1990-91
6	R.C.Russell	England v South Africa	Johannesburg	1995-96
6	I.A.Healy	Australia v England	Birmingham	1997
6	A.J.Stewart	England v Australia	Manchester	1997

 † Including one stumping

FIVE STUMPINGS IN AN INNINGS

5	K.S.More	India v West Indies	Madras	1987-88

NINE DISMISSALS IN A TEST

11	R.C.Russell	England v South Africa	Johannesburg	1995-96
10	R.W.Taylor	England v India	Bombay	1979-80
9†	G.R.A.Langley	Australia v England	Lord's	1956
9	D.A.Murray	West Indies v Australia	Melbourne	1981-82
9	R.W.Marsh	Australia v England	Brisbane	1982-83
9	S.A.R.Silva	Sri Lanka v India	Colombo (SSC)	1985-86
9†	S.A.R.Silva	Sri Lanka v India	Colombo (PSS)	1985-86
9	D.J.Richardson	South Africa v India	Port Elizabeth	1992-93
9	Rashid Latif	Pakistan v New Zealand	Auckland	1993-94
9	I.A.Healy	Australia v England	Brisbane	1994-95
9	C.O.Browne	West Indies v England	Nottingham	1995
9‡	R.C.Russell	England v South Africa	Port Elizabeth	1995-96

 † Including one stumping ‡ Including two stumpings

25 DISMISSALS IN A SERIES

28	R.W.Marsh	Australia v England	1982-83
27 (inc 2st)	R.C.Russell	England v South Africa	1995-96
27 (inc 2st)	I.A.Healy	Australia v England (6 Tests)	1997
26 (inc 3st)	J.H.B.Waite	South Africa v New Zealand	1961-62
26	R.W.Marsh	Australia v West Indies (6 Tests)	1975-76
26 (inc 5st)	I.A.Healy	Australia v England (6 Tests)	1993
25 (inc 2st)	I.A.Healy	Australia v England	1994-95

100 DISMISSALS IN TESTS

Total			Tests	Ct	St
355	R.W.Marsh	Australia	96	343	12
329	I.A.Healy	Australia	94	307	22
272†	P.J.L.Dujon	West Indies	81	267	5
269	A.P.E.Knott	England	95	250	19
228	Wasim Bari	Pakistan	81	201	27
219	T.G.Evans	England	91	173	46
198	S.M.H.Kirmani	India	88	160	38

Total			Tests	Ct	St
189	D.L.Murray	West Indies	62	181	8
187	A.T.W.Grout	Australia	51	163	24
176	I.D.S.Smith	New Zealand	63	168	8
174	R.W.Taylor	England	57	167	7
152	R.C.Russell	England	49	141	11
141	J.H.B.Waite	South Africa	50	124	17
135	D.J.Richardson	South Africa	37	134	1
130	K.S.More	India	49	110	20
130	W.A.S.Oldfield	Australia	54	78	52
119†	A.J.Stewart	England	69	112	7
114†	J.M.Parks	England	46	103	11
104	Salim Yousuf	Pakistan	32	91	13

The most dismissals for other countries are:

54†	A.Flower	Zimbabwe	22	50	4
34	S.A.R.Silva	Sri Lanka	9	33	1
34	R.S.Kaluwitharana	Sri Lanka	16	31	3

† Including catches taken in the field

FIELDING RECORDS

FIVE CATCHES IN AN INNINGS

5	V.Y.Richardson	Australia v South Africa	Durban	1935-36
5	Yajurvindra Singh	India v England	Bangalore	1976-77
5	M.Azharuddin	India v Pakistan	Karachi	1989-90
5	K.Srikkanth	India v Australia	Perth	1991-92

SEVEN CATCHES IN A TEST

7	G.S.Chappell	Australia v England	Perth	1974-75
7	Yajurvindra Singh	India v England	Bangalore	1976-77
7	H.P.Tillekeratne	Sri Lanka v New Zealand	Colombo (SSC)	1992-93

15 CATCHES IN A SERIES

15	J.M.Gregory	Australia v England	1920-21

100 CATCHES IN TESTS

Total			Tests	Total			Tests
156	A.R.Border	Australia	156	110	R.B.Simpson	Australia	62
123	M.A.Taylor	Australia	87	110	W.R.Hammond	England	85
122	G.S.Chappell	Australia	87	109	G.St A.Sobers	West Indies	93
122	I.V.A.Richards	West Indies	121	108	S.M.Gavaskar	India	125
120	I.T.Botham	England	102	105	I.M.Chappell	Australia	75
120	M.C.Cowdrey	England	114	103	G.A.Gooch	England	118

The most catches in the field for other countries are:

93	Javed Miandad	Pakistan	124	46	R.S.Mahanama	Sri Lanka	45
71	M.D.Crowe	New Zealand	77	17	A.D.R.Campbell	Zimbabwe	22
56	B.Mitchell	South Africa	42				

APPEARANCE RECORDS

100 TEST MATCH APPEARANCES

156	A.R.Border	Australia		116	D.B.Vengsarkar	India
131	Kapil Dev	India		114	M.C.Cowdrey	England
125	S.M.Gavaskar	India		110	C.H.Lloyd	West Indies
124	Javed Miandad	Pakistan		108	G.Boycott	England
121	I.V.A.Richards	West Indies		108	C.G.Greenidge	West Indies
118	G.A.Gooch	England		107	D.C.Boon	Australia
117	D.I.Gower	England		102	I.T.Botham	England
116	D.L.Haynes	West Indies				

The most appearances for other countries are:

86	R.J.Hadlee	New Zealand		22	A.D.R.Campbell	Zimbabwe
71	A.Ranatunga	Sri Lanka		22	A.Flower	Zimbabwe
50	J.H.B.Waite	South Africa		22	G.W.Flower	Zimbabwe

100 CONSECUTIVE TEST APPEARANCES

153	A.R.Border	Australia	March 1979 to March 1994
106	S.M.Gavaskar	India	January 1975 to February 1987

75 TESTS AS CAPTAIN

93	A.R.Border	Australia	December 1984 to March 1994

50 TEST UMPIRING APPEARANCES

66	H.D.Bird	July 1973 to June 1996

SOUTH AFRICA v AUSTRALIA (1st Test)

At The Wanderers, Johannesburg on 28 February, 1, 2, 3, 4 March 1997.
Toss: South Africa. Result: **AUSTRALIA** won by an innings and 196 runs.
Debuts: None.

SOUTH AFRICA

A.C.Hudson	c Healy b McGrath	0	run out		31
G.Kirsten	c Healy b McGrath	8	b Warne		8
J.H.Kallis	c M.E.Waugh b McGrath	6	b Warne		39
D.J.Cullinan	c Healy b McGrath	27	c Healy b Warne		0
*W.J.Cronje	c M.E.Waugh b Warne	76	c Healy b S.R.Waugh		22
J.N.Rhodes	c Healy b Gillespie	22	lbw b Warne		8
S.M.Pollock	c S.R.Waugh b Bevan	35	not out		14
L.Klusener	c Taylor b Bevan	9	c Hayden b Bevan		0
†D.J.Richardson	not out	72	c Hayden b Bevan		2
A.A.Donald	c Healy b Gillespie	21	b Bevan		0
P.R.Adams	lbw b Warne	15	b Bevan		0
Extras	(B 1, LB 3, W 3, NB 3)	10	(B 4, LB 2)		6
Total		**302**			**130**

AUSTRALIA

*M.A.Taylor	b Pollock	16
M.L.Hayden	c Cullinan b Pollock	40
M.T.G.Elliott	c Adams b Donald	85
M.E.Waugh	c Richardson b Donald	26
S.R.Waugh	c Richardson b Kallis	160
G.S.Blewett	c Adams b Klusener	214
M.G.Bevan	not out	37
†I.A.Healy	c Kirsten b Adams	11
S.K.Warne	b Cronje	9
J.N.Gillespie		
G.D.McGrath		
Extras	(B 1, LB 15, W 4, NB 10)	30
Total	(8 wickets declared)	**628**

AUSTRALIA	O	M	R	W	O	M	R	W	FALL OF WICKETS			
										SA	A	SA
McGrath	26	8	77	4	10	5	17	0	*Wkt*	*1st*	*1st*	*2nd*
Gillespie	17	6	66	2	11	4	24	0	1st	0	33	36
Warne	27.4	9	68	2	28	15	43	4	2nd	15	128	41
Bevan	17	1	64	2	15	3	32	4	3rd	25	169	46
Blewett	4	0	23	0					4th	78	174	90
S.R.Waugh					(5)	4	1	4	1	5th	115	559	108
M.E.Waugh					(6)	1	0	4	0	6th	165	577	127
									7th	183	613	128
SOUTH AFRICA									8th	195	628	130
Donald	35	7	136	2					9th	253	–	130
Pollock	32	3	105	2					10th	302	–	130
Klusener	37	10	122	1								
Kallis	21	4	54	1								
Adams	52	7	163	1								
Cronje	16.4	5	32	1								

Umpires: C.J.Mitchley (16) and S.Venkataraghavan (*India*) (17).
Referee: R.Subba Row (*England*) (19).   **Test No. 1356/60 (SA 207/A 564)**

SOUTH AFRICA v AUSTRALIA (2nd Test)

At St George's Park, Port Elizabeth on 14, 15, 16, 17 March 1997.
Toss: South Africa. Result: **AUSTRALIA** won by 2 wickets.
Debuts: None.

SOUTH AFRICA

Batsman	First innings		Second innings	
G.Kirsten	c Hayden b Gillespie	0	b Gillespie	43
A.M.Bacher	c Elliott b McGrath	11	c McGrath b Gillespie	49
J.H.Kallis	c Blewett b Gillespie	0	run out	2
D.J.Cullinan	c Warne b Gillespie	34	lbw b Gillespie	2
*W.J.Cronje	b McGrath	0	c Healy b Bevan	27
H.H.Gibbs	b Gillespie	31	c M.E.Waugh b McGrath	7
B.M.McMillan	c S.R.Waugh b Warne	55	lbw b Bevan	2
S.M.Pollock	lbw b Gillespie	0	lbw b Warne	17
†D.J.Richardson	c McGrath b Warne	47	not out	3
A.A.Donald	c and b Warne	9	c Warne b Bevan	7
P.R.Adams	not out	5	c Taylor b Warne	1
Extras	(B 8, LB 8, W 1)	17	(B 1, LB 5, NB 2)	8
Total		**209**		**168**

AUSTRALIA

Batsman	First innings		Second innings	
M.L.Hayden	c Cullinan b Pollock	0 (2)	run out	14
*M.A.Taylor	c Richardson b Pollock	8 (1)	lbw b McMillan	13
M.T.G.Elliott	run out	23	c and b Adams	44
M.E.Waugh	lbw b Cronje	20	b Kallis	116
S.R.Waugh	c Richardson b McMillan	8	c Cronje b Kallis	18
G.S.Blewett	b Donald	13	b Adams	7
M.G.Bevan	c Richardson b McMillan	0	c Cullinan b Cronje	24
†I.A.Healy	c Bacher b Cronje	5	not out	10
S.K.Warne	lbw b Adams	18	lbw b Kallis	3
J.N.Gillespie	not out	1	not out	0
G.D.McGrath	c Richardson b Kallis	0		
Extras	(B 1, LB 7, W 2, NB 2)	12	(B 11, LB 8, W 3)	22
Total		**108**	(8 wickets)	**271**

AUSTRALIA	O	M	R	W		O	M	R	W
McGrath	22	7	66	2		13	3	43	1
Gillespie	23	10	54	5		18	4	49	3
Warne	23.4	5	62	3	(5)	17.4	7	20	2
Blewett	4	2	3	0		7.3	3	16	0
Bevan	2	0	8	0	(6)	13	3	18	3
S.R.Waugh				(3)		4.3	0	16	0

SOUTH AFRICA	O	M	R	W		O	M	R	W
Donald	23	13	18	1		26	6	75	0
Pollock	6	3	6	2					
Adams	4	0	5	1	(5)	21	4	66	2
McMillan	14	2	32	2	(2)	21	5	46	1
Cronje	14	7	21	2	(3)	9.3	1	36	1
Kallis	9.4	2	18	1	(4)	16	7	29	3

FALL OF WICKETS

Wkt	SA 1st	A 1st	SA 2nd	A 2nd
1st	13	1	87	23
2nd	17	13	98	30
3rd	21	48	99	113
4th	22	64	100	167
5th	70	66	122	192
6th	95	70	137	258
7th	95	85	152	258
8th	180	86	156	265
9th	204	106	167	–
10th	209	108	168	–

Umpires: R.E.Koertzen (3) and S.Venkataraghavan (*India*) (18).
Referee: R.Subba Row (*England*) (20).   **Test No. 1357/61 (SA 208/A 565)**

SOUTH AFRICA v AUSTRALIA (3rd Test)

At Centurion Park, Pretoria on 21, 22, 23, 24 March 1997.
Toss: South Africa. Result: **SOUTH AFRICA** won by 8 wickets.
Debuts: None.

AUSTRALIA

*M.A.Taylor	c Richardson b Klusener	38	c Richardson b Donald	5
M.L.Hayden	b Schultz	10	lbw b Schultz	0
M.T.G.Elliott	c Schultz b Donald	18	b Donald	12
M.E.Waugh	b Donald	5	b Symcox	42
S.R.Waugh	c Richardson b Schultz	67	not out	60
G.S.Blewett	c Richardson b Symcox	37	b Donald	0
M.G.Bevan	lbw b Schultz	6	b Symcox	5
†I.A.Healy	c Richardson b Donald	19	c Richardson b Schultz	12
S.K.Warne	lbw b Schultz	0	lbw b Donald	12
J.N.Gillespie	not out	6	b Donald	0
G.D.McGrath	b Klusener	0	b Klusener	11
Extras	(B 1, LB 4, W 7, NB 9)	21	(B 2, LB 6, W 4, NB 14)	26
Total		**227**		**185**

SOUTH AFRICA

G.Kirsten	c Healy b McGrath	16	c Taylor b Blewett	6
A.M.Bacher	lbw b McGrath	96	c Elliott b Gillespie	5
B.M.McMillan	c Hayden b M.E.Waugh	55	not out	7
D.J.Cullinan	b McGrath	47	not out	12
P.L.Symcox	c Blewett b Gillespie	16		
J.H.Kallis	c S.R.Waugh b McGrath	2		
*W.J.Cronje	not out	79		
†D.J.Richardson	b McGrath	0		
L.Klusener	b Gillespie	30		
A.A.Donald	c Healy b Gillespie	8		
B.N.Schultz	c Healy b McGrath	2		
Extras	(B 11, LB 16, W 1, NB 5)	33	(W 1, NB 1)	2
Total		**384**	(2 wickets)	**32**

SOUTH AFRICA	O	M	R	W	O	M	R	W	FALL OF WICKETS			
										A	SA	A	SA
Donald	20	5	60	3	18	5	36	5	*Wkt*	*1st*	*1st*	*2nd*	*2nd*
Schultz	20	4	52	4	17	4	39	2	1st	23	26	5	11
Cronje	5	3	5	0					2nd	60	128	10	15
Klusener	14.5	4	23	2	(3)14.4	1	40	1	3rd	72	229	28	–
Symcox	23	4	62	1	19	5	49	2	4th	110	252	94	–
Kallis	7	2	20	0	(4) 5	1	13	0	5th	190	255	99	–
									6th	197	262	108	–
AUSTRALIA									7th	212	262	131	–
McGrath	40.4	15	86	6					8th	212	330	164	–
Gillespie	31	13	75	3	(1) 3.4	0	19	1	9th	226	367	164	–
Blewett	5	0	19	0	(2) 3	0	13	1	10th	227	384	185	–
Warne	36	11	89	0									
Bevan	15	3	54	1									
M.E.Waugh	7	1	34	1									

Umpires: M.J.Kitchen (*England*) (13) and C.J.Mitchley (17).
Referee: R.Subba Row (*England*) (21).   **Test No. 1358/62 (SA 209/A 566)**

SOUTH AFRICA v AUSTRALIA 1996-97

SOUTH AFRICA – BATTING AND FIELDING

	M	I	NO	HS	Runs	Avge	100	50	Ct/St
W.J.Cronje	3	5	1	79*	204	51.00	–	2	1
D.J.Richardson	3	5	2	72*	124	41.33	–	1	12
A.M.Bacher	2	4	–	96	161	40.25	–	1	1
B.M.McMillan	2	4	1	55	119	39.66	–	2	–
D.J.Cullinan	3	6	1	47	122	24.40	–	–	3
S.M.Pollock	2	4	1	35	66	22.00	–	–	–
G.Kirsten	3	6	–	43	82	13.66	–	–	1
L.Klusener	2	3	–	30	39	13.00	–	–	–
J.H.Kallis	3	5	–	39	49	9.80	–	–	–
A.A.Donald	3	5	–	21	45	9.00	–	–	–
P.R.Adams	2	4	1	15	21	7.00	–	–	3

Played in one Test: H.H.Gibbs 31, 7; A.C.Hudson 0, 31; J.N.Rhodes 22, 8; B.N.Schultz 2 (1 ct); P.L.Symcox 16.

SOUTH AFRICA – BOWLING

	O	M	R	W	Avge	Best	5wI	10wM
B.N.Schultz	37	8	91	6	15.16	4-52	–	–
W.J.Cronje	45.1	16	94	4	23.50	2-21	–	–
B.M.McMillan	35	7	78	3	26.00	2-32	–	–
J.H.Kallis	58.4	16	134	5	26.80	3-29	–	–
S.M.Pollock	38	6	111	4	27.75	2- 6	–	–
A.A.Donald	122	36	325	11	29.54	5-36	1	–
P.L.Symcox	42	9	111	3	37.00	2-49	–	–
L.Klusener	66.3	15	185	4	46.25	2-23	–	–
P.R.Adams	77	11	234	4	58.50	2-66	–	–

AUSTRALIA – BATTING AND FIELDING

	M	I	NO	HS	Runs	Avge	100	50	Ct/St
S.R.Waugh	3	5	1	160	313	78.25	1	2	3
G.S.Blewett	3	5	–	214	271	54.20	1	–	2
M.E.Waugh	3	5	–	116	209	41.80	1	–	3
M.T.G.Elliott	3	5	–	85	182	36.40	–	1	2
M.G.Bevan	3	5	1	37*	72	18.00	–	–	–
M.A.Taylor	3	5	–	38	80	16.00	–	–	3
I.A.Healy	3	5	1	19	57	14.25	–	–	11
M.L.Hayden	3	5	–	40	64	12.80	–	–	4
S.K.Warne	3	5	–	18	42	8.40	–	–	3
J.N.Gillespie	3	4	3	6*	7	7.00	–	–	–
G.D.McGrath	3	3	–	11	11	3.66	–	–	2

AUSTRALIA – BOWLING

	O	M	R	W	Avge	Best	5wI	10wM
M.G.Bevan	62	10	176	9	19.55	4-32	–	–
J.N.Gillespie	103.4	37	287	14	20.50	5-54	1	–
G.D.McGrath	111.4	38	289	13	22.23	6-86	1	–
S.K.Warne	133	47	282	11	25.63	4-43	–	–

Also bowled: G.S.Blewett 23.3-5-74-1; M.E.Waugh 8-1-38-1; S.R.Waugh 8.3-1-20-1.

WEST INDIES v INDIA (1st Test)

At Sabina Park, Kingston, Jamaica on 6, 7, 8, 9, 10 March 1997.
Toss: West Indies. Result: **MATCH DRAWN.**
Debuts: West Indies – R.I.C.Holder, F.A.Rose; India – A.Kuruvilla.

WEST INDIES

Batsman	1st innings		2nd innings	
S.L.Campbell	c Mongia b Joshi	40	b Kumble	43
S.C.Williams	b Kuruvilla	23	b Kumble	26
S.Chanderpaul	c Mongia b Prasad	52	c Tendulkar b Kuruvilla	48
B.C.Lara	c Mongia b Kuruvilla	83	c Mongia b Kumble	78
C.L.Hooper	c Prasad b Kuruvilla	129	not out	12
I.R.Bishop	c Joshi b Kumble	24		
R.I.C.Holder	c Azharuddin b Kumble	17	(6) not out	21
†J.R.Murray	lbw b Kumble	1		
C.E.L.Ambrose	c Ganguly b Kumble	23		
F.A.Rose	not out	14		
*C.A.Walsh	b Kumble	4		
Extras	(LB 9, NB 8)	17	(B 4, LB 9)	13
Total		**427**	(4 wickets declared)	**241**

INDIA

Batsman	1st innings		2nd innings	
V.V.S.Laxman	b Rose	64	c Holder b Rose	27
N.S.Sidhu	lbw b Bishop	10	c Holder b Walsh	0
R.Dravid	c Murray b Rose	43	not out	51
*S.R.Tendulkar	b Rose	7	not out	15
S.C.Ganguly	c Lara b Rose	42		
M.Azharuddin	c Lara b Rose	5		
†N.R.Mongia	c Holder b Walsh	78		
A.Kumble	b Bishop	7		
S.B.Joshi	b Bishop	43		
A.Kuruvilla	b Rose	0		
B.K.V.Prasad	not out	10		
Extras	(B 5, LB 9, NB 23)	37	(LB 1, NB 5)	6
Total		**346**	(2 wickets)	**99**

INDIA	O	M	R	W		O	M	R	W
Prasad	28	5	104	1		15	2	46	0
Kuruvilla	30	6	82	3		17	2	56	1
Kumble	42.4	5	120	5		23	6	76	3
Joshi	27	6	81	1		6	1	27	0
Ganguly	7	1	17	0					
Laxman	3	0	14	0	(5)	3	0	14	0
Tendulkar					(6)	2	0	9	0

FALL OF WICKETS

Wkt	WI 1st	I 1st	WI 2nd	I 2nd
1st	41	32	68	6
2nd	96	127	81	68
3rd	143	140	203	–
4th	290	145	203	–
5th	357	153	–	–
6th	368	234	–	–
7th	370	248	–	–
8th	408	315	–	–
9th	423	320	–	–
10th	427	346	–	–

WEST INDIES	O	M	R	W		O	M	R	W
Ambrose	25	10	35	0		6	3	7	0
Bishop	24.5	4	62	3					
Rose	33	7	100	6		9	1	23	1
Walsh	32	6	73	1	(2)	8	3	7	1
Hooper	21	9	40	0	(4)	16	6	27	0
Chanderpaul	11	3	22	0	(5)	6	0	18	0
Lara					(6)	3	0	16	0

Umpires: S.A.Bucknor (27) and M.J.Kitchen (*England*) (14).
Referee: P.L.van der Merwe (*South Africa*) (15). **Test No. 1359/66 (WI 328/I 306)**

WEST INDIES v INDIA (2nd Test)

At Queen's Park Oval, Port-of-Spain, Trinidad on 14, 15, 16, 17, 18 March 1997.
Toss: West Indies. Result: **MATCH DRAWN.**
Debuts: West Indies – M.V.Dillon.

WEST INDIES

S.L.Campbell	c Prasad b Kumble	8	lbw b Kuruvilla		4
S.C.Williams	c Dravid b Kumble	18	c Kumble b Joshi		128
S.Chanderpaul	c Mongia b Prasad	42	c Azharuddin b Joshi		79
B.C.Lara	c Azharuddin b Joshi	14	c Azharuddin b Kumble		19
C.L.Hooper	c Azharuddin b Kumble	40	c Laxman b Kumble		14
R.I.C.Holder	b Joshi	91	c Laxman b Joshi		9
†J.R.Murray	c and b Kumble	11	not out		12
C.E.L.Ambrose	c Dravid b Kumble	16	not out		10
F.A.Rose	c Dravid b Joshi	34			
*C.A.Walsh	c Mongia b Ganguly	0			
M.V.Dillon	not out	0			
Extras	(LB 20, NB 2)	22	(B 8, LB 13, NB 3)		24
Total		**296**	(6 wickets)		**299**

INDIA

V.V.S.Laxman	lbw b Ambrose	0
N.S.Sidhu	b Ambrose	201
R.Dravid	b Ambrose	57
*S.R.Tendulkar	run out	88
S.C.Ganguly	c Chanderpaul b Rose	6
M.Azharuddin	b Ambrose	1
†N.R.Mongia	b Dillon	17
A.Kumble	not out	12
S.B.Joshi	c Walsh b Ambrose	24
A.Kuruvilla	c Murray b Dillon	2
B.K.V.Prasad	c Lara b Dillon	0
Extras	(B 9, LB 11, NB 8)	28
Total		**436**

INDIA	O	M	R	W	O	M	R	W		FALL OF WICKETS		
										WI	I	WI
Prasad	26	9	54	1	20	7	38	0	*Wkt*	*1st*	*1st*	*2nd*
Kuruvilla	22	9	36	0	23	6	47	1	1st	26	0	25
Kumble	39	8	104	5	40	9	109	2	2nd	29	171	201
Joshi	22.3	2	79	3	36	11	57	3	3rd	59	345	244
Ganguly	5	3	3	1	3	0	6	0	4th	99	370	252
Laxman					9	3	21	0	5th	149	371	271
									6th	169	382	273
WEST INDIES									7th	220	401	—
Ambrose	41.4	10	87	5					8th	289	420	—
Walsh	36	11	71	0					9th	290	420	—
Rose	35	6	93	1					10th	296	436	—
Dillon	35	6	92	3								
Hooper	28	9	53	0								
Chanderpaul	8	1	20	0								

Umpires: L.H.Barker (26) and S.G.Randell (*Australia*) (28).
Referee: P.L.van der Merwe (*South Africa*) (16).   **Test No. 1360/67 (WI 329/I 307)**

WEST INDIES v INDIA (3rd Test)

At Kensington Oval, Bridgetown, Barbados on 27, 29, 30, 31 March 1997.
Toss: India. Result: **WEST INDIES** won by 38 runs.
Debuts: None.

WEST INDIES

Batsman	1st innings		2nd innings	
S.L.Campbell	c Azharuddin b Prasad	6	c Mongia b Ganesh	18
S.C.Williams	c Laxman b Ganesh	24	b Prasad	0
S.Chanderpaul	not out	137	lbw b Kuruvilla	3
*B.C.Lara	c Tendulkar b Prasad	19	c Azharuddin b Prasad	45
C.L.Hooper	c Mongia b Ganesh	19	lbw b Ganesh	4
R.I.C.Holder	c Azharuddin b Prasad	5	c Mongia b Prasad	13
†C.O.Browne	c Tendulkar b Kumble	24	c Mongia b Kuruvilla	1
I.R.Bishop	b Prasad	4	lbw b Kuruvilla	6
C.E.L.Ambrose	c Tendulkar b Kuruvilla	37	not out	18
F.A.Rose	run out	11	c Ganguly b Kuruvilla	4
M.V.Dillon	lbw b Prasad	0	b Kuruvilla	21
Extras	(LB 5, NB 7)	12	(LB 5, NB 2)	7
Total		298		140

INDIA

Batsman	1st innings			2nd innings	
V.V.S.Laxman	b Ambrose	6		b Rose	19
N.S.Sidhu	c Browne b Rose	26		c Williams b Rose	3
R.Dravid	b Bishop	78		c Browne b Rose	2
*S.R.Tendulkar	c Campbell b Bishop	92		c Lara b Bishop	4
S.C.Ganguly	c Browne b Dillon	22		b Ambrose	8
M.Azharuddin	c Browne b Rose	17		b Ambrose	9
†N.R.Mongia	c Williams b Bishop	1		b Bishop	5
A.Kumble	not out	23		c Holder b Bishop	1
A.Kuruvilla	b Ambrose	0	(10)	c Holder b Ambrose	9
D.Ganesh	c Browne b Rose	8	(9)	not out	6
B.K.V.Prasad	c Holder b Rose	0		b Bishop	0
Extras	(B 2, LB 12, W 2, NB 30)	46		(B 2, LB 2, NB 11)	15
Total		319			81

INDIA	O	M	R	W	O	M	R	W
Prasad	31.4	9	82	5	18	6	39	3
Kuruvilla	28	5	88	1	21	5	68	5
Ganesh	21	2	70	2	6	1	28	2
Kumble	16	1	44	1				
Ganguly	2	1	9	0				
WEST INDIES								
Ambrose	29	8	74	2	15	3	36	2
Bishop	28	6	70	3	11.5	4	22	4
Dillon	19	5	56	1				
Rose	22	4	77	4	(3) 9	2	19	3
Hooper	8	1	28	0				

FALL OF WICKETS

Wkt	1st WI	1st I	2nd WI	2nd I
1st	10	23	9	3
2nd	40	42	18	16
3rd	88	212	37	32
4th	118	253	65	32
5th	131	273	86	45
6th	187	295	87	51
7th	193	295	91	57
8th	258	296	95	66
9th	290	319	107	80
10th	298	319	140	81

Umpires: L.H.Barker (27) and S.G.Randell (*Australia*) (29).
Referee: P.L.van der Merwe (*South Africa*) (17). **Test No. 1361/68 (WI 330/I 308)**

WEST INDIES v INDIA (4th Test)

At Recreation Ground, St John's, Antigua on 4 (*no play*), 5 (*no play*), 6 (*no play*), 7, 8 April 1997.
Toss: West Indies. Result: **MATCH DRAWN.**
Debuts: None.

WEST INDIES

S.L.Campbell	run out	10
S.C.Williams	c Tendulkar b Kuruvilla	0
S.Chanderpaul	c Laxman b Kumble	24
B.C.Lara	c Mongia b Prasad	103
C.L.Hooper	c Azharuddin b Joshi	26
R.I.C.Holder	c Mongia b Kumble	56
†C.O.Browne	not out	39
I.R.Bishop	c Dravid b Joshi	17
C.E.L.Ambrose	c Mongia b Kumble	22
*C.A.Walsh	c Dravid b Joshi	21
F.A.Rose	absent ill	
Extras	(B 1, LB 5, NB 9)	15
Total		**333**

INDIA

A.Jadeja	run out	96
V.V.S.Laxman	c Browne b Walsh	56
R.Dravid	not out	37
S.B.Joshi	not out	10
*S.R.Tendulkar		
S.C.Ganguly		
M.Azharuddin		
†N.R.Mongia		
A.Kumble		
A.Kuruvilla		
B.K.V.Prasad		
Extras	(LB 3, NB 10)	13
Total	(2 wickets)	**212**

INDIA	O	M	R	W
Prasad	24	4	65	1
Kuruvilla	24	1	69	2
Kumble	36	14	93	2
Joshi	23.4	7	76	3
Ganguly	3	0	24	0

WEST INDIES	O	M	R	W
Ambrose	9	1	26	0
Bishop	16	3	47	0
Walsh	15	3	37	1
Hooper	15	4	40	0
Chanderpaul	11	0	40	0
Williams	3	0	19	0

FALL OF WICKETS

	WI	I
Wkt	*1st*	*1st*
1st	0	97
2nd	32	198
3rd	40	–
4th	82	–
5th	224	–
6th	230	–
7th	252	–
8th	295	–
9th	333	–
10th	–	–

Umpires: S.A.Bucknor (28) and B.C.Cooray (*Sri Lanka*) (10).
Referee: P.L.van der Merwe (*South Africa*) (18).   **Test No. 1362/69 (WI 331/I 309)**

WEST INDIES v INDIA (5th Test)

At Bourda, Georgetown, Guyana on 17, 18 (*no play*), 19 (*no play*), 20, 21 April 1997.
Toss: India. Result: **MATCH DRAWN.**
Debuts: None.

INDIA

A.Jadeja	c Browne b Bishop	8
N.S.Sidhu	c Hooper b Walsh	36
R.Dravid	c Hooper b Rose	92
*S.R.Tendulkar	c and b Bishop	83
M.Azharuddin	c Browne b Rose	31
†N.R.Mongia	c Hooper b Rose	39
A.Kumble	c Walsh b Hooper	15
S.B.Joshi	c Browne b Chanderpaul	7
D.Ganesh	c Browne b Hooper	7
A.Kuruvilla	c Bishop b Hooper	5
B.K.V.Prasad	not out	0
Extras	(B 8, LB 8, W 3, NB 13)	32
Total		**355**

WEST INDIES

S.C.Williams	lbw b Kumble	44
S.Chanderpaul	not out	58
B.C.Lara	c Sidhu b Joshi	30
C.L.Hooper	run out	1
†C.O.Browne	not out	0
S.L.Campbell		
R.I.C.Holder		
C.E.L.Ambrose		
I.R.Bishop		
F.A.Rose		
*C.A.Walsh		
Extras	(B 7, LB 2, W 1, NB 2)	12
Total	(3 wickets)	**145**

WEST INDIES	O	M	R	W
Ambrose	29	14	36	0
Bishop	31	9	61	2
Rose	33.1	7	90	3
Walsh	28.2	9	62	1
Hooper	18	7	34	3
Chanderpaul	29	8	56	1
INDIA				
Prasad	7	0	37	0
Kuruvilla	7	1	34	0
Ganesh	7	2	24	0
Kumble	4	1	30	1
Joshi	5	1	11	1

FALL OF WICKETS

	I	WI
Wkt	1st	1st
1st	32	72
2nd	68	127
3rd	231	145
4th	241	–
5th	280	–
6th	303	–
7th	320	–
8th	343	–
9th	355	–
10th	355	–

Umpires: E.G.Nicholls (1) and G.Sharp (*England*) (3).
Referee: P.L.van der Merwe (*South Africa*) (19).   **Test No. 1363/70 (WI 332/I 310)**

WEST INDIES v INDIA 1996-97

WEST INDIES – BATTING AND FIELDING

	M	I	NO	HS	Runs	Avge	100	50	Ct/St
S.Chanderpaul	5	8	2	137*	443	73.83	1	3	1
B.C.Lara	5	8	–	103	391	48.87	1	2	4
R.I.C.Holder	5	7	1	91	212	35.33	–	2	6
C.L.Hooper	5	8	1	129	245	35.00	1	–	3
S.C.Williams	5	8	–	128	263	32.87	1	–	2
C.O.Browne	3	4	2	39*	64	32.00	–	–	10
C.E.L.Ambrose	5	6	2	37	126	31.50	–	–	–
F.A.Rose	5	4	1	34	63	21.00	–	–	–
S.L.Campbell	5	7	–	43	129	18.42	–	–	1
I.R.Bishop	4	4	–	24	51	12.75	–	–	2
J.R.Murray	2	3	1	12*	24	12.00	–	–	2
M.V.Dillon	2	3	1	21	21	10.50	–	–	–
C.A.Walsh	4	3	–	21	25	8.33	–	–	2

WEST INDIES – BOWLING

	O	M	R	W	Avge	Best	5wI	10wM
I.R.Bishop	111.4	26	262	12	21.83	4- 22	–	–
F.A.Rose	141.1	27	402	18	22.33	6-100	1	–
C.E.L.Ambrose	154.4	49	301	10	30.10	5- 87	1	–
M.V.Dillon	54	11	148	4	37.00	3- 92	–	–
C.A.Walsh	119.2	32	250	4	62.50	1- 7	–	–
C.L.Hooper	106	36	222	3	74.00	3- 34	–	–

Also bowled: S.Chanderpaul 65-13-156-1; B.C.Lara 3-0-16-0; S.C.Williams 3-0-19-0.

INDIA – BATTING AND FIELDING

	M	I	NO	HS	Runs	Avge	100	50	Ct/St
R.Dravid	5	7	2	92	360	72.00	–	4	5
S.R.Tendulkar	5	6	1	92	289	57.80	–	3	5
A.Jadeja	2	2	–	96	104	52.00	–	1	–
N.S.Sidhu	4	6	–	201	276	46.00	1	–	1
V.V.S.Laxman	4	6	–	64	172	28.66	–	2	4
N.R.Mongia	5	5	–	78	140	28.00	–	1	13
S.B.Joshi	4	4	1	43	84	28.00	–	–	1
S.C.Ganguly	4	4	–	42	78	19.50	–	–	2
A.Kumble	5	5	2	23*	58	19.33	–	–	2
M.Azharuddin	5	5	–	31	63	12.60	–	–	9
D.Ganesh	2	3	1	8	21	10.50	–	–	–
B.K.V.Prasad	5	5	2	10*	10	3.33	–	–	2
A.Kuruvilla	5	5	–	9	16	3.20	–	–	–

INDIA – BOWLING

	O	M	R	W	Avge	Best	5wI	10wM
S.B.Joshi	120.1	28	331	11	30.09	3- 57	–	–
A.Kumble	200.4	44	576	19	30.31	5-104	2	–
D.Ganesh	34	9	122	4	30.50	2- 28	–	–
A.Kuruvilla	172	34	480	13	36.92	5- 68	1	–
B.K.V.Prasad	169.4	43	465	11	42.27	5- 82	1	–

Also bowled: S.C.Ganguly 20-5-59-1; V.V.S.Laxman 15-3-49-0; S.R.Tendulkar 2-0-9-0.

NEW ZEALAND v SRI LANKA (1st Test)

At Carisbrook, Dunedin on 7, 8, 9, 10 March 1997.
Toss: Sri Lanka. Result: **NEW ZEALAND** won by an innings and 36 runs.
Debuts: Sri Lanka – D.N.T.Zoysa.

NEW ZEALAND

B.A.Young	not out	267
B.A.Pocock	c Mahanama b Vaas	18
M.J.Horne	c Mahanama b Ranatunga	66
*S.P.Fleming	c Zoysa b Wickremasinghe	51
N.J.Astle	b Vaas	27
D.L.Vettori	c Mahanama b Vaas	1
C.L.Cairns	c Mahanama b Zoysa	70
†A.C.Parore	c Wickremasinghe b Vaas	19
D.N.Patel	not out	30
S.B.Doull		
H.T.Davis		
Extras	(LB 14, W 2, NB 21)	37
Total	(7 wickets declared)	**586**

SRI LANKA

S.T.Jayasuriya	b Doull	0	c Parore b Doull		50
R.S.Mahanama	lbw b Doull	26	b Doull		21
M.S.Atapattu	lbw b Doull	25	b Patel		22
P.A.de Silva	c Patel b Davis	3	lbw b Astle		0
*A.Ranatunga	c Young b Doull	14	c Horne b Vettori		13
H.P.Tillekeratne	not out	55	run out		8
†R.S.Kaluwitharana	c Fleming b Patel	43	c and b Vettori		103
W.P.U.C.J.Vaas	c Horne b Patel	2	c and b Davis		57
G.P.Wickremasinghe	c Parore b Davis	43	c Doull b Astle		0
D.N.T.Zoysa	c Young b Davis	0	not out		16
M.Muralitharan	c Cairns b Doull	0	c and b Doull		26
Extras	(LB 10, W 1)	11	(LB 9, NB 3)		12
Total		**222**			**328**

SRI LANKA	O	M	R	W	O	M	R	W
Vaas	35	6	144	4				
Zoysa	40	6	112	1				
Wickremasinghe	25	4	117	1				
Muralitharan	33	6	136	0				
Ranatunga	5	0	29	1				
Jayasuriya	8	0	34	0				

NEW ZEALAND	O	M	R	W	O	M	R	W
Doull	21.2	5	58	5	20.3	5	82	3
Davis	19	6	34	3	22	2	79	1
Horne	6	5	4	0	4	2	18	0
Astle	3	0	11	0	15	3	51	2
Patel	22	4	67	2	10	3	36	1
Vettori	14	5	38	0	15	3	53	2

FALL OF WICKETS

	NZ	SL	SL
Wkt	1st	1st	2nd
1st	55	4	49
2nd	195	55	82
3rd	271	58	85
4th	337	58	99
5th	343	79	115
6th	466	135	133
7th	512	141	270
8th	–	214	271
9th	–	215	285
10th	–	222	328

Umpires: C.E.King (3) and I.D.Robinson (*Zimbabwe*) (15).
Referee: P.J.P.Burge (*Australia*) (21).   **Test No. 1364/14 (NZ 251/SL 69)**

NEW ZEALAND v SRI LANKA (2nd Test)

At Trust Bank Park, Hamilton on 14, 15, 16, 17 March 1997.
Toss: New Zealand. Result: **NEW ZEALAND** won by 120 runs.
Debuts: Sri Lanka – K.S.C.de Silva.

NEW ZEALAND

B.A.Pocock	c Tillekeratne b Muralitharan	85	(2)	c Mahanama b Zoysa	7
B.A.Young	run out	4	(1)	c Ranatunga b Dharmasena	62
M.J.Horne	b Zoysa	21		st Kaluwitharana b Muralitharan	16
*S.P.Fleming	c Mahanama b Zoysa	2		b Muralitharan	59
N.J.Astle	lbw b Zoysa	0		c Mahanama b Vaas	52
C.L.Cairns	c Ranatunga b Dharmasena	10		c sub‡ b Muralitharan	4
†A.C.Parore	run out	23		run out	2
D.N.Patel	c Dharmasena b Muralitharan	13		c P.A.de Silva b Dharmasena	4
D.L.Vettori	b Muralitharan	4		b Zoysa	6
S.B.Doull	c P.A.de Silva b Vaas	20		c Mahanama b Zoysa	25
H.T.Davis	not out	8		not out	2
Extras	(B 11, LB 9, NB 10)	30		(B 9, LB 11, W 7, NB 7)	34
Total		**222**			**273**

SRI LANKA

S.T.Jayasuriya	c Astle b Davis	20		run out	3
R.S.Mahanama	lbw b Vettori	45		lbw b Doull	65
H.P.Tillekeratne	c Young b Doull	2		b Vettori	10
P.A.de Silva	c Parore b Vettori	1	(5)	lbw b Doull	5
*A.Ranatunga	lbw b Davis	4	(6)	c Doull b Vettori	33
†R.S.Kaluwitharana	c Parore b Davis	11	(7)	lbw b Doull	13
H.D.P.K.Dharmasena	c Fleming b Davis	27	(8)	not out	38
W.P.U.C.J.Vaas	c Pocock b Vettori	28	(4)	c Patel b Vettori	8
D.N.T.Zoysa	c Doull b Vettori	14		c Parore b Vettori	13
K.S.C.de Silva	not out	0		c Young b Davis	0
M.Muralitharan	c Parore b Davis	5		c Cairns b Vettori	7
Extras	(LB 9, W 1, NB 3)	13		(B 4, LB 5, W 1)	10
Total		**170**			**205**

SRI LANKA	O	M	R	W		O	M	R	W	FALL OF WICKETS			
										NZ	SL	NZ	SL
Vaas	12.4	1	32	1		15	3	34	1				
Zoysa	18	3	47	3		22.4	7	53	3	*Wkt*	*1st*	*1st*	*2nd*	*2nd*
K.S.C.de Silva	15	4	36	0	(4)10	2	29	0	1st	19	39	14	5
Dharmasena	22	7	39	1	(3)24	5	75	2	2nd	88	57	64	16
Muralitharan	22	4	43	3		26	7	62	3	3rd	96	58	108	40
Jayasuriya	1	0	5	0						4th	100	76	183	50
										5th	126	87	198	129
										6th	172	93	201	147
NEW ZEALAND										7th	172	144	211	152
Doull	13	4	19	1		15	4	34	3	8th	178	154	239	185
Davis	20.2	3	63	5		17	4	35	1	9th	203	165	243	186
Astle	3	1	8	0	(5)	3	1	9	0	10th	222	170	273	205
Vettori	24	8	46	4	(3)29.2	8	84	5					
Patel	8	2	25	0	(4)12	5	34	0					

Umpires: D.B.Cowie (5) and Mahboob Shah (*Pakistan*) (28). ‡ (U.D.U. Chandana)
Referee: P.J.P.Burge (*Australia*) (22). **Test No. 1365/15 (NZ 252/SL 70)**

NEW ZEALAND v SRI LANKA 1996-97

NEW ZEALAND – BATTING AND FIELDING

	M	I	NO	HS	Runs	Avge	100	50	Ct/St
B.A.Young	2	3	1	267*	333	166.50	1	1	4
S.P.Fleming	2	3	–	59	112	37.33	–	2	2
B.A.Pocock	2	3	–	85	110	36.66	–	1	1
M.J.Horne	2	3	–	66	103	34.33	–	1	2
C.L.Cairns	2	3	–	70	84	28.00	–	1	2
N.J.Astle	2	3	–	52	79	26.33	–	1	1
D.N.Patel	2	3	1	30*	47	23.50	–	–	2
S.B.Doull	2	2	–	25	45	22.50	–	–	4
A.C.Parore	2	3	–	25	46	15.33	–	–	6
D.L.Vettori	2	3	–	6	11	3.66	–	–	1
H.T.Davis	2	2	2	8*	10	–	–	–	1

NEW ZEALAND – BOWLING

	O	M	R	W	Avge	Best	5wI	10wM
S.B.Doull	69.5	18	193	12	16.08	5-58	1	–
D.L.Vettori	82.2	24	221	11	20.09	5-84	1	–
H.T.Davis	78.2	15	211	10	21.10	5-63	1	–
D.N.Patel	52	14	162	3	54.00	2-67	–	–

Also bowled: N.J.Astle 24-5-79-2; M.J.Horne 10-7-22-0.

SRI LANKA – BATTING AND FIELDING

	M	I	NO	HS	Runs	Avge	100	50	Ct/St
R.S.Kaluwitharana	2	4	–	103	170	42.50	1	–	–/1
R.S.Mahanama	2	4	–	65	157	39.25	–	1	8
H.P.Tillekeratne	2	4	1	55*	75	25.00	–	1	1
W.P.U.C.J.Vaas	2	4	–	57	95	23.75	–	1	1
S.T.Jayasuriya	2	4	–	50	73	18.25	–	1	1
A.Ranatunga	2	4	–	33	64	16.00	–	–	2
D.N.T.Zoysa	2	4	1	16*	43	14.33	–	–	1
M.Muralitharan	2	4	–	26	38	9.50	–	–	–
P.A.de Silva	2	4	–	5	9	2.25	–	–	1

Played in one Test: M.S.Atapattu 25, 22; K.S.C.de Silva 0*, 0; H.D.P.K.Dharmasena 27, 38* (1 ct); G.P.Wickremasinghe 43, 0 (1 ct).

SRI LANKA – BOWLING

	O	M	R	W	Avge	Best	5wI	10wM
D.N.T.Zoysa	80.4	16	212	7	30.28	3- 47	–	–
W.P.U.C.J.Vaas	62.4	10	210	6	35.00	4-144	–	–
H.D.P.K.Dharmasena	46	12	114	3	38.00	2- 75	–	–
M.Muralitharan	81	17	241	6	40.16	3- 43	–	–

Also bowled: K.S.C.de Silva 25-6-65-0; S.T.Jayasuriya 9-0-39-0; A.Ranatunga 5-0-29-1; G.P.Wickremasinghe 25-4-117-1.

SRI LANKA v PAKISTAN (1st Test)

At Premadasa Stadium (Khetterama), Colombo on 19, 20, 21, 22, 23 April 1997.
Toss: Sri Lanka. Result: **MATCH DRAWN.**
Debuts: Sri Lanka – R.P.Arnold.

SRI LANKA

S.T.Jayasuriya	b Mushtaq Ahmed	31	(7)	c Salim Elahi b Saqlain	62
R.P.Arnold	b Mushtaq Ahmed	24		c Shahid b Saqlain	15
M.S.Atapattu	c Salim Elahi b Saqlain	0	(1)	c Shahid b Saqlain	25
P.A.de Silva	st Moin b Mushtaq Ahmed	23	(3)	c Saqlain b Mushtaq Ahmed	168
*A.Ranatunga	c Salim Elahi b Asif	49	(4)	c Ramiz b Mushtaq Ahmed	58
H.P.Tillekeratne	c Asif b Saqlain	103	(5)	c Ramiz b Saqlain	54
†R.S.Kaluwitharana	b Saqlain	57	(6)	c Moin b Shahid	17
H.D.P.K.Dharmasena	b Saqlain	1		not out	11
W.P.U.C.J.Vaas	c Moin b Zahid	17		c sub‡ b Mushtaq Ahmed	1
D.N.T.Zoysa	lbw b Saqlain	0			
M.Muralitharan	not out	8			
Extras	(B 3, LB 9, W 1, NB 4)	17		(B 3, LB 4, NB 5)	12
Total		**330**		(8 wickets declared)	**423**

PAKISTAN

Salim Elahi	lbw b Vaas	0
*Ramiz Raja	c Ranatunga b Dharmasena	50
Ijaz Ahmed	c Dharmasena b Muralitharan	113
Salim Malik	run out	58
Inzamam-ul-Haq	c sub (R.S.Kalpage) b Muralitharan	12
Asif Mujtaba	c and b Muralitharan	21
†Moin Khan	b Muralitharan	0
Saqlain Mushtaq	run out	58
Mushtaq Ahmed	c Ranatunga b Muralitharan	26
Shahid Nazir	c Ranatunga b Muralitharan	2
Mohammad Zahid	not out	6
Extras	(B 11, LB 7, NB 14)	32
Total		**378**

PAKISTAN	O	M	R	W	O	M	R	W
Mohammad Zahid	17	2	44	1	11	1	60	0
Shahid Nazir	18	6	37	0	12	0	61	1
Saqlain Mushtaq	44.2	10	89	5	63	13	137	4
Mushtaq Ahmed	34	2	123	3	39.1	9	94	3
Asif Mujtaba	9	2	25	1	30	5	64	0

SRI LANKA	O	M	R	W
Vaas	32	6	75	1
Zoysa	10	0	55	0
Dharmasena	52.5	19	93	1
Muralitharan	53	19	98	6
Jayasuriya	3	0	15	0
De Silva	4	0	16	0
Ranatunga	3	1	5	0
Arnold	2	1	3	0

FALL OF WICKETS

	SL	P	SL
Wkt	1st	1st	2nd
1st	61	0	38
2nd	62	102	53
3rd	84	219	182
4th	90	247	265
5th	179	248	315
6th	268	248	390
7th	280	298	420
8th	322	336	423
9th	322	349	–
10th	330	378	–

‡ (Mohammad Hussain)

Umpires: D.R.Shepherd (*England*) (34) and W.A.U.Wickremasinghe (3).
Referee: J.R.Reid (*New Zealand*) (28).   **Test No. 1366/18 (SL 71/P 236)**

SRI LANKA v PAKISTAN (2nd Test)

At Sinhalese Sports Club, Colombo on 26, 27, 28, 29, 30 April 1997.
Toss: Sri Lanka. Result: **MATCH DRAWN.**
Debuts: None.

SRI LANKA

S.T.Jayasuriya	b Mushtaq Ahmed b Saqlain	72	c sub‡ b Saqlain		113
R.P.Arnold	run out	37	b Mushtaq Ahmed		50
M.S.Atapattu	c Salim Elahi b Mushtaq Ahmed	14	run out		4
P.A.de Silva	not out	138	not out		103
*A.Ranatunga	c Salim Elahi b Saqlain	4	st Salim Elahi b Mushtaq Ahmed		66
H.P.Tillekeratne	b Zahid	10	not out		24
†R.S.Kaluwitharana	b Asif	22			
R.S.Kalpage	c Salim Elahi b Saqlain	5			
W.P.U.C.J.Vaas	c Salim Elahi b Saqlain	17			
K.S.C.de Silva	st Moin b Mushtaq Ahmed	0			
K.J.Silva	run out	0			
Extras	(B 6, LB 3, NB 3)	12	(B 12, LB 6, W 7, NB 1)		26
Total		**331**	(4 wickets declared)		**386**

PAKISTAN

Salim Elahi	c Tillekeratne b Vaas	0	(2) c Arnold b Vaas		14
*Ramiz Raja	c Arnold b K.S.C.de Silva	36	(1) c Kaluwitharana b Vaas		0
Ijaz Ahmed	c Arnold b Vaas	4	c Vaas b Silva		47
Salim Malik	c Ranatunga b K.S.C.de Silva	24	c Kaluwitharana b Silva		155
Inzamam-ul-Haq	c Kaluwitharana b Vaas	43	not out		54
Asif Mujtaba	c P.A.de Silva b Vaas	49	c Ranatunga b Atapattu		6
†Moin Khan	c Atapattu b Silva	98			
Saqlain Mushtaq	b K.S.C.de Silva	23	(7) not out		5
Mushtaq Ahmed	c Atapattu b K.S.C.de Silva	1			
Mohammad Zahid	c Kaluwitharana b K.S.C.de Silva	0			
Shahid Nazir	not out	0			
Extras	(LB 4, W 4, NB 6)	14	(LB 3, NB 1)		4
Total		**292**	(5 wickets)		**285**

PAKISTAN	O	M	R	W	O	M	R	W
Mohammad Zahid	12	1	44	1				
Shahid Nazir	8	1	50	0				
Mushtaq Ahmed	32	6	90	2	(4)33	4	113	2
Saqlain Mushtaq	45	12	115	4	(3)42.5	4	171	1
Asif Mujtaba	15	3	23	1	6	0	33	0
Salim Malik					(1) 9	2	33	0
Ijaz Ahmed					(2) 5	0	18	0

FALL OF WICKETS

Wkt	SL 1st	P 1st	SL 2nd	P 2nd
1st	95	0	157	0
2nd	124	13	171	19
3rd	124	59	203	146
4th	129	83	308	267
5th	144	147	–	279
6th	204	238		
7th	224	276		
8th	300	283		
9th	321	283		
10th	331	292		

SRI LANKA	O	M	R	W	O	M	R	W
Vaas	27	7	60	4	16	7	40	2
K.S.C.de Silva	24.2	5	85	5	19	2	73	0
Silva	25	5	91	1	28	10	71	2
Kalpage	23	8	42	0	20	6	60	0
Ranatunga	4.1	1	8	0				
Arnold	5	3	2	0	(7) 6	0	26	0
Atapattu					(5) 4	0	9	1
Tillekeratne					(6) 2	1	3	0

Umpires: P.Manuel (2) and I.D.Robinson (*Zimbabwe*) (16). ‡ (Abdul Razzak)
Referee: J.R.Reid (*New Zealand*) (29). **Test No. 1367/19 (SL 72/P 237)**

SRI LANKA v PAKISTAN 1996-97

SRI LANKA – BATTING AND FIELDING

	M	I	NO	HS	Runs	Avge	100	50	Ct/St
P.A.de Silva	2	4	2	168	432	216.00	3	–	1
S.T.Jayasuriya	2	4	–	113	278	69.50	1	2	–
H.P.Tillekeratne	2	4	1	103	191	63.66	1	1	1
A.Ranatunga	2	4	–	66	177	44.25	–	2	4
R.S.Kaluwitharana	2	3	–	57	96	32.00	–	1	4
R.P.Arnold	2	4	–	50	126	31.50	–	1	3
W.P.U.C.J.Vaas	2	3	–	17	35	11.66	–	–	1
M.S.Atapattu	2	4	–	25	43	10.75	–	–	2

Played in one Test: K.S.C.de Silva 0; H.D.P.K.Dharmasena 1, 11* (1 ct); R.S.Kalpage 5; M.Muralitharan 8* (1 ct); K.J.Silva 0; D.N.T.Zoysa 0.

SRI LANKA – BOWLING

	O	M	R	W	Avge	Best	5wI	10wM
M.Muralitharan	53	19	98	6	16.33	6-98	1	–
W.P.U.C.J.Vaas	75	20	175	7	25.00	4-60	–	–
K.S.C.de Silva	43.2	7	158	5	31.60	5-85	1	–
K.J.Silva	53	15	162	3	54.00	2-71	–	–

Also bowled: R.P.Arnold 13-4-31-0; M.S.Atapattu 4-0-9-1; P.A.de Silva 4-0-16-0; H.D.P.K.Dharmasena 52.5-19-93-1; S.T.Jayasuriya 3-0-15-0; R.S.Kalpage 43-14-102-0; A.Ranatunga 7.1-2-13-0; H.P.Tillekeratne 2-1-3-0; D.N.T.Zoysa 10-0-55-0.

PAKISTAN – BATTING AND FIELDING

	M	I	NO	HS	Runs	Avge	100	50	Ct/St
Salim Malik	2	3	–	155	237	79.00	1	1	–
Ijaz Ahmed	2	3	–	113	164	54.66	1	–	–
Inzamam-ul-Haq	2	3	1	54*	109	54.50	–	1	–
Moin Khan	2	2	–	98	98	49.00	–	1	2/2
Saqlain Mushtaq	2	3	1	58	86	43.00	–	1	1
Ramiz Raja	2	3	–	50	86	28.66	–	1	2
Asif Mujtaba	2	3	–	49	76	25.33	–	1	–
Mushtaq Ahmed	2	2	–	26	27	13.50	–	–	1
Mohammad Zahid	2	2	1	6*	6	6.00	–	–	–
Salim Elahi	2	3	–	14	14	4.66	–	–	7/1
Shahid Nazir	2	2	1	2	2	2.00	–	–	2

PAKISTAN – BOWLING

	O	M	R	W	Avge	Best	5wI	10wM
Saqlain Mushtaq	195.1	39	512	14	36.57	5-89	1	–
Mushtaq Ahmed	138.1	21	420	10	42.00	3-94	–	–

Also bowled: Asif Mujtaba 60-10-145-2; Ijaz Ahmed 5-0-18-0; Mohammad Zahid 40-4-148-2; Salim Malik 9-2-33-0; Shahid Nazir 38-7-148-1.

WEST INDIES v SRI LANKA (1st Test)

At Recreation Ground, St John's, Antigua on 13, 14, 15 June 1997.
Toss: West Indies. Result: **WEST INDIES** won by 6 wickets.
Debuts: West Indies – F.L.Reifer.

SRI LANKA

Batsman	First innings	R		Second innings	R
S.T.Jayasuriya	b Hooper	85		c Hooper b Ambrose	0
R.S.Mahanama	c Browne b Ambrose	1		c Browne b Ambrose	14
R.P.Arnold	c Williams b Ambrose	0		c Browne b Ambrose	12
P.A.de Silva	c Walsh b Ambrose	0		c Browne b Bishop	47
*A.Ranatunga	run out	42		c Rose b Bishop	13
H.P.Tillekeratne	retired hurt	1		absent hurt	
†R.S.Kaluwitharana	hit wicket b Bishop	23	(6)	c Browne b Walsh	16
H.D.P.K.Dharmasena	c Browne b Ambrose	29	(7)	c Walsh b Rose	31
K.R.Pushpakumara	c Reifer b Bishop	1	(8)	c Williams b Rose	8
K.S.C.de Silva	c Reifer b Ambrose	6	(9)	not out	2
M.Muralitharan	not out	6	(10)	c Williams b Rose	0
Extras	(B 4, LB 11, NB 14)	29		(LB 2, NB 7)	9
Total		**223**			**152**

WEST INDIES

Batsman	First innings	R		Second innings	R
S.L.Campbell	c Muralitharan b K.S.C.de Silva	50		c Mahanama b Muralitharan	79
S.C.Williams	c Arnold b Pushpakumara	21		c sub‡ b Muralitharan	83
F.L.Reifer	c Kaluwitharana b Pushpakumara	29		b Dharmasena	1
B.C.Lara	c Kaluwitharana b Pushpakumara	4		c sub‡ b Muralitharan	4
C.L.Hooper	lbw b Muralitharan	27		not out	6
R.I.C.Holder	c and b Dharmasena	28		not out	0
†C.O.Browne	c Jayasuriya b Muralitharan	0			
I.R.Bishop	b Muralitharan	5			
C.E.L.Ambrose	not out	11			
F.A.Rose	b Muralitharan	0			
*C.A.Walsh	b Muralitharan	0			
Extras	(B 4, LB 6, NB 8)	18		(B 4, LB 2, W 1, NB 9)	16
Total		**189**		(4 wickets)	**189**

WEST INDIES	O	M	R	W		O	M	R	W
Ambrose	13.1	3	37	5		9	0	41	3
Bishop	15	3	44	2	(4)	17	0	29	2
Walsh	11	0	46	0	(2)	10	0	37	1
Rose	10	2	32	0	(3)	9	1	43	3
Hooper	19	2	49	1					

SRI LANKA	O	M	R	W		O	M	R	W
K.S.C.de Silva	13	1	56	1		9	2	35	1
Pushpakumara	15	2	62	3		8	0	38	0
Dharmasena	8	4	19	1	(4)	7	1	21	1
Muralitharan	23.4	13	34	5	(3)	21.2	5	72	3
Jayasuriya	1	0	8	0		4	0	17	0

FALL OF WICKETS

	SL	WI	SL	WI
Wkt	1st	1st	2nd	2nd
1st	19	40	0	160
2nd	19	94	17	178
3rd	23	97	41	182
4th	133	122	85	183
5th	171	168	91	–
6th	206	168	113	–
7th	210	172	140	–
8th	216	189	151	–
9th	223	189	152	–
10th	–	189	–	–

Umpires: L.H.Barker (28) and R.S.Dunne (*New Zealand*) (24). ‡ (D.K.Liyanage)
Referee: Talat Ali (*Pakistan*) (1). **Test No. 1368/2 (WI 333/SL 73)**

WEST INDIES v SRI LANKA (2nd Test)

At Arnos Vale, Kingstown, St Vincent on 20, 21, 22, 23, 24 June 1997.
Toss: Sri Lanka. Result: **MATCH DRAWN.**
Debuts: None.

WEST INDIES

Batsman	1st innings		2nd innings	
S.L.Campbell	c Mahanama b Dharmasena	20	b Pushpakumara	33
S.C.Williams	c Kaluwitharana b Pushpakumara	0	c Jayasuriya b Muralitharan	46
F.L.Reifer	lbw b Pushpakumara	0	(4) c Kalu'rana b Pushpakumara	18
B.C.Lara	c and b K.S.C.de Silva	1	(3) c Jayasuriya b Dharmasena	115
C.L.Hooper	c Atapattu b Pushpakumara	81	c Kaluwitharana b Dharmasena	34
R.I.C.Holder	c Atapattu b Muralitharan	16	hit wicket b Muralitharan	0
I.R.Bishop	b Muralitharan	11	lbw b Muralitharan	34
†C.O.Browne	lbw b Pushpakumara	0	lbw b Muralitharan	0
C.E.L.Ambrose	b Pushpakumara	7	c Kaluwitharana b K.S.C.de Silva	31
F.A.Rose	b Muralitharan	1	not out	0
*C.A.Walsh	not out	1	b Muralitharan	0
Extras	(B 3, LB 3, NB 3)	9	(B 4, LB 21, NB 7)	32
Total		**147**		**343**

SRI LANKA

Batsman	1st innings		2nd innings	
S.T.Jayasuriya	lbw b Hooper	90	b Walsh	17
R.S.Mahanama	c Browne b Rose	28	c Browne b Bishop	29
M.S.Atapattu	c Hooper b Rose	7	b Walsh	10
P.A.de Silva	c Lara b Hooper	35	b Walsh	78
*A.Ranatunga	c Lara b Walsh	13	not out	72
S.Ranatunga	c Hooper b Walsh	9	(7) run out Browne	0
†R.S.Kaluwitharana	c Browne b Ambrose	7	(6) hit wicket b Walsh	2
H.D.P.K.Dharmasena	b Hooper	10	c Browne c Ambrose	7
K.R.Pushpakumara	c Browne b Hooper	0		
K.S.C.de Silva	not out	4	not out	1
M.Muralitharan	c Reifer b Hooper	4	(9) c Holder b Ambrose	0
Extras	(B 2, LB 3, NB 10)	15	(LB 3, NB 14)	17
Total		**222**	(8 wickets)	**233**

SRI LANKA	O	M	R	W	O	M	R	W
K.S.C.de Silva	13	2	46	1	17	1	62	1
Pushpakumara	12.4	1	41	5	19	2	81	2
Dharmasena	7	0	26	1	25	4	62	2
Muralitharan	12	1	28	3	(3) 41	13	113	5

WEST INDIES	O	M	R	W	O	M	R	W
Ambrose	9	1	34	1	15	1	51	2
Walsh	22	3	62	2	24	2	73	4
Rose	12	1	44	2	6	1	24	0
Bishop	7	0	51	0	14	1	61	1
Hooper	13.4	5	26	5	9	3	21	0

FALL OF WICKETS

	WI	SL	WI	SL
Wkt	1st	1st	2nd	2nd
1st	2	63	62	26
2nd	2	75	92	55
3rd	5	151	143	118
4th	34	178	240	189
5th	92	185	272	193
6th	126	196	276	208
7th	133	211	286	231
8th	140	211	339	231
9th	145	215	343	—
10th	147	222	343	—

Umpires: S.A.Bucknor (30) and D.B.Cowie (*New Zealand*) (6).
Referee: Talat Ali (*Pakistan*) (2). Test No. 1369/3 (WI 334/SL 74)

WEST INDIES v SRI LANKA 1996-97

WEST INDIES – BATTING AND FIELDING

	M	I	NO	HS	Runs	Avge	100	50	Ct/St
C.L.Hooper	2	4	1	81	148	49.33	–	1	3
S.L.Campbell	2	4	–	79	182	45.50	–	2	–
S.C.Williams	2	4	–	83	150	37.50	–	1	3
B.C.Lara	2	4	–	115	120	30.00	1	–	2
R.I.C.Holder	2	4	1	34	78	26.00	–	–	1
C.E.L.Ambrose	2	3	1	31	49	24.50	–	–	–
F.L.Reifer	2	4	–	29	48	12.00	–	–	3
I.R.Bishop	2	3	–	11	16	5.33	–	–	–
C.A.Walsh	2	3	1	1*	1	0.50	–	–	2
F.A.Rose	2	3	1	1	1	0.50	–	–	1
C.O.Browne	2	3	–	0	0	0.00	–	–	11

WEST INDIES – BOWLING

	O	M	R	W	Avge	Best	5wI	10wM
C.E.L.Ambrose	46.1	5	163	11	14.81	5-37	1	–
C.L.Hooper	41.4	10	96	6	16.00	5-26	1	–
F.A.Rose	37	5	143	5	28.60	3-43	–	–
C.A.Walsh	67	5	218	7	31.14	4-73	–	–
I.R.Bishop	43	4	185	5	37.00	2-29	–	–

SRI LANKA – BATTING AND FIELDING

	M	I	NO	HS	Runs	Avge	100	50	Ct/St
S.T.Jayasuriya	2	4	–	90	192	48.00	–	2	3
A.Ranatunga	2	4	1	72*	140	46.66	–	1	–
P.A.de Silva	2	4	–	78	160	40.00	–	1	–
H.D.P.K.Dharmasena	2	4	–	31	77	19.25	–	–	1
R.S.Mahanama	2	4	–	29	72	18.00	–	–	2
K.S.C.de Silva	2	4	3	6	13	13.00	–	–	1
R.S.Kaluwitharana	2	4	–	23	48	12.00	–	–	6
M.Muralitharan	2	4	1	6*	10	3.33	–	–	1
K.R.Pushpakumara	2	3	–	8	9	3.00	–	–	–

Played in one Test: R.P.Arnold 0, 12 (1 ct); M.S.Atapattu 7, 10 (2 ct); S.Ranatunga 9, 0; H.P.Tillekeratne 1*.

SRI LANKA – BOWLING

	O	M	R	W	Avge	Best	5wI	10wM
M.Muralitharan	98	32	247	16	15.43	5-34	2	–
K.R.Pushpakumara	54.4	5	222	10	22.20	5-41	1	–
H.D.P.K.Dharmasena	47	9	128	5	25.60	2-62	–	–
K.S.C.de Silva	52	6	199	3	66.33	1-46	–	–

Also bowled: S.T.Jayasuriya 5-0-25-0.

ENGLAND v AUSTRALIA (1st Test)

At Edgbaston, Birmingham on 5, 6, 7, 8 June 1997.
Toss: Australia. Result: **ENGLAND** won by 9 wickets.
Debuts: England – M.A.Butcher.

AUSTRALIA

Batsman	1st innings	R		2nd innings	R
*M.A.Taylor	c Butcher b Malcolm	7	(2)	c and b Croft	129
M.T.G.Elliott	b Gough	6	(1)	b Croft	66
G.S.Blewett	c Hussain b Gough	7		c Butcher b Croft	125
M.E.Waugh	b Gough	5	(6)	c Stewart b Gough	1
S.R.Waugh	c Stewart b Caddick	12	(4)	lbw b Gough	33
M.G.Bevan	c Ealham b Malcolm	8	(5)	c Hussain b Gough	24
†I.A.Healy	c Stewart b Caddick	0		c Atherton b Ealham	30
J.N.Gillespie	lbw b Caddick	4	(10)	run out	0
S.K.Warne	c Malcolm b Caddick	47	(8)	c and b Ealham	32
M.S.Kasprowicz	c Butcher b Caddick	17	(9)	c Butcher b Ealham	0
G.D.McGrath	not out	1		not out	0
Extras	(W 2, NB 2)	4		(B 18, LB 12, W 2, NB 5)	37
Total		**118**			**477**

ENGLAND

Batsman	1st innings	R	2nd innings	R
M.A.Butcher	c Healy b Kasprowicz	8	lbw b Kasprowicz	14
*M.A.Atherton	c Healy b McGrath	2	not out	57
†A.J.Stewart	c Elliott b Gillespie	18	not out	40
N.Hussain	c Healy b Warne	207		
G.P.Thorpe	c Bevan b McGrath	138		
J.P.Crawley	c Healy b Kasprowicz	5		
M.A.Ealham	not out	53		
R.D.B.Croft	c Healy b Kasprowicz	24		
D.Gough	c Healy b Kasprowicz	0		
A.R.Caddick	lbw b Bevan	0		
D.E.Malcolm				
Extras	(B 4, LB 7, W 1, NB 15)	27	(B 4, LB 4)	8
Total	(9 wickets declared)	**478**	(1 wicket)	**119**

ENGLAND	O	M	R	W	O	M	R	W
Gough	10	1	43	3	35	7	123	3
Malcolm	10	2	25	2	21	6	52	0
Caddick	11.5	1	50	5	(4)30	6	87	0
Croft					(3)43	10	125	3
Ealham					15.4	3	60	3

AUSTRALIA	O	M	R	W	O	M	R	W
McGrath	32	8	107	2	7	1	42	0
Kasprowicz	39	8	113	4	7	0	42	1
Gillespie	10	1	48	1				
Warne	35	8	110	1	(3)7.3	0	27	0
Bevan	10.4	0	44	1				
S.R.Waugh	12	2	45	0				

FALL OF WICKETS

	A	E	A	E
Wkt	1st	1st	2nd	2nd
1st	11	8	133	29
2nd	15	16	327	–
3rd	26	50	354	–
4th	28	338	393	
5th	48	345	399	
6th	48	416	431	
7th	48	460	465	
8th	54	463	465	
9th	110	478	477	
10th	118	–	477	

Umpires: S.A.Bucknor (*West Indies*) (29) and P.Willey (6).
Referee: R.S.Madugalle (*Sri Lanka*) (5).   **Test No. 1370/286 (E 735/A 567)**

ENGLAND v AUSTRALIA (2nd Test)

At Lord's, London on 19 (*no play*), 20, 21, 22, 23 June 1997.
Toss: Australia. Result: **MATCH DRAWN**.
Debuts: None.

ENGLAND

M.A.Butcher	c Blewett b McGrath	5	b Warne		87
*M.A.Atherton	c Taylor b McGrath	1	hit wicket b Kasprowicz		77
†A.J.Stewart	b McGrath	1	c Kasprowicz b McGrath		13
N.Hussain	lbw b McGrath	19	c and b Warne		0
G.P.Thorpe	c Blewett b Reiffel	21	not out		30
J.P.Crawley	c Healy b McGrath	1	not out		29
M.A.Ealham	c Elliott b Reiffel	7			
R.D.B.Croft	c Healy b McGrath	2			
D.Gough	c Healy b McGrath	10			
A.R.Caddick	lbw b McGrath	1			
D.E.Malcolm	not out	0			
Extras	(B 4, NB 5)	9	(B 8, LB 14, W 1, NB 7)		30
Total		**77**	(4 wickets declared)		**266**

AUSTRALIA

*M.A.Taylor	b Gough	1	
M.T.G.Elliott	c Crawley b Caddick	112	
G.S.Blewett	c Hussain b Croft	45	
M.E.Waugh	c Malcolm b Caddick	33	
S.K.Warne	c Hussain b Gough	0	
S.R.Waugh	lbw b Caddick	0	
M.G.Bevan	c Stewart b Caddick	4	
†I.A.Healy	not out	13	
P.R.Reiffel	not out	1	
M.S.Kasprowicz			
G.D.McGrath			
Extras	(B 1, LB 3)	4	
Total	(7 wickets declared)	**213**	

AUSTRALIA	O	M	R	W	O	M	R	W	FALL OF WICKETS			
										E	A	E
McGrath	20.3	8	38	8	20	5	65	1	*Wkt*	*1st*	*1st*	*2nd*
Reiffel	15	9	17	2	13	5	29	0	1st	11	4	162
Kasprowicz	5	1	9	0	15	3	54	1	2nd	12	73	189
Warne	2	0	9	0	19	4	47	2	3rd	13	147	197
Bevan					8	1	29	0	4th	47	147	202
S.R.Waugh					4	0	20	0	5th	56	147	–
									6th	62	159	–
ENGLAND									7th	66	212	–
Gough	20	4	82	2					8th	76	–	–
Caddick	22	6	71	4					9th	77	–	–
Malcolm	7	1	26	0					10th	77	–	–
Croft	12	5	30	1								

Umpires: D.R.Shepherd (35) and S.Venkataraghavan (*India*) (19).
Referee: R.S.Madugalle (*Sri Lanka*) (6). Test No. 1371/287 (E 736/A 568)

ENGLAND v AUSTRALIA (3rd Test)

At Old Trafford, Manchester on 3, 4, 5, 6, 7 July 1997.
Toss: Australia. Result: **AUSTRALIA** won by 268 runs.
Debuts: England – D.W.Headley.

AUSTRALIA

*M.A.Taylor	c Thorpe b Headley	2	(2)	c Butcher b Headley	1
M.T.G.Elliott	c Stewart b Headley	40	(1)	c Butcher b Headley	11
G.S.Blewett	b Gough	8		c Hussain b Croft	19
M.E.Waugh	c Stewart b Ealham	12		b Ealham	55
S.R.Waugh	b Gough	108		c Stewart b Headley	116
M.G.Bevan	c Stewart b Headley	7		c Atherton b Headley	0
†I.A.Healy	c Stewart b Caddick	9		c Butcher b Croft	47
S.K.Warne	c Stewart b Ealham	3		c Stewart b Caddick	53
P.R.Reiffel	b Gough	31		not out	45
J.N.Gillespie	c Stewart b Headley	0		not out	28
G.D.McGrath	not out	0			
Extras	(B 8, LB 4, NB 3)	15		(B 1, LB 13, NB 6)	20
Total		**235**		(8 wickets declared)	**395**

ENGLAND

M.A.Butcher	st Healy b Bevan	51		c McGrath b Gillespie	28
*M.A.Atherton	c Healy b McGrath	5		lbw b Gillespie	21
†A.J.Stewart	c Taylor b Warne	30		b Warne	1
N.Hussain	c Healy b Warne	13		lbw b Gillespie	1
G.P.Thorpe	c Taylor b Warne	3		c Healy b Warne	7
J.P.Crawley	c Healy b Warne	4		hit wicket b McGrath	83
M.A.Ealham	not out	24		c Healy b McGrath	9
R.D.B.Croft	c S.R.Waugh b McGrath	7		c Reiffel b McGrath	7
D.Gough	lbw b Warne	1		b McGrath	6
A.R.Caddick	c M.E.Waugh b Warne	15		c Gillespie b Warne	17
D.W.Headley	b McGrath	0		not out	0
Extras	(B 4, LB 3, NB 2)	9		(B 14, LB 4, W 1, NB 1)	20
Total		**162**			**200**

ENGLAND	O	M	R	W	O	M	R	W	FALL OF WICKETS			
									A	E	A	E
Gough	21	7	52	3	20	3	62	0	*Wkt*	*1st*	*1st*	*2nd*	*2nd*
Headley	27.3	4	72	4	29	4	104	4	1st	9	8	5	44
Caddick	14	2	52	1	(5)21	0	69	1	2nd	22	74	33	45
Ealham	11	2	34	2	13	3	41	1	3rd	42	94	39	50
Croft	4	0	13	0	(3)39	12	105	2	4th	85	101	131	55
									5th	113	110	132	84
AUSTRALIA									6th	150	111	210	158
McGrath	23.4	9	40	4	21	4	46	4	7th	160	122	298	170
Reiffel	9	3	14	0	(3) 2	0	8	0	8th	230	123	333	177
Warne	30	14	48	6	(4)30.4	8	63	3	9th	235	161	–	188
Gillespie	14	3	39	0	(2) 12	4	31	3	10th	235	162	–	200
Bevan	8	3	14	1	3	2	34	0					

Umpires: G.Sharp (4) and S.Venkataraghavan (*India*) (20).
Referee: R.S.Madugalle (*Sri Lanka*) (7).   **Test No. 1372/288 (E 737/A 569)**

ENGLAND v AUSTRALIA (4th Test)

At Headingley, Leeds on 24, 25, 26, 27, 28 July 1997.
Toss: Australia. Result: **AUSTRALIA** won by an innings and 61 runs.
Debuts: England – A.M.Smith.

ENGLAND

M.A.Butcher	c Blewett b Reiffel	24	c Healy b McGrath		19
*M.A.Atherton	c Gillespie b McGrath	41	c Warne b McGrath		2
†A.J.Stewart	c Blewett b Gillespie	7	b Reiffel		16
N.Hussain	c Taylor b McGrath	26	c Gillespie b Warne		105
D.W.Headley	c S.R.Waugh b Gillespie	22	lbw b Reiffel	(8)	3
G.P.Thorpe	b Gillespie	15	c M.E.Waugh b Gillespie	(5)	15
J.P.Crawley	c Blewett b Gillespie	2	b Reiffel	(6)	72
M.A.Ealham	not out	8	c M.E.Waugh b Reiffel	(7)	4
R.D.B.Croft	c Ponting b Gillespie	6	c Healy b Reiffel		5
D.Gough	b Gillespie	0	c M.E.Waugh b Gillespie		0
A.M.Smith	b Gillespie	0	not out	–	4
Extras	(B 4, LB 4, W 1, NB 12)	21	(B 6, LB 4, NB 13)		23
Total		**172**			**268**

AUSTRALIA

*M.A.Taylor	c Stewart b Gough	0
M.T.G.Elliott	b Gough	199
G.S.Blewett	c Stewart b Gough	1
M.E.Waugh	c and b Headley	8
S.R.Waugh	c Crawley b Headley	4
R.T.Ponting	c Ealham b Gough	127
†I.A.Healy	b Ealham	31
S.K.Warne	c Thorpe b Ealham	0
P.R.Reiffel	not out	54
J.N.Gillespie	b Gough	3
G.D.McGrath	not out	20
Extras	(B 9, LB 10, NB 35)	54
Total	(9 wickets declared)	**501**

AUSTRALIA	O	M	R	W	O	M	R	W	FALL OF WICKETS			
										E	A	E
McGrath	22	5	67	2	22	5	80	2	Wkt	1st	1st	2nd
Reiffel	20	4	41	1	21.1	2	49	5	1st	43	0	23
Gillespie	13.4	1	37	7	23	8	65	2	2nd	58	16	28
Blewett	3	0	17	0					3rd	103	43	57
Warne	1	0	2	0	(4)21	6	53	1	4th	138	50	89
S.R.Waugh					(5) 4	1	11	0	5th	154	318	222
									6th	154	382	252
ENGLAND									7th	163	383	256
Gough	36	5	149	5					8th	172	444	263
Headley	25	2	125	2					9th	172	461	264
Smith	23	2	89	0					10th	172	–	268
Ealham	19	3	56	2								
Croft	18	1	49	0								
Butcher	2	0	14	0								

Umpires: M.J.Kitchen (15) and C.J.Mitchley (*South Africa*) (18).
Referee: C.W.Smith (*West Indies*) (12).　　　　**Test No. 1373/289 (E 738/A 570)**

ENGLAND v AUSTRALIA (5th Test)

At Trent Bridge, Nottingham on 7, 8, 9, 10 August 1997.
Toss: Australia. Result: **AUSTRALIA** won by 264 runs.
Debuts: England – A.J.Hollioake, B.C.Hollioake.

AUSTRALIA

M.T.G.Elliott	c Stewart b Headley	69	(2)	c Crawley b Caddick	37
*M.A.Taylor	b Caddick	76	(1)	c Hussain b B.C.Hollioake	45
G.S.Blewett	c Stewart b B.C.Hollioake	50		c Stewart b Caddick	60
M.E.Waugh	lbw b Caddick	68		lbw b Headley	7
S.R.Waugh	b Malcolm	75		c A.J.Hollioake b Caddick	14
R.T.Ponting	b Headley	9		c Stewart b A.J.Hollioake	45
†I.A.Healy	c A.J.Hollioake b Malcolm	16		c Stewart b A.J.Hollioake	63
S.K.Warne	c Thorpe b Malcolm	0		c Thorpe b Croft	20
P.R.Reiffel	c Thorpe b Headley	26		c B.C.Hollioake b Croft	22
J.N.Gillespie	not out	18		c Thorpe b Headley	4
G.D.McGrath	b Headley	1		not out	1
Extras	(B 4, LB 10, W 1, NB 4)	19		(B 1, LB 11, NB 6)	18
Total		**427**			**336**

ENGLAND

*M.A.Atherton	c Healy b Warne	27		c Healy b McGrath	8
†J.Stewart	c Healy b Warne	87		c S.R.Waugh b Reiffel	16
J.P.Crawley	c Healy b McGrath	18		c Healy b Gillespie	33
N.Hussain	b Warne	2		b Gillespie	21
G.P.Thorpe	c Blewett b Warne	53		not out	82
A.J.Hollioake	c Taylor b Reiffel	45		lbw b Gillespie	2
B.C.Hollioake	c M.E.Waugh b Reiffel	28		lbw b Warne	2
R.D.B.Croft	c Blewett b McGrath	18		c McGrath b Warne	6
A.R.Caddick	c Healy b McGrath	0		lbw b Warne	0
D.W.Headley	not out	10		c Healy b McGrath	4
D.E.Malcolm	b McGrath	12		c M.E.Waugh b McGrath	0
Extras	(B 2, LB 6, NB 5)	13		(B 6, LB 2, NB 4)	12
Total		**313**			**186**

ENGLAND	O	M	R	W	O	M	R	W		FALL OF WICKETS			
Malcolm	25	4	100	3	16	4	52	0		A	E	A	E
Headley	30.5	7	87	4	19	3	56	2	*Wkt*	*1st*	*1st*	*2nd*	*2nd*
Caddick	30	4	102	2	(4)20	2	85	3	1st	117	106	51	25
B.C.Hollioake	10	1	57	1	(5) 5	1	26	1	2nd	160	129	105	25
Croft	19	7	43	0	(3)26.5	6	74	2	3rd	225	135	134	78
A.J.Hollioake	7	0	24	0	12	2	31	2	4th	311	141	156	99
									5th	325	243	171	121
AUSTRALIA									6th	355	243	276	144
McGrath	29.5	9	71	4	13.5	4	36	3	7th	363	272	292	150
Reiffel	21	2	101	2	11	3	34	1	8th	386	290	314	166
Gillespie	11	3	47	0	8	0	65	3	9th	419	290	326	186
Warne	32	8	86	4	16	4	43	3	10th	427	313	336	186

Umpires: C.J.Mitchley (*South Africa*) (19) and D.R.Shepherd (36).
Referee: C.W.Smith (*West Indies*) (13).   **Test No. 1374/290 (E 739/A 571)**

ENGLAND v AUSTRALIA (6th Test)

At Kennington Oval, London on 21, 22, 23 August 1997.
Toss: England. Result: **ENGLAND** won by 19 runs.
Debuts: Australia – S.Young.

ENGLAND

M.A.Butcher	b McGrath	5	lbw b M.E.Waugh		13
*M.A.Atherton	c Healy b McGrath	8	c S.R.Waugh b Kasprowicz		8
†A.J.Stewart	lbw b McGrath	36	lbw b Kasprowicz		3
N.Hussain	c Elliott b McGrath	35	c Elliott b Warne		2
G.P.Thorpe	b McGrath	27	c Taylor b Kasprowicz		62
M.R.Ramprakash	c Blewett b McGrath	4	st Healy b Warne		48
A.J.Hollioake	b Warne	0	lbw b Kasprowicz		4
A.R.Caddick	not out	26	not out		0
P.J.Martin	b McGrath	20	c and b Kasprowicz		3
P.C.R.Tufnell	c Blewett b Warne	1	c Healy b Kasprowicz		0
D.E.Malcolm	lbw b Kasprowicz	0	b Kasprowicz		0
Extras	(B 2, LB 6, NB 10)	18	(B 6, LB 10, NB 4)		20
Total		**180**			**163**

AUSTRALIA

M.T.G.Elliott	b Tufnell	12	(2)	lbw b Malcolm	4
*M.A.Taylor	c Hollioake b Tufnell	38	(1)	lbw b Caddick	18
G.S.Blewett	c Stewart b Tufnell	47		c Stewart b Caddick	19
M.E.Waugh	c Butcher b Tufnell	19		c Hussain b Caddick	1
S.R.Waugh	lbw b Caddick	22		c Thorpe b Caddick	6
R.T.Ponting	c Hussain b Tufnell	40		lbw b Tufnell	20
†I.A.Healy	c Stewart b Tufnell	2		c and b Caddick	14
S.Young	c Stewart b Tufnell	0		not out	4
S.K.Warne	c Stewart b Tufnell	30		c Martin b Tufnell	3
M.S.Kasprowicz	lbw b Caddick	0		c Hollioake b Caddick	4
G.D.McGrath	not out	1		c Thorpe b Tufnell	1
Extras	(LB 3, W 1, NB 5)	9		(B 3, LB 4, W 1, NB 2)	10
Total		**220**			**104**

AUSTRALIA	O	M	R	W	O	M	R	W
McGrath	21	4	76	7	17	5	33	0
Kasprowicz	11.4	2	56	1	15.5	5	36	7
Warne	17	8	32	2	26	9	57	2
Young	7	3	8	0	(5) 1	0	5	0
M.E.Waugh					(4) 7	3	16	1

ENGLAND	O	M	R	W	O	M	R	W
Malcolm	11	2	37	0	3	0	15	1
Martin	15	5	38	0	4	0	13	0
Caddick	19	4	76	3	(4)12	2	42	5
Tufnell	34.3	16	66	7	(3)13.1	6	27	4

FALL OF WICKETS

Wkt	1st E	1st A	2nd E	2nd A
1st	18	49	20	5
2nd	24	54	24	36
3rd	97	94	26	42
4th	128	140	52	49
5th	131	150	131	54
6th	132	164	138	88
7th	132	164	160	92
8th	158	205	163	95
9th	175	205	163	99
10th	180	220	163	104

Umpires: L.H.Barker (*West Indies*) (29) and P.Willey (7).
Referee: C.W.Smith (*West Indies*) (14).   **Test No. 1375/291 (E 740/A 572)**

ENGLAND v AUSTRALIA 1997

ENGLAND – BATTING AND FIELDING

	M	I	NO	HS	Runs	Avge	100	50	Ct/St
G.P.Thorpe	6	11	2	138	453	50.33	1	3	8
N.Hussain	6	11	–	207	431	39.18	2	–	8
M.A.Ealham	4	6	3	53*	105	35.00	–	1	3
J.P.Crawley	5	9	1	83	243	30.37	–	2	3
M.A.Butcher	5	10	–	87	254	25.40	–	2	8
A.J.Stewart	6	12	1	87	268	24.36	–	1	23
M.A.Atherton	6	12	1	77	257	23.36	–	2	2
A.J.Hollioake	2	4	–	45	51	12.75	–	–	4
A.R.Caddick	5	8	2	26*	59	9.83	–	–	1
D.W.Headley	3	6	2	22	39	9.75	–	–	1
R.D.B.Croft	5	8	–	24	75	9.37	–	–	1
D.E.Malcolm	4	5	1	12	12	3.00	–	–	2
D.Gough	4	6	–	10	17	2.83			

Played in one Test: B.C.Hollioake 28, 2 (1 ct); P.J.Martin 20, 3 (1 ct); M.R.Ramprakash 4, 48; A.M.Smith 0, 4*; P.C.R.Tufnell 1, 0.

ENGLAND – BOWLING

	O	M	R	W	Avge	Best	5wI	10wM
P.C.R.Tufnell	47.4	22	93	11	8.45	7- 66	1	1
M.A.Ealham	58.4	11	191	8	23.87	3- 60	–	–
A.R.Caddick	179.5	27	634	24	26.41	5- 42	2	–
D.W.Headley	131.2	20	444	16	27.75	4- 72	–	–
D.Gough	142	27	511	16	31.93	5-149	1	–
D.E.Malcolm	93	19	307	6	51.16	3-100	–	–
R.D.B.Croft	161.5	41	439	8	54.87	3-125	–	–

Also bowled: M.A.Butcher 2-0-14-0; A.J.Hollioake 19-2-55-2; B.C.Hollioake 15-2-83-2; P.J.Martin 19-5-51-0; A.M.Smith 23-2-89-0.

AUSTRALIA – BATTING AND FIELDING

	M	I	NO	HS	Runs	Avge	100	50	Ct/St
P.R.Reiffel	4	6	3	54*	179	59.66	–	1	1
M.T.G.Elliott	6	10	–	199	556	55.60	2	2	4
R.T.Ponting	3	5	–	127	241	48.20	1	–	1
S.R.Waugh	6	10	–	116	390	39.00	2	1	4
G.S.Blewett	6	10	–	125	381	38.10	1	2	9
M.A.Taylor	6	10	–	129	317	31.70	1	1	6
I.A.Healy	6	10	1	63	225	25.00	–	1	25/2
M.E.Waugh	6	10	–	68	209	20.90	–	2	6
S.K.Warne	6	10	–	53	188	18.80	–	1	2
G.D.McGrath	6	8	6	20*	25	12.50	–	–	2
J.N.Gillespie	4	7	2	28*	57	11.40	–	–	3
M.G.Bevan	3	5	–	24	43	8.60	–	–	1
M.S.Kasprowicz	4	4	–	17	21	5.25	–	–	2

Played in one Test: S.Young 0, 4*.

AUSTRALIA – BOWLING

	O	M	R	W	Avge	Best	5wI	10wM
G.D.McGrath	249.5	67	701	36	19.47	8-38	2	–
J.N.Gillespie	91.4	20	332	16	20.75	7-37	1	–
M.S.Kasprowicz	93.3	19	310	14	22.14	7-36	1	–
S.K.Warne	237.1	69	577	24	24.04	6-48	1	–
P.R.Reiffel	112.1	28	293	11	26.63	5-49	1	–

Also bowled: M.G.Bevan 34.4-6-121-2; G.S.Blewett 3-0-17-0; M.E.Waugh 7-3-16-1; S.R.Waugh 20-3-76-0; S.Young 8-3-13-0.

SRI LANKA v INDIA (1st Test)

At R.Premadasa (Khettarama) Stadium, Colombo on 2, 3, 4, 5, 6 August 1997.
Toss: India. Result: **MATCH DRAWN.**
Debuts: Sri Lanka – D.P.M.Jayawardene; India – N.M.Kulkarni.

INDIA

†N.R.Mongia	c Jayawardene b Pushpakumara	7
N.S.Sidhu	c Kaluwitharane b Vaas	111
R.Dravid	c and b Jayasuriya	69
*S.R.Tendulkar	c Jayawardene b Muralitharan	143
M.Azharuddin	c and b Muralitharan	126
S.C.Ganguly	c Mahanama b Jayasuriya	0
A.Kumble	not out	27
R.K.Chauhan	c Vaas b Jayasuriya	23
A.Kuruvilla	c Atapattu b Pushpakumara	9
N.M.Kulkarni		
B.K.V.Prasad		
Extras	(B 10, NB 12)	22
Total	**(8 wickets declared)**	**537**

SRI LANKA

S.T.Jayasuriya	c Ganguly b Chauhan	340
M.S.Atapattu	c Mongia b Kulkarni	26
R.S.Mahanama	lbw b Kumble	225
P.A.de Silva	c Prasad b Ganguly	126
*A.Ranatunga	run out	86
D.R.M.Jayawardene	c Kulkarni b Ganguly	66
†R.S.Kaluwitharana	not out	14
W.P.U.C.J.Vaas	not out	11
K.R.Pushpakumara		
M.Muralitharan		
K.J.Silva		
Extras	(B 28, LB 9, W 7, NB 14)	58
Total	**(6 wickets declared)**	**952**

SRI LANKA	O	M	R	W
Vaas	23	5	80	1
Pushpakumara	19.3	2	97	2
Jayawardene	2	0	6	0
Muralitharan	65	9	174	2
Silva	39	3	122	0
Jayasuriya	18	3	45	3
Atapattu	1	0	3	0

INDIA	O	M	R	W
Prasad	24	1	88	0
Kuruvilla	14	2	74	0
Chauhan	78	8	276	1
Kumble	72	7	223	1
Kulkarni	70	12	195	1
Ganguly	9	0	53	2
Tendulkar	2	1	2	0
Dravid	2	0	4	0

FALL OF WICKETS

	I	SL
Wkt	1st	1st
1st	36	39
2nd	183	615
3rd	230	615
4th	451	790
5th	451	921
6th	479	924
7th	516	–
8th	537	–
9th	–	–
10th	–	–

Umpires: K.T.Francis (19) and S.G.Randell (*Australia*) (30).
Referee: J.R.Reid (*New Zealand*) (30).   **Test No. 1376/15 (SL 75/I 311)**

SRI LANKA v INDIA (2nd Test)

At Sinhalese Sports Club, Colombo on 9, 10, 11, 12, 13 August 1997.
Toss: India. Result: **MATCH DRAWN.**
Debuts: India – D.S.Mohanty.

SRI LANKA

S.T.Jayasuriya	c Tendulkar b Mohanty	32	b Kuruvilla	199
M.S.Atapattu	c Azharuddin b Prasad	19	c Azharuddin b Kumble	29
R.S.Mahanama	c Azharuddin b Mohanty	37	st Mongia b Kumble	35
P.A.de Silva	c Mongia b Mohanty	146	c sub (V.G.Kambli) b Kumble	120
*A.Ranatunga	c Mongia b Ganguly	14	run out	1
D.R.M.Jayawardene	c Mongia b Prasad	16 (7)	c Mongia b Kuruvilla	7
†R.S.Kaluwitharana	b Kuruvilla	7 (6)	run out	2
W.P.U.C.J.Vaas	b Kuruvilla	10	not out	5
M.Muralitharan	c Azharuddin b Kumble	39		
K.R.Pushpakumara	b Mohanty	0		
K.S.C.de Silva	not out	0		
Extras	(B 4, LB 4, NB 4)	12	(B 1, LB 4, W 1, NB 11)	17
Total		**332**	(7 wickets declared)	**415**

INDIA

A.Jadeja	c Kaluwitharana b Vaas	1	c Atapattu b K.S.C.de Silva	73
N.S.Sidhu	st Kaluwitharana b Muralitharan	29	c Jayasuriya b Vaas	16
R.Dravid	c Vaas b K.S.C.de Silva	2	c Atapattu b Muralitharan	6
*S.R.Tendulkar	c Muralitharan b Pushpakumara	139	c K.S.C.de Silva b Muralitharan	8
M.Azharuddin	c Mahanama b Vaas	22	not out	108
S.C.Ganguly	c Vaas b K.S.C.de Silva	147	c Kaluwitharana b Muralitharan	45
†N.R.Mongia	b Muralitharan	15	not out	10
A.Kumble	c Jayawardene b Muralitharan	0		
A.Kuruvilla	c Jayawardene b Muralitharan	0		
B.K.V.Prasad	c Kaluwitharana b K.S.C.de Silva	2		
D.S.Mohanty	not out	0		
Extras	(B 2, LB 3, NB 13)	18	(B 1, LB 7, NB 7)	15
Total		**375**	(5 wickets)	**281**

INDIA	O	M	R	W	O	M	R	W
Prasad	26	5	104	2	(2)16	1	72	0
Kuruvilla	20	5	68	2	(3)24	3	90	2
Mohanty	20.4	5	78	4	(1)16	0	72	0
Kumble	25	8	51	1	38.4	2	156	3
Ganguly	4	0	23	1	3	0	18	0
Dravid					1	0	2	0

SRI LANKA	O	M	R	W	O	M	R	W
Vaas	27	5	69	2	17	3	42	1
Pushpakumara	19	3	79	1	(4)14	1	50	0
K.S.C.de Silva	31.1	6	101	3	(2)16	5	32	1
Muralitharan	48	17	99	4	(3)35	5	96	3
Jayasuriya	10	6	15	0	10	4	24	0
Jayawardene	1	1	0	0	8	1	29	0
P.A.de Silva	5	2	7	0				

FALL OF WICKETS

Wkt	SL 1st	I 1st	SL 2nd	I 2nd
1st	53	2	65	55
2nd	59	9	145	75
3rd	121	81	363	100
4th	192	126	369	138
5th	230	276	374	248
6th	249	328	394	–
7th	274	334	415	–
8th	322	342	–	
9th	332	359	–	
10th	332	375	–	

Umpires: B.C.Cooray (11) and R.E.Koertzen (*South Africa*) (4).
Referee: J.R.Reid (*New Zealand*) (31).   **Test No. 1377/16 (SL 76/I 312)**

SRI LANKA v INDIA 1997-98

SRI LANKA – BATTING AND FIELDING

	M	I	NO	HS	Runs	Avge	100	50	Ct/St
S.T.Jayasuriya	2	3	–	340	571	190.33	2	–	2
P.A.de Silva	2	3	–	146	392	130.66	3	–	–
R.S.Mahanama	2	3	–	225	297	99.00	1	–	2
M.Muralitharan	2	1	–	39	39	39.00	–	–	2
A.Ranatunga	2	2	–	86	101	33.66	–	1	–
D.R.M.Jayawardene	2	3	–	66	89	29.66	–	1	4
W.P.U.C.J.Vaas	2	3	2	11*	26	26.00	–	–	3
M.S.Atapattu	2	3	–	29	74	24.66	–	–	3
R.S.Kaluwitharana	2	3	1	14*	23	11.50	–	–	4/1
K.R.Pushpakumara	2	1	–	0	0	0.00	–	–	–

Played in one Test: K.S.C.de Silva 0* (1 ct); K.J.Silva did not bat.

SRI LANKA – BOWLING

	O	M	R	W	Avge	Best	5wI	10wM
S.T.Jayasuriya	38	13	84	3	28.00	3- 45	–	–
K.S.C.de Silva	47.1	11	133	4	33.25	3-101	–	–
M.Muralitharan	148	31	369	9	41.00	4- 99	–	–
W.P.U.C.J.Vaas	67	13	191	4	47.75	2- 69	–	–
K.R.Pushpakumara	52.3	6	226	3	75.33	2- 97	–	–

Also bowled: M.S.Atapattu 1-0-3-0; P.A.de Silva 5-2-7-0; D.R.M.Jayawardene 11-2-35-0; K.J.Silva 39-3-122-0.

INDIA – BATTING AND FIELDING

	M	I	NO	HS	Runs	Avge	100	50	Ct/St
M.Azharuddin	2	3	1	126	256	128.00	2	–	4
S.R.Tendulkar	2	3	–	143	290	96.66	2	–	1
S.C.Ganguly	2	3	–	147	192	64.00	1	–	1
N.S.Sidhu	2	3	–	111	156	52.00	1	–	–
A.Kumble	2	2	1	27*	27	27.00	–	–	–
R.Dravid	2	3	–	69	77	25.66	–	1	–
N.R.Mongia	2	3	1	15	32	16.00	–	–	5/1
A.Kuruvilla	2	2	–	9	9	4.50	–	–	–
B.K.V.Prasad	2	1	–	2	2	2.00	–	–	1

Played in one Test: R.K.Chauhan 23; A.Jadeja 1, 73; N.M.Kulkarni did not bat (1 ct); D.S.Mohanty 0*.

INDIA – BOWLING

	O	M	R	W	Avge	Best	5wI	10wM
S.C.Ganguly	16	0	94	3	31.33	2- 53	–	–
D.S.Mohanty	36.4	5	150	4	37.50	4- 78	–	–
A.Kuruvilla	58	10	232	4	58.00	2- 68	–	–
A.Kumble	135.4	17	430	5	86.00	3-156	–	–

Also bowled: R.K.Chauhan 78-8-276-1; R.Dravid 3-0-6-0; N.M.Kulkarni 70-12-195-1; B.K.V.Prasad 66-7-264-2; S.R.Tendulkar 2-1-2-0.

ZIMBABWE v NEW ZEALAND (1st Test)

At Harare Sports Club on 18, 19, 20, 21, 22 September 1997.
Toss: New Zealand. Result: **MATCH DRAWN**.
Debuts: Zimbabwe – A.G.Huckle, G.J.Rennie; New Zealand – S.B.O'Connor.

ZIMBABWE

G.J.Rennie	c Fleming b Cairns	23	c Harris b O'Connor		57
G.W.Flower	c Parore b Cairns	104	c Fleming b O'Connor		151
†A.Flower	c Spearman b Cairns	8	c Parore b O'Connor		20
G.J.Whittall	c Fleming b O'Connor	33	run out		4
*A.D.R.Campbell	c Pocock b Astle	18	c Fleming b Davis		21
D.L.Houghton	lbw b Davis	23	c Davis b Astle		1
P.A.Strang	c Fleming b Davis	42	c Horne b Davis		17
H.H.Streak	c Fleming b Cairns	0	run out		0
J.A.Rennie	c Fleming b Davis	22	c and b Astle		16
B.C.Strang	lbw b Cairns	1	not out		4
A.G.Huckle	not out	0			
Extras	(B 1, LB 5, W 4, NB 14)	24	(LB 12, NB 8)		20
Total		**298**	(9 wickets declared)		**311**

NEW ZEALAND

C.M.Spearman	c Campbell b B.C.Strang	23 (2)	c A.Flower b Huckle		33
B.A.Pocock	run out	21 (1)	lbw b Streak		52
M.J.Horne	c Whittall b Streak	24	c A.Flower b P.A.Strang		0
*S.P.Fleming	c A.Flower b B.C.Strang	52	lbw b B.C.Strang		27
N.J.Astle	c A.Flower b B.C.Strang	7	c G.W.Flower b B.C.Strang		0
C.L.Cairns	run out	12	not out		71
†A.C.Parore	not out	42	lbw b Huckle		51
C.Z.Harris	lbw b Huckle	16	lbw b Streak		41
D.L.Vettori	c J.A.Rennie b P.A.Strang	2	c G.J.Rennie b Huckle		13
S.B.O'Connor	c Houghton b P.A.Strang	2	not out		1
H.T.Davis	c G.J.Rennie b Huckle	1			
Extras	(B 4, LB 1)	5	(B 6, LB 6, W 1, NB 2)		15
Total		**207**	(8 wickets)		**304**

NEW ZEALAND	O	M	R	W		O	M	R	W
O'Connor	26	1	104	1		26	3	73	3
Davis	20	1	57	3		13	2	45	2
Cairns	28.1	9	50	5		9	0	44	0
Astle	23	12	40	1	(6) 25.5	2	86	2
Vettori	4	0	14	0	(4) 13	2	40	0
Harris	13	5	27	0	(5) 5	3	11	0
ZIMBABWE									
Streak	23	2	63	1		21	3	52	2
J.A.Rennie	8	1	32	0	(6) 3	1	5	0
B.C.Strang	19	10	29	3	(2) 26	10	56	2
P.A.Strang	15	2	31	2		42	17	76	1
Whittall	5	0	15	0	(3) 5	1	19	0
Huckle	14	3	32	2		31	9	84	3

FALL OF WICKETS

	Z	NZ	Z	NZ
Wkt	1st	1st	2nd	2nd
1st	47	44	156	63
2nd	57	44	218	64
3rd	117	89	231	116
4th	144	96	263	116
5th	214	135	264	122
6th	244	147	290	200
7th	244	189	290	266
8th	295	198	290	296
9th	298	204	311	–
10th	298	207	–	–

Umpires: B.C.Cooray (*Sri Lanka*) (12) and I.D.Robinson (17).
Referee: S.Wettimuny (*Sri Lanka*) (1).   **Test No. 1378/5 (Z 23/NZ 253)**

ZIMBABWE v NEW ZEALAND (2nd Test)

At Queens Sports Club, Bulawayo on 25, 26, 27, 28, 29 September 1997.
Toss: Zimbabwe. Result: **MATCH DRAWN**.
Debuts: New Zealand – D.G.Sewell.

ZIMBABWE

G.J.Rennie	c Harris b O'Connor	57	lbw b Astle		24
G.W.Flower	c Fleming b Vettori	83	run out		49
†A.Flower	c Harris b Vettori	39	c and b Harris		7
G.J.Whittall	not out	203	run out		45
*A.D.R.Campbell	c Astle b O'Connor	7	not out		59
D.L.Houghton	b Cairns	32	c Harris b Vettori		13
P.A.Strang	c Harris b Vettori	5	lbw b Vettori		2
H.H.Streak	lbw b Cairns	17	run out		1
B.C.Strang	c Fleming b Cairns	0	b Cairns		10
A.G.Huckle	c Parore b Vettori	0	not out		0
E.Matambanadzo	c Fleming b O'Connor	4			
Extras	(LB 10, W 2, NB 2)	14	(B 2, LB 7, W 3, NB 5)		17
Total		**461**	(8 wickets declared)		**227**

NEW ZEALAND

C.M.Spearman	c Huckle b P.A.Strang	47 (2)	c Campbell b Huckle		27
B.A.Pocock	lbw b P.A.Strang	27 (1)	c P.A.Strang b Huckle		62
M.J.Horne	lbw b P.A.Strang	5	c Campbell b Huckle		29
*S.P.Fleming	c P.A.Strang b Huckle	27	run out		75
N.J.Astle	c sub (A.R.Whittall) b Huckle	96	c G.W.Flower b P.A.Strang		21
C.L.Cairns	c Rennie b Huckle	0	c Houghton b Huckle		8
†A.C.Parore	c G.W.Flower b Huckle	17	c Whittall b Huckle		23
C.Z.Harris	b Huckle	71	not out		12
D.L.Vettori	c B.C.Strang b Huckle	90	run out		7
S.B.O'Connor	run out	7	not out		0
D.G.Sewell	not out	1			
Extras	(B 1, LB 9, NB 5)	15	(B 6, LB 3, NB 2)		11
Total		**403**	(8 wickets)		**275**

NEW ZEALAND	O	M	R	W	O	M	R	W	FALL OF WICKETS				
										Z	NZ	Z	NZ
Sewell	19	4	81	0	4	0	9	0	*Wkt*	*1st*	*1st*	*2nd*	*2nd*
O'Connor	27	9	80	3	5	0	34	0	1st	144	60	75	41
Cairns	36	11	97	3	11	1	49	1	2nd	148	76	80	89
Vettori	58	11	165	4	18	3	69	2	3rd	218	92	91	138
Harris	14	6	13	0 (6)	17	4	41	1	4th	244	130	172	207
Astle	7	2	15	0 (5)	9	6	16	1	5th	322	130	202	221
									6th	343	162	204	240
ZIMBABWE									7th	416	259	205	260
Streak	15	5	26	0					8th	420	371	219	275
Matambanadzo	15	4	52	0 (1)	2	0	14	0	9th	421	389	–	–
P.A.Strang	47	18	110	3 (4)	23	1	81	1	10th	461	403	–	–
Huckle	40.3	10	109	6 (3)	32	2	146	5					
B.C.Strang	26	12	50	0 (2)	8	4	15	0					
Whittall	6	1	14	0									
G.W.Flower	10	2	19	0 (5)	3	1	10	0					
Campbell	2	0	13	0									

Umpires: R.B.Tiffin (4) and S.Venkataraghavan (*India*) (21).
Referee: S.Wettimuny (*Sri Lanka*) (2).   **Test No. 1379/6 (Z 24/NZ 254)**

ZIMBABWE v NEW ZEALAND 1997-98

ZIMBABWE – BATTING AND FIELDING

	M	I	NO	HS	Runs	Avge	100	50	Ct/St
G.W.Flower	2	4	–	151	387	96.75	2	1	3
G.J.Whittall	2	4	1	203*	285	95.00	1	–	2
G.J.Rennie	2	4	–	57	161	40.25	–	2	3
A.D.R.Campbell	2	4	1	59*	105	35.00	–	1	3
A.Flower	2	4	–	39	74	18.50	–	–	4
D.L.Houghton	2	4	–	32	69	17.25	–	–	2
P.A.Strang	2	4	–	42	66	16.50	–	–	2
B.C.Strang	2	4	1	10	15	5.00	–	–	1
H.H.Streak	2	4	–	17	18	4.50	–	–	
A.G.Huckle	2	3	2	0*	0	0.00	–	–	1

Played in one Test: E.Matambanadzo 4; J.A.Rennie 22, 16 (1 ct).

ZIMBABWE – BOWLING

	O	M	R	W	Avge	Best	5wI	10wM
A.G.Huckle	117.3	24	371	16	23.18	6-109	2	1
B.C.Strang	79	36	150	5	30.00	3- 29	–	–
P.A.Strang	127	38	298	7	42.57	3-110	–	–
H.H.Streak	59	10	141	3	47.00	2- 52	–	–

Also bowled: A.D.R.Campbell 2-0-13-0; G.W.Flower 13-3-29-0; E.Matambanadzo 17-4-66-0; J.A.Rennie 11-2-37-0; G.J.Whittall 16-2-48-0.

NEW ZEALAND – BATTING AND FIELDING

	M	I	NO	HS	Runs	Avge	100	50	Ct/St
C.Z.Harris	2	4	1	71	140	46.66	–	1	6
S.P.Fleming	2	4	–	75	181	45.25	–	2	10
A.C.Parore	2	4	1	51	133	44.33	–	1	3
B.A.Pocock	2	4	–	62	162	40.50	–	2	1
C.M.Spearman	2	4	–	47	130	32.50	–	–	1
N.J.Astle	2	4	–	96	124	31.00	–	1	2
C.L.Cairns	2	4	1	71*	91	30.33	–	1	–
D.L.Vettori	2	4	–	90	112	28.00	–	1	–
M.J.Horne	2	4	–	29	58	14.50	–	–	1
S.B.O'Connor	2	4	2	7	10	5.00	–	–	

Played in one Test: H.T.Davis 1 (1 ct); D.G.Sewell 1*.

NEW ZEALAND – BOWLING

	O	M	R	W	Avge	Best	5wI	10wM
H.T.Davis	33	3	102	5	20.40	3- 57	–	–
C.L.Cairns	84.1	21	240	9	26.66	5- 50	1	–
N.J.Astle	64.5	22	157	4	39.25	2- 86	–	–
S.B.O'Connor	84	13	291	7	41.57	3- 73	–	–
D.L.Vettori	93	16	288	6	48.00	4-165	–	–

Also bowled: C.Z.Harris 49-18-92-1; D.G.Sewell 23-4-90-0.

PAKISTAN v SOUTH AFRICA (1st Test)

At Rawalpindi Cricket Stadium on 6, 7, 8, 9, 10 October 1997.
Toss: Pakistan. Result: **MATCH DRAWN**
Debuts: Pakistan – Ali Naqvi, Azhar Mahmood, Mohammad Ramzan.

PAKISTAN

*Saeed Anwar	c Richardson b Donald	16	c sub (J.N.Rhodes) b Donald	4
Ali Naqvi	c Kirsten b Donald	115	c Richardson b Kallis	19
Mohammad Ramzan	lbw b Pollock	29	c Cronje b Kallis	7
Ijaz Ahmed	b Symcox	11	b Symcox	16
Inzamam-ul-Haq	c Richardson b Schultz	8	c Symcox b Cronje	56
Mohammad Wasim	c Kirsten b Symcox	11	c Pollock b Symcox	10
†Moin Khan	lbw b Donald	12	(8) not out	6
Azhar Mahmood	not out	128	(7) not out	50
Saqlain Mushtaq	lbw b Pollock	0		
Waqar Younis	lbw b Pollock	45		
Mushtaq Ahmed	b Cronje	59		
Extras	(B 2, LB 7, NB 13)	22	(B 2, LB 2, NB 10)	14
Total		**456**	(6 wickets)	**182**

SOUTH AFRICA

G.Kirsten	c Ijaz b Saqlain	98
A.M.Bacher	c Ramzan b Saqlain	50
J.H.Kallis	lbw b Saqlain	61
D.J.Cullinan	lbw b Saqlain	16
*W.J.Cronje	c Ijaz b Azhar	24
B.M.McMillan	c Ijaz b Saqlain	7
S.M.Pollock	c Wasim b Azhar	48
†D.J.Richardson	not out	45
P.L.Symcox	st Wasim b Mushtaq Ahmed	5
A.A.Donald	c Saeed b Mushtaq Ahmed	0
B.N.Schultz	lbw b Mushtaq Ahmed	1
Extras	(B 20, LB 9, W 4, NB 15)	48
Total		**403**

SOUTH AFRICA	O	M	R	W	O	M	R	W		FALL OF WICKETS		
										P	SA	P
Donald	33	3	108	3	11	4	25	1		1st	1st	2nd
Schultz	15	4	58	1					Wkt	45	107	5
Pollock	37	13	74	3 (2)	8	1	22	0	1st	45	107	5
McMillan	17	5	36	0 (3)	8	1	24	0	2nd	114	221	33
Symcox	46	12	130	2	16	2	56	2	3rd	135	228	42
Kallis	7	3	15	0 (4)	7.4	1	21	2	4th	152	249	66
Cronje	7.4	0	26	1 (6)	6	1	28	1	5th	196	278	80
Cullinan					1	0	2	0	6th	206	282	148
									7th	230	388	–
PAKISTAN									8th	231	393	–
Waqar Younis	20	8	45	0					9th	305	399	–
Azhar Mahmood	27	1	74	2					10th	456	403	–
Mushtaq Ahmed	58.5	16	126	3								
Saqlain Mushtaq	62	13	129	5								

Umpires: Javed Akhtar (14) and S.Venkataraghavan (*India*) (22).
Referee: R.S.Madugalle (*Sri Lanka*) (8).   **Test No. 1380/2 (P 238/SA 210)**

PAKISTAN v SOUTH AFRICA (2nd Test)

At Sheikhupura Stadium on 17, 18, 19, 20, 21 October 1997.
Toss: South Africa. Result: **MATCH DRAWN.**
Debuts: Pakistan – Ali Rizvi; South Africa – M.V.Boucher.

SOUTH AFRICA

G.Kirsten	b Wasim Akram	56
A.M.Bacher	c Moin b Mushtaq Ahmed	96
B.M.McMillan	c Moin b Mushtaq Ahmed	7
D.J.Cullinan	c Mohammad Wasim b Saqlain	1
*W.J.Cronje	c sub‡ b Mushtaq Ahmed	50
J.N.Rhodes	b Mushtaq Ahmed	11
S.M.Pollock	c Naqvi b Rizvi	82
L.Klusener	lbw b Azhar	58
†M.V.Boucher	b Azhar	6
P.L.Symcox	c Mohammad Wasim b Rizvi	17
P.R.Adams	not out	3
Extras	(B 7, LB 3, NB 5)	15
Total		**402**

PAKISTAN

Ali Naqvi	not out	30
*Saeed Anwar	b Symcox	17
Saqlain Mushtaq	not out	0
Ijaz Ahmed		
Inzamam-ul-Haq		
Mohammad Wasim		
Azhar Mahmood		
Wasim Akram		
†Moin Khan		
Mushtaq Ahmed		
Ali Rizvi		
Extras	(B 4, NB 2)	6
Total	(1 wicket)	**53**

PAKISTAN	O	M	R	W
Wasim Akram	13	3	26	1
Azhar Mahmood	14	3	52	2
Mushtaq Ahmed	38	12	122	4
Saqlain Mushtaq	32	6	120	1
Ali Rizvi	18.3	1	72	2

SOUTH AFRICA				
Pollock	7	1	35	0
Klusener	6	1	14	0
Adams	2	2	0	0
Symcox	2	2	0	1

FALL OF WICKETS

	P	SA
Wkt	1st	1st
1st	135	53
2nd	152	–
3rd	155	–
4th	179	–
5th	215	–
6th	252	–
7th	348	–
8th	356	–
9th	397	–
10th	402	–

Umpires: K.T.Francis (*Sri Lanka*) (20) and Mohammad Nazir jr (1). ‡ (Waqar Younis)
Referee: R.S.Madugalle (*Sri Lanka*) (9).   **Test No. 1381//3 (P 239/SA 211)**

PAKISTAN v SOUTH AFRICA (3rd Test)

At Iqbal Stadium, Faisalabad on 24, 25, 26, 27 October 1997.
Toss: South Africa. Result: **SOUTH AFRICA** won by 53 runs.
Debuts: None.

SOUTH AFRICA

Batsman	1st innings	R		2nd innings	R
G.Kirsten	not out	100	(2)	c Mushtaq Ahmed b Wasim	4
A.M.Bacher	c sub‡ b Wasim	1	(1)	lbw b Mushtaq Ahmed	14
B.M.McMillan	c sub‡ b Wasim	2		c Moin b Mushtaq Ahmed	21
D.J.Cullinan	lbw b Waqar	0	(5)	lbw b Mushtaq Ahmed	15
*W.J.Cronje	lbw b Waqar	9	(6)	c Azhar b Waqar	21
S.M.Pollock	c Aamir b Mushtaq Ahmed	5	(7)	not out	21
†D.J.Richardson	c Saqlain b Mushtaq Ahmed	8	(8)	lbw b Waqar	0
L.Klusener	c Ijaz b Mushtaq Ahmed	18	(3)	lbw b Saqlain	38
P.L.Symcox	b Wasim	81	(4)	lbw b Saqlain	55
A.A.Donald	c Mushtaq Ahmed b Wasim	2		b Saqlain	8
P.R.Adams	lbw b Azhar	1		c Saeed b Mushtaq Ahmed	0
Extras	(B 4, LB 3, NB 5)	12		(B 3, LB 13, NB 1)	17
Total		**239**			**214**

PAKISTAN

Batsman	1st innings	R		2nd innings	R
Ali Naqvi	b Donald	11		c Cullinan b Pollock	6
*Saeed Anwar	lbw b Pollock	3	(3)	c Richardson b Pollock	0
Ijaz Ahmed	lbw b Adams	16	(4)	lbw b Pollock	0
Inzamam-ul-Haq	c McMillan b Cronje	96	(5)	c McMillan b Pollock	5
Azhar Mahmood	b Klusener	19	(6)	c Richardson b Klusener	0
Wasim Akram	c Richardson b Klusener	2	(8)	c Kirsten b Symcox	9
†Moin Khan	b Cronje	80		c Donald b Symcox	32
Aamir Sohail	c Donald b Pollock	38	(2)	c Bacher b Donald	14
Saqlain Mushtaq	c Bacher b Adams	6		c Bacher b Symcox	0
Waqar Younis	c Cronje b Donald	34		b Pollock	0
Mushtaq Ahmed	not out	0		not out	4
Extras	(LB 1, W 1, NB 1)	3		(B 4, LB 6, W 1, NB 5)	16
Total		**308**			**92**

PAKISTAN	O	M	R	W	O	M	R	W
Wasim Akram	16	6	42	4	11	0	46	1
Waqar Younis	10	1	36	2	14	2	43	2
Mushtaq Ahmed	22	3	81	3	22	6	57	4
Azhar Mahmood	10.4	2	36	1	(5) 7	2	16	0
Saqlain Mushtaq	10	2	37	0	(4)15	6	36	3
SOUTH AFRICA								
Donald	17.4	1	79	2	(4) 6	1	14	1
Pollock	20	5	64	2	(3)11	1	37	5
Adams	23	5	69	2	(1) 5	2	10	0
Symcox	9	2	39	0	9.3	5	8	3
Klusener	8	1	30	2	6	1	13	1
McMillan	7	1	20	0				
Cronje	5	3	6	2				

FALL OF WICKETS

	S	P	SA	P
Wkt	1st	1st	2nd	2nd
1st	2	10	16	23
2nd	11	18	21	24
3rd	12	42	63	24
4th	30	74	97	29
5th	40	80	140	31
6th	64	224	140	68
7th	98	229	140	85
8th	222	246	187	87
9th	230	304	201	88
10th	239	308	214	92

‡ (Mohammad Wasim)

Umpires: R.S.Dunne (*New Zealand*) (25) and Mian Mohammad Aslam (4).
Referee: R.S.Madugalle (*Sri Lanka*) (10). Test No. 1382/4 (P 240/SA 212)

PAKISTAN v SOUTH AFRICA 1997-98

PAKISTAN – BATTING AND FIELDING

	M	I	NO	HS	Runs	Avge	100	50	Ct/St
Azhar Mahmood	3	4	2	128*	203	101.50	1	1	1
Mushtaq Ahmed	3	3	2	59	63	63.00	–	1	2
Ali Naqvi	3	5	1	115	181	45.25	1	–	1
Moin Khan	3	4	1	80	130	43.33	–	1	3
Inzamam-ul-Haq	3	4	–	96	165	41.25	–	2	–
Waqar Younis	2	3	–	45	79	26.33	–	–	–
Ijaz Ahmed	3	4	–	16	43	10.75	–	–	4
Mohammad Wasim	2	2	–	11	21	10.50	–	–	3/1
Saeed Anwar	3	5	–	17	40	8.00	–	–	2
Wasim Akram	2	2	–	9	11	5.50	–	–	–
Saqlain Mushtaq	3	4	1	6	6	2.00	–	–	1

Played in one Test: Aamir Sohail 38, 14 (1 ct); Ali Rizvi did not bat; Mohammad Ramzan 29, 7 (1 ct).

PAKISTAN – BOWLING

	O	M	R	W	Avge	Best	5wI	10wM
Wasim Akram	40	9	114	6	19.00	4- 42	–	–
Mushtaq Ahmed	140.5	37	386	14	27.57	4- 57	–	–
Waqar Younis	44	11	124	4	31.00	2- 36	–	–
Azhar Mahmood	58.4	8	178	5	35.60	2- 52	–	–
Saqlain Mushtaq	119	27	322	9	35.77	5-129	1	–

Also bowled: Ali Rizvi 18.3-1-72-2.

SOUTH AFRICA – BATTING AND FIELDING

	M	I	NO	HS	Runs	Avge	100	50	Ct/St
G.Kirsten	3	4	1	100*	258	86.00	1	2	3
S.M.Pollock	3	4	1	82	156	52.00	–	1	1
A.M.Bacher	3	4	–	96	161	40.25	–	2	3
P.L.Symcox	3	4	–	81	158	39.50	–	2	1
L.Klusener	2	3	–	58	114	38.00	–	1	–
D.J.Richardson	2	3	1	45*	53	26.50	–	–	6
W.J.Cronje	3	4	–	50	104	26.00	–	1	2
B.M.McMillan	3	3	–	21	37	9.25	–	–	2
D.J.Cullinan	3	4	–	16	32	8.00	–	–	1
A.A.Donald	2	3	–	8	10	3.33	–	–	2
P.R.Adams	2	3	1	3*	4	2.00	–	–	–

Played in one Test: M.V.Boucher 6; J.H.Kallis 61; J.N.Rhodes 11; B.N.Schultz 1.

SOUTH AFRICA – BOWLING

	O	M	R	W	Avge	Best	5wI	10wM
W.J.Cronje	18.4	4	60	4	15.00	2- 6	–	–
L.Klusener	20	3	57	3	19.00	2- 30	–	–
S.M.Pollock	83	21	232	10	23.20	5- 37	1	–
P.L.Symcox	82.3	23	233	8	29.12	3- 8	–	–
A.A.Donald	67.4	9	226	7	32.28	3-108	–	–

Also bowled: P.R.Adams 30-9-79-2; D.J.Cullinan 1-0-2-0; J.H.Kallis 14.4-4-36-2; B.M.McMillan 32-7-80-0; B.N.Schultz 15-4-58-1.

AUSTRALIA v NEW ZEALAND (1st Test)

At Woolloongabba, Brisbane on 7, 8, 9, 10, 11 November 1997.
Toss: New Zealand. Result: **AUSTRALIA** won by 186 runs.
Debuts: New Zealand – C.D.McMillan.

AUSTRALIA

*M.A.Taylor	c Young b Doull	112	(2)	c Astle b Cairns	16
M.T.G.Elliott	c Young b Cairns	18	(1)	c Fleming b Vettori	11
G.S.Blewett	c Vettori b Cairns	7	(4)	c Fleming b Cairns	91
M.E.Waugh	c Vettori b Cairns	3	(5)	c Fleming b Vettori	17
S.R.Waugh	lbw b Cairns	2	(6)	c Parore b Cairns	23
R.T.Ponting	c Pocock b Doull	26	(7)	not out	73
†I.A.Healy	b Doull	68	(3)	c Fleming b Allott	25
P.R.Reiffel	c Parore b Allott	77		not out	28
S.K.Warne	c Fleming b Vettori	21			
M.S.Kasprowicz	not out	13			
G.D.McGrath	c Fleming b Doull	6			
Extras	(B 4, LB 9, W 1, NB 6)	20		(B 1, LB 4, NB 5)	10
Total		**373**		(6 wickets declared)	**294**

NEW ZEALAND

B.A.Young	c Taylor b Kasprowicz	1	(2)	lbw b McGrath	45
B.A.Pocock	c Taylor b Warne	57	(1)	c Taylor b Reiffel	3
N.J.Astle	run out	12		c Blewett b McGrath	14
*S.P.Fleming	lbw b Kasprowicz	91		c Healy b Reiffel	0
D.L.Vettori	c S.R.Waugh b Blewett	14	(9)	c Taylor b Warne	0
C.D.McMillan	lbw b Warne	54	(3)	lbw b McGrath	0
C.L.Cairns	b McGrath	64	(6)	b Reiffel	21
†A.C.Parore	c Taylor b Warne	12	(7)	not out	39
C.Z.Harris	b Warne	13	(8)	b Warne	0
S.B.Doull	not out	2		c Healy b McGrath	2
G.I.Allott	c Elliott b McGrath	4		lbw b Warne	0
Extras	(B 4, LB 4, NB 17)	25		(LB 2, NB 6)	8
Total		**349**			**132**

NEW ZEALAND	O	M	R	W	O	M	R	W
Doull	30	6	70	4	19	5	44	0
Allott	31	3	117	1	19.5	4	60	1
Cairns	24	5	90	4	16	4	54	3
Vettori	21	5	46	1	36	13	87	2
Astle	11	2	20	0	(6) 1	0	14	0
Harris	4	1	17	0	(5) 9	0	30	0

AUSTRALIA	O	M	R	W	O	M	R	W
McGrath	32.2	6	96	2	17	6	32	5
Kasprowicz	24	6	57	2	8	1	17	0
Warne	42	13	106	4	(4) 25	6	54	3
Reiffel	21	6	53	0	(3) 12	4	27	2
M.E.Waugh	7	2	18	0				
Blewett	6	2	11	1				

FALL OF WICKETS

Wkt	A 1st	NZ 1st	A 2nd	NZ 2nd
1st	27	2	24	4
2nd	46	36	36	55
3rd	50	134	72	68
4th	52	173	105	68
5th	108	210	163	69
6th	225	299	217	112
7th	294	317	–	115
8th	349	343	–	117
9th	359	343	–	126
10th	373	349	–	132

Umpires: V.K.Ramaswamy (*India*) (21) and S.G.Randell (31).
Referee: C.W.Smith (*West Indies*) (15). **Test No. 1383/33 (A 573/NZ 255)**

AUSTRALIA v NEW ZEALAND (2nd Test)

At WACA Ground, Perth on 20, 21, 22, 23 November 1997.
Toss: New Zealand. Result: **AUSTRALIA** won by an innings and 70 runs.
Debuts: Australia – S.H.Cook.

NEW ZEALAND

B.A.Young	c S.R.Waugh b Kasprowicz	9	(2)	run out	23
B.A.Pocock	c Healy b Cook	15	(1)	c Blewett b Kasprowicz	1
†A.C.Parore	c Blewett b Reiffel	30		lbw b Kasprowicz	63
*S.P.Fleming	c Blewett b Warne	10	(5)	c Blewett b Warne	4
N.J.Astle	c Healy b Reiffel	12	(6)	lbw b Cook	19
C.D.McMillan	c Taylor b Kasprowicz	54	(7)	lbw b Cook	23
C.L.Cairns	c M.E.Waugh b Warne	52	(8)	b Cook	7
D.L.Vettori	not out	14	(4)	c Taylor b Warne	7
S.B.Doull	c Taylor b Warne	8		c S.R.Waugh b Cook	17
S.B.O'Connor	c S.R.Waugh b Cook	7		c Taylor b Cook	7
G.I.Allott	b Warne	0		not out	2
Extras	(LB 3, NB 3)	6		(LB 2, NB 5)	7
Total		**217**			**174**

AUSTRALIA

*M.A.Taylor	lbw b O'Connor	2
M.T.G.Elliott	c O'Connor b Cairns	42
G.S.Blewett	c Astle b O'Connor	14
M.E.Waugh	c Parore b Doull	86
S.R.Waugh	b O'Connor	96
†I.A.Healy	c Fleming b Cairns	85
R.T.Ponting	c Fleming b Cairns	16
P.R.Reiffel	c Fleming b Cairns	54
S.K.Warne	c O'Connor b Vettori	36
M.S.Kasprowicz	run out	9
S.H.Cook	not out	3
Extras	(B 6, LB 5, NB 7)	18
Total		**461**

AUSTRALIA	O	M	R	W		O	M	R	W	FALL OF WICKETS			
Kasprowicz	20	9	40	2		16	5	43	2		NZ	A	NZ
Reiffel	20	6	46	2		12	4	26	0	*Wkt*	*1st*	*1st*	*2nd*
Cook	10	5	36	2	(4)	10.2	3	39	5	1st	12	3	2
Warne	22.4	3	83	4	(3)	26	4	64	2	2nd	31	53	53
Blewett	2	1	9	0						3rd	51	71	55
										4th	72	224	84
NEW ZEALAND										5th	87	262	102
Doull	21	3	78	1						6th	161	287	137
O'Connor	31.4	7	109	3						7th	187	403	145
Cairns	28	9	95	4						8th	197	449	160
Vettori	29	7	84	1						9th	214	450	165
Allott	22	3	84	0						10th	217	461	174

Umpires: D.B.Hair (21) and G.Sharp (*England*) (5).
Referee: C.W.Smith (*West Indies*) (16).   Test No. 1384/34 (A 574/NZ 256)

AUSTRALIA v NEW ZEALAND (3rd Test)

At Bellerive Oval, Hobart on 27, 28, 29, 30 November, 1 December 1997.
Toss: Australia. Result: **MATCH DRAWN**.
Debuts: None.

AUSTRALIA

M.T.G.Elliott	c Young b McMillan	114			
*M.A.Taylor	b O'Connor	18	(1)	not out	66
G.S.Blewett	b Doull	99		b Vettori	56
M.E.Waugh	c Parore b O'Connor	81	(2)	lbw b O'Connor	9
S.R.Waugh	c McMillan b Doull	7	(4)	not out	2
R.T.Ponting	c Parore b Cairns	4			
†I.A.Healy	c Young b O'Connor	16			
P.R.Reiffel	c Young b Doull	19			
S.K.Warne	st Parore b Vettori	14			
M.S.Kasprowicz	c Doull b Cairns	20			
S.H.Cook	not out	0			
Extras	(LB 6, W 1, NB 1)	8		(B 4, LB 1)	5
Total		**400**		(2 wickets declared)	**138**

NEW ZEALAND

B.A.Young	b Reiffel	31	(6)	c Ponting b Warne	10
M.J.Horne	c Elliott b Reiffel	133	(1)	lbw b Reiffel	31
†A.C.Parore	lbw b S.R.Waugh	44	(7)	c Elliott b Warne	41
*S.P.Fleming	c Healy b S.R.Waugh	0		st Healy b Warne	0
R.G.Twose	lbw b Warne	2	(8)	run out	29
C.D.McMillan	lbw b S.R.Waugh	2	(5)	c Taylor b Warne	41
N.J.Astle	not out	22	(2)	c Ponting b Reiffel	40
C.L.Cairns	not out	10	(3)	st Healy b Warne	18
D.L.Vettori				c Healy b S.R.Waugh	3
S.B.Doull				not out	1
S.B.O'Connor				not out	0
Extras	(B 1, LB 2, NB 4)	7		(B 2, LB 7)	9
Total	(6 wickets declared)	**251**		(9 wickets)	**223**

NEW ZEALAND	O	M	R	W	O	M	R	W	FALL OF WICKETS				
Doull	33	11	87	3	8	1	28	0		A	NZ	A	NZ
O'Connor	34	8	101	3	9	2	32	1	*Wkt*	*1st*	*1st*	*2nd*	*2nd*
Cairns	35.1	13	86	2					1st	41	60	14	72
Astle	12	5	32	0	7	0	25	0	2nd	238	192	106	93
McMillan	15	4	43	1					3rd	238	192	–	93
Vettori	12	1	45	1	(3) 14	1	48	1	4th	246	195	–	95
									5th	266	198	–	137
AUSTRALIA									6th	291	229	–	152
Kasprowicz	13	1	43	0	3	0	33	0	7th	326	–	–	218
Reiffel	14	8	27	2	14	2	47	2	8th	353	–	–	221
Warne	27	4	81	1	28	6	88	5	9th	400	–	–	222
Cook	13	2	50	0	(5) 4	0	17	0	10th	400	–	–	–
M.E.Waugh	8	2	17	0	1	1	0	0					
Blewett	5	1	10	0									
S.R.Waugh	9	2	20	3	(6) 6	4	10	1					
Elliott	1	1	0	0									

Umpires: S.J.Davis (1) and R.B.Tiffin (*Zimbabwe*) (5).
Referee: C.W.Smith (*West Indies*) (17).   **Test No. 1385/35 (A 575/NZ 257)**

AUSTRALIA v NEW ZEALAND 1997-98

AUSTRALIA – BATTING AND FIELDING

	M	I	NO	HS	Runs	Avge	100	50	Ct/St
P.R.Reiffel	3	4	1	77	178	59.33	–	2	–
M.A.Taylor	3	5	1	112	214	53.50	1	1	10
G.S.Blewett	3	5	–	99	267	53.40	–	3	5
I.A.Healy	3	4	–	85	194	48.50	–	2	6/2
M.T.G.Elliott	3	4	–	114	185	46.25	1	–	4
R.T.Ponting	3	4	1	73*	119	39.66	–	1	2
M.E.Waugh	3	5	–	86	196	39.20	–	2	1
S.R.Waugh	3	5	1	96	130	32.50	–	1	4
S.K.Warne	3	3	–	36	71	23.66	–	–	–
M.S.Kasprowicz	3	3	1	20	42	21.00	–	–	–
S.H.Cook	2	2	2	3*	3	–	–	–	–

Played in one Test: G.D.McGrath 6.

AUSTRALIA – BOWLING

	O	M	R	W	Avge	Best	5wI	10wM
S.R.Waugh	15	6	30	4	7.50	3-20	–	–
G.D.McGrath	49.2	12	128	7	18.28	5-32	1	–
S.H.Cook	37.2	10	142	7	20.28	5-39	–	–
S.K.Warne	170.4	36	476	19	25.05	5-88	1	–
P.R.Reiffel	93	30	226	8	28.25	2-27	–	–
M.S.Kasprowicz	84	22	233	6	38.83	2-40	–	–

Also bowled: G.S.Blewett 13-4-30-1; M.T.G.Elliott 1-1-0-0; M.E.Waugh 21-5-54-0.

NEW ZEALAND – BATTING AND FIELDING

	M	I	NO	HS	Runs	Avge	100	50	Ct/St
A.C.Parore	3	6	1	63	229	45.80	–	1	5/1
C.L.Cairns	3	6	1	64	172	34.40	–	2	–
C.D.McMillan	3	6	–	54	174	29.00	–	2	1
N.J.Astle	3	6	1	40	119	23.80	–	–	2
B.A.Young	3	6	–	45	119	19.83	–	–	5
B.A.Pocock	2	4	–	57	76	19.00	–	1	1
S.P.Fleming	3	6	–	91	105	17.50	–	1	9
S.B.Doull	3	5	2	17	30	10.00	–	–	1
D.L.Vettori	3	5	1	14*	32	8.00	–	–	2
S.B.O'Connor	2	3	1	7	14	7.00	–	–	2
G.I.Allott	2	4	1	4	6	2.00	–	–	–

Played in one Test: C.Z.Harris 13, 0; M.J.Horne 133, 31; R.G.Twose 2, 29.

NEW ZEALAND – BOWLING

	O	M	R	W	Avge	Best	5wI	10wM
C.L.Cairns	103.1	31	325	13	25.00	4- 90	–	–
S.B.O'Connor	74.4	17	242	7	34.57	3-101	–	–
S.B.Doull	111	26	307	8	38.37	4- 70	–	–
D.L.Vettori	112	27	310	6	51.66	2- 87	–	–

Also bowled: G.I.Allott 72.5-10-261-2; N.J.Astle 31-7-91-0; C.Z.Harris 13-1-47-0; C.D.McMillan 15-4-43-1.

PAKISTAN v WEST INDIES (1st Test)

At Arbab Niaz Stadium, Peshawar on 17, 18, 19, 20 November 1997.
Toss: West Indies. Result: **PAKISTAN** won by an innings and 19 runs.
Debuts: Pakistan – Arshad Khan; West Indies – R.N.Lewis.

WEST INDIES

S.C.Williams	c Moin b Nazir	4	lbw b Wasim Akram	2
S.L.Campbell	lbw b Mushtaq	15	lbw b Wasim Akram	66
S.Chanderpaul	b Nazir	0	c Ijaz b Mushtaq	14
B.C.Lara	c Mushtaq b Wasim Akram	3	lbw b Azhar	37
C.L.Hooper	c Mohammad Wasim b Mushtaq	26	c sub‡ b Mushtaq	23
P.V.Simmons	b Mushtaq	1	c Wasim Akram b Mushtaq	1
†D.Williams	b Azhar	31	c Ijaz b Mushtaq	20
R.N.Lewis	b Mushtaq	4	lbw b Wasim Akram	0
I.R.Bishop	b Azhar	20	lbw b Wasim Akram	21
C.E.L.Ambrose	lbw b Mushtaq	30	st Mohammad Wasim b Mushtaq	6
*C.A.Walsh	not out	9	not out	6
Extras	(LB 6, NB 2)	8	(B 9, LB 4, NB 7)	20
Total		**151**		**211**

PAKISTAN

Saeed Anwar	c D.Williams b Hooper	65
Aamir Sohail	c Lara b Walsh	4
Ijaz Ahmed	c Hooper b Bishop	65
Mohammad Wasim	b Walsh	28
Inzamam-ul-Haq	not out	92
†Moin Khan	c Walsh b Bishop	58
*Wasim Akram	st D.Williams b Hooper	5
Azhar Mahmood	c Hooper b Walsh	16
Arshad Khan	c Lara b Bishop	4
Shahid Nazir	b Walsh	18
Mushtaq Ahmed	b Walsh	4
Extras	(B 2, LB 7, W 2, NB 11)	22
Total		**381**

PAKISTAN	O	M	R	W	O	M	R	W
Wasim Akram	14	5	29	1	23.2	5	65	4
Shahid Nazir	10	1	32	2	7.5	1	27	0
Azhar Mahmood	14	2	35	2	10.1	1	17	1
Mushtaq Ahmed	18.3	7	35	5	23	5	71	5
Arshad Khan	4	1	14	0	6	2	18	0

WEST INDIES	O	M	R	W
Ambrose	25	4	76	0
Walsh	32	9	78	5
Bishop	29	6	76	3
Simmons	2	0	9	0
Lewis	24	6	93	0
Hooper	20	7	40	2

FALL OF WICKETS

	WI	P	WI
Wkt	1st	1st	2nd
1st	9	10	14
2nd	9	143	56
3rd	16	145	102
4th	29	193	145
5th	45	207	147
6th	50	250	163
7th	58	294	167
8th	106	304	195
9th	129	347	201
10th	151	381	211

Umpires: Said Shah (1) and D.R.Shepherd (*England*) (37).   ‡ (Saqlain Mushtaq)
Referee: R.Subba Row (*England*) (22).   **Test No. 1386/32 (P 241/WI 335)**

PAKISTAN v WEST INDIES (2nd Test)

At Rawalpindi Cricket Stadium on 29, 30 November, 1, 2, 3 December 1997.
Toss: Pakistan. Result: **PAKISTAN** won by an innings and 29 runs.
Debuts: Pakistan – Shoaib Akhtar; West Indies – P.A.Wallace.

WEST INDIES

S.L.Campbell	c Shoaib b Azhar	78		b Mushtaq	34
P.A.Wallace	lbw b Wasim Akram	5		lbw b Waqar	8
S.C.Williams	c Mushtaq b Waqar	8		c Azhar b Wasim Akram	1
B.C.Lara	b Waqar	15		c and b Wasim Akram	1
C.L.Hooper	c Moin b Azhar	0		not out	73
S.Chanderpaul	lbw b Waqar	95		lbw b Wasim Akram	7
†D.Williams	c Moin b Shoaib	48		run out	0
I.R.Bishop	b Shoaib	10		run out	2
C.E.L.Ambrose	not out	10	(11)	b Waqar	0
F.A.Rose	b Azhar	7	(9)	c Mushtaq b Wasim Akram	6
*C.A.Walsh	lbw b Azhar	0	(10)	run out	0
Extras	(B1, LB 16, W 3, NB 7)	27		(NB 7)	7
Total		**303**			**139**

PAKISTAN

Saeed Anwar	c D.Williams b Ambrose	16
Aamir Sohail	c sub (P.V.Simmons) b Walsh	160
Ijaz Ahmed	c Wallace b Rose	10
Inzamam-ul-Haq	c Campbell b Walsh	177
Mohammad Wasim	c Hooper b Walsh	26
*Moin Khan	c D.Williams b Rose	1
Azhar Mahmood	c D.Williams b Rose	14
*Wasim Akram	b Bishop	11
Waqar Younis	lbw b Walsh	2
Shoaib Akhtar	c Hooper b Walsh	1
Mushtaq Ahmed	not out	0
Extras	(B 13, LB 9, W 6, NB 25)	53
Total		**471**

PAKISTAN	O	M	R	W	O	M	R	W	FALL OF WICKETS			
										WI	P	WI
Wasim Akram	22	6	40	1	14	5	42	4	*Wkt*	*1st*	*1st*	*2nd*
Waqar Younis	27	3	99	3	12	0	44	2	1st	15	41	9
Shoaib Akhtar	15	2	47	2	7	2	21	0	2nd	37	64	10
Azhar Mahmood	20.5	7	53	4	2	1	4	0	3rd	53	387	26
Mushtaq Ahmed	17	3	47	0	6	3	28	1	4th	58	414	67
									5th	205	415	98
WEST INDIES									6th	249	437	98
Walsh	43.1	6	143	5					7th	264	459	112
Ambrose	19	2	63	1					8th	291	469	126
Bishop	24	3	80	1					9th	303	469	138
Rose	33	7	92	3					10th	303	471	139
Hooper	17	1	71	0								

Umpires: Javed Akhtar (15) and D.R.Shepherd (*England*) (38).
Referee: R.Subba Row (*England*) (23).   **Test No. 1387/33 (P 242/WI 336)**

PAKISTAN v WEST INDIES (3rd Test)

At National Stadium, Karachi on 6, 7, 8, 9 December 1997.
Toss: West Indies. Result: **PAKISTAN** won by 10 wickets.
Debuts: None.

WEST INDIES

S.L.Campbell	c Wasim b Saqlain	50		c Inzamam b Waqar	5
S.C.Williams	run out	33		lbw b Waqar	12
B.C.Lara	b Saqlain	36		c Mohammad Wasim b Saqlain	37
C.L.Hooper	lbw b Mushtaq Ahmed	0		b Wasim Akram	106
S.Chanderpaul	lbw b Wasim Akram	21		c Moin b Saqlain	16
R.I.C.Holder	b Saqlain	26		c Aamir b Saqlain	5
†D.Williams	not out	22		b Saqlain	2
I.R.Bishop	st Moin b Saqlain	2	(9)	not out	6
F.A.Rose	lbw b Wasim Akram	13	(8)	c Moin b Wasim Akram	5
*C.A.Walsh	c Inzamam b Saqlain	1		b Wasim Akram	0
M.V.Dillon	b Wasim Akram	0		lbw b Wasim Akram	4
Extras	(B 4, LB 7, NB 1)	12		(B 7, LB 2, NB 5)	14
Total		**216**			**212**

PAKISTAN

Aamir Sohail	lbw b Chanderpaul	160			
Ijaz Ahmed	c D.Williams b Dillon	151			
Saaed Anwar	c D.Williams b Dillon	15			
Inzamam-ul-Haq	lbw b Dillon	4			
Mohammad Wasim	lbw b Dillon	12	(1)	not out	0
†Moin Khan	b Walsh	5			
Azhar Mahmood	not out	26	(2)	not out	13
*Wasim Akram	lbw b Walsh	0			
Saqlain Mushtaq	c Lara b Walsh	0			
Mushtaq Ahmed	b Walsh	1			
Waqar Younis	c S.C.Williams b Dillon	12			
Extras	(B 3, LB 9, W 2, NB 17)	31		(NB 2)	2
Total		**417**		(0 wickets)	**15**

PAKISTAN	O	M	R	W	O	M	R	W	FALL OF WICKETS			
										WI	P	WI	P
Wasim Akram	17.1	2	76	3	16.4	7	42	4		*1st*	*1st*	*2nd*	*2nd*
Waqar Younis	9	3	21	0	6	0	31	2	*Wkt*				
Azhar Mahmood	10	3	14	0	3	0	32	0	1st	47	298	14	—
Mushtaq Ahmed	13	2	40	1	8	0	72	0	2nd	109	329	19	—
Saqlain Mushtaq	24	6	54	5	19	9	26	4	3rd	114	333	140	—
									4th	126	359	182	—
									5th	160	374	186	—
WEST INDIES									6th	188	388	191	—
Walsh	23	2	74	4	0	0	11	0	7th	194	390	193	—
Rose	12	1	44	0	2	0	4	0	8th	209	390	207	—
Dillon	29.4	4	111	5					9th	211	396	208	—
Bishop	15	0	68	0					10th	216	417	212	—
Hooper	32	10	74	0									
Chanderpaul	7	0	34	1									

Umpires: C.J.Mitchley (*South Africa*) (20) and Salim Badar (4).
Referee: R.Subba Row (*England*) (24).   **Test No. 1388/34 (P 243/WI 337)**

PAKISTAN v WEST INDIES 1997-98

PAKISTAN – BATTING AND FIELDING

	M	I	NO	HS	Runs	Avge	100	50	Ct/St
Inzamam-ul-Haq	3	3	1	177	273	136.50	1	1	2
Aamir Sohail	3	3	–	160	324	108.00	2	–	1
Ijaz Ahmed	3	3	–	151	226	75.33	1	1	2
Azhar Mahmood	3	4	2	26*	69	34.50	–	–	1
Saeed Anwar	3	3	–	65	96	32.00	–	1	–
Mohammad Wasim	3	4	1	28	66	22.00	–	–	2/1
Moin Khan	3	3	–	58	64	21.33	–	1	5/1
Waqar Younis	2	2	–	12	14	7.00	–	–	–
Wasim Akram	3	3	–	11	16	5.33	–	–	3
Mushtaq Ahmed	3	3	1	4	5	2.50	–	–	3

Played in one Test: Arshad Khan 4; Saqlain Mushtaq 0; Shahid Nazir 18; Shoaib Akhtar 1 (1 ct).

PAKISTAN – BOWLING

	O	M	R	W	Avge	Best	5wI	10wM
Saqlain Mushtaq	43	15	80	9	8.88	5-54	1	–
Wasim Akram	107.1	30	294	17	17.29	4-42	–	–
Azhar Mahmood	60	14	155	7	22.14	4-53	–	–
Mushtaq Ahmed	85.3	20	293	12	24.41	5-35	2	1
Waqar Younis	54	6	195	7	27.85	3-99	–	–

Also bowled: Arshad Khan 10-3-32-0; Shahid Nazir 17.5-2-59-2; Shoaib Akhtar 22-4-68-2.

WEST INDIES – BATTING AND FIELDING

	M	I	NO	HS	Runs	Avge	100	50	Ct/St
C.L.Hooper	3	6	1	106	228	45.60	1	1	4
S.L.Campbell	3	6	–	78	248	41.33	–	3	1
S.Chanderpaul	3	6	–	95	153	25.50	–	1	–
D.Williams	3	6	1	48	123	24.60	–	–	6/1
B.C.Lara	3	6	–	37	129	21.50	–	–	3
C.E.L.Ambrose	2	4	1	30	41	13.66	–	–	–
I.R.Bishop	3	6	1	21	61	12.20	–	–	–
S.C.Williams	3	6	–	33	60	10.00	–	–	1
F.A.Rose	2	4	–	13	31	7.75	–	–	–
C.A.Walsh	3	6	2	9*	16	4.00	–	–	1

Played in one Test: M.V.Dillon 0, 4; R.I.C.Holder 26, 5; R.N.Lewis 4, 0; P.V.Simmons 1, 1; P.A.Wallace 5, 8 (1 ct).

WEST INDIES – BOWLING

	O	M	R	W	Avge	Best	5wI	10wM
C.A.Walsh	101.1	17	306	14	21.85	5- 78	2	–
M.V.Dillon	29.4	4	111	5	22.20	5-111	1	–
F.A.Rose	47	8	140	3	46.66	3- 92	1	–
I.R.Bishop	68	9	224	6	37.33	3- 76	–	–

Also bowled: C.E.L.Ambrose 44-6-139-1; S.Chanderpaul 7-0-34-1; C.L.Hooper 69-18-185-2; R.N.Lewis 24-6-93-0; P.V.Simmons 2-0-9-0.

INDIA v SRI LANKA (1st Test)

At Punjab CA Stadium, Mohali, Chandigarh on 19, 20, 21, 22, 23 November 1997.
Toss: India. Result: **MATCH DRAWN.**
Debuts: Sri Lanka – S.K.L.de Silva.

SRI LANKA

S.T.Jayasuriya	c Chauhan b Srinath	53	c Mongia b Srinath		17
M.S.Atapattu	lbw b Srinath	108	c Chauhan b Kuruvilla		31
R.S.Mahanama	lbw b Kumble	42	lbw b Srinath		11
P.A.de Silva	b Kuruvilla	33	not out		110
*A.Ranatunga	c Chauhan b Srinath	30	c Dravid b Kuruvilla		3
H.P.Tillekeratne	c Dravid b Kumble	14	c Tendulkar b Chauhan		9
†S.K.L.de Silva	b Kuruvilla	5	(8) not out		11
H.D.P.K.Dharmasena	not out	37	(7) b Srinath		25
W.P.U.C.J.Vaas	b Kuruvilla	2			
M.Muralitharan	c Srinath b Kuruvilla	10			
K.S.C.de Silva	b Srinath	6			
Extras	(B 4, LB 13, NB 12)	29	(B 13, LB 9, NB 12)		34
Total		**369**	(6 wickets)		**251**

INDIA

†N.R.Mongia	b Muralitharan	57
N.S.Sidhu	run out	131
R.Dravid	c Ranatunga b Jayasuriya	34
*S.R.Tendulkar	c Dharmasena b Jayasuriya	23
M.Azharuddin	lbw b Vaas	53
S.C.Ganguly	c Tillekeratne b Vaas	109
A.Kumble	c Dharmasena b Muralitharan	22
J.Srinath	c Mahanama b K.S.C.de Silva	6
R.K.Chauhan	c Dharmasena b Muralitharan	4
A.Kuruvilla	not out	35
D.S.Mohanty		
Extras	(B 19, LB 10, W 6, NB 8)	43
Total	(9 wickets declared)	**515**

INDIA	O	M	R	W	O	M	R	W
Srinath	27.2	4	92	4	22	3	75	3
Kuruvilla	27	7	88	4	(3)15.1	4	29	2
Mohanty	19	1	57	0	(2)16	4	32	0
Kumble	34	8	81	2	19	5	66	0
Ganguly	2	2	0	0	(6) 2	2	0	0
Chauhan	16	2	34	0	(5)18	11	23	1
Azharuddin					1	0	4	0

SRI LANKA	O	M	R	W
Vaas	36.5	11	107	2
K.S.C.de Silva	28	5	81	1
Dharmasena	34	11	65	0
Muralitharan	75	30	174	3
Jayasuriya	30	9	59	2
Ranatunga	3	3	0	0

FALL OF WICKETS

	SL	I	SL
Wkt	1st	1st	2nd
1st	98	120	22
2nd	202	214	40
3rd	254	259	67
4th	254	274	82
5th	301	353	106
6th	307	400	209
7th	307	419	–
8th	313	426	–
9th	333	515	–
10th	369	–	–

Umpires: S.A.Bucknor (*West Indies*) (31) and S.Venkataraghavan (23).
Referee: R.B.Simpson (*Australia*) (1).   **Test No. 1389/17 (I 313/SL 77)**

INDIA v SRI LANKA (2nd Test)

At Vidarbha CA Ground, Nagpur on 26, 27, 28, 29 (*no play*), 30 (*no play*) November 1997.
Toss: India. Result: **MATCH DRAWN**.
Debuts: None.

INDIA

†N.R.Mongia	c Muralitharan b Pushpakumara	11
N.S.Sidhu	c Atapattu b Vaas	79
R.Dravid	c Atapattu b Vaas	92
*S.R.Tendulkar	b Pushpakumara	15
M.Azharuddin	lbw b Pushpakumara	62
S.C.Ganguly	c Tillekeratne b Pushpakumara	99
A.Kumble	run out	78
J.Srinath	lbw b Jayasuriya	11
R.K.Chauhan	c Vaas b Jayasuriya	1
A.Kuruvilla	lbw b Pushpakumara	0
N.M.Kulkarni	not out	1
Extras	(B 8, LB 13, W 3, NB 12)	36
Total		**485**

SRI LANKA

S.T.Jayasuriya
M.S.Atapattu
R.S.Mahanama
P.A.de Silva
*A.Ranatunga
H.P.Tillekeratne
†S.K.L.de Silva
W.P.U.C.J.Vaas
K.R.Pushpakumara
M.Muralitharan
K.J.Silva

SRI LANKA	O	M	R	W
Vaas	31	3	80	2
Pushpakumara	32	3	122	5
Silva	28	6	81	0
Muralitharan	46	8	137	0
Ranatunga	1	0	8	0
Jayasuriya	16	4	32	2
Atapattu	1	0	4	0

FALL OF WICKETS

	I
Wkt	*1st*
1st	15
2nd	152
3rd	182
4th	272
5th	303
6th	462
7th	476
8th	484
9th	484
10th	485

Umpires: C.J.Mitchley (*South Africa*) (21) and V.K.Ramaswamy (22).
Referee: R.B.Simpson (*Australia*) (2).   **Test No. 1390/18 (I 314/SL 78)**

INDIA v SRI LANKA (3rd Test)

At Wankhede Stadium, Bombay on 3, 4, 5, 6, 7 December 1997.
Toss: Sri Lanka. Result: **MATCH DRAWN**.
Debuts: None.

INDIA

†N.R.Mongia	b Wickremasinghe	1	(6)	not out	9
N.S.Sidhu	c Mahanama b Dharmasena	35		c Pushpakumara b Jayasuriya	43
R.Dravid	c Mahanama b Ranatunga	93		c P.A.de Silva b Dharmasena	85
S.C.Ganguly	c S.K.L.de Silva b Dharmasena	173	(1)	c Tillekeratne b Wickremasinghe	11
*S.R.Tendulkar	b Pushpakumara	148	(4)	c P.A.de Silva b Jayasuriya	13
M.Azharuddin	lbw b Pushpakumara	0	(5)	c P.A.de Silva b Dharmasena	4
A.Kumble	b Pushpakumara	6		c Mahanama b Dharmasena	1
R.K.Chauhan	lbw b Dharmasena	4	(9)	run out	0
A.Kuruvilla	c Pushpakumara b Wickremasinghe	6	(10)	c P.A.de Silva b Dharmasena	0
J.Srinath	not out	15	(8)	c sub‡ b Dharmasena	5
B.K.V.Prasad	run out	3			
Extras	(B 3, LB 15, W 4, NB 6)	28		(B 3, LB 6, NB 1)	10
Total		**512**		(9 wickets declared)	**181**

SRI LANKA

S.T.Jayasuriya	c Azharuddin b Kumble	50		c Tendulkar b Kumble	37
M.S.Atapattu	c sub (A.Jadeja) b Chauhan	98		c Kumble b Chauhan	31
H.D.P.K.Dharmasena	c Kumble b Chauhan	40	(6)	c Azharuddin b Kumble	8
R.S.Mahanama	c Kumble b Prasad	20	(3)	lbw b Chauhan	35
P.A.de Silva	c Mongia b Chauhan	66	(4)	c Chauhan b Srinath	18
*A.Ranatunga	c Azharuddin b Chauhan	1	(5)	b Chauhan	12
H.P.Tillekeratne	lbw b Kuruvilla	25		not out	18
†S.K.L.de Silva	retired hurt	20		c Prasad b Kumble	0
W.P.U.C.J.Vaas	c sub (N.M.Kulkarni) b Kuruvilla	4		not out	0
G.P.Wickremasinghe	b Srinath	2			
K.R.Pushpakumara	not out	0			
Extras	(B 7, LB 12, W 4, NB 12)	35		(LB 2, NB 5)	7
Total		**361**		(7 wickets)	**166**

SRI LANKA	O	M	R	W	O	M	R	W	FALL OF WICKETS			
										I	SL	I	SL
Vaas	26	4	86	0	5	1	19	0				
Wickremasinghe	31.1	10	76	2	5	0	20	1	*Wkt*	*1st*	*1st*	*2nd*	*2nd*
Pushpakumara	28	5	108	3	5	0	28	0	1st	1	65	15	58
Dharmasena	48	11	144	3	(5)12.4	0	57	5	2nd	55	180	103	73
Ranatunga	17	7	35	1					3rd	215	219	136	106
Jayasuriya	12	2	45	0	(4)15	1	48	2	4th	471	259	149	133
									5th	475	269	173	146
INDIA									6th	476	312	175	160
Srinath	28.2	4	107	1	15	5	25	1	7th	481	351	181	166
Prasad	18	6	30	1	8	3	23	0	8th	487	359	181	
Kuruvilla	19	2	62	2	(4) 3	2	1	0	9th	502	361	181	
Kumble	41	19	76	1	(5)28	12	56	3	10th	512			
Chauhan	34	13	48	4	(3)26	9	59	3					
Ganguly	3	0	19	0									
Tendulkar					(6) 2	0	10	0					

‡ (D.R.M.Jayawardene)

Umpires: S.A.Bucknor (*West Indies*) (32) and A.V.Jayaprakash (1).
Referee: R.B.Simpson (*Australia*) (3).   **Test No. 1391/19 (I 315/SL 79)**

INDIA v SRI LANKA 1997-98

INDIA – BATTING AND FIELDING

	M	I	NO	HS	Runs	Avge	100	50	Ct/St
S.C.Ganguly	3	4	–	173	392	98.00	2	1	–
R.Dravid	3	4	–	93	304	76.00	–	3	2
N.S.Sidhu	3	4	–	131	288	72.00	1	1	–
S.R.Tendulkar	3	4	–	148	199	49.75	1	–	2
M.Azharuddin	3	4	–	62	119	29.75	–	2	3
A.Kumble	3	4	–	78	107	26.75	–	1	3
N.R.Mongia	3	4	1	57	78	26.00	–	1	2
A.Kuruvilla	3	4	1	35*	41	13.66	–	–	–
J.Srinath	3	4	1	15*	37	12.33	–	–	1
R.K.Chauhan	3	4	–	4	7	1.75	–	–	4

Played in one Test: N.M.Kulkarni 1*; D.S.Mohanty did not bat; B.K.V.Prasad 3 (1 ct).

INDIA – BOWLING

	O	M	R	W	Avge	Best	5wI	10wM
R.K.Chauhan	94	35	164	8	20.50	4-48	–	–
A.Kuruvilla	64.1	15	180	8	22.50	4-88	–	–
J.Srinath	92.4	16	299	9	33.22	4-92	–	–
A.Kumble	122	44	279	6	46.50	3-56	–	–

Also bowled: M.Azharuddin 1-0-4-0; S.C.Ganguly 7-4-19-0; D.S.Mohanty 35-5-89-0;
B.K.V.Prasad 26-9-53-1; S.R.Tendulkar 2-2-0-0.

SRI LANKA – BATTING AND FIELDING

	M	I	NO	HS	Runs	Avge	100	50	Ct/St
P.A.de Silva	3	4	1	110*	227	75.66	1	1	4
M.S.Atapattu	3	4	–	108	268	67.00	1	1	2
S.T.Jayasuriya	3	4	–	53	157	39.25	–	2	–
H.D.P.K.Dharmasena	2	4	1	40	110	36.66	–	–	3
R.S.Mahanama	3	4	–	42	108	27.00	–	–	4
H.P.Tillekeratne	3	4	1	25	66	22.00	–	–	3
S.K.L.de Silva	3	4	2	20*	36	18.00	–	–	1
A.Ranatunga	3	4	–	30	46	11.50	–	–	1
M.Muralitharan	2	1	–	10	10	10.00	–	–	1
W.P.U.C.J.Vaas	3	3	1	4	6	3.00	–	–	1
K.R.Pushpakumara	2	1	1	0*	0	–	–	–	2

Played in one Test: K.S.C.de Silva 6; K.J.Silva did not bat; G.P.Wickremasinghe 2.

SRI LANKA – BOWLING

	O	M	R	W	Avge	Best	5wI	10wM
S.T.Jayasuriya	73	16	184	6	30.66	2- 32	–	–
G.P.Wickremasinghe	36.1	10	96	3	32.00	2- 76	–	–
K.R.Pushpakumara	65	8	258	8	32.25	5-122	1	–
H.D.P.K.Dharmasena	94.4	22	266	8	33.25	5- 57	1	–
W.P.U.C.J.Vaas	98.5	19	292	4	73.00	2- 80	–	–
M.Muralitharan	121	38	311	3	103.66	3-174	–	–

Also bowled: M.S.Atapattu 1-0-4-0; K.S.C.de Silva 28-5-81-1; A.Ranatunga
21-10-43-1; K.J.Silva 28-6-81-0.

AUSTRALIA v SOUTH AFRICA (1st Test)

At Melbourne Cricket Ground on 26, 27, 28, 29, 30 December 1997.
Toss: Australia. **MATCH DRAWN**.
Debuts: None.

AUSTRALIA

M.T.G.Elliott	c Richardson b Klusener	6	(2)	lbw b Donald	1
*M.A.Taylor	c Kirsten b McMillan	20	(1)	c Cullinan b Symcox	59
G.S.Blewett	st Richardson b Symcox	26		c McMillan b Donald	6
M.E.Waugh	c Richardson b Donald	0		b Donald	1
S.R.Waugh	c Cullinan b Donald	96		c Richardson b Pollock	17
R.T.Ponting	b Symcox	105		c and b Pollock	32
†I.A.Healy	b Donald	16		b Donald	4
P.R.Reiffel	b Symcox	27		not out	79
S.K.Warne	c and b Pollock	1		c Symcox b Donald	10
M.S.Kasprowicz	c Bacher b Symcox	0		c Kirsten b Donald	19
G.D.McGrath	not out	0		c McMillan b Pollock	18
Extras	(B 1, LB 6, NB 5)	12		(B 4, LB 3, NB 4)	11
Total		**309**			**257**

SOUTH AFRICA

A.M.Bacher	c Healy b Kasprowicz	3	(2)	c Taylor b Warne	39
G.Kirsten	c Healy b M.E.Waugh	83	(1)	b Reiffel	0
J.H.Kallis	c Healy b McGrath	15		b Reiffel	101
D.J.Cullinan	run out	5		b Warne	0
*W.J.Cronje	c Blewett b Warne	0		c Taylor b S.R.Waugh	70
B.M.McMillan	c Healy b Kasprowicz	48		c Taylor b Warne	16
S.M.Pollock	lbw b Warne	7		not out	15
†D.J.Richardson	lbw b M.E.Waugh	1		lbw b McGrath	11
L.Klusener	lbw b Warne	11		not out	6
P.L.Symcox	b Kasprowicz	4			
A.A.Donald	not out	0			
Extras	(LB 2, W 1, NB 6)	9		(B 5, LB 4, NB 6)	15
Total		**186**		(7 wickets)	**273**

SOUTH AFRICA	O	M	R	W	O	M	R	W
Donald	29	6	74	3	27	8	59	6
Pollock	28	6	76	1	21.2	5	56	3
Klusener	19	3	48	1	(5) 9	2	28	0
McMillan	10	3	19	1	2	0	6	0
Symcox	27.2	4	69	4	(3)35	9	90	1
Kallis	4	2	5	0				
Cronje	4	2	11	0	(6) 2	0	11	0
AUSTRALIA								
McGrath	17	9	20	1	28	11	57	1
Reiffel	14	5	32	0	18	8	24	2
Kasprowicz	13.5	3	28	3	14	1	45	0
Warne	42	15	64	3	44	11	97	3
M.E.Waugh	18	8	28	2	10	0	25	0
S.R.Waugh	2	0	12	0	7	2	12	1
Blewett					1	0	4	0

FALL OF WICKETS

Wkt	1st A	1st SA	2nd A	2nd SA
1st	18	28	4	2
2nd	42	62	10	88
3rd	44	75	12	88
4th	77	76	44	211
5th	222	138	106	229
6th	250	155	128	241
7th	302	158	128	260
8th	309	182	146	–
9th	309	182	208	–
10th	309	186	257	–

Umpires: S.A.Bucknor (*West Indies*) (33) and S.G.Randell (32).
Referee: R.S.Madugalle (*Sri Lanka*) (11). **Test No. 1392/63 (A 576/SA 213)**

AUSTRALIA v SOUTH AFRICA (2nd Test)

At Sydney Cricket Ground on 2, 3, 4, 5 January 1998.
Toss: South Africa. Result: **AUSTRALIA** won by an innings and 21 runs.
Debuts: None.

SOUTH AFRICA

A.M.Bacher	lbw b Blewett	39	(2)	c Ponting b Reiffel	2
G.Kirsten	c Taylor b McGrath	11	(1)	lbw b McGrath	0
J.H.Kallis	run out	16		b Warne	45
*W.J.Cronje	c Taylor b Warne	88		c Ponting b Warne	5
H.H.Gibbs	c Healy b Warne	54		c Blewett b Warne	5
B.M.McMillan	c Elliott b Bevan	6		b Warne	11
S.M.Pollock	c Taylor b Warne	18		c Taylor b Warne	4
†D.J.Richardson	b Warne	6		c and b Warne	0
P.L.Symcox	c Healy b Warne	29		b Reiffel	38
A.A.Donald	not out	4		c Healy b Reiffel	2
P.R.Adams	c S.R.Waugh b Warne	0		not out	1
Extras	(B 4, LB 4, W 1, NB 7)	16		(B 2, LB 1, NB 1)	4
Total		**287**			**113**

AUSTRALIA

M.T.G.Elliott	c McMillan b Symcox	32
*M.A.Taylor	c Richardson b Pollock	11
G.S.Blewett	b McMillan	28
M.E.Waugh	lbw b Pollock	100
S.R.Waugh	b Donald	85
R.T.Ponting	c and b Adams	62
M.G.Bevan	c McMillan b Symcox	12
†I.A.Healy	not out	46
P.R.Reiffel	b Donald	0
S.K.Warne	lbw b Pollock	12
G.D.McGrath	c Richardson b Donald	14
Extras	(B 1, LB 12, NB 6)	19
Total		**421**

AUSTRALIA	O	M	R	W		O	M	R	W		FALL OF WICKETS		
McGrath	20	6	51	1	(2)	5	2	8	1		SA	A	SA
Reiffel	24	7	48	0	(1)	12	3	14	3	*Wkt*	*1st*	*1st*	*2nd*
Warne	32.1	8	75	5		21	9	34	6	1st	25	35	1
Bevan	23	3	56	2	(5)	3	0	18	0	2nd	70	59	3
Blewett	13	5	30	1	(4)	2	1	1	0	3rd	70	103	21
S.R.Waugh	8	4	10	0						4th	167	219	27
M.E.Waugh	3	1	5	0	(6)	10	2	35	0	5th	174	317	41
Elliott	1	0	4	0						6th	228	337	55
										7th	236	354	55
SOUTH AFRICA										8th	276	357	96
Donald	30.4	5	81	3						9th	287	385	112
Pollock	33	8	71	3						10th	287	421	113
Symcox	39	11	103	2									
Adams	38	9	66	1									
McMillan	18	5	55	1									
Kallis	8	1	30	0									
Cronje	1	0	2	0									

Umpires: D.B.Hair (22) and P.Willey (*England*) (8).
Referee: R.S.Madugalle (*Sri Lanka*) (12).   Test No. 1393/64 (A 577/SA 214)

AUSTRALIA v SOUTH AFRICA (3rd Test)

At Adelaide Oval on 30, 31 January, 1, 2, 3 February 1998.
Toss: South Africa. Result: **MATCH DRAWN**.
Debuts: Australia – S.C.G.MacGill.

SOUTH AFRICA

A.M.Bacher	c Warne b Bichel	64	(2)	c MacGill b Warne	41
G.Kirsten	c Warne b Kasprowicz	77	(1)	not out	108
J.H.Kallis	lbw b MacGill	15		b Kasprowicz	15
*W.J.Cronje	b Warne	73		c Warne b Kasprowicz	5
H.H.Gibbs	c Healy b Blewett	37	(7)	st Healy b MacGill	2
†D.J.Richardson	c Taylor b Warne	15			
J.N.Rhodes	c Bichel b Kasprowicz	6	(8)	not out	19
B.M.McMillan	not out	87			
S.M.Pollock	c Blewett b Kasprowicz	40			
L.Klusener	c Warne b MacGill	38	(5)	b MacGill	0
P.L.Symcox	lbw b S.R.Waugh	54	(6)	c Healy b MacGill	2
Extras	(LB 8, W 2, NB 1)	11		(NB 1)	1
Total		**517**		(6 wickets declared)	**193**

AUSTRALIA

*M.A.Taylor	not out	169	(2)	b Klusener	6
M.T.G.Elliott	c Kallis b Pollock	8	(1)	c Richardson b Pollock	4
G.S.Blewett	c Bacher b Pollock	31		b Pollock	16
M.E.Waugh	c Gibbs b Pollock	63		not out	115
S.R.Waugh	c Richardson b Pollock	6		c Richardson b Klusener	34
R.T.Ponting	b Klusener	26		c Symcox b Klusener	23
†I.A.Healy	c and b Pollock	1		c Richardson b Kallis	10
A.J.Bichel	c Symcox b Pollock	0		lbw b Klusener	7
S.K.Warne	c Richardson b Pollock	0		not out	4
M.S.Kasprowicz	c Symcox b Kallis	17			
S.C.G.MacGill	b Symcox	10			
Extras	(B 2, LB 12, NB 5)	19		(B 2, NB 6)	8
Total		**350**		(7 wickets)	**227**

AUSTRALIA	O	M	R	W		O	M	R	W		FALL OF WICKETS			
Kasprowicz	39	7	125	3		18	5	55	2			SA	A	SA	A
Bichel	35	10	103	1		14	2	51	0	*Wkt*	*1st*	*1st*	*2nd*	*2nd*
Warne	33	6	95	2	(4)	15	2	52	1	1st	140	15	80	6
MacGill	29	7	112	2	(5)	7	1	22	3	2nd	148	71	133	17
M.E.Waugh	6	1	21	0						3rd	160	197	155	54
Blewett	14	5	26	1						4th	269	207	155	112
S.R.Waugh	10	3	27	1	(3)	4	1	13	0	5th	275	263	157	185
										6th	286	273	165	202
SOUTH AFRICA										7th	305	279	–	215
Pollock	41	11	87	7		30.4	12	61	2	8th	374	279	–	–
McMillan	23	5	60	0	(5)	13	2	33	0	9th	442	317	–	–
Kallis	18	5	45	1		16	10	20	1	10th	517	350	–	–
Klusener	27	6	104	1	(2)	30	10	67	4					
Symcox	13.5	3	40	1	(4)	18	2	42	0					
Cronje						1	0	2	0					

Umpires: D.B.Cowie (*New Zealand*) (7) and S.G.Randell (33).
Referee: R.S.Madugalle (*Sri Lanka*) (13).   **Test No. 1394/65 (A 578/SA 215)**

AUSTRALIA v SOUTH AFRICA 1997-98

AUSTRALIA – BATTING AND FIELDING

	M	I	NO	HS	Runs	Avge	100	50	Ct/St
M.E.Waugh	3	5	1	115*	279	69.75	2	1	–
M.A.Taylor	3	5	1	169*	265	66.25	1	1	8
P.R.Reiffel	2	3	1	79*	106	53.00	–	1	–
R.T.Ponting	3	5	–	105	248	49.60	1	1	2
S.R.Waugh	3	5	–	96	238	47.60	–	2	1
G.S.Blewett	3	5	–	31	107	21.40	–	–	3
I.A.Healy	3	5	1	46*	77	19.25	–	–	9/1
G.D.McGrath	2	3	1	18	32	16.00	–	–	–
M.S.Kasprowicz	2	3	–	19	36	12.00	–	–	1
M.T.G.Elliott	3	5	–	32	51	10.20	–	–	1
S.K.Warne	3	5	1	12	27	6.75	–	–	5

Played in one Test: M.G.Bevan 12; A.J.Bichel 0, 7 (1 ct); S.C.G.MacGill 10 (1 ct).

AUSTRALIA – BOWLING

	O	M	R	W	Avge	Best	5wI	10wM
S.K.Warne	187.1	51	417	20	20.85	6-34	2	1
P.R.Reiffel	68	23	118	5	23.60	3-14	–	–
S.C.G.MacGill	36	8	134	5	26.80	3-22	–	–
M.S.Kasprowicz	84.5	16	253	8	31.62	3-28	–	–
G.D.McGrath	70	28	136	4	34.00	1- 8	–	–

Also bowled: M.G.Bevan 26-3-74-2; A.J.Bichel 49-12-154-1; G.S.Blewett 30-11-61-2;
M.T.G.Elliott 1-0-4-0; M.E.Waugh 47-12-114-2; S.R.Waugh 31-10-74-2.

SOUTH AFRICA – BATTING AND FIELDING

	M	I	NO	HS	Runs	Avge	100	50	Ct/St
G.Kirsten	3	6	1	108*	279	55.80	1	2	2
B.M.McMillan	3	5	1	87*	168	42.00	–	1	4
W.J.Cronje	3	6	–	88	241	40.16	–	3	–
J.H.Kallis	3	6	–	101	207	34.50	1	–	1
A.M.Bacher	3	6	–	64	188	31.33	–	1	2
P.L.Symcox	3	5	–	54	127	25.40	–	1	4
H.H.Gibbs	2	4	–	54	94	23.50	–	1	1
S.M.Pollock	3	5	1	40	84	21.00	–	–	3
L.Klusener	2	4	1	38	55	18.33	–	–	–
D.J.Richardson	3	5	–	15	33	6.60	–	–	10/1
A.A.Donald	2	3	2	4*	6	6.00	–	–	–

Played in one Test: P.R.Adams 0, 1* (1 ct); D.J.Cullinan 5, 0 (2 ct); J.N.Rhodes 6, 19*.

SOUTH AFRICA – BOWLING

	O	M	R	W	Avge	Best	5wI	10wM
A.A.Donald	86.4	19	214	12	17.83	6-59	1	–
S.M.Pollock	154	42	351	16	21.93	7-87	1	–
L.Klusener	85	21	247	6	41.16	4-67	–	–
P.L.Symcox	133.1	29	344	8	43.00	4-69	–	–

Also bowled: P.R.Adams 38-9-66-1; W.J.Cronje 8-2-26-0; J.H.Kallis 46-18-100-2;
B.M.McMillan 66-15-173-2.

ECB TOURS PROGRAMME

1998-99
England to Australia
England A to ?†

1999
World Cup/New Zealand (4)
Sri Lanka A

1999-2000
England to South Africa/Zimbabwe
England A to New Zealand

2000
West Indies (5)/†Zimbabwe (1)
New Zealand A

2000-01
England to Pakistan (3)/Sri Lanka (3)
England A to West Indies

† *To be confirmed*
Tests in brackets (where confirmed)

SECOND XI FIXTURES 1998

Abbreviations: (SEC)   Second Eleven Championship matches
(Three days unless marked * which are four days)
(AONT) AON Trophy (One day)

APRIL

Wed 22	(SEC)	Kent v Yorks	Canterbury	01227 456886
	(SEC)	Notts v Derbys	Trent Bridge	0115 982 1525
Tue 28	(SEC)	Leics v Glos	Hinckley Town CC	01455 615336
	(SEC)	*Warwicks v Hants	Knowle & Dorridge CC	01564 774338
	(AONT)	Essex v Kent	Saffron Walden	01799 522683
Wed 29	(SEC)	Essex v Kent	Saffron Walden	01799 522683
	(SEC)	Surrey v Notts	Oxted CC	01883 712792
	(SEC)	Sussex v Derbys	Eastbourne	01323 724328
Thu 30	(AONT)	Lancs v Yorks	Old Trafford	0161 282 4000

MAY

Fri 1	(AONT)	Glos v Somerset	Bristol	0117 924 5216
Tue 5	(SEC)	*Derbys v Yorks	Chesterfield	01246 273090
	(SEC)	*Worcs v Northants	New Road	.01905 748474
	(AONT)	Glam v Somerset	Cardiff	01222 343478
	(AONT)	MCC YC v Essex	Shenley	01923 859022
Wed 6	(SEC)	Glos v Durham	Bristol University	0117 968 1460
	(SEC)	Lancs v Surrey	Old Trafford	0161 282 4000
	(SEC)	Warwicks v Kent	Stratford-upon-Avon CC	01789 297968
	(AONT)	Leics v Middx	Hinckley Town	01455 615336
Thu 7	(AONT)	Somerset v Hants	Taunton	01823 272946
Mon 11	(AONT)	Lancs v Notts	Old Trafford	0161 282 4000
	(AONT)	Leics v Minor C	Grace Road	0116 2832128
	(AONT)	MCC YC v Sussex	Shenley	01923 859022
	(AONT)	Warwicks v Middx	West Bromich Dartmouth CC	0121 533 0168
Tue 12	(AONT)	Minor C v Middx	Dunstable	01582 663735
	(AONT)	Somerset v Glam	Taunton	01823 272946
	(AONT)	Surrey v Essex	The Oval	0171 582 6660
	(AONT)	Yorks v Notts	Castleford	01977 553627
Wed 13	(SEC)	Essex v Glos	Chelmsford	01245 252420
	(SEC)	Somerset v Northants	Taunton	01823 272946
	(SEC)	Surrey v Leics	The Oval	0171 582 6660
	(SEC)	Yorks v Notts	Bradford (Park Ave)	01274 391564
Thu 14	(AONT)	Lancs v Derbys	Old Trafford	0161 282 4000
Mon 18	(AONT)	Derbys v Notts	Belper Meadows	01773 824900

270

	(AONT)	Essex v MCC YC	Saffron Walden	01799 522683
Tue 19	(SEC)	Glos v Lancs	Bristol	0117 924 5216
	(AONT)	Hants v Glam	Southampton	01703 333788
Wed 20	(SEC)	Derbys v Essex	Abbotsholme School	01889 5902178
	(SEC)	Hants v Glam	Southampton	01703 333788
	(SEC)	Notts v Warwicks	Trent Bridge	0115 982 1525
	(SEC)	Sussex v Worcs	Hove	01273 827100
	(SEC)	Yorks v Leics	Bingley	01274 775441
	(AONT)	Middx v Minor C	Uxbridge	01895 237571
Mon 25	(AONT)	Derbys v Lancs	Duffield CC	01332 842610
	(AONT)	Worcs v Somerset	New Road	01905 784874
Tue 26	(SEC)	*Worcs v Glos	Kidderminster	01562 824175
	(SEC)	Yorks v Glam	Marske	01642 484361
	(AONT)	Derbys v Durham	Glossop	01457 869755
	(AONT)	Kent v Surrey	Maidstone	01622 754545
	(AONT)	Middx v Leics	Uxbridge	01895 237571
Wed 27	(SEC)	Derbys v Warwicks	Abbotsholme School	01889 5902178
	(SEC)	Kent v Surrey	Maidstone	01622 754545
	(SEC)	Northants v Hants	Campbell Park	01908 694820
Thu 28	(AONT)	Lancs v Durham	Urmston	0161 748 4660

JUNE

Mon 1	(AONT)	MCC YC v Surrey	Shenley	01923 859022
	(AONT)	Somerset v Worcs	Taunton	01823 272946
Tue 2	(SEC)	*Sussex v Kent	Hove	01273 827100
	(AONT)	Leics v Warwicks	Hinckley Town	01455 615336
	(AONT)	Yorks v Lancs	Elland	01422 372682
Wed 3	(SEC)	Glam v Durham	Abergavenny	01873 852350
	(SEC)	Glos v Middx	Bristol	0117 924 5216
	(SEC)	Notts v Hants	Trent Bridge	0115 982 1525
	(SEC)	Worcs v Somerset	New Road	01905 784874
Thu 4	(AONT)	Warwicks v Minor C	Griff & Coton CC	01203 386798
Mon 8	(AONT)	Derbys v Yorks	Dunstall	01283 712677
	(AONT)	Kent v Sussex	Maidstone	01622 754545
	(AONT)	Notts v Lancs	Worksop College	01909 472286
Tue 9	(SEC)	*Derbys v Glos	Chesterfield	01246 273090
	(SEC)	*Middx v Essex	Southgate CC	0181 886 8381
	(AONT)	Minor C v Leics	Banbury CC	01295 264368
Wed 10	(SEC)	Lancs v Somerset	Northern CC	0151 924 1594
	(SEC)	Northants v Durham	Campbell Park	01908 694820
	(SEC)	Sussex v Yorks	Horsham	01403 254 628
	(SEC)	Worcs v Glam	Halesowen	0121 550 2744
	(AONT)	Kent v MCC YC	Maidstone	01622 754545
Thu 11	(AONT)	Warwicks v Leics	Leamington CC	01926 423854
Fri 12	(AONT)	Minor C v Warwicks	Wolverhampton	01902 754053
	(AONT)	Surrey v MCC YC	The Oval	0171 582 6660
Mon 15	(AONT)	Glam v Glos	Ebbw Vale	01495 305368
	(AONT)	Hants v Somerset	Southampton	01703 333788
	(AONT)	Sussex v MCC YC	East Grinstead	01342 321210
	(AONT)	Yorks v Durham	Marske	01642 484361
Tue 16	(SEC)	*Notts v Leics	Trent Bridge	0115 982 1525
	(SEC)	*Yorks v Durham	Middlesbrough	01642 818567
	(AONT)	Middx v Northants	Lensbury	0181 977 8821
		Lancs (SEC Winners) v England	Ramsbottom	01706 822799
		U19 (4 days)		
Wed 17	(SEC)	Glam v Essex	Panteg	01495 763605
	(SEC)	Hants v Derbys	Finchampstead CC	01734 732890
	(SEC)	Middx v Worcs	Lensbury	0181 977 8821

	(SEC)	Somerset v Kent	Taunton	01823 272946
	(SEC)	Surrey v Northants	The Oval	0171 582 6660
	(SEC)	Warwicks v Sussex	Coventry & N Warwicks	01203 451426
Mon 22	(AONT)	Durham v Lancs	Seaton Carew	01429 260945
	(AONT)	Glam v Worcs	Newport	01633 281236
	(AONT)	Hants v Glos	Southampton	01703 333788
	(AONT)	Sussex v Surrey	Hove	01273 827100
	(AONT)	Warwicks v Northants	Solihull	0121 705 5271
	(AONT)	Yorks v Derbys	Bradford (Park Avenue)	01274 391564
Tue 23	(SEC)	*Durham v Lancs	Hartlepool	01429 260945
	(SEC)	Hants v Glos	Southampton	01703 333788
	(SEC)	Northants v Middx	Dunstable Town	01582 663735
	(AONT)	Notts v Yorks	Welbeck CC	
	(AONT)	Sussex v Kent	Hove	01273 827100
Wed 24	(SEC)	Essex v Somerset	Chelmsford	01245 252420
	(SEC)	Glam v Derbys	Pontardulais	01792 882256
	(SEC)	Kent v Leics	Ashford	01233 611700
	(SEC)	Notts v Surrey	Worksop	01909 472681
Mon 29	(SEC)	*Glos v Somerset	Bristol	0117 924 5216
	(AONT)	Hants v Worcs	Southampton	01703 333788
	(AONT)	Northants v Minor C	Northampton	01604 632917
Tue 30	(AONT)	*Northants v Warwicks	Northampton	01604 623917
	(SEC)	*Yorks v Worcs	Harrogate	01423 561301
	(AONT)	Essex v Sussex	Chelmsford	01245 252420
	(AONT)	Notts v Durham	Farnsford CC	01623 882986
	(AONT)	Surrey v Kent	The Oval	0171 582 6660

JULY

Wed 1	(SEC)	Essex v Hants	Wickford	01268 763023
	(SEC)	Glam v Leics	Abergavenny	01873 852350
	(SEC)	Middx v Kent	Harrow	0181 422 0932
	(SEC)	Notts v Durham	Collingham CC	01636 892921
	(SEC)	Surrey v Sussex	The Oval	0171 582 6660
Fri 3	(AONT)	Somerset v Glos	Taunton	01823 272946
Mon 6	(AONT)	Durham v Notts	Boldon	0191 536 4180
	(AONT)	Kent v Essex	Canterbury	01227 456886
	(AONT)	Northants v Middx	Campbell Park	01908 694820
	(AONT)	Surrey v Worcs	The Oval	0171 582 6660
	(AONT)	Worcs v Hants	New Road	01905 748474
Tue 7	(SEC)	*Warwicks v Worcs	Studley CC	01527 853668
	(AONT)	Glos v Glam	Lydney CC	01594 529585
	(AONT)	Leics v Northants	Lutterworth	01455 554752
Wed 8	(SEC)	Durham v Sussex	Chester-le-Street	0191 388 3684
	(SEC)	Essex v Northants	Chelmsford	01245 252420
	(SEC)	Kent v Lancs	Canterbury	01227 456886
	(SEC)	Middx v Derbys	Harrow	0181 422 0932
	(SEC)	Somerset v Notts	Taunton	01823 272946
	(SEC)	Surrey v Glam	The Oval	0171 582 6660
	(SEC)	Yorks v Hants	Todmorden	01706 813140
Mon 13	(AONT)	Durham v Yorks	Stockton CC	01642 870650
	(AONT)	Northants v Warwicks	Northampton	01604 632917
	(AONT)	Notts v Derbys	Notts Unity Casuals CC	0115 986 8255
	(AONT)	Sussex v Essex	Haywards Heath	01444 451384
	(AONT)	Worcs v Glos	New Road	01905 748474
Tue 14	(SEC)	*Surrey v Middx	The Oval	0171 582 6660
Wed 15	(SEC)	Kent v Glam	Folkestone	01303 253366
	(SEC)	Lancs v Warwicks	Fleetwood	01253 872132
	(SEC)	Northants v Leics	Northampton	01604 632917

	(SEC)	Notts v Glos	Nottingham High School	0115 960 5605
	(SEC)	Sussex v Somerset	Middleton-on-Sea	01243 583157
Mon 20	(AONT)	Essex v Surrey	Coggeshall	01376 562988
	(AONT)	Minor C v Northants	North Runcton	
	(AONT)	Worcs v Glam	New Road	01905 748474
Tue 21	(SEC)	*Essex v Surrey	Coggeshall	01376 652988
	(SEC)	Lancs v Yorks	Blackpool	01253 393347
	(AONT)	Durham v Derbys	Riverside	0191 528 4536
	(AONT)	Glos v Worcs	Cheltenham College	01242 522000
Wed 22	(SEC)	Durham v Derbys	Riverside	0191 528 4536
	(SEC)	Glam v Warwicks	Usk	01291 673754
	(SEC)	Kent v Northants	Maidstone	01622 754545
	(SEC)	Leics v Worcs	Hinckley Town	01455 615336
	(SEC)	Sussex v Middx	Hastings	01424 424546
	(AONT)	Glos v Hants	Bristol	0117 924 5216
Mon 27	(SEC)	Glam v Hants	Ammanford	01269 594988
	(AONT)	Middx v Warwicks	Ealing	0181 810 5270
	(AONT)	MCC YC v Kent	Shenley	01923 859022
	(AONT)	Northants v Leics	Tring	01442 823080
Tue 28		Durham v England U19	Stockton CC	01642 870650
		Warwicks v Pakistan U19	Stratford-upon-Avon	01789 297968
Wed 29	(SEC)	Derbys v Lancs	Cheadle CC	
	(SEC)	Durham v Worcs	Stockton CC	01642 870650
	(SEC)	Hants v Surrey	Bournemouth Sports Club	01202 581933
	(SEC)	Leics v Essex	Oakham School	01572 722487
	(SEC)	Middx v Notts	Vine Lane, Uxbridge	01895 237144
	(SEC)	Northants v Glam	Wellingborough School	01933 222427
	(SEC)	Somerset v Yorks	Clevedon	01275 877585

AUGUST

Tue 4	(SEC)	*Hants v Sussex	Southampton	01703 333788
Wed 5	(SEC)	Glam v Middx	Cardiff	01222 343478
	(SEC)	Lancs v Worcs	Middleton	0161 643 3595
	(SEC)	Notts v Northants	Worksop College	01909 472286
	(SEC)	Somerset v Surrey	Taunton	01823 272946
	(SEC)	Warwicks v Essex	Moseley CC	0121 744 5694
Mon 10	(SEC)	*Kent v Hants	Eltham	0181 859 1579
	(SEC)	Leics v Sussex	Oakham School	01572 722487
Tue 11	(SEC)	*Somerset v Glam	North Perrott	01460 77953
Wed 12	(SEC)	Durham v Essex	Sunderland	0191 528 4536
	(SEC)	Glos v Warwicks	Hatherley & Reddings CC	01242 862608
	(SEC)	Middx v Yorks	Lensbury	0181 977 8821
	(SEC)	Worcs v Notts	Barnt Green CC	0121 445 1684
Mon 17 or Tue 18	(AONT)	*AON Trophy Semi-Finals (One day)*		
Wed 19	(SEC)	Derbys v Somerset	Derby	01332 383211
	(SEC)	Durham v Kent	South Shields	0191 456 1506
	(SEC)	Glos v Sussex	Bristol	0117 924 5216
	(SEC)	Notts v Lancs	Cleethorpes	01472 691271
	(SEC)	Warwicks v Surrey	Walmley CC	0121 351 1349
	(SEC)	Worcs v Essex	Ombersley	01905 621469
	(SEC)	Yorks v Northants	York	01904 623602
Tue 25	(SEC)	*Glam v Glos	Usk	01291 623754
	(SEC)	*Leics v Derbys	Grace Road	0116 2832128
Wed 26	(SEC)	Essex v Yorks	Chelmsford	01245 252420
	(SEC)	Kent v Notts	Tunbridge Wells	01892 520846
	(SEC)	Lancs v Middx	Old Trafford	0161 282 4000
	(SEC)	Somerset v Hants	Weston-super-Mare	01934 623101

SEPTEMBER

Tue 1	(SEC)	*Derbys v Notts	Chesterfield	01246 273090
	(SEC)	Northants v Glos	Northampton	01604 623917
Wed 2	(SEC)	Essex v Lancs	Colchester	01376 562988
	(SEC)	Surrey v Durham	Oxted CC	01883 712792
	(SEC)	Warwicks v Middx	Kenilworth Wardens CC	01926 852476
	(SEC)	Worcs v Hants	New Road	01905 748474
Mon 7	(AONT)	*AON Trophy Final*		
(Reserve day Tue 8)				
Wed 9	(SEC)	Derbys v Northants	Derby	01332 383211
	(SEC)	Hants v Lancs	Southampton	01703 333788
	(SEC)	Warwicks v Yorks	Edgbaston	0121 446 4422
Mon 14	(SEC)	Leics v Lancs	Grace Road	0116 2832128
Fri 11	(SEC)	*Sussex v Notts	Hove	01273 827100

MINOR COUNTIES FIXTURES 1998

MAY

Sun 24	Hurst CC	(W) Berkshire v Herefordshire
	Bovey Tracey	(W) Devon v Dorset
	Sleaford	(E) Lincolnshire v Bedfordshire
	Swindon CC	(W) Wiltshire v Wales
Tue 26	Marlow	(E) Buckinghamshire v Suffolk
Sun 31	Reading CC	†(W) Berkshire v Wales
	Askam	†(E) Cumberland v Hertfordshire
	Kington	†(W) Herefordshire v Dorset
	Bourne	†(E) Lincolnshire v Staffordshire
	Jesmond	†(E) Northumberland v Buckinghamshire
	Telford (St Georges)	†(W) Shropshire v Oxfordshire

JUNE

Tue 2	Toft	†(W) Cheshire v Oxfordshire
	Netherfield	(E) Cumberland v Buckinghamshire
	Benwell Hill	(E) Northumberland v Hertfordshire
Mon 8	Barrow	(E) Cumberland v Norfolk
Wed 10	Saffron Walden	(E) Cambridgeshire v Suffolk
	Stone	†(E) Staffordshire v Norfolk
Sun 14	Bedford CC	†(E) Bedfordshire v Cumberland
	Bournemouth	†(W) Dorset v Shropshire
	Grantham	†(E) Lincolnshire v Northumberland
	Banbury	(W) Oxfordshire v Wales
	Corsham	†(W) Wiltshire v Berkshire
Mon 15	Werrington	(W) Cornwall v Cheshire
Tue 16	Wisbech	†(E) Cambridgeshire v Northumberland
	Longton	(E) Staffordshire v Buckinghamshire
Wed 17	Plymouth (Mount Wise)	(W) Devon v Cheshire
Sun 28	Colwall	†(W) Herefordshire v Devon

JULY

Wed 1	March	(E) Cambridgeshire v Staffordshire
Sun 5	Henlow	(E) Bedfordshire v Northumberland
	Reading CC	(W) Berkshire v Cornwall
	Slough	†(E) Buckinghamshire v Norfolk
	Torquay	(W) Devon v Wiltshire
	Shenley Park	†(E) Hertfordshire v Suffolk
	Lincoln (Lindum)	(E) Lincolnshire v Cumberland
	Pontypridd	(W) Wales v Shropshire
Tue 7	Cambridge (Fenner's)	(E) Cambridge v Cumberland
	Oxford (Christ Church)	(W) Oxfordshire v Cornwall

Sun 12	New Brighton	(W) Cheshire v Berkshire
	St Austell	†(W) Cornwall v Dorset
	Long Marston	(E) Hertfordshire v Buckinghamshire
	Cleethorpes	(E) Lincolnshire v Cambridgeshire
	Ipswich School	†(E) Suffolk v Bedfordshire
	Salisbury (S Wilts CC)	(W) Wiltshire v Oxfordshire
Mon 13	Jesmond	(E) Northumberland v Staffordshire
Tue 14	Bridgnorth	(W) Shropshire v Berkshire
Wed 15	Millom	(E) Cumberland v Staffordshire
Wed 22	Cambridge (Fenner's)	†(E) Cambridgeshire v Buckinghamshire
	Lakenham	(E) Norfolk v Hertfordshire
Sun 26	Aylesbury	(E) Buckinghamshire v Bedfordshire
	Lakenham	†(E) Norfolk v Lincolnshire
	Thame CC	(W) Oxfordshire v Devon
	Oswestry	(W) Shropshire v Herefordshire
	Copdock CC	(E) Suffolk v Northumberland
	Swansea	†(W) Wales v Cornwall
	Marlborough	(W) Wiltshire v Cheshire
Mon 27	Cannock	†(E) Staffordshire v Hertfordshire
Tue 28	Finchampstead	†(W) Berkshire v Devon
	Weymouth	(W) Dorset v Cheshire
	Brockhampton	(W) Herefordshire v Cornwall
	Lakenham	(E) Norfolk v Northumberland

AUGUST

Sun 2	Southill Park	(E) Bedfordshire v Hertfordshire
	Chester (Boughton Hall)	†(W) Cheshire v Wales
	Exmouth	†(W) Devon v Shropshire
	Bournemouth	(W) Dorset v Oxfordshire
	Brockhampton	(W) Herefordshire v Wiltshire
Mon 3	Lakenham	(E) Norfolk v Cambridgeshire
Tue 4	Falmouth	(W) Cornwall v Shropshire
Wed 5	Ipswich (Ransome's)	(E) Suffolk v Lincolnshire
Sun 9	Dunstable CC	(E) Bedfordshire v Norfolk
	Camborne	†(W) Cornwall v Wiltshire
	Hitchin	(E) Hertfordshire v Lincolnshire
	Aston Rowant	†(W) Oxfordshire v Herefordshire
	Pontardulais	(W) Wales v Dorset
Tue 11	Carlisle	†(E) Cumberland v Suffolk
Thu 13	Brewood	(E) Staffordshire v Suffolk
Sun 16	Luton CC	†(E) Bedfordshire v Cambridgeshire
	Bowdon	(W) Cheshire v Herefordshire
	Bournemouth	(W) Dorset v Berkshire
	Wellington	(W) Shropshire v Wiltshire
	Colwyn Bay	(W) Wales v Devon
Sun 23	Falkland CC	(W) Berkshire v Oxfordshire
	Beaconsfield	(E) Buckinghamshire v Lincolnshire
	Alderley Edge	(W) Cheshire v Shropshire
	Truro	(W) Cornwall v Devon
	Leominster (Dales CC)	(W) Herefordshire v Wales
	Hertford	(E) Hertfordshire v Cambridgeshire
	Jesmond	(E) Northumberland v Cumberland
	Leek	(E) Staffordshire v Bedfordshire
	Mildenhall	(E) Suffolk v Norfolk
	Westbury	(W) Wiltshire v Dorset

SEPTEMBER

Sun 6	tba	*CHAMPIONSHIP FINAL (two days)*

† match to be played under 'Grade' Rules.

PRINCIPAL FIXTURES 1998

*Includes Sunday play

Tuesday 14 April

Fenner's:	Cambridge U v Northants
The Parks:	Oxford U v Sussex

Friday 17 April

Britannic Assurance Championship
*Derby:	Derbys v Notts
Bristol:	Glos v Glam
Canterbury:	Kent v Middx
The Oval:	Surrey v Northants
*Hove:	Sussex v Lancs
Edgbaston:	Warwicks v Durham
Worcester:	Worcs v Essex
Headingley:	Yorks v Somerset

Other Matches
*Fenner's:	Cambridge U v Leics
The Parks:	Oxford U v Hants

Sunday 19 April

AXA League
Bristol:	Glos v Glam
Canterbury:	Kent v Middx
The Oval:	Surrey v Northants
Edgbaston:	Warwicks v Durham
Worcester:	Worcs v Essex
Headingley:	Yorks v Somerset

Tuesday 21 April

AXA League
Derby:	Derbys v Notts
Hove:	Sussex v Lancs *(Floodlit)*

Thursday 23 April

Britannic Assurance Championship
Riverside:	Durham v Glos
Chelmsford:	Essex v Sussex
Cardiff:	Glam v Kent
Southampton:	Hants v Northants
Old Trafford:	Lancs v Middx
Leicester:	Leics v Worcs
Taunton:	Somerset v Notts
The Oval:	Surrey v Warwicks
Headingley:	Yorks v Derbys

Sunday 26 April

AXA League
Riverside:	Durham v Glos
Chelmsford:	Essex v Sussex
Cardiff:	Glam v Kent
Southampton:	Hants v Northants
Old Trafford:	Lancs v Middx
Leicester:	Leics v Worcs
Taunton:	Somerset v Notts
The Oval:	Surrey v Warwicks
Headingley:	Yorks v Derbys

Tuesday 28 April

Benson and Hedges Cup
Derby:	Derbys v Durham
Southampton:	Hants v Surrey
Taunton:	Somerset v Kent
Headingley:	Yorks v Worcs

Other Match
The Parks:	British Us v Northants
	(One day)

Wednesday 29 April

Benson and Hedges Cup
Cardiff:	Glam v Essex
Old Trafford:	Lancs v Warwicks
Lord's:	Middx v Sussex
Luton:	Minor C v Northants
(Wardown Pk)	

Thursday 30 April

Benson and Hedges Cup
Taunton:	Somerset v British Us
The Oval:	Surrey v Glos

Friday 1 May

Benson and Hedges Cup
The Parks:	British Us v Hants
Dublin:	Ireland v Glam
(Castle Ave)	
Leicester:	Leics v Lancs
Trent Bridge:	Notts v Minor C
Edgbaston:	Warwicks v Northants
Worcester:	Worcs v Derbys

Saturday 2 May

Benson and Hedges Cup
Canterbury: Kent v Glos
Trent Bridge: Notts v Leics
Hove: Sussex v Essex
Linlithgow: Scotland v Yorks

Sunday 3 May

AXA League
Lord's: Middx v Glam
Arundel: Sussex v Hants
Worcester: Worcs v Durham

Monday 4 May

Benson and Hedges Cup
Derby: Derbys v Yorks
Chelmsford: Essex v Ireland
Bristol: Glos v Somerset
Leicester: Leics v Warwicks
Northampton: Northants v Notts
The Oval: Surrey v British Us
Worcester: Worcs v Scotland

Tuesday 5 May

Benson and Hedges Cup
Lord's: Middx v Ireland
Lakenham: Minor C v Lancs
Taunton: Somerset v Hants
Hove: Sussex v Glam

Wednesday 6 May

Benson and Hedges Cup
Riverside: Durham v Scotland
Bristol: Glos v British Us
Canterbury: Kent v Surrey
Lakenham: Minor C v Warwicks
Northampton: Northants v Leics

Thursday 7 May

Benson and Hedges Cup
Riverside: Durham v Worcs
Chelmsford: Essex v Middx
Southampton: Hants v Kent
Trent Bridge: Notts v Lancs

Friday 8 May

Benson and Hedges Cup
Leicester: Leics v Minor C
Forfar: Scotland v Derbys
The Oval: Surrey v Somerset

Saturday 9 May

Benson and Hedges Cup
The Parks: British Us v Kent
Cardiff: Glam v Middx
Bristol: Glos v Hants
Eglinton: Ireland v Sussex
Old Trafford: Lancs v Northants
Edgbaston: Warwicks v Notts
Headingley: Yorks v Durham

Sunday 10 May

AXA League
Cardiff: Glam v Somerset
Bristol: Glos v Kent
Southampton: Hants v Essex
Old Trafford: Lancs v Derbys
Trent Bridge: Notts v Durham
Edgbaston: Warwicks v Leics
Headingley: Yorks v Surrey

Monday 11 May

The Parks: Oxford U v Worcs

Wednesday 13 May

Britannic Assurance Championship
Derby: Derbys v Warwicks
Riverside: Durham v Essex
Bristol: Glos v Leics
Southampton: Hants v Surrey
Canterbury: Kent v Lancs
Lord's: Middx v Somerset
Northampton: Northants v Yorks
Trent Bridge: Notts v Sussex
Other Match
Fenner's: Cambridge U v Glam

Thursday 14 May

Vodafone Challenge Series
Worcester: Worcs v South Africans
               (Three days)

Saturday 16 May

The Parks: Cambridge U v Oxford U
               (One day)

Sunday 17 May

AXA League
Derby: Derbys v Warwicks
Riverside: Durham v Essex
Bristol: Glos v Leics

Southampton: Hants v Surrey
Canterbury: Kent v Lancs
Lord's: Middx v Somerset
Northampton: Northants v Yorks
Trent Bridge: Notts v Sussex
Tourist Match
Arundel: Duke of Norfolk's XI v
South Africans (*One day*)

Monday 18 May

Fenner's: Cambridge U v Durham
The Parks: Oxford U v Warwicks

Tuesday 19 May

AXA League
Derby: Derbys v Leics
Cardiff: Glam v Yorks
Uxbridge CC: Middx v Essex
Trent Bridge: Notts v Glos
Taunton: Somerset v Northants
Worcester: Worcs v Sussex
Tourist Match
Canterbury: Kent v South Africans
(*One day*)

Thursday 21 May

TEXACO TROPHY
**The Oval: ENGLAND v SOUTH
AFRICA**
(*First Limited-overs International*)
Reserve day Fri 22 May
Britannic Assurance Championship
*Chelmsford: Essex v Lancs
*Gloucester: Glos v Yorks
*Canterbury: Kent v Durham
*Leicester: Leics v Hants
*Uxbridge CC: Middx v Worcs
*Northampton: Northants v Glam
*Taunton: Somerset v Surrey
*Horsham: Sussex v Derbys
*Edgbaston: Warwicks v Notts

Saturday 23 May

TEXACO TROPHY
**Old Trafford: ENGLAND v SOUTH
AFRICA**
(*Second Limited-overs International*)
No reserve day

Sunday 24 May

TEXACO TROPHY
**Headingley: ENGLAND v SOUTH
AFRICA**
(*Third Limited-overs International*)
Reserve day Mon 25 May

Monday 25 May

AXA League
Chelmsford: Essex v Lancs
Gloucester: Glos v Yorks
Canterbury: Kent v Durham
Leicester: Leics v Hants
Uxbridge CC: Middx v Worcs
Northampton: Northants v Glam
Taunton: Somerset v Surrey
Horsham: Sussex v Derbys
Edgbaston: Warwicks v Notts

Wednesday 27 May

Benson and Hedges Cup
Quarter-Finals (*Reserve day Thurs
28 May*)
Tourist Match
Stone: Minor Counties XI v
South Africans
(*One day*)

Friday 29 May

Britannic Assurance Championship
*Chesterfield: Derbys v Leics
*Lord's: Middx v Glam
*Trent Bridge: Notts v Durham
*Worcester: Worcs v Sussex
Vodafone Challenge Series
*Bristol: Glos v South Africans
(*Four days*)
Other Match
The Parks: Oxford U v Yorks

Sunday 31 May

AXA League
Ilford: Essex v Northants
Taunton: Somerset v Warwicks

Wednesday 3 June

Britannic Assurance Championship
Chesterfield: Derbys v Glos
Ilford: Essex v Notts
Southampton: Hants v Glam

Tunbridge W: Kent v Sussex
Lord's: Middx v Durham
Northampton: Northants v Lancs
Taunton: Somerset v Warwicks
The Oval: Surrey v Worcs
Headingley: Yorks v Leics

Thursday 4 June

FIRST CORNHILL INSURANCE TEST MATCH
*Edgbaston: ENGLAND v SOUTH AFRICA

Sunday 7 June

AXA League
Chesterfield: Derbys v Glos
Southampton: Hants v Glam
Tunbridge W: Kent v Sussex
Lord's: Middx v Durham
Northampton: Northants v Lancs
Headingley: Yorks v Leics

Tuesday 9 June

Benson and Hedges Cup
Semi-Finals *(Reserve day Wed 10 June)*

Wednesday 10 June

Tourist Match
Leicester or Leics or Notts v South
Trent Bridge: Africans *(One day)*
(Warwicks to play South Africans at Edgbaston if both Leics & Notts involved in B&H semi-finals)
Other Matches
Fenner's: Cambridge U v Derbys
(Subject to neither Derbys nor British Universities being involved in the B&H semi-finals)
The Parks: Oxford U v Notts
(Subject to neither Notts nor British Universities being involved in the B&H semi-finals. Subject also to Notts not playing v South Africans on Wed 10 June)

Thursday 11 June

Britannic Assurance Championship
Riverside: Durham v Northants
Chelmsford: Essex v Surrey
Cardiff: Glam v Worcs
Bristol: Glos v Warwicks
Old Trafford: Lancs v Somerset

Leicester: Leics v Kent
Headingley: Yorks v Hants

Friday 12 June

Vodafone Challenge Series
*Arundel: Sussex v South Africans
(Three days)

Saturday 13 June

The Parks: Oxford U v Middx

Sunday 14 June

AXA League
Derby: Derbys v Middx
Riverside: Durham v Northants
Chelmsford: Essex v Surrey
Cardiff: Glam v Worcs
Bristol: Glos v Warwicks
Old Trafford: Lancs v Somerset
Leicester: Leics v Kent
Headingley: Yorks v Hants

Wednesday 17 June

Britannic Assurance Championship
Riverside: Durham v Yorks
Cardiff: Glam v Leics
Basingstoke: Hants v Derbys
Canterbury: Kent v Notts
Northampton: Northants v Middx
Bath: Somerset v Essex
Hove: Sussex v Warwicks
(1.00pm start each day)
Worcester: Worcs v Glos
AXA League
Old Trafford: Lancs v Surrey *(Floodlit)*

Thursday 18 June

SECOND CORNHILL INSURANCE TEST MATCH
*Lord's: ENGLAND v SOUTH AFRICA
Britannic Assurance Championship
*Old Trafford: Lancs v Surrey

Sunday 21 June

AXA League
Riverside: Durham v Yorks
Pontypridd: Glam v Leics
Basingstoke: Hants v Derbys
Canterbury: Kent v Notts
Northampton: Northants v Middx

Bath: Somerset v Essex
Hove: Sussex v Warwicks
Worcester: Worcs v Glos

Wednesday 24 June

NatWest Trophy
First Round
Derby: Derbys v Cumberland
Lakenham: Norfolk v Durham
Chester: Cheshire v Essex
  (Boughton Hall CC)
Cardiff: Glam v Bedfords
Bristol: Glos v Northants
Bournemouth: Dorset v Hants
Canterbury: Kent v Cambs
Old Trafford: Lancs v Sussex
Leicester: Leics v Staffs
Lord's: Middx v Herefords
Colwyn Bay: Minor C Wales v Notts
Taunton: Somerset v Holland
The Oval: Surrey v Bucks
Edgbaston: Warwicks v Ireland
Edinburgh: Scotland v Worcs
Exmouth: Devon v Yorks
Tourist Match
Fenner's: British Us v South
                      Africans (*Three days*)

Friday 26 June

Britannic Assurance Championship
*Leicester: Leics v Sussex
*Southgate: Middx v Essex
*Trent Bridge: Notts v Glam
*Taunton: Somerset v Hants
*Edgbaston: Warwicks v Lancs

Saturday 27 June

*Canterbury: Kent v Oxford U
*Headingley: Yorks v Cambridge U

Sunday 28 June

AXA League
The Oval: Surrey v Worcs
Tourist Match
Northampton: Northants v South
                 Africans (*One day*)

Wednesday 1 July

Britannic Assurance Championship
Derby: Derbys v Essex
Darlington: Durham v Leics
Swansea: Glam v Surrey

Southampton: Hants v Glos
Maidstone: Kent v Yorks
Trent Bridge: Notts v Middx
Hove: Sussex v Somerset
                 (*1.00pm start each day*)
Worcester: Worcs v Northants
Other Match
Lord's: Oxford U v Cambridge U
                 (Varsity Match) (*Three
                 days*)
AXA League
Edgbaston: Warwicks v Lancs
                 (*Floodlit*)

Thursday 2 July

THIRD CORNHILL INSURANCE TEST MATCH
*Old Trafford: ENGLAND v SOUTH AFRICA

Sunday 5 July

AXA League
Derby: Derbys v Essex
Darlington: Durham v Leics
Swansea: Glam v Surrey
Southampton: Hants v Glos
Maidstone: Kent v Yorks
Trent Bridge: Notts v Middx
Hove: Sussex v Somerset
Worcester: Worcs v Northants

Wednesday 8 July

NatWest Trophy
Second Round
Cardiff or   Glam or Bedfords v Leics
  Luton: or Staffs
Bristol or   Glos or Northants v
  Northampton: Surrey or Bucks
Bournemouth or   Dorset or Hants v
  Southampton: Cheshire or Essex
Old Trafford   Lancs or Sussex v Devon
  or Hove: or Yorks
Southgate or   Middx or Herefords v
  Brockhampton: Norfolk or Durham
Swansea or   Minor C Wales or Notts
  Trent Bridge: v Somerset or Holland
Edgbaston or   Warwicks or Ireland v
  Belfast: Kent or Cambridgeshire
Edinburgh or   Scotland or Worcs v
  Worcester: Derbys or Cumberland
Tourist Match
Amsterdam: Holland v South Africa
                 (*One day*)

280

Friday 10 July

Tourist Match
Downpatrick: Ireland v South Africa
                    (One day)
Other Match
Scarborough: Tim Rice's Intl XI v The
                    Yorkshiremen
(Boyes Stores Challenge) (One day)

Saturday 11 July

**Lord's: BENSON AND HEDGES
                    CUP FINAL**
(One reserve day Sun 12 July)
Other Match
Scarborough: Yorks v Durham
(Northern Electric Trophy) (One day)

Sunday 12 July

AXA League
*(Matches involving the B&H finalists to
  be played on Mon 13 or Tues 14 July)*
Derby: Derbys v Worcs
Trent Bridge: Notts v Glam
The Oval: Surrey v Leics
Edgbaston: Warwicks v Kent
Tourist Matches
Dublin: Ireland v South Africa
  (Castle Ave)   *(One day)*
Southampton: Hants or Somerset v Sri
  or Taunton: Lankans *(One day)*
*(Glos to play Sri Lankans at Bristol if
  both Hants & Somerset in B&H Final)*
Women's International Match
Scarborough: England v Australia
*(First Limited-overs International)
  (McCain Challenge)*

Monday 13 July

Scarborough: Tim Rice's XI v Yorks
(Tetley Bitter Festival Trophy) (One day)

Tuesday 14 July

AXA League
Edgbaston: Warwicks v Hants
                    (Floodlit)
Britannic Assurance Championship
Cheltenham: Glos v Sussex
Lytham: Lancs v Worcs
Leicester: Leics v Northants

Vodafone Challenge Series
Riverside: Durham v South Africans
                    (Three days)
Taunton: Somerset v Sri Lankans
                    (Three days)
Other Match
Scarborough: Heartaches XI v Invitation
                    XI *(One day)*

Wednesday 15 July

Britannic Assurance Championship
Southend: Essex v Kent
Guildford: Surrey v Middx
Edgbaston: Warwicks v Hants
Scarborough: Yorks v Notts
Women's International Match
Derby: England v Australia
(Second Limited-overs International)

Saturday 18 July

AXA League
Cheltenham: Glos v Sussex
Leicester: Leics v Northants
Vodafone Challenge Series
*Derby: Derbys v South Africans
                    (Three days)*
*Cardiff: Glam v Sri Lankans
                    (Three days)*
Tourist Match
Riverside: Durham v Australia 'A'
                    (One day) TBC
Other Match
Lord's: MCC v Rest of the World
*(One day) (Diana Princess of Wales
  Memorial Match)*
Women's International Match
Hove: England v Australia
(Third Limited-overs International)

Sunday 19 July

AXA League
Southend: Essex v Kent
Cheltenham: Glos v Northants
Taunton: Somerset v Hants
Guildford: Surrey v Middx
Scarborough: Yorks v Notts
Tourist Match
Riverside: Durham v Australia 'A'
                    (One day) TBC
Women's International Match
Southampton: England v Australia
(Fourth Limited-overs International)

Monday 20 July

AXA League
Old Trafford: Lancs v Worcs *(Floodlit)*
Hove: Sussex v Middx *(Floodlit)*

Tuesday 21 July

AXA League
Edgbaston: Warwicks v Essex
(Floodlit)
Tourist Match
Canterbury: Kent v Australia 'A'
(Three days) TBC
Women's International Match
Lord's: England v Australia
(Fifth Limited-overs International)

Wednesday 22 July

Britannic Assurance Championship
Colwyn Bay: Glam v Lancs
Cheltenham: Glos v Surrey
Portsmouth: Hants v Notts
Lord's: Middx v Yorks
Northampton: Northants v Derbys
Taunton: Somerset v Durham

Thursday 23 July

**FOURTH CORNHILL INSURANCE
TEST MATCH**
*Trent Bridge: ENGLAND v SOUTH
AFRICA
Britannic Assurance Championship*
*Edgbaston: Warwicks v Essex

Friday 24 July

Vodafone Challenge Series
*Leicester: Leics v Sri Lankans
(Four days)
Tourist Match
*Hove: Sussex v Australia 'A'
(Three days) TBC

Sunday 26 July

AXA League
Colwyn Bay: Glam v Lancs
Cheltenham: Glos v Surrey
Portsmouth: Hants v Notts
Lord's: Middx v Yorks
Northampton: Northants v Derbys
Taunton: Somerset v Durham

Tuesday 28 July

NatWest Trophy
Quarter-Finals

Wednesday 29 July

Tourist Match
Chelmsford Essex or Worcs v South
or Worcester: Africans *(One day)*
*(Derbys to play South Africans at Derby
if both Essex and Worcs involved in
NatWest Trophy quarter-finals)*

Thursday 30 July

Britannic Assurance Championship
Derby: Derbys v Kent
Southampton: Hants v Durham
Old Trafford: Lancs v Leics
Trent Bridge: Notts v Northants
*The Oval: Surrey v Sussex
*Edgbaston: Warwicks v Glam
Worcester: Worcs v Yorks
NatWest Under-19 International Match
Harrogate: England U19 v Pakistan
U19 (1st LOI)

Friday 31 July

Vodafone Challenge Series
*Chelmsford: Essex v South Africans
(Three days)
*Lord's: Middx v Sri Lankans
(Four days)

Saturday 1 August

NatWest Under-19 International Match
Riverside: England U19 v Pakistan
U19 (2nd LOI)

Sunday 2 August

AXA League
Derby: Derbys v Kent
Southampton: Hants v Durham
Old Trafford: Lancs v Leics
Trent Bridge: Notts v Northants
Worcester: Worcs v Yorks

Monday 3 August

AXA League
The Oval: Surrey v Sussex *(Floodlit)*

Edgbaston: Warwicks v Glam
(Floodlit)
NatWest Under-19 International Match
Riverside: England U19 v Pakistan
U19 (3rd LOI)

Wednesday 5 August

AXA League
The Oval: Surrey v Derbys (Floodlit)
Britannic Assurance Championship
Chelmsford: Essex v Glam
Canterbury: Kent v Hants
Old Trafford: Lancs v Glos
Leicester: Leics v Somerset
Lord's: Middx v Warwicks
Eastbourne: Sussex v Durham
Kidderminster: Worcs v Notts
Tourist Match
Lakenham: ECB XI v Sri Lankans
(One day)
Women's International Match
Guildford: England v Australia
(1st Test Match) (Four days)

Thursday 6 August

**FIFTH CORNHILL INSURANCE
TEST MATCH**
***Headingley: ENGLAND v SOUTH
AFRICA**
Britannic Assurance Championship
*The Oval: Surrey v Derbys

Friday 7 August

Tourist Match
Northampton: Northants v Sri Lankans
(One day)

Sunday 9 August

AXA League
Chelmsford: Essex v Glam
Canterbury: Kent v Hants
Old Trafford: Lancs v Glos
Leicester: Leics v Somerset
Lord's: Middx v Warwicks
Eastbourne: Sussex v Durham
Worcester: Worcs v Notts
Tourist Match
Milton Keynes: Northants v Sri Lankans
(Campbell Pk) (One day)

Tuesday 11 and Wednesday 12 August

NatWest Trophy
Semi-Finals
*(Reserve days for 1st Semi-Final Wed 12
and Thu 13 Aug)*

Tuesday 11 August

Tourist Match
Canterbury or Kent or Lancs v Sri
Old Trafford: Lankans (One day)
*(Warwicks to play Sri Lankans at
Edgbaston if both Kent & Lancs
involved in NatWest Trophy)*
Women's International Match
Harrogate: England v Australia
(2nd Test Match) (Four days)

Wednesday 12 August

Vodafone Trophy
Old Trafford First Class Counties
or Headingley: Select XI v South
Africans (One day)
*(Venue dependent on Lancashire/
Yorkshire progress in NatWest Trophy)*

Friday 14 August

**TRIANGULAR TOURNAMENT
Trent Bridge: SOUTH AFRICA v SRI
LANKA**
(Reserve day Sat 15 Aug)
Britannic Assurance Championship
*Derby: Derbys v Worcs
*Riverside: Durham v Glam
*Bristol: Glos v Kent
*Portsmouth: Hants v Essex
*Taunton: Somerset v Northants
*Hove: Sussex v Middx
*Headingley: Yorks v Lancs
NatWest Under-19 International Match
*Worcester: England U19 v Pakistan
U19 (First Match) (Four
days)

Sunday 16 August

**TRIANGULAR TOURNAMENT
Lord's: ENGLAND v SRI
LANKA**
(Reserve day Mon 17 Aug)

Monday 17 or Tuesday 18 August

AON Trophy
Semi-Finals

Tuesday 18 August

TRIANGULAR TOURNAMENT
Edgbaston: ENGLAND v SOUTH
AFRICA
(Reserve day Wed 19 Aug)

Wednesday 19 August

Britannic Assurance Championship
Riverside: Durham v Lancs
Colchester: Essex v Glos
Canterbury: Kent v Worcs
Leicester: Leics v Middx
Northampton: Northants v Warwicks
Trent Bridge: Notts v Surrey
Taunton: Somerset v Derbys
Vodafone Challenge Series
Hove: Sussex v Sri Lankans
                       (TBC)
*(In the event Sri Lanka fail to qualify for
the Triangular Tournament final. May
be played as a two-day match Thu
20-Fri 21 Aug depending on when Sri
Lanka know whether they have
qualified for the final or not)*

Thursday 20 August

TRIANGULAR TOURNAMENT
Lord's: Final
(Reserve day Fri 21 Aug)
Britannic Assurance Championship
*Cardiff: Glam v Yorks

Friday 21 August

Women's International Match
*Worcester: England v Australia
(3rd Test Match) (Four days)

Saturday 22 August

Vodafone Challenge Series
*Southampton: Hants v Sri Lankans
                       (Three days)*

Sunday 23 August

AXA League
Riverside: Durham v Lancs
Colchester: Essex v Glos

Canterbury: Kent v Worcs
Leicester: Leics v Sussex
Northampton: Northants v Warwicks
Trent Bridge: Notts v Surrey
Taunton: Somerset v Derbys

Monday 24 August

AXA League
Headingley: Yorks v Lancs *(Floodlit)*

Tuesday 25 August

NatWest Under-19 International Match
Taunton: England U19 v Pakistan
                       U19 (Second Match)
                       (Four days)
AXA League
Bristol: Glos v Somerset
                       (Floodlit)

Wednesday 26 August

Britannic Assurance Championship
Derby: Derbys v Durham
Northampton: Northants v Kent
Worksop CC: Notts v Leics
Hove: Sussex v Hants
Worcester: Worcs v Warwicks
Scarborough: Yorks v Essex

Thursday 27 August

CORNHILL INSURANCE TEST
MATCH
*The Oval: ENGLAND v SRI
LANKA
Britannic Assurance Championship
*Bristol: Glos v Somerset

Sunday 30 August

AXA League
Derby: Derbys v Durham
Southampton: Hants v Middx
Northampton: Northants v Kent
Trent Bridge: Notts v Leics
Edgbaston: Warwicks v Worcs
Scarborough: Yorks v Essex
Britannic Assurance Championship
*Hove: Sussex v Glam

Monday 31 August

Britannic Assurance Championship
Southampton: Hants v Middx

NatWest Under-19 International Match
Chelmsford: England U19 v Pakistan
U19 (Third Match)
(Four days)

Tuesday 1 September

Britannic Assurance Championship
Bristol: Glos v Northants
Old Trafford: Lancs v Derbys
Taunton: Somerset v Worcs
Edgbaston: Warwicks v Leics
Headingley: Yorks v Surrey

Thursday 3 August

AXA League
Hove: Sussex v Glam *(Floodlit)*

Saturday 5 September

Lord's: **NATWEST TROPHY
                FINAL**
(One reserve day Sun 6 Sept)

Sunday 6 September

AXA League
*(Match involving the NWT finalists to be
played on Tue 8 Sept)*
Riverside: Durham v Glam
Chelmsford: Essex v Notts
Old Trafford: Lancs v Hants
Leicester: Leics v Middx
Taunton: Somerset v Worcs
The Oval: Surrey v Kent
Hove: Sussex v Yorks

Monday 7 September

AON Trophy
Final *(Reserve day Tues 8 Sept)*

Wednesday 9 September

Britannic Assurance Championship
Riverside: Durham v Surrey
Cardiff: Glam v Derbys
Canterbury: Kent v Somerset
Leicester: Leics v Essex
Lord's: Middx v Glos
Northampton: Northants v Sussex
Worcester: Worcs v Hants
Headingley: Yorks v Warwicks
AXA League
Trent Bridge: Notts v Lancs *(Floodlit)*

Friday 11 September

Britannic Assurance Championship
*Trent Bridge: Notts v Lancs

Sunday 13 September

AXA League
Riverside: Durham v Surrey
Cardiff: Glam v Derbys
Canterbury: Kent v Somerset
Leicester: Leics v Essex
Lord's: Middx v Glos
Northampton: Northants v Sussex
Worcester: Worcs v Hants
Headingley: Yorks v Warwicks

Thursday 17 September

Britannic Assurance Championship
*Derby: Derbys v Middx
*Chelmsford: Essex v Northants
*Cardiff: Glam v Somerset
*Old Trafford: Lancs v Hants
*Trent Bridge: Notts v Glos
*The Oval: Surrey v Leics
*Hove: Sussex v Yorks
*Edgbaston: Warwicks v Kent
*Worcester: Worcs v Durham

ECB 38 County Competition (MCC Trophy)

Regional Groups

Group 1	Group 2	Group 3	Group 4
Cornwall	Berkshire	Bedfordshire	Herefordshire
Devon	Buckinghamshire	Herefordshire	Wales
Dorset	Hampshire	Middlesex	Warwickshire
Gloucestershire	Kent	Surrey	Wiltshire
Somerset	Sussex	Worcestershire	

Group 5	Group 6	Group 7	Group 8
Huntingdonshire	Cheshire	Cambridgeshire	Durham
Leicestershire	Cumberland	Essex	Lincolnshire
Nottinghamshire	Derbyshire	Norfolk	Northumberland
Oxfordshire	Lancashire	Northamptonshire	Yorkshire
Staffordshire	Shropshire	Suffolk	

	Date	Venue	Group	Match
May	Sun 10	Budleigh Salterton	(1)	Devon v Dorset
		Taunton	(1)	Somerset v Cornwall
	Sun 17	Helston	(1)	Cornwall v Dorset
		Bristol University	(1)	Gloucestershire v Somerset
		Ascott Park, Wing	(2)	Buckinghamshire v Berkshire
		Metropolitan Police CC	(3)	Surrey v Bedfordshire
		Pontypridd	(4)	Wales v Warwickshire
		South Wilts CC	(4)	Wiltshire v Herefordshire
		Kimbolton Town CC	(5)	Huntingdonshire v Oxfordshire
		Mansfield	(5)	Nottinghamshire v Leicestershire
		Neston	(6)	Cheshire v Cumberland
		Shifnal	(6)	Shropshire v Lancashire
		March	(7)	Cambridgeshire v Norfolk
		Exning CC	(7)	Suffolk v Northamptonshire
		Grimsby CC	(8)	Lincolnshire v Durham
		Elland CC	(8)	Yorkshire v Northumberland
	Thu 21	RAF Vine Lane	(3)	Middlesex v Surrey
	Sun 24	Liphook	(2)	Hampshire v Kent
		TBA	(4)	Warwickshire v Worcestershire
		Oakham School (tbc)	(5)	Leicestershire v Huntingdonshire
		Walsall	(5)	Staffordshire v Oxfordshire
		Wrekin College	(6)	Shropshire v Cheshire
		Framlingham College	(7)	Suffolk v Norfolk
		Gateshead Fell CC	(8)	Durham v Northumberland
	Thu 28	Leyland	(6)	Lancashire v Cumberland
	Sun 31	Bristol University	(1)	Gloucestershire v Devon
		Canterbury	(2)	Kent v Sussex
		Bedford Town CC	(3)	Bedfordshire v Surrey
		Corsham CC	(4)	Wiltshire v Worcestershire
		Denby CC	(6)	Derbyshire v Cheshire
		RGS Colchester	(7)	Essex v Cambridgeshire
		Lakenham	(7)	Norfolk v Northamptonshire
June	Sun 7	Falmouth	(1)	Cornwall v Gloucestershire
		Sherborne School	(1)	Dorset v Somerset
		Burridge CC	(2)	Hampshire v Buckinghamshire
		Horsham CC	(2)	Sussex v Berkshire
		Dunstable Town CC	(3)	Bedfordshire v Middlesex
		Metropolitan Police CC	(3)	Surrey v Hertfordshire
		Bulmers CC, Hereford	(4)	Herefordshire v Warwickshire
		Newport CC	(4)	Wales v Wiltshire
		Grace Road (tbc)	(5)	Leicestershire v Staffordshire
		Challow & Childrey	(5)	Oxfordshire v Nottinghamshire
		Nantwich	(6)	Cheshire v Lancashire
		Abbotsholme School	(6)	Derbyshire v Shropshire

Date	Venue	Group	Match
	March	(7)	Cambridgeshire v Suffolk
	Great Oakley CC	(7)	Northamptonshire v Essex
	South N'land CC	(8)	Northumberland v Durham
	Sheffield United CC	(8)	Yorkshire v Lincolnshire
Mon 8	Ashford CC	(2)	Kent v Buckinghamshire
Sun 14	Taunton	(1)	Somerset v Devon
	Middleton CC	(2)	Sussex v Hampshire
	Shenley Park	(3)	Hertfordshire v Middlesex
	Worcester	(4)	Worcestershire v Herefordshire
Mon 15	Eastwood Town	(5)	Nottinghamshire v Huntingdonshire
Thu 18	Southport & Birkdale	(6)	Lancashire v Derbyshire
	Hartlepool CC	(8)	Durham v Yorkshire
Sun 21	Chagford CC	(1)	Devon v Cornwall
	Finchampstead	(2)	Berkshire v Hampshire
	Kingsland	(4)	Herefordshire v Wales
	Dunstall	(5)	Staffordshire v Nottinghamshire
	Penrith	(6)	Cumberland v Shropshire
	Lakenham	(7)	Norfolk v Essex
	Jesmond	(8)	Northumberland v Lincolnshire
Thu 25	Finchley	(3)	Middlesex v Hertfordshire
Sun 28	Dean Park, Bournemouth	(1)	Dorset v Gloucestershire
	Finchampstead	(2)	Berkshire v Kent
	Milton Keynes	(2)	Buckinghamshire v Sussex
	Shenley Park	(3)	Hertfordshire v Bedfordshire
	tba	(4)	Warwickshire v Wiltshire
	Worcester	(4)	Worcestershire v Wales
	Kimbolton School	(5)	Huntingdonshire v Staffordshire
	Aston Rowant CC	(5)	Oxfordshire v Leicestershire
	Barrow	(6)	Cumberland v Derbyshire
	Chelmsford	(7)	Essex v Suffolk
	Finedon Dolben CC	(7)	Northamptonshire v Cambridgeshire
	Sleaford	(8)	Lincolnshire v Yorkshire

July

19th July	**Quarter-Finals)** *(no reserve day)*
Match A	Winners of Group 1 v Winners of Group 4
Match B	Winners of Group 6 v Winners of Group 8
Match C	Winners of Group 5 v Winners of Group 7
Match D	Winners of Group 3 v Winners of Group 2
Thu 30 July	**Semi-Finals** *(Fri 31 July, Reserve)*
Match E	Winners of Match A v Winners of Match D
Match F	Winners of Match C v Winners of Match B

August

Wed 26 Aug	**FINAL at Lord's** *(Thurs 27 Aug, Reserve)*
	Winners of Match E v Winners of Match F

Typeset by
Letterpart Limited, Reigate, Surrey

Printed and bound in Great Britain by
Clays Ltd, St Ives plc.

HEADLINE BOOK PUBLISHING
A division of Hodder Headline PLC
338 Euston Road
London NW1 3BH